designing
instructional strategies
for young children

designing
instructional strategies
for young children

BELEN COLLANTES MILLS
Florida State University

and

RALPH AINSLEE MILLS
University of Georgia

WM. C. BROWN COMPANY PUBLISHERS
Dubuque, Iowa

Consulting Editor
Joe L. Frost
University of Texas at Austin

Copyright © 1972 by Wm. C. Brown Company Publishers

Library of Congress Catalog Card Number: 72-182313

ISBN 0—697—06110—8

Printed in the United States of America

CONTRIBUTORS

B. Othanel Smith, Professor of Education, Bureau of Educational Research, University of Illinois

Israel Scheffler

Hilda Taba

Robert M. Gagné, Professor of Educational Psychology, Florida State University

Thorwald Esbensen, Assistant Superintendent in charge of Instruction, Duluth, Minnesota

Albert F. Eiss, Associate Executive Secretary of the National Science Teachers Association

Beulah M. Hirschlein and John G. Jones, Adult Basic Education Project Coordinator, School and Community Services; Assistant Professor, College of Education—University of Oklahoma

C. Benjamin Cox

Joe L. Frost, Associate Professor of Curriculum and Instruction, the University of Texas at Austin

Madeline Hunter, Principal, University Elementary School, University of California, Los Angeles

Samuel A. Kirk and Barbara Bateman, Director; Research Associate—Institute for Research on Exceptional Children, University of Illinois

James R. Okey, Assistant Professor of Education, University of California, Santa Barbara

Ann E. Boehm

George Mannello, Associate Professor of Elementary Education at Hofstra University

Roger A. Kaufman, Professor of Education, Chapman College, Orange, California

Donald T. Tosti and John R. Ball, General Manager; Media Analyst—Behavior Systems Division of the Westinghouse Learning Corporation, Albuquerque, New Mexico

M. David Merrill, Visiting Assistant Professor of Educational Psychology at Stanford University

John W. Childs, Acting Director of the Department of Instructional Technology, Wayne State University, Detroit, Michigan

Francis P. Hunkins, Assistant Professor of Education, Bureau of Educational Research, Kent State University

Robert T. Pate and Neville H. Bremer, Texas Technological College, Lubbock, Texas

Kenneth Shrable and Douglas Minnis, Assistant Professor; Head of Teacher Education—University of California, Davis

Meredith D. Gall, Far West Laboratory for Educational Research and Development

Carol A. Cartwright and G. Phillip Cartwright, Assistant Professor of Education; Assistant Professor of Special Education—the Pennsylvania State University

Harvey F. Clarizio and Stephen L. Yelon, Doctor of Education; Doctor of Philosophy—Michigan State University

Don Bushell, Jr., Patricia Ann Wrobel, and Mary Louise Michaelis, University of Kansas and Webster College

Arthur P. Coladarci, Professor of Education and Psychology at Stanford University

Charles H. Madsen, Jr., Wesley C. Becker, and Don R. Thomas, Florida State University and University of Illinois

William H. Allen

Ruth E. Hartley, Professor of Human Development and Director, Human Development Program, the University of Wisconsin, Green Bay

Paul R. Wendt and Gordon K. Butts

Judith Weinthaler and Jay M. Rotberg, Learning Disabilities Specialist, Brookline Public Schools, Brookline, Massachusetts; Assistant Professor of Education, Department of Special Education, Boston University

Isabel L. Beck and John O. Bolvin, Research Assistant and Director of the Curriculum Staff in Reading; Associate Professor of Education and Associate Director— Learning Research and Development Center, University of Pittsburgh

Joseph I. Lipson, Learning Research and Development Center, University of Pittsburgh

Donald Deep

James L. Fejfar, Associate Professor of Elementary Education, University of Nebraska

Paul C. Berry

Philip G. Kapfer, Curriculum and Research Director, Valley High School, Las Vegas, Nevada

June M. Patterson

Jerry A. Jenkins, Research Associate, Institute for Educational Research, Downers Grove, Illinois

Roger Fall and Virginia L. Brown, Indiana University, Bloomington; University of Minnesota at Duluth

John Withall, Professor of Educational Psychology and Head, Department of Secondary Education, Pennsylvania State University

Thelma Harms, Head Teacher at the Harold E. Jones Child Study Center of the University of California at Berkeley

Belen C. Mills and Ralph A. Mills, Assistant Professor of Elementary Education, Florida State University, Tallahassee; Supervisor of Instruction, Georgia Center for Continuing Education, the University of Georgia, Waycross Center

H.M. Harmes, Director of the School Service Center, Division of Continuing Education, Florida Atlantic University, Boca Raton

Albert V. Mayrhofer, Assistant to the Associate Commissioner of Education, U.S. Office of Education

Contents

PART THREE. COMBINING STRATEGIES FOR INDIVIDUALIZED INSTRUCTIONAL PROGRAMS

Foreword

The concept of early childhood education is interpreted broadly in this book, encompassing the developmental range from infancy to pre-adolescence. Such a broad emphasis is deliberately posed to counter the present "hardening of the categories" characterizing the restricting domains of "nursery," "kindergarten," "first grade," "second grade," etc. The instructional strategies presented by Professors Mills and Mills are universal in nature, that is, they permeate instruction at all levels—early childhood through university—although at varying levels of complexity and for different purposes. Consequently, the material presented herein will be useful across a broad range of educational programs.

The collective selections of the editors present a strong base for the concept of "educational engineering" but it does not follow that a scientific approach to the teaching-learning process is essentially de-humanizing. Quite the contrary, such an approach to the education of teachers is a welcome alternative to the hit-or-miss programs of the past which often led to drop-out, alienation, and failure for large segments of society. History may well judge the sensitivity of science tempered with humanism to be the legacy of the 1970's for subsequent educational practice.

Although particular selections of this book deal with the planned manipulation of behavior (the typical pattern is improvised manipulation), the permeating emphasis is upon *individualization* and the *participative approach.* Frolic and joy are not inherently ruled out in the approaches described herein; such omission is likely to result from the actions of poorly prepared teachers who are insecure in their professional roles. This point is fundamental, for the merely intuitive, guessing teacher cannot hope to compete with the carefully prepared professional (other factors being equal) in building relevant matches between present developmental levels of children, instructional media, subject matter content, and instructional strategies. Such professional activity requires *skill;* the development of this valuable resource is the subject matter of this timely book.

Joe L. Frost
Series Editor
University of Texas at Austin

Preface

This book presents a scientific approach to classroom instruction. It is directed to prospective and in-service teachers for the purpose of providing them a new view of teaching—that teaching is not just exercising intuition or using a "bag of tricks," but involves a complex mental operation, the decision-making process.

The scientific method, as applied to decision making, consists of the definition of problems, diagnosis of needs and constraints, formulation of hypotheses, observation and experimentation, evaluation and analysis of results. This listing of the essential elements of the method does not imply that it is always necessary to implement them in the same order. In practice, the order of the steps enumerated is subject to considerable variation. For example, analysis of results may lead to a redefinition of the problem, to the implementation of a different experimental strategy, or to the discarding of the original hypothesis in favor of another formulation.

However, regardless of the exact methodology utilized in a particular activity, the performance of that function is subject to the personal philosophy of the doer. A scientist makes decisions on the basis of facts. A teacher, also, must decide on the basis of scientifically tested facts—what is known about the nature of the child, what is known about the teaching-learning process, and other bases for decision making. The decision-making behavior of a teacher—deciding which skills to teach certain children, which teaching strategies to use for certain types of learning, determining the types of instructional materials that will enhance learning for each child—is strongly related to her personal beliefs concerning teaching and learning. Part I, therefore, seeks to foster the development of a personal philosophy of teaching, on the part of each student, which will serve as a guide for action in all phases of the teaching process. This is done by presenting for the student's consideration and analysis some different views of teaching and new conceptions of learning.

In Part II an analytical approach to classroom instruction is presented for the student. Teaching is much too complicated a process to examine in its entirety. Therefore, this section attempts to analyze the teaching act by breaking it down into its basic components; namely, the identification and statement of instructional objectives, diagnosis and assessment of learning needs, promoting learning through questioning techniques, organization of learning experiences, strategies for the reinforcement of learning and utilization and management of instructional media. Using this technique, one is provided with essential elements of the teaching process that are of a size and complexity that facilitates investigation. This presentation should enhance the student's understanding of the teaching function, make her more conscious of her own role with respect to each component, and provide her the basis for a more scientific approach to the designing of instructional strategies for young children. In harmony with these objectives, a variety of teaching strategies are presented to develop an awareness on the part of the student that there is not one best method of teaching—that there exists as great a number of effective techniques as there are different types of teacher and pupil personalities. While a number of strategies are presented in this section, a concerted effort has been made to avoid showing any bias toward any one technique. It is hoped that the use of such an approach will facilitate the formulation of original teaching strategies which are designed to fit the special requirements and capabilities of each learner in the classroom.

Part III provides the student with several strategies for individualizing instruction. It attempts to develop a better understanding of the interrelatedness of the essential components of the teaching process and a greater awareness of the desirability of combining different strategies for effective teaching.

Finally, Part IV directs the student's attention toward the need for continuous evaluation for the purpose of ascertaining the extent to which instructional objectives have been attained, and for discovering ways of enhancing progress toward the achievement of these objectives through modification of classroom practices and alteration of the classroom environment. A number of different suggestions for developing and implementing systems for evaluation are presented and examined.

Inextricably interwoven with evaluation is the concept of accountability. In this last section, a number of questions are raised concerning the role of accountability in education. For example: What aspects of the teaching-learning process are, or should be, subject to accountability? How may systems of accountability be validly implemented? To whom is the educator ultimately accountable? Questions such as these are considered and various points of view are set forth for consideration—both to acquaint the student with the direction of current thought and to stimulate her own thinking concerning this crucial issue.

While this book is intended for use as a textbook in early childhood or elementary education, specifically in courses dealing with educational methods, its design and construction are such that much broader application is anticipated. For example, it can also be used as a supplementary text for education courses in such areas as elementary education, secondary education, habilitative sciences, educational administration, methods of evaluation and educational psychology. Finally, but certainly not least importantly, it can provide the in-service teacher a valuable guide for self-evaluation and the improvement of her own teaching effectiveness.

A unique feature of the book is its functional orientation. While numerous theories are presented and examined, some in considerable depth, the student is not, at any point, encouraged to go theory-gathering or to engage in mere speculation or arm-chair philosophizing. On the contrary, she is never permitted to forget that her ever-present purpose is to prepare for actual classroom teaching and that her every thought and action should be consistent with this aim. To intensify this awareness on the part of the student, and to encourage the development of a genuine interest and a personal commitment, the following format is utilized.

The selections in this book are introduced by three mutually reinforcing techniques. First, a general overview of each section and the articles which comprise it is provided by the editorial comments which precede the section. These comments are designed to arouse the student's interest and to make her aware of some of the more important topics and questions examined by the selections. In modern parlance, they are intended to "show her where it's *at!*"

The editors are not content, however, to consign the student to a potential "forty-year's wandering in the wilderness" and therefore attempt to provide light on the path in the form of motive questions which precede each selection. These questions are designed to provide more specific guidance, intensify interest, provoke thought and motivate the reader toward a critical approach of study of the article. Because of a deep-seated conviction that when summaries are provided they are altogether too likely to be *all* that is read, summarization of the selections presented has been deliberately avoided.

Finally, a means of self-evaluation and verification of achievement is provided by the inclusion of a statement of objectives for each section. By referring to these, the student may ascertain those areas in which she is deficient, take steps to alleviate such deficiencies and devise means for assessing her own progress. The objectives stated are ordered according to ascending levels of difficulty in achievement and it is not expected that the selections included in each section will, by themselves, provide the means of achieving all of them. The intent of the editors is to provide a means of accommodating individual differences. For example, the more advanced student may, through individual initiative, make use of the recommended readings to discover additional sources of information and thus attain a higher level of achievement. The beginning student, on the other hand, may wish to concentrate upon gaining a basic understanding of the essentials. Suggestions for further study, in the form of recommended readings, appear at the close of each section.

B.C.M.
R.A.M.

Acknowledgements

A book of this nature cannot be produced without the cooperation and support of many dedicated individuals. To the authors of the articles selected for inclusion in this volume and to the editors and publishers of the various professional journals, we are deeply grateful for their permission to reprint. To our colleagues and students for their many valuable comments and suggestions, we express our sincere appreciation. Special thanks go to Dr. Billy Guice and to Dr. Glennon Rowell for their professional criticisms of certain portions of the manuscript, and to our friend and colleague, Dr. Edwin Smith, for his continued support and assistance. A debt of gratitude is due to Professor Howard Lincoln, a source of constant inspiration and encouragement, and to Dr. Joe Frost for his generosity in providing the foreword of this book. Finally, to our own *Young Children,* Roger Ainslee and Belinda Lee, for their infinite patience and understanding and for their precocious acceptance of mature responsibilities in managing the household in the face of our abdication of that role during the preparation of this manuscript, we express our heartfelt apologies and loving thanks.

Dedicated to all teachers everywhere:
especially our first,

Epifania and Ricardo Collantes
Marilu and Reginald Mills

and our most recent,

Belinda and Roger

Understanding
the Teaching-Learning Process

INTRODUCTION

Introduction to Part I

Clarity of definition is an outstanding characteristic of all sciences. To treat teaching as a science, one must first clearly define its meaning, identify the processes it involves and specify the goals it seeks to achieve. Formulation of such a concept of teaching necessarily involves answering questions like "What is it?", "What is it intended to do?", "Whom is it intended to serve?". As soon as the student has developed a clear conception of the nature of teaching and its desired objectives, she can proceed with the designing of a plan for accomplishing its purposes. She can, in effect, provide herself with a road map for teaching that will enable her to determine whether she is moving efficiently toward stated objectives and whether her destination has been reached.

In order to aid the student in formulating her own operational definition of teaching, Part I presents different concepts of teaching for her consideration and analysis.

Smith views teaching, in a generic sense, as a "system of actions intended to induce learning," and distinguishes between teaching and learning as separate but parallel concepts. He presents a pedagogical model of the teaching-learning process for assessing teacher-pupil interactions which takes into account the differing backgrounds, capabilities and needs of pupils. A further contribution is his analysis of the teaching act on the basis of a logical classification of the verbal behavior of teachers.

Scheffler agrees with Smith that teaching is "an activity aimed at the achievement of learning." He further examines three historical teaching philosophies, pointing out their respective strengths and weaknesses. He implies that a current philosophy of teaching may validly abstract from each philosophical model certain elements to form a synthesis capable of application to contemporary problems. An interesting position is taken by Scheffler in his denunciation of the behaviorists whose view of teaching he characterizes as "shaping the student's behavior" or "controlling his mind." Such a view Scheffler finds unacceptable because of his own emphasis upon the importance of transmitting, through teaching, those traditions of principled thought and action which provide the basis for a reasoned approach to life.

Taba traces the evolution of the concept of teaching giving considerable attention to the inadequacy of current assumptions concerning the nature of the teaching process

3

and to the dearth of conclusive research studies dealing with this question. She indicates that the evolution of the concept of teaching has reached a state wherein it is realized that teaching cannot be evaluated without considering students' responses. Therefore, she favors the present trend toward studying teaching in the classroom situation since such an approach affords opportunities to observe teaching behavior, student behavior and the reciprocal interaction between the two. She presents a model designed to provide insights into the nature of teaching. While the target of the teaching examined was the development of cognitive processes, Taba suggests that the model may also be utilized to investigate teaching involving other objectives.

Cognizant of the important role that learning plays in the teaching process, Gagné discusses some new theories of learning and their implications for instruction. Viewed in the light of the modern conception of learning as "information-processing," instruction acquires a new meaning. It ceases to be regarded solely as a process of imparting knowledge and comes to mean the encouraging of the use of capabilities that the learner already possesses and ensuring that he has the "enabling conditions" for learning.

After reading Part I and its related readings, it is anticipated that the student will be able to:

1. Discuss the nature of the teaching process.
2. Compare and contrast the various definitions of teaching advanced by different authors.
3. Present her own definition of teaching and analyze its components.
4. Explore the implications of new conceptions of learning for teaching and the designing of instructional programs.
5. Formulate a viable personal philosophy of teaching that is capable of application in a dynamic environment.
6. Construct a teaching model of her own, illustrate diagrammatically the relationships between its major components, and state the rationale for its development.

A Concept of Teaching*

B. Othanel Smith

EDITORS' QUESTIONS:

1. Discuss the nature of teaching as presented by the author. Do you agree with his analysis of the teaching act? Support your answer.

2. What do you perceive the nature of teaching to be? Analyze the components of the teaching act and develop a rationale for your analysis.

3. Formulate a statement of what you consider to be the essential elements of an adequate definition of teaching. Using the elements designated as your criteria, evaluate the different definitions of teaching presented in this article.

4. Develop an operational definition of learning. Compare and contrast your definition with the ones presented in this article.

5. Do you agree with the author that teaching is independent from learning? Justify your position.

6. React to the analogy drawn between teaching and selling.

B. Othanel Smith, "A Concept of Teaching," *Teachers College Record*, LXI, No. 5 (February 1960), 229–241. Reprinted with the permission of the *Teachers College Record* and B. Othanel Smith.

It is well understood that words can be defined to satisfy the purpose of the individual who uses them. For this reason many controversies center in the meaning of terms. The literature of education is filled with claims and counter claims about the meaning of "education." One authority defines education as growth; another says it is the cultivation of intellectual virtues; and still another claims that education is the means by which civilization is transmitted from one generation to another. These definitions are controversial because each one is packed with a set of preferences about what is to be taught, how it is to be taught, who is to be educated, and so on. And conducting the controversy consists in unpacking the definitions—each side pointing out what the opposing view commits us to, what it denies or fails to include, and at the same time claiming its own conception to be more defensible and desirable.

The word "teaching" is used in various ways also, and definitions of it often lead to or underlie controversial discussions in pedagogical circles. While the unpacking of various definitions of "teaching" would be an interesting undertaking, it is not our purpose to do so in this article. We shall attempt to undercut conventional definitions by developing a descriptive rather than a normative concept of teaching and to distinguish it from other concepts with which it is often confused.

*The analysis reported herein was made pursuant to a contract with the United States Office of Education, Department of Health, Education, and Welfare.

Dr. Smith is the author of *Research on Teaching to Develop Critical Thinking,* a report published in 1960 by the University of Illinois Press.

Definitions of Teaching

Three uses of the word "teaching" are found in ordinary discourse. First, it is used to refer to that which is taught, as a doctrine or body of knowledge. In the expression "the teachings of the church" reference is made to a body of ideas or a system of beliefs. Second, "teaching" is used to refer to an occupation or a profession—the profession of one who instructs or educates. And finally, "teaching" is used to refer to ways of making something known to others, usually in the routine of a school.

We are concerned here with the third of these uses and shall disregard the first two altogether. "Teaching" in this third sense has been defined in the following ways:

Teaching: arrangement and manipulation of a situation in which there are gaps or obstructions which an individual will seek to overcome and from which he will learn in the course of doing so.[1]

Teaching: intimate contact between a more mature personality and a less mature which is designed to further the education of the latter.[2]

Teaching: impartation of knowledge to an individual by another in a school.[3]

From a generic standpoint, each of these definitions suffers from the same defect. It smuggles in its own particular view of how teaching is to be carried on. All are question-begging definitions, for they answer in advance the very question which research on teaching seeks to answer. The first of these definitions commits us to the view that the individual learns by engaging in problem solving, and that he is motivated to learn by involvement in an unsettled state of affairs for which he has no ready-made response. To teach is to engage and direct the pupil in problem-solving. Once we accept this definition, we commit ourselves to a chain of propositions identified with a particular theory of education.

The second definition just as surely, though perhaps less obviously, incorporates a theory of didactics. Teaching, we are told, consists in contacts between two individuals, one more mature than the other. The contacts are to be intimate and designed to advance the education of the less mature person. Education, in the view of the author of this definition, is the development of the individual through learning, and learning in turn is defined as an adaptive process. Intimate contact supposedly requires the presence of one person in the company of the other. To unpack this definition of teaching would again bring to view a theory of education.

We are no better off when we turn to the last of these three concepts. The definition of teaching as the impartation of knowledge is typically used by persons who think of education as the cultivation of the mind, the mind being thought of as an accumulation of information—factual, theoretical, and practical. Teaching, according to this definition, typically takes on the character of lecturing.

To say that the foregoing definitions are question-begging is to say that teaching is confused with didactics. The way in which teaching is or can be performed is mistaken for teaching itself. In its generic sense, teaching is a system of actions intended to induce learning. So defined, teaching is observed to be everywhere the same, irrespective of the cultural context in which it occurs. But these actions may be performed differently from culture to culture or from one individual to another within the same culture, depending upon the state of knowledge about teaching, and the teacher's peda-

1. Adapted from John Brubacher, *Modern Philosophies of Education* (New York: McGraw-Hill, 1939), p. 108.
2. Henry C. Morrison, *Basic Principles of Education* (Boston: Houghton Mifflin, 1934), p. 41.
3. Adapted from common usage.

gogical knowledge and skill. Didactics, or the science and art of teaching, are not the same as the actions which they treat. And a definition of teaching as such, which packs a set of biases about how these actions are to be conducted, confuses teaching with its science and its art.

Teaching and Learning Distinguished

Furthermore, teaching is frequently assimilated to learning. The belief that teaching necessarily entails learning is widely held, and is expressed in more than one book on pedagogical method. As one of our most distinguished authorities says, unless the child learns the teacher has not taught.[4] Then he goes ahead to say that teaching is to learning as selling is to buying, apparently on the assumption that if there is no buying, there can have been no selling. At first, this binding of teaching and learning together after the fashion of selling and buying seems plausible enough. But the analogy will not bear inspection, although it does highlight the responsibility of the teacher and the importance of active endeavor by the pupil.

To begin examination of the idea that teaching entails learning, let us note first of all that teaching and selling each involve some sort of interaction. We do, perform, or accomplish many acts unaided. We race, hunt, and sing without the assistance of anyone. But there are actions which can be performed only in association with other persons. We can do business only if there is somebody to do business with. We can negotiate if there is someone to carry on negotiations with, and not otherwise. Likewise we can carry on the activities of selling only if there is someone who will buy our product and we can teach only if there is somebody whom we may instruct. Were there no buyers, there could be no sellers.

Unless there were pupils, there could be no teachers. Such verbs as *negotiate, sell,* and *teach* signify proceedings between two or more individuals, involving some sort of deliberation with adjustment of mutual claims and interests in expectation that some result will issue. Lacking a process of interaction there can be neither teacher nor pupil just as there can be neither seller nor buyer.

Beyond this point, the analogy between teaching and selling begins to break down. To see how this is so, let us spell out the analogy. There are four elements in the selling-buying operation: a seller, a buyer, the act of selling, and the act of buying. Similarly, in the teaching-learning combination we find a teacher, a pupil, the action of teaching, and the activities of learning. To say that a teacher is to teaching as a seller is to selling, while not strictly correct, does not do violence to either of these relations. The qualifying expression "not strictly correct" is inserted because there are several different actions which we expect of a teacher: making assignments, grading papers, showing how to do something, telling why something is the case, and so on. But there is little more than one sort of behavior predictable from the statement that one is a seller; namely, that he gives something in return for a consideration, usually money. Looking further we find that learning is not coordinate with buying, because the relation of pupil to learning is not the same sort of thing as buyer to buying. We can say that a buyer is to buying as a pupil is to "pupiling," but the parallel breaks down when we say "as a pupil is to learning." "Pupiling," if there were such a word, would be required by the analogy to mean receiving instruc-

4. William H. Kilpatrick, *Foundations of Method* (New York: MacMillan, 1926, p. 268). See also John Dewey, *How We Think,* Rev. ed. (New York: D. C. Heath, 1934), p. 35f.

tion just as "buying" means receiving something in return for an agreed-upon price. Nor are we any better off if we substitute "learner" for "pupil," since "learner" is defined as one who receives instruction.

Furthermore, the relation between selling and buying is not the same as that between teaching and learning. The statement "I am selling X and someone is buying it from me" is implicitly tautological. It is clear from common usage that in order to be selling something someone must be buying. It would be contradictory to say "I am selling X but no one is buying it,"* or to say "I am buying X from so and so but he is not selling it." If you state "I am selling X" you are stating only part of what you mean, for implicit in this statement is the idea that someone is buying it. On the other hand, "I am teaching X (meaning, say, mathematics) to A and he is learning it" is not tautological. It is not contradictory to say "I am teaching X to A but he is not learning it." Nor is it contradictory to assert "A is learning X but no one is teaching it to him." "I taught X to A" means that I showed A how to do X, or told him such and such about X. This expression does not include the idea that A learned from me how to do X. It is thus not repeating the idea to add it to the expression. Hence "I taught X to A" says something differerent from "I taught X to A and he learned X." However, the parallel suggested in the paragraph above is logically similar to that between buying and selling. To assert "I am teaching X (mathematics) and he is 'pupiling' it" (meaning he is receiving my instruction), would be tautological. It would then be contradictory to say "I am teaching X (mathematics) and he is not 'pupiling' it" (meaning he is not receiving my instruction). To give instruction would seem to entail receiving it. It would likewise be contradictory to say "He received instruction, but no one gave him instruction."

The difference between teaching and learning may be further explored by reference to the distinction which Ryle makes between what he calls task words and achievement or success words.[5] Task words are those which express activities such as *racing, treating, traveling,* and *hunting.* The corresponding achievement words are *win, cure, arrive,* and *find. Teaching* is a task word and *learn* is the parallel achievement word. Achievement words signify occurrences or episodes. Thus one wins, arrives, or finds at a particular moment, or a cure is effected at a particular time. Nevertheless, some achievement verbs express a continued process. A boat is launched at a particular instant but it is held at the dock for inspection. On the other hand, task verbs always signify some sort of activity or extended proceedings. We can say of a task such as play, treat, or teach that it is performed skillfully, carefully, successfully, or ineffectively. We may play the game successfully or unsuccessfully, but we cannot win unsuccessfully. We may treat a patient skillfully or unskillfully, but the restoring of health is neither skillful nor unskillful. It makes sense to say that we teach unsuccessfully. But it is self-contradictory to say we learned French unsuccessfully.

Teaching as a System of Actions

That learning does not necessarily issue from teaching, that teaching is one thing and learning is quite another, is significant for pedagogical research. It enables us to

---

*There is a sense in which it would not be contradictory to say, "I am selling X but no one is buying it." For example, "I have been selling cars all day but nobody bought one" is not self-contradictory. But in this case it would be more precise to say "I have been *trying* to sell cars," etc., meaning I have been doing things intended to result in the sale of cars.
5.Gilbert Ryle, *The Concept of Mind* (London: Hutchinson House, 1952), pp. 149–52.

analyze the concept of teaching without becoming entangled in the web of arguments about the processes and conditions of learning; in short, to carry on investigations of teaching in its own right. Teaching, like learning, has its own forms, its own constituent elements, its own regularities. It takes place under specifiable conditions— time limits, authority relations, individual abilities, institutional structures, and so on. What is needed for scientific inquiry is a concept which recognizes teaching as a distinctive phenomenon general enough to embrace normative definitions (see page 6) as special cases.

The word "teacher" is a dispositional term in the sense that under specifiable conditions—classroom, pupils, and so forth— the individual referred to as a teacher tends to behave in characteristic ways. He may explain something with the expectation that what he says will be remembered by the pupil; he may draw a diagram and point out certain features of it, emphasizing that these are to be remembered; he may read from a book and ask a pupil to interpret the passage; and so on. When the teacher behaves in these and many other ways, we say he is teaching. To repeat, teaching thus conceived may be defined as a system of actions directed to pupils. These actions are varied in form and content and they are related to the

behavior of pupils, whose actions are in turn related to those of the teacher. From the execution of these actions and interactions of teacher and pupil, learning occurs. But learning, being an acquired disposition to behave in particular ways in particular circumstances, is neither action nor behavior, though it is exhibited in actions. The theoretical conception of teaching we propose to present will include all the actions of teachers necessary to explain and to predict the behavior of pupils and the occurrence of learning, though such explaining and predicting cannot be made from these actions alone.

It is to be kept in mind that the actions which constitute teaching, as defined in this discussion, take place in and are influenced by an environment which typically contains such social factors as mores, organizational structures, and cultural resources, as well as physical objects, persons, and so forth. But this environment is excluded from our conception of teaching, not because it is unimportant or irrelevant to teaching, but because it is not a part of the concept of teaching. Teaching is doubtless related to the mores and to social structures, but it is not the same sort of thing.

To explicate the concept of teaching we shall resort to a model which draws upon the psychological paradigm developed by

A Pedagogical Model

I Independent Variables (Teacher)	III Intervening Variables (Pupils)	II Dependent Variables (Pupils)
(1) Linguistic behavior	These variables consist of postulated explanatory entities and processes such as memories, beliefs, needs, inferences, and associative mechanisms.	(1) Linguistic behavior
(2) Performative behavior		(2) Performative behavior
(3) Expressive behavior		(3) Expressive behavior

Tolman,[6] although the psychological features of his model are of little interest to us here. All the variables involved in and related to the actions which make up teaching can be classified into three categories, but the actions themselves belong to only one of these. Although their particular contents continue to be controversial, the categories themselves have been well established in the behavioral sciences. They are (1) independent variables, (2) dependent variables, and (3) intervening variables. By referring to the model it can be easily seen that the actions of teaching belong to the first of these categories, and the actions of pupils to the second. Learning, as achievement, is an intervening variable. The index of its presence is pupil behavior, and this behavior is a dependent variable.

In the course of teaching, these variables are related in various ways. In so far as these relations can be postulated, described, and verified, teaching can be shaped in terms of empirically tested principles. While it is not possible here to deal concretely with these relations, we can discuss them in a very general way. In the model, the arrows indicate the direction of causal influences. The teacher's actions are followed by postulated states, events, or processes in the pupil and are represented by the intervening variables. Then, as a result of these variables, the pupil behaves in one or more of the ways indicated in the dependent variables column. The teacher can see the pupil's behavior, but he cannot see the postulated events and processes; that is, he cannot observe interests, motives, needs, beliefs, and the like. But these psychological entities and processes are present by implication in the behavior of the pupil. The teacher may therefore infer these psychological factors from the pupil's behavior, and in some instances he actually does infer them, although he may not be aware that he is doing so. Thus the teacher often infers from the reactions of the pupil that he is interested, or that he wants to do so and so, or the contrary.

Our model does not depict the ebb and flow of teaching, nor does it give a complete schema of the cycle of giving and taking instruction, hereafter referred to as the teaching cycle. To complete the picture the model must be extended to the right in duplicate form. Thus extended, the model would show that the pupil's actions bring into operation the teacher's intervening variables. These variables in turn lead to teacher actions, and at this point the whole cycle begins again. In this way the process of teaching is continued until the teacher believes either that the pupil has achieved what the teacher intended or that it is not profitable to continue teaching at the moment.

The foregoing analysis enables us to describe the teaching cycle, to mark off units of this cycle, and to distinguish the act of teaching from the act of receiving instruction. The teaching cycle is symbolized as follows:

$$\| P_t \to D_t \to R_t \mid \to P_p \to D_p \to R_p \parallel \to P_t \to D_t \to R_t \mid \to P_p \to D_p \to R_p \parallel \to$$
$$P_t \to D_t \to R_t \mid \to P_p \to D_p \to R_p \parallel \ldots \ldots \ldots \to \text{achievement,}$$

where P_t is the teacher's perception of the pupil's behavior; D_t is the teacher's diagnosis of the pupil's state of interest, readiness, knowledge, and the like, made by inference from the behavior of the pupil; and R_t is the action taken by the teacher in light of his diagnosis; and where P_p is the pupil's perception of the teacher's behavior; D_p is the pupil's diagnosis of the teacher's state of interest, what he is saying, and so on, as

6. Edward C. Tolman, "A Psychological Model," in *Toward a General Theory of Social Action,* Edited by Talcott Parsons and Edward A. Shils (Cambridge: Harvard University Press, 1952), pp. 279–302.

inferred from the teacher's behavior; and R_p is the reaction of the pupil to the actions of the teacher.

Each unit marked off by the double vertical lines is an instance of the teaching cycle. Each one consists of a teacher-pupil interaction. Within this teaching cycle are two subunits divided by the single vertical line. The subunit $|\ P_t \quad D_t \quad R_t\ |$ is what we refer to as an act of teaching; the subunit $|\ P_p \quad D_p \quad R_p\ |$ is what we call the act of taking instruction. These are reciprocating acts, and when performed under proper conditions they issue in achievement.

Teaching, according to our schema, does entail someone to give instruction as well as someone to take it. If a pupil is working on an assignment, he is probably learning. But no teaching is going on. No one is acting toward the pupil as a teacher. However, teaching acts can occur, though in abbreviated form, without the physical presence of pupils. For example, a teacher giving instruction over a television network is not in the physical presence of pupils. He can even be cut off the air by a mechanical difficulty, and being unaware that anything has happened, continue to teach. In a case like this the teacher is shaping his instructional behavior to some generalized group anyway, and the fact that he is off the air consequently makes no difference.

Of course actual classroom teaching is not as simple as our schema. For one thing, more than one pupil is usually involved in classroom teaching. The teacher typically addresses himself to the entire class rather than to a single pupil. Even when he appears to be talking to a single pupil, he usually speaks for the benefit of the whole class. His perception of pupil behavior is likely to be some sort of generalized picture, and his diagnosis a hunch as to the general state of the class as a whole. Finally, his actions are likely to be shaped more by these general considerations and by his habits than by the psychological requirements of any one pupil.

The fact that classroom teaching is more complex than our pedagogical model is no criticism of the model. One of the advantages of models is that they give a simplified picture of the phenomenon they depict. However, the fact that our symbolic schema and verbal performances in the classroom are isomorphic is borne out by our descriptive studies of classroom teaching. By taping classroom discourse and analyzing it into pedagogically neutral units called episodes we have established a context within which to view verbal exchanges comprising the teaching cycle.[7] Acts of teaching as well as acts of taking instruction can be clearly distinguished in the episodic structure.

Our knowledge of the act of teaching as well as that of taking instruction is meager. Neither of these acts has been investigated sufficiently to justify, from a scientific standpoint, fundamental changes in teaching. We have considerable knowledge of how human learning occurs, although much of it comes by extrapolation from studies of animal learning. The amount of adjustment in our current theories of learning which verbal behavior and cognitive processes may require is something about which we can only guess. We do not even know how accurately our learning theory describes what occurs in the act of taking instruction. Be that as it may, the act of teaching has received far less attention than its central role in pedagogy would seem to require.

7. B. Othanel Smith and Others, *A Study of the Logic of Teaching.* A report on the first phase of a five-year research project. United States Office of Education. Dittoed 1959.

For a more detailed treatment see "The Analysis of Classroom Discourse: A Method and Its Uses," by Mary Jane Aschner (Unpublished Doctor's Dissertation, University of Illinois, 1958).

The Variables

Intervening variables consist of constructs, or postulated entities and processes, which stand between the independent and dependent variables and are functionally related to them. The independent variables —the teacher's actions—are conceived to be causal factors which evoke or bring into operation postulated entities and processes, and these in turn are connected by a set of functions to the dependent variables—to the behavior of pupils. An account of these variables would involve us in psychological theory, and consequently, in one of the most controversial areas of the behavioral sciences. In the heyday of radical behaviorism, postulation of entities and processes between stimulus and response was frowned upon. Even Thorndike's postulation of physiological entities and processes was believed to be unnecessary to the explanation of learning. In recent years, however, different schools of psychology have assumed, each in its own way, whatever processes and entities seem to afford the most plausible explanation. To a large extent, differences in schools of psychology hinge upon differences in their conceptual postulations. Fortunately our task is a modest one, requiring us to delineate only the variables of our model. Were we to develop completely a general theory of teaching, we would be required to set forth a set of intervening variables, and to show their postulated causal connections with both independent and dependent variables of our model.

The independent variables consist of linquistic, performative, and expressive behaviors. These behaviors are essential elements of the concept of teaching and are not to be confused with the dependent variables, which are the behaviors identified with the act of taking instruction and are functionally associated with learning.

To continue our discussion of independent variables, teaching acts consist largely in verbal behavior, in what is done with and to pupils through the medium of words. But the fact that language is the primary medium of instruction is not as important as the things we do with language. For if we are to understand teaching, we must know what the actions are that we perform linguistically. Furthermore, it may be supposed that changes in the effectiveness of instruction will follow upon changes in the execution of such verbal actions.

What are the sorts of actions we perform with language in the classroom? First, there is a group of actions which have to do with the performance of what we shall call logically relevant—subject to logical appraisal —tasks. The teacher is called upon to deal with questions whose answers involve logical operations. For example, the teacher defines terms. To define a term is to perform a logical operation. If he gives a classificatory definition such as "A triangle is a plane figure with three sides," the teacher names the class of things (plane figure) to which triangles belong and then gives the attributes (three sides) which distinguish triangles from all other plane figures. We will describe only briefly a few of the logically relevant actions which are found in didactic verbal behavior.[8]

Defining. In general, definitions are rules for using words. There are several ways to define words, depending upon the rules. Among these ways are classificatory, opera-

8. For a more extended discussion of these verbal actions see Smith and Others, *op. cit.* It should be noted that there are different dimensions of verbal behavior which cannot be discussed here. The teacher not only makes assertions about objects, but also talks about language itself. To ask "What is the author comparing X to?" in a given passage is to direct the pupil's attention to an object, event, and so forth, while to ask "Is this passage a metaphor?" is to ask about language itself. To ask for a definition is one thing, and to ask what a definition *is* is quite another thing.

tional, relational, and nominal definitions.

Classifying. To classify is to put something in a category. The teacher classifies implicitly when he defines, describes, or explains. But the logic of classification is far more involved than the mere verbal act of asserting "*X* is a *Y.*" Its logic become explicit when the teacher attempts to tell why he classifies *X* as a *Y.* He is then expected to set forth the criteria (rules) he uses and to show that they apply in the particular case.

Explaining. Explanations are called for when an event or a state of affairs is to be accounted for. To explain is to set forth an antecedent condition of which the particular event to be accounted for is taken as the effect, or else to give the rules or facts which are used to tell why decisions or judgments were made or actions taken. There are at least six different kinds of explanations: mechanical, causal, sequent, procedural, teleological, and normative.

Conditional Inferring. In conditional inferring, a set of conditions is described and the teacher then gives the consequent—the effect, result, or outcome. Sometimes the conditions are fairly simple, so that the path from the conditions to a conclusion is easily followed and the logical connection between the conditions and the outcome is fairly explicit. In other instances the path is complex, involving a number of steps, and is difficult to connect logically with the conditions.

Comparing and Contrasting. In this sort of verbal action two or more things—actions, factors, objects, processes—are compared; or else something is given and the teacher attempts to interpret it by describing another familiar object or process to which it is compared. Such comparative relations can often be expressed in terms of transitivity and symmetry.

Valuating. To perform the act of valuating, the teacher rates some object, expression, event, or action, let us say, as to its truth and the like. If he gives the complete operation of valuating, the teacher will set forth the reasons for his rating.

Designating. To designate is to identify something by name, word, or symbol. The verbal action here consists in citing instances or examples of a group of things or in giving the name of a particular thing or class of things.

Other Actions. In addition to the foregoing actions, there are verbal actions less closely related perhaps to logical operations. The teacher states theorems, rules, beliefs. He reports what was stated in a book, or verbally by someone. He states something to be the case; for example, that the date and place of a particular event were thus and so.[9]

The second group of actions which teachers perform with words is called directive action. In the moment-to-moment tasks of the classroom the teacher is called upon to tell pupils what to do in the performance of some operation or the practice of a motor skill. He may observe a pupil's mistake in the practice of typing and tell him what to do to correct it, just as on the playing field he may tell a player what to do to improve his tackling. He may tell a pupil in the laboratory that a piece of apparatus is to be set up in a particular way, or that he has made an error in reasoning which can be corrected in such and such a way. These verbal actions are all directive in the sense that they instruct the pupil in what he is to do. There are other directive actions which are less specific and only suggest the direction in which the pupil is to move. Verbal

9. Our own studies of classroom discourse in English, social studies, science, and mathematics show that episodes involving definitions make up about 4 per cent of the total number of episodes; classifying about 3 per cent; explaining about 13 per cent; conditional inferring about 7 per cent; comparing and contrasting about 3 per cent; valuating about 5 per cent; designating about 15 per cent; and others 50 per cent.

actions of this sort always frame a situation in a general way. For example, a teacher may tell a group of pupils that they are to take a trip by automobile and that they need to know how much the gasoline will cost in order to pro-rate the expense among members of the class. He then asks what they need to know in order to find out the cost of the gasoline. In this case, the teacher sets a situation and suggests the line along which the pupils are to work.

In both of these sorts of saying and telling the teacher does not intend that the pupil learn what he says. The pupil is not expected to say back to the teacher, in either the same or different words, what the teacher himself said. In the case of learning motor skills, he does expect the pupil to do what he is told, and thereby to effect changes in his performance. If the pupil forgets entirely what the teacher said, it does not matter so long as the pupil's performance is improved. The same is true with respect to less specific directives, as in the case of the automobile trip. The pupils most certainly will forget all about the situation laid before them by the teacher. This is not what the teacher wishes them to remember. His hope is that the pupils will learn how to analyze a situation and to decide upon the relevant factors in the course of working it out. This use of language is quite different from the expository uses discussed above. There the pupil is expected to remember what the teacher says and to repeat it in his own words in a subsequent situation. If the teacher says that the law of gravity is so and so and that it can be expressed mathematically thus and so, he expects the pupil to remember what he has said and to be able to say the same thing in his own words when he is called upon to do it.

Finally, the teacher performs admonitory acts. He praises and commends; blames and

reprimands. He recommends, advises, and enjoins. He says to a pupil, "That is good." He may say to another, "That is not up to your ability. You could have done better." He may say, "You got yourself into this difficulty. You have only yourself to blame." He may suggest some course of action as the way out of the trouble. He may enjoin the pupil to remember so and so when he comes up against a particular sort of situation in the future. These kinds of verbal acts may effect psychological reinforcements or extinctions, depending upon the particular admonitory act and the circumstances in which it occurs. They are conventionally understood to be taken for their social or emotional impact upon the pupil rather than for their cognitive content.

We turn now to consider those independent variables of our model which are nonverbal. The first set of these we call performative actions; that is, actions which are performed for assumed or understood purposes but which are not linguistic. They may be accompanied by verbal behavior but they are themselves mere motor performances. These actions serve to *show* rather than to *tell* something to pupils, and the showing is done by manipulating objects. The teacher shows a pupil how to do something—say, how to regulate a Bunsen burner—by performing the act himself. At the same time, he may say, "Here is the way to do it—you turn this to control the amount of air," and so forth. But the saying is itself directive verbal behavior and not performative in our sense. The act of turning the element of the apparatus, and thus showing the relation between the turning and the color of the flame, is what we refer to as performative behavior. In such cases it is assumed that the pupil is to learn how to perform this action himself, so that the next time he will be able to adjust the burner without the aid of the teacher.

Numerous instances of this type of performative behavior can be found in the day-to-day work of the teacher. In some situations, however, the teacher engages in performative actions which the pupil is not expected to learn, for their purpose is to facilitate the learning of something else. For example, the teacher performs a demonstration in a science class to show the lines of force in a magnetic field. He goes through the usual operations of putting the appropriate piece of paper over a magnet and then sprinkling iron filings on the paper. Of course the pupils may learn from their observation of the teacher how to do the demonstration themselves. But the purpose of the performance is to show the magnetic field rather than how to carry out the demonstration.

The second set of nonverbal variables is what we call expressive behavior. These behaviors are illustrated in bodily posture, facial expression, tone of voice, expression of the eyes, and other ways. Typically they are neither purposeful nor addressed to anyone. In this respect they differ significantly from both verbal and performative actions, which we always understood as being directed to someone or to a group. Nevertheless, expressive behaviors function in teaching because they are taken by pupils as signs of the psychological state of the teacher. In this sense expressive behaviors are natural signs, like the things we call clouds, lightning, rivers. We take them as signifying something —as a cloud is a sign of rain.

Turning now to the dependent variables of our model—those which make up the instruction-taking part of the teaching cycle— we find a parallel between these variables and the independent ones. The pupil performs linguistic actions. He defines, explains, valuates, and so on, just as the teacher does. He performs these actions at the teacher's suggestion, or often even voluntarily. However, the pupil's purpose is not to instruct anyone, but to bear witness that he is taking instruction—that he understands what is happening or that he is taking part in (accepting or dissenting from) what is going on.

Directive verbal behavior of the pupil occurs infrequently, and usually on occasions when he plays the role of teacher, as chairman of class discussion, for example. The same observation holds for admonitory behavior. Classroom conventions do not permit the pupil to praise, blame, or advise the teacher with respect to his work, but this does happen on occasion. A pupil may complain that the teacher has been unfair, but he is not likely to say either to another pupil or to a teacher, "Your explanation was splendid." Such verbal behavior is odd and is likely to be ill received by the pupils as well as by the teacher.

While the pupil exhibits performative behavior (nonverbal behavior carried on for a purpose), he does so typically to practice the actions themselves rather than to instruct anyone. Thus he engages in performative actions when he sets up laboratory equipment, takes part in athletic events, and so on. Actions of this nature under the direct tutelage of the teacher are part of the teaching cycle. If they occur outside of teacher-pupil interaction, they are simply ways of study and practice.

The expressive behavior of the pupil is the same as that of the teacher. The pupil smiles or frowns; he slumps or sits erect in his seat; his voice is firm and convincing or weak and uncertain. Such behavior in the pupil, even more often than in the teacher, is not addressed to anyone. It is not typically intended to communicate. Nevertheless, it functions as signs to the teacher—as the skies, clouds, and winds are signs to the skipper at sea. The posture of the pupil, the light in his eyes, or the frown on his face tell the teacher who can read them about his feelings, intentions, and ideas.

The Language of Didactics

By "didactics" is meant, of course, the science or art of teaching, and not teaching itself. When we speak of what we know about how teaching is to be conducted we have reference to didactics. The language of didactics traditionally is marked by such terms as "method," "drill," "interest," "learning situation." Discussions of teaching as such are carried on in the terms of the lecture method, problem method, project method, supervised study method. Much of the research on teaching has been framed in terms of these various doctrines. Is the problem method more effective than the lecture method? Is the project method more effective than the recitation method?

Numerous experiments to find answers to these and similar questions have produced only inconclusive results. This fact is often attributed to inadequate control of experimental conditions and to the complexity of the phenomenon itself. No one can doubt the strength of these claims. Nevertheless, the fact that teaching itself has never been analyzed apart from the context of doctrine may contribute to failure to control relevant factors. Has not our theorizing about teaching, even for experimental purposes, become clouded with commitments to the very words we use to discuss teaching?

If what we just said about pedagogical theorizing is only partly correct, it suggests that a new way of talking about didactic questions is in order. Perhaps a new approach to the study of teaching will emerge if we abandon the term "method," which is associated with such heavy-laden terms as "induction," "deduction," and "problem-solving"—terms for which everyone had his own preconceptions and predilections. If we cut through the verbal curtain and look at actual instructional operations in the classroom, we find them to be different from what our linguistic commitments lead us to believe. We see that teachers do many things which cannot be neatly fitted into the traditional theories of pedagogy. For example, at one time a teacher sets up a verbal situation from which he can move in a number of directions, depending upon his assessment of the way his pupils are psychologically deployed. At another time he sets up a nonverbal state of affairs and invites his pupils to explore it, to tell how it can be handled, and so forth. On another occasion a pupil may execute a verbal maneuver to counter the teacher's move. The teacher may then outflank the pupil, leaving one or more members of the class to meet the challenge.

We need studies of the sorts of positions teachers assume, and what maneuvers and detailed actions they take under varying circumstances and with different sorts of materials. If these were made, it would be appropriate to speak of the strategies and tactics of teaching. From such descriptive studies we might then go on to develop experimental as well as more nearly adequate theoretical didactics.

Philosophical Models of Teaching *

Israel Scheffler

EDITORS' QUESTIONS:

1. Of what value to the in-service teacher is a knowledge of philosophical models of teaching such as those examined in this article? Justify your view.

2. Are the three models presented in this selection different in kind, or only in emphasis? Qualify your answer. What are some of the concepts of each model that are applicable to contemporary teaching practices?

3. Which of the theories of learning implicit in each model do you believe to be superior? Justify your answer by identifying the strengths and weaknesses of each view.

4. Reconsider your answer to question three. If your chief criterion was applicability to actual teaching situations, would you make the same response? If so, explain why. If not, specify the changes that you would make and state your reasons for making each alteration.

5. What are the implications for teaching of Augustine's view that all knowledge results from a process of internal illumination and cannot be directly communicated?

6. Scheffler suggests that multiple evolving traditions should provide an important focus for teaching. Would it be accurate to say that he is advocating a traditional approach to teaching? Substantiate your answer.

7. Formulate a teaching philosophy which incorporates the more valuable elements of each of the three models presented in this selection. Justify your choices of the components included in the synthesis.

Israel Scheffler, "Philosophical Models of Teaching," *Harvard Educational Review,* 35, Spring 1965, 188–200. Copyright © 1965 by President and Fellows of Harvard College.

I. Introduction

Teaching may be characterized as an activity aimed at the achievement of learning, and practiced in such manner as to respect the student's intellectual integrity and capacity for independent judgment. Such a characterization is important for at least two reasons: First, it brings out the intentional nature of teaching, the fact that teaching is a distinctive goal-oriented activity, rather than a distinctively patterned sequence of behavioral steps executed by the teacher. Secondly, it differentiates the activity of teaching from such other activities as propaganda, conditioning, suggestion, and indoctrination, which are aimed at modifying the person but strive at all costs to avoid a genuine engagement of his judgment on underlying issues.

This characterization of teaching, which I believe to be correct, fails, nevertheless, to answer certain critical questions of the

*This paper was presented at Brown University as the Marshall Woods lecture on Education for 1964. Variant versions were delivered to the Harvard-Lexington Summer Program for 1964, and to the Boston University Philosophy Club.

17

teacher: What sort of learning shall I aim to achieve? In what does such learning consist? How shall I strive to achieve it? Such questions are, respectively, normative, epistemological, and empirical in import, and the answers that are provided for them give point and substance to the educational enterprise. Rather than trying to separate these questions, however, and deal with each abstractly and explicitly, I should like, on the present occasion, to approach them indirectly and as a group, through a consideration of three influential models of teaching, which provide, or at any rate suggest, certain relevant answers. These models do not so much aim to *describe* teaching as to *orient* it, by weaving a coherent picture out of epistemological, psychological, and normative elements. Like all models, they simplify, but such simplification is a legitimate way of highlighting what are thought to be important features of the subject. The primary issue, in each case, is whether these features are indeed critically important, whether we should allow our educational thinking to be guided by a model which fastens upon them, or whether we should rather reject or revise the model in question. Although I shall mention some historical affiliations of each model, I make no pretense to historical accuracy. My main purpose is, rather, systematic or dialectical, that is, to outline and examine the three models and to see what, if anything, each has to offer us in our own quest for a satisfactory conception of teaching. I turn, then, first to what may be called the "impression model."

II. The Impression Model

The impression model is perhaps the simplest and most widespread of the three, picturing the mind essentially as sifting and storing the external impressions to which it is receptive. The desired end result of teaching is an accumulation in the learner of basic elements fed in from without, organized and processed in standard ways, but, in any event, not generated by the learner himself. In the empiricist variant of this model generally associated with John Locke, learning involves the input by experience of simple ideas of sensation and reflection, which are clustered, related, generalized, and retained by the mind. Blank at birth, the mind is thus formed by its particular experiences, which it keeps available for its future use. In Locke's words, (Bk. II, Ch. I, Sec. 2 of the *Essay Concerning Human Understanding*):

> Let us then suppose the mind to be, as we say, white paper, void of all characters, without any ideas; how comes it to be furnished? Whence comes it by that vast store, which the busy and boundless fancy of man has painted on it with an almost endless variety? Whence has it all the materials of reason and knowledge? To this I answer, in one word, From experience; in that all our knowledge is founded, and from that it ultimately derives itself. Our observation, employed either about external sensible objects, or about the internal operations of our minds, perceived and reflected on by ourselves, is that which supplies our understandings with all the materials of thinking. These two are the fountains of knowledge, from whence all the ideas we have, or can naturally have, do spring.

Teaching, by implication, should concern itself with exercising the mental powers engaged in receiving and processing incoming ideas, more particularly powers of perception, discrimination, retention, combination, abstraction, and representation. But, more important, teaching needs to strive for the optimum selection and organization of this experiential input. For potentially, the teacher has enormous power; by controlling the input of sensory units, he can, to a large degree, shape the mind. As Dewey remarked,[1]

> Locke's statements . . . seemed to do justice to both mind and matter. . . . One of the two supplied the matter of knowledge and the object upon which the mind should work. The other supplied definite mental powers, which were few in number and which might be trained by specific exercises.

The process of learning in the child was taken as paralleling the growth of knowledge generally, for all knowledge is constructed out of elementary units of experience, which are grouped, related, and generalized. The teacher's object should thus be to provide data not only useful in themselves, but collectively rich enough to support the progressive growth of adult knowledge in the learner's mind.

The impression model, as I have sketched it, has certain obvious strong points. It sets forth the appeal to experience as a general tool of criticism to be employed in the examination of all claims and doctrines, and it demands that they square with it. Surely such a demand is legitimate, for knowledge does rest upon experience in some way or other. Further, the mind is, in a clear sense, as the impression model suggests, a function of its particular experiences, and it is capable of increased growth with experience. The richness and variety of the child's experiences are thus important considerations in the process of educational planning.

The impression model nevertheless suffers from fatal difficulties. The notions of absolutely simple ideas and of abstract mental powers improvable through exercise have been often and rightly criticized as mythological:[2] Simplicity is a relative, not an absolute, concept and reflects a particular way of analyzing experience; it is, in short, not given but made. And mental powers or faculties invariant with subject matter have,

as everyone knows, been expunged from psychology on empirical as well as theoretical grounds. A more fundamental criticism, perhaps, is that the implicit conception of the growth of knowledge is false. Knowledge is not achieved through any standard set of operations for the processing of sensory particulars, however conceived. Knowledge is, first and foremost, embodied in language, and involves a conceptual apparatus not derivable from the sensory data but imposed upon them. Nor is such apparatus built into the human mind; it is, at least in good part a product of guesswork and invention, borne along by culture and by custom. Knowledge further involves *theory,* and theory is surely not simply a matter of generalizing the data, even assuming such data organized by a given conceptual apparatus. Theory is a creative and individualistic enterprise that goes beyond the data in distinctive ways, involving not only generalization, but postulation of entities, deployment of analogies, evaluation of relative simplicity, and, indeed, invention of new languages. Experience is relevant to knowledge through providing tests of our theories; it does not automatically generate these theories, even when processed by the human mind. That we have the theories we do is, therefore, a fact, not simply about the human mind, but about our history and our intellectual heritage.

In the process of learning, the child gets not only sense experiences but the language and theory of his heritage in complicated linkages with discriminable contexts. He is heir to the complex culture of belief built up

1. John Dewey, *Democracy and Education.* New York: The Macmillan Company, 1916, p. 62.
2. Dewey, *Ibid.,* "the supposed original faculties of observation, recollection, willing, thinking, etc., are purely mythological. There are no such ready-made powers waiting to be exercised and thereby trained."

out of innumerable creative acts of intellect of the past, and comprising a patterned view of the world. To give the child even the richest selection of sense data or particular facts alone would in no way guarantee his building up anything resembling what we think of as knowledge, much less his developing the ability to retrieve and apply such knowledge in new circumstances.

A *verbal* variant of the impression model of teaching naturally suggests itself, then, as having certain advantages over the *sensory* version we have just considered: What is to be impressed on the mind is not only sense experience but language and, moreover, accepted theory. We need to feed in not only sense data but the correlated verbal patterning of such data, that is, the *statements* about such data which we ourselves accept. The student's knowledge consists in his stored accumulation of these statements, which have application to new cases in the future. He is no longer, as before, assumed capable of generating our conceptual heritage by operating in certain standard ways on his sense data, for part of what *we* are required to feed into his mind is this very heritage itself.

This verbal variant, which has close affinities to contemporary behaviorism, does have certain advantages over its predecessor, but retains grave inadequacies still, as a model of teaching. To *store* all accepted theories is not the same as being able to *use* them properly in context. Nor, even if some practical correlation with sense data is achieved, does it imply an understanding of what is thus stored, nor an appreciation of the theoretical motivation and experimental evidence upon which it rests.

All versions of the impression model, finally, have this defect: They fail to make adequate room for radical *innovation* by the learner. We do not, after all, feed into the learner's mind all that we hope he will have as an end result of our teaching. Nor can we construe the critical surplus as generated in standard ways out of materials we do supply. We do not, indeed cannot, so construe insight, understanding, new applications of our theories, new theories, new achievements in scholarship, history, poetry, philosophy. There is a fundamental gap which teaching cannot bridge simply by expansion or reorganization of the curriculum input. This gap sets *theoretical* limits to the power and control of the teacher; moreover, it is where his control ends that his fondest hopes for education begin.

III. The Insight Model

The next model I shall consider, the "insight model," represents a radically different approach. Where the impression model supposes the teacher to be conveying ideas or bits of knowledge into the student's mental treasury, the insight model denies the very possibility of such conveyance. Knowledge, it insists, is a matter of vision, and vision cannot be dissected into elementary sensory or verbal units that can be conveyed from one person to another. It can, at most, be stimulated or prompted by what the teacher does, and if it indeed occurs, it goes beyond what is thus done. Vision defines and organizes particular experiences, and points up their significance. It is vision, or insight into meaning, which makes the crucial difference between simply storing and reproducing learned sentences, on the one hand, and understanding their basis and application, on the other.

The insight model is due to Plato, but I shall here consider the version of St. Augustine, in his dialogue, "The Teacher,"[3] for it

3. *Ancient Christian Writers*, No. 9, St. Augustine, "The Teacher," edited by J. Quasten and J. C. Plumpe, translated and annotated by J. M. Colleran, Newman Press, Westminster, Md: 1950; relevant passages may also be found in Kingsley Price, *Education and Philosophical Thought*, Boston: Allyn and Bacon, Inc., 1962, pp. 145–159.

bears precisely on the points we have dealt with. Augustine argues roughly as follows: The teacher is commonly thought to convey knowledge by his use of language. But knowledge, or rather *new* knowledge, is not conveyed simply by words sounding in the ear. Words are mere noises unless they signify realities present in some way to the mind. Hence a paradox: If the student already knows the realities to which the teacher's words refer, the teacher teaches him nothing new. Whereas, if the student does not know these realities, the teacher's words can have no meaning for him, and must be mere noises. Augustine concludes that language must have a function wholly distinct from that of the signification of realities; it is used to *prompt* people in certain ways. The teacher's words, in particular, prompt the student to search for realities not already known by him. Finding these realities, which are illuminated for him by internal vision, he acquires new knowledge for himself, though indirectly as a result of the teacher's prompting activity. To *believe* something simply on the basis of authority or hearsay is indeed possible, on Augustine's view; to *know* it is not. Mere beliefs may, in his opinion, of course, be useful; they are not therefore knowledge. For knowledge, in short, requires the individual himself to have a grasp of the realities lying behind the words.

The insight model is strong where the impression model is weakest. While the latter, in its concern with the conservation of knowledge, fails to do justice to innovation, the former addresses itself from the start to the problem of *new* knowledge resulting from teaching. Where the latter stresses atomic manipulable bits at the expense of understanding, the former stresses primarily the acquisition of insight. Where the latter gives inordinate place to the feeding in of materials from the outside, the former

stresses the importance of firsthand inspection of realities by the student, the necessity for the student to earn his knowledge by his own efforts.

I should argue, nevertheless, that the case offered by Augustine for the prompting theory is not, as it stands, satisfactory. If the student does not know the realities behind the teacher's words, these words are, presumably, mere noises and can serve only to prompt the student to inquire for himself. Yet if they *are* mere noises, how can they even serve to prompt? If they are not understood in any way by the student, how can they lead him to search for the appropriate realities which underlie them? Augustine, furthermore, allows that a person may believe, though not know, what he accepts on mere authority, without having confronted the relevant realities. Such a person might, presumably, pass from the state of belief to that of knowledge, as a result of prompting, under certain conditions. But what, we may ask, could have been the content of his initial belief if the formulation of it had been literally unintelligible to him? The prompting theory, it seems, will not do as a way of escaping Augustine's original paradox.

There is, however, an easier escape. For the paradox itself rests on a confusion of the meaning of *words* with that of *sentences*. Let me explain. Augustine holds that words acquire intelligibility only through acquaintance with reality. Now it may perhaps be initially objected that understanding a word does not always require acquaintance with its signified reality, for words may also acquire intelligibility through definition, lacking such direct acquaintance. But let us waive this objection and grant, for the sake of argument, that understanding a word *always* does require such acquaintance; it still does not follow that understanding a true sentence similarly requires acquaintance with the state of affairs which it represents.

We understand new sentences all the time, on the basis of an understanding of their constituent words and of the grammar by which they are concatenated. Thus, given a sentence signifying some fact, it is simply not true that, unless the student already knows this fact, the sentence must be mere noise to him. For he can understand its meaning indirectly, by a synthesis of its parts, and be led thereafter to inquire whether it is, in reality, true or false.

If my argument is correct, then Augustine's paradox of teaching can be simply rejected, on the ground that we *can* understand statements before becoming acquainted with their signified realities. It follows that the teacher can indeed *inform* the student of new facts by means of language. And it further seems to follow that the basis for Augustine's prompting theory of teaching wholly collapses. We are back to the impression model, with the teacher using language not to prompt the student to inner vision, but simply to inform him of new facts.

The latter conclusion seems to me, however, mistaken. For it does *not* follow that the student will *know* these new facts simply because he has been *informed;* on this point Augustine seems to me perfectly right. It is knowing, after all, that Augustine is interested in, and knowing requires something more than the receipt and acceptance of true information. It requires that the student earn the right to his assurance of the truth of the information in question. New *information,* in short, can be intelligibly conveyed by statements; new *knowledge* cannot. Augustine, I suggest, confuses the two cases, arguing in effect for the impossibility of conveying new knowledge by words, on the basis of an alleged similar impossibility for information. I have been urging the falsity of the latter premise. But if Augustine's

premise is indeed false, his conclusion as regards knowledge seems to me perfectly true: To *know* the proposition expressed by a sentence is more than just to have been told it, to have grasped its meaning, and to have accepted it. It is to have earned the right, through one's own effort or position, to an assurance of its truth.

Augustine puts the matter in terms of an insightful searching of reality, an inquiry carried out by oneself, and resting in no way on authority. Indeed, he is perhaps too austerely individualistic in this regard, rejecting even legitimate arguments from authority as a basis for knowledge. But his main thesis seems to me correct: One cannot convey new knowledge by words alone. For knowledge is not simply a storage of information by the learner.

The teacher does, of course, employ *language,* according to the insight model, but its primary function is not to impress his statements on the student's mind for later reproduction. The teacher's statements are, rather, instrumental to the student's own search of reality and vision thereof; teaching is consummated in the student's own insight. The reference to such insight seems to explain, at least partially, how the student can be expected to apply his learning to new situations in the future. For, having acquired this learning not merely by external suggestion but through a personal engagement with reality, the student can appreciate the particular fit which his theories have with real circumstances, and, hence, the proper occasions for them to be brought into play.

There is, furthermore, no reason to construe adoption of the insight model as eliminating the impression model altogether. For the impression model, it may be admitted, does reflect something genuine and important, but mislocates it. It reflects the increase of the culture's written lore, the growth of knowledge as a public and recorded possession. Furthermore, it reflects the primary importance of conserving such knowledge, as a collective heritage. But knowledge in this public sense has nothing to do with the process of learning and the activity of teaching, that is, with the growth of knowledge in the individual learner. The public treasury of knowledge constitutes a basic source of materials for the teacher, but he cannot hope to transfer it bit by bit in growing accumulation within the student's mind. In conducting his teaching, he must rather give up the hope of such simple transfer, and strive instead to encourage individual insight into the meaning and use of public knowledge.

Despite the important emphases of the insight model which we have been considering, there are, however, two respects in which it falls short. One concerns the simplicity of its constituent notion of insight, or vision, as a condition of knowing; the other relates to its specifically cognitive bias, which it shares with the impression model earlier considered. First, the notion that what is crucial in knowledge is a vision of underlying realities, a consulting of what is found within the mind, is far too simple. Certainly, as we have seen, the knower must satisfy *some* condition beyond simply being informed, in order to have the right to his assurance on the matter in question. But to construe this condition in terms of an intellectual inspection of reality is not at all satisfactory. It is plausible only if we restrict ourselves to very simple cases of truths accessible to observation or introspection. As soon as we attempt to characterize the knowing of propositions normally encountered in practical affairs, in the sciences, in politics, history, or the law, we realize that the concept of a *vision of reality* is impossibly

simple. Vision is just the wrong metaphor. What seems indubitably more appropriate in all these cases of knowing is an emphasis on the processes of deliberation, argument, judgment, appraisal of reasons *pro* and *con*, weighing of evidence, appeal to principles, and decision-making, none of which fits at all well with the insight model. This model, in short, does not make adequate room for principled deliberation in the characterization of knowing. It is in terms of such principled deliberation, or the potentiality for it, rather than in terms of simple vision, that the distinctiveness of knowing is primarily to be understood.

Secondly, the insight model is specifically cognitive in emphasis, and cannot readily be stretched so as to cover important aspects of teaching. We noted above, for example, that the application of truths to new situations is somewhat better off in the insight than in the impression model, since the appropriateness of a truth for new situations is better judged with awareness of underlying realities than without. But a judgment of appropriateness is not all there is to application; habits of proper execution are also required, and insight itself does not necessitate such habits. Insight also fails to cover the concept of character and the related notions of attitude and disposition. Character, it is clear, goes beyond insight as well as beyond the impression of information. For it involves general principles of conduct logically independent of both insight and the accumulation of information. Moreover, what has been said of character can be applied also to the various institutions of civilization, including those which channel cognition itself. Science, for example, is not just a collection of true insights; it is embodied in a living tradition composed of demanding principles of judgment and conduct. Beyond the cognitive insight, lies the fundamental commitment to principles by which insights are to be criticized and assessed, in the light of publicly available evidence or reasons. In sum, then, the shortcoming of the insight model may be said to lie in the fact that it provides no role for the concept of *principles,* and the associated concept of *reasons.* This omission is very serious indeed, for the concept of principles and the concept of reasons together underlie not only the notions of rational deliberation and critical judgment, but also the notions of rational and moral conduct.

IV. The Rule Model

The shortcoming of the insight model just discussed is remedied in the "rule model," which I associate with Kant. For Kant, the primary philosophical emphasis is on reason, and reason is always a matter of abiding by general rules or principles. Reason stands always in contrast with inconsistency and with expediency, in the judgment of particular issues. In the cognitive realm, reason is a kind of justice to the evidence, a fair treatment of the merits of the case, in the interests of truth. In the moral realm, reason is action on principle, action which therefore does not bend with the wind, nor lean to the side of advantage or power out of weakness or self-interest. Whether in the cognitive or the moral realm, reason is always a matter of treating equal reasons equally, and of judging the issues in the light of general principles to which one has bound oneself.

In thus binding myself to a set of principles, I act freely; this is my dignity as a being with the power of choice. But my own free commitment obligates me to obey the principles I have adopted, when they rule against me. This is what fairness or consistency in conduct means: if I could judge rea-

sons differently when they bear on my interests, or disregard my principles when they conflict with my own advantage, I should have no principles at all. The concepts of *principles, reasons,* and *consistency* thus go together and they apply both in the cognitive judgment of beliefs and the moral assessment of conduct. In fact, they define a general concept of rationality. A rational man is one who is consistent in thought and in action, abiding by impartial and generalizable principles freely chosen as binding upon himself. Rationality is an essential aspect of human dignity and the rational goal of humanity is to construct a society in which such dignity shall flower, a society so ordered as to adjudicate rationally the affairs of free rational agents, an international and democratic republic. The job of education is to develop character in the broadest sense, that is, principled thought and action, in which the dignity of man is manifest.

In contrast to the insight model, the rule model clearly emphasizes the role of principles in the exercise of cognitive judgment. The strong point of the insight model can thus be preserved: The knower must indeed satisfy a further condition beyond the mere receiving and storing of a bit of information. But this condition need not, as in the insight model, be taken to involve simply the vision of an underlying reality; rather, it generally involves the capacity for a principled assessment of reasons bearing on justification of the belief in question. The knower, in short, must typically earn the right to confidence in his belief by acquiring the capacity to make a reasonable case for the belief in question. Nor is it sufficient for this case to have been explicitly taught. What is generally expected of the knower is that his autonomy be evidenced in the ability to construct and evaluate fresh and alternative arguments, the power to innovate, rather than just the capacity to reproduce stale arguments earlier stored. The emphasis on innovation, which we found to be an advantage of the insight model, is thus capable of being preserved by the rule model as well.

Nor does the rule model in any way deny the psychological phenomenon of insight. It merely stresses that insight itself, wherever it is relevant to decision or judgment, is filtered through a network of background principles. It brings out thereby that insight is not an isolated, momentary, or personal matter, that the growth of knowledge is not be be construed as a personal interaction between teacher and student, but rather as mediated by general principles definitive of rationality.

Furthermore, while the previous models, as we have seen, are peculiarly and narrowly *cognitive* in relevance, the rule model embraces *conduct* as well as cognition, itself broadly conceived as including processes of judgment and deliberation. Teaching, it suggests, should be geared not simply to the transfer of information nor even to the development of insight, but to the inculcation of principled judgment and conduct, the building of autonomous and rational character which underlies the enterprises of science, morality and culture. Such inculcation should not, of course, be construed mechanically. Rational character and critical judgment grow only through increased participation in adult experience and criticism, through treatment which respects the dignity of learner as well as teacher. We have here, again, a radical gap which cannot be closed by the teacher's efforts alone. He must rely on the spirit of rational dialogue and critical reflection for the development of character, acknowledging that this implies the freedom to reject as well as to accept what is taught. Kant himself holds, however, that rational principles are somehow embedded in the structure of the human mind, so that education builds on a solid foundation. In any event, the stakes are high, for on such building by education depends the prospect of humanity as an ideal quality of life.

There is much of value in the rule model, as I have sketched it. Certainly, rationality is a fundamental cognitive and moral virtue and as such should, I believe, form a basic objective of teaching. Nor should the many historical connotations of the term "rationality" here mislead us. There is no intent to suggest a faculty of reason, nor to oppose reason to experience or to the emotions. Nor is rationality being construed as the process of making logical deductions. What is in point here is simply the autonomy of the student's judgment, his right to seek reasons in support of claims upon his credibilities and loyalties, and his correlative obligation to deal with such reasons in a principled manner.

Moreover, adoption of the rule model does not necessarily exclude what is important in the other two models; in fact, it can be construed quite plausibly as supplementing their legitimate emphasis. For, intermediate between the public treasury of accumulated lore mirrored by the impression model, and the personal and intuitive grasp of the student mirrored by the insight model, it places general principles of rational judgment capable of linking them.

Yet, there is something too formal and abstract in the rule model, as I have thus far presented it. For the operative principles of rational judgment at any given time are, after all, much more detailed and specific than a mere requirement of formal consistency. Such consistency is certainly fundamental, but the way its demands are concretely interpreted, elaborated, and supplemented in any field of inquiry or practice, varies with the field, the state of knowledge, and the advance of relevant methodological sophistication. The concrete rules governing inference and procedure in the special sciences, for example, are surely not all embedded in the human mind, even if the demands of formal consistency, as such, *are* universally compelling. These concrete rules and standards, techniques and methodological criteria evolve and grow with the advance of knowledge itself; they form a live tradition of rationality in the realm of science.

Indeed, the notion of tradition is a better guide here, it seems to me, than appeal to the innate structure of the human mind. Rationality in natural inquiry is embodied in the relatively young tradition of science, which defines and redefines those principles by means of which evidence is to be interpreted and meshed with theory. Rational judgment in the realm of science is, consequently, judgment which accords with such principles, as crystallized at the time in question. To teach rationality in science is to interiorize these principles in the student, but furthermore, to introduce him to the live and evolving *tradition* of natural science, which forms their significant context of development and purpose.

Scholarship in history is subject to an analogous interpretation, for beyond the formal demands of reason, in the sense of consistency, there is a concrete tradition of technique and methodology defining the historian's procedure and his assessment of reasons for or against particular historical accounts. To teach rationality in history is, in effect, here also to introduce the student to a live tradition of historical scholarship. Similar remarks might be made also with respect to other areas, e.g. law, philosophy

and the politics of democratic society. The fundamental point is that rationality cannot be taken simply as an abstract and general ideal. It is embodied in *multiple evolving traditions,* in which the basic condition holds that issues are resolved by reference to *reasons,* themselves defined by *principles* purporting to be impartial and universal. These traditions should, I believe, provide an important focus for teaching.

V. Conclusion

I have intimated that I find something important in each of the models we have considered. The impression model reflects, as I have said, the cumulative growth of knowledge in its *public* sense. Our aim in teaching should surely be to preserve and extend this growth. But we cannot do this by storing it piecemeal within the learner. We preserve it, as the insight model stresses, only if we succeed in transmitting the live spark that keeps it growing, the insight which is a product of each learner's efforts to make sense of public knowledge in his own terms, and to confront it with reality. Finally, as the rule model suggests, such confrontation involves deliberation and judgment, and hence presupposes general and impartial principles governing the assessment of reasons bearing on the issues. Without such guiding principles, the very conception of rational deliberation collapses, and the concepts of rational and moral conduct, moreover, lose their meaning. Our teaching needs thus to introduce students to those principles we ourselves acknowledge as fundamental, general, and impartial, in the various departments of thought and action.

We need not pretend that these principles or ours are immutable or innate. It is enough that they are what we ourselves acknowledge, that they are the best we know, and that we are prepared to improve them should the need and occasion arise. Such improvement is possible, however, only if we succeed in passing on, too, the multiple live traditions in which they are embodied, and in which a sense of their history, spirit, and direction may be discerned. Teaching, from this point of view, is clearly not, as the behaviorists would have it, a matter of the teacher's shaping the student's behavior or of controlling his mind. It is a matter of passing on those traditions of principled thought and action which define the rational life for teacher as well as student.

As Professor Richard Peters has recently written,[4]

The critical procedures by means of which established content is assessed, revised, and adapted to new discoveries have public criteria written into them that stand as impersonal standards to which both teacher and learner must give their allegiance. . . . To liken education to therapy, to conceive of it as imposing a pattern on another person or as fixing the environment so that he 'grows,' fails to do justice to the shared impersonality both of the content that is handed on and of the criteria by reference to which it is criticized and revised. The teacher is not a detached operator who is bringing about some kind of result in another person which is external to him. His task is to try to get others on the inside of a public form of life that he shares and considers to be worthwhile.

In teaching, we do not impose our wills on the student, but introduce him to the many mansions of the heritage in which we ourselves strive to live, and to the improvement of which we are ourselves dedicated.

4. *Education as Initiation,* an inaugural lecture delivered at the University of London Institute of Education, 9 December 1963; published for The University of London Institute of Education by Evans Brothers, Ltd., London.

Teaching Strategy and Learning

Hilda Taba

EDITORS' QUESTIONS:

1. Critically analyze the model of teaching presented by the author. Of what significance is this model to you as a classroom teacher?

2. Compare and contrast the different analyses of the teaching act done by Scheffler, Smith, Flanders, Hughes and Taba. In what ways are they similar? How are they different?

3. If you were to formulate your own description of teaching, which of the components presented by each author would you incorporate in your model? Which would you eliminate? Which would you modify or alter? Justify whatever modifications you make.

4. Develop your own model of teaching. Develop a visual representation of your model.

Hilda Taba, "Teaching Strategy and Learning," *The California Journal for Instructional Improvement,* (December 1963), 3–11. Reprinted with the permission of *The California Journal for Instructional Improvement.*

Recently, attention has been turning to one aspect of the educational process: the actual strategy of teaching or instruction in the classroom. Several research projects have been focused on investigating the teaching acts and teaching strategies in the classroom. The American Research Association has just published a voluminous handbook on research on teaching.[1] Suggestions have been appearing regarding the need for a theory of instruction.[2]

This aspect of the educational process has been somewhat neglected. In curriculum planning, a reasonable care is exercised in selecting and organizing the content. Whatever weaknesses exist in this process are caused by deficiencies in the theory and methodology of curriculum planning, not by lack of attention or effort. In contrast, the selection and organization of learning ac-

tivities, and the corresponding instructional strategy, are left to the judgment of individual teachers. The most one can find in curriculum guides are general injunctions regarding a suggested approach to a subject, occasionally an unorganized list of suggested learning activities—a smorgasbord from which the teacher is invited to select whatever pleases his or her fancy. Very little is provided regarding the principles of selection, let alone a methodology for the guidance of learning activities in the classroom.

According to some recent writers, research on teaching is in a similarly poor condition. It is pointed out, in fact, that there is

1. N. L. Gage, ed. *Handbook of Research on Teaching.* Rand McNally, 1963.
2. Elizabeth Z. Howard. Needed: A Conceptual Scheme for Teacher Education. *The School Review.* Spring, 1963, pp. 12–26.

no theory of instruction adequate enough to develop effective strategies of teaching. We know relatively little about the activities in which a teacher engages, the problems encountered in classroom instruction, and still less about the effect of teaching acts or of teaching strategies on learning. After reviewing the numerous studies of the relationship of teacher personality to effective teaching, Getzels and Jackson conclude that

> Despite the critical importance of the problem and a half-century of prodigious research effort, very little is known for certain about the nature and measurement of teacher personality, or about the relation between teacher personality and effectiveness. The regrettable fact is that many of the studies so far have not produced significant results. Many others have produced only pedestrian findings. For example, it is said after the usual inventory tabulation, that good teachers are friendly, cheerful, sympathetic, and morally virtuous rather than cruel, depressed, unsympathetic, and morally depraved. But when this has been said, not very much that is especially useful has been revealed. For what conceivable human interaction—and teaching implies first and foremost a human interaction—is not the better if the people involved are friendly, cheerful, sympathetic, and virtuous rather than the opposite? What is needed is not research leading to the reiteration of the self-evident, but to the discovery of specific and distinctive features of teacher personality and of the effective teacher.[3]

Sarason goes even as far as to say that teaching and teacher education is an unstudied problem.[4]

Assumptions Regarding Teaching

Some of the causes for this neglect may be found in the assumptions about teaching which have held stubbornly through decades of research data to the contrary. Throughout the history of professional concern about the processes of education, there has never been sufficient appreciation of the complexity of the job we call teaching. One or another simplified assumption has prevailed about the nature and function of teaching. Among the simplest and most stubborn has been the notion that the chief, if not the only function of teaching is to impart knowledge. Currently, this conception of teaching is again in vogue. Such a concept of teaching underlies, for example, the recent Conant report on teacher education.[5] Recent credential legislation in California, as well as a spate of plans for teacher education, testifies to the fact that the mastery of the liberal arts and sciences is regarded as a guarantee of effectiveness in teaching. The assumption seems to be that the knowledge of content areas to be taught bears a simple relationship to the effectiveness of teaching. While there is no doubt that extending the mastery of academic background would improve teaching, it would be foolhardy to assume that strengthening this background alone would assure effective teaching.[6]

Another widely accepted assumption about teaching is that it is the product of mastering certain specified methods for certain subjects, such as history, physics, and arithmetic. A large portion of teacher education—the methods courses—is predicated on this assumption. Often, the problem of methodology is furthermore narrowed down to *the* method. Acrimonious debates about teaching reading center largely on pitting one method against another as *the* one by which to teach children to read. This

3. J. W. Getzels and P. W. Jackson. "The Teacher Personality and Characteristics" in American Educational Research Assn., N. L. Gage, ed., *Handbook of Research on Teaching,* Rand McNally, 1963, p. 574.
4. K. Davidson Sarason and B. Blatt. *The Preparation of Teachers—an Unstudied Problem in Education.* John Wiley, 1962.
5. James B. Conant. *The Education of American Teachers.* McGraw-Hill Book Co., Inc., 1963.
6. Sarason *et al., op. cit.,* pp. 2–3.

conception of teaching not only takes for granted that there is one "right" method to teach anything, but that this method is equally effective in the hands of all teachers, for all kinds of children, and under all varieties of learning conditions.[7] It also implies that any particular method can be developed and applied apart from the larger rationale of the general learning process.

A third assumption is that good teachers are born, not made. Those operating on this assumption transform teaching into a sort of mystique: an art, the secrets of which a few "good" teachers grasp intuitively or stumble into accidentally. Such a conception practically bars an objective analysis of the processes of teaching or learning, and denies the possibility of imparting that "art" to prospective teachers by such ordinary means as education.

Research on Teaching

Criticisms are voiced also about the theoretical framework responsible for fruitless research on teaching and teacher education. The most basic of these criticisms is the charge that the concepts of method have been inferred from studies of learning carried on in situations which have little or no relationship to the classroom. Page, for example, suggests that there has been a gross misapplication of behavioral sciences, especially of psychology, and that both the psychologists and educators have engaged in verbal magic in translating findings applicable only to a very limited situation, such as reactions of hooded rats to electric shock, in a laboratory, first to behavior in general and then to learning in a classroom.[8]

Partly because of this verbal magic, models for conceptualizing teaching tend to be in global terms which makes it impossible to establish a relationship of a given method to a particular learning theory. The result is a lack of integration between descriptions of teaching methods and of the learning models. If one concedes, further, that the learning theories themselves do not differentiate between different types of learning, such as developing a skill, learning to think, and acquiring an attitude, it is not surprising that a principle of learning relevant to one category of learning is applied to all types of learning. Overgeneralizing from the particular learning principles with limited applicability has been a convenient pastime of both the learning theorists and the educators who apply the findings of research on learning. This is true of such recent developments as the use of the reinforcement principle, which encompasses a minute aspect of learning, in developing teaching machines with vastly broader functions.

Evaluation of teaching effectiveness for purposes of research on selection and retention is drawing a barrage of disparagement also. Medley and Mitzel describe one circular research process which goes as follows:

Research in teacher effectiveness began with studies in which large numbers of laymen were asked to recall great teachers they had once had, and tell the investigator what characteristics made them great. The investigator would then classify and summarize these characteristics and publish some sort of list. Later, researchers refined this method by asking only people qualified as experts, a large part of whose expertise must have consisted in familiarity with these very same lists, to identify the effective teachers. The final refinement was to have the experts rate teachers' possession of qualities which, according to the same lists, were characteristic of effective teachers. Nowhere in this circular process was there verification of the assumption that

7. Donald M. Medley and Harold E. Mitzel, "The Scientific Study of Teacher Behavior" in Arno Bellack, ed., *Theory and Research in Teaching,* Teachers College, Bureau of Publications, New York, 1963, pp. 85–88.
8. Ellis Batten Page. "Behavioral Theory, Verbal Magic, and Education," *Educational Theory,* V. 12, No. 2, April 1962, pp. 74–75.

teachers originally judged to be more effective were actually producing greater changes in pupils than teachers identified as less effective.[9]

Rating as a device of evaluating teaching effectiveness suffers in addition from the fact that different raters use different criteria of effectiveness, especially when these criteria or their observable indices are not too clearly defined.

The fundamental trouble with both the studies of teacher characteristics and the rating of teacher effectiveness is that both are based on an inappropriate conception of teaching as a series of discrete competencies, kinds of behavior, or characteristics. Teaching is an organic complex in which each specific behavior, such as the degree of affective response or of structuring, acquires a different meaning depending on the nature of the whole complex.

It is quite evident, also, that it is difficult to assess the effectiveness of teaching without comparing teacher behavior to the changes it produces in students, a criterion which is attempted only in a few studies. However, the results of these studies are usually inconclusive, partly because of defective analysis of teaching effectiveness, but largely because the measures of student achievement are limited in the scope of changes that they measure. Throughout the problem of studying teaching and evaluating its effectiveness runs the difficulty of a lack of differentiation between the processes required by different types of learning, such as learning facts, learning to think, developing attitudes. Consequently, the teaching strategies required by each type are not sharply enough articulated to accommodate the difficulties.

These difficulties have not only retarded research on teaching and handicapped experimentation with teaching strategies in school situations. They have also affected teacher training, which tends to center either on specific packaged devices offered as methods of various subjects, or on generalized philosophical principles offered as injunctions, without sufficient bridges to enable a teacher to implement them in classroom instruction. Neither of these approaches have affected prospective teachers sufficiently to prevent them from reproducing in their teaching the methods they experienced as learners, or from imitating the influential staff members in the schools into which they enter. Thus, both the conceptions of teaching and the ways of teacher training seem to conspire to regenerate the most tradition-bound (and often the least adequate) teaching styles, which are inadequate for coping with the complexities of the teaching-learning situation in schools of today.

Recent Signs of Rejuvenation

Under the twin impacts of continued criticism of education and an increased flow of money into research and experimentation, a new interest has been kindled in the theory of instruction and in the analysis of the teaching process. Conviction is growing that to understand either, we must study teaching as it occurs in the classroom, instead of inferring its effectiveness from the personality characteristics of teachers, or from a general list of *a priori* competencies.

In this shift of the focus of studying teaching and learning in the classroom, the description of teaching acts has become the chief tool for securing information. Recent studies of teaching focus on the description of teaching acts by grouping teacher behaviors from observation or the transcriptions of classroom interaction into certain functional categories. Different researchers use

9. Medley and Mitzel, *op. cit.*, pp. 83–84.

different categories or functions, depending upon their particular ideas about what is important about teaching.

Smith, one of the first students of teaching through an analysis of classroom interaction, maintains that in order to develop an adequate theory of didactics, a description of the actions of teachers must first be made, and then translated into tactics of teaching. He maintains that such description should cut through the verbal curtain represented in such terms as the "method," "problem solving," "induction," and "deduction," and free us to look at the actual instructional operations which may be different from what our linguistic commitments may have led us to believe. He classifies teaching acts according to certain logical characteristics, such as defining, classifying, comparing, contrasting, evaluating, directing, and admonishing.[10]

Flanders is more interested in distinguishing patterns of teacher influence on students, such as domination, integration, and freedom. In his interaction analysis, he uses the following categories to describe teacher behavior: accepting and clarifying feelings; praising and encouraging; accepting and using ideas of students; asking questions of procedure; lecturing; giving directions; criticizing and justifying authority.[11]

The first four he describes as indirect influence, and the last three as direct influences. The indirect influence is assumed to expand the freedom of the student and to make him less dependent on the teacher. By compiling these types of behaviors, in addition to identifying talk initiated by the teacher and talk initiated by students, into a matrix, Flanders plots the concentrations of direct and indirect influence, and from this infers their impact on students' behavior.[12]

Marie Hughes' analysis of the teaching acts is somewhat similar, in that she is also interested in control and freedom. Among the categories she uses to describe teacher acts are: *controlling,* or the acts which tell children what to do, how to go about it, and who should do what; *facilitating,* such as checking, demonstrating, and clarifying; *content development,* such as elaborating the structure of the problem under consideration, or building up data for generalization; *personal responsiveness; positive* and *negative affectivity.*[13] From the frequencies of the teacher acts falling into these categories, she infers certain qualities of teaching and their impact upon what students learn. For example, a large percentage of controlling acts in the repertory of teacher behavior indicates the tendency to limit students' intellectual activity to memory and recall, while a large percentage of acts designated as content development would imply that mental processes other than recall were being developed.[14]

One final step in the rather rapid evolution of the concept of teaching reflected in recent research is the idea that, since the student, equally with the teacher, is an agent of his learning, and hence also of his success or failure to learn, it is impossible to evaluate the effectiveness of teaching without at the same time determining what the student is doing.[15] This concept has led to

10. B. O. Smith. "A Concept of Teaching," *Teachers College Record,* V. 6, No. 5, February 1963, pp. 229–234.

11. Ned A. Flanders, "Intent, Action, and Feedback: A Preparation for Teachers," *J. of Teacher Education,* Vol. XIV, No. 3, Sept. 1963, p. 225.

12. Ned A. Flanders, "Teacher Influence, Pupil Attitudes, and Achievement." Pre-publication manuscript of a proposed Office of Education monograph, U. of Michigan, Ann Arbor, Michigan, 1962, p. 15.

13. Marie Hughes *et al. Development of the Means for the Assessment of the Quality of Teaching in the Elementary School.* U. of Utah, 1959, mimeo.

14. *Ibid.,* pp. 95–97.

15. Mary Jane McCue Aschner. "The Analysis of Verbal Interaction in the Classroom," in *Theory and Research in Teaching,* Arno H. Bellack, ed., Bureau of Publications, Teachers College, Columbia U., 1963, p. 53.

attempts to analyze classroom transactions in multidimensional terms: the behavior of the teacher, the behavior of the student, and the content of the product of their interaction. In other words, it has become necessary to conceive of teaching acts and student responses as being in a reciprocal relationship, in which one generates and influences the other, and both together are responsible for the end product or the quality of learning.

Teaching, then, is being viewed as an extremely complex process, which means a variety of things: giving and imparting knowledge, as well as asking questions; setting tasks and organizing the steps for accomplishing them; creating models for thought, and guiding discovery. Teaching is also viewed as a functional part of a transactional process which includes student response.

Teaching Strategies and Thought Processes

The study called *Thinking in Elementary School Children* might be used as one example of this last step in the evolution of specifying the concept of teaching.[16]

This study was based on the following rationale: first, it seemed evident that it is useless to study teaching in general, as a global process serving any and all objectives of education. Rather, it seemed necessary to identify the particular teaching strategies required by particular types of learning goals, such as generating certain cognitive operations, stimulating certain types of inquiry, and integrating certain bits of information into larger concepts.

These strategies must be composed in the light of some theoretical framework, in which the appropriate dimensions of the teaching-learning situations are staked out. (1) Account must be taken of the relevant

general learning principles, of the factors which predispose students to learning, and of the kinds of stimulation needed. (2) The teaching strategies must be related to the nature of the specific objective and be structured according to its requirements. For example, assigning reading in a text may be the most appropriate way of teaching if the sole aim is to transfer as much knowledge as possible from the book into the heads of the students. However, such a method of teaching is probably totally inappropriate if the purpose is to generate independent methods of inquiry, creative uses of knowledge, or the ability to draw inferences from data. Giving information may be a necessary function at some points of the learning process, while asking questions and seeking answers may be required at other points, and with other learning tasks. (3) Attention must be paid to the optimal structuring of the content, so that it retains its unique nature and is organized for learnability. (4) Finally, certain facts about learners, such as their ability, level of maturity, peculiarities of their mental structures, habits, and skills must be considered.

The role of these factors and how they combine in determining teaching strategy may be illustrated by a case study of developing cognitive skills on the elementary level in the study mentioned above. The description that follows is confined to social studies and to the methods of developing three major aspects of thought: concept formation, making inferences and forming generalizations from interpreting data, and the use of known facts and principles or generalizations to explain new phenomena or predict consequences from described conditions.

16. A research project supported by a grant from the Cooperative Research Branch, U.S. Office of Education, Department of Health, Education, and Welfare. Project No. 1574. Hilda Taba, Director.

Concepts of Cognitive Processes

Several concepts governed the analysis of the above cognitive processes, as well as the building of the appropriate teaching strategies. First, it was assumed that these processes are subject to training, and not in the category of powers which are inherent in the individual. Second, the data from the studies of development of thought indicate that thought follows certain developmental sequences, in which the mastery of each preceding step is a prerequisite to the mastery of the next one. In essence, thought matures through a continuous organization and reorganization of the conceptual structures. At each point of his experience, the individual fits the information he receives into the conceptual scheme he already possesses. This conceptual scheme may be adequate to organizing his environment, or not. However, when the requirements of the situation do not fit his current scheme, the individual is forced to alter, or to extend it to accommodate new information. Piaget calls the fitting process "assimilation" and the process of alteration "accommodation."[17]

The implications of these three concepts about cognitive development—those of developmental sequence, the organization and reorganization of conceptual structure, and the assimilation and accommodation—are many. First, they suggest a major cycle of learning tasks in which the simpler and the concrete cognitive operations precede the complex and abstract operations. For example, if the curriculum content is structured by organizing the concrete details around basic focusing ideas, the actual cycle of learning experiences should begin with the analysis of the concrete instances of these general ideas. These encounters with the specific instances of the general ideas should be frequent enough to enable students to grasp the idea, at least intuitively. This analysis should then be followed by learning tasks which permit the students to understand consciously that which they at first only perceived intuitively: namely, operations to produce generalizations. Finally, to assure that learning generates transfer, experiences are needed which call for the application of that which is learned to new events, or situations.

The fact that there is a developmental cycle suggests that the modification of thought is not in the class of instantaneous learning. Shifts in the patterns and styles or modes of thinking usually require both time and practice. Attainment of high levels of thinking is possible only if both the curriculum and the teaching strategies are shaped to aid a cumulative development over a period of time. This cumulative development requires not only an upward spiral in the content, but also the spiralling in the demands regarding the level of cognitive functioning—a greater degree of precision, a higher level of abstraction, a more refined analysis, etc.

The concept of assimilation and accommodation suggests the need for a systematic rotation of learning tasks which foster assimilation of new information into the existing conceptual scheme with those that require an extension and reorganization of the scheme.[18] A prolonged assimilation of facts without the corresponding reshaping of the conceptual schemes with which to organize them is bound to retard maturation of thought. On the other hand, a premature leap into a more complex or a higher level of thought is likely to immobilize mental activity and to cause reversion to rote learning,

17. Jean Piaget. *The Psychology of Intelligence.* London: Routledge and Kegan Paul, 1947.
18. J. McV. Hunt. *Experience and Intelligence.* New York: The Ronald Press, 1961.

or at any rate to a lower level of thought. Students need a sufficient amount of assimilation to have the "stuff" to think with. But they need, equally, a challenge to stretch their modes of thinking and their conceptual schemes. An appropriate transition from the one to the other requires a proper match between the current level and that which is required. When the level of learning tasks is below the level of thought, the effect is boredom. When questions and learning tasks are too far beyond the existing levels of thought, passive or rote learning is inevitable. Determining the proper match is perhaps one of the most difficult tasks in teaching, and constitutes in effect a new concept of readiness and pacing. This task is complicated by the fact that the mastery of abstract communications, such as language and number, often masks the actual level of thinking. Verbalization may deceive the teacher and lead him to assume that thinking is more advanced than it is, and hence to pushing the child's verbal habits of learning beyond his level of thinking.[19]

The strategy of rotating assimilation and accommodation is fundamentally different from "correcting" the student. The task of reorganization must fall on the student instead of being performed by the teacher, which is the case in correcting errors of thought on the spot, in place of providing experience which leads the student to self-correction. To the extent that the students are led to discover ideas and conceptual organizations on their own, they also acquire a progressively greater control over the information with which they deal.

It is possible, further, that the key to individual differences in learning may be found partially in the difference in the amount of concrete thinking an individual needs before formal thought can emerge.

This difference may distinguish the slow but capable learner from who is incapable of abstract thought. It is not beyond possibility that many a slow learner can achieve a high level of abstract thought, provided that he has the opportunity to examine a greater number of concrete instances than the teaching process now allows. The employment of teaching strategies which are scientifically designed for the development of cognitive skills may make it possible to develop cognitive processes at a much higher level, and in a greater number of students.

The Logic of Three Major Cognitive Tasks

The considerations of the logic of the three cognitive tasks—concept formation, inference, and application of principles—introduces still another cycle of sequences, within the major sequence. To form general concepts from a series of specific facts requires several categories of skills which must be mastered in the following sequence: (1) differentiation $\rightarrow$ (2) grouping $\rightarrow$ (3) labelling. For example, a class studying Latin America may be asked as an opening exercise to enumerate the differences they would expect to find in Latin America. This enumeration involves a differentiation among the various characteristics, such as "climate," "seasons are upside down," "language," "no electricity," "people are poor," etc. The greater the range of these characteristics, the more encompassing will be the eventual concept of "differences in Latin America."

The second step is that of grouping these differences according to "what goes together," such as grouping together climate, weather, and altitude. This operation

19. E. A. Peel. *The Pupil's Thinking*. London: Oldbourne, 1960.

requires the formulation of some basis for grouping. Essentially, the process of grouping is that of finding certain common characteristics, and discarding the divergent ones. Finally, the groupings must be labeled under some heading which denotes the common characteristic.

Interpretation of concrete data and drawing inferences from them requires first, assembling of the concrete information, either by instigating a process of recall and retrieval of previously learned information, or by presenting new information. Identifying and discriminating the various specific points in this information is the first step in the processing data. This step is followed by establishing relationships between the various points, which in turn should be followed by comparing and contrasting, which finally leads to generalizing.

The process involved in the application of known facts and generalizations to explain new events or to predict consequences from described conditions, such as predicting what will happen in the desert if it had enough water, is quite complex. It is composed of divergent lines of prediction as well as the chains of rationale with which these predictions are supported, as shown in the figure below.

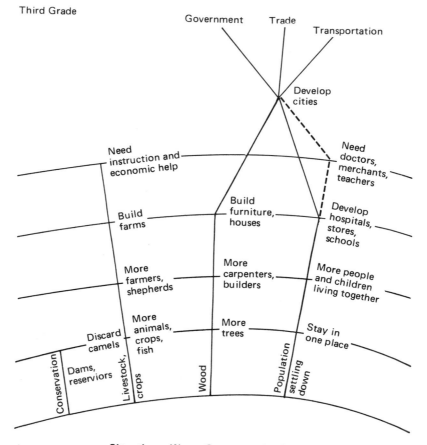

Situation: Water Comes to the Desert

Furthermore, each line of prediction can be extended to represent hierarchies of leaps from the most immediate consequences to the most remote. Individuals can either build on each other's chains or construct the entire chain on their own. The records of discussions show, however, that spontaneous chains by individuals are rather rare and not too long. Usually, the extended chains are products of group interaction.

The implications of the above for teaching strategies are startling. In the first place, the teacher must have a cognitive map of the logic of the content, and of the logic and psychology of the cognitive processes involved. For example, in the case of differences one would expect to find in Latin America, the teacher needs to know what are the important differences between the United States and Latin America, in order to help students to an orderly conceptualization of these differences. He must, further, understand the logical processes involved in the task. For example, the processes of grouping and classification must be known to the teacher in order to distinguish the vague from the precise statements, statements which represent verbal stereotypes from those which are specific enough to serve as adequate material for grouping; e.g., "climate," which only denotes an area of possible differences, as against "seasons are backwards," which actually describes a difference. Understanding the different orders of classification is involved also, such as recognizing that headings such as "transportation," "education," are different from headings such as "conditions and facilities" and that the mixing of the two will create confusion.

Decisions must be made regarding the adaptation of the sequential steps required for a particular cognitive task to the possibilities of the group: how to pace each step, or to combine certain processes, such as alternating specification and classification of information and generalizing; deciding when it is possible to shift the focus, or to lift the level of thought, such as shifting from description ("what") to explanation ("why?"), and so on. Attempts to lift thought prematurely to a higher level results either in confusion or regression to the more primitive level. The chief difficulty with the current teaching procedure is that while the subject moves on, there is no corresponding movement in the maturity of thought. Providing for cumulative growth in cognitive skills is a requirement against which the current teaching practice commits the greatest errors. The typical strategy in a classroom discussion moves illogically from one point to another, rather than moving systematically from one step to another and from one level of intellectual operation to another. This kind of teaching involves leaps in cognitive demands too large for students to follow, so that it is impossible for them to achieve higher levels of intellectual operation.

Decisions regarding pacing and progressive lifting of thought levels naturally depends upon accurate diagnosis of the group's quality of performance. Depending upon both their ability and previous habits of thought, some groups require a more prolonged enumeration before they can group similar items successfully, while others can do with less. Some students can readily grasp the idea that grouping must be done according to some definite basis, while others may need to "mess around" for a while until they "discover" this idea. In some classrooms a great deal of clarification may be needed in the process of establishing the "what" to avoid confusion, while others may hold to the focus easily, and proceed to generalizations early. In effect, then, diagnosis of the degree of readiness for the next step, and a continued testing of limits, is needed. Since the particular response patterns differ radically from class to class and even from individual to individual, these matters inevitably must be decided "on the spot," so to say. While the general principles of sequence can be established beforehand, their particular application and the ways of coping with the divergent student performance can be mastered only "in the process" and aided through analysis of feedback—through opportunities to examine their own teaching acts in the light of the principles and facts regarding the learning processes involved. *This is the aspect of teaching which is usually described as "art," chiefly because neither the means or the materials have been available to give teachers proper clinical experience with the process. Perhaps the time has come to transform this "art" into a science.*

As one considers teaching, especially in the light of the dual nature of the desired end product—that of discovering content ideas and knowledge, and of mastering complex cognitive skills—one is impressed with the complexity of the task of teaching. It requires a high quality of individual acts, such as a manner of asking questions. A focus set by questions determines which points students can explore and what modes of thought they learn. A question such as "What are the important cities in the Balkans?" provides a poor focus in several respects. In addition to training in arbitrary evaluation, such a question also develops an unproductive mode of thinking. It assumes, first, that one can judge the importance of cities without a criterion. For example, does one look for large cities, capitals, ancient ones, or what? Most students faced with such a question have only two alternatives: guessing what the teacher wants, or trying to recollect what the book says of the topic, both cognitive rather unproductive activities.

Asking questions to which only one right answer is possible builds, in addition, a highly convergent mind—one which looks for simple "right" answers, and which assumes that the "right" answers depend on authority rather than on rational judgment. If the development of autonomy in thinking is an important objective, the "seeking" functions of teaching assume a vastly greater importance than are the "giving" functions. But whatever the function, the teaching act must focus the task so that it is both concretely perceptible to the students and at the same time open-ended, to permit spontaneity and autonomy as well as participation in the search by students of different abilities and perceptions. Too often, the most frequent acts performed by the teacher are those which control and limit the responses of students and thereby inhibit their mental activity beyond that which is necessary for orderly development of thought.

However, the impact of teaching lies not alone in its single acts, but in the manner in which these acts are combined into a pattern. For example, the level of thought attained by a group seems to be determined by the way in which different teaching acts are combined: the particular combination of focusing, extending, and lifting; the length of time spent on a particular operation in preparation for another level, such as listing what the class has perceived in a film before proceeding to explain the phenomenon seen; diagnosis of the distance between the mental operations of the students and those required by the task set; how the functions of "giving" and "seeking" are distributed; the way in which the intake of information is alternated with processing, transforming, and synthesizing the information.

Finally, the teaching acts required by the logic of the task are only one segment of the total teaching strategy. Learning does not occur in a vacuum. The fact that teaching and learning occur in a group situation introduces the need for a host of so-called managerial functions. The teacher must do certain things to keep order in the discussion. He must recognize the limits between disorder and a control so great that it stifles expression. He must watch for opportunities to enlarge the students' participation, and not let the aggressive students absorb all the social space and opportunities for self-expression. In addition, there are functions which are necessary to establish the affective climate in the classroom. This involves diagnosis of students' ego needs and awareness of the great varieties and degrees of these needs. He must distinguish between approval and criticism, acts which cultivate dependence or independence, autonomy or conformity.

Viewed in this light, one does get the feeling that the scientific study of teaching has only begun. The purpose of the present article is to suggest the great need for further study, and that it is possible to combine in one process the analysis the three basic elements necessary to assess teaching: an account of (1) what the teacher does, (2) of what the student does, and (3) appraisal of the product of interaction between the two. In this article, the model of studying teaching was illustrated in connection with the development of cognitive processes as a target. However, it seems possible that teaching strategies appropriate for other targets, such as creation of mentally healthy classroom climate, the development of emotional maturity, or mastery of information, could be studied by a similar model.

Some New Views
of Learning and Instruction

Robert M. Gagné

EDITORS' QUESTIONS:

1. State, in your own words, the concept of learning as an information processing activity. What advantages does this approach have over the older view of learning as the establishment of connections between stimuli and responses?

2. Discuss the new conceptions of human learning and memory. What implications do they have for curriculum development and teaching?

3. Why do you suppose that a condition of specific readiness for learning tends to obviate the necessity for repetition? Indicate ways in which an understanding of the enabling conditions for learning can assist the classroom teacher in designing instructional strategies.

4. How does the fact that much of what has been learned may be forgotten complicate the task of providing learning experiences that are consistent with individual students' capabilities? What technique for overcoming this difficulty is suggested by Gagné? Assess the applicability of this procedure to actual classroom situations.

5. Make suggestions for the improvement of your own presentation of learning tasks on the basis of insights gained from studying this article. Indicate ways in which you might have proceeded previously and specify the changes you would now make. In each case, state your rationale for the modification.

Robert M. Gagné, "Some New Views of Learning and Instruction," *Phi Delta Kappan*, (May 1970), 468–472. Reprinted with the permission of Phi Delta Kappa, Inc. and Robert M. Gagné.

During recent years there has been an increased recognition of, and even emphasis on, the importance of principles of learning in the design of instruction for the schools. This recognition of the central role of learning in school-centered education seems to be accorded whether one thinks of the instruction as being designed by a teacher, by a textbook writer, or by a group of scholars developing a curriculum.

When the findings of research studies of learning are taken into account, one usually finds questions about instruction to be concerned with such matters as these:

1. For student learning to be most effective, how should the learning task be presented? That is, how should it be communicated to the student?

2. When the student undertakes a learning task, what kinds of activity on his part should be required or encouraged?

3. What provisions must be made to insure that what is learned is remembered and is usable in further learning and problem solving?

Robert M. Gagné is professor of educational psychology at Florida State University, Tallahassee. He is author of *The Conditions of Human Learning* (1965) and has co-authored or edited several other books on learning and instruction. This article is based on a paper he delivered before a seminar on recent scientific developments sponsored by the American Association of School Administrators last October 26-28 in Washington, D.C.

Questions such as these are persistent in education. The answers given today are not exactly the same as those given yesterday, and they are likely to be altered again tomorrow. The major reason for these changes is our continually deepening knowledge of human behavior and of the factors which determine it. One should not, I believe, shun such changes nor adopt a point of view which makes difficult the application of new knowledge to the design of novel procedures for instruction. The opportunities for improvement seem great and the risks small.

Status of Learning Research

As a field of endeavor, research on how human beings learn and remember is in a state of great ferment today. Many changes have taken place, and are still taking place, in the conception of what human learning is and how it occurs. Perhaps the most general description that can be made of these changes is that investigators are shifting from what may be called a *connectionist* view of learning to an *information processing* view. From an older view which held that learning is a matter of establishing *connections* between stimuli and responses, we are moving rapidly to acceptance of a view that stimuli are *processed* in a quite a number of different ways by the human central nervous system, and that understanding learning is a matter of figuring out how these various processes operate. Connecting one neural event with another may still be the most basic component of these processes, but their varied nature makes connection itself too simple a model for learning and remembering.

My purpose here is to outline some of these changes in the conception of human learning and memory, and to show what implications they may have for the design and practice of instruction. I emphasize that I am not proposing a new theory; I am simply speculating on what seems to me to be the direction in which learning theory is heading.

The Older Conception

The older conception of learning was that it was always basically the same process, whether the learner was learning to say a new word, to tie a shoelace, to multiply fractions, to recount the facts of history, or to solve a problem concerning rotary motion. Edward L. Thorndike held essentially this view. He stated that he had observed people performing learning tasks of varied degrees of complexity and had concluded that learning was invariably subject to the same influences and the same laws.[1] What was this model of learning that was considered to have such broad generalizability?

One prototype is the conditioned response, in which there is a pairing of stimuli, repeated over a series of trials. The two stimuli must be presented together, or nearly together, in time. They are typically associated with an "emotional" response of the human being, such as an eyeblink or a change in the amount of electrical resistance of the skin (the galvanic skin reflex). The size of the conditioned response begins at a low base-line level, and progressively increases as more and more repetitions of the two stimuli are given. Such results have been taken to indicate that repetition brings about an increasingly "strong" learned connection—with an increase in strength that is rapid at first and then more slow.

Learning curves with similar characteristics have been obtained from various other kinds of learned activities, such as simple motor skills like dart-throwing and memorization of lists of words or sets of word-pairs.

1. E. L. Thorndike, *Human Learning.* New York: Appleton-Century, 1931, p. 160.

Remembering. What about the remembering of such learned activities? Is learning retained better as a result of repetition? Is something that is repeated over and over at the time of learning better recalled after the passage of several weeks or months? The curve which describes forgetting is perhaps equally familiar. Forgetting of such things as lists of nonsense syllables is quite rapid in the beginning, and after several weeks descends to a point at which only about 20 percent is remembered. A motor task is usually retained a great deal better, and after the same amount of time its retention may be as much as 80 percent.

These are the basic facts about remembering. But how is it affected by repetition? Is retention better if the original learning situation has been repeated many times? Evidence is often cited that this is so. Increasing the number of trials of repetition during original learning has the effect of slowing down the "curve of forgetting," i.e., of improving the amount of retention measured at any particular time. Underwood,[2] for example, has stated that "degree of learning" of the task to be recalled is one of the two major factors which influence forgetting in a substantial manner. The second factor is interfering associations, whose strength is also determined by their degree of learning. It should be pointed out that when Underwood uses the phrase "degree of learning" he refers to amount of practice —in other words, to amount of repetition.

At this point, let me summarize what I believe are the important implications for instruction of what I call the "older" conceptions of learning and memory. The designer of instruction, or the teacher, had to do two major things: First, he had to arrange external conditions of presentation so that the stimulus and response had the proper timing—in other words, so that there was *contiguity* between the presentation of the

stimulus and the occurrence of the response. Second, he had to insure that sufficient *repetition* occurred. Such repetition was necessary for two reasons: It would increase the strength of the learned ⸱connections; the more the repetition, within limits, the better the learning. Also, repetition was needed to insure remembering—the greater the number of repetitions, the better the retention. Presumably, whole generations of instructional materials and teacher procedures have been influenced in a variety of ways by application of these conceptions of learning to the process of instruction.

Questioning Older Conceptions

During recent years, a number of significant experimental studies of learning and memory have been carried out which call into question some of these older conceptions. (Of course there have always been a certain number of individuals—voices in the wilderness—who doubted that these principles had the general applicability claimed for them.) I shall describe only a few of the crucial new studies here, to illustrate the perennial questions and their possible answers.

Does learning require repetition? A most provocative study on this question was carried out by Rock[3] as long ago as 1957. It has stimulated many other studies since that time, some pointing out its methodological defects, others supporting its conclusions.[4]

---

2. B. J. Underwood, "Laboratory Studies of Verbal Learning," in E. R. Hilgard (ed.), *Theories of Learning and Instruction. Sixty-third Yearbook, Part 1.* Chicago: National Society for the Study of Education, 1964, p. 148.
3. I. Rock, "The Role of Repetition in Associative Learning," *American Journal of Psychology,* June, 1957, pp. 186–93.
4. W. K. Estes, B. L. Hopkins, and E. J. Crothers, "All-or-None and Conservation Effects in the Learning and Retention of Paired Associates," *Journal of Experimental Psychology,* December, 1960, pp. 329–39.

The finding of interest is that in learning sets of verbal paired associates, practice does not increase the strength of each learned item; each one is either learned or not learned. To be sure, some are learned on the first practice trial, some on the second, some on the third, and so on; but an item once learned is fully learned.

So far as school subjects are concerned, a number of studies have failed to find evidence of the effectiveness of repetition for learning and remembering. This was true in an investigation by Gagné, Mayor, Garstens, and Paradise,[5] in which seventh-graders were learning about the addition of integers. One group of children was given four or five times as many practice problems on each of 10 subordinate skills as were given to another group, and no difference appeared in their final performance. A further test of this question was made in a study by Jeanne Gibson,[6] who set out to teach third- and fourth-graders to read decimals from a number line. First, she made sure that subordinate skills (reading a number in decimal form, writing a number in decimal form, locating a decimal number on a number line) were learned thoroughly by each child. One group of students was then given a total of 10 practice examples for each subordinate skill, a second group 25 for each, and a third none at all. The study thus contrasted the effects of no repetition of learned skills, an intermediate amount of repetition, and a large amount of repetition. This variable was not found to have an effect on performance, both when tested immediately after learning and five weeks later. Those students who practiced repeated examples were not shown to do better, or to remember better, than those who practiced not at all.

Still another study of fairly recent origin is by Reynolds and Glaser,[7] who used an instructional program to teach 10 topics in biology. They inserted frames containing half as many repetitions, in one case, and one-and-a-half times as many repetitions, in another, as those in a standard program. The repetitions involved definitions of technical terms. When retention of these terms was measured after an interval of three weeks, the investigators were unable to find any difference in recall related to the amount of repetition.

I must insert a caveat here. All of the studies I have mentioned are concerned with the effects of repetition immediately after learning. They do not, however, test the effect of repetition in the form of *spaced reviews*. Other evidence suggests the importance of such reviews; in fact, this kind of treatment was found to exert a significant effect in the Reynolds and Glaser study. Note, though, that this result may have quite a different explanation than that of "strengthening learned connections."

Modern Conceptions of Learning

Many modern learning theorists seem to have come to the conclusion that conceiving learning as a matter of strengthening connections is entirely too simple. Modern conceptions of learning tend to be highly analytical about the events that take place in learning, both *outside* the learner and also *inside*. The modern point of view about learning tends to view it as a complex of processes taking place in the learner's nervous system. This view is often called an "information-processing" conception.

5. R. M. Gagné, J. R. Mayor, H. L. Garstens, and N. E. Paradise, "Factors in Acquiring Knowledge of a Mathematical Task," *Psychological Monographs,* No. 7, 1962 (Whole No. 526).
6. J. R. Gibson, "Transfer Effects of Practice Variety in Principle Learning." Berkeley: University of California. Ph.D. Dissertation, 1964.
7. J. H. Reynolds and R. Glaser, "Effects of Repetition and Spaced Review upon Retention of a Complex Learning Task," *Journal of Educational Psychology,* October, 1964, pp. 297–308.

One example of an information processing theory is that of Atkinson and Shiffrin.[8] According to this theory, information is first registered by the senses and remains in an essentially unaltered form for a short period of time. It then enters what is called the short-term store, where it can be retained for 30 seconds or so. This short-term store has a limited capacity, so that new information coming into it simply pushes aside what may already be stored there. But an important process takes place in this short-term memory, according to Atkinson and Shiffrin. There is a kind of internal reviewing mechanism (a "rehearsal buffer") which organizes and rehearses the material even within this short period of time. Then it is ready to be transferred to long-term store. But when this happens it is first subjected to a process called *coding*. In other words, it is not transferred in raw form, but is transformed in some way which will make it easier to remember at a later time. Still another process is *retrieval*, which comes into play at the time the individual attempts to remember what he has learned.

It is easy to see that a much more sophisticated theory of learning and memory is implied here. It goes far beyond the notion of gradually increasing the strength of a single connection.

Prerequisites for learning. If repetition or practice is not the major factor in learning, what is? The answer I am inclined to give is that the most dependable condition for the insurance of learning is the prior learning of prerequisite capabilities. Some people would call these "specific readinesses" for learning; others would call them "enabling conditions." If one wants to insure that a student can learn some specific new activity, the very best guarantee is to be sure he has previously learned the prerequisite capabilities. When this in fact has been accom-

plished, it seems to me quite likely that he will learn the new skill without repetition.

Let me illustrate this point by reference to a study carried out by Virginia Weigand.[9] She attempted to identify all the prerequisite capabilities needed for sixth-grade students to learn to formulate a general expression relating the variables in an inclined plane. Without using the exact terminology of physics, let us note that the task was to formulate an expression relating the *height* of the plane, the *weight* of the body traversing downwards, and the *amount of push* imparted to an object at the end of the place. (Wiegand was not trying to teach physics, but to see if the children could learn to formulate a physical relationship which was quite novel to them.) The expression aimed for was, "Distance pushed times a constant block weight equals height of plane times weight of cart."

Initially, what was wanted was explained carefully to the students; the plane and the cart were demonstrated. Thirty students (out of 31) were found who could not accomplish the task; that is, they did not know how to solve the problem. What was it they didn't know? According to the hypothesis being investigated, they didn't know some *prerequisite* things. Figure 1 shows what these missing intellectual skills were thought to be.

What Wiegand did was to find out which of these prerequisite skills were present in each student and which were not present. She did this by starting at the top of the hierarchy and working downwards, testing

8. R. C. Atkinson and R. M. Shiffrin, "Human Memory: A Proposed System and Its Control Processes," in K. W. Spence and J. T. Spence (eds.), *The Psychology of Learning and Motivation: Advances in Research and Theory*, Vol. 2. New York: Academic Press, 1968, pp. 89–195.
9. V. K. Wiegand, "A Study of Subordinate Skills in Science Problem Solving." Berkeley: University of California. Ph.D. Dissertation, 1969.

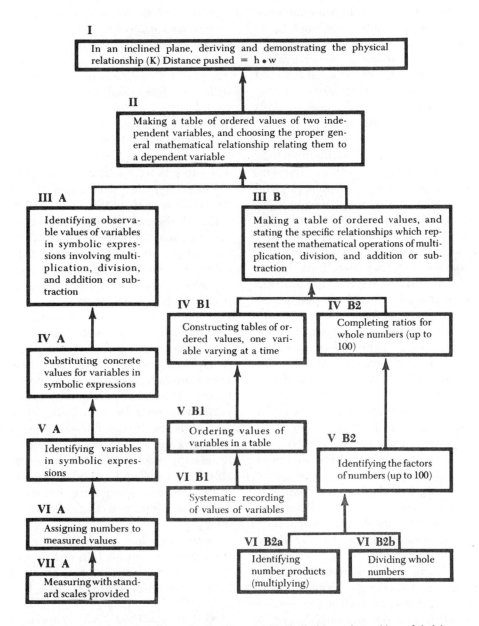

I

In an inclined plane, deriving and demonstrating the physical relationship (K) Distance pushed = h • w

II

Making a table of ordered values of two independent variables, and choosing the proper general mathematical relationship relating them to a dependent variable

III A

Identifying observable values of variables in symbolic expressions involving multiplication, division, and addition or subtraction

III B

Making a table of ordered values, and stating the specific relationships which represent the mathematical operations of multiplication, division, and addition or subtraction

IV A

Substituting concrete values for variables in symbolic expressions

IV B1

Constructing tables of ordered values, one variable varying at a time

IV B2

Completing ratios for whole numbers (up to 100)

V A

Identifying variables in symbolic expressions

V B1

Ordering values of variables in a table

V B2

Identifying the factors of numbers (up to 100)

VI A

Assigning numbers to measured values

VI B1

Systematic recording of values of variables

VII A

Measuring with standard scales provided

VI B2a

Identifying number products (multiplying)

VI B2b

Dividing whole numbers

Figure 1 A hierarchy of subordinate intellectual skills applicable to the problem of deriving a general expression relating variables in an inclined plane (Wiegand, 1969).

at each point whether the student could do the designated task or not. In some students, only two or three skills were missing; in others seven or eight. When she had worked down to the point where these subordinate capabilities *were* present, Wiegand turned around and went the other way. She now made sure that all the prerequisite skills were present, right up to, but not including, the final inclined plane problem.

The question being asked in this study was "If all the prerequisite skills are present, can the students now solve this physical problem which they were unable to solve previously?" Wiegand's results are quite clear-cut. Having learned the prerequisites, nine out of 10 students were able to solve the problem which they were initially unable to solve. They now solved the problem without hesitation and with no practice on the problem itself. On the other hand, for students who did not have a chance to learn the prerequisites, only three of 10 solved the problem (and these were students who had no "missing" skills). This is the kind of evidence that makes me emphasize the critical importance of prerequisite intellectual skills. Any particular learning is not at all difficult if one is truly prepared for it.

Coding and remembering. Quite a number of studies appear in the experimental literature pertaining to the effects of coding of information on its retention. I choose as an illustration a study by Bower and Clark.[10] These investigators studied the recall by college students of 12 lists of 10 nouns apiece. In learning each list, each student was encouraged to make up a story connecting the nouns. For each student there was a yoked control who was not encouraged to make up a story but who was permitted the same amount of time to learn each list of nouns.

Here is an example of a story which one of the subjects constructed for the words *vegetable, instrument, college, nail, fence, basin, merchant, queen, scale,* and *goat:* "A vegetable can be a useful instrument for a college student. A carrot can be a nail for your fence or basin. But a merchant of the queen would scale that fence and feed the carrot to a goat."

The subjects were asked to recall each list immediately after their study of it. They recalled 99 percent under both conditions. The subjects were later asked to recall all of the lists, after they had learned all 12. In this case there was an enormous difference: The recall of the narrative group averaged 93 percent, that of the non-narrative group only 13 percent. In other words, deliberate coding had increased recall by seven times.

Retrieval and remembering. Suppose that learning has indeed occurred; what will insure that whatever has been learned will be remembered? There seems to be at least some absence of evidence that simply practicing or repeating things after they have been learned has the effect of improving retention. What the individual does when he is asked to remember something is to *retrieve* it; that is, he brings to bear a process of searching and finding, in his memory, something he is looking for. This process is probably very little understood at present, but there is increasing evidence that it does occur and that it plays a crucial role in remembering.

Some interesting work has been done on the subject of retrieval. In one experiment, Tulving and Pearlstone[11] had groups of high school students learn lists of words of

10. G. H. Bower and M. C. Clark, "Narrative Stories as Mediators for Serial Learning," *Psychonomic Science,* April, 1969, pp. 181–82.
11. E. Tulving and Z. Pearlstone, "Availability Versus Accessibility of Information in Memory for Words," *Journal of Verbal Learning and Verbal Behavior,* August, 1966, pp. 381–91.

various lengths: 12 words, 24 words, or 48 words. The words themselves were instances of categories, such as four-footed animals (cow, rat); weapons (bomb, cannon); forms of entertainment (radio, music); professions (lawyer, engineer), and so on. The words were presented one at a time in mixed-up order. Different lists also used one, two, or four words in each category.

Once the lists of words had been learned, recall was measured under two different conditions. In the first, the learners were simply told to write down all the words they could remember. In the second, the category names were used as cues to recall; that is, the learners were asked to write down all the words they remembered which were "forms of entertainment," all which were "four-footed animals," and so on. These extra cues worked wonders on recall. The effect was more marked the greater the number of words that had to be recalled. The differences among those learning 48 words was striking, amounting to a twofold increase.

These results show in a rather clear way how powerful is the effect of such extra cues on retrieval of information that has been learned. In this study, the words themselves can be said to have been "equally well learned" in all the groups. What was different between the groups was the aid they were given in retrieving what they had learned. This is only one of the accumulating pieces of evidence that remembering is markedly affected by retrieval at the time of recall, more than it is, perhaps, by events taking place at the time of learning.

Implications for Instruction

The contrasts between older and newer conceptions of learning and memory seem to me quite remarkable. What implications do they have for instruction? If there are

indeed newly discovered ways to affect learning and remembering, how might they be put to use in the classroom and in materials of the curriculum?

First, there is the very fundamental point that each learner approaches each new learning task with a different collection of previously learned prerequisite skills. To be effective, therefore, a learning program for each child must take fully into account what he knows how to do already, and what he doesn't know how to do already. One must find out what prerequisites he has already mastered—not in a general sense, but in a very precise sense for each learner. Does this mean one must do "diagnostic testing"? Yes, that's exactly what it means. To do so, of course, one must first develop the requisite diagnostic tests. By and large, we don't have them.

Second, the most important guide to the learning that needs to be accomplished is the set of prerequisites that the student has not yet mastered. Remember here Wiegand's experiment. When she systematically saw to it that students climbed the hierarchy, skill by skill, this was what was specifically needed to get them to engage in the problem solving they were originally unable to do.

Third, do students need additional practice to insure retention? If by this is meant, "Should they be given many additional examples so that what they have learned will be 'strengthened'?," I think the evidence says it probably won't work this way. Periodic and spaced reviews, however, are another matter, and it seems likely that these have an important role to play in retention. Notice that when a review is given the student has to exercise his strategies of retrieval.

This brings me to the final point, which concerns the processes of coding and retrieval. Probably what should be aimed for here is the learning by students of strategies of coding. These are by no means the same as what are called "mnemonic systems," although it is possible that such systems have a contribution to make in teaching us how coding might be done. For meaningful learning, it appears even more likely that notions like "advance organizers" and "anchoring ideas," as studied by Ausubel,[12] may be particularly powerful.

Similarly, retrieval strategies are also a class of objective that might be valued for instruction. From the evidence we have, I should say that retrieval strategies might very well consist in networks of superordinate categories into which newly learned specific information, or specific intellectual skills, can be placed. Having students learn to retrieve information by a process of search which first locates such superordinate networks may be a major way of providing them with the capability of good retention.

Even these two or three aspects of modern learning conceptions, it seems to me, lead to a very different view of what instruction is all about. In the most general sense, instruction becomes not primarily a matter of communicating something that is to be stored. Instead, it is a matter of stimulating the use of capabilities the learner already has at his disposal, and of making sure he has the requisite capabilities for the present learning task, as well as for many more to come.

12. D. P. Ausubel, *Educational Psychology: A Cognitive View.* New York. Holt, Rinehart and Winston, 1968.

Recommended Readings: Understanding the Teaching-Learning Process

Allen, Dwight W. and Seifman, Eli, eds. *The Teacher's Handbook*. Glenview, Illinois: Scott, Foresman, 1971.

Anderson, Harold and Brewer, Helen M. "Studies of Teachers' Classroom Personalities. 1. Dominative and Socially Integrative Behavior of Kindergarten Teachers," *Applied Psychology Monograph*, No. 6 (1945).

Boy, Angelo V. and Pine, Gerald J. *Expanding the Self: Personal Growth for Teachers*. Dubuque, Iowa: Wm. C. Brown Company Publishers, 1971.

Brubaker, Dale L. *The Teacher as a Decision-Maker*. Dubuque, Iowa: Wm. C. Brown Company Publishers, 1970.

Carpenter, Finlay and Haddan, Eugene E. *Systematic Application of Psychology to Education*. New York: The Macmillan Co., 1964.

Ellis, Henry C. *Fundamentals in Human Learning*. Dubuque, Iowa: Wm. C. Brown Company Publishers, 1972.

Frankena, William K. *Three Historical Philosophies of Education*. Glenview, Illinois: Scott, Foresman, 1968.

Hadden, Eugene E. *Evolving Instruction*. New York: The Macmillan Co., 1970.

Hough, John B. and Duncan, James K. *Teaching: Description and Analysis*. Reading, Massachusetts: Addison-Wesley Publication Co., 1970.

Hyman, Ronald T. *Contemporary Thought on Teaching*. Englewood Cliffs, New Jersey: Prentice-Hall, Inc., 1971.

Johansen, John H., Collins, Harold W., Johnson, James A., and Carley, Frank. *American Education: The Task and the Teacher*. Dubuque, Iowa: Wm. C. Brown Company Publishers, 1971.

Kuethe, James L. *The Teaching-Learning Process*. Glenview, Illinois: Scott, Foresman, 1965.

Logan, Frank A. *Introduction to Learning and Motivation*. Dubuque, Iowa: Wm. C. Brown Company Publishers, 1970.

Lucas, Christopher J., ed. *What is Philosophy of Education?*. New York: The Macmillan Co., 1969.

MacMillan, C. J. B. and Nelson, Thomas W., eds. *Concepts of Teaching*. Chicago, Illinois: Rand McNally & Co., 1969.

Marx, M. H., ed. *Learning: Processes*. New York: The Macmillan Co., 1965.

Morse, William C. and Wingo, Max G. *Classroom Psychology: Readings in Educational Psychology*. Glenview, Illinois: Scott, Foresman, 1970.

Raths, Louis E. *Teaching for Learning*. Columbus, Ohio: Charles E. Merrill Publishing Co., 1969.

Simon, Henry W. *What is a Teacher?*. New York: A Collier Book, 1964.

Skinner, B. F. *Science and Human Behavior*. New York: The Macmillan Co., 1965.

Smith, Othanel and Associates. *A Study of the Logic of Teaching*. U.S. Office of Education Cooperative Research Project, No. 258 (7257), Urbana: University of Illinois, 1960.

Torrance, Paul. *Encouraging Creativity in the Classroom*. Dubuque, Iowa: Wm. C. Brown Company Publishers, 1970.

Weiss, Thomas M. and Hoover, Kenneth H. *Scientific Foundations of Education*. Dubuque, Iowa: Wm. C. Brown Company Publishers, 1970.

PART
TWO

Strategies for Teaching

Identifying and Stating Instructional Objectives

The value of having clearly defined objectives in any human activity is forcefully illustrated by the following from *Alice's Adventures in Wonderland:*

> "Cheshire-Puss," she began, . . . "Would you tell me, please, which way I ought to go from here?" "That depends a good deal on where you want to get to," said the Cat. "I don't much care where—" said Alice. "Then it doesn't matter which way you go," said the Cat.[1]

The current emphasis upon educational accountability has given impetus to efforts to improve the effectiveness of classroom instruction. In recognition of the relevance of a clear definition of objectives to effective instruction, educators have posed the following question: How should instructional objectives be stated in order to provide maximal utility in evaluating learning achievement? While few would deny the need for this innovation, there is, as yet, no general agreement as to precisely how it should be accomplished. Nevertheless, the critical ex-

amination of the points of view introduced by Section 1 should provide the student a basis for decision making which is consistent with her knowledge of the nature of learning and behaving.

The behaviorists stipulate that, since one cannot see inside the pupil to ascertain whether learning is taking place, the only indication of learning is a change in the child's overt behavior. They advocate, therefore, the stating of objectives in behavioral terms. Numerous examples of this approach are provided by Esbensen in the article "Writing Instructional Objectives." Esbensen forcefully asserts the proposition that stating instructional objectives in behavioral terms facilitates measurement of the extent to which objectives have been achieved. By stating the purpose of instructional objectives and postulating three criteria for identifying a well-written objective, he illustrates by comparative examples how

[1]Lewis Carroll. *Alice's Adventures in Wonderland.* New York, N.Y.: Random House, Inc., 1946. pp. 71–72.

statements of instructional objectives can be evaluated. His emphasis, throughout, is upon the statement of objectives in terms of observable performance with considerable attention being given to the need for precision in defining the desired behavior.

On the basis of insights resulting from an examination of a model of the learning process, Eiss seeks to develop a rationale for the use of performance objectives stated in behavioral terms. The model, a diagram representing a learner's mind, depicts the mental processing of educational stimuli and illustrates an interaction between the affective and cognitive levels of reaction resulting in the elicitation of an observable psychomotor response indicative of the learning achieved. Eiss indicates, however, that the preparation and use of behavioral objectives is not without pitfalls, and a number of these are enumerated. He admits that defining goals is a very difficult task—especially when one is confronted with the necessity of specifying behaviors which cannot be evoked "on demand" such as those occurring within the affective domain. However, he asserts that, rather than perpetuating the haphazard manner of working which is characteristic of many school systems, educators must take the initiative in clarifying and specifying the goals of instruction, before others expropriate this function.

The difficulty of identifying and expressing behaviors in the affective domain is recognized readily by Hirschlein and Jones. However, they state that "difficulty is not a license for neglect." In their article the authors illustrate, with an example, how a teacher might evaluate progress toward the achievement of a behavior in the affective realm.

The article by Cox constitutes a comprehensive overview of the nature, uses and kinds of behavioral objectives, as well as providing, for the more astute reader, a veritable treasure trove of opportunities for further study. Of particular value to the student are the check list for evaluating statements of instructional objectives, the many illustrative examples of the stating and sequencing of behavioral objectives and a student's performance scale which demonstrates the interrelatedness of the affective and cognitive domains.

The article by Frost provides a framework for the analysis of early childhood education programs on the basis of their educational objectives. The hierarchy of educational objectives he develops has potentially immense value to the writer of instructional objectives. While this selection is somewhat broader in scope than other articles included in Section 1, the insights it provides into the interrelationships which exist among levels of objectives, content, curriculum and methodologies make it required reading for anyone concerned with ensuring that the statement of instructional objectives contributes directly to the realization of overall program goals.

In this section, the following objectives are proposed for accomplishment. The student should be able to:

1. Explain the need for clear, specific instructional objectives.
2. Write instructional objectives in behavioral terms.
3. State an instructional objective and suggest learning experiences which would contribute to its realization.
4. Distinguish among the three levels of objectives and illustrate, through the use of a diagram, their interrelatedness.
5. Identify a program objective and its related instructional objectives.

6. Suggest ways of stating desired affective learnings in terms of behavioral objectives.
7. Offer alternative methods of stating instructional objectives and state the rationale for each approach indicated.

Writing Instructional Objectives

Thorwald Esbensen

EDITORS' QUESTIONS:

1. To what extent do the examples of instructional objectives offered by Esbensen provide for the measurement of affective learning? In implementing a system of instruction utilizing behavioral criteria for assessing learning achievement, how can objectives be stated in a way that enables the teacher to distinguish between behavior that is based upon concept formation and that which is simply parroted?

2. What is implied by the statement "If it is to be of use to us, a statement of performance must specify some sort of behavior that can be observed."? Do you agree? Justify your position.

3. This article indicates that only observable behavior can be used to measure learning and that attempts to measure comprehension or understanding directly are not worthwhile since mental activity is not subject to observation. Can you think of any instances in which this approach would fail to reveal learning that had, in fact, taken place? Are such occurrences sufficiently numerous to significantly limit the effectiveness of this approach? Support your answer logically, using research findings as appropriate.

4. What, in your opinion, is the author's reason for stressing, in the writing of performance objectives, the use of specific lists of words, particular tests or lessons, minute segments of behavior and percentage levels of accuracy? Could such practices limit the range and quality of educational experiences available to pupils? Explain.

5. If you are not completely satisfied with the behavioral approach to the statement of instructional objectives, develop your own procedure and indicate why you prefer this alternative approach.

6. Write a learning objective which meets Esbensen's criteria for the identification of "good" instructional objectives.

Thorwald Esbensen, "Writing Instructional Objectives," *Phi Delta Kappan*, XLVIII, (January 1967), 246–247. Reprinted with the permission of Phi Delta Kappa, Inc. and Thorwald Esbensen.

For many years, educators have talked about the importance of instructional objectives. The purpose of an instructional objective is to make clear to teachers, students, and other interested persons *what it is that needs to be taught*—or what it is that *has been taught.*

A well-written instructional objective should say three things: (1) what it is that a student who has mastered the objective will be able to *do,* (2) under what *conditions* he will be able to do it, and (3) to what *extent* he will be able to do it. To put the matter in a single sentence, a well-written instructional objective should specify under what

Mr. Esbensen (211, University of Minnesota-Duluth Chapter) is assistant superintendent in charge of instruction, Duluth, Minn.

conditions and to what extent a certain kind of student performance can be expected to take place.

Performance—conditions—extent. Let us consider first the word *performance.* Performing means doing. A student who performs something does something.

Here are two statements. Which one is expressed in terms of student performance?

A. *The student will have a good understanding of the letters of the alphabet, A through Z.*

B. *The student will be able to pronounce the names of the letters of the alphabet, A through Z.*

Statement B tells what it is that the student will be able to *do.* He will be able to *pronounce* the names of the letters of the alphabet, A through Z.

Statement A tells us that the student will have a good *understanding* of the letters of the alphabet. But this is not very clear. We cannot tell what it is that the student is supposed to be able to *do* as a result of this understanding.

Let's try another pair of statements. Which one is expressed in terms of student performance?

A. *The student will have an adequate comprehension of the mechanics of punctuation.*

B. *Given a sentence containing an error in punctuation, the student will correct the mistake.*

Statement B tells what it is that the student will *do.* Statement A, which says that the student will have an adequate *comprehension* of the mechanics of punctuation, is pretty vague. We cannot tell what it is that the student is supposed to be able to *do* as a result of his comprehension.

At this point, an objection may be raised. Isn't the person who is comprehending something doing something? Isn't intellectual performance an acceptable kind of student performance?

Certainly. The difficulty is that mental activity, as such, is not directly observable.

We cannot literally open up a person's head and see the thinking that is going on inside. If it is to be of use to us, a statement of performance must specify some sort of behavior that can be observed.

This does not mean that we are not concerned about intellectual performance. It does mean that since mental activity, as such, is not directly observable, some sort of behavior that is observable will have to stand for or represent the intellectual performance we have in mind.

For example, suppose that we are interested in having students know something about the writing style of Ernest Hemingway. Whatever may be intellectually involved in the attainment of this goal, it should be apparent that the language of our aim as stated leaves much to be desired.

What is the student who *knows* able to do that the student who does *not know* is not able to do? This is the important question, because we cannot measure the accomplishment of our instructional purpose until we have worked out a clear answer to it. Although there is no single answer (our objective of "knowing something" is too vague for that), here is a possible statement of desired performance: *Given 10 pairs of short prose passages—each pair having one selection by Ernest Hemingway and one by a different author —the student is able, with at least 90 percent accuracy, to choose the 10 selections written by Hemingway.*

Performance—conditions—extent. We have been talking about *performance.* Let us now consider *conditions.*

Here is one of our earlier statements concerning the alphabet: *The student will be able to pronounce the names of the letters of the alphabet, A through Z.* We have said that this statement is expressed in terms of student performance. Does this statement also set forth the *conditions* under which the performance is to take place?

It does not. For one thing, we cannot tell from our statement whether the student is to pronounce the names of the letters *at sight* or *from memory*. If the letters are to be shown, we do not know whether the student is to work with capital letters, small letters, or both. Nor do we know whether the student is to work with these letters in regular sequence or in random order. Obviously, each set of conditions is substantially different from the rest, and will make its own special demands upon the student who attempts to accomplish the objective.

Let's examine two more statements. Which one sets forth the *conditions* under which a certain kind of performance is to take place?

A. *Given the Dolch list of the 95 most common nouns, the student will be able to pronounce correctly all the words on this list.*

B. *The student will be able to pronounce correctly at least 90 percent of all words found in most beginning reading books.*

Statement A, which tells us that the Dolch list will be used, sets the conditions for the demonstration of student mastery. We are told that these particular words, and no others, are the ones at issue for this objective.

Statement B, offering us only the dubious clue of "words found in most beginning reading books," does not tell us enough. Our conditions need to be defined more precisely than this.

We come now to the matter of the *extent* and *level* of performance. A well-written instructional objective will establish an acceptable minimum standard of achievement.

Look at this objective: *Given 20 sentences containing both common and proper nouns, the student will be able to identify with very few mistakes both kinds of nouns.* Does this objective establish a minimum standard of achievement?

It does not. It leaves open the question, How many mistakes are "a very few"?

Here is the Hemingway objective we looked at earlier: *Given 10 pairs of short prose passages—each pair having one selection by Ernest Hemingway and one by a different author—the student is able, with at least 90 percent accuracy, to choose the 10 selections written by Hemingway.* Does this objective establish a minimum standard of achievement?

It does. The student is expected to be able to make at least nine correct choices out of the 10. This constitutes a minimum standard of achievement.

Let's try one more objective: *The student should be able to pronounce from memory, and in sequence, the names of the letters of the alphabet, A through Z.* Does this objective establish a minimum standard of achievement?

It does. The objective implies that we are looking for 100 percent mastery. However, we could, if we wanted to be explicit, restate our objective in this way: *The student should be able to pronounce from memory, in sequence, and with 100 percent accuracy, the names of the letters of the alphabet, A through Z.*

An instructional objective should not ordinarily be limited to specific *means* (particular materials or methods), but should be stated in terms that permit the use of various procedures. Look at this statement of an objective: *Given the California Test Bureau's E-F level programmed booklet on capitalization, the student is able to work through the exercises in this booklet with at least 90 percent accuracy.* Is this objective limited to the use of a particular instructional item or procedure?

It is. The objective is expressed exclusively in terms of performance with a specific booklet. Although the particular kind of skill development that is promoted by this booklet is presumably also fostered by other instructional materials and methods, no such options are available under the terms of our objective as it is now written.

Look at this statement of an objective: *Given 20 sentences containing a variety of mistakes in capitalization, the student is able, with at least 90 percent accuracy, to identify and rewrite correctly each word that has a mistake in capitalization.* Is this objective limited to the use of a particular instructional item or procedure?

It is not. The objective as expressly stated permits us to use a number of instructional items that show promise of being able to help students attain the desired performance. Among these items are not only the California Test Bureau's E-F level material but the somewhat simpler C-D level presentation, a programmed booklet by D. C. Heath, Unit 11 of English 2200, Unit 9 of English 2600, Lessons 87 and 88 of English 3200, several filmstrips on capital letters, and so on.

Finally, a well-written instructional objective will suggest how its accomplishment can be measured. This follows from our view that a well-written objective specifies under what *conditions* and to what *extent* a certain kind of student *performance* can be expected to take place.

Look at this objective: *The student should know the alphabet.* Does this objective suggest how its accomplishment can be measured?

It does not. The reason for this judgment is that *knowing the alphabet* can mean different things to different people. Therefore, depending upon what is meant, the measuring of this knowing will take different forms.

Suppose we elaborate upon our objective so that it reads: *Shown the letters of the alphabet in random order (in both upper and lower case form), the student is able to say the name of each letter with 100 percent accuracy.* Does our objective now suggest how its accomplishment can be measured?

It does. The objective as stated makes plain how its accomplishment can be measured.

If teachers at all levels of schooling would be this explicit in writing instructional objectives, they might reasonably hope to eliminate almost immediately one major cause of learning failure among students: the traditional fuzziness of classroom assignments.

Performance Objectives

Albert F. Eiss

EDITORS' QUESTIONS:

1. What is the difference in meaning of the following terms? educational objectives; performance objectives; behavioral objectives.

2. Discuss the rationale for the writing of performance objectives advanced by the author. Do you agree with his justifications?

3. Identify the different problems in preparing and using behavioral objectives. Suggest ways of counteracting these difficulties.

4. Critically analyze Eiss's model for learning. Assess its relevance to the designing of instructional strategies and the measurement of learning achievement.

5. What suggestions can you offer, in addition to those provided by the author, for clarifying our goals and processes of instruction.

Albert F. Eiss, "Performance Objectives," *National Association of Secondary School Principals Bulletin,* LIV, (January 1970), 51–57. Reprinted with the permission of the National Association of Secondary School Principals and Albert F. Eiss.

". . . No evaluation of the outcomes of learning can occur until some overt behavior is shown by the student. It therefore seems logical to state the objectives of learning in terms of the behavioral outcomes that are desired."

The first step in discussing performance objectives should be a definition of the term. It is evident that we are dealing with a semantic problem. Mager uses the term *educational objectives* as a synonym for *performance objectives.* The National Science Teachers Association and the National Science Supervisors Association have used the term *behavioral objectives* in referring to performance objectives. What, if any, difference is there in the meaning of these terms?

Mager gives the most specific definition. According to him, an *educational objective* should specify (1) the student behavior that is desired, (2) the conditions under which the behavior will be exhibited, and (3) the

level of performance required. Individuals writing such objectives frequently find that these criteria tend to produce formalized statements that are sometimes rather awkward. Some prefer to make general statements about the condition under which the desired behaviors will be shown and the performance level desired and then, when writing specific objectives, state only the behaviors that are sought.

Although the term *performance objectives* is frequently used synonymously with educational objectives, it leaves something to be desired when writing objectives in the affective domain. Affective behaviors frequently cannot be produced "on demand" as easily

Albert F. Eiss, associate executive secretary of the National Science Teachers Association, gave this paper at the NSTA convention held in Dallas, Texas, last March.

as cognitive behaviors can. The term behavioral objectives seems to be the most comprehensive and useful, but it has fallen into disuse to some extent because of the extreme opposition of individuals who read into the term an identification with the ideas of some behavioral psychologists—ideas that these critics will not accept. There is little need to deal further with the semantic differences of these terms, except to point out that listeners should be reasonably sure that they understand what meaning the speaker is giving to the particular term he is using.

Furthermore, it is discouraging to note that only a small fraction of so-called performance objectives (or educational or behavioral—whichever term you choose to use) are expressed in behavioral terms. Many people claiming to write such objectives lack an understanding of suitable ways of expressing student behaviors, with the result that they merely restate the more traditional type of objectives in different terms.

Rationale for Performance Objectives

Every instructional system is based upon some type of educational objectives, either explicitly stated or implied. In the past, many of these objectives have taken two forms: vague generalizations that no one will dispute, but with little meaning, or unstated objectives that teachers frequently deny if accused of having them. Examples of generalized statements are "the student will learn to appreciate science" or "the student will gain an understanding of the principles of science." Examples of unstated objectives are: (a) to "cover" the textbook, or (b) to pass the College Boards.

Performance objectives (or behavioral objectives, as I prefer to call them—a term

that I will use during the remainder of this presentation) require more specific statements of the desired outcomes of the instructional program. The necessity for determining the student behaviors that are desired is apparent if we consider the way a student learns.

In the diagram, which represents the individual's mind, all input must come through the level of awareness in the affective domain, where the individual considers (a cognitive process) whether or not he wishes to continue to give his attention to the stimulus. If the answer is "no," the stimulus is simply "turned off" unless it is so strong or insistent that it cannot be ignored. If the conscious mind decides to continue to examine the stimulus, the input interacts with the storage capacity of the mind, and associations begin to be made. Before long, the psychomotor aspect of the individual's mind must come into play if the learning process is to continue.

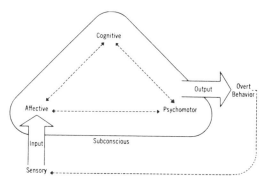

Figure 1 A Model for Learning

It is at these levels—in the affective domain (willingness to respond) and in the psychomotor (the actual response) and in the cognitive (content of the response)—that the first indication is evident to an observer that the learning process is taking place. The only way in which a teacher can determine that the individual has learned, or how he feels, or what he thinks, is to provide a stimulus that will elicit a psychomotor response and then to evaluate this response for evidence that the desired learning has occurred.

There is no alternative to this process. As long as thoughts and learning are "locked up" in the individual's mind, there is no evidence of what is happening. It is only when the individual responds in some way that the teacher can tell what has happened.

The conclusion, then, is that no evaluation of the outcomes of learning can occur until some overt behavior is shown by the student. It therefore seems logical to state the objectives of learning in terms of the behavioral outcomes that are desired. This produces clear, specific statements of objectives that lend themselves readily to the evaluation of learning outcomes. The entire idea seems so simple that many people wondered why it took so long to move from the intuitive process that teachers have frequently used to a more carefully studied and more formalized process that can be examined objectively.

Hazards in Using Behavioral Objectives

But it is not all this simple. The use of behavioral objectives will not produce an educational millenium. There are many hazards that must be guarded against if behavioral objectives are to be used effectively.

(1) *As behavioral objectives are now written, many, if not most of them, tend to be trivial.* It is easy to write objectives describing student behaviors that demonstrate skills and knowledge of specific facts; it is much more difficult to write objectives describing behaviors that demonstrate the student's ability to think and reason.

This brings us full circle. Unless we can write objectives that deal with the more important goals of learning in terms of students' behaviors, we are still forced to deal either with vague generalities that are of little value, or with specific trivia that together do not make up the real objectives of the learning process.

(2) *The list of objectives may become encyclopedic.* A "telephone book" of well-written behavioral objectives may be useful to someone who wishes to program a course of study, but they are of little value to the individual teacher. Yet it is the individual teacher who frequently determines the course of study, unless the course has been completely programed. And there is little, if any, evidence that completely programed courses achieve many of the more important goals of education.

(3) *There are too many examples of objectives at the lower levels of the cognitive domain, and too few examples of objectives in the affective domain.* In fact, there are many educators who claim that it is impossible to write behavioral objectives in the affective domain. This is why the National Science Supervisors Association, in cooperation with NSTA, has spent two years in studying this topic, resulting in the publication which NSSA has just prepared, *Behavioral Objectives in the Affective Domain.*[1] Still there is need for more work on writing objectives for the higher levels of the cognitive domain, as well as much more work on objectives in the affective domain.

(4) *Developing a catalog of objectives may limit the goals of teaching, with the result that some of the spontaneity and value of education may be lost.* At the present time, it is not possible to write behavioral objectives for

1. *Behavioral Objectives in the Affective Domain.* Albert F. Eiss and Mary Blatt Harbeck. Washington: National Science Supervisors Association. 1969, pp. vi 42.

all of the educational outcomes that are desired. To my knowledge, no one has ever claimed to be able to verbalize all of the desirable outcomes of learning. Some individuals use this as a reason for resisting the verbalization of *any* of the goals of education, claiming that teaching is an art rather than a science.

Personally, I believe that there is both an art and a science to teaching, just as I believe that both art and science are employed by composers, painters, sculptors, and individuals working in any other type of career. However, we must not let the mechanics of the scientific process delimit our goals or dim our vision to the fact that there are goals that cannot yet be expressed in specific terms.

Problems in Preparing and Using Behavioral Objectives

There are many problems involved in avoiding these and other hazards in the learning process. One of the important problems is the psychological block experienced by many people in dealing with behavioral objectives. This is sometimes evidenced by opposition to the use of the term itself. This psychological block produces a related philosophical block that may prevent some people from examining the other problems from an unbiased, objective viewpoint.

Another problem is the difficulty experienced by many people in writing behavioral objectives. Some people need to know the distance from New York to San Francisco precisely, while others only wish to know the distance within 50 or 100 miles. The same thing is true with behavioral objectives. Just as a surveyor takes a great amount of time to measure a given distance precisely, so a writer of behavioral objec-

tives may require more time to prepare a more precise statement. The time required to obtain the desired precision must be balanced against the need for that degree of precision, once it has been obtained. An encouraging observation is that writing behavioral objectives does become easier and more rapid with practice.

The "inference gap" that exists between the desired objective (the behavior that is accepted as evidence of its attainment) and the development of a valid measure of its attainment will always be a problem. The use of behavioral objectives does not create this problem—it only makes it more obvious.

The difficulty in defining goals is a very real difficulty. Behavioral objectives were first used in the military, where the desired outcomes often were skills, making it easy to describe and measure outcomes. It is nearly as easy to state objectives of vocational courses in behavioral terms. Even correspondence courses have specific aims that are easier to describe than objectives of many general education courses. It becomes exceedingly difficult to prepare objectives for general courses, where goals are sometimes very fuzzy. One useful result is that the difficulty of writing such objectives is forcing those of us in education to examine more closely our reasons for teaching and to become more explicit in stating the goals that we hope to achieve.

Suggestions for Action

Is the situation hopeless? Must we continue to work in the haphazard fashion that is characteristic of many school systems? The answer is an emphatic NO. If we, as educators, do not take steps to clarify our goals of instruction, do not develop an adequate rationale for curriculum development, and fail to take immediate steps to implement the process, others will act for us. There is a distinct danger—even a probability—that unless teachers and administrators take immediate action our initiative will be lost.

What steps, then, can we take in developing immediate action on clarifying the goals and processes of education? We cannot afford another "bandwagon syndrome." There is a need for a psychologically sound and carefully planned approach to the problem. This cannot be done by starting to run before we know where we want to go, nor by sitting down and going nowhere. There are at least five crucial processes which ought to be initiated immediately.

1. A statement of a viewpoint on education that all, or at least a majority of, educators can agree upon is essential. It sometimes appears that the "educational establishment" does not want anyone to question or challenge their thinking. We need more classroom teachers who have learned from years of experience how children act and learn, to tell us how the process can be facilitated. Most of all, we need to examine the real goals of education—as contrasted with the stated goals—and the outcomes that we are now achieving.

2. We need to place much more emphasis and study on the affective domain. What good is it to teach students a lot of information about science if they learn to dislike it in the process? Yet there is mounting evidence that this is just what is happening in many of our present science courses.

3. We must give careful attention to the interdisciplinary aspects of education. Research scientists, as well as the ordinary layman, may show evidence of scientific illiteracy and intellectual myopia. Statements of what a scientifically literate citizen should be like are not often enough reflected either in our courses of study or in the outcomes of our instruction, and almost never in the form of performance objectives.

4. We need long-range plans, and they need to be open-ended. We cannot afford, in this time of rapid change, to "freeze" the curriculum. We must work toward a flexible, individualized learning environment that will produce the type of individual that we claim to want to produce.

5. And most of all, we need action—immediate action! This will mean that some dedicated professionals will need to forget the thirty-hour week, or even the forty-hour week, and attempt to develop intensive, well planned, and effective approaches to solving our problems. What do you propose to do about it?

The Function of Stated Objectives in Teaching for Affective Learning

Beulah M. Hirschlein
and John G. Jones

EDITORS' QUESTIONS:

1. Critically analyze the different procedures for stating behavioral objectives described by Childs, Burns, and Mager. Which of these methods would you be more inclined to follow? Support your answer.

2. Assess the feasibility of the suggested method of "letting students choose what they desire to learn." Discuss the educational benefits which can be derived from this approach. What difficulties can you anticipate as a result of its implementation?

3. Assess the procedure illustrated by the author for evaluating progress toward the achievement of the sample objective—an appreciation of the worth and dignity of individuals of all races.

4. Choose an objective in the affective domain. Identify a series of behaviors which would give evidence that such objective has been reached.

5. Construct a device similar to that presented by the author. Use such a device to rate the behavior of a group of children. Determine its applicability and modify or alter it as necessary.

Beulah M. Hirschlein and John G. Jones, "The Function of Stated Objectives in Teaching for Affective Learning," *Educational Technology*, (June 1971), vol. XI, No.6, 47–49. Reprinted with the permission of *Educational Technology*.

Education is minus a systematic effort to develop and collect evidence of growth of affective objectives which in any way parallels the systematic and continuing efforts to develop and evaluate cognitive achievement.

The development of a more systematic approach toward the achievement of affective objectives includes at least two prerequisites: (1) the ability of the teacher to establish a positive climate for affective growth and (2) the ability of the teacher to identify affective objectives as an integral part of curriculum planning. It is assumed that whatever the specific goals of classroom instruction might be, the affective tone can facilitate or interfere with their attainment

(Ripple, 1965). What could be more absurd than to attempt the development of affective objectives in a climate of hostility and duress? For treatment within the confines of this paper, the establishment of an affective climate will be generally assumed, and major attention will be focused on the identification and implementation of affective objectives within the curriculum framework.

As stated by Kelley (1965), "Everyone who learns something has some feeling about it . . . No matter what we do, affective

Beulah M. Hirschlein is adult basic education project coordinator, School and Community Services, the University of Oklahoma. John G. Jones is assistant professor, College of Education, the University of Oklahoma.

learning goes on anyway." In this context the function of identifying and consciously attempting to provide opportunity for the achievement of affective objectives is to ensure that affective learning will be positive; that changed behavior will be constructive. Both Kelley (1965) and Mager (1968) suggest that a student should complete a course feeling more able and courageous than when he began it. If the contrary is true, then the class has damaged him rather than helped him.

In the words of Slack (1967), "When learning is inefficient, educational objectives tend to be 'broad' and unclear. For learning to become efficient, objectives must be stated with behavioral precision." Burns, Childs and Mager have each outlined the components of specific behavioral objectives. To Burns (1967b), all specific objectives are expressed from the learner's point of view and essentially are composed of three major parts:

(1) type of behavior,
(2) name of behavior, and
(3) behavioral description.

Childs' (1968) interpretation varies slightly. He includes:

(1) a statement of a learner's observable performance.
(2) a statement of the conditions under which the performance will be observed, and
(3) a statement of the level of performance or criterion for the performance.

Mager (1962) outlines the following specifications for instructional objectives:

(1) describes what the learner will be doing when he is demonstrating that he has reached the objective,
(2) describes the important conditions (givens or restrictions, or both) under which the learner will be

expected to demonstrate his competence, and
(3) indicates how the learner will be evaluated by describing lower limits of acceptable performance.

Essentially, the three authors are in agreement as to the basic elements of behavioral objectives. Examples of objectives which adhere to their specifications are as follows:

> Burns (1967b)—"A learner is to develop a knowledge of 25 technical terms so that he can write, from memory, sentences correctly using a minimum of 24 of the terms."
> Childs (1968)—"At the end of this unit a student will be able to differentiate between the initial sounds of 'M' and 'B.' "
> Mager (1962)—"The student must be able to solve at least seven simple linear equations within a period of 30 minutes."

The sample objectives shown above are obviously from the cognitive domain. Upon analyzing the objectives against the criteria given by Burns, Childs and Mager, one finds them complete. The elements prescribed are present, but an important affective element which is not present is that of helping the learner to understand the value of the objective to him. The attachment of an affective element (value) to the Burns objective would alter it as follows:

> A learner is to develop a knowledge of 25 technical terms so that he can write, from memory, sentences correctly using a minimum of 24 of the terms. *A knowledge of technical terms enables the learner to . . .*

The addition of the *value* of the objective, whether or not it is actually stated, enables the learner to know why a certain behavior is expected of him. This provides one additional piece of information useful in determining whether or not the objective in question is really desirable for him. From the learner's point of view, he now knows what he is expected to do, under what conditions, how well and why. Much of the criticism of cognitive learning is that it is simply void of perceived relevance by the learner. If the teacher can do no more toward the development of affective learning than to assist learners in seeing the value of knowledge and allow students to participate in the selection of objectives which ultimately control them, he has still made a tremendous contribution to education. To paraphrase the words of Slack (1967), when learning is inefficient, educational objectives tend to be broad, ambiguous and *irrelevant.*

As teachers become more able to identify and articulate cognitive behavioral objectives that are comprehensible to students, a giant step toward the development of affective objectives has been accomplished. Krathwohl *et al.* (1964) have developed a continuum of affective behaviors which, when integrated with a theory of expressing objectives in specific behavioral terms, may enable the teacher to become quite proficient in establishing goals for affective learning. The affective taxonomy was developed to cover a range of objectives, including interests, attitudes, values, appreciation and adjustment. Each objective is viewed as having to become internalized prior to becoming a part of the person's behavioral repertoire. This internalization process proceeds through five steps: (1) awareness, (2) responding, (3) valuing, (4) organization and (5) characterization by value or value complex.

To some, it is clearly unreasonable to suggest that a teacher consider such a detailed process as this, plus an even more lengthy classification of cognitive behaviors as set forth by Bloom (1956) and various theories of stating objectives, as he sits down to plan learning experiences. A better suggestion might be one that advises a study of taxonomies as a means of understanding the various aspects of cognition and affect in

order that objectives may be arranged in logical and orderly sequence.

Perhaps more important than a logical, orderly sequence somewhat arbitrarily assigned by a teacher is student acceptance or rejection of the objectives. What good is the application of a taxonomy in ordering objectives if the end result is one repulsive to the students? No matter how refined or scientific the procedure of arriving at objectives, little can be gained without the cooperation of the learner. Burns (1967a) suggests that teachers should experiment with lists of objectives, letting the learner choose the sequence in which he wishes, to achieve. Alternate, yet similar, objectives should be provided—*letting students choose what they desire to learn.* The observation and recording of the choosing behavior of the learners should produce insight into the learning process.

The difficulty of expressing objectives which deal with attitudes, interests and appreciations is readily acknowledged. Let it be immediately stated, however, that difficulty is not a license for neglect. Even though the behaviors people demonstrate (when they, for example, appreciate the uniqueness of each individual or have an attitude of open-mindedness toward individuals of other races) cannot be universally described, the teacher is advised to do the best he can and then continually revise behaviors in light of added experience.

An affective behavioral objective intended to illustrate the above point is as follows:

> The learner shows an appreciation for the worth and dignity of people of both minority and majority races as evidenced by non-discriminating interaction with both groups in casual classroom situations.

This objective is somewhat ambiguous in that the term "non-discriminating" lacks a common definition in most groups. The objective is limited when compared to the criteria suggested by Burns (1967b). For example, the student is not able to tell from the objective how well he is to achieve; he only knows that he is to evidence non-discriminating behavior which he really may not understand. The attachment of a proficiency level statement to the objective alters it in the following manner:

> The learner shows an appreciation for the worth and dignity of people of both minority and majority races as evidenced by non-discriminating interaction with both groups in *four out of five* casual classroom situations.

The criterion, "four out of five," is arbitrary and misleading. The objective has not been strengthened by this type of proficiency level statement. To refer again to Slack (1967), "When learning is inefficient, educational objectives tend to be 'broad' and unclear." Admittedly, the sample objective above is very broad, it is ambiguously stated, but it may be very relevant; therefore, some effort to provide learning experiences leading toward its achievement are warranted.

It seems appropriate at this point to suggest that objectives dealing with affect can not be formulated with the same degree of specificity as those dealing with cognition. The more specific affective objectives become, the more trivial they are. To dissect behaviors to the point where affective objectives can meet the same criteria as that suggested for the cognitive domain is to become needlessly mechanized. Affective objectives so developed would seem sterile or insignificant when compared to original purpose or intent.

Attitudes, appreciations and values are highly complex systems involving a multitude of observable behaviors. As an example, an appreciation of the worth and dignity of individuals of both minority and majority races might be manifested by a number of overt behaviors. In attempting to evaluate progress toward the achievement of the sample objective, a teacher, with the help of students, might develop a series of behaviors which seem to provide overt evidence of reaching the objective. Behaviors might be placed on a continuum for student self-rating before and after learning experiences related to the objective. An example follows:

Behaviors Related to Appreciation of the Worth
and Dignity of Individuals of All Races

withdraws upon being touched by a member of a minority (majority) race	0 1 2 3 4	initiates and tolerates normal contact with students of minority (majority) group
avoids sitting near minority (majority) students when choice is available	0 1 2 3 4	sits near (next to) minority (majority) when choice is available
makes negative comments about minority (majority) students in their absence	0 1 2 3 4	makes positive comments about minority (majority) students in their absence
responds to discussion of minority (majority) student's problems with trite statements	0 1 2 3 4	open-mindedly participates in discussion of problems and issues involving minority (majority) students
nominates only majority (minority) students for status or class leadership roles	0 1 2 3 4	nominates minority (majority) students for status or class leadership roles
limits casual conversation to members of own race	0 1 2 3 4	chats amiably with minority (majority) students in casual situations

NOTE: A minority student using this self-rating device would substitute "majority" for "minority."

The construction and use of a device such as this could be a valuable experience for students and teachers. It is not suggested as an instrument for collection of objective data about progress toward the same goal; neither is it recommended for obtaining data which feed into a student's score or grade in class. It is merely illustrative of how a teacher might attempt to guide self-evaluation of student progress toward or achievement of an affective objective, recognizing that 100 percent achievement is neither likely not observable in ordinary classroom situations. The fact that the above instrument is not objective should not devalue it for the purpose intended. The criticism by Buethe (1968), that an overemphasis on objectivity is a curse, is worth noting in this respect. The sample objective discussed above is broad and very difficult to measure. The following objective offered by Eisele (1967) is more specific:

> To show appreciation for the plight of the minority group in America by selecting a minority group and comparing their living conditions with those of a majority group in America.

This objective, while more specific, is questionable in that it seems to infer that the behavior, "comparing minority group living conditions with those of a majority group," is an evidence of appreciation for the plight of a minority group. As pointed out many years ago by John Dewey, the assumption that the knowledge of ethical and moral choices necessarily leads to ethical and moral conduct has little basis in fact (Raths, 1964). The Eisele objective also seems to imply a one-to-one relationship between an appreciation and an evidencing behavior, when in reality a cluster of behaviors may be related to an appreciation. Other criticisms could also be made of this objective, if its adequacy is to be evaluated against that established for writing cognitive objectives. Many more examples of objectives could be selected from the affective taxonomy and criticized in a similar manner, which merely reinforces the notion of difficulty associated with stating, implementing and evaluating affective objectives.

Difficulty in deciding upon and stating objectives is reflected by the recognition that many schools operate without objectives and most educational materials are prepared without behavioral outcomes. To expect educators to immediately define and use behavioral objectives in either the cognitive or affective domains would be like expecting a revolution. Perhaps a revolution is needed, but slow evolutionary progress in that direction is all that can be reasonably expected.

Burns (1968) offers one approach toward resolving part of the difficulty. He suggests that objectives be classified into two types. Type I objectives are knowledges, understandings and skills. These objectives can be expressed in specific behavioral terms and can be measured at the end of the instructional period. Type II objectives are interests, attitudes and appreciations. These objectives cannot be expressed in specific behavioral terms or, at best, only partially described. Burns believes that Type II objectives may be listed as goals of instruction, but the teacher should be extremely cautious about claiming that these objectives are obtainable by instruction. In regard to the value of Type II objectives, Burns (1968) points out that the primary problems that schools have in implementing these objectives develop because they must be stated in general rather than specific terms.

In spite of all the difficulties, teacher activity in attempting to identify and implement affective curricular objectives is desirable, mainly because it focuses attention upon a very crucial part of a child's education. In other words, it represents a *planned* attempt to educate affect *rather than simply depending upon chance alone.* The pursuit of skill in identifying and implementing affective objectives is believed to be a step toward achieving a better balance in curriculum goals.

REFERENCES

Bloom, Benjamin, ed. *Taxonomy of Educational Objectives, Handbook I: Cognitive Domain.* New York: David McKay Company, 1956.

Buethe, Chris. "A Curriculum of Value,"

Educational Leadership. Vol. 26, No. 1 (October, 1968), pp. 31–33.

Burns, Richard W. "Measuring Objectives and Grading," *Educational Technology.* Vol. 7, No. 17 (September 15, 1967), pp. 1–3.(a)

——"The Theory of Expressing Objectives," *Educational Technology.* Vol. 7, No. 20 (October 30, 1967), pp. 1–3.(b)

——"Objectives Involving Attitudes, Interests and Appreciations," *Educational Technology.* Vol. 8, No. 8 (April 30, 1968), pp. 14–15.

Childs, John W. "A Set of Procedures for the Planning of Instruction," *Educational Technology.* Vol. 8, No. 16 (August 30, 1968), pp. 7–14.

Eisele, James E. "Computers in Curriculum Planning," *Educational Technology.* Vol. 7,

No. 22 (November 30, 1967), pp. 9–16.

Kelley, Earl C. "The Place of Affective Learning," *Educational Leadership,* Vol. 22, No. 7 (April, 1965), pp. 455–57.

Krathwohl, David R. *et al. Taxonomy of Educational Objectives, Handbook II: Affective Domain.* New York: David McKay Company, 1964.

Mager, Robert F. *Preparing Objectives for Programmed Instruction.* Palo Alto, California: Fearon Publishers, 1962.

——*Developing Attitude Toward Learning.* Palo Alto, California: Fearon Publishers, 1968.

Raths, James. "A Strategy for Developing Values," *Educational Leadership.* Vol. 21, No. 8 (May, 1964), pp. 509–14, f.

Ripple, Richard E. "Affective Factors Influence Classroom Learning," *Educational*

Behavior as Objective in Education

C. Benjamin Cox

EDITORS' QUESTIONS:

1. Critically evaluate the following statement. "The idea of behavioral objectives, according to Broudy, is linked also with 'an earlier, more positivistic, and on the whole, a more naively inductive view of science' than is now in vogue."

2. Assess the value to the classroom teacher of Gronlund's set of general instructional objectives in the affective domain.

3. Evaluate the advisability and the feasibility of stating desired learnings within the affective domain in behavioral terms. Include a discussion of the factors which are involved in any attempt to measure learnings in this realm.

4. Analyze the differing methods of structuring behavioral objectives advanced by Gagné, Plowman and Mager. After reading the articles of these authors referenced by Cox, develop a set of behavioral objectives for classroom use based upon a synthesis of these approaches.

5. Construct a set of instructional objectives for teaching a unit in science. Use Gronlund's check list for evaluating the adequacy of your objectives. Make whatever changes are necessary and appraise the benefits derived from the use of this technique.

C. Benjamin Cox, "Behavior as Objective in Education," *Social Education,* 35, No. 5 (May, 1971), pp. 435–449. Reprinted with permission of the National Council for the Social Studies and C. Benjamin Cox.

Through uncertain, changing, and growing endeavors, issues and controversies parade endlessly. Not only is it often the case that there are unsettling questions and dilemmas, but also too often the necessary dimensions of inquiry are unknown. As a result, issues are drawn erratically and solutions are cast capriciously. In such a climate, fads offer hard competition for solidly grounded innovations, for sometimes they are indistinguishable and very often both elements are active in a single idea.

This article will attempt to examine such an idea. The supposition is that the current popularity of behavioral objectives, the idea in question, is both warranted on solid grounds and mindlessly promoted. This examination will try to discriminate between the disparate elements in the idea. The approach, in the main, will be to assess the nature, uses, and kinds of behavioral objectives following a brief survey of the sources of objectives in the curriculum.

It should be noted at the outset that the statement does not talk exclusively to social studies practitioners, though they are the target population. The assumption is made that the issues should be dealt with broadly.

Their resolution, however, may be unique in each field of instruction.

I. Sources of Educational Objectives

Educational planners, including teachers and curriculum makers, are always deeply involved in the identification and clarification of their goals and purposes. Objectives of every kind emerge from such planning operations, though ordinarily they reflect such limitations as the life uses of the learnings, the materials selected, the target population, the life expectancy of the plan, the nature of the bodies of knowledge used to support the project, as well as the perspicacity of the planners.

Society, Knowledge, and Learners as Sources

The sources of such objectives, however, are limited. In very general terms, there are three sources of objectives for educational programs. These include descriptive and predictive statements about children and adolescents, the society, and the disciplines that provide the content of the curriculum. Largely, educational objectives are derived from organized bodies of knowledge about individuals, groups, and culture including the literature on the goals of education and the political and socioeconomic goals of the nation, the information we possess about the characteristics of children, and the literature of developmental psychology and the various disciplines from which school subjects are derived. Textbooks themselves are an appropriate source of certain kinds of educational objectives.[1]

While the extraction of objectives for the educational enterprise would seem to be quite complex, given the variety of sources from which they may be generated, it is also recondite. Atkin locates the fundamental problem as lying in the easy assumption that we know or can readily identify either the educational objectives for which we strive or the outcomes that result from whatever programs we invent.[2] Further frustrating this situation is the perplexing occurrence of often selecting for emphasis in school programs those goals that are ephemeral, socio-degradable, or trivial. While few intend to spend their energies and time in educational work committed to the trifles of the culture and to the perpetuation of the profane and the mythological, it is too often the case.

The problem grows more complex at every glance and turn. Not only must teachers and curriculum makers work with bodies of knowledge that are variant in their quality and generality and in which are embedded a remarkable range of values and predictions, but also the clientele which they serve is as variable as the society itself ranging through the spectrums of personality, intelligence, social class, color, age, and the like. Each new variable bewilders the attempts toward generalizability. Some variables, of course, are more bewildering than others. Bialek, for example, found that 750 teachers rated a number of educational objectives as imperative for accelerated learners; but most of these same teachers rated no educational objectives as imperative for slow learners. Apparently teachers, as represented by this sample, are uncertain what to teach the intellectually less gifted clientele of the school.[3]

1. Paul D. Plowman, *Behaviorial Objectives,* Chicago: Science Research Associates, 1971, p. xxiv.
2. J. Myron Atkin, "Behavioral Objectives in Curriculum Design: A Cautionary Note," *The Science Teacher,* 35:28, May, 1968.
3. Hilton M. Bialek, "A Measure of Teachers' Perceptions of Bloom's Educational Objectives." Paper presented to AERA Annual Meeting, New York, 1967. See also William D. Johnson, "Use of Behaviorally Stated Educational Objectives," mimeo., University of Illinois, 1970, p. 3.

Content vs. Behavior

In contemporary curriculum development, there is at least one additional complication. In very gross terms, the curriculum development function in the schools has come to be dominated by two varying and, at times, antithetical cultures. On the one hand are the content scholars who represent the society's commitment to the venerable research disciplines that supply to most school subjects their life source of fact and concept. On the other hand are the evaluators, the behavior specifiers who represent in the curriculum a particular interpretation of the psychological foundations of learning.[4] It is unfortunate that the problem has become dichotomized in this fashion. For, from one point of view, the behaviorists and the discipline specialists make compatible bed partners. The psychological presuppositions which support the position of the behavior specifiers are quite similar to those that support the learning of disciplinary content, as this preoccupation has developed in the schools. Fortunately, the treatment of this false dichotomy is not central to this article.

It would be appropriate to deal with the Dewey-like question posed in Louise Tyler's suggestion that educational curriculum discussions ought to be about the consideration of the place and meaning of objectives in curriculum and instruction.[5] Some incisive minds should attack such a question; but that is too grand a task to undertake here. Rather, this statement will be an examination of the behavioral half of the dichotomy identified above. It will barely reach the edge of Tyler's directive. The primary occupation of this statement will be with the limited task of examining the nature, the uses, and the kinds of objectives preferred by behavioristic curriculum theorists and developers, evaluators, and teachers.

II. The Nature of Behavioral Objectives

This section shall attempt to review the grounds and justifications for behavioral objectives, the effect of behavioral objectives on instructional and curriculum decisions and operations, and some prescriptive statements on the production of behavioral objectives.

The Grounds in Behavioralism and Connectionism

The idea of behavioral objectives emerges from behavioristic and connectionist learning theories and their variants. While behavioral objectives represent a fairly simple adaptation of a fairly simple interpretation of learning, their popularity in schools is likely reflective of the utilization of behavioristic and connectionist theories of learning by educational practitioners.

The idea of behavioral objectives, according to Broudy, is linked also with "an earlier, more positivistic, and on the whole, a more naively inductive view of science" than is now in vogue. If this view is a correct one, and the imaginative, intuitive, and discovery features that are presently prominent in science continue to gain in importance, then the pressures to produce educational objectives and outcomes in behavioral terms may recede. Come what new devotions and notions may, behavioral objectives probably will be with us for many years to come. Though theories wax and wane with the temper of the times and are shaped by the kind of knowledge believed important at the time, educational ideas seldom die and few practices fade entirely away.[6]

4. Atkin, *op. cit.,* p. 29.
5. Louise L. Tyler, "Symposium on the Instructional Objectives Controversy." Paper presented to AERA Annual Meeting, Chicago, 1968, p. 5.
6. Harry S. Broudy, "Research and the Dogma of Behavioral Objectives," mimeo., University of Illinois, 1969, p. 3.

For some types of learning, behaviorism offers a believable and reliable explanation. Within this concept, learning is inferred from a change of behavior. That is, "people do not learn in a general sense, but always in the sense of a change in behavior that can be described in terms of an observable type of human performance." "A successful act of learning is inferred from the fact that the individual can now do something he could not do before."[7] Therefore, objectives referring to these acts have their counterparts in the behavior of individuals. Furthermore, these descriptive statements referring to the learned behavior of individuals can be classified in a number of ways.[8]

The assumption is made that these statements of behavioral goals take cognizance of the individual's understanding and attitudes. While the statement emphasizes the action itself, it is assumed that the described behavior is or will be the result of the learning individual's reasoned conclusion, his disciplined feelings, and his awareness of the situation at hand.[9]

In most references to these behavioral learnings, e.g., in Ralph W. Tyler's and Robert F. Mager's definitions of behavioral objectives, the concept of change is either stated or implied. And, as in the case of these examples, there is the further implication that the change is brought about by an external force. That suggests that some instrument of the curriculum is presumed to act upon the learner as he pursues the activities of the program. There are theoretical disagreements at this point by those who believe the exclusive reference to an external force defines the ground too narrowly. As one alternative, education and specific acts of learning may be thought of as freeing what is within the individual.[10]

Adapters and users of educational theories are prone to simplify the concepts in their practical application. The learning theories of the behaviorists have suffered their share of vulgarization at the hands of the proponents of behavioral objectives in the schools. Behavioral learning, though demonstrable by a simple combination of motions and symbols, is a complex concept as expressed by the theorists. Krathwohl quotes Martin Scheerer as saying that no true separation of behavior is possible. No matter how it is sliced for convenience, "the ingredients or motivation-emotion-cognition are present in one order or another."[11] For the purposes of research, evaluation, or instruction, however, the concept is too complex to deal with in all its dimensions at once. Consequently, researchers and analysts have attempted to conceptualize behavior more advantageously by teasing it apart, e.g., into affective and cognitive components, while keeping in mind the interrelations of the components.[12] The common error among the behavioral objectifiers is the neglect of the interrelations.

Views and Relationships of Objectives

Educational goals, obviously, may be stated from a number of points of view, e.g., an educational system, a particular school, the teacher, or the learner.[13] For the most part, behavioral objectives focus on pupil-learners, though occasionally, the teacher is identified as the behaver in the situation. Also, there are several levels of educational

7. Robert M. Gagné, *The Conditions of Learning,* New York: Holt, Rinehart and Winston, Inc., 1965, p. 172.
8. Benjamin S. Bloom, editor, *Taxonomy of Educational Objectives; Handbook I: Cognitive Domain.* New York: David McKay Company, Inc., 1956, p. 5.
9. Harry D. Berg, editor, *Evaluation in Social Studies,* Thirty-fifth Yearbook of the National Council for the Social Studies, Washington, D.C.: NCSS, 1965, p. 158.
10. Tyler, *op. cit.,* p. 3.
11. David R. Krathwohl, Benjamin S. Bloom, and Bertram B. Masia, *Taxonomy of Educational Objectives; Handbook II: Affective Domain,* New York: David McKay, Inc., 1964, p. 45.
12. *Ibid.,* p. 46.
13. Berg, *op. cit.,* p. 158.

goals. Very global goals may relate to the purposes of education in a society. Still at a very general level, goals may anticipate the effects of prolonged periods of instruction. There are multifarious course level objectives and very specific objectives at the lesson level.

Another way to look at objectives is with respect to their contingency relationship. That is, the achievement of some objectives depends upon the prior achievement of some other objectives. This relationship may be implied by the designation of terminal and interim objectives. Terminal objectives would state mastery behaviors or whole steps along the educational path. Statements referring to half-step subordinate skills and knowledge to be acquired before the students can master the terminal objective would be called interim objectives.[14] The linear hypothesis that supports this contingency relationship between terminal and interim or en route objectives has a limited validity in social studies and, therefore, should be applied judiciously. It is understood, for example, in mathematics that the operations of subtraction and multiplication are essential prior behaviors to the operation of division. Division could be designated as the terminal behavior with multiplication and subtraction designated as the en route or interim behaviors. In history, on the other hand, an understanding of the relationship between the separate states and the central government under the Articles of Confederation would not have to precede the understanding of the relationship between the states and the federal government as defined by the Constitution. In other instances in social studies contingency relationships may be hypothesized. Students could be required as an interim objective to learn the various logical forms of explanation prior to identifying these forms of ex-

planation in social material or judging the most adequate explanation in a given social situation.

Actually, the concept of terminality has little stability. Terminal behavior in one construction may be construed as interim in another. An objective maintains its interim or terminal position largely because the curriculum maker or the teacher has so designed it. From the learner's point of view, all behaviors are both terminal and interim; any learning can be thought of as an end in itself and as supporting or leading to further learnings. The notion is compelling enough, however, to argue for some kind of sequencing of activities in a curriculum.

Sequencing Objectives

Plowman deals with the questions of contingency behaviors by prescribing steps to be followed in the sequencing of behavioral objectives. This series of decisions provides for preparatory or cumulative behaviors to facilitate the performance of the terminal behavior. First, there is the decision about what the learner is to do when he has completed the sequence. Second, this terminal behavior is defined as a behavioral objective. Third, the decision is made on what preparatory tasks the learner must complete prior to his demonstration of the terminal behavior. Fourth, these preparatory, interim tasks are then cast as behavioral objectives and ordered along a continuum. If the objectives defined for this behavior system contain elements at different psychological or logical levels, then the sequencing of the behaviors should be arranged on the basis of the taxonomic or hierarchical structure that is presumed to contain the different elements.[15] Some of

14. F. Coit Butler, "Preparing Instructional Objectives," mimeo., American Institutes for Research, 1968, p. 8.
15. Plowman, *op. cit.*, p. 31.

these structures are treated later but, for the moment, one example is the taxonomy of the cognitive domain developed by Bloom and his associates.

The procedure outlined by Plowman attends to some but not all of the decisions identified by Gagné as affecting an educational "system." Besides decisions about objectives and the structure of the knowledge to be learned, Gagné insists that a systems approach demands attention to the motivation of the learner, the conditions in which the learning is to take place, and the transferability of the knowledge to be learned in the program. Both Gagné and Plowman emphasize decisions about assessment, an inherent aspect of behavioral objectives.[16]

The point to be made in this discussion is that in the more sophisticated statements about behavioral objectives, the idea is conceived as a complex and systematized approach to curriculum development as well as classroom instruction. Besides being means by which the teacher can infer specific learning, behavioral objectives are seen as the guidelines and signposts of the instructional program of the school.

Gronlund has attempted to encapsulate most of the decisions relative to the use of behavioral objectives in school programs in the following checklist. While some of his points have not been discussed the entire checklist is included here to help establish the context for the specifications of behavioral objectives which follow in the next section.

Check List[17]

                      Yes   No

Adequacy of the List of General Objectives

1. Does each general instructional objective indicate an appropriate outcome for the instructional unit? (See recommendations of curriculum and subject experts.) ____ ____

2. Does the list of general instructional objectives include all logical outcomes of the unit (knowledge, understanding, skills, attitudes, etc.)? ____ ____

3. Are the general instructional objectives attainable (do they take into account the ability of the students, facilities, time available, etc.)? ____ ____

4. Are the general instructional objectives in harmony with philosophy of the school? ____ ____

5. Are the general instructional objectives in harmony with sound principles of learning (e.g., are the outcomes those that are most permanent and transferable)? ____ ____

Statement of General Objectives

6. Does each general instructional objective begin with a *verb* (e.g., knows, understands, appreciates, etc.)? ____ ____

7. Is each general instructional objective stated in terms of *student performance* (rather than teacher performance)? ____ ____

8. Is each general instructional objective stated as a learning product (rather than in terms of the learning process)? ____ ____

9. Is each general instructional objective stated in terms of

16. Gagné, *op. cit.,* p. 263.
17. Norman E. Gronlund, *Stating Behavioral Objectives for Classroom Instruction,* New York: The Macmillan Company, 1970, pp. 51-52.

the students' *terminal behavior* (rather than the subject matter to be covered)? ____ ____

10. Does each general instructional objective include only one general learning outcome? ____ ____

11. Is each general instructional objective stated at the proper level of generality (i.e., is it clear, concise, and readily definable)? ____ ____

12. Is each general instructional objective stated so that it is relatively independent (i.e., free from overlap with other objectives)? ____ ____

Behavioral Definition of General Objectives

13. Is each general instructional objective defined by a list of specific learning outcomes that describes the terminal behavior students are expected to demonstrate? ____ ____

14. Does each specific learning outcome begin with a *verb* that specifies definite, *observable behavior* (e.g., identifies, describes, lists, etc.)? ____ ____

15. Is the behavior in each specific learning outcome relevant to the general instructional objective it describes? ____ ____

16. Is there a sufficient number of specific learning outcomes to adequately describe the behavior of students who have achieved each of the general instructional objectives? ____ ____

During the reading of the next section, the reader may wish to refer to Gronlund's list for a comparison of criteria.

Definition of Behavioral Objectives

In this section a working definition of behavioral objectives will be attempted. Generally speaking, objectives of any ilk serve similar purposes in curriculum and in instruction. They are primarily destinations or intended states toward which the educational process is to tend. They declare the hoped-for conditions, the expectancies, the anticipated consequences of the educational system. Within this definition, behavioral objectives are a subclass of the class concept objectives. As such, they are presumed to function within the curriculum as would objectives of any definition. The argument is, however, that objectives of the garden variety are possessed of ambiguity and vagueness. They are often expressed in global, indefinite, or imprecise terms and fail to provide guidance for the teacher or the student.

Broudy insists that the basic import of the move toward behavioral objectives is objectivity rather than behaviorality. Primarily, he says, "the motive is to exorcise the evils of fuzziness and idiosyncracy from subjective judgments."[18] The high priests of behavioral objectives go a step further in their stipulation, however. They assert that the only way to achieve clarity in statements of objectives is to couch them in behavioral terms. Such a statement, according to Gagné, is an operational definition "that communicates reliably to any individual . . . the set of circumstances that identifies a class of human performances." These operational definitions, according to Gagné, are comprised of four basic components: (1) a verb denoting observable action; (2) a description of the class of stimuli being responded to; (3) a word or words denoting the object used for action, unless implied by the verb; and (4) a description of the class of

18. Broudy, *op. cit.*, p. 1.

correct responses.[19] These four components are reflected in both Mager's and Plowman's criterial steps for framing behavioral objectives. Mager's formula, perhaps the most famous of the prescriptions for preparing behavioral objectives, is included here for examination.

> First, identify the terminal behavior by name; we can specify the kind of behavior which will be accepted as evidence that the learner has achieved the objective.
>
> Second, try to further define the desired behavior by describing the important conditions under which the behavior will be expected to occur.
>
> Third, specify the criteria of acceptable performance by describing how well the learner must perform to be considered acceptable.[20]

Plowman's framing steps, fair replications of Mager's, additionally prescribe the prior determination of the method to be used in judging the performance.[21]

Assuming that objectives perform a significant function in the curriculum and that there is a useful place for objectives in the design of instruction, this discussion has proposed that the clear and unambiguous statement of objectives can increase their benefit. It was further hypothesized in this section that a way to make objectives pellucid is to state them in behavioral terms. Furthermore, the decisions to be made and the steps and procedures to be followed in framing statements of objectives of this order were specified. Such statements were represented as operational definitions that claim the qualities of observability and measurability.

Meaningfulness vs. Worthwhileness

A major objection to the idea of behavioral objectives is a reaction to the dogmatic insistence that objectives having observable and measurable behavioral counterparts are meaningful and worthwhile. Critics such as Atkin, for example, declare that the as-

sumption that measurable goals are most worthwhile is untenable. Rather, the judgment of worthwhileness of an objective comes first, not the methods for assessing progress. Goals, says Atkin, need to be derived in terms of their significance, not their measurability.[22] The requirements for stating behavioral objectives have the effect of shifting objectives toward the trivial. Typical criteria necessitate overt behavior, the prediction of situations which the learner must respond to, and an evaluation procedure. It is doubtful whether the application of these criteria alone will result in significant statements of instructional goals.[23]

Raths suggests that a loosening of these criteria might help matters inasmuch as no goal is ever absolutely specific anyway. Some degree of ambiguity is inherent in all statements of objectives, no matter how carefully and precisely they are defined. Furthermore, Raths declares, the criteria proposed for behavioral objectives lead to statements that are more specific than teachers use in practice.[24] Critics Eisner and Haberman believe that only the simplest of aspects of instruction are readily stated in behavioral terms. The dynamics of classroom interaction are much too complex and reflect too many important affective considerations to be predicted by specific behavioral objectives.[25]

19. Gagné, *op. cit.,* pp. 242-243.
20. Robert F. Mager, *Preparing Instructional Objectives,* Palo Alto: Fearon Publishers, 1962, p. 12.
21. Plowman, *op. cit.,* p. 15.
22. Atkin, *op. cit.,* p. 30.
23. Tyler, *op. cit.,* p. 4.
24. James D. Raths, "Specificity as a Threat to Curriculum Reform." Paper presented to AERA Annual Meeting, Chicago, 1968, mimeo., pp. 3-4.
25. Elliot W. Eisner, "Educational Objectives: Help or Hindrance?" *The School Review,* 75:250-260, Autumn, 1967. Martin Haberman, "Behavioral Objectives: Bandwagon or Breakthrough?" *The Journal of Teacher Education,* 19:91-94, Spring, 1968. See also William D. Johnson, *op. cit.,* p. 1.

While the behavioralists have answers for most of these charges, the indictments warrant careful examination. In the perception of these critics, promotion of behavioral objectives has prompted undue attention to the insignificant, the trivial, and the simpler operations in education.

III. Uses for Behavioral Objectives

In the previous section the nature of behavioral objectives as defined by their proponents was examined in some detail. Also, a cursory hearing was given to some of the objections raised to the employment of behavioral objectives. This part will look at some additional claims for behavioral objectives in terms of the uses that are suggested for them. Additionally, a few of the abuses for which behavioral objectives have been blamed will be examined. The supposition is that the utilization of behavioral objectives provides both benefits and detriments. Potential users and producers of behavioral systems should examine both the claims and the blames.

Behavioral Objectives as an Empirical Base

The popularity of behavioral objectives has grown with the increasing demand for the development of an empirical demonstration of educational improvement. Credibility and accountability are the new clichés which couch the demands made upon teachers, schools, and curriculums by parents, newly militant groups, and society itself. Either procedures for laying an empirical foundation must be developed and marketed widely or believable reasons for not doing so must be forthcoming. Though he sees no simple solution for this dilemma, Baker predicts that if we continue on a whimsical, guesswork basis in the development of our educational program, our school curriculums will be overloaded with phantom objectives that cannot be anticipated or even identified.[26]

The behavioral objectivists tend to see effectiveness and efficiency as the twin criteria of improvement. Reflecting these criteria, instruction is viewed as basically the management of the conditions of learning pointed toward producing the greatest possible change in performance in the shortest possible time. Linked to this definition of instruction is the dictum that clearly stated behavioral objectives are the essential first step towards sound instructional design.[27] The road to an adequate response to the demands of the society for an empirical demonstration of improvement in education is paved with behavioral objectives.

At the whimsical level of operations in the schools, the learning of children is regularly and consistently compromised. Schooling is related to learning in a most obscure and vague way. In this quagmire of uncertainty the behavioralists propose to lay stepping stones of consistent reliability and dependability. They opt for the direct measurement of outcomes, according to Gagné, to insure that instructional objectives have been met. Building on his concept of the hierarchical nature of knowledge, which he poses as a useful structure on which to construct behavioral objectives, Gagné explains that it is useless for the learner to proceed to advanced levels of the hierarchy if earlier objectives are unmet.[28]

Applications of Behavioral Objectives

Proponents of behavioral objectives assert that in the classroom the motivations

26. Robert L. Baker, "The Educational Objectives Controversy." Paper presented to AERA Annual Meeting, Chicago, 1968, pp. 1-3.
27. Butler, *op. cit.,* pp. 9-10.
28. Gagné, *op. cit.,* p. 260.

and performance of the student are directly related to his knowing what to do and how well he did. Some teachers, operating under a different understanding of motivation, try to prevent students from knowing exactly what is expected assuming that students left in the dark will study more than what is minimally required and thus learn more. Classroom behavioralists see this both as a false assumption and as an inefficient exercise. Students shouldn't have to guess; they will waste time studying the wrong things.[29]

That is not to say that these individuals see the classroom as a totally mechanized operation. For Gagné, at least, the use of behavioral objectives in classrooms is differentiated for extemporaneous and predesigned instruction. Ordinary classroom interaction is considered by Gagné as extemporaneous inasmuch as decisions concerning the direction of discourse are made in response to unanticipated events. Predesign, on the other hand, is a general characteristic of mediated instruction which is less flexible and subject to more prior decisions concerning expected performances.[30]

At the point of evaluation, behavioral objectives can help the teacher design appropriate test items and discriminate among relevant and irrelevant test items. The objective, "To develop a knowledge of American history," for example, would offer the teacher no guidance in designing or selecting items to test his students.[31]

It should be noted that these positive arguments are not represented as being inclusive. While the uses expressed in the above discussion appear to be advantageous and defensible, there are obviously many other supportive statements that can be made concerning the use of behavioral objectives. Haberman, for example, whose list is included below as a summation of this section,

identifies seven advantageous uses of behavioral objectives in the design of curriculum and in the instruction in classrooms as well as in the training of teachers and in the process of research.

1. Behavioral objectives give both teachers and pupils a *clear sense of purpose.*

2. Behavioral objectives facilitate the fragmenting of content into *meaningful and manageable* pieces.

3. Behavioral objectives facilitate the *organizing of content* into hierarchies and therefore instructional sequence.

4. Behavioral objectives simplify *evaluative procedures.*

5. Behavioral objectives simplify the *training of teachers.*

6. Behavioral objectives *clarify the relevance* of particular pieces of instructional material.

7. Behavioral objectives open the educative process to *research and planning.*[32]

In the next section some of the more critical detriments of behavioral objectives in the process of education will be analyzed.

Detriments of Behavioral Objectives

Opposition to the employment of behavioral objectives in the schools does not extend, for the most part from the judgment that the idea is actually fraudulent or that it does not produce reliable, empirical data or permit the development of sound instructional designs. Rather, the objections are grounded largely in the claim that devotion to specific goals in the process of education precludes attention to other important mat-

29. Butler, *op. cit.,* p. 2.
30. Gagné, *op. cit.,* p. 251.
31. Mager, *op. cit.,* pp. 33, 37.
32. Haberman, *op. cit.;* see also Johnson, *op. cit.,* p. 1.

ters in education. Raths expresses the objection in terms of the typical values of teachers. The requirements of specificity now being advanced by Mager, Popham, Walbesser and others, he asserts are in direct conflict with the traditional values of teachers. Teaching for such limited goals is not only an unappealing task for classroom teachers, but also is antagonistic to their spirit of humanitarianism and, in addition, runs counter to their values of intellectualism.[33] Teaching, from this point of view, is something of an art form possessing a high affective tone that successfully integrates compassion and romanticism with the intellect. Devoting one's energies and requiring the devotion of the energies of hundreds of students to the performance of niggling pieces of behavior is a dehumanizing commitment. Furthermore, in this view, teachers are seen as perceiving themselves as intellectuals who prefer to deal with specific content and information primarily as a means to clarify the powerful ideas of a general nature in the culture. The extreme preoccupation with the particles of learning, presumably demanded in a behavioral system, averts the teacher and his student from this grander involvement.

At a more practical level, in the day-to-day interaction of the classroom, rigid goals, according to Atkin, inhibit the teacher's accommodation to his classroom and to the teaching situation. The incorporation of this new master in the classroom, the behavioral system, produces a mechanical pedagogical style on the part of the teacher and results in his loss of spontaneity in his work with students.[34] As expressed by Broudy, behavioral objectives put a premium on teaching information and on the rote recall of definitions, rules and principles, particular operations, and the solution of problems having only one solution.[35] Atkin further clarifies

this behavioralistic syndrome suggesting that when the identification of outcomes is accepted and even expected, the curriculum will naturally tend to emphasize these. As a result, those outcomes that are identified only with difficulty or are rarely translated into behavioral terms will tend to atrophy.[36] The syndrome, again within the conception of Broudy, is characterized by a preoccupation with the replicative uses of knowledge. The overemphasis on the replicative use of knowledge has had the unfortunate consequence of making relatively unpopular within the educational system the interpretive, associative, and applicative uses of knowledge, though these are particularly important in life after school.[37]

Broudy further claims that our excessive concern with behavioral objectives is accompanied by a belittling of the important life-use aspect of schooling embodied in the concept of tacit knowledge. Tacit knowledge, according to Broudy and Polanyi, is a kind of social wisdom made up of a mysterious amalgam of once known, but unattended specifics that allows one to judge, to understand, or to explain without being able to recall the particulars that support the judgment or without being able to identify the many specific behaviors that comprise the judgment.[38] That some such knowledge function does obtain seems fairly evident on the observance of highly trained professionals, for example, who regularly make diagnoses, prognoses, and analyses that theoretically require the application of complex principles and concepts without being able to recall the source of their knowledge

33. Raths, *op. cit.*, pp. 3-4.
34. Atkin, *op. cit.*, p. 29.
35. Broudy, *op. cit.*, p. 1.
36. Atkin, *op. cit.*, p. 28.
37. Broudy, *op. cit.*, p. 2.
38. *Ibid.*, p. 7.

or being able to identify the particular conceptual inputs into the judgment or even being able to express them on demand in a coherent way. Broudy does not appear to claim, in this instance, that attention to behavioral specifics prevents the appearance of tacit knowledge; but he is suggesting that excessive attention to one aspect of learning precludes an appropriate interest in the development of the other.

In the development of curriculum, a task in which he is both accomplished and experienced, Atkin declares that the early articulation of behavioral objectives by the curriculum developer limits the range of his exploration. The curriculum developer becomes so committed to designing a program that will achieve these particular goals that he is unable to see the delicate and fascinating opportunities that shimmer fitfully in the periphery of his vision. Furthermore, certain types of curricular innovations are hampered or even frustrated by the early demands for behavioral statements of objectives.[39]

There are additional objections to behavioral objectives, some stemming from other frames of reference, e.g., Broudy's contention that the behavioralistic orientation of research has produced a dangerous accumulation of anomalies in educational theory and practice.[40] But the arguments included in the discussion above are perhaps sufficient to express the critical tone of much of the opposition in the school setting.

In a recent AERA conference, Popham listed the 11 most common objections raised against the employment of behavioral objectives in the schools. To each of these criticisms he expressed his own response as a strong proponent of behavioral systems in curriculum and instructional programs. Epitomizations of the 11 criticisms and Popham's responses are paralleled in the

columns following and are offered here without further comment as a suitable summation of this section.[41]

Reasons given in opposition to behavioral objectives	Popham's responses to the objections
1. Trivial behaviors are easiest to operationalize. Really important outcomes will be underemphasized.	1. Explicit goals allow easier attention to the important goals.
2. Prespecification prevents teacher capitalization of unexpected instructional opportunities.	2. Ends do not necessarily specify means. Serendipity is always welcome.
3. There are other types of educational outcomes that are also important, e.g., for parents, staff, community.	3. Schools can't do everything. Primary responsibility is to pupils.
4. Objectively, mechanistically measured behaviors are dehumanizing.	4. Broadened concept of evaluation includes "human" elements.
5. Precise, preplanned behavior is undemocratic.	5. Society knows what it wants. Instruction is naturally undemocratic.
6. Behaviorally described teaching is not natural, is unrealistic of teachers.	6. Identifying the status quo is different than applauding it.
7. In certain areas, e.g., fine arts and humanities, it is more difficult to measure behaviors.	7. Sure it's tough; but still a responsibility.
8. General statements appear more worthwhile to outsiders. Precise goals appear innocuous.	8. We must abandon the ploy of "obfuscation by generality."

39. Atkin, *op. cit.,* pp. 2-3.
40. Broudy, *op. cit.,* pp. 12-13.
41. W. James Popham, "Probing the Validity of Arguments Against Behavioral Goals." Paper presented to AERA Annual Meeting, Chicago, 1968, pp. 1-7, *passim.*

Reasons given in opposition to behavioral objectives	Popham's responses to the objections
9. Measurability implies accountability. Teachers might be judged on their ability to produce particular results rather than being judged on many bases.	9. Teachers *should* be held accountable for producing changes.
10. It is more difficult to generate precise objectives than to talk of them in vague terms.	10. We should allocate the necessary resources to accomplish the task.
11. Unanticipated results are often most important. Prespecification may cause inattentiveness.	11. Dramatic unanticipated outcomes cannot be overlooked. Keep your eyes open!

IV. Kinds of Behavioral Objectives

In earlier sections of this article occasional references to kinds and levels of objectives were made. In one instance the concept of terminality was examined with its categories of terminal objectives and interim or en route objectives. In another instance, specifically in Gronlund's checklist, reference was made to general objectives and their meaning specifiers, specific objectives. In each of these instances it was indicated that some controlling concept ordered the relationship between the large and the small objectives, e.g., contingency, cumulation, entailment, or sequence. That is, the accomplishment of the large objective is contingent upon the prior successful accomplishment of the smaller objectives; or the performance of the larger objective is accomplished by the putting-all-together of the prior smaller objectives; or the meaning of the larger objectives is simply specified by the behaviors identified in smaller objectives; and so forth. The logic of these various relationships deserves a more careful

examination than is offered in this statement. However, if behavioral objectives are to remain with us with any degree of permanency as a part of our curriculum and instructional language, then both the psychological and logical dimensions of these relationships should be pursued with considerable deliberateness.

Structuring Behavioral Objectives

One attempt to provide a structure by which behavioral objectives can be sequenced is Gagné's hierarchy of learning types. Gagné hypothesizes that there are several types or levels of learning that can be ordered along a hierarchy whose controlling concept is complexity. At the base of Gagné's hierarchy is *signal* learning or conditioned response. At the second level is *stimulus response* learning or precise response to discriminated stimuli. The third type of learning is the *chaining* of stimulus response bonds. At Gagné's fourth level, *verbal associations* or verbal chains are formed. Next is *multiple discrimination,* defined as very complex stimulus responses. At a still higher level is *concept learning* where the individual learns a common response to a class of stimuli. At the seventh level chains of concept are put together in the performance of *principle learning.* Finally, at the apex of Gagné's hierarchy is *problem solving.* This level of learning requires that the individual manage a number of internal events called thinking.[42]

The supposition is that the application of such a conceptual structure to the preparation of behavioral objectives would add legitimacy and respectability to the process. Behavioral objectives could be classified according to the level of learning involved and sequenced appropriately, e.g., a level seven

42. Gagné, *op. cit.,* pp. 58-59.

objective should be preceded in the instructional program by a level six behavior. The example is only illustrative, for a number of hypothesized structures are available as guidelines for the preparation of behavioral objectives.

Plowman lists 14 types of learning sequences which could serve to establish the sequence in behavioral systems. His list is included here as evidence of the variability possible in the design of these systems.

TYPES OF LEARNING SEQUENCES[43]

1. Fact #1 → Fact #2 → Fact #3. . . .
2. Fact → Concept
3. Concrete Experience → Abstract Representation of Experience
4. Skill #1 → Skill #2 → Skill #3. . . .
5. Maturative or Developmental Level #1 → #2 → #3. . . .
   Personal or Societal Developmental Task #1 → #2. . . .*
6. Level of Awareness #1 → #2 → #3. . . .
   6.1 Through sensitizing a person to his environment.
   6.2 Through sensitizing a person to relationships among persons, among institutions, and among data.
   6.3 Through multi-sensory experience.
   6.4 Through using and developing all the senses.
7. Level of Rationality #1 → #2 → #3. . . .
   e.g., Comprehension and proposed solution to problem.
   7.1 Using additional facts, possibly from different subject-matter disciplines, to achieve successively higher levels of comprehension.
   7.2 Formulating more sophisticated definitions of the problem.
   7.3 Generating a number of possible solutions to the problems.
8. Ways of gathering data, solving problems, or of bringing about change.
   8.1 Various strategies and processes, usually starting with gathering data and organizing it in some way and ending with either verification of solutions or institutionalization of an innovation.
9. Knowledge → Comprehension → Application → Analysis → Synthesis → Evaluation†
10. Cognition → Memory → Divergent Thinking → Evaluative Thinking**

Creative Process††

11. Preparation → Incubation → Illumination → Revision

Creative Skill

12. Awareness and sensitivity to a situation → Cognitive reordering of elements of the situation → Search model formation → Verification of product and worth of product and testing
13. Conceptualizing an object of art → Preparing a plan → Selecting medium and materials Choosing tools → Producing an object of art → Evaluating the product

Leadership

14. Getting other persons to engage in an activity or to carry out a task with few or no objections or interruptions.

   Planning → Motivating → Organizing → Coordinating → Protecting Followers → Evaluating

The Cognitive Taxonomy as Structure

Among the types of learning sequences identified by Plowman is the cognitive taxonomy developed by Bloom and nearly three dozen of his examiner and evaluator colleagues across the United States.[44] The taxonomy has proved of special value in the evaluation process and has remarkably direct application for the curriculum maker or the teacher attempting to design behavorial systems for classroom employment. The taxonomy is especially useful because it deals with behavioral phenomena that teachers have typically been concerned with. Its conceptualizations of behavior, especially in the first three levels, are reflected in their own language about the classroom. Furthermore, the taxonomy has enjoyed many rich interpretations and varied applications in the literature.

*Robert J. Havighurst, *Developmental Tasks and Education*, New York: McKay, 1952.
†See reference Bloom *et al.*
**J. P. Guilford, "Creativity: Its Measurement and Development," *A Source Book for Creative Thinking*, edited by Sidney J. Parnes and Harold F. Harding. New York: Scribner's, 1962.
‡Graham Wallas, *The Art of Thought*, New York: Harcourt, Brace & World, Inc., 1926. From E. Paul Torrance, *Guiding Creative Talent*, Englewood Cliffs, New Jersey: Prentice-Hall, Inc., 1962, p. 17.
43. Plowman, *op. cit.*, pp. 34-35.
44. Bloom, *op. cit.*

Gronlund has applied the cognitive taxonomy to the statement of general instructional objectives and specific learning outcomes. The vertical components of his table reproduced below reflect the six categories of cognitive objectives: knowledge, comprehension, application, analysis, synthesis, and evaluation. The verbs on the right-hand side of the table refer to specific behaviors sought for in the cognitive realm. A behavioral objective in the cognitive domain would begin appropriately with one of these verbs.

Examples of General Instructional Objectives and Behavioral Terms for the Cognitive Domain of the Taxonomy[45]

Illustrative General Instructional Objectives	Illustrative Behavioral Terms for Stating Specific Learning Outcomes
Knows common terms Knows specific facts Knows methods and procedures Knows basic concepts Knows principles	Defines, describes, identifies, labels, lists, matches, names, outlines, reproduces, selects, states
Understands facts and principles Interprets verbal material Interprets charts and graphs Translates verbal material to mathematical formulas Estimates future consequences implied in data Justifies methods and procedures	Converts, defends, distinguishes, estimates, explains, extends, generalizes, gives examples, infers, paraphrases, predicts, rewrites, summarizes
Applies concepts and principles to new situations Applies laws and theories to practical situations Solves mathematical problems	Changes, computes, demonstrates, discovers, manipulates, modifies, operates, predicts, prepares, produces, relates, shows, solves, uses
Constructs charts and graphs Demonstrates correct usage of a method of procedure	
Recognizes unstated assumptions Recognizes logical fallacies in reasoning Distinguishes between facts and inferences Evaluates the relevancy of data Analyzes the organizational structure of a work (art, music, writing)	Breaks down, diagrams, differentiates, discriminates, distinguishes, identifies, illustrates, infers, outlines, points out, relates, selects, separates, subdivides
Writes a well organized theme Gives a well organized speech Writes a creative short story (or poem, or music) Proposes a plan for an experiment Integrates learning from different areas into a plan for solving a problem Formulates a new scheme for classifying objects (or events, or ideas)	Categorizes, combines, compiles, composes, creates, devises, designs, explains, generates, modifies, organizes, plans, rearranges, reconstructs, relates, reorganizes, revises rewrites, summarizes, tells, writes
Judges the logical consistency of written material Judges the adequacy with which conclusions are supported by data Judges the value of a work (art, music, writing) by use of internal criteria Judges the value of a work (art, music, writing) by use of external standards of excellence	Appraises, compares, concludes, contrasts, criticizes, describes, discriminates, explains, justifies, interprets, relates, summarizes, supports

45. Gronlund, *op. cit.,* p. 21.

The Affective Taxonomy as Structure

Potentially useful in subject areas as value tumescent as social studies is the taxonomy of objectives in the affective domain produced by Krathwohl, Bloom, and Masia in association with the evaluators who had helped on the cognitive taxonomy. To date, the affective taxonomy and affective goals in general have received comparably less coverage in educational literature. The reasons for this relative neglect are fairly evident. For one thing, there is a lack of general theory to account for the various kinds of affective outcomes. Unlike the cognitive domain that is blessed with numerous concepts, principles, generalizations, and laws organized variously into a half-dozen or so coherent theories, there are few, if any, accepted generalizations in this realm.[46] The absence of a general affective theory presents a major obstacle in identifying, observing, and measuring affective behaviors.

Also an aura of privacy tends to enshroud the realm of the affective. Persons in this culture are expected to claim the right to their own opinions, many of which are laced with affect. Children are rather carefully taught from the moment they express their first distaste of the adult world that, especially in their communications with their elders, they should keep their feelings to themselves, particularly if they are negative ones. Mystical conceptualizations of affective behaviors have caused the domain to be imbued with a special sanctity. Not only are attitudes, appreciations, tastes, feelings, interests, opinions, values, and the like thought to be private possessions, but also they are viewed as almost inviolable. Teachers are taught to abhor indoctrination and to resist making wholesale assaults on their students' values.

At the same time, positive valences are expressed toward rather rigid conceptualizations of good art, good music, and good behavior and attitudes, such as decency, nonprejudice, and acceptance. Similarly, negative valences are expressed toward pornography, bad music and other noises, ribaldry, prejudice, rejection, and the like. Fraught as it is with unreliable concepts and uncertain relationships, the domain is approached with ambivalence and escaped in dilemma.

The behaviors of the affective realm seem to be more elusive and ephemeral than the behaviors of the cognitive realm. The child can be asked his attitude (an approach not essentially different than that used in assaying his knowledge); but he may not know it, or he may not be able to verbalize it, or he may not want to tell it. Furthermore, his response may change capriciously over time and circumstance.[47]

Situational observations of affective behavior, as with cognitive behavior, is the most reliable means of evaluation. Short of that, the individual can only be asked what he would do in a given situation, again, a condition not appreciably different from that in the cognitive domain.

The difference that does make a difference in the preparation and evaluation of objectives in the two realms is that a cognitive objective is always a *can-do* response, while an affective objective is always a *does-do* response. Behaviors of the can-do variety are traditionally and relatively easily triggered and evaluated. But behaviors of the does-do variety, while highly valued, tend to be more difficult to trigger reliably and standardize.[48]

Gronlund has applied the affective tax-

46. Berg, *op. cit.*, p. 119.
47. *Ibid.*, p. 164.
48. Krathwohl, pp. 60-61.

onomy also to the statement of general instructional objectives and specified learning outcomes. The vertical components of his table refer to the five categories of affective objectives, receiving, responding, valuing, organization, and characterization, as defined in the taxonomy. As in the exemplary table for the cognitive domain, the verbs on the right-hand side of the table refer to appropriate behaviors sought for in the affective realm. According to the prescriptions offered earlier for the preparation of behavioral objectives, the statement of a behavioral objective in the affective domain would appropriately begin with one of these verbs.

Examples of General Instructional Objectives and Behavioral Terms for the Affective Domain of the Taxonomy[49]

Illustrative General Instructional Objectives	*Illustrative Behavioral Terms for Stating Specific Learning Outcomes*
Listens attentively Shows awareness of the importance of learning Shows sensitivity to human needs and social problems Accepts difference of race and culture Attends closely to the classroom activities	Asks, chooses, describes, follows, gives, holds, identifies, locates, names, points to, selects, sits erect, replies, uses
Completes assigned homework Obeys school rules Participates in class discussion Completes laboratory work Volunteers for special tasks Shows interest in subject Enjoys helping others	Answers, assists, complies, conforms, discusses, greets, helps, labels, performs, practices, presents, reads, recites, reports, selects, tells, writes
Demonstrates belief in the democratic process Appreciates good literature (art or music) Appreciates the role of science (or other subjects) in everyday life	Completes, describes, differentiates, explains, follows, forms, initiates, invites, joins, justifies, proposes, reads, reports, selects, shares, studies, works
Shows concern for the welfare of others Demonstrates problem-solving attitude Demonstrates commitment to social improvement	
Recognizes the need for balance between freedom and responsibility in a democracy Recognizes the role of systematic planning in solving problems Accepts responsibility for his own behavior Understands and accepts his own strengths and limitations Formulates a life plan in harmony with his abilities, interests, and beliefs	Adheres, alters, arranges, combines, compares, completes, defends, explains, generalizes, identifies, integrates, modifies, orders, organizes, prepares, relates, synthesizes
Displays safety consciousness Demonstrates self-reliance in working independently Practices cooperation in group activities Uses objective approach in problem solving Demonstrates industry, punctuality and self-discipline Maintains good health habits	Acts, discriminates, displays, influences, listens, modifies, performs, practices, proposes, qualifies, questions, revises, serves, solves, uses, verifies

The Relationship of the Cognitive and Affective

The dichotomization of behavior into cognitive and affective realms, as practiced in the above discussion and in most of the literature, is a conceptual convenience. It reflects a human incapacity for dealing simultaneously with all aspects of behavior at an

49. Gronlund, *op. cit.,* p. 23.

adequate level of sophistication. Underlying this analysis is the assumption that somewhere it can be put all together. Meanwhile, the glimmer of an interrelationship is grasped when it appears to be useful to the purpose of the moment. For example, it seems useful for a student to experience the affective behavior of awareness as a prelude to his demonstrations of the cognitive behavior of knowing.

Similarly, curriculum guides and course syllabi are replete with interest objectives. Bruner suggests in an expression of the rationale of much of the curriculum movement of the 1960's that we must develop "in the child an interest in what he is learning and with it an appropriate set of values and attitudes about intellectual activities in general."[50] Teachers are poignantly aware of the relationship between motivation and learning. Motivation, a concept that reflects many affective particulars, is a major way that the affective domain is used as a means to the cognitive. As Krathwohl expresses it, the influence of hedonic tone on memory and learning is appreciable.[51]

Teachers often intuitively use cognitive behaviors and the achievement of cognitive goals as a means to attain affective behavior. For example, a teacher who challenges his students' beliefs or discusses issues in class may be satisfied with the interaction only when students commit themselves emotionally to a point of view or ground their opinions in a value position. Sometimes cognitive objectives are prerequisite to affective goals. For example, an appreciation of art or music at a sophisticated level would need to be preceded by an understanding of art and music, at least at the level of analysis.[52]

The inference to be drawn from this discussion is that in the designing of a behavioral system in a curriculum or in an instructional setting, the designer should attend to both cognitive and affective behaviors. It should not be inferred, however, that the conceptualizations and the sequencing pattern need be those presented in the two taxonomies.

One attempt to draw these two realms together in the evaluation of students is seen in the performance scale of Leppert and Payette. In this instance the affective is represented by the concept willingness while the cognitive is represented by the concept ability. The specific behaviors intended are categorized under the general behaviors of communicating, thinking, and acting.

DESCRIPTION OF STUDENT PERFORMANCE ASPECTS[53]

Date: _____

Class: _____

Name of student: _____

Evaluator: *Teacher* *Group member* *Self*
(Circle one)

Directions: The assessment of the person's behavior may be made at any point along the scale. H represents High; M, Medium; L, Low. Check ( ) the appropriate point on the scale for each of the behaviors observed.

WILLINGNESS TO COMMUNICATE

The person described

1. shares facts	H / M / L
2. shares personal beliefs about people and institutions	H / M / L
3. shares interpretations	H / M / L
4. shares personal experiences	H / M / L
5. shares vicarious experiences, i.e., learning based on the experiences of others	H / M / L
6. shares rating experiences	H / M / L
7. shares feelings	H / M / L

50. Jerome Bruner, *The Process of Education*, Cambridge, Massachusetts: Harvard University Press, 1960, p. 73.
51. Krathwohl, *op. cit.*, p. 57.
52. *Ibid.*, pp. 55-56.
53. Ella Leppert and Roland F. Payette, "Description of Student Performance Aspects," mimeo., University of Illinois, 1970–71.

ABILITY TO COMMUNICATE

The person described communicates

8. clearly rather than vaguely	H	/ M	/	L
9. accurately rather than erroneously	H	/ M	/	L
10. freely rather than reluctantly	H	/ M	/	L
11. sensitively rather than insensitively	H	/ M	/	L
12. deliberately rather than compulsively	H	/ M	/	L

WILLINGNESS TO THINK

The person described

13. formulates hypotheses	H	/ M	/	L
14. defines terms	H	/ M	/	L
15. examines how terms are used	H	/ M	/	L
16. searches out all related information	H	/ M	/	L
17. establishes logically necessary conclusions	H	/ M	/	L
18. rates events on the basis of standards	H	/ M	/	L
19. identifies values pertinent to social issues or problems	H	/ M	/	L

ABILITY TO THINK

The person described

20. tests hypotheses, beliefs, conclusions against appropriate information	H	/ M	/	L
21. tests the adequacy of terms by reference to customary usage by offering explicit reasons for new uses of terms.	H	/ M	/	L
22. applies tests to determine whether conclusions follow necessarily from the reasons provided in an argument	H	/ M	/	L
23. revises conclusions as required by new information	H	/ M	/	L

WILLINGNESS TO ACT

The person described

24. participates in the resolution of issues and problems	H	/ M	/	L

ABILITY TO ACT

The person described

25. acts consistently with tested beliefs	H	/ M	/	L
26. stresses negotiation rather than arbitrariness	H	/ M	/	L

Summary

This statement has looked primarily at the description, uses, and kinds of behavioral objectives. While arguments for and against behavioral objectives have been offered, it is presumed that neither a conclusion that they are either good or bad nor the judgment that they should or should not be used can be made on the basis of this review. If the teacher decides to employ behavioral objectives in his teaching, there are significant hazards which he should attempt to avoid. If he decides, on the other hand, that he should not make use of behavioral systems in his classroom, then for him, too, there are significant perils to which he should attend.

Perhaps the issue is prematurely drawn that requires the teacher at our present level of understanding to choose either one option or the other. Rather, the teacher should ask himself what goals the employment of behavioral objectives will enable him to achieve and to what extent he wishes to commit his teaching to those goals.

Analyzing Early Childhood Education Programs: The Nature of Educational Objectives

Joe L. Frost *

EDITORS' QUESTIONS:

1. Diagram the hierarchy of educational objectives described by Frost and explain the relationships which exist among levels of objectives. Stipulate ways in which this approach is helpful in the planning of instruction.

2. Design a program for "disadvantaged" 5-year-old children. Be sure that you have specified desired objectives at the program, intermediate and instructional levels. Then, choose a particular program objective and identify the instructional objectives which contribute to its achievement.

3. State an instructional objective in mathematics. Specify the different instructional activities which would contribute to the attainment of such an objective.

4. Distinguish between product-, process- and content-oriented educational programs. What purposes are served by making such distinctions?

Joe L. Frost. "The Nature of Educational Objectives." *EDUCATIONAL LEADERSHIP* 28(8): 797–801; May 1971. Reprinted with permission of the Association for Supervision and Curriculum Development and Joe L. Frost. Copyright © 1971 by the Association for Supervision and Curriculum Development.

Educators and other professionals are confronted with a renewed concern for the development of early childhood education programs. A preliminary process leading to local program development is the examination of existing types of early childhood education programs. This process is facilitated and objectified to some extent through analysis of the various types of goals related to these programs. The scheme for analysis of objectives characteristic of individual programs may be represented by a triadic hierarchy (Figure 1).

Program Goals

The objectives of a particular program may be described at any one of these levels: program, intermediate, or instructional.

Some statements, in fact, contain a mixture of unrelated objectives at several levels.

Program Objectives

Program objectives are extremely broad in nature, serving to describe the major intent of a program. Program sponsors may communicate their intent as *custodial*, though this is unlikely, given current emphasis on educational child care; or they may publicize their major intent as *educational*.

Publicized objectives are not always true indicators of actual practice, and the operational program should be examined before making final judgments about program ob-

* Joe L. Frost, Associate Professor of Curriculum and Instruction, The University of Texas at Austin, and Member, ASCD Early Childhood Education Council

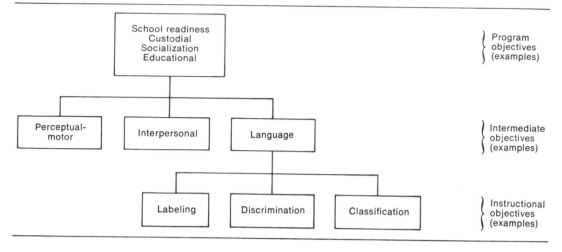

Figure 1 Analysis of Objectives of Individual Programs

jectives. If the program is truly *custodial,* concerned only with keeping children confined while parents work, no further analysis of educational objectives is needed. Such a program is indefensible from a child development-education point of view. Given an early childhood *education* program emphasis or objective, the evaluator may examine the reports and/or operational procedures of the program to determine *precise* objectives.

Intermediate Objectives

Intermediate objectives are selected on the basis of existing knowledge about human development—how humans develop intelligent behavior or the incremental evolution of the individual's abilities to control the environment. For educational purposes, the major dimensions of development are typically categorized as cognitive, affective, and psychomotor. Such categorization is highly artificial, particularly the cognitive-affective dichotomy, for increase in control over one's environment is affected when emotional *or* psychological damage *or* benefit is effected.

Similarly, typical curriculum process-content-product dichotomies are highly artificial for these are, in the strictest sense, inseparable. Nonetheless, it seems essential for communication that certain of the intermediate-type objectives be identified and described in relation to common classificatory patterns (Figure 2).

The identification of intermediate objectives and their categorization into a systematic framework help to assure that important dimensions—for example, socialization, language—are not under- or over-emphasized, though a strong case may be made for switching, adding, or deleting elements of the particular categorization system.

Instructional Objectives

Broad goals are appropriate as directives for programs or units of study. Systematic analysis of program and intermediate objectives leads to specific instructional objectives, for program goals are logical outcomes of instructional goals. Specific instructional goals actually define program goals. A prevalent pattern in curriculum development is to base instruction and evaluation on broad program goals. Educators with a behavioral-environmental orientation see this practice as evidence of a vast leap of faith and logic, while those with a cognitive-transactional view may consider specific statements of instructional objectives far too narrow and restricting.

Support that instructional objectives are linked to psychological evidence is most clearly seen in reply to the question, "Should instructional objectives be stated in behavioral terms?" A number of books have been published on this issue in recent months (McAshan, 1970; Popham and Baker, 1970; Armstrong *et al.,* 1970; Kibler *et al.,* 1970), and arguments for and against behavioral objectives are accumulating (see Popham, 1970; Macdonald and Wolfson, 1970).

Educators deal with the child's behavior by necessity because they have no direct control over genetics and neurophysiology, at least for the present. Such important global dimensions as knowing, understanding,

and valuing cannot be directly observed, so the educator acts and reacts (teaches) on the basis of what he or she can observe, that is, the direct behavior of the student (what he does, says, or writes). From such observations the teacher can only *infer* knowing, understanding, and valuing.

The range of present early childhood programs is extremely broad in nature, including, at one end of the continuum, the day care-custodial-socially oriented-therapeutic types, and, at the other extreme, academically oriented-concentrated instruction types, with many possible varieties in between. Each type may conceivably have the same ultimate goal: the development, in general terms, of a "fully functioning" individual. The perpetuators of each program may simply have a different point of view regarding the proper procedure for assisting in the development of such a person.

Objectives do not inherently fix methodologies. The personnel of the socially oriented schemes may feel that logical procedure is to provide a variety of materials and socializ-

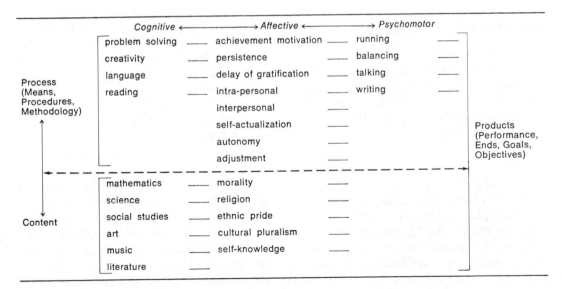

Figure 2 Intermediate Objectives (Representative)

ing opportunities and to guide the child to explore and discover relevant social and intellectual behaviors for himself. In such situations, instructional objectives usually are either unspecified or are stated in very general terms. This places a great burden of interpretation upon the observer, who attempts to conceptualize operational bases and procedures, and it severely limits communication to others who would attempt replication.

Some operational instructionally-oriented programs use precise behavioral goals, usually ordered in a hierarchical manner; evaluation is sometimes constructed to match these goals. Precise objectives allow for precise definition of a program, assuming, of course, that methodology and other major curricular dimensions are defined. The fact that socially oriented programs are not typically defined by precise objectives does not necessarily mean that they could not be or should not be, but rather that social ends are not as amenable to precise definition as are cognitive ones.

Characteristics of Objectives

In addition to a determination of the levels at which objectives are described, analysis can be continued by examining: (a) the range and priority of objectives; (b) the degree of relatedness seen among them; and (c) their process-content-product focus.

Range and Priority

The range of objectives may vary from almost total emphasis upon one objective (for example, language) to a broadly-based program encompassing most or all of the types of objectives shown in Figure 2. Three interrelated factors are influential here: (a) how the sponsors of the program view the nature and needs of the children for whom

the program is intended; (b) what relationships are assumed to exist among various categories of behavior; and (c) the underlying view (implicit or explicit) of human development and learning.

Many current preschool programs are intended for "disadvantaged" children. Therefore, selection of objectives for such programs is based on analyses of the ways in which children from such families differ from those that are more "advantaged." (The use of this basis for selection cuts across all views of development and learning.) Some educators see the "disadvantaged" as lacking certain behavior patterns such as impulse control, ability to follow the rules of classroom conduct, specific language skills or vocabulary, or auditory and visual discrimination skills, and believe that each of these patterns can be taught separately.

Others focus on broader characteristics such as attention span, delay of gratification, self-concept, and achievement motivation or on more inclusive objectives such as competence. Each program gives priority to the objectives considered most crucial to the child it serves, while assuming that other objectives: (a) are achieved in other ways (for example, through home or family); or (b) will be fulfilled as secondary or concomitant learnings.

Careful examination of representative programs shows that objectives may be unspecified yet inherent in ongoing methodology and in the outcome measure used. If a relatively consistent methodology is employed, these inherent objectives may be derived through systematic analysis. For example, motivation and persistence, though not specified as objectives, may result from the careful sequencing of tasks, the social reinforcement (verbal) from the teacher, and the consistent success of pupils in performing increasingly complex tasks.

Degree of Relatedness

Another influence on the range of behavior dimensions identified in objectives and the levels (program, intermediate, instructional) at which they are described is the sponsor's view of the degree of interdependence among these dimensions. If individual behaviors are seen as responses to be associated with other behaviors through the proper programming of cues and reinforcement contingencies, then the objectives, at the instructional level, tend to be quite specific and focused on those behaviors considered relevant to the attainment of broader goals.

Objectives tend to be more general (intermediate level) if specific behaviors or learnings are viewed as closely related to one another within broad mental structures, and thus dependent upon the development of these structures.

The *products* of educational intervention, for example, abilities to perform given tasks, result from *processes,* and processes require *content* —an inseparable relationship. Given a desired product, the ability to discriminate between four shapes, one teacher may choose language drill as a teaching medium, requiring the child to repeat over and over, "A square has four equal sides," or "A triangle has three sides." In isolation this would represent an extreme version of the "teaching English as a foreign language" technique, and the alert teacher would learn that parroting words for which insufficient conceptual referents or prerequisite abilities had been established is wasteful.

A second teacher might provide a set of wooden shapes and allow the children to explore them, in either a leisurely or a structured fashion. Yet the language referents may not be developed, teacher questioning may be limited, and pupil talk may not be systematically encouraged. Such a situation may be found in some Montessori programs

enrolling "disadvantaged" children.

A third teacher may provide for both systematic language interaction and object exploration but choose to allow children to abuse one another verbally and physically, and she may produce certain other undesirable behaviors through punitive or coercive actions. Certain objectives may be emphasized and others deemphasized in the early childhood program, but not to the extent that fundamental interrelationships between process, content, techniques, and objectives are jeopardized.

Process-Content-Product Focus

The writer rejects the notion of *unequivocal* differentiation of "process," "content," and "product." However, he presents here an operational scheme for program analysis, since programs tend to emphasize one or more of the three factors in their statements of objectives. For purposes of program analysis, "process" may be defined as: (a) the systematic series of actions (teaching methodology and learning activities) directed toward some end (objective), for example, the set of teacher-child behaviors characteristic of "discovery" learning; and (b) a series of progressive and interdependent steps by which an end is attained, for example, the cumulative acquisition of abilities or competencies in the evolution of language or, in a broader sense, intelligent behavior. In the most elementary terms, process refers to "how" an objective is to be achieved.

"Content" is defined as the substance or matter of the educative process, for example, mathematics, science, music. Referring to Figure 2, it is seen that certain elements, for example, "religion," "ethnic pride," readily fit in the categories of "process" *and* "content," for they obviously include more than mere subject matter to be learned.

"Product" refers to that which is produced by, or results from, an action or operation (process). "Product" may be defined as the achievement of a given objective evidenced by measured performance of particular tasks or skills, or in simplest terms, "what" is to be achieved.

The process-oriented program emphasizes procedures or means, "how" things are done, for example, how to identify objects, how to construct with blocks, how to discriminate and classify, how to get along with one's peers. Also involved is learning what to look for in certain situations and subject areas when certain kinds of operations, for example, classification or seriation, are applicable, and how to check one's answers.

Some process-oriented programs lack specific instructional objectives. The early Head Start programs, for example, relied upon a series of 12 broad program goals.

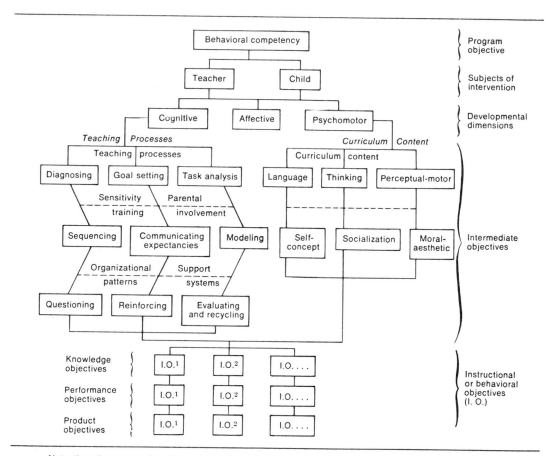

Note that the two major dimensions of the model are (a) *teaching processes* and (b) *curriculum content* (which may be considered processes). In teacher education, curriculum content is mastered primarily through the use of *knowledge objectives*; teaching processes are mastered primarily through the use of *performance objectives*; and the ultimate worth of the teacher education program is measured by means of criterion referenced *product objectives* or the performance of pupils.

Figure 3 A Dyadic Model for Teacher Education—Early Childhood Curriculum

Consequently, guidelines were subject to almost infinite interpretation. Similarly, a number of experimental program developers seem to confuse objectives (ends) with procedures (means). Examples of stated "instructional objectives" gleaned from the Follow Through models are: "to involve children" and "to encourage participation." These are merely broad statements of desired teaching *procedures* and should not be construed as objectives or ends.

Figure 3 illustrates how teaching procedures are integrated with curriculum variables. This model shows the inseparable relationships among various types of objectives, teaching processes, curriculum content, developmental processes, and support systems. None of these elements alone represents a complete program for young children. Process-oriented programs are more consistent with the cognitive-transactional view of development than with the behavioral-environmental view.

The content-oriented program emphasizes what is to be learned, for example, the numerals to ten, selections of verses or songs, names of body parts, role of community helpers, or the letters of the alphabet. Kindergartens geared to developing "readiness for school" usually emphasize content to be learned. The maturational-normative view is typically held by those who produce programs with a content emphasis.

The product-oriented program emphasizes observable outcomes. In contemporary programs, outcomes are defined in terms of behavioral change. Behaviorally stated objectives are specified in advance of teaching. The act of teaching is viewed as hypothesis testing (X teaching should produce Y behavior), and the success of the selected methodology (hypothesis) is judged by the child's performance on a given task. Emphasis upon product (getting to the desired end as soon as possible) is more consistent with the behavioral-environmental view of learning and development than with the other views described.

REFERENCES

R. J. Armstrong *et al. The Development and Evaluation of Behavioral Objectives.* Worthington, Ohio: Charles A. Jones Publishing Co., 1970.

J. L. Frost and G. T. Rowland. *Compensatory Programming: The Acid Test of American Education.* Dubuque: William C. Brown Company, 1971.

R. J. Kibler *et al. Behavioral Objectives and Instruction.* Boston: Allyn and Bacon, Inc., 1970.

J. B. Macdonald and B. J. Wolfson. "A Case Against Behavioral Objectives," *The Elementary School Journal* 71 (3): 119–28; December 1970.

J. H. McAshan. *Writing Behavioral Objectives.* New York: Harper & Row, Publishers, 1970.

W. J. Popham. "Probing the Validity of Arguments Against Behavioral Goals," Paper presented at the annual American Educational Research Association meeting, Chicago, Illinois, February 1968. In: R. J. Kibler *et al. Behavioral Objectives and Instruction.* Boston: Allyn and Bacon, Inc., 1970.

W. J. Popham and F. L. Baker. *Establishing Instructional Goals.* Englewood Cliffs, New Jersey: Prentice-Hall, Inc., 1970.

D. P. Weikart. "A Comparative Study of Three Preschool Curricula," Paper presented at the annual American Educational Research Association meeting, Santa Monica, California, March 1969. In: J. L. Frost and G. R. Hawkes. *The Disadvantaged Child: Issues and Innovations.* Second edition. Boston: Houghton Mifflin Company, 1970.

Recommended Readings: Identifying and Stating Instructional Objectives

Ammons, M. "Definition, Function and Use of Educational Objectives," *The Elementary School Journal* 62 (1962):432–436.

Atkins, J. M. "Behavioral Objectives in Curriculum Design: A Cautionary Note," *The Science Teacher* 35 (1968):27–30.

Bloom, Benjamin S., ed. *Taxonomy of Educational Objectives; The Classification of Educational Goals. Handbook 1: Cognitive Domain* New York: Longmans, Green & Co., 1956.

Burns, Richards *New Approaches to Behavioral Objectives.* Dubuque, Iowa: Wm. C. Brown Company Publishers, 1972.

————"The Theory of Expressing Objectives," *Educational Technology* 7 (1967): 1–3.

————"Objectives Involving Attitudes, Interests and Appreciations," *Educational Technology* VIII (1968):14–15.

Canfield, Albert A. "A Rationale for Performance Objectives," *Audio-visual Instruction* 13 (1968):127–129.

Eiss, Albert F. and Harbeck, Mary Blatt *Behavioral Objectives in the Affective Domain.* Washington: National Science Supervisors, Asso., (1969). pp. vi–42.

Grieder, C. "Is it Possible to Word Educational Goals?" *Nations Schools* 68 (1961): 10.

Gronlund, Norman E. *Stating Behavioral Objectives for Classroom Instruction.* New York: The Macmillan Company, 1970.

Hearn, Edell M. *Simulated Behavioral Teaching Situations.* Dubuque, Iowa: Wm. C. Brown Company Publishers, 1971.

Jarolimek, J. "Taxonomy: Guide to Differentiated Instruction," *Social Education* 26 (1962):445–447.

Kapfer, Philip G. "Behavioral Objectives in the Cognitive and Affective Domains," *Educational Technology* VIII (1968):11–13.

Kibler, Robert J., Barker, Larry L., and Miles, David T. *Behavioral Objectives and Instruction.* Boston: Allyn and Bacon, 1970.

Krathwohl, David R., Bloom, Benjamin S. and Masia, Bertram B. *Taxonomy of Educational Objectives; The Classification of Educational Goals. Handbook II. Affective Domain.* New York: David McKay Company, Inc., 1964.

MacDonald, James B. and Wolfson, Bernice J. "A Case Against Behavioral Objectives," *The Elementary School Journal* 71 (1970):119–128.

Mager, R. F. *Preparing Instructional Objectives.* Palo Alto: Fearon Publishers, 1962.

McAshan, H. H. *Writing Behavioral Objectives: A New Approach.* New York: Harper & Row, Publishers, 1970.

Ojemann, R. H. "Should Educational Objectives Be Stated in Behavioral Terms?" *The Elementary School Journal* 68 (1968): 223–231.

Palmer, R. R. "Evaluating School Objectives," *Educational Research Bulletin* 37 (1958):60–66.

Popham, James W., Eisner, Elliot W., Sullivan, Howard J., Tyler, Louise L. *Instructional Objectives.* Chicago, Illinois: Rand McNally & Company, 1969.

Rahmlow, Harold F. "Specifying Useful Instructional Objectives," *NSPI Journal* VII (1968):7.

Strategies for Diagnosing and Assessing a Child's Learning Needs

The growing commitment to individualized instruction has intensified the need for teachers to devise better classroom diagnostic procedures. Section 2, therefore, is devoted to the presentation of different diagnostic strategies in order to provide teachers with an understanding of the process of diagnosis and to foster their acquisition of the technical competence to apply it in the classroom.

Hunter proposes a series of diagnostic questions designed to aid teachers in discovering the pupil's degree of prior achievement, learning capabilities, interests and attitudes. She also indicates that diagnosis is a continuous process and that evaluation-based diagnostic questions can provide the means of furthering learning progress. Great care is taken to indicate that any diagnostic procedure should provide information which can serve as a basis for decision making in connection with the development of teaching strategies, the motivation of individual learners and the assessment of learning achievement.

A procedure for the diagnosis of reading disabilities is outlined by Kirk and Bateman. Though the article is written for teachers of exceptional children, the diagnostic procedures suggested can be utilized by classroom teachers in general. The authors of this selection stress the importance of going beyond initial diagnosis by including, as a vital step in the procedure, the planning of specific remedial procedures. They further propose a plan for the development of a scientific pedagogy in the area of learning difficulties involving (1) the development of behavioral diagnostic instruments for assessing psycholinguistic disabilities, (2) empirical validation of these instruments and (3) the determination of the educability of children having such disabilities. Particularly helpful is the use of case studies to illustrate the diagnosis and remediation of learning difficulties. The use of this technique permits the student to examine how the steps in the diagnostic procedure can be applied in actual situations.

Okey stresses the need for a high degree

of precision in diagnosis. He contends that it is not enough for the teacher to have a knowledge of the general capabilities of each student but that she must be able to pinpoint the specific learning difficulties requiring alleviation. Two kinds of diagnoses which teachers may be required to make are examined in detail and are categorized in accordance with the observed learning characteristics of the students being examined. These two kinds of diagnosis are (1) diagnosis aimed at students with learning problems and (2) diagnosis aimed at "successful" learners.

The use of a hierarchy of learning objectives or an "instructional map" is suggested as an aid in diagnosing students' capabilities and deficiencies. The procedure given for constructing such a learning hierarchy and applying it to the diagnostic process is one of the major contributions of this selection.

Boehm relates the experience of developing an assessment procedure for measuring pupil progress during the school year in a New York State funded experimental pre-kindergarten program. A valuable outgrowth of this process was the development of an Inventory of Cognitive Skills and Visual-Motor Functioning. The author stresses the beneficial effects of teacher, aide and parent cooperation upon the development of this instrument and suggests that this same approach can be used as a model for evolving additional assessment procedures.

Section 2 is designed to enhance the student's capacity to:

1. Discuss the significance of assessing pupils' abilities, interests and attitudes.
2. Construct a learning hierarchy and illustrate it through the use of a flow diagram.
3. Demonstrate the functional utility of a learning hierarchy.
4. Develop a check list consisting of diagnostic questions for determining a pupil's degree of prior achievement, for discovering his learning capabilities and for determining his interests and attitudes.
5. Develop instruments for assessing those strengths and/or weaknesses of a particular child which might facilitate or impede his learning progress.
6. Predict the possible effects of the child's weaknesses upon his learning behavior and devise specific ways of alleviating such weaknesses.
7. Recommend specific ways of using a child's strengths as bases for remedial instruction.
8. Devise her own original methods of gathering information about the capabilities of each learner and illustrate through examples how such information can be used for making instructional decisions.

When the Teacher Diagnoses Learning

Madeline Hunter

EDITORS' QUESTIONS:

1. Enumerate and discuss the factors which must be given consideration in determining appropriate learning objectives for individual pupils.

2. Is diagnosis properly regarded as a prelude to teaching activities or as a pervasive component of the instructional process itself? Provide examples which substantiate your answer.

3. Assume a set of observations resulting from diagnosis of a particular pupil's needs and capabilities. Indicate how each of these observations affects the development of a strategy for teaching a particular skill.

4. It has been suggested that not every piece of information obtained through diagnosis is necessarily relevant to the teaching-learning process. Suggest criteria for distinguishing between relevant and irrelevant diagnostic information.

5. How does a knowledge of the pupil's physical condition, psychological profile and his home environment assist the teacher in structuring learning experiences?

6. Suggest materials and techniques, other than classroom observation and objective diagnostic tests, which might be useful in assessing pupils' learning needs and capabilities.

7. In what ways does a teacher's choice of learning objectives affect the diagnostic process? Substantiate your answer.

Madeline Hunter. "When the Teacher Diagnoses Learning." *EDUCATIONAL LEADERSHIP* 23(7): 545–49; April 1966. Reprinted with permission of the Association for Supervision and Curriculum Development and Madeline Hunter. Copyright © 1966 by the Association for Supervision and Curriculum Development.

What kind of a boy is Johnny? What has he already learned? What "next" learning tasks are appropriate for him? How can a teacher increase the efficiency and economy of his accomplishment?

As the teacher confronts these questions for each learner under his supervision, small wonder he is tempted to murmur, "Please pass the crystal ball!" Fortunately, crystal balls and divining rods are not available on supply requisition lists, so professional rigor is beginning to replace folklore and fantasy as the basis for diagnosis of and for educational prescription for the learner.

This shift from routinized application of the currently recommended panacea (what is it this year, look-say or phonics?) to decision making based on critical evaluation of each learner has been the major factor in the change from the technology of teaching to the profession of education.

Madeline Hunter is principal, University Elementary School, University of California, Los Angeles.

101

No longer is diagnosis restricted to or reserved for only the educationally "sick." Rather, such diagnosis has become an intrinsic part of the teaching act for *all* learners. Out of such diagnosis are created educational prescriptions. The repertoire of competencies of the teacher and alternatives offered by the school constitute a pharmacy from which such prescriptions are filled.

We first must identify the questions such diagnosis is designed to answer. Only then can we seek instruments whose validity, reliability and precision give us confidence in the accuracy of the assessment on which diagnosis is based.

Diagnostic Questions

Identification of the essential and relevant has as its irrefutable and logical counterpart identification of the nonessential and irrelevant. The latter, no matter how fascinating and tempting (with *that* home situation what can you expect of me?), must be discarded. We also must discard many of our most easily collected but relatively worthless "test results" on learners.

Each datum we use in our diagnostic procedure must pass the screen of contributing to the answer to one of the following questions:

1. What objective is appropriate for this learner to achieve? (Notice the change from "*I* am seeking to attain with this learner.")

2. What is his present status in relation to that objective?

3. What is the next learning step in attainment of that objective?

4. Based on data about this particular learner, what can the teacher do to help him take that step efficiently and economically?

5. Was he successful?

6. If so, what is the next appropriate step?

7. If not, what changes should be made?

Questions 1, 2, and 3 are content-based. Knowledge of the learning task (reading, math, or ball playing) must be related to the assessment of the learner's present degree of achievement.

Question 4 is learner-based. An assessment of the intellectual, physical, social, and emotional factors that contribute to or detract from the learning process provides the data for the answer.

Questions 5, 6, 7 are evaluation-based, where "at this moment in time" must become the qualifying phrase for any answer.

Let us begin with an inspection of these questions as they relate to a physical activity so we will not get trapped in the value-imbued educational platitudes ("competency in reading," "appreciation of the democratic process"), which are so emotionally charged. Suppose we are trying to determine the appropriate high jump objective for a boy of a given age. The first factor that becomes obvious is that other data may be more critical than his age. Does he have long or short legs? Is he fat or thin? How well is he muscled and coordinated? (It makes you stop to reconsider the statement that ten-year-old boys should be reading at a fifth grade level, does it not?)

Suppose we agree that this boy should be able to clear a five-foot bar. Now we turn to our second question—how high can he actually jump? We find (possibly to our horror) that he can comfortable clear only a 3' 8" bar, although on occassions he can jump a 4' one. Obviously, at this point we are not going to insist he keep trying the 5' bar, but plan to start teaching so he can consistently clear the 4' one. (Hammering away at 5th grade work that is too difficult is as obviously unsound.)

Our fourth question is concerned with

the use of data about the learner that will guide us in planning the learning opportunity and teaching strategy to help him accomplish his task. Will competition with other jumpers stimulate or retard his effort? What for him is the optimum ratio of success to failure? If he responds well to performance heavily weighted with success, we had better keep the bar at 3' 10". If he is motivated by the frustration of some failure, let us start at 4'. What does he need in the way of teacher support? Shall we stand by to encourage or let him work by himself? Does he respond well to his own perception of growth or does he need public recognition of his achievement? Will his parents contribute to his achievement motivation or do they think high jumping is a waste of time? (His parents may be getting a divorce or his father may be an alcoholic; however, these dramatic bits of information are not relevant unless we find evidence that they contribute to or detract from his accomplishment of the learning task.)

Now that we have defined the task, and applied a teaching strategy to help him accomplish it, did it work? If the answer is "yes," we are ready to move on to the next task, raise the height of the bar and proceed. If the answer is "no," we must look for factors that may need to be changed. Have we correctly assessed his jumping ability or should we have started with a lower bar? Could there be something wrong of which we were not aware (fatigue, low energy, movement or coordination difficulties)? Was our teaching strategy ineffective? Should we have given more encouragement? Should we have been "tougher" and insisted he "get at it" with consequences if he did not? Would making him the high-jump coach for less able jumpers do the trick? Are there other factors operating which we had not taken into consideration?

By practicing, he may miss the opportunity to talk with fascinating girls or perhaps he may be attempting to insure our continued attention by his lack of success.

Our estimate of the correct answer to all of these diagnostic questions becomes the basis for an adjusted educational prescription. Again we fill the prescription from the pharmacy of teaching competency and the alternatives possible in the school and again assess its effectiveness by the performance of the jumper.

Diagnosis in Reading

Let us now pose these same questions in the diagnosis of a learner we find in every classroom.

Bill is not performing well in reading. While not so remedial that he needs special help, he is dragging at the bottom of his group. We have the uncomfortable feeling that the only thing he is learning is that reading is a bore to be avoided whenever possible.

We begin our diagnosis with the first question, "What goal is appropriate for this learner?" Notice by using goal in the singular, we are being forced to give priority to "enjoyment of reading" or "skills in reading" or "appreciation of literature" or "more active participation in the reading program." Once we identify the primary goal we are able to deal with or eliminate the incompatibility of other goals. (Chaucer and enjoyment may not be compatible at this point.) Unidentified, their counter-directions can neutralize our teaching efforts.

If we select "enjoyment of reading" as the goal basic to the achievement of all others, this becomes our criterion for answering subsequent questions. (It also eliminates such temptations as having his dad make him read an hour each night.)

Our second question, "What is his present status in relation to that goal?" involves a valid assessment of Bill. The eyes and ears of a well prepared teacher continue to be among the best instruments of appraisal; however, we can validate or supplement these observations with objective tests. There is a relationship (but not one to one correspondence) between enjoyment of and skill in an activity, so we need carefully to assess Bill's reading skills. We look beyond the homogenized 5.3 grade placement score on the fact sheet of a reading test because the information we are seeking is inside the test and we will find it only if we inspect Bill's responses.

What kinds of items did he miss? Did he do the easy ones correctly and then quit? Were careless errors responsible for missing easy items while he passed harder ones? Could his errors indicate an attempt to respond correctly or was he simply filling in the blanks? Most important, how does his test performance compare with our daily perception of him? If he performs significantly better in either the test or classroom, what factors might be responsible? Obviously, a numerical grade placement score does not begin to answer these questions.

Let us assume our answer is: Bill *can* read 5th grade material with understanding but the vocabulary load slows him down. Fourth grade material insures a more comfortable pace; however, the content of both 4th and 5th grade material he finds uninteresting. When the reading is difficult he seems to turn off his effort and make wild guesses. When the content is uninteresting, he withdraws into daydreaming with a resultant lack of focus on the learning task.

Our assessment of Bill's performance should direct us to the answer to the question, "What is the next appropriate learning step?"

Now we have two criteria to guide us. The material must be easy enough to encourage his progress and interesting enough to hold his focus. This may involve abandoning, for a time, the state series and selecting a book with a low vocabulary load and exciting content. Remember, "enjoyment of reading" is the goal with highest priority at this point in time. (We are adjusting the high jump bar so he can get over it.) We have not abandoned word attack skills and extraction of meaning but we are concentrating on first things first.

Having selected an appropriate task, we now turn to our design to help him accomplish it. Here our diagnosis of the learner requires professional literacy in learning theory and personality theory. To what reward system will he respond? Will his accomplishment be positively reinforcing or do we need to add the social rewards of praise and recognition? Do we need to suppress any behavior (such as avoidance of reading) by negative reinforcement? Will *in*creasing or *de*creasing anxiety result in better motivation? How long a reading period can he tolerate before negative feelings take over? How might we extend this period?

These are samples of the questions we must answer for a valid diagnosis. The questions determine whether we skillfully entice him into the reading task or arbitrarily assign it with a time limit and consequences. We may make him the star performer in a book review or may quietly converse with him when the rest of the group are busy. We may make reading a definite assignment or a leisure-time activity. We may "keep after him" or turn him loose.

Diagnosis must lead to action. As mere intellectual exercise it is useless. Consequently, based on our best judgment, we will do *something*. The results determine the validity of our diagnosis and prescription. If all goes well we will proceed to the next learning task. If not, we will reassess our answers to each of the questions, revise our diagnosis and prescription, and try again.

Many people are seeking an instrument that will diagnose, then will "tell us what to do." It is important that we remember this has not been accomplished in any profession that deals with the intricacies of a human being. The thermometer registers with considerable accuracy the temperature of the patient but a doctor must decide which medication to use. In spite of his best and learned judgment, some patients are allergic to the dose and some are beyond his ability to help. Still we have seen tremendous advances in the skill and precision of the medical diagnostician.

As educators, we too are increasing the skill and precision of our assessment of the learner, so we no longer need to keep interminable records and stockpile useless data to stuff cumulative folders. By identification of the critical elements of an assessment we may be sure that instruments will be devised so their objectivity and precision will augment but never replace the highly trained observation that guides educational decisions.

Diagnosis and Remediation of Learning Disabilities

Samuel A. Kirk
and Barbara Bateman

EDITORS' QUESTIONS:

1. What are some of the limitations of the Illinois Test of Psycholinguistic Abilities (ITPA) as a diagnostic instrument? Suggest ways in which this device can be combined with other diagnostic procedures to develop a comprehensive program for the diagnosis of learning needs and capabilities.

2. What advantages are offered by the case study method of diagnosing learning difficulties which are not readily obtainable through the use of an alternative approach?

3. It is indicated that one of the objectives of current research is the development of instruments for the discovery of specific psycholinguistic disabilities. Once this has been accomplished, would it be advantageous to go a step further and attempt to differentiate between organic dysfunctions and psychosomatic disabilities? Support your view.

4. What do you believe to be the authors' reasons for excluding from the definition of a "learning disability" any condition which is the result of mental retardation, sensory deprivation or cultural or instructional factors? Does this proviso augment or diminish the applicability of this concept to the diagnosis of learning capabilities? Support your position.

5. Using as a guide the steps enumerated for diagnosing a reading disability, describe a procedure for identifying a learning disability in another subject-matter area.

6. One of the approaches to rehabilitation is to utilize the strengths of an individual as a basis for any remedial program. Give an example of this method.

Samuel A. Kirk and Barbara Bateman, "Diagnosis and Remediation of Learning Difficulties," *Exceptional Children*, XXIX, (1962), 73–78. Reprinted with the permission of The Council for Exceptional Children and the authors.

Disabilities and disturbances in learning processes have long been of interest to various professions. The medical professions, especially neurologists, have been concerned with finding physiological and structural correlates of specific learning disorders. Pathology in particular brain areas has been related to certain disabilities.

While the medical specialist is concerned with the relation between communication disorder and the location of cerebral dys-

function in children, the special educator is concerned primarily with assessment of the behavioral symptoms and with designing the special methods of remediation required to ameliorate the disability. Since it is often

Samuel A. Kirk is Director and Barbara Bateman is a Research Associate, Institute for Research on Exceptional Children, University of Illinois. The investigations described in this paper were supported in part by a grant from the Psychiatric Training and Research Foundation of the Illinois Department of Mental Health.

difficult to determine whether or not there is a cerebral dysfunction except by inferences from behavior, the educator is concerned primarily with behavioral symptoms of deficits rather than with the location or extent of brain damage. The knowledge of whether a reading disability, for example, is caused by an injury to the angular gyrus or to some other brain area does not usually alter the remedial procedures. Remediation is generally determined by the behavioral symptoms, not by the neurological findings.

Dyslexia is a label meaning that the person has difficulty learning to read. A dyslexic may have a lesion in the angular gyrus, or had his handedness changed, or perhaps his father rejected him. But none of these kinds of analyses tells us what to do to improve the reading of our particular subject. Our interest is in the kind and extent of diagnosis of learning problems, that lead directly to a formulation of what should be done about the disability.

While there are a substantial number of children who are delayed or retarded in learning to talk, read, write, spell, or do arithmetic, not all children with these problems are considered to have learning disabilities *per se.* A *learning disability* refers to a retardation, disorder, or delayed development in one or more of the processes of speech, language, reading, writing, arithmetic, or other school subjects resulting from a psychological handicap caused by a possible cerebral dysfunction and/or emotional or behavioral disturbances. It is not the result of mental retardation, sensory deprivation, or cultural or instructional factors.

Quite a bit is known about learning disability in the area of reading, and the kind of diagnosis we have been discussing can be illustrated by describing the steps in diagnosing a reading disability.

The first step is to determine the child's capacity for reading. Mental age, arithmetic achievement, and years in school are among the factors used in estimating this reading capacity. Next, actual reading achievement is determined, and the discrepancy between the capacity for reading and actual achievement in reading is examined.

The processes of reading are analyzed to determine which symptoms of poor reading are present and to describe fully the way the child approaches reading. Method of word attack and types of errors made are but two important aspects of the reading processes which must be fully examined.

The next step is to study related disabilities in the child to determine why he has failed to learn by the normal procedures. Mixed dominance or laterality, poor auditory fusion or sound blending ability, difficulties in visualization, poor visual or auditory memory, closure problems, and so forth, may provide important clues to the psychological disabilities underlying reading failure. The last step, and a most vital one, is the recommendation or planning of specific remedial procedures and techniques, based on a knowledge of the child's disabilities, and designed to correct the particular faulty patterns of reading.

For the past several years, interest at the Institute for Research on Exceptional Children has been concentrated on the development of a scientific pedagogy in the area of learning disabilities. Psychological factors in language (psycholinguistic) functions with young children has been the specific concern. A scientific pedagogy in this field requires (a) the development of behavioral diagnostic instruments of such a nature that the specific psycholinguistic disabilities can be differentiated and identified; (b) validation of these tests by research studies; and (c) determination of the educability of psycholinguistic disabilities through longitudinal training of a select group of children.

At the present time the experimental edition of the Illinois Test of Psycholinguistic Abilities is itself being extensively tested, and a few children are receiving tutoring.

The test, its theoretical background, rationale, and illustrations of its diagnostic uses are discussed by Kirk and McCarthy (1961). The present edition of the ITPA assesses six psycholinguistic abilities involving meaningful use of language (auditory decoding, vocal encoding, auditory-vocal association, visual decoding, motor encoding, and visual-motor association) and three abilities involving automatic usage (auditory-vocal automatic, auditory-vocal sequential, and visual-motor sequential).

Three recent studies using the ITPA have demonstrated its usefulness and validity as a differential diagnostic test, and have also pointed out its limitations. Olson (1960) found that the test differentiates children who are deaf, sensory aphasic, and expressive aphasic. Bateman's (1962) study established the usefulness of this test with children who have severe visual defects, short of legal blindness, and thus suggested that the test primarily measure central psychological processes which appear to be relatively independent of sensory processes or acuity. A study by Kass (1962) found that children with normal intelligence, but with severe learning disabilities in the area of reading, show deficits in the automatic-sequential, or second-level abilities, while they perform normally on the tests at the representational or meaning level. That is, their comprehension and association abilities to deal meaningfully with language are not deficient, but their performance on the automatic aspects of language usage is inferior. In addition to providing new, useful knowledge about some psychological corre-

lates of severe reading disabilities, Kass's study also pointed up the desirability of expanding the ITPA to include more tests at the automatic usage level.

The present problem is to determine whether children who show significant deficits in some areas of psycholinguistic functions can improve in these functions if special training on their deficits is offered. Currently a case-study method is used to (a) make a study of the child, (b) determine whether the child has a specific learning disability in the psycholinguistic area, (c) organize a tutorial remedial program for the purpose of ameliorating his deficits, and (d) re-examine the child with psychometric tests and with the ITPA. Through a series of such case studies, in a sense using a child as his own contrast, the investigators hope to define more clearly the patterns of disabilities found in children and the correlation of these clinical disabilities to other characteristics, and to determine the extent and the rate at which one can help to ameliorate these deficits.

To illustrate the present stage of research and the methods currently employed in a field in which conventionally controlled research is not feasible, two case studies are given.

Case 1

WH was referred to the institute by his parents when he was four years of age. He had been excluded from a nursery school because of his inability to adjust, and because the authorities felt he was mentally defective. He was the only child of parents of professional status. Observations and test reports by other agencies suggested that he was quite severely retarded in social development, motor coordination, and speech. Both walking and talking had been developmentally delayed. No physical abnormalities were noted by the medical examiners.

When initially tested, WH was 4-7. His Binet IQ was 82 and his Minnesota Preschool verbal IQ was 83. However, he obtained scores in the average range on the non-verbal Minnesota Preschool (103) and the Peabody Picture Vocabulary Test (97). The solid line in Figure 1 shows these psychometric results, converted to age scores, and his ITPA profile.

It will be noted from Figure 1 that his primary psycholinguistic deficits appear in the visual-motor association, motor encoding, and visual-motor sequential abilities. All of these disabilities involve the visual-motor language channel. Because his visual decoding ability was average and other observations suggested that perhaps the motor encoding difficulty was primary, it was decided to plan tutorial remediation in the area of motor encoding.

Early tutoring activities were planned to elicit gross motor activities such as marching, running, jumping, and hopping in a manner suggested by Kephart (1960) for brain-damaged children. Stages in developing these activities included alternately moving arms and legs, imitating the tutor's movements in such games as "Follow the Leader," and moving by verbal command and in response to music.

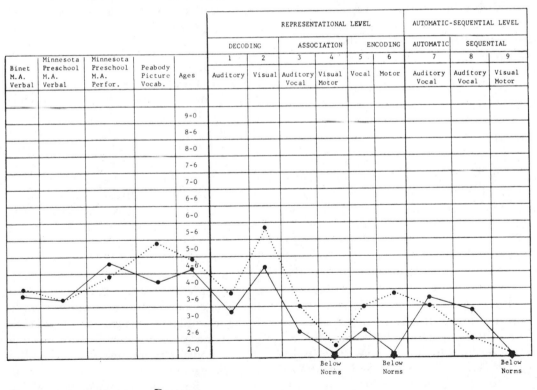

Pretest •———————•   Posttest •..........•

Figure 1 Comparison of Illinois Test of Psycholinguistic Abilities pretest and posttest profile for WH.

Readiness for motor encoding itself (expressing ideas motorically) included drawing, finger painting, directional drawing, and building with and arranging blocks.

WH was retested after three and one-half months of remedial work, as shown by the dotted line in Figure 1. Figure 1 shows that the only area in which WH showed appreciable gain in the test after the brief three and one-half months of remediation was in motor encoding. (At this stage in research, we feel that a change of two years is the minimum that can be accepted as significant with children in WH's age range.) It is interesting to note that neither of the other abilities improved beyond the gain expected from maturation, in spite of the improvement shown in motor encoding. WH's tutoring will continue and perhaps, at a later date, it will be determined whether work on his motor encoding disability will irradiate to the presumably related disabilities, or whether it will be necessary to plan instruction for these areas directly.

Case II

Figure 2 shows ITPA profiles for three educable mentally retarded siblings from a family of a low socio-economic status in which the parents and grandparents are also retarded. The two older children are girls, ages 8-0 (MC) and 6-7 (P), and the youngest is a boy age 5-1 (D). At the time of initial testing MC had spent a year in a class for the educable mentally retarded, P had just entered a class for the retarded, and D remained at home. It may be noted that the three profiles show striking similarities in assets and deficits: (a) all show deficits in auditory-vocal automatic and auditory-vocal association (tests 3 and 7); (b) all are stronger in motor encoding than in vocal encoding; and (c) in each case visual decoding is superior to auditory decoding. This similarity in profiles of the three children raises the question of genetic or cultural factors.

The oldest girl (MC) received remedial tutoring in the auditory-vocal automatic and auditory-vocal association areas while the other two siblings received no special tutoring. MC showed significant gains in the two areas tutored while retests revealed no significant changes in these areas (greater than two years) in the ITPA profiles of the two siblings. However, D, the youngest child, showed a significant gain in visual decoding, even though his IQ dropped during the same period. A possible explanation of this phenomenon can be found in his concentration on watching television and working puzzles during the time his sisters were in school.

The cases presented above are illustrations of a psychodiagnostic approach to some forms of learning disabilities in children, and the use of this diagnosis in deciding on the appropriate techniques of remediation for the child's major deficits.

There are two basic approaches to rehabilitation. One approach is to capitalize on the assets of an individual rather than to pay direct attention to his handicaps or deficits. For example, since mentally retarded children have difficulty in learning to read or to do arithmetic but presumably can accomplish handwork, the programs for the mentally retarded for years have emphasized handwork and minimized academic work. In the education of the deaf, teaching speech is a major area of difficulty. The tendency in some schools is to minimize speech and to emphasize manual forms of communication.

The philosophy of remediation which has been adopted here is to emphasize the development of the areas of major deficits found in the psycholinguistic profile. The hypothesis is that, although the child may have a biological or emotional factor which has inhibited the development of some functions, a part of the deficit in the child is the result of psychological withdrawal from activities requiring use of the deficient ability.

It is likely that during the growing stages the child exercises functions in which he can be successful, and avoids activities in which he faces failure. As a result he later shows marked deficits in some areas and normal performance in others. If a child has difficulty in speech and obtains his desired ends through motor encoding his profile may show low vocal encoding and high motor encoding. If he learns by and exercises his auditory decoding abilities, but does not succeed at an early age in understanding

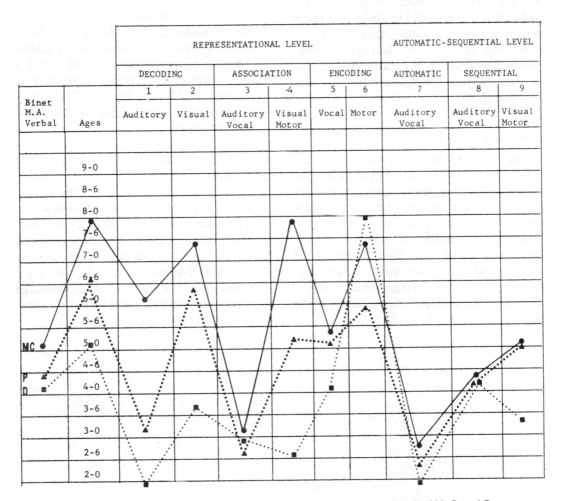

Figure 2 Comparison of Illinois Test of Psycholinguistic Abilities profiles for MC, P, and D.

what is seen, or visual decoding, he will later have higher auditory than visual decoding ability.

The present problem is to determine whether the marked deficits found in some children can be developed, and to what extent these disabilities can be ameliorated. The remedial procedures that have been used are based upon two factors; (a) the major disability or disabilities that need amelioration, and (b) the level of functioning at which we have to initiate remediation. If the child shows, as did WH in Figure 1, a major deficit in motor encoding, that is one area that needs development. But the activities required to develop this ability had to start at the two year level where he was then functioning.

Summary

The current research reported here has dealt with a psychoeducational system of diagnosing those learning disabilities in children which result from a possible cerebral dysfunction and/or emotional disturbance. This method of diagnosis of psycholinguistic functions yields a profile of abilities and disabilities which in turn suggests cues for developing remedial procedures for the purpose of ameliorating the deficits.

Further development and refinement of this and similar procedures are needed in many areas of special education to enable us to fit our training programs more efficiently and accurately to specific disabilities found in exceptional children. When we are able to diagnose disabilities accurately and then to prescribe appropriate remedial instruction to ameliorate these disabilities, we will have arrived one step closer to our goal—the development of a scientific pedagogy.

REFERENCES

Bateman, Barbara, D. *Reading and Psycholinguistic Processes of Partially Seeing Children.* Monogr. Council Except. Child., 1, No. 5.

Kass, Corrine E. "Some Psychological Correlates of Severe Reading Disability." Unpublished doctoral dissertation. Univer. of Illinois, 1962.

Kephart, N. *The Slow Learner in the Classroom.* Columbus, Ohio: Charles E. Merrill Books, Inc., 1960.

Kirk, S. A. & McCarthy, J. J. "The Illinois Test of Psycholinguistic Abilities—An Approach to Differential Diagnosis," *Amer. J. ment. Defic.,* 1961, 66, 399–412.

Olson, J. L. "A Comparison of Sensory Aphasia, Expressive Aphasia, and Deaf Children on the Illinois Test of Language Ability." Unpublished doctoral dissertation. Univer. of Illinois, 1960.

Diagnosing Learning Difficulties

James R. Okey

EDITORS' QUESTIONS:

1. Assess the validity of the analogy between medical practice and instructional activities. Be sure to include in your answer all stages of both processes.

2. Use the organizational format portrayed in Figure 1 of this selection to develop a learning hierarchy for reading. Use, as an example, an objective stated in terms of a specific reading task pupils are required to perform.

3. What information is provided by the use of a pass/fail technique of analysis within the framework provided by a learning hierarchy? How can such information be utilized in the planning of instruction?

4. Explain fully how the learning hierarchy approach to diagnosis is superior to the practice of relying solely upon scores achieved on diagnostic tests.

5. Evaluate the wisdom of the following hypothetical remarks. "A teacher must make certain assumptions concerning readiness. For example, if one wishes to teach a certain skill in arithmetic—such as the subtraction of two digit numbers—it is necessary for her to assume that most of her pupils are already familiar with less complicated forms of subtraction."

12

James R. Okey, "Diagnosing Learning Difficulties," *The Science Teacher*, XXXVII, (May 1970), pp. 59–61. Reprinted with the permission of the National Science Teachers Association.

In some respects the job of a teacher and that of a physician are similar. Both are charged with the responsibility of diagnosing ailments and prescribing treatments. In the domain of the physician, the ailments are often physical and the patient is advised to take certain therapy. For the teacher, the ailments to be diagnosed are often intellectual, and the student is advised to study certain instructional materials as a treatment.

The trend toward individualizing instruction has increased the demand for diagnostic capabilities in teachers. Among the reasons given for individualizing instruction are differences in students' capabilities and their rates and styles of learning. [3] In order to individualize instruction, then, it is essential that specific knowledge is available about the different capabilities of students. If these different capabilities can be determined for each student by some diagnostic procedure, instruction can be designed accordingly.

Several questions can be raised. First, how can the teacher acquire knowledge about the capabilities of each student? Precisely what kind of knowledge does the teacher need? Finally, what kind of instructional decisions can be made if such knowledge is available?

Dr. Okey is an assistant professor of education at the University of California on the Santa Barbara campus.

Presumably, we need to know more than the fact that Student X is having trouble in arithmetic. Rather, the diagnosis must be as precise as: Student X is incapable of adding fractions with unlike denominators. [2] If the area is science: Rather than say that Student Y is not doing well in a unit on electricity, we need to say that Student Y cannot construct a workable series circuit, or whatever deficiency is found. Precise learning difficulties must be pinpointed if students' learning ailments are to be diagnosed and treated, whether or not instruction is individualized.

There are several kinds of diagnoses that teachers may be requested to make. One kind of diagnosis is aimed at the unsuccessful student, the person who isn't "getting it." If a student fails some learning task, it may mean that the prerequisite behaviors have not been acquired. The teacher will need to know the learning tasks that precede the one which the student has failed. An example would be the identification of a student incapable of solving work problems in which the speed of an object is to be calculated, given distance and time data. Probable prerequisite tasks here include the ability to multiply numbers and to substitute numerical values in symbolic expressions. Finding out whether the student can do either of these prerequisite tasks is a first step in diagnosing and treating this learning problem.

Diagnostic capabilities are also required with successful students. Consider a classroom in which the long-range goal is to have students discover the principle that heat lost is equal to heat gained when liquids of different temperature are mixed. Suppose that some students in this class have just learned to measure the mass of a liquid. What should they learn next? The teacher has to decide on the next step in the learning pro-

cess. This, too, can be considered a problem of diagnosis.

Another kind of diagnosis associated with successful learners concerns the initial placement of students. Consider the case of an algebra teacher about to begin his course by having students learn the nomenclature and operations associated with "sets." In all likelihood, some students have learned these things long before. Others may be capable of generating specific sets of objects or numbers but incapable of finding the union or intersection of two sets. For a few students, the subject of "sets" may be completely new. The teacher's problem in this situation, if the school is seriously interested in individualizing instruction, is to start each student in the instructional program at the appropriate place. Clearly, this is a problem requiring an educational diagnosis and prescription.

In each of the three instances just described, it is clear that the teacher needs an instructional map. The map should specify which capabilities need to be acquired enroute to desired goals and the sequence in which they should be learned. In the three diagnostic problems cited, one teacher needed to know the prerequisites for a task; another, the next task to be learned on the way to a specific goal; and the third needed to know the entire sequence of tasks leading to a final goal in order to place students with widely differing capabilities. An instructional map showing the sequence of tasks from entering behavior to final performance would have been a powerful tool to aid each of these teachers.

The procedure used in deriving an instructional map, usually called a learning hierarchy, has been described by Gagné. [1] The first step in the procedure is to specify in performance terms what the final task is to be. Following this, the question is asked,

"What would the student have to know how to do already in order to learn this final task with a minimum of instruction?" One or more prerequisite or subordinate tasks may be identified in this way. The same question is then asked of the subordinate tasks and still more lower-order tasks may be identified. An example will probably best illustrate the procedure of "deriving a learning hierarchy."

Suppose students are to learn to calculate the work done in lifting an object by using the expression, work = force X distance. What we have in mind is placing a block on the floor and requiring the student to calculate the work done in moving it vertically to the desk top. What would the student already have to know in order to learn this final task with a minimum of instruction? Probably three capabilities would be valuable. The student should already know how to: solve equations of the form $X = A \times B$; experimentally measure the distance traveled and force required to move an object over a specified pathway; and translate written work problems into mathematical relationships. Therefore, in analyzing this final task, three subordinate tasks have been identified. There is no great mystery about where the subordinate tasks come from; they are components of the final task itself. In order to perform the final task, values for force and distance are first determined; next, the values are substituted into the expression $W = F \times D$; and finally, the obtained expression is solved. These three component parts of solving the final task are represented by the three subordinate tasks.

The three subordinate tasks just discussed are now subjected to the same questioning procedures as before. In order to solve an equation of the form $W = F \times D$, students must know how to multiply. As the analysis procedure continues, therefore, more lower-order tasks are derived. The analysis procedure stops when the subordinate tasks being derived are almost surely ones that could be performed by any member of the intended student population. Figure 1 shows what a learning hierarchy might look like for the task just analyzed. The lines in the chart designate the subordinate relationships tasks have to one another. What the chart represents is a series of hypotheses of the tasks students should learn in order to reach a specific goal and the sequential relationship the tasks have to one another.

How can a learning hierarchy (or, instructional map) similar to the one just described aid in answering the following three questions, which were raised at the beginning of this paper?

1. How can the teacher acquire knowledge about the capabilities of each student? One or more items to test each task in a learning hierarchy can be devised and administered to students. The scores on the test will show, for each individual, what tasks can or cannot be performed.

2. What kind of knowledge does the teacher need (about the capabilities of individual students)? Composite scores, such as that the class mean was 82 percent, are not of primary interest. Neither are composite scores for an individual; it does not help much to say that a student passed six of nine test items. Instead, what is needed is knowledge of how each student did on each task in the learning hierarchy; specifically, which tasks were passed and which were failed.

3. What kind of instructional decisions can be made with knowledge of each student's capabilities? Sup-

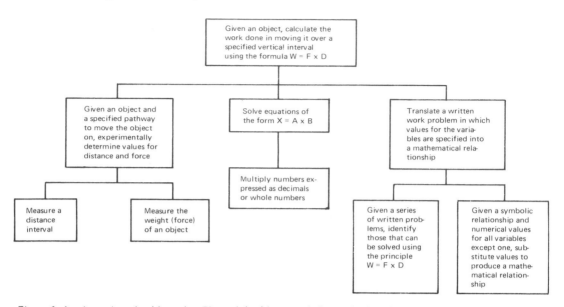

Figure 1 A science learning hierarchy. The task in this example is to calculate the work done in lifting an object.

pose that as a result of the testing just described, the pattern of scores for two students are as shown in Figure 2. A plus (+) mark means that a task was passed and a minus (–) mark means that it was failed. With the information shown in Figure 2, the teacher can decide which tasks each of the students needs to work on next in order to reach the final task. Each of the students will be assigned different learning tasks in this case because there is evidence that they have different capabilities.

Of course, the information obtained about individual students by using a learning hierarchy does not solve all the teachers' problems. Discipline problems, lack of motivation, inability to read, inadequate facilities, and a host of other factors may still stand in the way of student success. However, the information does pinpoint, for both teachers and students, where effort

must ultimately be directed in order to reach the final goal.

Few learning hierarchies exist. The elementary school science project sponsored by the American Association for the Advancement of Science [4] and the Individually Prescribed Instruction project at the University of Pittsburgh [3] have learning hierarchies for their instructional materials. These are exceptions, however, and the teacher expecting to find a learning hierarchy accompanying a newly purchased set of instructional materials will most often be disappointed. Over time this situation may change. If teachers are expected to do a more thorough diagnostic job they may, in turn, bring pressure to bear regarding the kind of instructional materials they wish purchased for their use.

In summary, to diagnose and treat learning ailments requires precise knowledge about the capabilities of individual students. Administering tests to students on the tasks in a learning hierarchy is a means

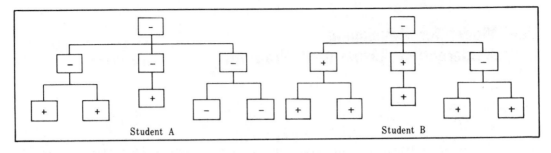

Figure 2 Pass-fail patterns for two students on the tasks in a learning hierarchy.

of obtaining such knowledge. A learning hierarchy shows the sequence of tasks from entering behavior to final performance and is derived by starting the final task in performance terms and working backward to determine subordinate tasks. Decisions regarding the selection of appropriate learning tasks for students based on their demonstrated capabilities are described.

REFERENCES

1. Gagné, R. M. "Learning Hierarchies," *Educational Psychologist* 6: 1–9; November 1968.

2. Hunter, Madeline. "When the Teacher Diagnoses Learning," *Educational Leadership* 23:545–549; 1966.

3. Lindvall, C. M., and R. C. Cox. "The Role of Evaluation in Programs for Individualized Instruction," In R. Tyler (Editor), *Educational Evaluation: New Roles, New Means.* University of Chicago Press, Chicago, Illinois, 1969.

4. *Science—A Process Approach,* Parts 1-7. American Association for the Advancement of Science, Washington, D.C. 1965.

One Model for Developing
a Prekindergarten Assessment Program

Ann E. Boehm

EDITORS' QUESTIONS:

1. Discuss the limitations of the practice of comparing I.Q. test results before and after instruction as an indication of the success of a program.

2. Indicate the difficulties which are apt to be encountered in devising a system for evaluating the achievement of the educational goals which the author indicates were specified by teachers in their curriculum reports.

3. Assess the value of teacher, aide and parent interaction in developing evaluative procedures. Do you believe this approach to be superior to one in which a single individual is entirely responsible for the system developed? Justify your response.

4. Why do you suppose that the Inventory developed by the experimental kindergarten was restricted to the evaluation of cognitive skills and visual-motor functioning? If you were developing an inventory of this sort, what other kinds of learning achievement would you attempt to measure? Justify your response.

5. How does the breaking down of tasks in the inventory into successive levels of difficulty enhance this instrument's value to the planner of instructional strategies?

6. Suggest an alternative scheduling of the Inventory's use which would further enhance its value as an evaluative instrument.

Ann E. Boehm, "One Model for Developing A Prekindergarten Assessment Program," *Exceptional Children*, XXXVII, No. 7 (March 1971) 523–527. Reprinted with the permission of the Council for Exceptional Children and Ann E. Boehm.

With the recent growth of prekindergarten programs for the disadvantaged has come increasing concern regarding their effectiveness. It has been questioned whether such programs "work"—whether in fact they improve children's overall readiness for school. Another question centers around the type of program that is most effective.

The majority of current research studies assessing the effectiveness of prekindergarten intervention programs have based their evaluation on changes in scores on standardized tests of intelligence, reading readiness, or language abilities (Deutsch, 1965; Gray & Klaus, 1965; Kohlberg, 1965; Weikart, 1967). Generally, positive gains have been reported as a result of such programs. However, followup studies dealing with the long range effect of prekindergarten programs after kindergarten or first grade have demonstrated conflicting and often disappointing results (DiLorenzo, Salter, & Bradley, 1968; Green, 1969).

Serious doubts have been raised as to the value of changes in IQ scores as measures of program success. Glick (1968) discussed the variability in IQ scores on the part of deprived children, and suggested that the change in scores may be the result of motivation or understanding how to take the tests. Furthermore, such testing measures assess only part of a program's overall goals. Passow noted at the National Conference on the Education of the Disadvantaged (1966) that although new program ideas are being attempted, old and inappropriate evaluation techniques are still employed. The nature and appropriateness of experiences are other factors in determining a program's effectiveness.

Evaluation of prekindergarten programs and assessment procedures rarely have been utilized by prekindergarten programs which *match* teaching and curricular materials to the individual needs of the pupils. Such a goal has been fundamental to the development of the assessment program to be described.

History and Goals

The question of program effectiveness has been an important issue facing a prekindergarten program located in an urban setting near New York City. This program encountered many of the same problems as those found in the larger urban setting. Of the approximately 900 children who reach the age of 4 during any one year and live in this city, 150 children from low income families are served by the prekindergarten program. This program is one of 48 New York State funded experimental prekindergarten programs. There are 10 classes of 15 children, each meeting for a half-day session 4 days per week. On the fifth day, inservice courses are held for the teachers and other staff members. A teacher certified in early childhood education and a teacher aide work with each class. Classrooms are located in four elementary school buildings and the program is considered an integral part of that school.

In order to evaluate the effectiveness of this prekindergarten program, it was necessary to raise the question, "Effective in relationship to what?" Better performance on standardized intelligence tests or readiness tests? The attainment of curricular goals? While these two questions are not mutually exclusive, the problem of assessment has been approached from the second point of reference.

The first source of information used was the teachers' written curricular reports. In these reports, the teachers' educational goals for children were indicated and grouped into the following categories: (a) improved social interactions, (b) emotional development, (c) cognitive development, (d) increased ability to cope with the problems of classroom life, (e) increased expression of ideas and thoughts through language, and (f) physical-motor development.

Another source of information was an investigation of the conditions and/or skills necessary for success in kindergarten and first grade. Based on teacher interviews and a survey of curricular materials, such conditions and skills included: (a) following directions consisting of multiple components, e.g., color all of the little triangles green, (b) comprehending what is read and heard, (c) understanding basic concepts such as "big" and "small," (d) differentiating beginning and ending sounds of words, (e) meeting success with beginning reading, (f) learning basic mathematical concepts, (g) expressing thoughts in spoken words and through the written symbol, and (h) developing emotional and social maturity.

Through discussions with teachers, aides, and other staff personnel, the goals of the prekindergarten assessment program were set to:

1. Select or devise measurement instruments relevant to 3 and 4 year old chil-

dren from many backgrounds.

2. Measure those aspects of children's functioning which appear related to later school success.

3. Utilize measures in a diagnostic manner so that the levels of children's functioning can be determined with regard to strengths and weaknesses.

4. Provide information to teachers which will help the teacher modify and/or develop curricula to meet specific needs of children.

5. Devise a series of teacher administered tasks which are adequately delineated to measure some of the above goals.

Other major purposes of the assessment program have been to compare the growth of a child *with himself* during the course of the school year, compare the functioning of the individual child with that of his prekindergarten class as a whole, and evaluate the success of the program in attaining selected curricular goals.

Inventory of Skills and Functioning

Integrating the information gained from teachers' curriculum reports, the survey of curricular materials used in prekindergarten, kindergarten, and first grade, and discussions with teachers, an Inventory of Cognitive Skills and Visual-Motor Functioning* was developed.

The following areas were covered in the Inventory.

    I. Knowledge of body parts

    II. Identification of color and shapes

    III. Number concepts such as the recognition of the number of concrete or pictured objects presented

    IV. Information from pictures and comprehension of simple stories

    V. Relational concepts such as "same" and "different"

    VI. Following directions containing multiple components such as "Find the ball that is big and red"

    VII. Copying geometric forms

    VIII. Gross motor functioning.

The final section of the inventory deals with the child's overall behavior during testing. A rating scale dealing with behavioral factors —such as "attention span" and "ease of relationship"—which might affect the child's performance, is therefore an integral part of each inventory.

The design of the inventory was such that each of the major areas tested was broken down into levels of difficulty. Therefore, if a child encountered difficulty at one level, the task was broken down into simpler levels so that the point of difficulty could be determined, particularly in terms of materials or instructions. For example, a child was asked to identify a number of basic colors with the question at level 3 being, "What color is this dress?" At level 3, it was necessary for the child to make an identification among colors and provide the color label. If the child met difficulty at level 3, the label was provided and the evaluator moved to level 2 with the question, "Show me the dress that is red." The child at level 2 was expected to make only the correct identification of the color. If difficulty continued to be met at level 2, the evaluator then moved to level 1 and placed a colored square before the child and asked him to, "Find me another one like this" or "Where does this go?" At level 1, the child needed

*Additional information about the *Inventory of Cognitive Skills and Visual-Motor Functioning* may be obtained from The Experimental Pre-kindergarten Program, City School District, New Rochelle, New York.

only to match the color correctly. He did not have to identify a specific color or provide a label.

Aspects of a child's cognitive development, approach to learning, physical-motor development, and verbal expression are assessed in part by the inventory (corresponding to points *c* through *f* of the teacher's educational goals for children). Observational reports and teacher conferences are used to supply further information regarding the social and emotional growth of the child.

The Development Process

The first form of the inventory was administered individually by the writer to a sample of 50 children during October and November (pretest) and May and June (posttest) of the 1966–67 school year. Upon completion of the fall testing, the results were reported to teachers, aides, and other prekindergarten personnel. They, in turn, questioned the meaning, necessity, and representativeness of the questions.

During a number of inservice sessions, the nature and meaning of "assessment" was discussed. Assessment was defined as evaluating the level of a child's functioning, both his strengths and his weaknesses, in areas related to the curriculum.

Assessment procedures employed a task analysis approach which broke down the same task into levels of difficulty so that if a child did not meet success at one level, he might enjoy success at another. Thus tasks involved in the assessment were viewed not as an "all or none" entity but as containing several degrees of attainment. The inventory was not just "another test" which would yield another intelligence quotient; it was a source of data useful for program planning. After completion of the end of

year testing, teachers were able to compare the child's functioning against himself from the beginning to the end of the school year. Teachers indicated that although daily interactions with children provided insight into many of the areas assessed, the inventory provided a systematic check for all children in the class.

Teacher Administration

Next in the process of development (1967–68) was the refinement of the inventory, instructions, and scoring criteria so that teacher administration would be feasible. Administration of the inventory by teachers was desirable because teachers and aides would have immediate feedback regarding the functioning of each child, his style and approach to the tasks presented, and his reactions to success and difficulty. The psychologist and supervisor could then discuss the results in terms of the child's strengths and areas needing development, teacher impressions of the child, and program planning for that child. Thus the goal of *matching* a curricular program to the needs of the child could be fostered by this procedure.

Before administering the inventory, teachers and classroom aides attended a one day training session. Directions and scoring criteria were clarified where possible. For example, teachers pointed out that a child would never see a "group" of ice cream cones, and he would be more familiar with the word "pile." The direction was changed to read: "Show me the piles of boxes that are the same." Teachers were also requested to note suggestions or areas of difficulty which occurred during testing.

It was anticipated that the total testing time per child would range between 12-15 minutes. The teachers and aides administered the inventory during the first 2 weeks of school, testing 3 or 4 children during any one day in their classroom setting. Complaints arose about the length of the test, inadequacy of the pictured material, and the disruptive aspects of testing during class time. Suggestions were also made to clarify directions, eliminate items which yielded inadequate information, and provide ideas for better pictorial representations. At this point, the prekindergarten staff began to view the assessment inventory as *their* inventory, one that reflected their recommendations and criticisms.

A major criticism of the form of the inventory described above (1967–68) was the difficulty which occurred as a result of administration during class sessions at the beginning of the school year. Children were in the process of adjusting to the routines of classroom life at this time and teachers stated that it was difficult to devote the necessary time to assessment. As a result of the criticisms and suggestions made, in the 1968–69 school year the inventory was administered during the registration period the week before classes began.

Parent Interaction

An important modification suggested by the teaching staff was to have parents present during the testing session. This modification was made an integral part of the assessment procedures during the 1969–70 school year. This gave the teacher the opportunity to interpret to the parent that:

1. No child is expected to answer all questions correctly, since the tasks assessed are among the skills to be developed during the prekindergarten year. Furthermore, the same battery will be administered at the end of the child's

prekindergarten experience. In such a manner the child's progress in relation to himself can be determined.
2. The prekindergarten experience involves more than play, for it has specific cognitive goals.
3. Each child has strengths and areas needing development in planning his curriculum.

Some parents were pleased to observe their children's levels of learning. Others were concerned that their children should know everything, viewing the inventory as a test to be "passed."

Parent and teacher communication was facilitated by this interaction with the inventory providing a stimulus for the discussion of curricular goals. Many parents indicated that they did not know the areas measured were important for success in school. Parent interaction with younger children in these families should benefit from this exposure.

End of Year Testing

The end of year testing takes place during the last 2 weeks of school. Two days are set aside for the testing with half of the children in any one class present each day. The teacher and aide are able to manage the smaller class group successfully as well as to test each of the seven or eight children present.

Comparing the child's progress from the beginning to the end of the school year on each of the subareas assessed has enabled the prekindergarten teacher to specify factually gains made as well as areas in need of further development. Such information has been passed on to kindergarten teachers so that more meaningful follow-through programs can be developed.

Results

Teacher, aide, and parent interaction in the development of a prekindergarten assessment program has facilitated the development of a workable inventory which provides meaningful information to teachers. The prekindergarten staff has moved from viewing testing as a task to provide data which slots children into groups to viewing testing as an assessment procedure and a basis for educational communication with parents. Discussions regarding the fairness of items have now moved to discussions in which questions are raised such as, "How representative is the inventory of what is taught in your classroom?" and "What doesn't the test measure that would be useful?" Another benefit of this interaction has been additional concentration on the learning process. The task analysis approach of breaking down tasks into their multiple components is now used by the teaching staff in developing curricular approaches and materials.

The assessment consultant has gained insight into the curricular goals and concerns of the prekindergarten staff. An ongoing dialog with the staff has resulted. This same approach, although requiring considerable time, can serve as a model for developing other assessment procedures.

REFERENCES

Deutsch, M. *Institute for Developmental Studies: Annual Report.* New York: New York Medical College, 1965.

DiLorenzo, L., Salter, R., & Bradley, J. *Prekindergarten Programs for the Disadvantaged. A Third-year Report on an Evaluative Study.* New York: State Education Department, December 1968.

Glick, J. "Some Problems in the Evaluation of Preschool Intervention Programs," In R. D. Hess and R. M. Bear, eds. *Early Education.* Chicago: Aldine, 1968, pp. 215–222.

Gray, S. W., & Klaus, R. A. "An Experimental Preschool Program for Culturally Deprived Children," *Child Development.* 1965, 36, 887–898.

Green, M. "Follow-through Study of Children Who Attended the Great Neck Prekindergarten Center for Disadvantaged Pre-schoolers during 1967–68 School Year and are Attending Kindergarten in the Great Neck Schools during 1968–69," Great Neck, N.Y.: Great Neck Public Schools, 1969 (duplicated).

Kohlberg, L. "Montessori with the Culturally Disadvantaged: A Cognitive-Developmental Interpretation and Some Research Findings," In R. D. Hess and R. M. Bear, eds. *Early Education.* Chicago: Adline, 1968, pp. 105–118.

US Department of Health, Education, and Welfare. *National Conference on Education of the Disadvantaged.* Report of a national conference held in Washington, D.C., July 18–20, 1966. Washington, D.C.: US Government Printing Office, 1966.

Weikart, D. P. "Preschool Programs: Preliminary Findings," *Journal of Special Education,* 1967, 1, 163–181.

Recommended Readings: Strategies for Diagnosing and Assessing a Child's Learning Needs

Beatty, W. H., ed. *Improving Educational Assessment.* Washington, D.C.: Association for Supervision and Curriculum Development, 1969.

Broudy, Harry S. and Palmer, John R. *Exemplars of Teaching Method.* Chicago, Illinois: Rand McNally & Company, 1965.

Burnett, R. "Classroom Teacher as a Diagnostician," *International Reading Association. Conference Proceedings.* 13, Part 4, (1970):1–10.

Carter, Homer L. J. and McGinnis, Dorthy J. *Diagnosis and Treatment of the Disabled Reader.* New York: The Macmillan Co., 1970.

Eisele, James E. "Diagnostic Teaching: Can the Curriculum Specialist Help?" *Educational Leadership* 24 (1967):331–335.

Falcone, J. *"Diagnostic Classroom,"* *Catholic Education Review* 67 (1969):139–144.

Florence, C. and Valletutti, P. "Defining Behavior Modification," *Educational Technology,* (1969): 328–330.

Freeman, W. "Diagnostic Teaching," *Audiovisual Instruction* 13 (1968):858–860.

Gagné, R. M. "Learning Hierarchies," *Educational Psychologist* 6 (1968):1–9.

Grobman, Hulda *Evaluation Activities of Curriculum Projects.* Chicago, Illinois: Rand McNally & Co., 1969.

Gronlund, Norman E. *Measurement and Evaluation in Teaching.* New York: The Macmillan Co., 1965.

Lindvall, C. M. and Cox, R. C. (with the collaboration of John O. Bolvin). *Evaluation as a Tool in Curriculum Development: The IPI Evaluation Program.* Chicago, Illinois: Rand McNally & Co., 1970.

Mial, D. J. and Jacobson, S. "Diagnosing a Classroom Problem," *Today's Education* 57 (1968):79–80.

Palmer, J. O. *The Psychological Assessment of Children.* New York: John Wiley & Sons, Inc., 1970.

Prouty, R. W. and Prillman, D. "Diagnostic Teaching: A Modest Proposal," *The Elementary School Journal* 70 (1970):265–270.

Rice, D. B. "Learning Disabilities, An Investigation: Evaluation Procedures and Findings," *Journal of Learning Disabilities* 3 (1970):149–155.

Schubert, Delwyn G. and Torgerson, Theodore L. *Improving Reading Through Individualized Correction.* 2nd ed. Dubuque, Iowa: Wm. C. Brown Company Publishers, 1968.

Serio, M. "Know the Child to Teach the Child: A Checklist," *Academic Therapy Quarterly* 5 (1970):222–227.

Silvaroli, Nicholas J. *Classroom Reading Inventory.* rev. ed. Dubuque, Iowa: Wm. C. Brown Company Publishers, 1969.

Tyler, Ralph, Gagné, Robert M. and Scriven, Michael *Perspectives of Curriculum Evaluation.* Chicago, Illinois: Rand McNally & Co., 1967.

Managing the
Teaching-Learning Process

What is the best method of managing the teaching-learning process? Is there, in fact, any one best method or is one method more efficient given a particular set of circumstances and another more efficient in a different setting? This section presents a number of selections dealing with the management of learning experiences in order to assist the student in discovering answers to questions such as these.

Two alternative systems of educational planning are examined by Mannello. The resource unit model is compared and contrasted with the more recent instructional systems model and an alternative formulation is suggested for combining the desirable features of both approaches. The author suggests that such a synthesis might be labeled a resource unit-systems approach. He indicates that the maintenance of educational efficiency requires the retention of the central role of the teacher and the adaptation for classroom use those elements of each approach that will "enable teachers

to organize efficient instructional systems (teaching units) of their own."

Kaufman's article recommends the use of a systems approach as a means of analyzing and managing the educational process. The implementation of this approach, as illustrated by the selection, is an excellent example of the application of the scientific method to educational problem solving. This view of the educational process as a system—composed of interrelated subsystems like teaching, administration and mission support—supplies the student with a valuable tool for analysis. Furthermore, comprehension of the interrelated nature of educational processes and the effects of certain constraints should enable her to effect a continual evaluation of the feasibility of specified learning objectives and of the strategies she has devised for achieving them.

A model intended to provide a more rigorous approach to the designing of instructional systems is presented by Tosti and

Ball. Special attention is given to the analytical effects of distinguishing between the system component designated the "presentation form" and the medium or media utilized to implement it. A thorough analysis of the process of behavioral modification with emphasis upon the structuring of the presentation, the selection of compatible media and the designing and managing of the operational instructional system make this selection a most thought-provoking offering.

Merrill has provided the student with a new and different method for the structuring of learning experiences—a cybernetic systems approach. One of the inherent advantages of such a system is that it necessitates the utilization of feedback from the learner as a basis for modification of the instructional program. Too often student responses as a basis for improving instructional effectiveness are ignored in classroom situations. The student's attention is directed, in particular, to the flow chart in Figure 2 which provides a comprehensive view of the interrelationships among the elements of a cybernetic instructional system.

A flow chart, such as a computer programmer might construct, is utilized by Childs to represent his suggested set of procedures for the planning of instruction. The major advantages of this approach are that it provides a guide for the sequencing of decisions, allows for the reevaluation of previously-made decisions on the basis of currently received feedback and permits the reaccomplishment of certain functions as necessary. Such a format is also useful in ensuring that crucial decisions are actually made and are not merely overlooked.

Perusal of the diagram itself should intensify the student's awareness of the central role of decision making in the planning of instruction. The recommended set of procedures may also be useful to the student as a guide for intelligent participation in the development of a set of planning procedures that are responsive to local needs and circumstances.

It is anticipated that a thorough analysis of the materials presented in this section will provide the student the necessary background and insight to:

1. Write a resource unit and make a valid comparison between this preparatory technique and a systems approach to the planning of instruction.

2. Utilize a systems approach in the planning, organizing and implementing of learning processes.

3. Apply a cybernetic approach to the structuring of learning experiences, intelligently utilizing feedback in modifying teaching strategies to provide for the needs and capabilities of individual pupils.

4. Implement the behavioral approach to instructional design recommended by Tosti and Ball by selecting presentation forms and media that are compatible, thereby enhancing the achievement of instructional objectives.

5. Adapt techniques normally used by computer programmers to provide guides for the planning of instruction that will ensure that essential elements of the process are not inadvertently omitted.

Resource Unit verses Instructional System

George Mannello

14

EDITORS' QUESTIONS:

1. What is a resource unit? Discuss its components.
2. Define an instructional system. Discuss the interrelatedness of its parts.
3. Compare and contrast the two models of educational planning: the resource-unit model and the instructional-systems model. Discuss the advantages and disadvantages of each model.
4. The author discusses some of the disadvantages of the instructional-systems approach. Do you agree with his position? Justify your answer.
5. Evaluate the alternative approach to educational planning suggested by the author, the "resource unit-systems approach." Do you find this to be a superior system? Qualify your position.
6. Devise an educational planning model of your own which incorporates the advantages of both the resource-unit model and the instructional-systems model.

George Mannello, "Resource Unit versus Instructional System," *THE EDUCATIONAL FORUM,* XXXV, No. 1 (November 1970), 83–91. Used by permission of Kappa Delta Pi, An Honor Society in Education, owners of the copyright.

It has been said that the curriculum is what happens when the teacher steps into the classroom and shuts the door. As the Englishman's home is his castle, the teacher's classroom is his realm. Despite the fine philosophies, the careful curriculum guides, and the rich resources, what really matters in the educational enterprise is what the teacher does. He is an important decision maker, and programming proceeds according to what in this paper will be called the "resource unit model."

This position of the lordship of the teacher, if it ever really existed, is being encroached upon today by a new movement. Closed door or not, its adherents say, what occurs in the classroom depends upon a number of interacting factors in a predetermined total program of learning of which the teacher is only one part. A type of educational programming is growing in which the teacher no longer is a central decision maker; it is known as the "instructional system model."

The purpose of this article is to examine and compare the nature of these two models of educational planning and then suggest a third model that incorporates desirable features of each.

The question as to what happens to the traditional role of the teacher when the educational industries undertake to supply him with highly organized and carefully worked instructional packages is the theme of this article. The author is Associate Professor of Elementary Education at Hofstra University and has written extensively in a wide variety of educational journals.

The Resource Unit Model

The resource unit method of planning instruction embodies a vertical relationship of three levels of planning: resource unit, teaching unit, and daily lesson. Let us examine these plans that move from the general to the specific and see how each step spawns the next.

A resource unit is a statement of possibilities concerning a given area of learning. It is a comprehensive guide from which the teacher may select to organize his instruction, a rich reservoir of alternative ideas some of which will be chosen by the teacher in preference to others. Different teachers will select different options or the same teacher may make different selections from year to year as perceptions, emphases, and the composition of his classes change.

Although there are variations the resource unit usually contains the following elements.

A title. This is a short descriptive statement defining the substantive focus of the unit.

A statement of possible objectives. This may include a philosophical position as well as a number of broad goals to be functionally realized. The objectives may be divided into cognitive, affective, and skill attainments. They answer the question, "Why?"

A statement of possible content. This is organized in some fashion around basic facts, concepts, generalizations, questions, problems, and issues. It is the "what" of the unit.

A statement of possible activities. This is replete with suggested instructional procedures for the teacher and learning experiences for the student, including research, creative, construction, problem solving, and drill activities. It tells "how" the objectives may be achieved.

A statement of possible learning materials. Specific instructional media of all types bearing on the topic are listed—textbooks, trade books, magazines, fugitive materials, audio and visual aids, simulation games, places to visit, and guest speakers.

A statement of possible evaluation procedures. These include sample test questions, student self-evaluation techniques, teacher observations, product evaluation techniques, attitude and value questionnaires, and interviews.

The resource unit is constructed for the general school population rather than for a specific class. The wealth of alternatives makes it adaptable to a variety of teaching situations, and the unit may even bracket a number of adjoining grade levels. Thus, resource units are frequently drawn up by persons external to the particular class in which they are used. They may be prepared by faculty committees, state departments of education, university or government research and development projects, teachers' associations such as the NCSS, and commercial companies. Today, academic scholars, classroom teachers, and educationists team up in the effort to construct units that are authentic, practical, and psychologically sound.

Teaching units derive from resource units. Much of what has been said about the latter applies to the former. That is, a teaching unit will contain statements of title, objectives, content, activities, learning materials, and evaluation techniques. But there are important differences, too.

A teaching unit is constructed by the teacher for his own class. Objectives, content, etc., are drawn from the resource unit with a particular group of youngsters in mind. In making the selection the teacher considers his own on-going curriculum, the interest and abilities of the students, and the amount of time that he wishes to spend on the unit. Sometimes the children are invited to help plan the curriculum, a practice that encourages relevance, motivation, and commitment. Thus, for the model presented here, teaching units are drawn up by persons *internal* to a given learning situation rather than by outsiders.

What emerges, then, is a blue print of expectations: the actual concepts, skills, and attitudes that the teacher hopes will be achieved behaviorally through selected teaching-learning activities. Ideally, provision will be made for the differing interests, needs, and abilities of the children. It can be seen, therefore, that no two classes will follow the same blue print. Also, the teaching unit will be articulated with both the preceding and following units to incorporate sensible sequence and the reiteration of organizing concepts.

Daily lesson plans take off from the teaching unit. They are more closely tailored to immediate classroom situations than any other type of planning. In his daily work the teacher once again identifies the standard categories of goal, content, method, material, and evaluation. At this point he must differentiate between common learning for the entire group and individual experiences. Once more, he may permit children to help in deciding what will be studied and how it may be done. Again, the specific design of the immediate curriculum is determined by local persons rather than by external specialists.

In summary, then, the resource unit model of planning provides a rich statement of instructional alternatives from which the teacher chooses for his own situation. There are two underlying assumptions: that the individual teacher should be the one to plan his own units and that he is capable of doing so.

The Instructional System Model

The world is rapidly changing. The sciences multiply and become more complex. Citizenship roles transcend local and national boundaries to encompass a global community. Mass communications bring every domestic riot and every international "brush fire" into each living room. Effective economic or career choice is complicated by an abundance of alternatives. So much assails the senses that we are often left confused. How can we possibly equip people with the knowledge, attitudes, and skills to deal successfully with this seemingly impossible world? To live with continual rapid change?

Not by the old methods of education, say the systems analysts. The typical hit-or-miss learning of the past is inadequate today; it is uncoordinated, unfocused, inefficient, and confusing to the learner. Random roaming in the classroom leaves the child uneducated concerning the essentials of his society. The teacher still operates at a handicraft stage in a culture that has become technologically sophisticated and where specialization, expertise, and automation prevail. What is needed to cope with the knowledge explosion is a carefully planned, coordinated system of instruction deliberately organized to realize selected goals. Moreover, educators must interweave into this system the new offerings of science and technology such as computers, teletypewriters, television, programmed materials, and single concept film loops. It is apparent, the systems analysts conclude, that we cannot expect the ordinary classroom teacher to take major responsibility for modern educational planning and programming. The teacher simply does not have the time, the knowledge, the skill, nor the resources to do the comprehensive, meticulous, and expert programming required for effective education. He needs massive assistance and specific direction. The answer is the systems approach, similar in structure to the military and industrial complexes of American society; it is the engineer's model.

What is an instructional system? It is the totality of all the interacting components of an educational program designed to achieve efficiently some clearly identified goal. The functioning of each part affects the entire apparatus as well as the performance of each of the other parts. For example, in the system of an automobile engine every part interacts with the whole and with other parts. Thus, a defective water hose threatens the entire engine. Similarly, in an instructional system, if the parts mesh with each other and are mutually supportive, the educational output is efficient and smooth. However, if one or more of the parts fails to function, according to the system design, educational efficiency decreases.

The significant interacting components (which can be considered sub-systems) of an instructional system include the following.

1. *Objectives.* The purposes of instruction are delineated.
2. *The learner.* Both the general characteristics of children at a given stage of development and individual differences are considered.
3. *The teacher.* Personality, training, experience, and teaching modes are factors.
4. *The content.* Facts, concepts, and generalizations are carefully selected to realize the goals.
5. *Resources.* These include both the hardware and software of education selected with precision to fit the system.
6. *Teaching-learning methods.* Specific teaching techniques and learning activities are identified to achieve the objectives most efficiently.
7. *Deployment.* Administrators, teachers, and children are organized and grouped for efficient achievement.
8. *Evaluation.* Suitable instruments are constructed and techniques outlined to measure progress towards goals.

While it is true that all of these are the elements of any educational program, in the systems approach the components are more studiously integrated to create a smoothly operating whole.

In organizing an instructional system two basic departures from older planning practices occur: (1) the planning role of the individual classroom teacher is considerably reduced, and (2) the resource unit is eliminated. Most of the important decisions as to what should happen in each class are made by research and development teams outside the classroom. Instructional systems are constructed by specialists such as academic scholars, media experts, methods and curriculum specialists, child psychologists, and a few selected teachers who will pilot the trial program through their own classes prior to general distribution. Moreover, since curriculum decisions are now made by a high-powered planning and programming team, the resource unit with its wide choice of options to individual teachers becomes obsolete. Instead, systems analysts devote their attention to programming teaching units and even daily lesson plans, both formerly considered the exclusive province of the classroom teacher. They concentrate on the expected rather than the possible.

The planning team employs the methods of science and technology. First there is *analysis* in which an existing system is broken down to identify its parts and their relationships. These parts are separated, and the limits of the specific system are noted. Questions such as the following are answered: What is the system under study? What is it supposed to do? How is it supposed to do it? What are the parts which achieve what is to be done? By what criteria do we measure excellence of performance? Then there is *synthesis,* a process in which previously non-related components may be combined in a meaningful relationship to produce a new whole system. The following question is answered: What plan will improve performance beyond existing approaches? The instructional systems analyst has adopted the vocabulary of technology: input, output, signal path, feed-back, and closed loop system.

The culmination of all this is a complete package. It may include:

Teaching units and specific lesson plans published in a teacher's guide; specially prepared learning materials such as textbooks, booklets, films, recordings, simulation games, and realia; and evaluation instruments.

The teacher is regarded as one component in this system, albeit an important one, and if he needs to be re-educated for the new program, this may be done through summer workshops and on-the-job supervision.

Such packages may be developed through research and development projects, (whether foundation supported or publicly funded), state departments of education, local school districts, and commercial companies. It is conceivable that local school authorities who wish to revamp their curriculum may evaluate a number of competing systems on the market and buy the package that comes closest to their demands.

We can summarize by saying that an instructional system is a tightly organized program of interacting parts in which outside specialists do much of the planning formerly done by the individual classroom teacher. Actually, the instructional system model and the resource unit model both are systems. But resource unit teaching evolves more loosely and hapazardly through the classroom teacher. The psychologies and modes that operate might be compared with Soviet five-year plans and British muddling through—top-level, comprehensive planning versus struggling with crises as they occur on the local level and shoring up cave-ins when desperately needed.

Discussion

Package programs possess great attraction. The roster of recognized scholars and other specialists stamp the systems with a seal of authority. Moreover, the learning materials are fascinating; they are often produced with great artistry. Also, the teacher's job is made easier through a guide that details daily lesson plans. Further teacher assistance is provided through workshop courses specifically designed for the particular program. Another attractive feature is the tighter structuring for cumulative, sequential learning leading to the understanding of key concepts and generalizations. All in all the systems approach is intellectually enchanting. Yet, as with any innovation, one must look beyond the siren call of positive attributes enthusiastically publicized.

The question that most disturbs this writer is, "What happens to the classroom teacher as a self-motivated, inner-directed person?" What about creative teaching? In the resource unit model the teacher is a key decision maker. He determines the final selection of goals, content, and activity for his class. But in the systems approach the classroom practitioner is regarded as one of several operating components all of which mesh together in the entire apparatus largely predetermined by the system planners. True, there is some room in which to move around, but it is limited. For example, one package producer suggests that, ". . . we hope teachers will add their own ideas and adapt the lessons for their students." However, invitations such as "add" and "adapt" imply minimal variation in contrast with, "Select what you think is important for your group and develop it in a manner that appears most suitable."

This suggests that, despite its attractiveness, the systems model may not turn out to be as efficient as expected. We must not presume that because the systems approach works well in its innovative stage, when enthusiasm runs high among volunteer teachers and their students who welcome a change of routine, when specialists and university professors personally confer with teachers, and when money is poured into the research and development project, it will continue to succeed in its mass education phase. As innovation is transformed into universal practice, new routine is generated. It must be remembered that most of the pilot teachers who first try out a new program more or less elect to do so. Hence, they still exercise some decision making power and feel a sense of commitment. But once the system is established, the thousands of teachers who follow them may not have this choice, nor the same feelings of excitement and adventure.

Thus, we come back to the teacher, not as an important component of an instructional system but as the hub of the entire program. Without such teacher qualities as caring, commitment, responsibility, and creativity, no educational program, no matter how well organized, can succeed—not in the long run.

For example, we can visualize a situation in which an instructional system has been generally established for some time and its novelty has worn off. It is quite conceivable that a large number of teachers may follow, cookbook recipe style, the teaching units and lesson plans constructed by experts in just as mechanical and dissociated a manner as in the textbook teaching that systems analysts inveigh against. There is no point in substituting for one "slavish" method (going through the textbook page by page) another method that is apt to become equally slavish (ticking off the teaching unit). At least in the former the teacher can be less slavish if he is so motivated. In the systems approach, however, with everything so neatly laid out, with materials and strategies so explicit, with the built-in expectation of conformity, the tendency will be to fall into one's place, to become "other-directed." When the teacher loses his feeling of centrality in the teaching-learning act, the qualities of good teaching previously mentioned diminish. Instead, he may come to regard himself, just as the analysts say, one of a number of interacting parts, and as in and standardized machine replaceable by another identical part. It is dehumanizing.

It is also deprofessionalizing. The teacher who no longer creates, organizes, and directs according to his own perceptions cannot be regarded as a full-fledged professional. He becomes a technician who implements some one else's design.

It has been said that one of the advantages of the complete package is that the rest of the system can carry the learning program reasonably well even though there is a poor teacher, a defective part in a sense. Indeed, the unfortunate expression "teacher-proof materials" has been used, meaning that simply putting the materials in the hands of the students results in great educational benefit irrespective of the particular teacher.

My argument, then, is this: educational efficiency is not so much a matter of over-all organization but rather continuing personal, intelligent involvement by teachers. Any system that discourages this becomes less efficient. If we want teachers to perform well, we must give them every opportunity to learn how to do so. Some years ago, while a supervisor, I found one of my student teachers following a textbook teacher's manual word for word. This student was instructed not to look at the manual for the remainder of the semester until *after* she had prepared each lesson. Then she could compare.

"But," she protested, "there are so many good ideas in the manual. I cannot make up such fine lessons!"

I answered, "Is it better to teach a lesson of your own that turns out poorly than to follow on faith a fine plan drawn up by someone else."

The act of organizing one's own teaching from beginning to end was a better, more educative experience than parroting a well laid out prescription. The dynamic teacher constantly tries out new things. He makes mistakes, he fumbles, he corrects himself, he becomes inspired, he is inconsistent, but he is alive and is the central force of his classroom. His students come alive, too, because he, himself, throbs with vitality. His teaching may lack the fine organization of an instructional system but it is *his* organization, and this sense of personal identification may more than compensate for any loss of efficiency provided by the specialists. A dynamic, autonomous teacher will probably achieve more in his less refined program than an indifferent, other-directed one in a well-organized instructional system.

Then there are the students. We know that when learners have a say in what will be learned, when their concerns and interest are incorporated into the program, they are more likely to generate their own study activity. This is the value of cooperative planning. Yet, the systems approach may deter this practice. It is true that many of the instructional systems emphasize student involvement through inductive, self-discovery strategies, but this usually is on the terms of the planners and within the limits of the system. Students are not invited to help draw up the plan; it is done for them. Thus, the teacher who closely follows an "authoritative" guide will probably do less cooperative planning than one who habitually composes his own lessons. The growing revolt on college and high school campuses tells us that students want to help determine their educational programs, not peripherally, but starting at the foundations. Student demand for participation in basic educational planning and the systems approach are on a collision course.

Finally, there is the question of change. Once an instructional system had been adopted by a local school district, what happens if its basic assumptions are later found to be wanting? Systems analysts point out that change is a natural process in any instructional system, that constant feedback and adjustment are built in to insure efficient production in terms of the over-all objectives. But suppose the objectives are wrong?

Here is where the "muddling through" and the "five-year plan" modes differ. In the resource unit approach individual teachers who find selected objectives inadequate can shift to other ones. Or they may expand on what they consider the more important aspects of the unit and hurry over the less significant parts. They may discard a unit altogether. These changes can take place informally at no great cost to the school system. Administrative resistance to change will tend to be minimal.

However, a proposal to substitute one instructional system for another will meet much greater opposition. The adoption of a system means total involvement: acceptance of the philosophy and objectives of the system, purchase of specially designed materials, a training program to enable teachers to understand and become skillful in teaching the content of the system, and appropriate evaluation instruments. This investment in time, toil, and treasure will not be easily discarded no matter how lacking the system may prove to be. It is quite probable that an instructional system will survive long after its basic foundations are considered unsatisfactory.

An Alternative Approach

Perhaps the saving feature of any model is that its practice is seldom "pure." Indeed, it might be possible to have the best of both worlds, to combine the efficient unitary structure of a systems approach with the centrality of the individual classroom teacher. Let us see how this might be done.

First, the resource unit should be retained as the base from which planning begins, but "beefed up" with more particular and articulated assistance to the teacher as found in an instructional system, perhaps called a "resource unit-system" approach. Thus, the resource unit would not only present statements of possibility, it would also provide many specific aids from which the teacher could select. For example, a unit on Eskimo life might include several films specifically developed for the various objectives of the unit, as well as a listing of films that can be found in general sources. This combination could apply to all categories of materials: booklets, recordings, games, tests, etc. Some

would be produced especially for the unit and some would come from other sources.

Moreover, resource unit-systems could take the form of teaching guides (but not teaching units) wherein the basic premises, knowledge structure, and principles of the unit are developed. Although a sequential program of daily lesson plans would not be included, such a guide could contain several demonstration lessons of different types illustrating and analyzing for the teacher the varying modes that could be employed in developing the unit. And if a number of workshop sessions are deemed desirable to help teachers think through the content and to see the possible approaches for one or more resource unit-systems, by all means have them.

Then, enable teachers to organize efficient instructional systems (teaching units) of their own. The answer to random roaming in the classroom is not traffic lights but intelligent self-direction. One of the glaring deficiencies of current teacher education programs is the failure to develop planning skills. Students have repeatedly complained to this author that while theory is coming out their ears, only lip service is paid to planning. Certainly the sophisticated programming of the instructional system model requires training, and if our teachers cannot program well, one reason is that we have not taught them. Teachers must be taught how to create more deliberately their own instructional systems, integrating the eight interacting components presented earlier in this article. At appropriate times they will invite students to participate in this planning.

Lastly, the complaint that the teacher cannot do the job because he has no time need not deter us. Finding the time often has been a matter of motivation. If a school system believes that effective teacher planning is important the authorities will find ways to help him put a block of time together for such purpose: through the use of para-professionals, team teaching, summer stipends, and class scheduling. Rather than dependence upon the experts, the heart of teaching must remain within the person of the teacher.

A System Approach to Education: Derivation and Definition[1]

Roger A. Kaufman

EDITORS' QUESTIONS:

1. What advantages may be gained from the use of a systems approach in planning and implementing learning experiences?

2. Identify and define the steps in a systems analysis procedure. Give an example of the application of each of these steps to the management of the teaching-learning process.

3. Explain how a knowledge of the mission profile assists the teacher in problem solving.

4. Assess the importance of the need assessment procedure in a systems approach to instruction. Explain how the meaning of need assessment differs, in this context, from that of diagnosis.

5. Evaluate the following statement: "A system approach requires that problems be solved so that the sum total of separate parts of the system working independently and together will achieve previously specified objectives."

6. It has sometimes been alleged that the utilization of a systems approach is "dehumanizing" and discourages initiative and creativity on the part of the classroom teacher. Is this necessarily the case? Justify your position.

Roger A. Kaufman, "A System Approach to Education: Derivation and Definition," *Audio Visual Communication Review,* XVI, (Winter 1968), 415–425. Reprinted with the permission of the *Audio Visual Communication Review.*

The terms *system* and *system approach* are quite popular in the literature of education today (e.g., Bern, 1967; Corrigan & Kaufman, 1966; Barson & Heinich, 1966; Kaufman, Corrigan, Corrigan, & Goodwin, 1967; Mauch, 1962; Silvern, 1968). Many people use the terms but the essence and the concept seem to have multiple referents. This paper attempts to define a system approach in terms of a problem-solving process, and to identify the characteristics of the general sequence of steps involved in applying a system approach to education.

Problem Solving—A Description of a Process

In education, we are attempting to meet needs: needs of society, needs of learners, and needs of educators to be responsive to

Roger A. Kaufman is professor of education at Chapman College, Orange, California.

1. This is a revision of a paper originally presented to California Teacher's Association Staff Conference on Problem Solving; Asilomar, California, January 30, 1968. Much of the contents of this paper was developed for use in the Experienced Teacher Fellowship Program at Chapman College and for Operation PEP and thus reflects contributions of Robert E. Corrigan, Donald Goodwin, and Betty O. Corrigan.

requirements placed upon us by those we strive to serve. A *need* is here defined as the discrepancy between *what is* and *what is required*—a definition that indicates that a need is a measurable difference or distance between a present state or condition and what is required to be accomplished.

For the purposes of this discussion, a *problem* is defined as the requirement to reduce or eliminate a discrepancy between *what is* and *what is required* to a specified level. In this context, then, needs are identified as discrepancies, and problems are derived from the identified needs. An example of a hypothetical discrepancy in education might be: Children in State X have a mean reading score of Q on valid test Y which is F% below mandated performance. A problem which could be derived from this hypothetical need might be: To raise reading skill level so that mean reading score on valid test Y by State X's children will be raised to required level. Needs may be identified through a process called *need assessment* wherein all discrepancies are identified relative to a given area (such as within a specified school district or a community) and priorities placed on each of the needs relative to one another. This need assessment procedure will increase the probability of obtaining valid needs and thus relevant problems which will allow the educator to reduce or eliminate the "true" needs.

By the above definition, a problem has both a beginning and an end. The beginning is what presently exists (what is) and the end is what the conditions will be when the problem is solved (what is required). Problem solving is a process by which one may get from *what is* to *what is required*. For purposes of demonstration, following is a simplified example of a problem and a process by which this or more complex problems may be attacked and solved.

Step 1: Identify and Define What Is

In this example, $X + 3 = 4$, we define our starting conditions and assumptions, including that of the number system in which we are working (assume a number system to the base 10) and that a person solving the problem knows the rules of working in that number system. Here all assumptions and starting conditions are defined.

Step 2: Identify and Define What Is Required

Here the criteria for acceptable problem solution are identified and defined in operational or measurable terms. For the example, the correct solution will be achieved when the equation is symmetric ($X + 3 = 4$ and $4 = X + 3$).

Step 3: Select Process Steps for Getting From Step 1 to Step 2

Eldridge (1965) in *Maxims for a Modern Man* states that "wisdom is the ability to discover alternatives." Here, the best process or procedure for solving the problem is selected from identified viable alternatives. For this example, alternatives might include, (a) count on fingers or count physical objects, (b) guess, (c) ask the teacher or look on someone else's paper, (d) keep substituting numbers for the X, (e) count mentally to derive answer, and (f) use mathematical logic. System people frequently use a criterion of cost-effectiveness or cost-benefit as the selection criterion for solution strategies.

Step 4: Implement Process

Here, the selected process (or methods-means) is implemented and the product obtained.

Step 5: Determine Validity

Here the characteristics of the outcome or product are compared to determine the extent to which the outcome meets the criteria identified in Step 2.

Step 6: Re-do if Necessary

This final step provides the critical feature of self-correction so that any or all steps in getting from *what is* to *what is required* may be re-done or modified so that the required output will reduce or eliminate the identified need as required. Allowing modifications to meet requirements is a characteristic of a self-correcting or *closed-loop* problem solving model. Figure 1 shows this six-step problem solving model with examples related to the simplified problem of solving the equation $X + 3 = 4$.

A System Approach to Education

The above derived problem solving model is the basic model for a System Approach to Education (Kaufman et al., 1967) which is process oriented rather than simply descriptive in nature. If one were to arrange the steps differently the result would be something called a *functional flow block diagram* such as that shown in Figure 2. This type of presentation shows the steps for process functions for going from *what is* to a relevant *what is required,* and it may be read by following the order of the numbers (1.0 to 2.0 to 3.0, etc.) and by following the solid lines and arrows. Each function (or

STEP 1:	WHAT IS:	$x + 3 = 4$
STEP 2:	WHAT IS REQUIRED:	DETERMINE "x" SUCH THAT x+3=4 AND 4=x+3
STEP 3:	SELECT PROCESS STEPS FOR GETTING FROM STEP 1 TO STEP 2:	(A) SUBTRACT THREE FROM BOTH SIDES, OR (B) ADD NEGATIVE THREE TO BOTH SIDES,
STEP 4:	IMPLEMENT SOLUTION STRATEGY:	x + 3 = 4 x + 3 - 3 = 4 - 3 x + 0 = 1 x = 1
STEP 5:	DETERMINE VALIDITY OF OUTCOME:	LET x = 1, THEN x + 3 = 4 BECAUSE 1 + 3 = 4, 4 = 4, THEREFORE 1 + 3 = 4 AND 4 = 1 + 3
STEP 6:	RE-DO IF NECESSARY	IF WE HAD SELECTED AN INCORRECT STRATEGY AND ARRIVED AT x = 5, THEN IN CHECKING WE WOULD HAVE ARRIVED AT 5 + 3 ≠ 4, SO RE-DOING OF ALL OR PART OF THE PROCESS IS REQUIRED.

A Possible Generic Problem Solving Model And The Application Of Its Process To Solving A Simple Problem. It Is Suggested That The Same Process May Be Applied To The Almost Infinitely Complex Problems Of Education.

Figure 1

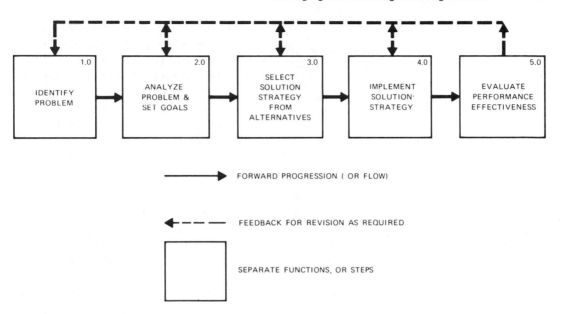

FORWARD PROGRESSION (OR FLOW)

FEEDBACK FOR REVISION AS REQUIRED

SEPARATE FUNCTIONS, OR STEPS

A Diagramatic Representation Of A Problem Solving Process. Note That This Is A Six-Step Process · 1.0 Through 5.0 Plus The Sixth Step Of "Re-do" Noted By The Broken Line Requiring Revision As Necessary.

Figure 2

step in the problem solving process) is identified as independent by enclosure in a box. The broken or dotted lines indicate the requirement to re-do a previous function if it is necessary.

It is quite obvious that in education, our problems are almost infinitely more difficult than $X + 3 = 4$, but this same basic model may be applied to any problem, no matter how simple or how complex. By formally following this type of model (a System Approach to Education) we may be more assured that a self-correcting strategy is being applied and that relevant and cogent variables will be considered. The formality of the approach, its openness, and its objectivity, reduce the risk of overlooking important elements or using inappropriate solution strategies.

This approach is a tool *for* educators; it is not mechanical and it is not dehumanizing when applied. It does minimize the likelihood of adopting prepackaged solutions before the requirements for solution have been identified. This system approach requires that the problem be identified and specified before solutions are tried. Frequently, educational agencies have had unfortunate experience with the application of solutions which have turned out to be inappropriate to the problem—simply because there was a logic leap from *what is* to the selection of the strategy before the *what is required* had been identified and defined. Perhaps the reader can think of examples of rushing into a panacea only to find out that it was a solution all right, but not to the problem at hand!

What Is a System?

A system may be defined as "the sum total of separate parts working independently and in interaction to achieve previously specified objectives." Like the model of a System Approach to Education in Figure 2, which may be called a system (a problem solving system), education also may be viewed as a system. Some of the components of an educational system could be: Teaching and instruction, management and administration, facilities and support, community, and learners.

Each of these parts, when considered alone, may be classified as individual systems. Remembering that, as here defined, these components may be considered as independent, if one had a new problem to solve relative to any one of these individual systems alone, one could use a system approach to identify and derive the most appropriate solution within each.

Most educators realize that it is artificial to think of any of the systems above as independent; all of these components actually interact together in the operational world. Therefore, any educational unit (classroom, school, district, county, state, nation) may be viewed as an integrated whole of the above identified individual systems. When these parts are put together to form an educational system, these components become subsystems of the overall educational system. Thus, any educational operation may be viewed as a system, and any problems relating to it must consider the fact that all components, or subsystems, must operate both independently and together to achieve a specified outcome. To solve problems relating to such an educational system, a system approach would seem to be an effective and efficient tool to assure that the complex interactions will be properly considered. A system approach requires that problems be solved so that the sum total of separate parts of the system working independently and together will achieve previously specified objectives. The educational world is complex, and it would seem that this formal problem solving model may serve it well.

A Brief Introduction to the Tools of a System Approach

Given the six-step problem solving model which describes the process of a System Approach to Education (Figure 2), there are a number of tools and techniques for implementing a system approach. These formal methods may be summarized into two arbitrary categories called *system analysis,* and *system synthesis.* Oversimplifying, system analysis deals primarily with the first two problem solving steps (shown in Figure 2) of: 1.0 identify problem, and 2.0 analyze problem and set goals. System synthesis techniques are useful for the balance of the problem solving steps (3.0 through 5.0 and including the broken line requiring re-doing if necessary). The system analysis procedure (Figure 3) includes a number of steps and their associate techniques (Kaufman et al., 1967). These include: mission analysis, functional analysis, task analysis, and methods-means analysis.

Mission analysis is a determination of where are we going and how do we know when we've arrived. Recalling that the definition of a system, as used here, included "to achieve previously specified objectives," an analyst needs to identify the elements of the problem solving process which specify what is required. Mission analysis includes the steps of identifying an overall mission objective and the specific measurable performance requirements for satisfactory completion of the mission. The mission is what has to be accomplished, or what is required.

The mission objective is a precise, specific statement of what is required; the performance requirements give the criteria for successful completion. With the statement of what has to be accomplished in measurable performance terms, constraints may be identified. A *constraint* is anything that will prevent the accomplishment of the mission objective in whole or in part. These constraints must be reconciled before further analysis is continued. By identifying the mission objective, performance requirements, and reconciling constraints, the system analysis process continually identifies all of the feasible *whats* for problem solution. The system analysis process provides information relative only to *what* must be done and provides the data base of feasible *whats* for use in system synthesis where *how* determinations are made. Thus, the use of this system approach virtually eliminates the possibility of solutions being introduced before the problem has been identified and defined.

After the mission objective and its per-

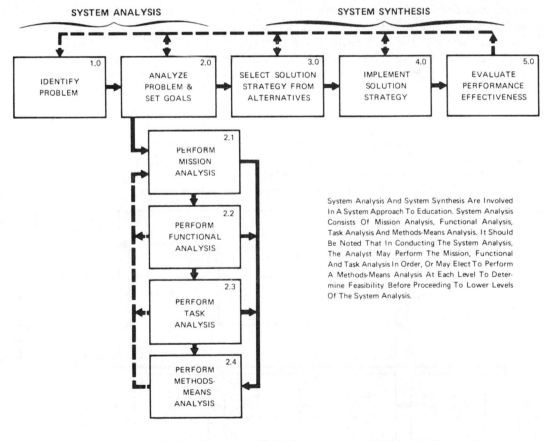

System Analysis And System Synthesis Are Involved In A System Approach To Education. System Analysis Consists Of Mission Analysis, Functional Analysis, Task Analysis And Methods-Means Analysis. It Should Be Noted That In Conducting The System Analysis, The Analyst May Perform The Mission, Functional And Task Analysis In Order, Or May Elect To Perform A Methods-Means Analysis At Each Level To Determine Feasibility Before Proceeding To Lower Levels Of The System Analysis.

Figure 3

formance requirements have been identified and the constraints reconciled, a management plan is derived to identify the steps for getting from *what is* to *what is required.* This central path for problem solution is called a *mission profile.* A mission profile has already been presented in Figure 2—a mission profile for solving educational problems using a system approach. Actually, each problem will have a different mission profile depending upon the *what is* and the *what is required* (Figure 4 shows a possible mission profile for preparing instructional materials using a system approach).

Mission analysis, then, identifies what is required, and derives the central path for achieving valid feasible problem solution.

Functional analysis and *task analysis* are quite closely related to mission analysis, and consist of breaking down all of the func-

tions identified in the mission profile into its constituent component functions. Functional and task analyses may be viewed as vertical expansions of the mission profile, and continue until units of performance are identified—these being called *tasks.* The difference between mission analysis and functional analysis is a difference of degree rather than of kind. Figure 5 shows a hypothetical functional analysis.

The remaining system analysis step is called *methods-means analysis.* This analysis step identifies for each performance requirement or family of performance requirements (identified in mission, functional, and task analysis) *possible* strategies and vehicles for accomplishing the performance requirements. In practice, the methods-means analysis may begin at any point in the system analysis procedure, and thus may be con-

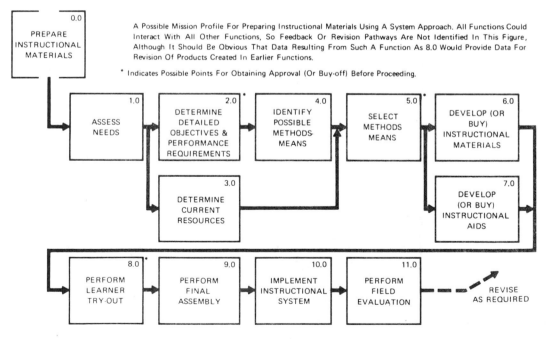

Figure 4

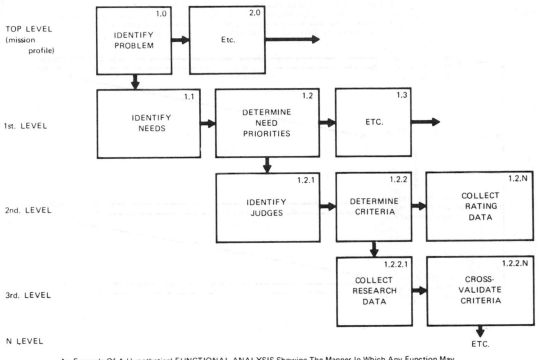

An Example Of A Hypothetical FUNCTIONAL ANALYSIS Showing The Manner In Which Any Function May Be Analyzed Into Lower Level Constituent Functions.

Figure 5

tinually refined as more detailed performance requirements are identified. For each of the methods-means identified, the advantages and disadvantages of each are listed. Again, like all of the other steps of the system analysis, this only identifies *what* is available, not *how*. The total system analysis provides the data for selecting and implementing the most effective and efficient solution strategies and vehicles for getting from *what is* to *what is required.*

The process by which a system analysis may be accomplished is shown in the process chart in Figure 6. The questions to be answered by a system analysis may be reviewed in Figure 7.

Once this data base of feasible *whats* is obtained through the system analysis process, system synthesis utilizes this data to select solution strategies and vehicles for the identified performance requirements, making and/or buying the system components that are required, trying them out to determine their effectiveness, and implementing them and evaluating the total system product in the environment for which they were designed (Kaufman et al., 1967). Generally system synthesis consists of: 3.0 select solution strategy, 4.0 implement solution strategy, 5.0 determine performance effectiveness, and 6.0 revise and correct as required (as described in Figure 3).

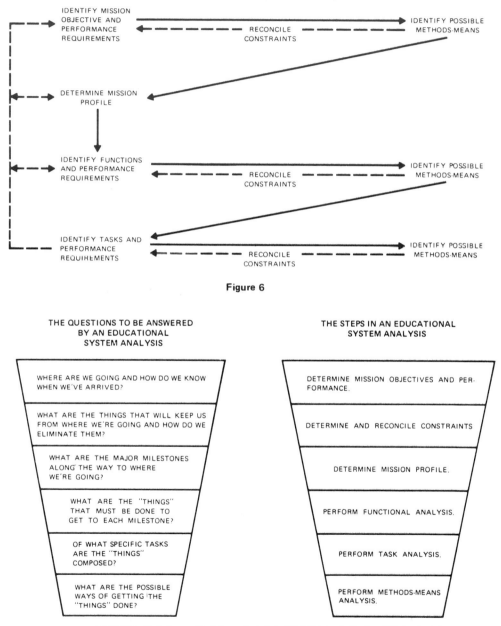

A System Analysis Process Model Which Identifies The Relationship Between The Various Steps In The Process. Note That A Continous Feasibility Check Is Being Made During The Process By Identifying Requirements In The Mission, Functional And Task Analysis And Determining If There Are Any Methods-Means Available For Accomplishing Each Performance Requirement Or Family Of Performance Requirements.

IDENTIFY MISSION OBJECTIVE AND PERFORMANCE REQUIREMENTS

IDENTIFY POSSIBLE METHODS-MEANS

RECONCILE CONSTRAINTS

DETERMINE MISSION PROFILE

IDENTIFY FUNCTIONS AND PERFORMANCE REQUIREMENTS

IDENTIFY POSSIBLE METHODS-MEANS

RECONCILE CONSTRAINTS

IDENTIFY TASKS AND PERFORMANCE REQUIREMENTS

IDENTIFY POSSIBLE METHODS-MEANS

RECONCILE CONSTRAINTS

IDENTIFY POSSIBLE METHODS-MEANS

Figure 6

THE QUESTIONS TO BE ANSWERED BY AN EDUCATIONAL SYSTEM ANALYSIS

THE STEPS IN AN EDUCATIONAL SYSTEM ANALYSIS

WHERE ARE WE GOING AND HOW DO WE KNOW WHEN WE'VE ARRIVED?

WHAT ARE THE THINGS THAT WILL KEEP US FROM WHERE WE'RE GOING AND HOW DO WE ELIMINATE THEM?

WHAT ARE THE MAJOR MILESTONES ALONG THE WAY TO WHERE WE'RE GOING?

WHAT ARE THE "THINGS" THAT MUST BE DONE TO GET TO EACH MILESTONE?

OF WHAT SPECIFIC TASKS ARE THE "THINGS" COMPOSED?

WHAT ARE THE POSSIBLE WAYS OF GETTING THE "THINGS" DONE?

DETERMINE MISSION OBJECTIVES AND PERFORMANCE.

DETERMINE AND RECONCILE CONSTRAINTS

DETERMINE MISSION PROFILE.

PERFORM FUNCTIONAL ANALYSIS.

PERFORM TASK ANALYSIS.

PERFORM METHODS-MEANS ANALYSIS.

The Questions To Be Answered In A System Analysis And Their Relation To The Steps Of Performing A System Analysis.

Figure 7

The foregoing brief description of system analysis and system synthesis is obviously too hurried for detailed examination. It is designed to show its relationship to a generic problem solving model and a system approach. The steps and tools of system analysis and system synthesis do derive from the suggested generic model and thus constitute tools to be used to solve educational problems using a system approach.

Implications for Educators

Educators deal with perhaps the most complex problems confronting man today. Everything that can affect people is included in education and the educational process. Complex problems involving the future of our fellow humans must not be left to chance or to hunches. The steps and tools of A System Approach to Education, although still relatively crude, are being improved and refined as required by the system approach itself. Implementation of this approach by educators, and its correction through experience and validation, should continuously improve education.

REFERENCES

Barson, J. & Heinich, R. *The Systems Approach to Instruction,* DAVI 1966 Convention, San Diego (audiotape). Boulder: National Tape Repository, University of Colorado. Also reported in "The System Approach," *Audiovisual Instruction,* 1966, *11,* 431–433.

Bern, H. A. "Wanted: Educational Engineers," *Phi Delta Kappan,* 1967, *48,* 230–236.

Corrigan, R. E. & Kaufman, R. A. *Why System Engineering.* Palo Alto, Calif.: Fearon, 1966.

Eldridge, P. *Maxims for a Modern Man.* Cranbury, N.J.: A. S. Barnes, 1965.

Kaufman, R. A., Corrigan, R. E., Corrigan, B. O., & Goodwin, D. L. Steps and Tools of System Analysis as Applied to Education; Steps and Tools of the System Synthesis Process in Education; Mission Analysis in Education; Functional Analysis in Education; Task Analysis in Education; Methods-means Analysis in Education; An Interim Generic Problem Solving Model; An Exercise in the Analysis of Planned Change in Education. (Eight pamphlets prepared for Operation PEP) San Mateo, Calif.: San Mateo County Department of Education, 1967.

Mauch, J. A. "Systems Analysis Approach to Education," *Phi Delta Kappan,* 1962, *43,* 158–161.

Silvern, L. C. "Cybernetics and Education K-12," *Audiovisual Instruction,* 1968, *13,* 267–275.

A Behavioral Approach to Instructional Design and Media Selection[1]

Donald T. Tosti
and John R. Ball

EDITORS' QUESTIONS:
1. Discuss the advantages which result from distinguishing between the presentation form and the medium or media by which it is conveyed.
2. Construct an example which illustrates the application of the guide presented in Figure 3 for the structuring of the presentation form.
3. Explain why media limitations are considered more appropriate criteria for media selection than media advantages.
4. State an objective in behavioral terms, select a presentation form which is both reasonable and adequate and discuss the advisability of using several different types of media either singly or in combination.
5. Indicate ways in which the management of the presentation dimension can be used to facilitate the attainment of instructional objectives.

Donald T. Tosti and John R. Ball, "A Behavioral Approach to Instructional Design and Media Selection," *Audio Visual Communication Review*, XVII, (Spring 1969), 5–25. Reprinted with the permission of the *Audio Visual Communication Review*.

This paper proposes a new model for instructional system design and develops a system component called a presentation form. Presentation form is designed to be independent of media and content so that media forms may be paired to educational requirements and theories in a rigorous manner.

A significant feature of the developmental model proposed here is the distinction between medium and presentation form. A presentation design theory leading to the generation of presentation form is discussed in detail, and six dimensions of the presentation form are proposed: stimulus (encoding, duration), response (response demand, response frequency), and management (frequency, purpose). After presentation forms have been specified and media choices are to be made, media limitations are proposed as the basic selection criteria instead of media advantages.

Developmental Procedure

According to Webster, a medium is "a means of effecting or conveying something." Since in education we are obviously very concerned with effecting a change in learning behavior, it follows that educational media research should be important. But to date research in media effects has not produced practical results. It could be, as

1. This paper is an adaptation of a 90-page monograph prepared for the Westinghouse Learning Corporation. Donald T. Tosti is general manager and John R. Ball is media analyst in the Behavior Systems Division of the Westinghouse Learning Corporation, Albuquerque, New Mexico.

146

some writers have pointed out, that fault lies in the nature of the experimentation we conduct in media research. Or it may be that media effects in themselves are not significant enough in the teaching-learning process to warrant investigation.

This last statement must be considered rationally and not emotionally. There is already too much emotion centered around media. Organizations devoted to the spread of new media information and excitement have appeared. Defense of the traditional media of lecture, laboratory, and text is also voiced. However, when the extant literature is examined from the standpoint of what is actually known about the learning process, ineligible data, faulty generalizations from learning theory, and appeals to the emotions or artistic inclinations are apparent. If procedures for learning are to be improved at a reasonable pace, then more solid theory and less of the above must be forthcoming.

The major fault in instructional design today is the frequent failure to recognize the distinction between three separate design elements: the medium, the presentation form, and the content.

The key to establishing such a distinction lies in taking a behavioral view. Although such an approach is still questioned in educational circles, its support in learning research and instructional design is such that

no alternatives seriously rival it. The behavioral approach elicits the inevitable conclusion that the quality of an educational system must be defined primarily in terms of change in student behaviors. Thus every factor in the educational system must be evaluated as to its ability to modify either directly or indirectly the behavior of the student. In designing a behavioral change system, several classes of variables must be considered (see Figure 1). Generally, educational research attempts to control task variables and student variables and directly relate these to operational variables without controlling those intervening events which we call presentational variables. However, psychology and learning research has taken quite a different trend. In learning experiments the presentational variables are primary. Thus most experiments in human behavior learning can be classified into those dealing with (1) stimulus factors, (2) response factors, or (3) consequential or contingent factors. What we have attempted to do in this paper is to sort through these behavioral factors to select those which have the maximum impact in determining the operational system or media mix. Concepts like response-similarity may have no direct media selection implication, while a concept like response-type definitely does. As an example of the effect of

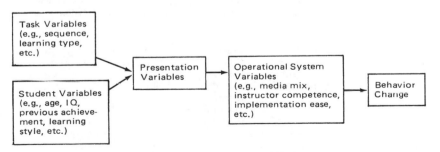

Figure 1 Important Variables in a Behavioral Change System

the latter, certain media such as films cannot accept a written response, while other media such as workbooks can.

It is important for us to examine all the steps leading to the design of the operational system (which includes considerations of the medium) and also to include shaping of student repertoire as a parallel development. (By *shaping student repertoire* we mean deliberate instruction in observational sets, learning style, syntax of presentation, etc.) Such a developmental procedure is shown in Figure 2 and summarized as follows:

Step 1. Determine the nature of the problem by interview, observation, or research. Establish general goals to solve the problem.

Step 2. Determine the specific behaviors to be established and the entering behaviors of the students.

Step 3. Deduce the presentation factors which produce the desired behavioral effect employing established evidence in learning; then analyze or synthesize the generalized response sets which may be employed by the student in his response to the presentation.

Step 4. Select media which fit the presentation requirements. Media selection must be done in terms of eliminating media which limit or otherwise adversely affect the presentation design rather than specifying advantageous media. Then assemble an operational instructional systems package (media-mix).

Step 5. Determine strategy for introduction of the operational system into the instructional environment.

If possible, each step should impose as few constraints as possible on the preceding step. The final system must be extended to handle all constraints, but the fewer constraints imposed, such as prior medium selection, etc., the better and less expensive will be the resulting system.

Given the inputs of behavioral objectives and environmental information, presentation design theory will be used to prepare one or more presentation forms for those inputs. Then media selection may proceed, considering the medium's limitations in conveying the presentation form intact rather than some unsupported advantages claimed for it.

A significant part of the behavioral approach to instructional design is the design of a presentation form (Step 3). Presentation

Step 1	Step 2	Step 3	Step 4	Step 5
Determine general goals	Determine behavior objectives	Design presentation	Develop operational system (media mix)	Implementation
	Assess entering student repertoire	Design student shaping procedures (behavior modification)	(materials preparation)	

Figure 2 Developmental Procedure

design is discussed in terms of the following six dimensions:

stimulus $\begin{cases} \text{1. encoding form} \\ \text{2. duration} \end{cases}$

response $\begin{cases} \text{3. demand form} \\ \text{4. demand frequency} \end{cases}$

management $\begin{cases} \text{5. management form} \\ \text{6. management frequency} \end{cases}$

Presentation versus Medium

Media researchers to date have not chosen to distinguish a presentation form from the media which carry that form. This new model requires that such a separation be made. The media in instructional systems carry not only the data of the instructional message but also data on students' responses and various other bits of data necessary to maintain the operating systems. It is the structure by which the information is carried by a medium that is called the presentation form. A student does not learn from the media. He learns from the presentation form. Media do little more than deliver the information to be learned in whatever presentational form previously decided upon.

As an example of the relationship between presentation and media, consider that a picture of an elephant in a book versus a verbal description of an elephant by a teacher differ in both media and presentation form. However, a picture of the elephant on a slide and the one in the book have the same presentation form but are being delivered by two different media. It is also possible for a given medium to be able to deliver several presentation forms. It is doubtful if all presentation forms can be delivered equally well since media have differing limitations. To illustrate presentation form and point out the existing confu-

sion between presentation form and medium, let us examine the technique known as programed instruction (PI).

The term *programed instruction* is commonly used both for the presentation form and for a particular type of workbook often employed as a medium. The basic PI presentation form is as follows:

1. The stimuli are presented in a verbal or illustrated form.
2. A demand of a written or selection response is made.
3. The presentation lasts as long as the student desires.
4. The student must make some response before proceeding to the next item.

The four characteristics given above define a format or procedure for teaching that is independent (to a first approximation) of both content and media. Although all pertinent stimulus forms, response demands, and timing have been specified in the PI presentation form, no mention was made of the medium to be employed.

An obvious medium that could be used to implement the PI presentation form is the printed frame-by-frame workbook. But other media such as slide-tapes, laboratory-workbooks, TV-problem booklets, peer-tutor scripts, and sound films with Edex-like feedback devices could be used to implement this same presentation form. Some of these media choices will impose limitations upon the intent of the presentation form or upon other system components. Where medium-based limitations exist, value judgments must be used for final selection. Further research is necessary to give some structure to media choice situations or at least to provide guidelines for value judgments.

Media Experiments

In examining current media research we frequently see that presentation variables are either ignored, confused with content, or "controlled" by grouping them under gross media classifications such as "printed" or "projected." Results of such experiments cannot be generalized to produce reliable course designs.

A typical approach in media experiments is to use the same or similar course content with an experimental and a control medium. Usually the control medium becomes a human lecturer. Such a situation ignores the different presentation forms present in the lecture session and the experimental media session. It is the form of the presentation which influences learning rather than the media employed (to a first approximation). A direct comparison of any two such experimental situations is analogous to an engineer comparing two pipe materials for a delivery system without knowing that flow rate is dependent on pipe diameter and the friction coefficient of the inner surface. Media studies that confound the presentation form cannot be analytical nor extendible.

Yet researchers seem blissfully unaware of these implications. For example, in a recent experiment by Warner (1968) a mechanical medium, the Language Master, is compared to the human medium, the teacher. In her discussion, Warner admits that the two presentations are not equivalent in her statement:

> . . . the teacher allowed for assessment of the learning situation and appropriate modification of the pacing of the teaching program to suit individual difference.

However, later in the implication section she says:

> For first-graders in the initial phase of reading instruction, prompting and reinforcing may be more effective when provided by the teacher than by a mechanical device.

Presentation Design

Several years' experience in developing programed materials forced us into careful consideration of the stimulus and response aspects of the presentation, and for the most part any motivational factors were ignored. But as we began to actually use such material in classrooms we were amazed to find that other factors could compensate for poor stimulus control design. This realization forced us to cease thinking of PI as synonymous with the workbook medium, and to abstract the characteristics of PI as a presentation form.

Today, presentational design is used at the Behavior Systems Division (BSD) to generate presentation forms which allow a variety of media to be utilized in operating instructional systems.

Behavioral engineers, using presentational design theory and known techniques for behavior modification, have been able to develop a technology to work around most limitations of particular media. This effort has been so successful that today almost anything can be taught to anyone over the age of six using printed text with illustrations as the sole medium.

Of course, there is a danger in overgeneralizing this success, since it does not mean that such an operating instructional system will be efficient in terms of cost of preparation, student effort, or other criteria.

Media Limitations

On the surface, considering the limitations of media may seem to be nothing more than the reverse of stating the advantages of media. The difference is subtle but important. Two media may fit the general requirements of the presentation form, but each has different limitations. It may be easier to compensate for the limitations of Medium A than of Medium B. Hence, Medium A should be selected. Quite often, however, Medium B has an aura of advantage surrounding it. It is multisensory, it is new, it has been successfully used in other settings, or it has received great press reviews. The novice designer may, therefore, incorrectly select Medium B because of its extrinsic advantages which are really superficial to the learning task.

Since few researchers have even recognized that there is a distinction between media and presentation form, it is not yet known just what attributes of media may constitute inherent advantages. However, a reduction to practice of presentational analysis would allow the limitations of media to be easily distinguished. Such media attributes might be structured in behavioral terms, in operational terms, or in terms of inherent syntactical cues.

The assertion that media limitations are the key to proper media selection does not outlaw at least two special cases in which media advantages should be used. Suppose at least two media have almost equivalent limitations for a given presentation form. Then, if one medium has the advantage of greater student experience or preference over the other medium, this should be a consideration in the actual media selection. A second special case also assumes two media more or less equivalent from the standpoint of limitations but the accompanying advantages are weighed differently. A common practice in manufacturing is to compare a suggested product improvement in two situations: factory-added, or to be acquired by the consumer at a later date. In the media situation, the presentation form may call for a particular component to be added by the student from other media or at

another time. However, a consideration of the advantages of the media may suggest that this component may better be provided now.

To use an analogy, if salt enhances the flavor of asparagus, it is easier to add salt during processing of the asparagus when it is delivered to the consumer by the medium of the can, than when delivered fresh. Interestingly, the person who prefers canned asparagus over fresh may really be responding to salt which is not inherent in the medium of the can nor impossible to implement via the fresh medium. Similarly, many learners and educators are superstitiously conditioned to prefer one medium over another because one "packager" may have added a desirable form of presentation not used by the other.

Designing Student Shaping Procedures

Engineering of student behavior is considered to be an important part of any instructional system implemented by BSD. Perhaps the basic reason that student engineering has assumed such prominence at BSD derives from the equipment used in early instruction experiments. Typically available equipment was unreliable, was frequently out of service, had poor resolution, and often required additional simulation support by humans behind a curtain. Since these media limitations were so obvious and because human simulation is a difficult task, many ways were found to engineer the student's behavior to compensate for the limitations of the media devices used.

In designing equipment for educational purposes, two ideas are important. First, equipment doesn't necessarily have to be sophisticated. That is, equipment does not need to be designed around the limitations of human behavior as the equipment engineers might see them. Many equipment features, such as embellishment of student response modes, are bad because they attempt to replace simple behavioral tasks that could be more easily handled with a behavioral engineering approach. Second, many of the design engineers apparently assume that the conventional classroom is an ideal medium since most educational devices could be described as simulations of a teacher, a blackboard, and a writing tablet. This is not necessarily bad since the information receptors that students possess are standard equipment and do not change when the student is moved from the classroom to media devices. However, such devices usually and unnecessarily carry over the same bias for or against certain presentation forms that exist in the classroom. Two examples of this carry-over are the classroom preference for constructed rather than selective responses and sequential display of content rather than simultaneous media usage.

It is not unusual to find that individuals, even psychologists specializing in automated learning and learning aids, overemphasize the mechanical aspects of their system and ignore all but the most obvious behavioral considerations as a result. Their actions have been not so much to design an integrated instructional system as to simulate the desirable features of an individual tutor.

The Engineering of Presentation

It is convenient and essential to the theory of presentation design that a classification system be as independent of media device, content, and external constraints as possible. The classification scheme presented here does not necessarily meet the above criteria, but it is sufficiently structured so that experimental verification of the theory of presentation design can begin now.

From a list of almost 100 variables in the area of structuring and producing educational materials, six attributes relating to structuring presentation form from given behavioral objectives were derived. These attributes, called the dimensions of presentation, are summarized as follows and diagramed in Figure 3.

Stimulus Factors
1. *Encoding forms.* Data must be encoded in some stimulus form. Although this dimension is nominal, the categories can be arranged in a hierarchy according to an increasing level of abstraction.
2. *Duration.* Presentation varies on this ordinal dimension from transient to persistent depending upon the duration of the stimulus. Movies usually are conveyors of more transient presentation, and texts display relatively persistent ones. In a classroom, presentation by lecture is more transient than one delivered via the blackboard.

Response Factor
3. *Response demand characteristics of the presentation.* This is another nominal dimension which includes covert, selective, constructed, verbal, motor, and affective responses.
4. *Response demand frequency.* This is an ordinal dimension concerned with the frequency with which some response is demanded from the student.

Instructional Management
5. *Presentational management frequency.* This dimension is ordinal and is ordered according to the relative frequency of the decision to modify the presentation. The activity of management in deciding to modify the presentation is made on the basis of

some assessment of the student or his environment.

6. *Management purpose.* One may manage objective-oriented activities by providing learning tasks, remedial exercises or enrichment activities, or one may manage motivation by providing high probability contingency activities.

Encoding Dimensions

Stimulus encoding is probably the most obvious of the presentational dimensions.

Man has invented encoding forms for many reasons. These forms enable him to convey data about the real world without the necessity of having objects available, to condense data and eliminate noise, to allow more rapid delivery of data, and to reduce the cost of data transmission.

Although there are many ways in which data have been encoded, the more important forms can be categorized as:

1. *Environmental structure.* This category requires real objects either alone or in cer-

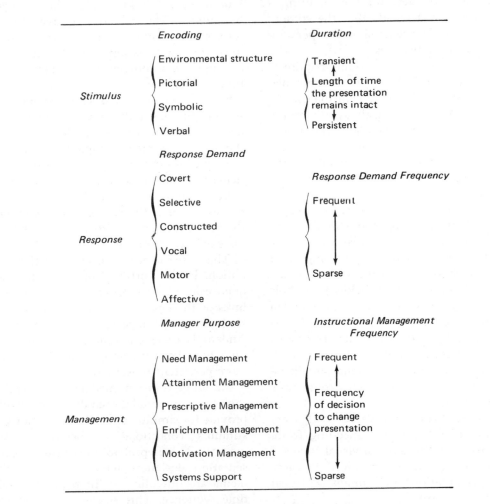

Figure 3 The Dimensions of Presentation

tain combinations. In an operational system the student may be examining a flower or counting a row of blocks. The flower and the row of blocks constitute media for the environmental structure which was selected. The media employed for the environmental structure may allow the student to utilize other senses or combinations of senses. He can see it, feel it, smell it, taste it, or hear it. There are, however, no data which indicate that a multiplicity of sensory events is necessarily superior to one sensation alone. The decision for requiring a medium which demands that the student use more than one sense should depend on the behavioral objectives.

2. *Pictorial.* Pictorial encoding requires a reproduction of either real or imagined visual aspects of objects. The media used to convey pictorial encoding always distort the various visual dimensions, e.g., resolution, color fidelity, size, etc. Some media used for pictorial presentation, such as paintings and illustrations, eliminate or exaggerate various parts of an object.

3. *Symbolic.* Man has created many stimuli which stand for other stimuli which may be more complex, less abstract, or more difficult to manipulate. (A very important class of such symbols is the verbals which are considered separately below.) Symbols range from graphics to schematics and from numerals to equations. Most symbolic encoding is in the visual dimension; but some, such as that delivered by fire sirens, is aural. But again, the sensory demand should be related to the external systems constraints and objectives.

4. *Verbal.* Words and verbal syntax are the stimuli of the verbal encoding form. These may be either aural or visual. Some of the media most often employed to carry verbal presentations are humans (lectures) and books (prose).

Duration Dimension

Duration is an ordinal dimension that varies according to the length of time a given presentation remains unchanged. Presentations vary from transient to persistent. Persistent implies that the presentation can last unchanged for an indefinite period. Certain media convey transient presentations better than others. For example, the presentation conveyed by motion pictures is usually transient although persistent presentations (such as a six-hour movie of the Empire State Building) can also be conveyed by movies. The primary disadvantage of transient presentations is that the student must store information, since it is not available in the environment for a long period of time. Transient presentations present difficulties when a response is demanded to several stimuli simultaneously. The requirement of storing information places limits on the ability of media employing transient presentation to generate new learning particularly if the tasks involve both discriminations and new information to be processed, or if the student must combine the new information with associations from his existing repertoire.

There are further implications in this limitation. In the portrayal of a dynamic sequence in which the individual behavioral links of the chain are unfamiliar or at low strength, the storage level required of the student is too great unless the individual links have been previously established in a more persistent presentation.

Although transient media have potential, their presentational design does not usually provide for simultaneous discriminations of stimulus conditions in behavioral sequences. This is probably because the presentation designers who work with the media are unwilling to interrupt the real-time sequence. This suggests that educational film and ITV makers should follow neither the techniques of the lecturers nor the techniques of the entertainment producers, but develop a new form based on a knowledge of learning conditions. Discrimination learning in a more persistent medium prior to exposure to the dynamic medium would shape observing behaviors necessary to elicit the covert response to the transient medium associated with the correct stimulus elements of those presentations.

Although a more transient presentation may be a higher level simulation, it may be preferable to specify a more persistent presentation. Often when a situation is duplicated, the sequence is too rapid or too complex to allow the student to discriminate the subtasks and their controlling stimuli. By going to a more persistent presentation, the action can be stopped, and the operation can be simplified to isolate those particular stimuli to which the student should attend. This storage-demand disadvantage is offset somewhat where the information is already at some strength, i.e., where the presentation is already familiar. As is discussed in the encoding dimension section, the meaningfulness of the presentation can be enhanced via mediated transfer by relating the new information to familiar analogies. The storage limitation indicates why there are no films teaching calculus.

However, it may be practical to use a film presentation to teach an understanding of calculus by relating principles of calculus to analogous situations that are highly familiar. The two main considerations in selecting more transient presentations are the possible closer simulation of the criterion situation and the increased speed at which information may be presented.

A disadvantage of persistent media is its inability to indicate real-time contiguous associations between individual member links of a behavioral sequence chain.

In some cases, this has been overcome by employing syntactical cues to indicate time or motion. Illustrations, such as showing arrows or providing a fixed sequential pattern as in comic books, have the potential of providing a contiguous association between behavioral links. Even in these cases, however, there are no real time constraints imposed on the system, and in many cases the response speed is the desired conditioned component.

Another way to overcome disadvantages of persistent media is to combine persistent and transient presentations. The lecture and blackboard are the most common examples. In teaching a behavioral chain such as welding, it is best to strengthen the individual behavioral links with a persistent presentation as in a PI workbook followed by a transient one displayed by a slide-tape device. A second disadvantage of most persistent media, their lack of any response-time demand, can be offset by presentational management techniques such as contingency management.

Response Demand Dimension

For use in the theory of presentation design, student responses have been classified into the following categories:

1. *Covert.* Those behaviors that are normally not directly observed. Examples are attending (listening, reading, observing), meditation, imagining, thinking through, etc.

2. *Selective.* The selection between alternatives as in multiple-choice or the pairing of alternatives as in matching.

3. *Constructed.* Writing, drawing, or typing.

4. *Vocal.* Saying something. Vocal is also a constructed response, but it is of sufficient

importance to justify a separate listing.

5. *Motor.* All nonvocal activities which employ the striated muscles but are not included under constructed.

6. *Affective.* Emotional respondings primarily defined in terms of the smooth muscles but often inferred from certain subcategories of the vocal, selective, and motor forms. Thus, it is often said that the student is making a positive affective response toward an activity if he says he likes it, if he selects it or rates it over several other alternatives, or if he engages in it enthusiastically.

Some of the more important factors in structuring and using the response demand dimension are summarized as follows:

Response Integration

Responses already well learned require less effort to be hooked up with stimuli than those which are less well integrated. Well learned responses also allow for greater response form equivalence. Thus, with familiar responses, it may make little difference if the student writes it, types it, chooses it from among others, or thinks it to himself.

Response-Produced Stimuli

The act of responding always makes modifications in the environment. Chaining, where the response-produced stimuli control the emission of further responses, is one outcome of this. Other response-produced stimuli have feedback properties, i.e., they act to modify the form of the response on its emission. External confirmation is one such class of response-produced stimuli.

Discrimination

Feedback discrimination tasks have recently been used in place of response practice. Evans (1961) hypothesized that discrimination practice could shape the student's ability to guide his own behaviors into the desired response pattern. He gave preschool children practice in discriminating well formed numbers from those badly formed. It was found that these children were able to write the numbers much sooner than those who had been given either response guidance or response practice. Similar techniques have been employed to teach machine operation. By using discrimination training to show proper equipment setup, the students first learn the proper appearance of the outcome and thus are able to monitor their own behavior in acquiring the skill.

Response Demand Frequency

At this time little can be said about this dimension since in most studies the frequency of response demand is confounded with the frequency of confirmation or frequency of reinforcement (both are management considerations). However, some data in PI research where confirmation has been removed indicates that just calling for the response is equivalent to calling and confirming. There also may be an interaction effect between demand frequency and demand type since some data show that in PI with a high response demand frequency it makes no difference what type of response is called for.

Management of Presentation Dimension

In designing an educational system, one of the most important tasks is the presentational dimension of management. Management refers to the decision to alter the presentation as a function of an assessment of the student or of the environment. Management involves three activities, all of which take place in every instructional system:

1. Appraisal of data,
2. Selection of an assignment as a result of a decision based on the data,
3. Specification of the various actions that may be assigned.

Some of the reasons for presentational management are considered below.

Management for Need

This type of management usually involves bypassing activities which would only strengthen already acquired behaviors. Some of the simplest forms of this management can be seen in the skip ahead options on material the student may already know. On the more complex level, achievement test data can be used to indicate proper placement in an instructional sequence. A summary typical of need management activities in an operational instruction system follows:

Appraisal	Selection Decision	Action
Examination of student repertoire	Comparison of student achievement scores with prescriptive flowchart	Student shifts to those instructional tasks appropriate for him
Medium—diagnostic, pretests	Medium—teacher or teacher aid	Medium—Workbooks and exercise sheets

Management for Attainment

It frequently happens that the student responds to the presentation in a manner which does not allow him to reach the objective. There are four strategic subclasses of management activity appropriate for such situations.

1. *Redundancy.* If the student fails to reach the objective, repeat the same or continue through as many similar presentations until he does.

2. *Multiform.* If the student fails to reach the objective with one presentation form, select a parallel but different form.

3. *Multilevel.* If the student fails to reach the objectives with the presentation form, select a lower level (more expanded) form.

4. *Error-Diagnostic.* If an error is made at any point within the presentation, an action designed to correct that specific error is selected. It is necessary when using this error-diagnostic strategy to classify errors as (a) *input errors*—due to poor presentational design; (b) *processing errors*—due to the student's lack of the assumed appropriate repertoire on which the learning material was built, or the student's use of an inappropriate approach to the solution; or (c) *output errors*—due to carelessness, poor attention, or chance error (failed to attend to a significant stimulus).

Following is a summary typical of attainment management activities:

Appraisal	Selection Decision	Action
Examination of student error	Comparison of present level of achievement to final behavior objective	Student goes through alternate form of instructional task
Medium—curriculum imbedded tests	Medium—teacher or teacher aid	Medium—text or workbook

Management for Enrichment

This refers to the selection of presentations designed to produce behaviors which although related to the specific behavioral objectives are not required for their attainment. Some reasons for enrichment management are that it provides time fillers, helps motivate the student, and provides for greater generalization of behaviors. This type of management will undoubtedly become more important as systems become more refined.

Management for Motivation

To keep the student in the learning environment, or to keep him responding at a satisfactory rate, his learning activity should lead to some positive consequence. Laboratory studies of reinforcement typically use the positive consequence of eating or drinking to motivate animal behavior. Equivalent kinds of reinforcement can be used with children. However, it is awkward to use this kind of payoff for learning activities in the classroom. Students cannot be starved, nor can candy be placed in their mouths for correct responses. This creates the impossible position that standard laboratory rewarding consequences are necessary but impractical. There are, however, many other kinds of preferred activities which can be employed in the classroom. The formal administrative technique employed to provide positive consequences for learning activities has been termed "contingency management" (Homme & Tosti, 1965).

Motivational management uses the same approach as other management forms. That is, a decision for the student to engage in some activities is made on the basis of some data. In motivational management, those data are usually the student's score on some progress check test, and the selection possibilities include activities the student may prefer, e.g., playing games, talking with friends, working on algebra, viewing an entertaining movie, reading a novel, or engaging in a guided group discussion with peers and the teacher.

Designing the Operational Instructional System

Once the presentation has been designed, it is necessary to design the operational instructional system to carry it. This involves selection and sequencing of the media. It is essential to use a medium that can carry the specified presentation with as little distortion as possible. Of course, every medium will limit the presentation in some effect or fine detail, and when the presentation is stuffed into the "can" of a particular medium, it is often necessary to sacrifice some of the effectiveness.

Using the dimensions of presentation, media can be classified with some psychological sense. Figures 4 and 5 show the classification of some instructional media in two-dimensional matrices. It may be noted that many media appear in several places since several encoding forms can be carried by those media. For example, flash cards can have words or equations on them, texts may display pictorial and verbal presentations, and sound motion pictures usually convey both pictorial and verbal presentations simultaneously.

Also, with enough prior instruction and follow-up, one can demand almost any response to any medium. Figure 5 indicates those responses most frequently demanded in practice.

For a complete analysis of the media selection possibilities of the six presentation design dimensions, a six-dimensional matrix would have to be imagined or constructed, or another tabular technique would have to be developed for selecting media from a prior choice of intersections along the presentation design axis.

Depending on the particular intersection choices on each dimension, there may be none, one, or several media choices listed at the common intersection point of all dimensions. Where not enough media choices are available, one or more of the dimensional intersections must be expanded to include more of the axis, or media-mix possibilities must be investigated.

Presentation Design Example

Consider the following objective statement. Given a coin minted in England during the period 1200 AD—1400 AD, the student will be able to name and characterize the purpose or origin of each mark on the coin.

Since the marks on the coin must be seen

Encoding Dimension	Transient		Persistent
Environmental	Demonstration	Laboratory / Field-Trip	Object
Pictorial	Film / Video	Slide / Pi-Workbook	Photograph / Illustrated-Text / Painting
Symbolic	Animation	Flash-Card	Diagram / Blackboard
Verbal	Conversation / Lecture	Flash-Card / Pi-Workbook	Text / Manual
	Group Discussion		
	Tutor		

Duration Dimension

Figure 4 Media Classified by Encoding versus Duration

Encoding Dimension	Covert	Selective	Vocal	Constructed	Motor
Environmental	Demonstration / Field-Trip	Item-Sort			
Pictorial	Film / Video / Slide / Painting / Photograph	Multiple-Choice-Teaching Machine		Illustrated-Pi-Text	Laboratory
Symbolic	Blackboard / Diagram	Card-Sort	Flash-Card		Diagram
Verbal	Lecture / Audiotape	Pi-Workbook	Conversation / Roel-Playing / Audiotape		
	Text	Tutor	Tutor	Tutor	Tutor

Response Demand Dimension

Figure 5 Media Classified by Encoding versus Response Demand

to be identified, some sort of pictorial encoding must be used. The objective does not specify the response form but again, a reasonable choice would be vocal. The duration would be toward the transient end of the duration scale since the amount of detail on the coin is small. A proper choice for the management type and frequency of this objective would be to give feedback or error diagnosis after each response. A tabulation of these choices would appear as follows:

	Presentation Form	Film	Book	Audiotape
Encoding	Pictorial			No
Response Demand	Vocal			X
Duration	Momentary		No	X
Management	Feedback after each response	No	1/2	1/2

The choices in the center of the table constitute the presentation form. One technique for continuing from these intersections on the dimensional axis to find media common to all requirements is to extend the above table by listing several plausible media choices to the right, as shown. Then the spaces can be filled in with checks or scaled numbers representing the applicability of the medium choice to the dimensional intersection.

None of the medium choices listed meet all of the requirements. Often there is no one best medium or media-mix for a given objective. Several alternative operational systems may convey equivalent presentational designs within the constraints specified. The final selection between these operational systems should then be based on external considerations such as: (1) *cost,* including developmental costs, purchase costs of media devices, initial setup costs, and the cost of maintaining the system; (2) *availability* of various media, e.g., tutors, AV devices; and (3) *market or user preference.*

Perhaps the model can be extended to include additional dimensions but only after more is known about the existing six dimensions. Conceivably, sets of curves or even linear programing techniques could be developed to optimize the instructional design for various operational constraints.

Let us consider a second exercise in media selection where a media mix can be evaluated. Suppose it is determined from a behavioral analysis that the best presentation form to meet the objectives is as follows: the stimuli are to be presented in a verbal and illustrated form; a demand of a written or selection response is to be made; the presentation must last as long as the student desires it; and the student must make some response before proceeding to the next item.

Figure 6 shows the limitation of the medium of motion pictures against these requirements. The presentation is by necessity distorted. A better fit in some areas can occur if a human tutor is used (Figure 7), but still there is much distortion. If a mixed-media system is used (Figure 8), the presentation remains intact.

There are considerations in the selection of media other than presentation form. Such factors as the cost of making a movie or the instructional reliability of a tutor have to be considered. But this new model of presentation design allows us to examine on a systematic basis most of the important

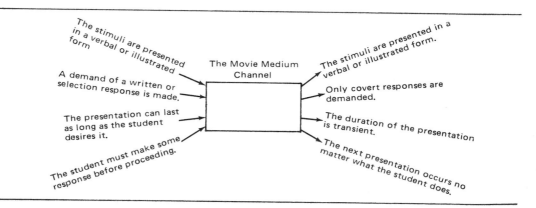

Figure 6 Distortion of the Presentation by the Single Medium of Motion Pictures

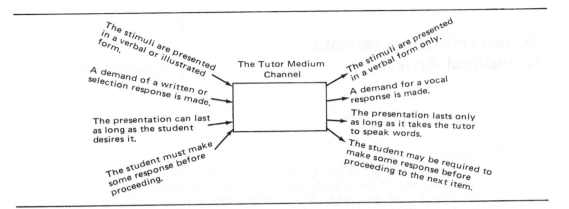

Figure 7 The Presentation by the Single Medium of Tutor

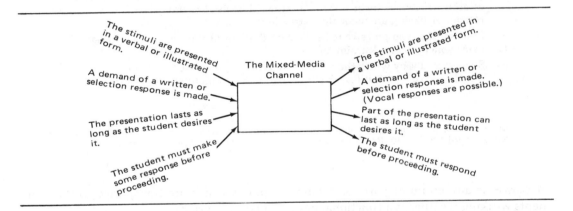

Figure 8 The PI Presentation by the Mixed-Media Instructional System of Tutor + Blackboard + Writing Tablet

trade-offs which are possible.

As can be seen, the process of presentation design is not foolproof. Much more work on the subject must be done. However, the promise of defining a form of presentation—independent of media, content, and learner—and the technology for its use is very exciting. Such research work must be continued.

REFERENCES

Evans, J. L. "Multiple-Choice Discrimination Programing." Paper presented at the American Psychological Association Annual Convention, New York, 1961.

Homme, L. E., & Tosti, D. T. "Contingency Management and Motivation," *NSPI Journal,* 1965, *4,* 14–16.

Warren, D. "A Beginning Reading Program with Audiovisual Reinforcement: An Experimental Study." *Journal of Educational Research,* 1968, *61,* 5.

Components of a Cybernetic Instructional System

M. David Merrill

EDITORS' QUESTIONS:

1. Define "cybernetic."
2. Discuss the components of a cybernetic instructional system. Describe the functions of each component and show how each interacts with others to promote learning efficiency. Provide your own visual representation of the process.
3. React to this idea: "Instructional theory must be prescriptive rather than merely descriptive." Do you agree or disagree? Justify your position.
4. The author suggests two research strategies which would facilitate the development of an instructional theory. What are they? Discuss the importance to a classroom teacher of having an adequate instructional theory.
5. Discuss what you perceive to be the contributions of the cybernetic approach to the management of the learning process.
6. Suggest means by which the classroom teacher can increase her awareness of instructional feedback and utilize this information to promote effective learning.

M. David Merrill, "Components of a Cybernetic Instructional System," *Educational Technology*, VIII, No. 7, (April 1968), 5–10. Reprinted with the permission of *Educational Technology*.

A *System* is any group of parts or components working together as a functional unit. All systems include at least three basic elements. The *input* unit provides some process by which material or information is entered into the system. The *processor* acts on the material or information to modify it in some way. The *output* unit consists of some procedure for discharging the results of the process from the system. One useful way to describe the process of learning is to consider the learner as a system.

Learner as a System

The learner system can be subdivided into various components. The senses convert physical energy input into nervous impulses which are transported to the central nervous system.

Perception is a process which interprets the nervous energy and sometimes distorts the representation of the physical environment as a result of the learner's previous experiences, feelings and attitudes.

The memory component is a mechanism for storing a representation of the physical input as modified by the perception component. This unit also involves some mechanism for retrieving the information once it is stored.

Dr. Merrill is visiting assistant professor of educational psychology at Stanford University and research associate at Stanford's Center for Research and Development on Teaching. He is on leave from Brigham Young University.

The thinking component is a process which enables the learner to manipulate what has been stored by combining, modifying and restructuring the content of memory to produce predictions concerning future physical events in the environment and to represent imaginary stimulation which does not exist in the environment.

The muscles and skeletal system provide the output unit which enables the learner to express the results of the processing conducted by the other components. This expression of behavior represents the output of the system.

The learner system described to this point has been an open loop system, which means that the output of the system has no effect on future input nor on subsequent output. In a *closed loop system* the output is returned to the system and consequently affects future output of the system. Closed loop systems are often referred to as cybernetic systems.

Cybernetic comes from the Greek word *kybernetes,* meaning pilot or governor and *kybernan,* meaning to steer or govern. Cybernetic systems are systems which have some mechanism for controlling or governing themselves.

The most familiar and frequently used example of a cybernetic system is the home heating system. The output is heat, which raises the room temperature. The room temperature is put back into the system by a thermostat which compares it with some preset standard. When the temperature in the room is less than the preset standard, an electrical current starts the furnace. When the room temperature is equal to the present temperature the furnace shuts off. Output from a system which is returned as input to control future output is called *feedback.*

A more accurate description of a learner system is illustrated in Fig. 1. Three kinds of

sensory input are indicated. The stimulus situation indicates some physical energy from the environment acting on the senses of the learner and to which, through the process of learning, he develops a reaction or response.

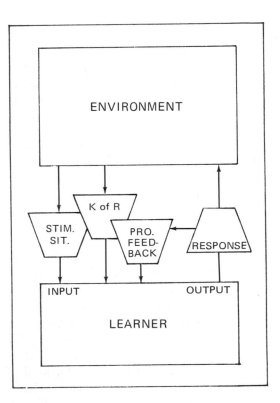

Figure 1 The Learner as a Cybernetic System

When a learner makes a response, two additional kinds of stimuli are produced. First, the learner feels, sees, hears or in some other way senses the fact that he has made a response. Stimulus input resulting from making some response is called *proprioceptive feedback.*

Second, the response made by the learner usually produces some change in the environment. The stimulus input which indicates to the learner the nature of the change produced in the environment is called *knowledge of results.*

Both of the sensory inputs which result from making a response provide feedback to the learner. This feedback is used by the learner to modify his subsequent responses. The process of response modification as a result of proprioceptive feedback and knowledge of results is called *learning.*

Learning theories are attempts by scientists, who are studying the learning process, to identify the component parts of the learner system and to explain how each of these components operate to produce a modification of responses. While scientists do not always describe their theories in system notation, it is usually possible to make such a translation.

An Instructional System

The discussion to this point has been concerned with the learner system. The description of the environment in relation to the learner system has been ambiguous.

It was established earlier that learning occurs whenever the learner interacts with the environment. *Instruction,* however, involves only interactions with a particular kind of environment and only when there is a deliberate attempt to produce a particular kind of behavior. Instruction represents a subset of all learning situations. An instructional situation requires a particular kind of environment which might be conceptualized as an instructional system.

An instructional system may be any of a number of kinds of environments including classrooms with live teachers, audiovisual presentations, books, machines or any combination of these elements. Like all previously discussed systems, an instructional system also has three major elements.

Outputs of an open instructional system consist primarily of a structured display to the student.

A cybernetic instructional system would also include K of R to the learner and some record of student responses. Inputs to an open instructional system include library material (subject matter content), an indication of learner characteristics and objectives.

A cybernetic instructional system would also include student responses as feedback input. The processor controls the presentation and in a cybernetic system modifies the presentation of the display and/or K of R on the basis of student response correspondence to the objectives.

Fig. 2 illustrates a cybernetic instructional system. The first essential input is the content or material to be presented or displayed to the student. It is convenient to refer to all such material as *library input* and realize that this input may include written material, audiovisual materials of all kinds, programmed instruction frames, diagrams, models, actual events or things, and even information stored in the head of the teacher if the teacher is part of the system.

Perhaps the most important input to an instructional system is the objectives (performance standards) which the system is designed to accomplish.

A third input for a cybernetic instructional system is information concerning the individual characteristics of the students who will interact in the system. This information is essential if the rules for operation of the various components are to be adequate for teaching individuals. This input will be referred to as *learner traits.*

Because this is a cybernetic system, the fourth type of input consists of the feedback from the learner in the form of learner response. Without this feedback input, an instructional system is not able to adjust the

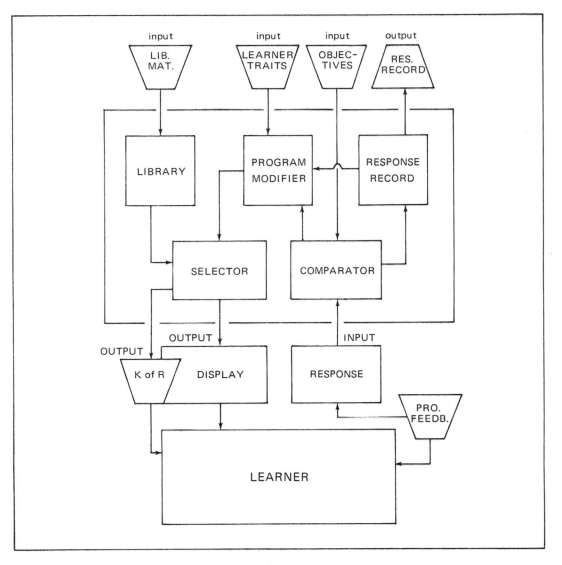

Figure 2 Components of Cybernetic Instructional System

presentation to produce the changes in behavior specified by the objectives input.

It should be recognized that in much instruction in schools and elsewhere the input from student response is ignored.

The first essential output from an instructional system is the display to the learner. A *display* can take many forms and does not necessarily infer written material. A given display may be aural, such as a lecture or explanation; visual, such as a picture, movie, model; written, such as a book, frame of programmed instruction, words on the blackboard; tactual, such as an object for the learner to feel; olfactory, such as an odor for the learner to smell; in short, a display is any stimulus situation structured and presented to the learner for the purpose of establishing some response or potential for response.

In a cybernetic system a second output presented to the learner is some form of *knowledge of results.* This may be simple information such as right or wrong or may include lengthy demonstrations or explanations of the probable cause of error. The knowledge of results may be immediate or delayed for several hours, days, or longer.

If student response is input to the system, a third type of output which may or may not be used in a particular instructional situation is some *record* of each student's responses. This record may be lengthy and detailed, such as the amount of time required and response chosen on every frame of a machine program or it may be abbreviated, such as the mid-term and final grades in a course.

In an open loop instructional system, the processor is some selection mechanism which presents displays in a linear fashion, one following the other. Movie or filmstrip presentations are good examples of such an open loop system. Books and other types of presentations may be more or less cybernetic depending on how they are written or on how the learner uses them.

A cybernetic system such as the one illustrated in Fig. 2 is much more flexible. In operation the system must first make some display to the student, who then reacts to the display by making some response. The *comparator* component compares the response with the objective entered into the system.

A record of the comparison and/or the response is recorded in the response record.

The results of the comparison are fed to the *selector,* which determines the type of K of R to be presented and to the *modifier,* which makes a decision concerning the adequacy of the presentation and determines if the selection sequence will be altered.

If the student did not make the expected response, the Modifier changes the sequence and indicates that a new sequence is to be followed or that some review sequence is to be introduced to the learner.

If the student made the expected response, control will be returned to the selector, which selects the next display in the sequence from the library and presents it to the student.

Instructional Theory

A theory of instruction consists of the identification of the component parts of the instructional system and a description of the principles which are used by the components to select, modify, and present the display and knowledge of results so as to produce particular kinds of responses in the learner.

To be useful, instructional theory must be prescriptive rather than merely descriptive.

Principles specified by such a theory should include rules specifying the display and knowledge of results requirements for producing particular responses (presentation rules); rules specifying the requirements for measuring particular responses and for comparing responses with objectives (evaluation rules); rules for altering the presentation to adapt to the particular requirements of individual students (individualization rules), and rules indicating modification required when feedback from the student indicates that a particular presentation failed to produce the desired behavior (modification rules).

Since instruction aims at behavior change in some specified direction, the first requirement for establishing an operating instructional system is the identification of the desired outcomes or objectives.

If every objective represents a unique behavior, then the establishment of presentation and evaluation rules becomes a difficult if not impossible task. On the other hand, if objectives can be classified into a finite number of types and an appropriate set of presentation and evaluation rules identified for each type, the task is greatly simplified.

An instructional theory, therefore, requires a classification system for objectives such that for each category in the classification a unique set of presentation and evaluation rules can be identified.

It is anticipated that each presentation and evaluation rule thus identified will require a number of parameters for its specification.

It is further postulated that the function of individualization rules will be to specify the values of the parameters required for individuals with similar relevant characteristics.

If all such rules were known, it would be possible to specify the techniques required to establish any behavior in any individual. Because it is unlikely that all the parameters required by such a theory will be identified in the foreseeable future, it is necessary to specify modification rules so that the system can learn how to teach a particular behavior to a given individual.

This implies that not only must the system modify the instruction for given individuals who fail to attain the objectives but also that it remembers such modifications and implements these same changes when other individuals with similar characteristics are encountered. This leads to a discussion of research strategy with a cybernetic instructional system.

Research on Instruction

Perhaps two research strategies can be identified which facilitate the development of an instructional theory. The first approach emphasizes *modification* rules. A program is developed to produce in the learner a specified response or series of responses. As learning proceeds, a record of student responses is accumulated. At given intervals or after a certain number of responses, the record is compared with the performance standards.

If the learner's record does not compare adequately with the performance standards, the presentation rules are modified. After another segment of the presentation, another comparison is made. Modification continues until an adequate procedure is discovered for the particular learner.

If a careful aptitude profile is collected for each student and the individual response records of many students are collected and the strategy changes are carefully identified, then students for whom a given presentation proved effective can be grouped together and their aptitude profiles examined for common elements.

This procedure should yield individualization rules which can subsequently be verified by administering the appropriate strategy to other students who have a similar aptitude profile.

The procedure is generalizable only to the extent that the number of classes of students is small in number and the aptitudes used as a basis for classification are appropriate to other presentations designed to develop similar behaviors in other subject areas.

The value of the strategy changes used is related also to the generalizability of the strategy to other tasks having similar characteristics but teaching different content.

A second research approach might be characterized as a model building or theoretical approach. (It should be noted that the previous approach is not really a sans theory approach, since the number of strategy changes possible and/or the number of aptitude records collected can not be infinite and whatever basis is used for their selection must to some extent reflect theoretical notions.)

In this latter approach a careful analysis is made of the various components of the instructional system, and classification schemes are hypothesized. A given behavioral objective is identified as a member of a particular class of responses. Presentation rules and evaluation rules are hypothesized for each such response class. Individualization rules are postulated and empirically investigated to determine values and qualities for the parameters of the presentation rules.

The emphasis in this approach is on presentation rules rather than modification rules.

This second research technique can proceed at various levels. First, the adequacy of response classification can be checked by comparison of presentation rules. If the presentation rules for one kind of response class are not different from those of another class, there is no value in postulating different response classes.

Second, alternative sets of presentation and evaluation rules can be proposed for a particular behavioral outcome and their relative effectiveness in establishing the desired behavior compared.

Third, various values can be assigned to the parameters of the presentation and evaluation rules and the relative effectiveness compared for different categories of individuals classified on various aptitude measures.

While research on learning is primarily concerned with the identification and description of various components of the learner, research on instruction is primarily concerned with the identification and description of the various components of the instructional system. These two research concerns are closely related but do not represent mirror images.

Learning research often has instructional implications, but understanding the learner system may not be sufficient for prescribing instructional strategies.

Furthermore, a completely adequate description of the learner system is not yet available. But in spite of its absence it is still possible to develop and experimentally validate prescriptive descriptions of an instructional system.

A Set of Procedures for the Planning of Instruction

John W. Childs

EDITORS' QUESTIONS:

1. Write a lesson plan for teaching a learning skill in a particular subject matter area. Teach the skill to a group of not more than three pupils and evaluate results. With a matched group of pupils follow the procedure outlined by Childs in Figure 1 through every step from planning to evaluation. Enlist the aid of other students for those steps requiring group participation. Which technique is more efficient in promoting learning? Why?

2. Explain how the built-in loops of Childs' procedure refine the quality of planning decisions.

3. Is the planning procedure described by this article properly regarded as a cybernetic system? What provisions are made for program modification on the basis of feedback?

4. Prepare a flow chart representing a procedure for the diagnosis of learning capabilities. What elements of this process were you made more aware of as a result? Cite specific examples.

18

John W. Childs, "A Set of Procedures for the Planning of Instruction," *Educational Technology*, VIII, No. 16, (August 1968), 7–14. Reprinted with the permission of *Educational Technology*.

The purpose of this paper is to describe a specific set of procedures for the planning of instruction.

A flow chart is provided in *Figures 1 to 9*. This is intended to aid the reader in following the sequential decisions, activities and feedback functions of the proposed set of procedures.

Discussion on Developmental Model

The first activity block in the flow chart is traditional with the education profession. It allows for the inclusion in the developmental process of a number of significant inputs to the design system.

The basic goals and purposes of education, as drawn from the total society, must become a part of the educational enterprise. This initial block suggests that the designer can explicitly recognize the goals of his particular schools, its purposes and aims.

Given a reasonably precise set of statements concerning the general goals and purposes of the school, the designer moves to the specification of the behavioral components of each of the goals.

The task of translating the content and experiences of the school into precise statements of behavior is an arduous and lengthy one. In an effort to develop individuals who can do the job of preparing behavior specifications for something called a course, the author's experience has been that it takes two individuals working together to do a

Dr. Childs is acting director of the Department of Instructional Technology, Wayne State University, Detroit, Michigan.

good job. The lone individual is inclined, by the nature of his thinking processes, to miss some significant aspect of the behavior to be learned or the conditions under which it will be learned as he prepares a behavioral specification. When the work is done by a team, the immediacy of feedback concerning missing elements in the specification produces a better behavioral specification in less time.

The meaning of the term "behavioral specification" as used here should be reviewed at this point. The first component of a good behavioral specification is a statement of a learner's observable performance. Examples of some observable performance statements are given below:

> Given a map with a printed compass rose of the streets and main buildings surrounding a fictitious school building, the student will be able to answer at least six of ten questions based upon the identification of certain main buildings that would be reached if he followed the ten sets of walking directions from the school (like: walk two blocks west and three blocks north from the school) during a twenty minute period with the map and questions.
> At the end of this unit a student will be able to differentiate between the initial sounds of "M" and "B"

There are several ways to construct observable performance statements. These statements are only representative of some behavior areas which may be found within a school.

The second component of the complete behavioral specification called for at this point in the flow chart is a statement of the conditions under which the performance will be observed.

The third component of a behaviorally stated objective is a statement of the level of performance, or criterion for the performance.

Returning now to the flow chart, we need to add a further comment about the preparation of the terminal and intermediate objectives. Earlier, a case was made for the committee route to the specification, due to the need of having design teams of individuals interact in the process of drafting the behavioral specifications. The logistics of developing all of the behavioral specifications necessary for a total curriculum also suggests the need to pull together teams or committees to undertake the task of behavioral specification.

The third box in our flow chart *(Figure 3)* proposes to submit the specifications developed by the school committee of subject specialists to a team of full-time specialist programmers and materials evaluators. The intent here is to relieve the classroom teacher of the mundane and routine task of searching out or developing new materials with which to implement the objectives. This phase might well be deleted from the chart if one were applying the process to his own personal development behavior; however, this is the point at which the instructional (1) psychologist, (2) research analyst, (3) curriculum specialist, and (4) media specialist enter the design process with their particular expertise. In the development of instruction, this is the point at which the programmer and materials evaluator must make initial judgments based on experience, knowledge, and learning research about the feasibility of mediating the learning leading to the specific objectives. Here is where input constraints are considered.

If there are limitations in what is available in terms of mediating machinery or mediating software, this is the point in the design process where the limitations can be considered. As a result of the information gathering activity in this block, a decision

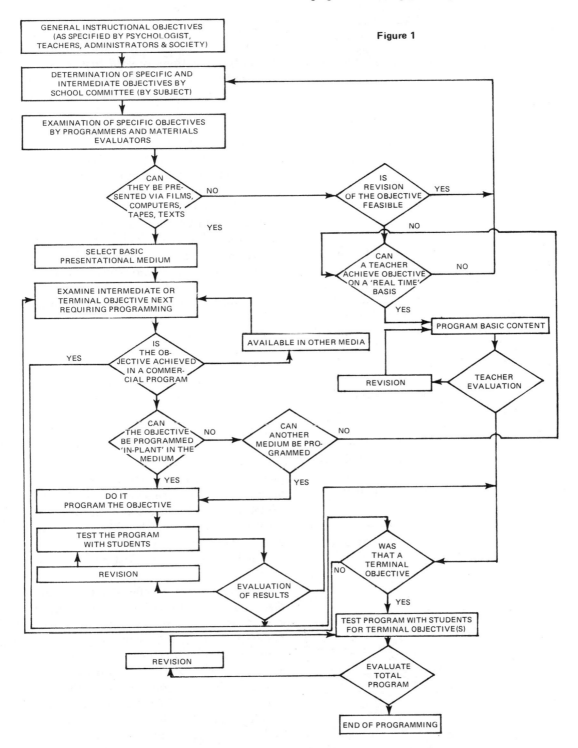

Figure 1

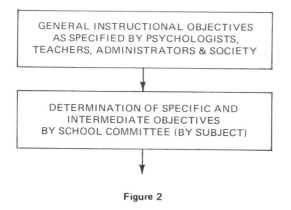

Figure 2

point is reached concerning the direction of future activity.

Figure 3 shows the "go, no-go" decision that must be made concerning the attempt to conduct the instruction in a mediated form. A negative decision at this point will lead to a sequence in the model calling for examination of the objective for possible revision. If a positive decision is reached at this point, then a sequence of development activity follows that selects or produces mediated forms of instruction.

What choices are available if a negative decision chain results from an objective which the design team believes cannot be programmed in a mediated form? It has al-

ready been suggested that the first alternative in this situation is the possible revision of the objective; therefore, the first block on the negative chain is one of further decision making on the nature of the objective itself *(Figure 4)*.

Two alternatives are available in the flow chart: first, the positive decision for revision and second, the negative decision, which leads to additional decision activity *(Figure 4)*. If the design team believes that revision is possible, the proposed revision is fed back to the objective preparation team and a substitute objective is drafted and begins its way through the design process. If the design team believes that no revision is possible, or ascertains from the objective preparation group that no revision is possible, then the next block in the flow chart raises the question of real-time teacher instruction.

Why, in *this* model, was it decided to put the decision for teacher handling of the objective in real-time after the question of other forms of mediation?

If the decision block for teacher handling of the objectives is placed before the mediation question, teacher handling will frequently occur when some other form might do equally well. It is believed that in the end the teacher *can* do just about any instructional task. But should he? Thus, it seems wise to raise the question of mediated individualized instruction first in the flow chart.

Returning to the teacher decision chain *(Figure 4)*, two alternative decisions again occur. One, the teacher *can* do it on a real-time basis; or two, the teacher *cannot* do it. In the event that the negative decision is made, the model shows a feedback to the objectives determination block. If the first decision is made for teacher handling, then a move is made to a design sequence which produces or secures the content resources

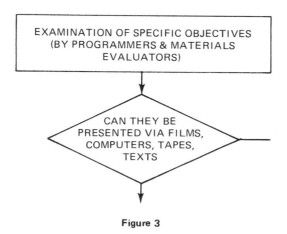

Figure 3

the teacher will need to handle the objective.

A return to the main sequence of the developmental flow chart *(Figure 5)*, picks up at the mediation decision block. A positive decision at this point results in a task activity labeled "select the basic presentational medium." This particular block implies the full means for the completion of this task.

At this date, the media field knows far too little about the decision structure to use in carrying out this task. Some fairly good specifications of the media characteristics exist, but there is no evidence to tie these characteristics to the learning suggested by the specific objectives. Decisions can be made here by considering such things as logistical requirements, ease of preparation of material, visual or audio nature of the learning experience or the availability of the medium. What is needed is a classification structure that will allow the designer to *match the medium to the behavioral objective.*

Two efforts at this type of matching have been widely distributed. Robert Gagné, in Chapter XI of his book, *The Conditions of Learning,* (Holt, 1965) supplies a chart relating his eight learning types (into which behavioral objectives may be fitted) to the specific medium of communication that may be appropriate for that type of learning.

Leslie J. Briggs wrote of another procedure for achieving this end in the March, 1967, issue of "Audiovisual Instruction" under the title "A Procedure for the Design of Multimedia Instruction." He drew upon the work of Gagné for his learning-type classification, but chose to approach the media selection process on an overall basis for a series of objectives rather than an objective by objective base. Both Gagné and Briggs indicate a need for considerable additional research on the media-matching variables.

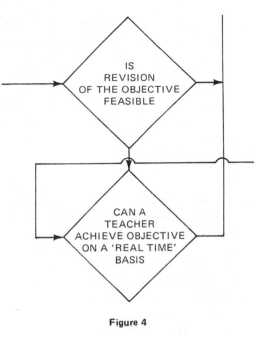

Figure 4

Once the basic presentational medium is selected, further efforts must be conducted to develop the medium in line with the objectives of the mediated sequence *(Figure 5).*

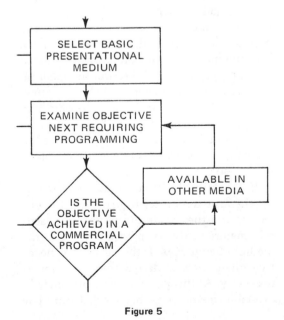

Figure 5

The next activity block on the flow chart indicates this need by suggesting that each objective be taken on for examination of its implications for the design of the instructional material within the selected medium. It results in a decision block in which the designer must answer the question of programming the objective with the design team or selecting the program from a commercially available source.

This decision block is essential to the function of the media specialist. Neither the time nor the funds are available to buy time to create the wheel all over again. If an objective is embodied in the material prepared by an outside agency, then we must make use of the material in order to have the energy and time to create the many resources that do *not* exist.

This decision block has three alternatives: First, a positive response that indicates the objective exists in a mediated form, in which case there is a skip ahead to the trial testing of the mediated form; second, the possibility exists that the objective is met in commercially available form but in a medium other than that selected in the previous sequence. In this case, the feedback is to the medium selection activity to check the appropriateness of altering the medium selection. The third alternative here is a new decision block to determine if the objective can be met through the preparation of a mediated unit in the medium selected within the confines of the design team's development resources.

If a positive decision is made here *(Figure 6)*, then the design team turns over the objective and the specifications for the learning material to the programmer for the medium being used. If the decision is negative, then another design team decision is necessary. At this point, other commercially available media have been ruled out. The remaining decision must be to program in another medium or to feed the objective back for revision or reconsideration of teacher handling.

If the decision is to go back to teacher handling *(Figure 4)*, then we enter again our secondary decision chain. Given that the decision is made to have a teacher handle the objective *(Figure 7)*, the basic program content for the teacher must be prepared along with any additional supplementary materials. An addition to this decision chain (that does not occur in regular teaching patterns as we now know them) is the planned teacher tryout and revision cycle for the development of teacher handled objectives.

Returning to the main decision chain and the other alternate decision on programming in another medium *(Figure 6)*, the DO IT activity block appears once again.

Perhaps next to the stress placed on objectives in this model of instructional development is the stress placed on the pretesting of materials for their ability to produce the changes in student behavior called for by the objectives. Thus, the activity block following the act of preparing the mediated material in the selected medium is the testing of the mediated instruction with students *(Figure 8)*.

If this phase of instructional development is treated rigorously, and sufficient tests are conducted to "debug" the instruction, it may be expected that the mediated instruction will be adequately developed for a major trial without damaging results to a large segment of the students for which the instruction is designed. This stage of pilot testing and revision should be an integral part of the design team's activity during the preparation of the material to meet each objective.

Next *(Figure 9)*, the flow chart leads to the activity block of revision. After enough cy-

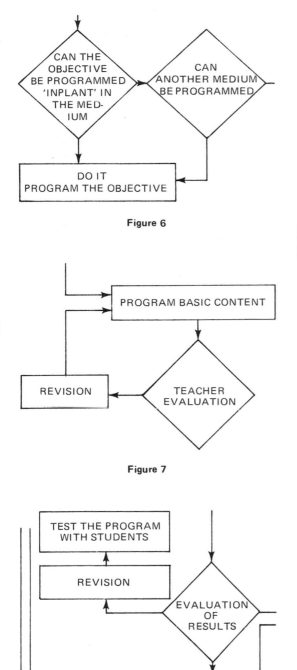

Figure 6

Figure 7

Figure 8

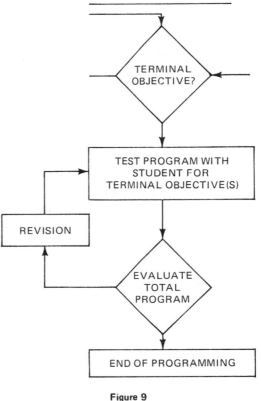

Figure 9

cles of pilot evaluation followed by revision, two alternative decisions can be made concerning further activity; *(Figure 9)* the design team may reach a decision to completely recycle to consider other instructional strategies, such as teacher handling. The intent is that the evaluation of the mediated instruction will be satisfactory and thus the design effort will move into another decision situation.

The second alternative will be taken if the objective the team has programmed is a terminal one; hence, the developed mediated instruction will move to full scale testing with a large group of students. This test may result in some revision *(Figure 9)*. A cycle for this activity is shown on the flow chart. Following total program review, the instructional planning comes to an end.

In the event that the objective(s) under design consideration is not a terminal objective at the pilot test point, the system recycles to pick up and carry through a new objective(s) until a terminal one is reached *(Figure 9)*.

Summary

The complex description of the functions depicted by the flow chart can be summarized in a set of procedural steps. The procedural steps are, in essence, the decision activities that must go on in the process of instructional design.

1. Determine general objectives.
2. Determine the behavioral objectives.
3. Specify the learning types for each objective.
4. Determine the feasibility of mediated instruction or teacher-handled instruction: if neither, revise objectives.
5. Select the basic presentational medium.
6. Examine each objective and develop programming specifications.
7. Choose between in-house programming and selecting from commercial sources of mediated programs which meet the objectives.
8. Program the objective in-house.
9. Test the program with students.
10. Revise the mediated program.
11. Evaluate the mediated program with a large student population.
12. Revise and conclude the instructional development sequence for any given set of behavioral objectives.

Recommended Readings: Managing the Teaching-Learning Process

Baird, Hugh, et. al. *A Behavioral Approach to Teaching.* Dubuque, Iowa: Wm. C. Brown Company Publishers, 1972.

Banghart, Frank W. *Educational Systems Analysis.* New York: The Macmillan Co., 1969.

Berman, Louise *From Thinking to Behaving.* Teachers College, Columbia University, New York: Teachers College Press, 1967.

Chamberlin, Leslie J. *Team Teaching: Organization and Administration.* Columbus, Ohio: Charles E. Merrill Publishing Co., 1969.

Craig, Robert C. *The Psychology of Learning in the Classroom.* New York: The Macmillan Co., 1966.

Flanders, Ned A. *Teacher Influence, Pupil Attitudes, and Achievement: Studies in Interaction Analysis.* U.S. Office of Education Cooperative Research Project, No. 397, Minneapolis: University of Minnesota, 1960.

Flavell, J. H. *The Development of Role-Taking and Communication Skills in Children.* New York: John Wiley & Sons, Inc., 1968.

Haddan, Eugene E. *Evolving Instruction.* New York: The Macmillan Co., 1970.

Hearn, Edell M. and Reddick, Thomas L. *Simulated Behavioral Teaching Situations.* Dubuque, Iowa: Wm. C. Brown Company Publishers, 1971.

Kuethe, James L. *The Teaching-Learning Process.* Glenview, Illinois: Scott, Foresman, 1968.

Lindgren, H. C. *Educational Psychology in the Classroom.* 3rd ed. New York: John Wiley & Sons, Inc., 1967.

Mann, John *Education and the Human Poten-tial.* New York: The Free Press, A Division of The Macmillan Co., 1970.

McDonald, Blanche and Nelson, Leslie W. *Methods that Teach.* 2nd ed. Dubuque, Iowa: Wm. C. Brown Company Publishers, 1965.

Meyen, Edward L. *Unit Teaching.* Dubuque, Iowa: Wm. C. Brown Company Publishers, 1971.

Michaelis, John U. ed. *Teaching Units in the Social Sciences.* Chicago, Illinois: Rand McNally & Co., 1966.

Nelson, Leslie W. and McDonald, Blanche *Guide to Student Teaching,* 3rd ed. Dubuque, Iowa: Wm. C. Brown Company Publishers, 1958.

Olivero, James L. *Micro-Teaching: Medium for Improving Instruction.* Columbus, Ohio: Charles E. Merrill Publishing Co., 1970.

Parker, Ronald K. and Whitney, David C. "A System Approach to Early Education: The Discovery Program," *Educational Technology* XI (1971):22–28.

Silvern, L. C. "Cybernetics and Education, K-12," *Audiovisual Instruction* 13 (1968): 267–275.

Travers, Robert M. W. *Essentials of Learning.* 2nd ed. New York: The Macmillan Co., 1967;

Ulrich, Robert E., Louisell, Stephen E. and Wolfe, Marshall "The Learning Village: A Behavioral Approach to Early Education," *Educational Technology* XI (1971): 32–45.

Williams, Francine K. *Systems Analysis and Design.* Dubuque, Iowa: Wm. C. Brown Company Publishers, 1972.

Promoting Learning Through Questioning Techniques

Section 4 explores the role of questions in promoting thinking and learning, and offers practical guides and suggestions for improving the techniques of classroom questioning.

Hunkins states that questions have always been used by teachers as strategies for promoting learning. However, though teachers purport to encourage thinking among their students, the questions they ask often require only the recall of facts. He, therefore, stresses the need for improving questioning techniques of teachers and offers valuable ideas for implementing the process.

The responses of 190 elementary school teachers to the question, "What are three important purposes of teachers' questions?", were analyzed and categorized by Pate and Bremer. Based upon the responses of the teachers, the authors arrived at the following conclusions: (1) Questions are used by teachers to serve many purposes. (2) Insufficient thought is often given to the purposes of questions asked by teachers.

(3) The practice of asking questions that call for short answers robs pupils of the opportunity to use questions for making generalizations and inferences. An instrument called a Questions Analyzer is presented to aid the teacher who wishes to improve her questioning techniques.

Shrable and Minnis have also developed a system of classifying questions and a technique for analyzing questioning strategies for teachers. One of the purposes of this approach is to provide the teacher with a feedback device for studying her verbal interaction patterns within the classroom. Several suggestions are offered for the use of such a technique in teacher education, research and teaching.

Recognizing the importance of questions in teaching, Gall stresses the need for research that concentrates on the types of questions teachers should ask in the classroom. She points out that questions should be viewed as a means of producing desirable changes in the behavior of students. Research efforts, therefore, should also be directed toward the identification of the desired behaviors and determining whether questions teachers ask are instrumental in effecting behavioral changes. In addition, Gall stresses the need for teacher training programs designed to improve teachers' questioning techniques.

The articles and the recommended readings in this section are presented for the purpose of equipping the student to:

1. Analyze the different objectives that questioning strategies seek to accomplish and formulate questions consistent with each of these purposes.

2. Utilize one or both of the instruments provided for the analysis of teacher questioning behavior in order to improve her own questioning techniques.

3. Devise her own system for analyzing and evaluating questioning practices.

4. Demonstrate, through simulation or micro teaching, an example of a questioning strategy designed to achieve a specified instructional objective.

5. Devise her own system for the analysis of the verbal interactions of teachers and pupils.

6. Conduct in-class experiments designed to discover the relationship between certain questioning strategies and observable changes in pupil behavior.

Using Questions to Foster Pupils Thinking

Francis P. Hunkins

EDITORS' QUESTIONS:

1. Identify some learning objectives that questions can help achieve.
2. Formulate some questions and classify them according to what learning objectives they can best help achieve.
3. How does a teacher know whether her questions are effective or not? Develop some criteria for judging the effectiveness of questions.
4. Devise a procedure for improving your own questioning techniques.

19

Francis P. Hunkins, "Using Questions to Foster Pupils Thinking." Reprinted from the October, 1966, issue of EDUCATION. Copyright, 1966, by The Bobbs-Merrill Company, Inc., Indianapolis, Indiana. Used by permission.

Teachers are urged to utilize classroom methods which will enable pupils to become effective thinkers. New materials are being constructed; workshops are conducted to suggest ways to achieve this goal. Pupils, it is commonly asserted, should not be developed as mere possessors of knowledge, but, rather developed into individuals capable of thinking—individuals who can utilize knowledge.

Developing thinking individuals has become the slogan of the schools and the selling-point of educational materials, whether they be textbooks or tests. Some aspect of this goal of developing thinkers is mentioned in our lesson-plan objectives. Means of achieving this objective are listed. However, one procedure which is usually *not* mentioned in lesson plans, or in school slogans, or in educational materials is the effective use of the *question.*

Questions in teacher-talk and instructional material are significant in the guidance of/or guiding the teaching-learning situation toward the achievement of objectives. Questions which teachers ask substantiate stated objectives and reveal unverbalized aims. They may stress, for example, increasing pupils' knowledge of facts, increasing pupils' understandings and concepts, or increasing pupils' skills at interpreting materials. Yet, from current research, the predominant emphasis of teachers' questions seems to be on knowledge of facts—not thinking.

Some Typical Teacher Questions

An excerpt from a tapescript made in a fifth-grade social studies class is presented. It gives evidence of the poor quality of teacher questions and testifies, also, to their emphasis upon factual knowledge. The tapescript also reveals that teachers' verbal utterances are many times inappropriate to

Francis P. Hunkins is Assistant Professor of Education, Bureau of Educational Research, Kent State University, Kent, Ohio the subject area being discussed. This "bit" of dialogue should not suggest sweeping generalizations, but, rather, should give the reader an instance of discourse to stimulate his thinking.

> T.　(pointing to map): Is there anyone here who could not tell how we got all those chunks? (Chunks refers to the first states.) Well, let's go over them very briefly. Ah, what happened first, there?
> T.:　What was the first addition?
> T.:　The first, we started with what?
> T.:　Let's change our question.
> T.:　We started with what?
> T.:　What did we, our country start in 1789 when we were first organized as a country?
> T.:　When we first started to be a country?
> P.:　Thirteen colonies were made into thirteen states.
> T.:　And their western boundaries were to be what?
> P.:　The western boundaries of these thirteen states that grow out of the, they were to go west to the Mississippi.
> T.:　All right, then we and we and how was it that we acquired this?
> P.:　We fought a war with England. And that is the beginning of our country, this chunk right through here.
> T.:　And what was our first addition to this state?
> T.:　And how did we get Florida?
> T.:　And at that time if you will look in the book, Florida was clear over here. All right, what was the next big chunk we got?
> P.:　The Louisiana Purchase
> T.:　And from what country did we buy it?

If nothing else is gained from reading this discourse, one can see that the questions did not really demand that the pupils think. The teacher had not carefully contemplated the wording and emphasis of her questions; the questions had a spontaneous birth in the atmosphere of classroom discourse.

Questions Concerned with Facts

Teachers stress thinking, yet their classroom questions contradict their claims. Over the years, their questions have been primarily concerned with the same thing—memory of facts—specific facts.

Over fifty years ago, Stevens (9) noted a dominant emphasis on memory questions in both English and social studies classes, with social studies sections stressing this type of question more. Consequently, Stevens called for intelligent use of questions as instructional devices and stated that questions should stimulate reflective thought in addition to mere memorization of facts. Stevens' plea has been greatly ignored.

Recently, Floyd (5) studied questions asked by primary teachers and concluded that there existed a poor balance of question types with memory questions dominating the class activity.

Adams (1), developing a system of categories by which he classified the questions asked by secondary school English and social studies teachers, discovered a similar dominating emphasis of memory questions, although the overall proportion, when compared with Stevens' study, was somewhat less. Even so, the overall emphasis on memory questions proved memory to be still the cognitive objective receiving the most emphasis in the teaching situations of both groups of teachers.

Davis and Hunkins (4) discovered that questions in fifth-grade social studies textbooks reflected this emphasis on memory. Pfeiffer and Davis (8), in analyzing teacher-made examinations, found a similar factual emphasis.

An Effective Teaching Device

Even though actual practice has shown misuse of the question to emphasize knowledge, many books and articles have been written which extol the merits of the question as a device of effective teaching. For example, Loughlin (7) stated that effective questioning is effective teaching. Klebaner (6) adds agreement to Loughlin's claim by stating that the carefully thought out question used effectively is vital to achieving the purposes of education.

Wellington and Wellington (10), while differing in their definition of teaching, advocate more effective use of questions in the teaching situation. Teaching, they stress, is not the teacher asking questions, but rather the teacher guiding the pupils so that they ask effective questions.

Carner (3) took somewhat the same emphasis in stating that teachers must be cognizant of the types of thinking required before they can frame effective questions to assist children in such cognitive development. Teachers need to be aware of the level, concrete or abstract, of questions which is most suited to a particular learning situation. Carner stated that present teacher-emphasis is on questions which are supported by facts.

Questions Have Many Uses

The evidence of the past points accusingly at teachers' uses of questions. Teachers have been and are hampered in their use of questions by considering them primarily as instruments of testing what facts pupils

have learned. But they need not rest on this misconception. Questions have other uses: as tools to assist in diagnosing pupil difficulties and as motivators to learning. Too, questions may be tools to foster thinking to guide learning of higher cognitive processes. Questions which stimulate thinking are difficult to construct; they demand of the teacher careful planning with respect to the goals of the lesson or unit. These questions should be as carefully thought out as are the objectives, for if the questions are poor the objectives will not be achieved.

Many Forms and Emphases

Questions have varying forms and varying emphases. An extremely helpful guide was issued ten years ago (2). This guide, *Taxonomy of Educational Objectives: Cognitive Domain*, presents six hierarchically-arranged categories: knowledge, comprehension, application, analysis, synthesis, and evaluation.

Most classroom questions seem to get bogged down in the knowledge category. The *who, when, where, what* questions ably represent this category—the necessity of learning facts. Teachers must not hastily, and unwisely, conclude that our present plight may be remedied simply by de-emphasizing the *who, when, where, what* questions and by bringing in the *how* and the *why* question. The form of question does play a major role in determining its emphasis or emphases, but the purpose of the question must also be known in relation to context.

If the question's form is employed as the sole rationale for judging questions, misinterpretation will result many times. To exhort teachers to use more *why* than *what* questions without an understanding of the relation of form and purpose would be, in substance, no change at all. For example, "Why are olives grown in this particular part of California?" might well be expected to call for "thinking" rather than "memorization." But if one considers the question in relation to its context in a particular book, he might discover that this question is just asking for a listing of specifics which support the fact that olives are grown in this particular geographic region.

To judge questions with regard to form without consideration of their relation to context is only half the picture. Questions neither stand alone in materials, nor can they be judged alone according to a single criterion of form. Also, the cognitive response which a question elicits depends to a great extent upon the information which an individual brings to the question. A pupil, lacking some particular information, may be stimulated by a question to analyze information. However, if the pupil already knows the information, the cognitive response might be only in the realm of knowledge.

Form Not Only Cue to Emphasis

The examples of questions below give evidence that form of question is not the sole cue to its emphasis. These questions also show that one must make certain assumptions about the prior information which pupils bring to the questions.

1. What was and is today the major factor in determining a man's standing in the herding community? (knowledge)
2. Why didn't the Africans of the past produce much of their own food? (knowledge—specific facts in book)
3. Why were iron tools and weapons valuable? (comprehension)
4. How did the Africans make iron? (comprehension)
5. Locate on the map the two capitals of South Africa. (application)
6. Look at your map and determine the major landscape type of Ethiopia. (application)
7. The author states that Africa is a land of contrasts. Does the author present enough information to support this statement? (analysis)
8. Explain why the major trading cities in Western Africa were located along the western edge of the Sahara. (analysis)
9. Australia needs additional water. Describe as many ways as you can which will supply water more efficiently to this country. (synthesis)
10. Describe several plans which you propose to assist in bringing peace to the world. (synthesis)
11. Do you feel that the type of farming practices carried on by these people was efficient? (evaluation)
12. What do you think of our foreign policy? (evaluation)

These examples illustrate that questions can have either simple or complex form. There are no "pat" questions which immediately inform the teacher that he has constructed an analysis question to stimulate his class to the heights of thinking.

The difficulty of constructing good questions should not deter us in attempting improvement. Questions can be effective in fostering pupils' thinking. The time is propitious to convert our slogans about thinking into deeds and actually stimulate our pupils.

REFERENCES

1. Adams, Thomas Howard. *The Development of a Method for Analysis of Questions Asked by Teachers in Classroom Discourse.* Doctor's thesis (New Bruns-

wick, New Jersey: Rutgers, The State University, 1964).

2. Bloom, Benjamin S., Ed. *Taxonomy of Educational Objectives, The Classification of Educational Goals: Handbook I. Cognitive Domain* (New York: David McKay Co., Inc., 1956).

3. Carner, Richard L. "Levels of Questioning." *Education* Vol. 83 (May 1963) pp. 546–550.

4. Davis, O. L. Jr., and Hunkins, Francis P. "Textbook Questions: What Thinking Processes Do They Foster?" *Peabody Journal of Education,* in press.

5. Floyd, William D. *An Analysis of the Oral Questioning Activity in Selected Colorado Primary Classrooms,* Doctor's thesis (Greeley, Colorado: Colorado State College, 1960).

6. Klebaner, Ruth Perlman. "Questions That Teach." *Grade Teacher,* Vol. 81 (March 1964), pp. 10, 76–77.

7. Loughlin, Richard L. "On Questioning." *The Educational Forum,* Vol. 25 (May 1961), pp. 481–482.

8. Pfeiffer, Isobel and Davis, O. L. Jr. "Teacher-Made Examinations: What Kind of Thinking Do They Demand?" NASSP *Bulletin* Vol. 49 (September 1965), pp.1–10.

9. Stevens, Romiett. *The Question as a Measure of Efficiency in Instruction.* (New York: Teachers College, Columbia University, 1912).

10. Wellington, Jean, and Wellington, Burleigh. "What is a Question?" *The Clearing House* Vol. 36 (April 1962), pp. 471–472.

Guiding Learning through Skilful Questioning

Robert T. Pate
and Neville H. Bremer

EDITORS' QUESTIONS:

1. Critically analyze the research design used by Pate and Bremer for discovering the purposes of teachers' questions. What is the relevance of their findings to efforts designed to improve teachers' questioning strategies?

2. Why do the authors suggest that questions not be classified until the child has attempted to answer them? How would such a procedure aid the teacher in individualizing instruction?

3. Assess the utility of the Questions Analyzer as a device for increasing the effectiveness of questioning techniques.

4. Tape record one of your micro teaching experiences and analyze your own questioning practices to (a) determine the number of questions you ask and (b) classify them according to the categories provided by the Questions Analyzer. On the basis of this analysis, make suggestions for improving your questioning behavior.

5. Offer suggestions for using questioning techniques to foster learnings in the affective domain.

Robert T. Pate and Neville H. Bremer, "Guiding Learning through Skilful Questioning," *The Elementary School Journal,* Vol. 67, No. 8 (May 1967) pp. 417–422. Published monthly October through May *by* the University of Chicago Press with the Department of Education and the Graduate School of Education of the University of Chicago. Copyright 1967 by the University of Chicago. Reprinted with the permission of the University of Chicago and Robert T. Pate.

Joe waved his hand impatiently. He was eagerly waiting for a chance to respond to the teacher's question. As he waited, he continued to work over his ideas. When the teacher finally called on Joe, his response had reached the sophistication level of a question: "Can't we change the form of the problem to one we already know?" he asked. The teacher's reply was disappointing: "A good thought, Joe. Now let's look at the example in the book."

This brief sample is typical of exchanges in several classrooms observed during a recent research project (1). As a result of these observations, the writers have become concerned about improving the quality and the use of questions in guiding children's learning—questions that require an oral response as well as questions that require a written response.

Joe was eager when he asked his question. Would his eagerness have been enhanced if the teacher had countered with another question: "How would you change it, Joe?" or simply, "What do you mean?"

Before suggesting a technique for improving the quality and the use of questions in guiding children's learning, it seems appropriate to consider why teachers ask questions.

The authors are affiliated with Texas Technological College, Lubbock, Texas.

Recently 190 elementary-school teachers in Grades 1 through 6 were asked to respond to the question: "What are three important purposes of teachers' questions of pupils?" The responses were analyzed and categorized. The results are summarized in Table 1.

One hundred and twenty-nine teachers (68 per cent) said that an important purpose of teachers' questions is to check on the effectiveness of teaching by checking on what pupils have learned. What these teachers consider *learning* was not apparent from the responses. It seems likely that teachers' ideas of learning differed: 89 teachers (47 per cent) said that an important purpose of questions is to check pupils' ability to recall specific facts; other teachers said that an important purpose is to require the use of facts in generalizing and in making inferences. Few teachers listed both purposes.

One hundred and two teachers (54 per cent) said that teachers' questions serve the important purpose of diagnosing pupils' difficulties. Does this mean that the remaining 46 per cent of the teachers do not consider diagnosis as an important function of teachers' questions? Or does it mean that teachers have not given much thought to the purposes their questions serve? Some teachers who said that tests "check on the effectiveness of teaching" may have had in mind instructional adjustments in the light of the answers. These teachers would be indicating a diagnostic use.

Sixteen of the teachers (8 per cent) gave as an important purpose that of having pupils check their own learning. Two teachers (1 per cent) said that discovering pupils' interests is an important purpose. Two teachers said that questions check pupils' proficiency in expression. Thirty-one teachers (16 per cent) said that an important function of questions is "to determine grades,"

Table 1

Purposes of Teachers' Questions as Indicated by Responses of 190 Elementary-School Teachers to the Question, "What Are Three Important Purposes of Teachers' Questions of Pupils?"

Purpose	Number of Teachers	Per Cent of Teachers Responding
Check on effectiveness of teaching by checking on pupils' learning	129	68
Diagnosis	102	54
Check pupils' recall of specific facts	89	47
Meet individual needs	33	17
Determine grades (marks)	31	16
Require pupils to use facts in generalizing and in making inferences	19	10
Check on pupils' progress	17	9
Provide for pupils to check their own learning	16	8
Motivation	13	7
Determine grade-level placement of materials	8	4
Acquaint pupils with different kinds of questions	7	4
Discover pupils' interests	2	1
Check pupils' proficiency in expression	2	1
Help pupils retain knowledge	1	1

and 33 (17 per cent) said that teachers' questions "meet individual needs." Other purposes given were "motivation," "check on pupils' progress," "help pupils retain knowledge," and "acquaint pupils with different kinds of questions."

Only 19 teachers (10 per cent) gave responses which seemed to indicate that an important purpose of teachers' questions is "to require pupils to use facts in generalizing and in making inferences." In the opinion of these writers, this is one of the most important uses that can be made of questions, written as well as oral. The nature of the responses and the small number of teachers who listed this purpose may mean that teachers are thinking of questions that require "short answers."

If learning is seen as not only the acquiring of knowledge, but also as skill in using this knowledge, teachers need to recognize that questions offer an excellent means of checking on pupils' skill in organizing facts and on pupils' understanding of relationships among facts. We recognize that written answers are difficult to score. They take time and a great amount of judgment. The fact that written answers take time to evaluate must be accepted; little can be done to help. On the problem of judgment, it should be said that teachers are capable of passing judgment in subjects on which they are expert and should not have to apologize for their judgment in such matters.

A surprising number of the teachers who responded were apparently unable to give readily as many as three purposes served by questions. Several teachers listed only one or two purposes. Some gave two or three, which, when analyzed, were placed in a single category. If each of the 190 teachers had given three responses, the total number of responses would have been 570. Actually, only 469 responses were tabulated. Perhaps many teachers have not considered carefully the purposes that questions may serve.

From the teachers' responses to the question, "What are three important purposes of teacher questions?" it may be concluded that:

1. Teachers use questions for a number of purposes.
2. Some teachers apparently have not given much thought to the purposes their questions can serve.
3. Most teachers ask questions that require short answers, thus missing opportunities to give pupils practice in the skill of using facts to generalize and make inferences.

Though no teacher said that one purpose of teacher's questions is to guide pupils' learning, this purpose appears to be implicit in most of the responses.

The teacher who wants to improve his questioning might begin by assessing the types of inquiry he is using. The authors have developed a technique and an instrument to help in the analysis (2). The instrument has nine categories that encompass various types of questions that might be asked during teaching. The categories are divided into two major types, convergent and divergent. Convergent questions generally call for a particular response; they are designed to evoke one possible answer. Divergent questions call for a response that has several facets or involve more than one possible answer. The kinds of questions a teacher asks during a given period may be tallied on the Questions Analyzer, which is reproduced here. A teacher may have a colleague keep the record during an observation period, or the teacher may use a tape recorder and do his own tallying during a replay of the lesson.

Questions are tallied in the appropriate

categories based on the following descriptions:

Simple Recall—One Item

This category calls for the greatest amount of convergence. The child is asked to recall one item of information. The response involves only recalling and repeating what was previously stated in class in one way or another. The following questions might fall into this group: "What is the capital of our state?" "Name the town he visited." "What baseball club made the run?"

Recall—Choice of Multiple Items

This category calls for a level of convergent thinking that is slightly below the level required for the category "simple recall—one item." The category "recall—choice of multiple items" involves recall of information previously given the pupil in one way or another, but requires a greater organiza-

tion of thinking in that he will have to recall several items. The following questions might fall into this category: "Who were the culprits?" "What were the names of the towns?" "When did these things happen?" "What were their destinations?" "Who were the leaders?"

Determination of Skills Abilities (Demonstrate)

This category calls for a lower level of convergence than either of the two previous categories. The category "determination of skills abilities (demonstrate)" requires the pupil to exhibit a higher degree of skill in assimilating information than any of the other convergent categories listed. The questions in this category require the pupil to demonstrate his skill, knowledge, or proficiency in an area by demonstrating before a group at the chalkboard or on paper.

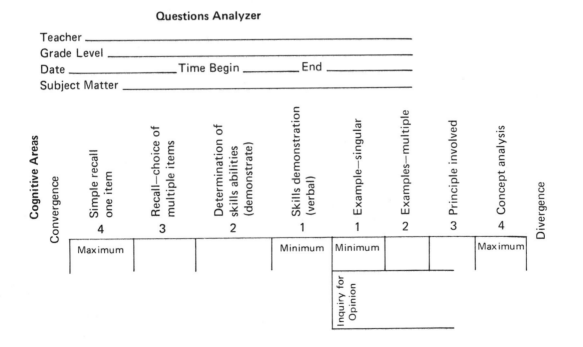

Skills Demonstration (Verbal)

This category calls for the least amount of convergence. Questions tallied in this column call for a verbal (only) demonstration of skills in some area. This category requires of the pupil a higher level of thought than the previous category. The following questions asked by the teacher would be tallied in this column: "How would you work this?" "Will you explain this problem to the class?" (verbal explanation).

Example—Singular

This category involves the least amount of divergence. A question in this category requires of the child a higher degree of assimilation and analysis than called for by questions in any of the categories described to this point. A question tallied in this column would require the child to have an idea so well developed that he could give an example of the area under discussion. Questions that might fit into this category are: "What will we do now?" "Will you give me an example of what you mean?" The pupil must analyze the situation to the point that he can present at least one example of the idea under discussion.

Examples—Multiple

This category involves a level of thought more demanding of the child's thought process. He must understand and be capable of illustrating, with more than one example. The examples must be different enough to illustrate a deeper level of understanding on the part of the child than the preceding category calls for. The following might fit this category: "Give me some examples of what you mean."

Principle Involved

This is the category for questions that exhibit near maximum divergence. A question fits in this category only when the teacher has asked the child to use his maximum potential in the area under discussion. The questions give the child an opportunity to see relationships in the area, to compare one principle with another, and to discuss potential relationships.

Concept Analysis

This category calls for thought that involves maximum divergence, drawing of inferences, and a more critical view of the facts and ideas available. The teacher's question should call for an answer that exhibits a depth of understanding that will allow the pupil to use the various processes of analysis and bring forth ideas related to the concept under discussion as well as alien ideas. Questions in this category might be: "Can we develop a basic idea from the information we have?" "What is another way to approach this problem?"

Inquiry for Opinion

Questions fit in this category when the teacher attempts to involve as many pupils as possible in the discussion. The teacher may ask: "What do you think?" "What is your opinion?" "How would you do it?" These questions involve a type or form of divergence and are, therefore, tallied in the column associated with divergence, but they are not tallied in the other divergence categories unless it appears that the teacher's intent was other than merely to ask for an opinion.

The professional educator who uses the *Questions Analyzer* may find the following suggestions helpful:

1. Become familiar with the general outline of the instrument and the location of the various categories.

2. Study the description of each of the broad categories and try to develop questions that fit each category.

3. Make a few trial observations with the instrument to assure complete familiarity with the instrument and the categories.

4. Do not classify a question until the child has answered or tried to answer it. The child's response will help clarify the teacher's intent, as the child sees it. The value of the form lies in the opportunity to consider the teacher's question as the child interprets it.

5. It is important that the observer realize that all levels of questions can be asked at all grade levels.

The teacher's effectiveness in questioning depends on an awareness of various purposes that questions may serve and an awareness of different types of questions for achieving these purposes. Skilful guidance through questioning can result in greater depth of learning.

References

1. Robert T. Pate, "Transactional Pattern Differences between School Mathematics Programs," *Arithmetic Teacher, 13* (January, 1966) 21–25.
2. Robert T. Pate. *Questions Analyzer.* Copyright by Robert T. Pate, 1966.

Interacting in the Interrogative

Kenneth Shrable
and Douglas Minnis

21

EDITORS' QUESTIONS:

1. What purposes are served by classifying the types of questions asked by teachers? Of what value to the classroom teacher is the information thus provided?

2. Give examples of ways in which questioning strategies may be used to foster achievement of learning objectives.

3. How can the Cognitive Levels Analysis Interaction Model (CLAIM) be used to assist teachers in improving their question-framing skills? Give examples.

4. Devise a micro–teaching experiment designed to assess the differences in impact upon pupils of two different levels of questioning. Report and analyze your results.

Kenneth Shrable and Douglas Minnis, "Interacting in the Interrogative," *The Journal of Teacher Education*, XX, (Summer 1969), 201–212. Reprinted with the permission of the National Commission on Teacher Education and Professional Standards, National Education Association.

This paper describes a method for analyzing teacher questioning strategies. It is frequently asserted that skillful questioning is one of the most valuable techniques available to the teacher for stimulating and guiding thinking. Furthermore, it is assumed that the teacher can control, in large measure, the quality and direction of classroom dialogue by means of questioning strategies (9, 10, 11, 20).

Although teachers have often been criticized for using too many short-answer questions emphasizing recall, observation of teachers in training indicates that they do attempt to utilize broad, abstract questions. However, the teacher's initial efforts may result in irrelevant or scattered responses from the class; frustrated by their inability to move the class to higher levels of interaction, teachers may come to rely largely on the use of recall questions as a means of involving students in the discussion. One major reason for such failures in questioning strategies is that student teachers frequently commit the error of attempting to lift the level of thinking too soon (20).

Another problem from an instructional standpoint is that higher-level questions may be used by the teacher in a random fashion or without a defined strategy. These questions may be answered by a few students with special background or high ability, without the teacher's awareness of the lack of movement to more abstract levels of thinking on the part of the majority of the class. Taba (20) has described this pattern of erratic movement among cognitive levels and suggests that it reflects inappropriate pacing of questions aimed at lifting levels of classroom discourse.

Teachers are generally aware of the above

Dr. Shrable is assistant professor, and Dr. Minnis is head of teacher education, University of California, Davis.

problems. However, in studying patterns of teacher-pupil verbal behavior, Flanders (12) found that, though teachers could describe varying models of classroom interaction, they had difficulty in initiating changes in their own behavior. For example, when a student stops talking, teachers know that certain critical decisions must be made as to whether the instructor expresses his own ideas, praises the student's response, accepts the affective aspects of student talk, gives further directions, or asks a question. In general, teachers are aware that differences in these critical decisions lead to different styles of classroom interaction. Yet, Flanders found that on the average teachers do not make these decisions easily; they do not move from one mode of interaction to another in response to the different purposes of classroom communication. Similarly, teachers can readily attain a conceptual understanding of different types of questions and of the cognitive processes they are assumed to elicit in the student; the difficulty is for them to demonstrate that they not only understand but can transform this understanding into control over their own behavior. Research with the system of interaction analysis developed by Amidon and Flanders (2) has shown that such behavior change can be facilitated by a method of feedback for the teacher concerning his own classroom interaction patterns (13, 16, 18).

As a means of providing training in questioning skill, we have developed a system for classifying questions and a method for analyzing a teacher's questioning strategies. Our initial task involved devising a means of categorizing questions reliably. In recent years, various systems of classifying questions have been proposed. For example, Bloom (8) has provided a six-stage classification scheme as a corollary of his set of educational objectives in the cognitive domain. His question types are memory or recall, comprehension, application, analysis, synthesis, and evaluation, which are considered to form a continuum ranging from simple to complex behavior. Taba (20), though primarily concerned with specifying levels of cognitive tasks as part of her definition of thinking, describes the teacher's questioning strategies as being concerned with concrete information (data) or abstract principles and generalization. Gallagher and Aschner (14) have classified questions into four types based on certain theoretical categories of thinking (15): memory, convergent, divergent, and evaluation questions. Gallagher and Aschner also make the assumption that different levels of cognitive complexity or abstraction are involved in their classification framework. Recent modifications of the interaction analysis system for classifying teacher-pupil verbal behavior have included categories for different types of questions by expanding the original ten-category system (2) to sixteen different classifications for teacher-pupil behavior (4, 5). This enables the observer to classify questions as to type and level of abstraction, but produces a complex system that is unwieldy for focusing on training in questioning strategies. In addition, the modified system does not use the same classification categories for teacher-pupil behavior in cataloging teacher questions, student responses, and teacher reaction to the pupil's handling of questions.

In considering various classifications of questions, one communality that emerged was the underlying assumption of a hierarchical order of cognitive operations. In each of the above systems, it is assumed that the cognitive operations required in responding to the question types at various levels can be ordered on a scale of complexity. A common assumption seems to be that, when proceeding up the scale from concrete to abstract or simple to complex questions, responses in a given class are likely to make use of and be built on the behavior found in the preceding class. Generally, it is assumed that the more abstract- or complex-level operations cannot be performed until the prior steps have been completed (8:18, 20). We have utilized this notion of levels of complexity in thinking in devising a schema for analyzing questions. After a tryout of various systems of classification, we adopted one utilizing three levels of question types. In our classification system, questions are categorized as being at the level of data recall, data processing, and application or generalization (cf. 20, 19:10). These categories, which are defined below, follow closely the definitions developed by Taba in specifying levels of cognitive tasks:

1. *Data recall* cues the student to respond with a descriptive type statement. Recalling and reciting previously acquired information are typical tasks at this level.
2. *Data processing* involves the student in using data to show cause and effect relationships, to group, classify, synthesize, define, analyze, compare, contrast, and infer from data.
3. *Application* cues the student to do some divergent thinking, to make predictions, to develop theories, and to apply principles learned in other contexts.

These categories are similar to those previously noted. For example, our level one (data recall) is found in most of the above classification systems and needs no further clarification. Our level two category (data processing) is more general than some of the other categories in the systems noted previously. For instance, the categories labeled interpretation, analysis, synthesis, and some types of evaluation in Bloom's taxonomy of questions would be classified level two in our system; the convergent category and part of the evaluation classification of Gal-

lagher and Aschner would also be found at this level. We reserved level three for teacher questions aimed at eliciting responses relevant to the use of data or inferences in new situations, such as predictions or applications to different conditions from those under which the original learning took place. This level is comparable to Bloom's application and extrapolation categories and to the divergent category of Gallagher and Aschner. The present classification system is selective with respect to the areas of classroom dialogue considered. Our intention is to provide a maximum amount of feedback, with as simple a system as possible, in order to provide a reliable feedback instrument for use by teachers in studying their own classroom interaction.

Having adopted a classification system for questions, we were faced with a second major task. Questions occur in the context of a larger dialogue between the teacher and the student. To deal adequately with questioning strategies, especially with those aimed at initiating movement among cognitive levels, it was necessary to devise a classification system for teacher-pupil verbal behavior that would capture changes in levels of thinking and also enable us to examine questioning skill in the light of sequences of teacher-pupil interaction. Because of the complexity of verbal behavior, the study of classroom dialogue requires certain arbitrary decisions about which aspects of this behavior will be studied (7). We have arbitrarily chosen as our unit of analysis an interaction sequence consisting of a teacher's initiatory response (primarily direct questions, or implied questions, as in directions or commands), student response to the teacher, and the teacher's reaction to the student response. The findings of Bellack and others (6) in their study of teacher-pupil interaction indicate that this particular pattern of verbal behavior tends to be the most common one in classroom dialogue. Generally, classroom interaction is initiated by what Bellack calls a teacher's soliciting move, i.e., the teacher asks a question or directs the student to respond. This is followed by a pupil's responding move, which, in turn, is generally followed by a teacher reaction to the student response. Briefer forms of interaction involving a teacher solicitation closed by a student response can be treated as simply a variant of the general pattern above. Dialogue initiated by the student, an important but infrequent phenomenon (6), is not the central focus of the present system and is arbitrarily categorized as part of the student's responsive behavior.

·In review, our system of analysis of classroom dialogue focuses on teacher-pupil interaction sequences and on levels of cognitive operation. First, with respect to type of behavior, our analysis focuses on soliciting moves by the teacher, responding moves by the student, closed by responding moves on the part of the teacher. The soliciting move is primarily concerned with the teacher's direct or implied questions. Directions and instructions cuing the student to respond are treated as implied questions. The teacher's soliciting move may be initiatory, in that it sets the focus for a topic of discussion, or responsive, i.e., follows up the discussion in the student response. Second, with regard to the analysis of levels of thinking, our classification system recognizes that teacher-pupil moves can occur at different levels of complexity or abstraction. Our classification of questions, i.e., soliciting moves, specifies three levels for classroom dialogue. Since we have focused on both level of dialogue and interaction behavior, our classification system is labeled "Cognitive Levels Analysis, Interaction Model" (CLAIM).

With this background in mind, we now turn to a description of the coding of type of behavior and level of cognitive operation. With respect to type of behavior, the letter "A" is used to designate the teacher's initiatory behavior (i.e., a soliciting move which sets the focus for a topic of discussion); "B," to classify student responsive behavior; and "C," to designate teacher responsive behavior. A teacher's responsive behavior (C) can also be a soliciting move, as in the instance in which the teacher uses a question to follow up the student's response. An example of the coding of a segment of classroom dialogue is given below.

Teacher: (A) John, define a noun.
Student: (B) A noun is the name of something.
Teacher: (C) Good.

With regard to the level of thinking, the three levels specified in the present system are data recall, data processing, and application of principles. In order to differentiate level, our classification system uses the subscript "1" to designate the data recall level, "2" for data processing, and "3" for application level. Table 1 presents the three levels and the three types of responses to be coded, along with abbreviated definitions.

Recording

In recording tallies, it is necessary that the sequence of events in the classroom be retained. In developing the scoring system, typescripts of lessons were employed. The rule adopted for coding behavior called for rating each consecutive ten-word segment of dialogue or coding each interaction change (i.e., the speaker in the dialogue shifts). When a segment of verbal behavior was less than 10 (but 5 or more) words in length the section was scored as a complete unit; segments less than 5 words in length were disregarded when they did not represent a single speaker's comment. Consecutive interaction sequences of approximately

10 to 20 minutes in length are desirable for obtaining patterns for analysis.

The tallies should be recorded in a column to facilitate the preparation of a matrix for analysis (cf. 2). The following segment of dialogue with coding symbols illustrates the way a rater would tally it.

1st Pair ... A_1	(T) What are some of the things you know about hippies?
2nd Pair ... B_1	(S) They have long hair
3rd Pair ... C_1	(T) O.K.
4th Pair ... B_1	(S) They wear beards
C_1	(T) All right.

The tallies are entered on a matrix following the system utilized by Amidon and Flanders (2). Once the symbols for classifying responses are made, these are marked off in pairs. The first pair above is A_1B_1; the second, B_1C_1; the third C_1B_1, etc. We are now ready to enter the observations in the 9 by 9 matrix shown in Table 2. The particular cell in which tabulation of the pair of symbols is made is determined by using the first symbol in the pair to indicate the row; and the second, the column in the matrix (Table 2). Thus, A_1B_1 would be shown by a tally in the cell formed by row A_1 and column B_1. The second pair, B_1C_1, would be shown in the cell formed by row B_1 and column C_1. The third pair, C_1B_1, is entered in the cell formed by row C_1 and column B_1. Notice that each pair of symbols overlaps with the previous pair; each symbol, except the first and last, is used twice.

Analysis

For meaningful analysis, the matrix (Table 2) should represent an observer's tallying of a single type of activity, i.e., a discussion of a social studies topic rather than of social studies combined with one relating to an arithmetic lesson. After recording the tallies on the matrix, it is possible to describe different kinds of classroom interaction.

One of the simplest ways of depicting the interaction tallied in Table 2 is to examine the column totals (C_3, B_3, A_3, etc., reading from left to right) in terms of percentages of total verbal behavior. In order to do this, the percentage of tallies in each of the columns is computed by dividing each of the column totals by the total number of tallies in the matrix. This computation provides us with the proportion of the total interaction observed in each category of behavior (A_1, A_2, A_3, B_1, B_2, etc.). In other words, we can determine the percentage of teacher verbal behavior devoted to initiating dialogue at level one (A_1), level two (A_2), and level three (A_3), or the amount of interaction in which the teacher is responding to student talk at the various levels (C_1, C_2, C_3). The percentage of student talk at the various levels of classroom dialogue can also be noted by reading the percentages in columns labeled B_1, B_2, and B_3.

The column totals also provide information about the proportion of teacher-student verbal behavior (cf. 2). The sum of the total tallies in the A and C columns (teacher initiatory and responsive behavior), divided by the total tallies in the matrix, yields a ratio of the amount of teacher talk in this dialogue segment. For example, in Table 2 the sum of the A and C columns is 34, and the total number of tallies in the matrix is 154. This yields a ratio of .22, which means that the teacher's verbal behavior constituted less than one-fourth of the verbal behavior in this particular lesson. Since student talk makes up the remainder of the behavior tallied, it comprises 78 percent of this classroom interaction, which indicates a high level of student participation.

A visual inspection of Table 2 gives other information. At the lower right-hand side of the matrix, a heavy shaded area is marked

Table 1

Cognitive Levels Analysis Interaction Model[1]

Behavior Level	Behavior Type		
	Teacher Initiatory	Student Responsive	Teacher Responsive
Data Recall	(A_1) Question or instructions cue the student to respond with a descriptive statement, to use recall, to recite, enumerate, list. For example: "Name the presidents of the United States;" or, "Who invented the electric light?"	(B_1) Student responds by recalling facts, i.e., answers A_1 question as directed. Includes, "I don't know."	(C_1) Teacher maintains descriptive level. Cues the student that recall is accepted (e.g., "good," "correct," etc.) or cues student to continue by instructions or follow-up questions on the topic.
Data Processing	(A_2) Question or directions cue the student to use data to show relationships or cause and effect; to synthesize, classify, analyze, compare, contrast data. For example: "Compare the strength of steel and copper." "Why couldn't you keep this acid in a metal container?"	(B_2) Student responds by explaining, inferring, or showing relationships among bits of information. Uses the cognitive operations called for in teacher's A_2 or C_2 response.	(C_2) Teacher maintains inference level by accepting student response, elaborating or using student's B_2 behavior. Includes follow-up questions at level two, i.e., questions on the same topic as student response. If the teacher shifts the topic, score as A_2 (initiatory behavior, level two).
Application	(A_3) Question directs the student to respond by predicting, theorizing, or applying a principle in a new situation; to do divergent thinking. For example: "What would happen if the nomads of the desert had all the water they could use?" or, "What do you think would happen if we were to use a larger test tube?"	(B_3) Student responds by predicting, hypothesizing, or applying a principle to a new situation. Performs the cognitive operations implied in the teacher's A_3 response.	(C_3) Teacher's verbal behavior cues the student that predicting, theorizing is accepted, to be continued, or follow-up question on same focus as the B_3 response.

1. Additional instructions and examples of scoring are contained in the CLAIM manual (17).

off and labeled "Level One." The tallies in this part of the matrix comprise the behavior of both teacher and student emphasizing recall of information. Level two behavior is found in the center areas of the matrix; level three behavior will be tallied in the upper left-hand corner. By inspection of the matrix, it can readily be determined whether the lesson remained primarily at level one or moved upward. In this instance, where a

Table 2
Cognitive Levels Analysis Interaction Model

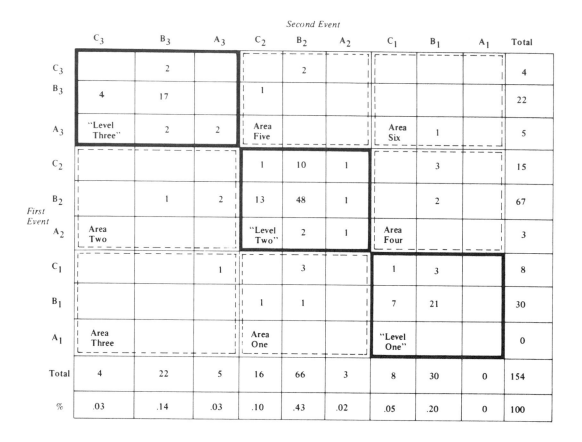

Second Event

First Event	C₃	B₃	A₃	C₂	B₂	A₂	C₁	B₁	A₁	Total
C₃		2			2					4
B₃	4	17		1						22
A₃	"Level Three"	2	2	Area Five			Area Six	1		5
C₂				1	10	1		3		15
B₂		1	2	13	48	1		2		67
A₂	Area Two			"Level Two"	2	1	Area Four			3
C₁			1		3		1	3		8
B₁				1	1		7	21		30
A₁	Area Three			Area One			"Level One"			0
Total	4	22	5	16	66	3	8	30	0	154
%	.03	.14	.03	.10	.43	.02	.05	.20	0	100

lesson remains at level one, the tallies would tend to be clustered in the rectangular area at the lower right-hand corner of the matrix. The lesson tallied in Table 2 moves upward from the lower right-hand corner toward the center and upper left-hand area, indicating that teacher and student behavior move to higher levels of dialogue. This particular lesson is heavily concentrated at level two, indicating that the teacher emphasized data processing, i.e., required students to use data in drawing conclusions, analyzing, synthesizing, or making comparisons among the items of information. Table 2 also illus-

trates movement to level three in classroom interaction. The piling up of tallies in the B_3B_3 cell indicates sustained student response at the level of prediction-, generalization-, or hypothesis-making stage.

For ease in noting other bits of information, the matrix in Table 2 has been marked off into six areas which represent points of transition in classroom dialogue. Tallies in areas one and two represent teacher-pupil responses shifting the dialogue upward one step (level). For example, the C_1B_2 cell in area one contains three tallies or three instances in which a pupil thrusts the level of interaction up from recall of information to making inferences about relationships in the data. Area two captures moves from data processing (level two) to generalization (level three), a one-step move upward. Area three reflects a broader leap, in that the single tally in this cell indicates a shift from data recall to prediction (level one to level three), or a two-step upward shift. The coding system enables us to ascertain immediately who made this move. Note that it occurs in the C_1A_3 cell (Table 2). The coding order preserves the behavioral sequence in the classroom and tells us that following a level one response by the teacher the instructor immediately attempted to initiate behavior at level three (A_3), i.e., attempted to move the dialogue from data recall to application of principles or generalization. By way of contrast, areas four and five represent one-step downward focus moves on the part of the participants. Area four tallies reflect moves from level two back down to level one, whereas area five contains tallies representing moves downward from application (level three) to data processing (level two). Area six, which has only one tally for the lesson coded in Table 2, designates shifts two steps downward in the dialogue. In the present instance, the single tally in the A_3B_1 cell of area six informs us that following an initiatory focusing move at level three (A_3) by the teacher the pupil responded with data recall (B_1) rather than the anticipated prediction or application level.

Coding Reliability

Two scorers were trained in the use of the classification system using typescripts of lessons, the description of categories, and illustrations of scoring contained in the manual (16). Three lessons were tallied and comparisons made of the independent rat-

ings. Areas of agreement and disagreement were studied until a high level of consensus was reached on the meaning of categories. A typescript of a sixth-grade social studies discussion (approximately ten minutes in length) was then scored independently by the raters and the percentage of agreement computed. Agreement on behavior type, whether A (teacher initiatory) or C (teacher responsive) or B (student responsive) between the two scorers was 97 percent. With respect to assignment of teacher-pupil behavior to levels (one, two, three), agreement was 79 percent. The overall agreement on assignment of verbal behavior by type and level was 78 percent, which was considered sufficiently high for interpretation of movement among cognitive levels in a lesson. Using typescripts, the two scorers then tallied selections of dialogue from four other lessons taught by four different teachers. The interrater agreement on type and level of verbal behavior was 91 percent for a fourth-grade social studies lesson, 100 percent for a primary-grade safety discussion, 84 percent for a third-grade reading lesson, and 85 percent for a discussion of an art experience in the primary grades. Rater agreement tends to vary directly with lesson complexity. The higher percentages (100, 91) reflect agreement on lessons that tend to contain primarily one level of cognitive behavior. The lower percentages (78, 84, 85) reported above were obtained with lessons containing all three levels of cognitive operations tallied in the scoring procedure. In general, the level of agreement obtained is quite high and indicates essential concurrence on overall patterning of the lessons.

Implications

The classification system introduced in this paper is concerned with verbal behavior only. Research with the interaction analysis technique (3) has shown the usefulness of approaches limited to cataloging verbal behavior for studying classroom learning. The present system was designed:

1. To provide teachers with structured, objective feedback about their interaction patterns with pupils with respect to levels of cognition and questioning techniques.
2. To provide a common language for teacher-supervisor interaction during training in the planning of teaching strategies and the evaluation of lessons taught from these plans.
3. To provide a method for obtaining reliable, quantifiable data in the limited but important domain of questioning behavior for research on classroom learning.

Implications for Teacher Education

The analysis and planning of classroom dialogue should be an integral part of teacher education. Those who provide this experience for teachers can develop skill sessions where strategies are planned and executed in a microteaching situation (1). As part of a preservice or staff development program, this approach would allow the teacher to develop a repertoire of basic dialogue patterns involving the use of questions to serve as a basis for further experimentation in actual classroom teaching.

Some possible teaching patterns derived from the mode of questioning and levels of thinking are described as follows: One type of pattern, which can be illustrated from dialogue analysis, is one in which the teacher keeps tight control over the discussion. For example, a sequence such as $A_1B_1A_1B_1$, etc., would be an interaction pattern in which the teacher sets each initial focus (A_1) by a data recall move. Student responses are not followed up directly, in that the teacher returns each time to initiatory behavior (A_1) rather than following up or building on student behavior. This pat-

tern would be appropriate in the instance in which a teacher sets the purpose of the interaction as one of giving directions or instructions for an activity and simply seeks from the students information as to whether they have complied with the teacher's instructions. It might also be the pattern for a teacher-directed quick drill in which the teacher wished a brief review before initiating new learning. In this strategy, the teacher does not wish to give attention to student comments not directly in response to the teacher's solicitations, e.g., pupil responses that expand the topic to new material or raise issues not covered previously. Another pattern can be described which shows teacher control over focus but illustrates the teacher's concern with feedback to the student; for example, a pattern such as $A_1B_1C_1A_1B_1C_1$ could reflect the teacher's concern with motivating students by praise or acceptance of student ideas.

Moving away from close teacher control, a pattern of the type $A_1B_1C_1B_1C_1B_1C_1$ illustrates the teacher behavior oriented toward following up student ideas. The teacher responds to student comment (C_1) without shifting the focus. Still other patterns illustrate movement among cognitive levels. A pattern of the type $A_1B_1C_2B_2$ depicts a sequence of interactions in which the teacher makes use of the student's response to lift the level of dialogue from data recall to data processing. In the following sequence of tallies, $A_1B_2C_2$, the student initiated the upward movement and the teacher responded by maintaining the level of dialogue. In other instances, the teacher may be concerned with maintaining focus at a given level, as in the sequence $A_1B_2C_1$ where the student shifted the discussion upward from recall to processing information and the teacher refocused the discussion (C_1) by returning to level one. Refocusing would be necessary if the teacher wished to gather more information for later use or wanted to involve slower students in the discussion (19). Sequences of interaction may provide clues as to appropriateness of timing the movement among cognitive levels by teacher solicitations. A series of interactions consisting of $A_2B_1C_1$, $A_3B_2C_2$, A_3B_1 would suggest that students are not yet able to operate at the level required by the teacher's initiatory behavior. In each of the preceding interactions, the student behavior (B) drops one or two steps below that of the teacher's focus.

Implications for Research

The above teaching patterns described by the CLAIM categories are useful for research dealing with the effect of teaching behavior on learning. For example, a teacher can practice theoretical patterns, as in the microteaching system (1). By varying the pattern from one focused at level one to one utilizing levels one and two, it then becomes possible to determine whether a teacher who works primarily at the data recall level in classroom dialogue has a different impact on students from that of one who initiates and responds to student processing of data in a variety of ways. One hypothesis would be that students who have been encouraged to engage in the use of data in drawing inferences, teasing out cause-effect relationships, or predicting outcomes of actions in new contexts would show greater skill in decision making or problem solving. Another hypothesis would be that the teacher's classroom interaction pattern sets a style for students in the area of thinking. If the teacher emphasizes level one behavior, this should set a pattern of thinking before the student as normative that is different from one in which the student is engaged directly in data processing or making generalizations from data. It should be noted that inferences, generalizations, and comparisons can be taught to students in such a fashion that their own use of these reflects recall of the teacher's behavior rather than their own processing of information.

Implications for Teaching

When the CLAIM classification system is used as a descriptive tool, it serves as a self-help method of making explicit the current pattern of classroom interaction used by a teacher. With the aid of a tape recorder, the classification system provides a means of feedback concerning the teaching act along the dimensions in the model. The teacher has the information needed to judge the "fit" of his own behavior in the class hour with that anticipated in planning the lesson. It also enables him to compare his classroom performance with the model concerning levels of thinking. He can readily identify both the behaviors he is currently using and those he is neglecting. Once he has acquired adequate skill in using the CLAIM system, he can monitor his classroom behavior without the necessity of supervisory assistance.

The CLAIM system helps the teacher to become conscious of different models of classroom interaction and provides a means of making behavior more explicit for study. When these patterns of interaction are made explicit, their differences become apparent and clearly distinguishable. When they are thus delineated, they can be identified; judgments can then be made about their appropriateness for a given purpose or objective in the classroom.

REFERENCES

1. Allen, D. W. "A New Design for Teacher Education: The Teacher Intern Program at Stanford University." *The*

Journal of Teacher Education 17: 296–300; Fall 1966.

2. Amidon, E. J., and Flanders, N. A. *The Role of the Teacher in the Classroom.* Minneapolis, Minn.: Amidon and Associates, 1963.

3. Amidon, E. J., and Hough, J. B., editors. *Interaction Analysis: Theory, Research and Application.* Reading, Mass. Addison-Wesley, 1967.

4. Amidon, E. J., and Hunter, E. "Interaction Analysis: Recent Developments." *Interaction Analysis: Theory, Research and Application.* (Edited by E. J. Amidon and J. B. Hough.) Reading, Mass.: Addison-Wesley, 1967. pp. 388–92.

5. ———. "Verbal Interaction in the Classroom: The Verbal Interaction Category System." *Interaction Analysis: Theory, Research and Application.* (Edited by E. J. Amidon and J. B. Hough.) Reading, Mass.: Addison-Wesley, 1967. pp. 141–49.

6. Bellack, A. A., and others. *The Language of the Classroom: Meanings Communicated in High School Teaching.* Part Two. U.S. Department of Health, Education, and Welfare, Office of Education, Cooperative Research Project No. 2023. New York: Teachers College, Columbia University, 1965.

7. Biddle, B. J. "Methods and Concepts in Classroom Research." *Review of Educational Research* 37: 337–57; June 1967.

8. Bloom, B. S., editor. *Taxonomy of Educational Objectives: The Classification of Educational Goals.* Handbook 1—*Cognitive Domain.* New York: Longmans, 1956.

9. Carner, R. L. "Levels of Questioning." *Education* 83: 546–50; May 1963.

10. Clements, R. D. "Art Student-Teacher Questioning." *Studies in Art Education* 6: 14–19; Autumn 1964.

11. Eisner, E. W. "Critical Thinking: Some Cognitive Components." *Teachers College Record* 66: 624–34; April 1965.

12. Flanders, N. A. "Interaction Models of Critical Teaching Behaviors." *Interaction Analysis: Theory, Research and Application.* (Edited by E. J. Amidon and J. B. Hough.) Reading, Mass.: Addison-Wesley, 1967. pp. 360–74.

13. Furst, N. "The Effects of Training in Interaction Analysis on the Behavior of Student Teachers in Secondary Schools." *Interaction Analysis: Theory, Research and Application.* (Edited by E. J. Amidon and J. B. Hough.) Reading, Mass.: Addison-Wesley, 1967. pp. 315–28.

14. Gallagher, J. J., and Aschner, M. J. "A Preliminary Report: Analysis of Classroom Interaction." *Merrill-Palmer Quarterly* 9: 183–94; 1963.

15. Guilford, J. P. "Three Faces of Intellect." *American Psychologist* 14: 469–79; 1959.

16. Hough, J. B., and Ober, R. "The Effect of Training in Interaction Analysis on the Verbal Teaching Behavior of Pre-service Teachers." *Interaction Analysis: Theory, Research and Application.* (Edited by E. J. Amidon and J. B. Hough.) Reading, Mass.: Addison-Wesley, 1967. pp. 329–45.

17. Minnis, D. L., and Shrable, K. *Cognitive Levels Analysis Training Manual.* Davis: University of California, 1968. (Mimeographed)

18. Moskowitz, G. "The Attitudes and Teaching Patterns of Cooperating Teachers and Student Teachers Trained in Interaction Analysis." *Interaction Analysis: Theory, Research and Application.* (Edited by E. J. Amidon and J. B. Hough.) Reading, Mass.: Addison-Wesley, 1967. pp. 271–82.

19. Simon, A., and Boyer, E. G., editors. *Mirrors for Behavior: An Anthology of Classroom Observation Instruments.* Philadelphia, Pa.: Research for Better Schools, 1967.

20. Taba, H., and Elzey, F. F. "Teaching Strategies and Thought Processes." *Teachers College Record* 65: 524–34; March 1964.

The Use of Questions in Teaching

Meredith D. Gall[1]

EDITORS' QUESTIONS:

1. Discuss the findings of research concerning the use of questions in teaching. Show how you can utilize the data furnished by research for improving your own questioning technique.

2. Identify areas in questioning which need further investigation, the results of which would assist classroom teachers in refining their skills in questioning.

3. Discuss the effects of teachers' questions on student behavior. Of what value is this knowledge to you as a classroom teacher?

4. Evaluate the programs for changing teachers' questioning behavior mentioned in this article. Compare these programs with some other programs that you know. If you note limitations in these programs, suggest ways of alleviating such weaknesses.

Meredith D. Gall, "The Use of Questions in Teaching," *Review of Educational Research,* XL, No. 5 (December 1970), 707–721. Copyright by American Educational Research Association, Washington, D.C. Used by permission.

It is a truism for educators that questions play an important role in teaching. Aschner (1961), for example, called the teacher "a professional question maker" and claimed that the asking of questions is "one of the basic ways by which the teacher stimulates student thinking and learning." Also, asking questions is one of the 10 major dimensions for studying teachers' behavior in the widely used System for Interaction Analysis (Flanders, 1970).

Certainly teachers ask many questions during an average school day. A half-century ago, Stevens (1912) estimated that four-fifths of school time was occupied with question-and-answer recitations. Stevens found that a sample of high-school teachers asked a mean number of 395 questions per day. High frequencies of question use by teachers were also found in recent investigations: 10 primary-grade teachers asked an average of 348 questions each during a school day (Floyd, 1960); 12 elementary-school teachers asked an average of 180 questions each in a science lesson (Moyer, 1965); and 14 fifth-grade teachers asked an average of 64 questions each in a 30-minute social studies lesson (Schreiber, 1967). Furthermore, students are exposed to many questions in their textbooks and on examinations.

Granting the importance of questions in teaching, researchers still do not know much about them. What educational objectives can questions help students to achieve? What are the criteria of an effective question and how can effective questions be identified? How can teacher's question-framing skills be improved? Until researchers find answers to questions such as these, hopes

[1] The author wishes to thank Dr. Walter R. Borg for his helpful suggestions and criticism during the writing of this paper.

for a viable behavioral technology of teaching will remain unrealized. The purpose of this paper is to define the present state of research knowledge in this area and to suggest some contributions which can be made by researchers who are interested in improving the quality of classroom teaching. Although textbook and examination questions undoubtedly make a contribution to the learning process, I will limit my review for the most part to studies of spoken questions which occur during regular classroom teaching, particularly classroom discussions.

The Classification of Questions by Type

Many researchers have attempted to describe the types of question asked by teachers. To quantify their descriptions, some have found it helpful to develop sets of categories into which teachers' questions can be classified. At least 11 classification systems have been proposed in recent years (Adams, 1964; Aschner, 1961; Bloom, 1956; Carner, 1963; Clements, 1964; Gallagher, 1965; Guszak, 1967; Moyer, 1965; Pate & Bremer, 1967; Sanders, 1966; Schreiber, 1967).

Several systems, such as Bloom's, Gallagher's, and Carner's, consist of a limited number of general categories which can be used to classify questions irrespective of context. This feature enables the researcher to investigate issues such as the different types of question emphasized in various school curricula (Pfeiffer & Davis, 1965) or in traditional or new curricula (Sloan & Pate, 1966). However, these systems are of limited utility if the researcher is interested in more detailed descriptions of questions asked in a specific context.

For detailed descriptions a classification system developed for a specific curriculum is preferable. One such system (Clements, 1964) was designed to classify the questions asked by art teachers as they talked with students about their artwork. For example, the "suggestion-order" category includes questions such as: "Why don't you make the hands larger?"; "Why not put some red over here?"; "Why don't you use freer lines?" This type of question, which occurs frequently in art classes, is not adequately described by any of the categories in the more general systems.

Guszak's Reading-Comprehension Question-Response Inventory is a specific classification system designed for the analysis of question that teachers ask elementary school reading groups. The specificity of the categories is typified by the "recognition question" category, which includes questions requiring students to locate information from the reading context (e.g., "Find what Little Red Ridinghood says to the wolf.") In Schreiber's system for classifying social science questions, there are also a number of fairly curriculum-specific categories, such as Use of Globes (e.g., "Will you find Greenland on the globe?") and Stating of Moral Judgments (e.g., "Do you think it is right to have censorship of the news?").

Most of the question-classification systems are composed almost entirely of categories based on the type of cognitive process required to answer the question. For example, in Bloom's *Taxonomy,* the question "What is your opinion of our present stance on the Vietnam War?" is classified an Evaluation question because it requires evaluative thinking, whereas "What assumptions does the author make in criticizing New Deal politics?" is classified an Analysis question because it requires that students engage in analytic thinking. The categories of representative question-classification systems are shown in Table 1. I have organized the categories to show similarities between the

Table 1

Representative Question-Classification System

Author	Classification				
	Recall	Analytic thinking	Creative thinking	Evaluative thinking	Other
Adams (1964)	Memory	Ratiocinative (logical reasoning)	—	Evaluative	Associative, clarifying, neutral
Aschner (1961)	Remembering	Reasoning	Creative thinking	Evaluating	—
Bloom (1956)[a]	Knowledge	Analysis	Synthesis	Evaluation	Comprehension, application
Carner (1963)	Concrete	Abstract	Creative	—	—
Clements (1964)	Past experience, process recall	—	Planning	Product judgment	Present experience, rule, opening, identification, suggestion, order, acceptance
Guszak (1967)	Recognition, recall	Explanation	Conjecture	Evaluation	Translation
Pate & Bremer (1967)	Simple recall of one item, recall-choice of multiple items	Principle involved, concept analysis	Divergence	—	Determination of skills abilities (demonstrate), skills demonstration(verbal), example-singular, examples-multiple
Schreiber (1967)	Recall of facts, arranging facts in sequential order	Making comparisons, identifying supporting facts, drawing conclusions	Speculating on outcomes	Identifying main part & important parts, stating moral judgment, stating judgment based on personal experience, evaluating quality of source material, evaluating adequacy of data	Describing situations, defining & clarifying information, using globes, using maps, uncovering information & raising questions for study

[a]In the complete system, each category is divided into sub-categories.

systems. It appears that Bloom's *Taxonomy* best represents the commonalities that exist among the systems.

A weakness of the cognitive-process approach to question classification is that these processes are inferential constructs. Therefore, they cannot be observed directly. Bloom (1956) acknowledged this difficulty in his statement that it is not always possible to know whether a student answered a particular question by using a high-level cognitive process, such as analysis or synthesis, or by using the relatively low-level process of knowledge recall. The question, "What are some similarities between the Greek and American forms of democracy?" probably stimulates critical thinking in some students. However, this question may only elicit rote recall if students answer by recalling similarities they have read in a textbook.

To deal with this problem, the researcher can control the lesson material on which the teacher bases his questions. For example, he might have a sample of teachers give the same reading assignment to their students. Preferably the assignment would be on a subject new to the students. The teachers would then ask discussion questions on this assignment and the questions could be classified as recall or higher-cognitive depending on whether the answer was given directly in the assignment. Furthermore, if the researcher is studying differences between teachers in question-asking skill or is studying improvement in this skill as a result of a training program, the use of a constant lesson topic makes it possible to attribute variance in question-asking to the teachers rather than to differences in the lessons. With two exceptions (Gall, Dunning, Galassi & Banks, 1970; Hunkins, 1966, 1967), the studies reviewed here did not make use of this important control technique.

It seems evident that existing taxonomies classify questions which cover only a few important educational objectives. These are the types of questions which teachers ask to test students' recall of information and to develop their critical thinking processes. Yet there are several other worthwhile question types which are treated scantily, if at all, in existing taxonomies: (*a*) questions which cue students to improve on an initally weak response to a question ("Can you tell me a little more?"; "What do you mean by that?"); (*b*) questions which create a discussion atmosphere ("Billy, do you agree with Sue's position?"); (*c*) questions which stimulate students' sense of curiosity and inquiry ("What would you like to know about this manuscript?"; "How would you propose to find an answer to this question?"); and (*d*) questions which guide students' learning of a problem-solving, behavioral or affective skill ("What do you think we do next to solve this problem?"; "Mark, what is your response to these drawings?").

Another limitation of existing classification systems is that they were designed primarily to investigate the types of question which teachers actually use in the classroom, not the types of question which teachers should use. Researchers have shown relatively little interest in identifying effective types of questions. There have been only a scattering of opinion articles, and these have emphasized the formal characteristics of a "good question, e.g., clarity of phrasing, rather than the educational purposes which good questions serve.

Much of what has been learned about the merits and pitfalls of descriptive systems should provide guidance for identifying effective question types. For example, it would seem preferable to identify questions which are effective for a specific curriculum and classroom setting rather than to search for general question types. Research might be done to identify effective question types in mathematics tutoring, introducing concepts in the science curriculum, discussing controversial issues, role playing in social studies, etc. These specific question types, as compared to the categories of a general classification system such as Bloom's *Taxonomy,* would have two advantages: they would provide a more precise and possibly clearer description of what constitutes effective questioning in a particular teaching situation; and they would be more useful than general question types in training teachers to improve their classroom instruction.

Prior to defining effective types of question, the researcher needs to identify valued educational objectives in a specific setting. Once objectives are identified, the task of constructing questions which enable the student to reach each objective can be started. It would help in this task if groups of expert teachers and curriculum developers composed questions for each objective and then selected the most effective questions. In this type of research, effective question types would be defined in terms of whether or not they enabled the student to achieve desired educational objectives.

Another task for the researcher is to consider whether there are effective question sequences. Should teachers start a discussion by asking recall questions to test students' knowledge of facts and then ask higher-cognitive questions that require manipulation of these facts? This was the approach taken by Taba (1964, 1966), who attempted to identify questioning strategies that stimulate students to reflect on curriculum materials on an increasingly abstract level. In Shaver's model of Socratic teaching (1964), another type of question sequence was proposed: the teacher asks the student for a statement of his position on an issue, then asks appropriate follow-up questions to probe the student's stated position.

Further research on teachers' "follow-up" questions is needed. Consider a typical situation which occurs in classroom discussions. The teacher asks a question such as, "What do you think can be done to solve the problem of air pollution?"; this would be classified as a higher-cognitive question in most question-classification systems. A student answers, "Make sure all cars and trucks have smog control devices." Did the student really have to think to answer this question? He may have considered the problem in depth and decided that smog control is the best solution. However, it is more likely that the student is repeating a solution he has heard or read about. To really test the student's ability to think about the problem and to stimulate the development of his thinking processes, the teacher should probably ask follow-up questions such as, "How would that solve the problem?"; "Isn't that being done already?"; "Is that a better solution than converting to electric or steam-powered cars?" We know very little about teachers' use of such questions in discussions. In fact, most question-classification systems do not take them into account since the systems are not concerned with question sequence. However, I suggest the hypothesis that follow-up questioning of the student's initial response has substantial impact on student learning in classroom teaching situations.

Studies of Teachers' Questioning Practices

Educators generally agree that teachers should emphasize the development of students' skill in critical thinking rather than in learning and recalling facts (Aschner, 1961;

Carner, 1963; Hunkins, 1966). Yet research spanning more than a half-century indicates that teachers' questions have emphasized facts.

Probably the first serious study of this issue was done by Stevens (1912). She found that, for a sample of high-school classes varying in grade level and subject area, two-thirds of the teachers' questions required direct recall of textbook information. Two decades later, Haynes (1935) found that 77% of teachers' questions in sixth-grade history classes called for factual answers; only 17% were judged to require students to think. In Corey's study (1940), three judges classified all questions asked by teachers in a one-week period in a laboratory high school. The judges classified 71% of the questions as factual and 29% as those which required a thoughtful answer.

Studies conducted in the last several years indicated that teachers' questioning practices are essentially unchanged. Floyd (1960) classified the questions of a sample of 40 "best" teachers in elementary classrooms. Specific facts were called for in 42% of the questions. I summed Floyd's percentages of questions in categories which appear to have required thoughtful responses from students; these accounted for about 20% of the questions asked. In two other studies conducted at the elementary-school level (Guszak, 1967; Schreiber, 1967), similar percentages of fact and thought questions were asked. At the high-school level, Gallagher (1965) and Davis and Tinsley (1967) classified the questions asked by teachers of gifted students and by student teachers. More than half of the questions asked by both groups were judged to test students' recall of facts.

The findings in studies on teachers' questioning practices are fairly consistent (though in some instances there are meth-

odological flaws such as failure to report inter-rater reliability in classification of questions and lack of clarity in the definition of question categories). It is reasonable to conclude that in a half-century there has been no essential change in the types of question which teachers emphasize in the classroom. About 60% of teachers' questions require students to recall facts; about 20% require students to think; and the remaining 20% are procedural.

Why has the primary objective of American education, as revealed by an analysis of teachers' questions, been the learning and recall of facts? One explanation is that although higher-cognitive objectives are valued in American education, teachers need to ask many fact questions to bring out the data which students require to answer thought questions. Even though this explanation has merit, it can be argued that instruction in facts is best accomplished by techniques (such as programmed instruction) that do not require teacher intervention. The teacher's time is better spent in developing students' thinking and communication skills during discussions after the students have demonstrated an acceptable level of knowledge on a written test.

Another explanation of the research findings is that although educators have for a long time advocated the pursuit of objectives such as critical thinking and problem solving, only recently were these objectives incorporated systematically into new curricula. The relationship between curriculum change and teachers' questioning practices is illustrated in a recent study comparing teachers in the School Mathematics Study Group (SMSG) with teachers in a traditional mathematics program (Sloan & Pate, 1966). The researchers hypothesized that the two groups would differ in their patterns of questioning since the SMSG program emphasizes the objectives of inquiry and discovery. They found that, compared to the traditional math teachers, the "new math" teachers asked significantly fewer recall questions and significantly more comprehension and analysis questions.

Sloan and Pate's study suggested the interesting hypothesis that teachers' use of fact and higher-cognitive questions is dependent on the type of curriculum materials available to them. This hypothesis could be easily tested by asking teachers to lead discussions based on different lesson topics assigned to students: for example, a poem, a traditional textbook chapter, a newspaper editorial, a film. On the basis of my own preliminary research findings, I hypothesize that teachers ask more higher-cognitive questions about primary sources, e.g., poems and newspaper editorials, than about secondary sources (most school textbooks).

Still another reason why teachers have emphasized fact questions over a half-century, as indicated in research findings, is the lack of effective teacher training programs. In their study of questions in mathematics teaching, Sloan and Pate (1966, p. 166) observed:

> Although the School Mathematics Study Group teachers' use of questions evidenced their awareness of the processes of inquiry and discovery, these processes had not been fully implemented, as shown by the fact that these teachers used so few synthesis and opinion questions that the pupils were denied the opportunity to develop inferences from available evidence.

Therefore, Sloan and Pate advocated training teachers in effective questioning practices so the objectives of the "new math" can be realized. The issue of teacher training in questioning skills is discussed later in this paper.

Effect of Teachers' Questions on Student Behavior

Teachers' questions are of little value unless they have an impact on student behavior. Yet very few researchers have explored the relationship between teachers' questions and student outcomes.

The most important work in this area to date is the research by Hunkins (1967, 1968). The purpose of his research was to determine whether the variable of question type bears any relationship to student achievement. Two experimental groups of sixth-grade students worked daily for a month on sets of questions which were keyed to a social studies text. In one group the questions stressed knowledge; in the other, analysis and evaluation questions were stressed. Question types were defined in terms of Bloom's *Taxonomy*. Hunkins found that the analysis-evaluation group earned a significantly higher score on a specially constructed post-training test than did students who answered questions that stressed knowledge. The performance of the two groups was also compared on the six parts of the test which corresponded to the six main types of question in Bloom's *Taxonomy:* the analysis-evaluation group of students did not differ from the comparison group in achievement on subtests containing knowledge, comprehension, analysis, and synthesis questions; they scored significantly higher on the subtests containing application and evaluation questions.

Before the implications of these findings are considered, some possible limitations of Hunkin's research design should be noted. First, whereas the daily sets of questions required students to write out their answers, the students responded to multiple-choice questions on the post-training test. Therefore, one may question whether the achievement test provided an adequate comparison of the effectiveness of the two experimental conditions. Second, it seems a distortion of Bloom's Taxonomy to put the question types into a multiple-choice format since some types, such as evaluation questions, do not really have a "correct" answer. In other words, practice in answering certain types of questions may affect the quality of students' responses rather than their correctness. Third, students monitored their own responses using answer sheets provided with the daily sets of questions. Teacher monitoring of at least some of the student's responses might have enhanced the differences found between the experimental conditions.

In view of these methodological limitations, the Hunkins' findings should be viewed as only suggestive. It seems to be a reasonable hypothesis for further investigation, however, that if a group of students is exposed to certain types of question and if their responses are monitored to improve their quality (rather than correctness), then they will be able to answer similar types of question better than a group of students who have not had this exposure.

In testing this hypothesis, the researcher is confronted with the problem of defining qualitative differences in student responses. This is one of the important unsolved problems in the study of teachers' questioning practices. Although much is known about higher-cognitive questions and their classification, little is known about what constitutes good answers to these questions. It seems reasonable to state, though, that responses to fact questions can be evaluated by the simple criterion of correctness, but responses to higher-cognitive questions require several criteria to measure their qual-ity. On the basis of exploratory work on the problem I suggest these criteria as possibilities: (a) complexity of the response; (b) use of data to justify or defend the response; (c) plausibility of the response; (d) originality of the response; (e) clarity of the phrasing; and (f) the extent to which the response is directed at the question actually asked. It would seem reasonable to expect at least a moderate correlation between length of the response and its quality, particularly as judged by criteria (a) and (b). Dealing with a related problem, Corey and Fahey (1940) obtained a correlation of +.50 between judges' ratings of the "mental complexity" of student questions and number of words in the question.

Students' Questions

Some educators contend that our attention should be focused on questions asked by students rather than on teachers' questions (Carner, 1963; Wellington & Wellington, 1962). Certainly, it seems a worthwhile educational objective to increase the frequency and quality of students' questions in the context of classroom interaction. However, research findings consistently show that students have only a very limited opportunity to raise questions.

Houston (1938) observed 11 junior-high-school classes and found that an average of less than one question per class period was student-initiated. Corey (1940) recorded all talk in six junior-high and high-school classrooms for a period of one week. The ratio of student questions to total questions varied considerably between classes: in two English classes, students accounted for 1% of the questions asked; seventh-grade and ninth-grade science students asked 17% and 11% of the questions respectively. At the primary grade level, Floyd (1960) found that student questions were 3.75%, 5.14%, and 3.64% of the total number of questions asked during a taped class session for samples of first- second- and third-grade classrooms respectively. A low incidence of student questions was also reported for high-school English classes (Johns, 1968) and for social studies classes at the elementary-school (Dodl, 1966) and senior-high-school levels (Bellack, Kliebard, Hyman & Smith, Jr., 1966).

In investigating student questions in the classroom, researchers need to undertake several important tasks. First, although it would be of interest to investigate the types of question students ask (see Gatto, 1928), the more important task is to identify the types of question which students should be encouraged to ask. For example, when introducing a new topic for study, teachers should probably ask students what they want to know about it. Finley (1921) found that elementary-school students had an average of about five questions each to ask when presented with an unfamiliar animal in class. Another classroom situation in which student questions should probably be elicited occurs when a teacher has explained a new subject. Students should be queried about possible lack of understanding. In fact, one might offer the hypothesis that students encouraged to ask questions in this type of situation will learn more than a group of students deprived of this opportunity.

Another key area for educational innovation is the training of students in question-asking skills. For example, what types of question should students ask themselves when they read a poem, a social studies textbook, or a science lesson? It seems that the shaping of student questioning skills has been a neglected feature of classroom learning. There has been increasing attention given to this problem since inquiry and discovery methods of teaching became prominent, but as Cronbach (1966) and others pointed out, research and training in these methods remain limited by the failure to adequately operationalize the concept. Perhaps the approach of focusing on specific questioning skills in various classroom situations, as I did above, would provide the clarity needed to operationalize the inquiry method.

Programs to Change Teachers' Questioning Behavior

I have shown that the importance of questioning skills in teaching has been recognized by educators for more than a half-century. Yet relatively few programs have been implemented for the specific purpose of improving teachers' questioning practices. This does not mean that the need for such programs has been ignored. More than 30 years ago, Houston (1938) developed an inservice education program for the purpose of changing teachers' questioning practices. Among the techniques Houston used to effect behavioral change were group conferences, stenographic reports of each teacher's lessons, self-analysis, and supervisory evaluation. Examination of quantitative data yielded by pre- and post-training evaluations of 11 teachers indicated that most of the teachers were able to effect substantial changes in specific aspects of their questioning behavior. As a group the teachers increased the percentage of questions relevent to the purpose of the lesson from 41.6% to 67.6%, the percentage of student participation from 40.4% to 56.1%, and the percentage of questions requiring students to manipulate facts from 10% to 18%. There was also a reduction in a number of bothersome teaching habits such as repetition of one's questions (from 4.8 occurrences to none), repetition of students' answers (from 5.5 to .6 occurrences), answering of one's own questions (from 3.5 to .3 occurrences), and interruption of student responses (from 10.3 to 1.5 occurrences).

Recently a program was developed at the Far West Laboratory for Educational Research and Development (Borg, Kelley, Langer & Gall, 1970) to help teachers achieve similar changes in their questioning behavior. Called a minicourse, it is a self-contained, inservice training package requiring about 15 hours to complete. The minicourse relies on techniques such as modeling, self-feedback, and microteaching (Allen & Ryan, 1969) to effect behavioral change. In a field test with 48 elementary-school teachers, the minicourse produced many highly significant changes in teachers' questioning behavior, as determined by comparisons of pre- and post-course video-tapes of 20-minute classroom discussions: increase in frequency of redirection questions (questions designed to have a number of students respond to one student's original question) from 26.7 to 40.9; increase in percentage of thought questions from 37.3% to 52.0%; and increase in frequency of probing questions (questions which require students to improve or elaborate on their original response) from 8.3 to 13.9. As in Houston's program (1938), there was also a reduction in frequency of poor questioning habits: repetition of one's questions (from 13.7 to 4.7 occurrences); repetition of students' answers (from 30.7 to 4.4 occurrences); and answering of one's own questions (from 4.6 to .7 occurrences). The Far West Laboratory now supports the development of about 20 additional minicourses to deal with other types of classroom teaching such as tutoring, role-playing, lecturing, and the inquiry method. Many of these courses include training in questioning skills that are appropriate to the particular teaching-learning context.

Other programs for improving teachers' questioning practices have been developed, though these have generally had more limited objectives than the programs of Houston (1938) and Borg (1970). Shaver and Oliver (1964) trained teachers in the use of questioning methods appropriate to discussion of controversial issues in the social studies. Suchman (1958) identified inquiry skills for science classes; training teachers in their use resulted in a significant increase in the number of questions asked by students. In social studies, Taba (1966) and her co-workers (1964) developed a system of teacher training centered around questioning strategies. These questioning strategies were viewed as techniques which teachers could use to develop their students' abilities in forming concepts, explaining cause-and-effect relationships, and exploring implications.

Discussion

This survey of research on questions over a fifty-year period reveals that the main trend has been the development of techniques to describe questions used by teachers in classroom practice. There is now considerable data regarding the incidence of teachers' questions and the relative frequencies with which various types of questions are asked. I expect that researchers will now turn their attention more toward the improvement of teachers' questioning practices.

Efforts to improve existing practices will probably move in several directions. First, whereas in the past researchers have developed taxonomies to describe questions which teachers ask, they need now to develop taxonomies based on types of question which teachers *should* ask. This means that increasing attention must be paid to the definition of desirable educational objectives and to the identification of questions and question sequences which will enable students to achieve these objectives. It was pointed out above that there are certain advantages to developing systems of question types which are curriculum- and situation-specific. The chief advantage is that teacher training in questioning methods is likely to be facilitated if specific rather than general types of question are learned.

It is important that teachers' questions should not be viewed as an end in themselves. They are a means to an end—producing desired changes in student behavior. Therefore, researchers should give high priority to the tasks of identifying what these desired changes are and of determining whether new questioning strategies have the impact on student behavior which is claimed for them. Hunkins's investigation (1967, 1968), discussed above, may serve as the prototype for future research in this area. In line with the concern with student behavior, researchers should develop more programs directed at the shaping of student skills in questioning.

I would like to stress again the need for effective teacher training programs to implement desired questioning strategies in the classrooms. Sloan and Pate (1966), for example, called for strong inservice training programs in the questioning skills necessary for teaching the "new mathematics" (SMSG) curriculum. If these programs are to succeed, they need to incorporate two important features. First, teacher training should involve not only study of questioning strategies, but also guided practice in their use. As the findings of Borg and his colleagues (1970) seem to indicate, microteaching is an effective technique for providing this practice. Second, teachers cannot be expected to learn the inquiry method or any new pedagogy if it is presented to them in vague, general, undefined terms; they can be expected to learn new methods if the methods are presented, at least in part, as sets of specific types of questions asked in specific classroom situations.

In the last analysis, the value of focusing on teachers' questions is that they are the basic unit underlying most methods of classroom teaching. If this is true, then their continued study deserves the strong support of researchers.

REFERENCES

Adams, T. H. *The Development of a Method for Analysis of Questions Asked by Teachers in Classroom Discussion.* (Doctoral dissertation, Rutgers University) Ann Arbor, Mich.: University Microfilms, 1964. No. 64-2809.

Allen, D., & Ryan, K. *Microteaching.* Reading, Mass.: Addison-Wesley, 1969.

Aschner, M. J. "Asking Questions to Trigger Thinking," *NEA Journal,* 1961, 50, 44–46.

Bellack, A. A., Kliebard, H. M., Hyman, R. T., & Smith, F. L., Jr. *The Language of the Classroom.* New York: Teachers College Press, Columbia University, 1966.

Bloom, B. S., ed. *Taxonomy of Educational Objectives: Handbook I: Cognitive Domain.* New York: David McKay, 1956.

Borg, W. R., Kelley, M. L., Langer, P., & Gall, M. *The Minicourse: A Microteaching Approach to Teacher Education.* Beverly Hills, Calif.: Macmillan Educational Services, 1970.

Carner, R. L. "Levels of Questioning," *Education,* 1963, 83, 546–550.

Clements, R. D. "Art Student-teacher Questioning," *Studies in Art Education,* 1964, 6, 14–19.

Corey, S. M. "The Teachers Out-Talk the Pupils." *The School Review,* 1940, 48, 745–752.

Corey, S. M., & Fahey, G. L. "Inferring Type of Pupil Mental Activity from Classroom Questions Asked," *Journal of Education Psychology,* 1940, 31, 94–102.

Cronbach, L. J. "The Logic of Experiments on Discovery," In L. S. Shulman and E. R. Keislar, eds. *Learning by Discovery: A Critical Appraisal.* Chicago: Rand McNally, 1966.

Davis, O. L., & Tinsley, D. C. "Cognitive Objectives Revealed by Classroom Questions Asked by Social Studies Student Teachers," *Peabody Journal of Education,* 1967, 45, 21–26.

Dodl, N. R. *Pupil Questioning Behavior in the Context of Classroom Interaction.* (Doctoral dissertation, Stanford University) Ann Arbor, Mich.: University Microfilms, 1966. No. 66-2512.

Finley, C. "Some Studies of Children's Interests in Science Materials," *School Science and Mathematics,* 1921, 21, 1–24.

Flanders, N. A. *Analyzing Teaching Behavior.* Reading, Mass.: Addison-Wesley, 1970.

Floyd, W. D. *An Analysis of the Oral Questioning Activity in Selected Colorado Primary Classrooms.* (Doctoral dissertation, Colorado State College) Ann Arbor, Mich.: University Microfilms, 1960. No. 60-6253.

Gall, M. D., Dunning, B., Galassi, J., & Banks, H. "The Relative Effectiveness of Perceptual versus Symbolic Modeling in a Teacher Training Program on Higher-cognitive Questioning." Unpublished manuscript, Far West Laboratory for Educational Research and Development, Berkeley, California, 1970.

Gallagher, J. J. "Expressive Thought by Gifted Children in the Classroom," *Elementary English,* 1965, 42, 559–568.

Gatto, F. N. "Pupils' Questions: Their Nature and Their Relationship to the Study Process." Unpublished doctoral dissertation, University of Pittsburgh, 1928.

Guszak, F. J. "Teacher Questioning and Reading," *The Reading Teacher,* 1967, 21, 227–234.

Haynes, H. C. "The Relation of Teacher Intelligence, Teacher Experience, and Type of School to Types of Questions." Unpublished doctoral dissertation, George Peabody College for Teachers, 1935.

Houston, V. M. "Improving the Quality of Classroom Questions and Questioning," *Educational Administration and Supervision,* 1938, 24, 17–28.

Hunkins, F. P. "Using Questions to Foster Pupils Thinking," *Education,* 1966, 87, 83–87.

Hunkins, F. P. "The Influence of Analysis and Evaluation Questions on Achievement in Sixth Grade Social Studies." Paper presented at the annual meeting of the American Educational Research Association, New York, 1967.

Hunkins, F. P. "The Effects of Analysis and Evaluation Questions on Various Levels of Achievement." Paper presented at the annual meeting of the American Educational Research Association, Chicago, 1968.

Johns, J. P. "The Relationship Between Teacher Behaviors and the Incidence of Thought-provoking Questions by Students in Secondary Schools." *The Journal of Educational Research,* 1968, 62, 117–122.

Moyer, J. R. *An Exploratory Study of Questioning in the Instructional Processes in Selected Elementary Schools.* (Doctoral dissertation, Columbia University) Ann Arbor, Mich.: University Microfilms, 1966. No. 66-2661.

Pate, R. T., & Bremer, N. H. "Guiding Learning Through Skillful Questioning," *Elementary School Journal,* 1967, 67, 417–422.

Pfeiffer, L., & Davis, O. L. "Teacher-made Examinations: What Kind of Thinking do They Demand?" *NASSP Bulletin,* 1965, 49, 1–10.

Sanders, N. M. *Classroom Questions: What Kinds?* New York: Harper & Row, 1966.

Schreiber, J. E. *Teachers' Question-asking Techniques in Social Studies.* (Doctoral dissertation, University of Iowa) Ann Arbor, Mich.: University Microfilms, 1967. No. 67-9099.

Shaver, J. P. "Ability of Teachers to Conform to Two Styles of Teaching," *Journal of Experimental Education,* 1964, 32, 259–267.

Shaver, J. P., & Oliver, D. W. "Teaching Students to Analyze Public Controversy: A Curriculum Project Report." *Social Education,* 1964, 28, 191–194.

Sloan, F. A., & Pate, R. T. "Teacher-pupil Interaction in Two Approaches to Mathematics," *The Elementary School Journal,* 1966, 67, 161–167.

Stevens, R. "The Question as a Measure of Efficiency in Instruction: A Critical Study of Classroom Practice," *Teachers College Contributions to Education,* 1912, No. 48.

Suchman, J. R. *The Elementary School Training Program in Scientific Inquiry.* United States Office of Education Cooperative Research Project No. 216. Urbana: University of Illinois, 1958.

Taba, H. *Teaching Strategies and Cognitive Function in Elementary School Children.* United States Office of Education Cooperative Research Project No. 2404. San Francisco: San Francisco State College, 1966.

Taba, H., Levine, S., & Elzey, F. F. *Thinking in Elementary School Children.* United States Office of Education Cooperative Research Project No. 1574. San Francisco: San Francisco State College, 1964.

Wellington, J., & Wellington, B. "What Is a Question?" *The Clearing House,* 1962, 36, 471–472.

Recommended Readings: Promoting Learning through Questioning Techniques

Amidon, E. J. and Hough, J. B. eds. *Interaction Analysis: Theory, Research, and Application.* Reading, Massachusetts: Addison-Wesley, 1967.

Aschner, M. J. "Asking Questions to Trigger Thinking," *National Education Association Journal* 50 (1961):44–46.

Carner, R. L. "Levels of Questioning," *Education* 83 (1963):546–550.

Corey, S. M. and Fahey, G. L. "Inferring Type of Pupil Mental Activity from Classroom Questions Asked," *Journal of Educational Psychology* 31 (1940):94–102.

Dodl, N. R. "Pupil Questioning Behavior in the Context of Classroom Interaction," (Doctoral dissertation, Stanford University) Ann Arbor, Michigan: University Microfilms, No. 66-2512, 1966.

Eisner, E. W. "Critical Thinking: Some Cognitive Components," *Teachers College Record* 66 (1965):624–634.

Flanders, Ned A. *Interaction Analysis in the Classroom: A Manual for Observers.* Rev. ed. University of Michigan: Ann Arbor, 1966.

Gallagher, J. J. and Aschner, M. J. "A Preliminary Report: Analysis of Classroom Interaction," *Merrill-Palmer Quarterly* 9 (1963):183–194.

Guzak, Frank J. "Teacher's Questions and Reading," *The Reading Teacher* 21 (1967):227–234.

Houston, V. M. "Improving the Quality of Classroom Questions and Questioning," *Educational Administration and Supervision* 24 (1938):17–28.

Loughlin, R. L. "On Questioning," *The Educational Forum* 25 (1961):481–482.

Melnik, Amelia "Questions: An Instructional Diagnostic Tool," *Journal of Reading* 11 (1968):509–512.

Moyer, J. R. *An Exploratory Study of Questioning in the Instructional Processes in Selected Elementary Schools.* (Doctoral dissertation, Columbia University) Ann Arbor, Michigan: University Microfilms, 1966, No. 66-2661.

Pfeiffer, L. and Davis, O. L. "Teacher-made Examinations: What Kind of Thinking do they Demand?" *National Association of Secondary School Principals* 49 (1965):1–10.

Sanders, N. M. *Classroom Questions: What Kinds?* New York: Harper & Row, 1966.

Schneyer, J. W. "Class Verbal Interaction," *The Reading Teacher* 23 (1970):369–371.

Stevens, Romiett *The Question as a Measure of Efficiency in Instruction.* New York: Teachers College, Columbia University, 1912.

Taba, Hilda *Teaching Strategies and Cognitive Function in Elementary School Children.* United States Office of Education Cooperative Research Project, No. 2404, San Francisco: San Francisco State College, 1966.

Taba, H. and Elzey, F. F. "Teaching Strategies and Thought Processes," *Teachers College Record* 65 (1964):524–534.

Wellington, J. and Wellington, B. "What is a Question?" *The Clearing House* 36 (1962):471–472.

Promoting Learning Through Motivation and Reinforcement Strategies

It is widely agreed that learning achievement is enhanced through the application of motivational techniques. Usually less fully understood, however, is the fact that certain teacher behaviors may be reinforcing without her knowledge. For example, disruptive conduct may be reinforced by the teacher's immediate expression of anger or even by her acknowledgement of the disturbance. Therefore, a hit or miss approach to reinforcement based upon a dangerously small amount of knowledge concerning the nature of motivation can be disastrous. This section is designed to acquaint students with the essentials of motivational theory and to provide the basis for a reasoned approach to the selection and implementation of reinforcement strategies for motivating learning.

The utilization of the Modified Reward Preference Assessment Procedure (MRPA) as a means of determining the reward preferences of individual pupils is described in detail by Cartwright and Cartwright. They stress the importance of matching motivational strategies with the personal preferences of the individual child as a means of increasing the occurrence of desired behaviors.

A number of ways in which the principles of learning theory can be applied to effect desired changes in pupil behavior are examined by Clarizio and Yelon. The authors indicate that aggressive behavior, withdrawal, overdependency and other maladaptive behaviors may be partially or fully extinguished, and more desirable behaviors strengthened by the application of appropriate techniques for behavior modification. Extinction, positive reinforcement, modeling and punishment are the methods advocated for reinforcing desired behavior and diminishing the frequency of unwanted responses. Though the emphasis of the article is upon the modification of deviant behavior, many of the techniques discussed can be used equally well with children having no serious emotional problems.

Another method of reinforcing desired

behaviors is through the provision of extrinsic rewards. An interesting experiment investigating the applicability of this approach to groups of pupils in a classroom setting is reported by Bushell, Wrobel and Michaelis.

A change of pace is provided by the Coladarci article. In this selection, the negative effects upon learning achievement of the inhibitory self-fulfilling prophecy are examined. It would appear that, within limits, expectations on the part of the teacher and /or the pupil are capable of predetermining levels of pupils' achievement even though the basis of such expectations is entirely faulty. Because of the tremendous influence teachers exert upon the intellectual, moral, social and emotional development of the young, they, especially, need to develop an awareness of this phenomenon. Equipped with an understanding of its potentially debilitating influence, they may be able to prevent its operation, or at least diminish its crippling effects through the implementation of a positive program for the motivation of learning through reinforcement.

The experimental study reported by Madsen, Becker and Thomas indicates the existence of a significant relationship between the kinds of motivational and control techniques used by teachers and the types of behaviors exhibited by students. The authors conclude that teachers can be taught to apply systematic procedures which will enable them to obtain more effective behaviors from their pupils.

The articles and recommended readings in this section are provided for the purpose of preparing the student to:

1. Implement the Modified Reward Preference Assessment Procedure to determine the reward preferences of individual pupils.

2. Recognize examples of self-fulfilling prophecies and take steps to overcome their effects.

3. Discern the importance of timing in the implementation of the motivational strategies and discover ways in which the frequency and timing of rewards may be modified to obtain successively closer approximations of desired behaviors.

4. Devise ways of converting neutral stimuli into effective motivational incentives.

5. Replicate some reinforcement techniques utilized by the authors of the selections and evaluate the results obtained.

6. Develop her own behavioral modification strategies, making sure that they are consistent with the needs and personality structures of individual pupils.

7. Conduct in-class experiments to determine the feasibility and reliability of recommended behavioral-modification techniques.

Determining the Motivational Systems of Individual Children

Carol A. Cartwright
and G. Phillip Cartwright

23

EDITORS' QUESTIONS:

1. Give examples of how the matching of learning incentives with the reward preferences of individual children fosters the attainment of instructional objectives.

2. Explain how previously neutral activities of occurrences can be converted into effective incentives.

3. State the rationale for requiring, in the preparation of a set of reward preference testing cards, that the same sample reward be used to illustrate a particular reward category each time it appears.

4. Make suggestions for implementing the Modified Reward Preference Assessment Procedure (MRPA) in a prekindergarten program. Identify and discuss any special circumstances or difficulties that are likely to be encountered.

5. Once the reward preferences of individual pupils have been ascertained, is it advisable to continue using the same reward over and over for an extended period? Justify your response.

6. How can the frequency and timing of rewards be modified to obtain successively closer approximations of a desired behavior? Give examples which illustrate this process.

Carol A. Cartwright and G. Phillip Cartwright, "Determining the Motivational Systems of Individual Children," *Teaching Exceptional Children,* II (Spring 1970), 143–149. Reprinted with permission of The Council for Exceptional Children and the authors.

The Role of Rewards and Incentives in Learning

Increasing numbers of teachers and psychologists have found that using various rewards and incentives, determined by individual needs, helps to motivate children. This is especially applicable to exceptional children whose needs are even more individualized than usual because of their disabilities. Educators who have experimented with procedures for systematically determining and applying rewards and incentives in classroom situations are enthusiastic about the results they obtain.

A reward is a stimulus which is given to the child after the occurrence of a particular response in a given situation. The reward tends to increase the frequency of the response. The term incentive refers to the expectation that a particular reward will be obtained after behaving in a certain way. For example, when a child is promised a gold star on his paper if he finishes some work, the child's expectation that he will receive the gold star is his incentive. When the gold star is given, and if the star is satisfying, it is the reward.

Carol A. Cartwright is Assistant Professor of Education, and G. Philip Cartwright is Assistant Professor of Special Education and Assistant Director of the Computer-Assisted Instruction Laboratory. They are associated with The Pennsylvania State University, University Park, Pennsylvania.

Stimuli which function as rewards and incentives for a child were, at some point in the child's life, nonmeaningful, or neutral stimuli. Psychologists are in general agreement that previously neutral stimuli become meaningful rewards and incentives as a result of having been continually paired with satisfying stimuli. If it is known that a child likes candy, but is indifferent to adult praise, candy and adult praise can be given together several times as a reward, until eventually the adult approval becomes the satisfying reward and incentive in place of the candy.

Since each child has experienced a unique history of associations between neutral and satisfying stimuli, each child can be expected to attach different degrees of meaning to the rewards which are typically used in classroom situations. One child might be greatly rewarded by public praise, whereas another might despise getting public recognition.

Since the teacher establishes a child's reward expectancies and dispenses rewards, it is very important that he or she have some information about what individual children find satisfying. When a teacher does not know what a child's reward preferences are, any use of rewards will be on a trial-and-error basis. It is not sufficient to assume that most of the children will be motivated equally by the expectation of adult praise. Just as individualized instruction can be expected to result in improved learning, individually determined rewards can be expected to result in improved motivation. Improved motivation, in turn, should lead to an increase in learning and achievement.

An Inventory for Determining Individual Reward Preferences

One systematic way of determining individuals' preferences for rewards is the modified reward preference assessment procedure (MRPA) which is based on a model developed by King and Dunn-Rankin (1965). A complete description of the development and early experimentation with the King and Dunn-Rankin inventory can be found in Cartwright (in press). In order to implement MRPA, three steps should be taken.

Step 1 Choosing Appropriate Rewards

In the MRPA, rewards which teachers are able to apply in the classroom have been categorized into five areas: (a) Adult Approval, (b) Competition, (c) Consumable, (d) Peer Approval, and (e) Independence. The teacher should choose four examples of each reward category which he or she considers appropriate for the children in a given class. See Table 1 for a list of sample rewards for each reward category. The ages, needs, and abilities of the children involved, as well as classroom limitations and procedures should be taken into consideration here. For example, if a teacher does not think the marks "A," "100," "Perfect," or "Excellent" on children's papers will be effective for his or her children, but would prefer to use stars, he or she should use the statement, "Teacher puts a star on your paper," as a sample reward in the Adult Approval category. Similarly, other sample rewards listed in Table 1 could be replaced with rewards which are more appropriate to the children in question.

Handicapped children need special consideration. A visually impaired child will get little meaning from the marks on his paper; statements about receiving verbal praise might be used instead.

Step 2 Preparing Testing Cards and Scoring Sheets

After sample rewards for each of the five categories are chosen, prepare four sets of ten cards which illustrate the sample rewards. The cards can vary in size, depending on the teacher's judgement of what size would be most effective for the group in question. Each card should contain statements and illustrations depicting two sample rewards (See Figure 1). The categories depicted on the front of each card should be written on the back of the card. Categories to be paired on each card within a set and the order in which the ten pairings should be presented are as follows:

1. Adult Approval/Competition
2. Consumable/Peer Approval
3. Independence/Adult Approval
4. Peer Approval/Competition
5. Independence/Consumable
6. Adult Approval/Peer Approval
7. Competition/Independence
8. Consumable/Adult Approval
9. Peer Approval/Independence
10. Competition/Consumable

Table 1

Sample Rewards for the Five Categories of the Reward-Preference Inventory*

Category	Sample Rewards
Adult Approval	Teacher writes "100" on your paper.
	Teacher writes "A" on your paper.
	Teacher writes "perfect" on your paper.
	Teacher writes "excellent" on your paper.
Competition	Be first to finish your work.
	Be the only one that can answer a question.
	Have only your paper shown to the class.
	Have your paper put on the bulletin board.
Consumable	A package of bubble gum.
	A candy bar.
	An ice cream cone.
	A soft drink.
Peer Approval	Students ask you to be on their team.
	Friends ask you to sit with them.
	Classmates ask you to be class leader.
	Friends ask you to work with them.
Independence	Be free to do what you like.
	Be free to go outside.
	Be free to play outside.
	Be free to work on something you like.

*These sample rewards are those used by King and Dunn-Rankin (1965).

Illustrations for the reward statement may take the form of magazine pictures or simple line drawings.

In each ten card set, each reward category should be represented by the same sample reward on each of the four cards upon which it appears. For instance, if "a candy bar" is chosen as the sample reward which represents the Consumable category, every card presenting this category in this set should contain the picture of a candy bar and the phrase "a candy bar."

In each set of ten cards, use a different one of the four sample rewards in each category. For example, each sample consumable reward might be dealt with as follows:

Set 1—four bubble gum cards
Set 2—four candy bar cards
Set 3—four ice cream cone cards
Set 4—four soft drink cards

Prepare tally sheets for recording children's responses (See Figure 2).

Step 3 Administering the Inventory

The following directions should accompany the presentations of the cards: "After you finish some work, you are going to get something you like. Suppose you had your choice of these two (present card 1 and point to each half of the card). Which one of these kinds of things would you like?" After the child responds, either by pointing or by stating his choice, record his responses on the tally sheet. Then say "And suppose you had to choose between these things, (present card 2 and point to each half of the card). Which do you like best?" Record the response. This procedure is followed until each card in a set has been presented. It is important to be sure while giving the inventory that the child understands that the picture of the reward is only an indication or representation of the type of reward that he might receive, rather than one he will receive after answering your questions.

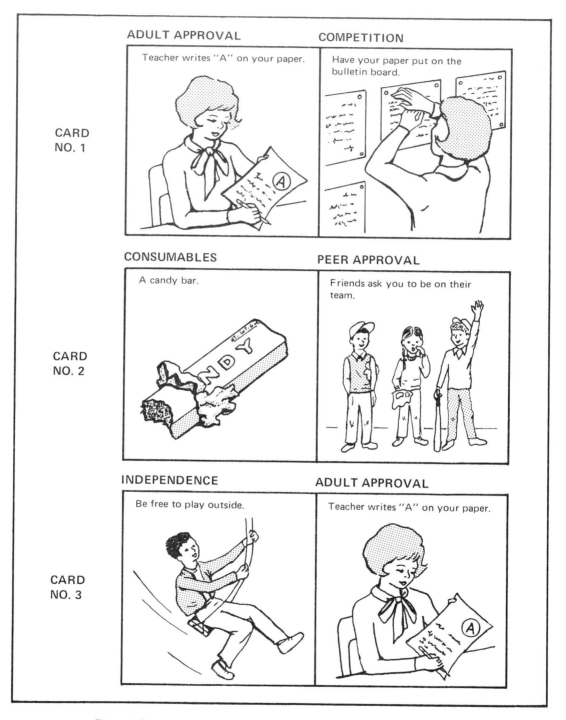

Figure 1 Examples of Cards for the Reward-Preference Assessment Procedure

Reward Preference Tally Sheet

Name _____ Date _____

Category	Frequency
Adult Approval	1111
Competition	~~1111~~ ~~1111~~ 11
Consumable	~~1111~~ 111
Peer Approval	~~1111~~ 111
Independence	~~1111~~ 111

Preferred Reward Category _____

Figure 2 Sample Tally Sheet

The child's most preferred type of reward is determined by counting the total number of tallies for each category: The category with the highest number of tallies is the most preferred. The sample tally sheet (see Figure 2) indicates Competition rewards are preferred.

Using Inventory Results in the Classroom

Once a child's preference for rewards has been established through the use of the card sets, it is a simple matter to test the validity of the results by trying out the preferred rewards in different situations. As rewards and incentives are varied from time to time, teachers can observe the effectiveness of the anticipated reward (incentive) on the task-related behavior of the child. Teachers should note that they need to experiment with different possible rewards within a child's preferred category. If a child prefers Adult Approval, for example, try different kinds of adult approval rewards such as: stars for seat work, a certificate of merit for a project, a few words of praise from the school principal, or a photograph of the child with his teacher.

How often are rewards required? Psychologists suggest that as a child is learning a new skill or behavior it is better to reward him liberally upon each instance of the desired behavior or upon each closer approximation to the desired behavior. Teachers can shape the behavior of a child and modify it in a positive direction by rewarding his early endeavors often. Then, as the child begins to show he is moving toward the desired behavior, closer approximations of the behavior should be required before a reward is given. Once a behavior or skill has been acquired by the child, and overlearned, gradually withdraw the rewards until the child receives only occasional rewards for the desired behavior.

As an example, a teacher might want to encourage a hyperactive child to sit down in his seat and stay in it for increasingly longer periods of time. At first, he would reward the child when he passed near the chair. Then he would reward him only if he touched the chair. Next he might reward him for sitting in the chair for a few seconds. Eventually he would reward the child only if he stayed seated throughout a given activity. Key principles are: (a) liberally reward behavior you wish to encourage, whether it is sitting quietly for a hyperactive child or attending to an arithmetic lesson for another child; and (b) occasionally reward a stable behavior pattern in order to maintain it; and (c) avoid rewarding undesirable behaviors.

Shaping reward preference patterns. It is important to note that by judiciously pairing neutral and desirable rewards, it may be possible to alter a child's reward preference patterns, over a period of time. The child who responds only to candy as a reward may eventually learn to value human praise much more than candy. In this case, the child's reward preference pattern could be switched from the Consumable category to the Adult Approval category. In the process, hopefully he has learned a more mature form of behavior and become less preoccupied with tangible rewards.

Some cautions. The MRPA procedure as outlined here is not an infallible measure of children's motivational structures. The use of the suggested procedure should give the teacher some ideas about motivation and the use of incentives. Periodic reappraisals of individual children's reward preference profiles and their responses to the actual rewards given should be undertaken by the teacher and revisions in the type of rewards used should be made if necessary.

Conclusions

Reward systems, to be truly effective, must capitalize on incentive motivation. That is, a child will work harder and longer at a task if he has some incentive. The MRPA helps teachers find out what kinds of rewards children like, and therefore what incentives will work best with them. Teachers should set up goals which are realistic. Also they should be certain that children are aware of what is expected of them and which reward they will receive. Finally it is important that, once the reward system has

been established, it be maintained in a highly consistent manner.

REFERENCES

Cartwright, C. A. "The Efficacy of Preferential Incentives with Elementary School Children," *Journal of Educational Psychology,* in press.

King, F. J., and Dunn-Rankin, P. "Reward Preference Inventory." Unpublished inventory, Florida State University, 1965.

RELATED READINGS

Neisworth, J. T., Deno, S. L. & Jenkins, J. R. *Student Motivation and Classroom Management: A Behavioristic Approach.* Newark, Delaware: Behavior Technics, 1969.

Becker, W. C., Thomas D. R., & Carnine, D. *Reducing Behavioral Problems: An Operant Conditioning Guide for Teachers.* Urbana, Illinois: ERIC Clearinghouse on Early Childhood Education, Nov., 1969.

Valett, R. E. *Modifying Children's Behavior.* Palo Alto, Calif.: Fearon Publishers, 1969.

Reese, E. P. *The Analysis of Human Operant Behavior.* Dubuque, Iowa: William C. Brown Company Publishers, 1966.

Learning Theory Approaches to Classroom Management: Rationale and Intervention Techniques

Harvey F. Clarizio
and Stephen L. Yelon

24

EDITORS' QUESTIONS:

1. Discuss the limitations of punishment as a means of preventing or discouraging undesirable behavior.

2. Give a brief but practical example of the implementation of each of the techniques suggested by the authors for the modification of pupil behavior.

3. Establish criteria for the selection of specific behavioral modification strategies which are consistent with the unique personality structures of individual pupils.

4. Recommend procedures which will enable teachers to avoid inadvertently reinforcing undesirable behaviors.

5. Suggest procedures or instruments for distinguishing between behavioral problems that should be referred to a specialist and those the classroom teacher should attempt to correct.

Harvey F. Clarizio and Stephen L. Yelon, "Learning Theory Approaches to Classroom Management: Rationale and Intervention Techniques," *Journal of Special Education,* I, (1967), 267–274. Reprinted with permission of the *Journal of Special Education.*

Today, more than ever before, there is acute concern about the mental health of children. Traditionally, we have modeled intervention efforts after the clinical concept of treatment. Dissatisfaction with the limitations of psychotherapeutic intervention (Levitt, 1957) together with the professional manpower shortage in the mental health field has led, however, to suggestions, e.g., Redl (1962), that we need new modes of treatment, closer to real-life situations, if we are to tackle children's problems more effectively.

When psychodynamic models were the preferred method of treatment, teachers were accorded at best a second-string status on the clinical team helping emotionally handicapped children. The increasing popularity of behavior therapy and other approaches based on learning theory now offers teachers opportunities for an integral role in the quest for better mental health for children. Indeed, it might well be the mental health specialist who will now assume the supportive role (Gallagher & Chalfant, 1966) in the "treatment" of children.

In the application of learning theory principles to the modification of deviant behavior, the emphasis is on the changing of behavior with little attention devoted to the etiology of the behavior. Why should teachers focus primarily on the behavior rather than on its causes? There are several reasons:

1. First, teachers by virtue of their orientation are not trained to probe the causes of behavior that even mental hygiene specialists often consider obscure and uncertain.

Authors are affiliated with Michigan State University.

227

Hence, is it really helpful to ask the teacher to understand the causes underlying children's disturbed behavior?

2. Teachers in any case are rarely in a position wherein they can directly manipulate the causes so as to modify their influence on the child's classroom adjustment. For example, if the problem lies in the parent-child relations or in a brain lesion, there are few if any constructive intervention techniques that the teacher can employ. Yet the child's troublesome behavior persists and must be handled as effectively as possible when it occurs in the classroom.

3. Even in such occasional cases where the causes can be identified and manipulated directly, the maladaptive behaviors may persist. Thus, despite the discovery and correction of the contributing role of poor vision and faulty child-rearing practices in a reading disability case, a pupil may continue to experience difficulty with his reading until attention is *specifically* devoted to his reading behavior, and unless he can experience success in this specific area, his mental health will continue to be impaired.

4. Behaviors or symptoms or habits may in their own right be incapacitating and disturbing, and current persisting symptoms may themselves be producing emotional disturbance (Franks, 1965) above and beyond the core disturbance from which the child is suffering. And, as research indicates (White & Harris, 1961), it is difficult to disentangle educational and emotional maladjustments in the school-age child (Gallagher & Chalfant, 1966).

5. There is little substantial evidence to indicate that if the teacher assists the child in modifying his behavior or symptoms, other undesirable behaviors will inevitably take their place in the manner of symptom substitution (Grossberg, 1964).

6. Finally, and most importantly, as already implied, the teacher most commonly has no resort other than to deal with the pupil's behavior as it appears in the here and now. As Lewis (1965) attests:

> If we cannot aspire to reconstruction of personality that will have long range beneficial effects, we can modify disturbing behavior in specific ways in present social contexts. This more modest aspiration may not only be more realistic but it may be all that is required of the child-helping professions in a society that is relatively open and provides a variety of opportunity systems in which a child can reconcile his personal needs with society's expectations of him.

Having argued that the teacher should be primarily concerned with behavior *per se* rather than with its causes, let us turn to techniques emanating from learning theory which have relevance to the modification of deviant behavior in the classroom (see Glossary of Terms). Although the techniques to be presented are discussed separately for the sake of clarity, it should be recognized that more than one of them may be operating at any given time in real-life attempts to modify behavior. Moreover, common to all of these techniques is the use of "systematic environmental contingencies to alter the object's responsiveness to stimuli" (Krasner & Ullman, 1965).

Glossary of Terms

Behavior Therapy. A therapeutic process in which the primary goal is to change overt behavior rather than to re-structure an individual's personality makeup. The process uses principles of learning for its methodological source.

Extinction. The decrease and eventual disappearance of a response learned under conditions of reinforcement when the reinforcement is withheld.

Reinforcement. Whatever serves to maintain the occurrence or increase the strength of a response, e.g., food, water or the avoidance of punishment.

Partial Reinforcement. A condition in which subjects receive reinforcement only at various time intervals or after a certain number of responses.

Positive Reinforcement. Much the same as reinforcement, i.e., *presenting* a pleasant stimulus when a response occurs, as opposed to negative reinforcement where an unpleasant stimulus is *removed* when a response occurs.

Modeling. A condition where the behavior to be acquired is demonstrated for the learner.

Punishment. A condition where a learner is made to feel uncomfortable by being presented an unpleasant stimulus, e.g., the infliction of pain by hitting, and/or a condition where a pleasant stimulus is withdrawn so that the learner is made to feel discomfort, e.g., having treats withdrawn.

The Techniques

Extinction

There is a growing body of research demonstrating that simple withdrawal of reinforcers can reduce or eliminate such troublesome behavior as excessive talking, tantrum behavior and academic errors (Warren, 1965; Williams, 1959; Zimmerman & Zimmerman, 1962). Extinction is not always, however, the most economic and effective means of producing behavioral change (Bandura & Walters, 1963). Certain cautions should be recognized:

1. Spontaneous remission—the return of undesirable behavior—may occur following the extinction trials, thus necessitating additional extinction sessions.

2. When behavior is maintained on a partial reinforcement schedule, removal of the reinforcers may actually produce an increase in the frequency and intensity of the deviant responses. Moreover, it is sometimes extremely difficult not to reinforce maladaptive behaviors in a school setting,

since circumstances may be beyond the teacher's control. The aggressive youngster who kicks the teacher or a classmate cannot help but be reinforced by the look of pain on the victim's face. The needed cooperation of classmates in the application of extinction procedures may also be difficult to secure, so that by necessity the deviant behavior is established on a partial reinforcement schedule.

3. General observation suggests that certain behaviors do not diminish and disappear simply because reinforcers are withdrawn, and sometimes teachers cannot or will not wait long enough to permit the completion of the extinction process. These limitations are particularly acute in situations in which emotional contagion is a distinct possibility. Behaviors seriously injurious to the self would also seemingly not lend themselves well to this technique. In brief, this method of behavior change has proven to be of value with acting-out as well as inhibited youngsters. Yet, its limitations suggest that other methods of behavioral modification are at times more economical and effective (see also Ausubel, 1957, Bandura, 1965).

Positive Reinforcement

Operant conditioning techniques constitute one of the main tools of behavior modification. In this technique, emphasis is placed on the response made by the individual, and only minimal attention is given to the stimuli eliciting the response. Essentially, the teacher presents a reward whenever the child emits the desired response. While teachers have been cognizant of the value of positively reinforcing "good" behavior, there is ample evidence to suggest that even "good" teachers not uncommonly reinforce undesirable behavior. One of the merits of the positive reinforcement technique stems from its applicability to antisocial youngsters as well as to withdrawn children (Bandura & Walters, 1963).

There has been a dearth of psychotherapeutic approaches designed for the conduct of the problem child, despite such pupils typically being the most disruptive of classroom procedures. The application of positive reinforcement principles to seriously aggressive children involves the manipulation of three variables: the schedules of reinforcement, the interval factor and the type of reward. With respect to the concept of reinforcement schedules, a distinction must be enforced between the acquisition and the maintenance of behavior. For the former, continuous or full-schedule reinforcement or reward after each appearance of the desired behavior is most effective, whereas for the latter, partial or intermittent reinforcement is most economical and effective. The interval variable merely refers to the passage of time between the production of a response and the presentation of the reward or reinforcer. The delay factor should usually be quite short initially, because acting-out children typically have difficulty in postponing gratification. Step by step, the interval can be lengthened as the child acquires more adequate behavioral controls.

The rewards for such pupils, at the start, may have to be tangible or physical in nature but should always be paired with verbal social reinforcers, e.g., "You handled yourself well in that situation today" (Quay, 1963). Gradually, the reinforcers can be shifted away from the concrete into language and other symbolic forms of reward until the child can respond satisfactorily to them. In deciding upon the most suitable reinforcers, consideration should be given to such factors as the child's developmental level and socio-cultural background.

The main unresolved question with the technique of positive reinforcement centers around the question of how to make the child initiate the response in the first place so that he can be rewarded (Franks, 1965). The technique of social modeling may well provide at least a partial answer to this problem (Baer, 1963; Ferster, 1961; Hewett, 1964; Slack, 1960; Wolf, Risley & Mees, 1964).

Modeling

Modeling is based on the premise that a child will imitate the behavior of others. Modeling is important in that children commonly acquire social skills through imitation of and identification with examples of socially approved behaviors presented by suitable models. School teachers thus have a unique opportunity to influence the behavior of entire groups of children. However, this technique has been typically overlooked in the management or modification of deviant behavior in schools. Modeling procedures may represent a more effective means than positive reinforcement of establishing new response patterns in children (Bandura, 1965). Moreover, a behavior pattern, once acquired through imitation, is often maintained without deliberate external reinforcement, because human beings learn to reinforce themselves for behaving in certain ways. Teacher training institutions have long recognized the importance of modeling procedures in the training of future teachers and, accordingly, attempt to provide adequate models in the form of critic teachers. However, attention should now be devoted to the teacher's use of modeling procedures in influencing the behavior of the pupils.

There are three effects of exposure to models: the *modeling effect,* the *inhibitory* or *disinhibitory effect,* and the *eliciting effect* (Bandura, 1965). Through the *modeling effect* children come to acquire responses that were not previously a part of their behavior. As noted earlier, modeling procedures may be considerably more economical in establishing new responses than the method of operant conditioning based on positive reinforcement, especially when a combination of verbalizing models and demonstration procedures are used. The strengthening or weakening of inhibitory responses already existing in the observer (the *inhibitory* or *disinhibitory effect*) can also be accomplished through modeling procedures. Children, for example, who see a model punished or rewarded for aggressive behavior tend to decrease or increase their aggressive behavior accordingly. The *eliciting* or *response facilitation effect* refers to the teacher's eliciting responses that precisely or approximately match those exhibited by the model. Thus, observation of the teacher's response provides discriminative clues that trigger similar responses already in the pupil's behavior repertoire. This eliciting effect is distinguished from the modeling and the disinhibiting effects in that the imitated behavior is neither new nor previously punished.

The probability that a child will imitate a model is a function of several variables. Modeling is partly dependent upon the reinforcing consequences of the model's behavior. Thus, if a model is rewarded for his socially approved behavior, the likelihood that the observer will behave in a socially approved manner is increased. Other factors include the process of attending to the model's behavior, e.g., previous training in observation, and various environmental stimuli, e.g., the complexity of the stimuli (Baldwin, 1967; Bandura, 1962b; Bandura & Hutson, 1961; Bandura & Kupers, 1964; Bandura, Ross & Ross, 1963).

Punishment

Aversive conditioning or punishment is an intervention technique which has been used primarily to discourage undesirable behavior. This technique consists in the presentation of either physically or psychologically painful stimuli or the withdrawal of pleasant stimuli when undesirable behavior occurs. The use of punishment as a technique for behavioral modification has been contraindicated for the following reasons:

1. Punishment does not eliminate the response; it merely slows down the rate at which the troublesome behaviors are emitted.

2. This technique serves notice to stop certain negative behaviors; it does not indicate what behaviors are appropriate in the situation.

3. Aggressive behaviors on the teacher's part may provide an undesirable model for the pupil.

4. The emotional side effects of punishment, such as fear, tenseness and withdrawal are maladaptive.

5. Punishment serves as a source of frustration which is apt to elicit additional maladaptive behaviors.

Some psychologists, who are currently reconsidering the concept of punishment, contend that it can have a beneficial effect if applied to specific responses rather than to general behavior (Marshall, 1965).

Teachers, whatever their motivations, use verbal reprimands and other forms of correction in their approach to classroom management, and the judicious use of punishment as an intervention technique is most likely necessary in that it is impossible to guide behavior effectively with positive reinforcement and extinction alone. As Ausubel (1957) asserts, "It is impossible for children to learn what is *not* approved and tolerated simply by generalizing in reverse from the approval they receive for the behavior that *is* acceptable." Thus, punishment of specific responses can have an informative and beneficial effect. A particular positive value that may accrue from the use of punishment is that undesirable behaviors are held in abeyance, thus permitting the teaching of desirable modes of behavior through such intervention techniques as social imitation or positive reinforcement. Although punishment techniques have been used primarily with acting-out pupils, they have also been found to be of value in certain cases of withdrawn behavior (Bandura, 1962a; Church, 1963; Lovaas, 1965; Meyer & Offenbach, 1962; Redl, 1965; Sears, Maccoby & Levin, 1957; Solomon, 1964).

Discrimination Learning

Children sometimes engage in maladaptive behavior because they have transferred behaviors acceptable in one setting to a second setting where these behaviors are considered inappropriate and maladaptive. Thus, for example, the child who is overly dependent upon his mother may behave in a very dependent way toward his teacher. Such cases of inappropriate generalization can sometimes be remediated through the use of discrimination learning. Essentially this process consists of labeling given behaviors as appropriate within a specific environmental context. The teacher in the above case, for example, may inform the child in a nonpunitive way that she is not his mother but his teacher and that as such she will require him to become more self-reliant. This labeling by the teacher makes the child more aware of both inappropriate and appropriate behaviors. Interestingly, children do not always have to be able to express such discriminations verbally in order to achieve "insight" into their behavior.

It is rather required, to insure effective results, that appropriate responses be rewarded and undesirable responses discouraged. Discrimination learning thus may be of service in conjunction with most other techniques in managing conduct and personality problems in the classroom (Ayllon & Michael, 1959; Barrett & Lindsley, 1962; Brackbill & O'Hara, 1958; Penny & Lupton, 1961; Stevenson, Weir & Zigler, 1959).

Desensitization

Desensitization as an intervention technique has been used principally with the fearful and phobic child. The basic objective is to have the child achieve a relaxed response in the presence of what were previously anxiety-producing stimuli. To accomplish this relaxed response, the subject is encouraged to perform approximations of previously punished acts within non-punishing or actually rewarding situations. Or through gradual exposure to the feared object or situation, a subject may become able to perform a formerly feared act or approach the feared object in a relaxed manner (Bentler, 1962; Garvey & Hegrenes, 1966; Jersild & Holmes, 1935; Lazarus, 1960; Wolpe, 1958).

Concluding Remarks

As evidenced by our discussion of the limitations of each technique, we do not envision management techniques emanating from learning theory as a panacea, but these intervention techniques do have certain potential advantages:

1. The fruitfulness of these techniques in modifying human behavior has been demonstrated in laboratory settings as well as in natural settings.

2. They are consistent with the teacher's role whereby she must reflect cultural ex-

pectations and set standards for her pupils' academic and social behavior.

3. Behavioral approaches offer specific and practical techniques for use in day-to-day classroom problems. While teachers already use some or all of these techniques, they frequently do so intuitively or inconsistently thereby reducing their efficacy.

4. These techniques enable the teacher to strive toward more realistic and obtainable goals relative to their pupils' mental health.

5. One of the most important attributes of these techniques is the fact that they can be taught to teachers. While there are few if any teacher training institutions currently offering didactic and practice training in such techniques, one can envision the time when teachers will acquire such skills through laboratory courses taken in conjunction with their formal course work or through in-service meetings and workshops.

REFERENCES

Ausubel, D. *Theory and Problems of Child Development.* New York: Grune & Stratton, 1957.

Ayllon, T. & Michael, J. "The Psychiatric Nurse as a Behavioral Engineer," *Journal of Experimental Analysis of Behavior,* 1959, 2, 323–334.

Baer, D. "Effect of Withdrawal of Positive Reinforcement on an Extinguishing Response in Young Children," *Child Development,* 1961, 32, 67–74.

Baer, D. "Social Reinforcement and Behavior Change," *American Journal of Orthopsychiatry,* 1963, 591–633.

Baldwin, A. "Theories of Child Development," *Critique of Social Learning Theory,* Chapter 16. New York: Wiley, 1967.

Bandura, A. "Punishment Revisited," *Journal of Consulting Psychology,* 1962, 26, 289–301(a).

Bandura, A. "Social Learning Through Imitation," In M. Jones ed. *Nebraska Symposium on Motivation,* Lincoln, Nebraska.: University of Nebraska Press, 1962. pp. 211–269(b).

Bandura, A. "Behavioral Modification Through Modeling Procedures," In L. Krasner & L. Ullman eds. *Research in Behavior Modification.* New York: Holt, Rinehart & Winston, 1965.

Bandura, A. & Hutson, A. "Identification as a Process of Incidental Learning," *Journal of Abnormal and Social Psychology,* 1961, 63, 311–318.

Bandura, A. & Kupers, C. "The Transmission of Patterns of Self-Reinforcement Through Modeling," *Journal of Abnormal and Social Psychology,* 1964, 69, 1–19.

Bandura, A., Ross, D. & Ross, S. "Imitation of Film Mediated Aggressive Models," *Journal of Abnormal and Social Psychology,* 1963, 66, 3–11.

Bandura, A., & Walters, R. *Social Learning and Personality Development.* New York: Holt, Rinehart & Winston, 1963.

Barrett, B. & Lindsley, O. "Deficits in Acquisition of Operant Discrimination and Differentiation Shown by Institutionalized Retarded Children," *American Journal of Mental Deficiency,* 1962, 67, 424–436.

Bentler, P. "An Infant's Phobia Treated with Reciprocal Inhibition Therapy," *Journal of Child Psychology and Psychiatry,* 1962, 3, 185–189.

Brackbill, Y. & O'Hara, J. "The Relative Effectiveness of Reward and Punishment for Discrimination Learning in Children," *Journal of Comparative and Physiological Psychology,* 1958, 51, 747–751.

Church, R. "The Varied Effects of Punishment on Behavior," *Psychological Review,* 1963, 70, 369–402.

Ferster, C. "Positive Reinforcement and Behavioral Deficits of Autistic Children," *Child Development,* 1961, 32, 437–456.

Franks, C. "Behavior Therapy, Psychology and the Psychiatrist: Contribution, Evaluation and Overview," *American Journal of Orthopsychiatry,* 1965, 35, 145–151.

Gallagher, J. & Chalfant, J. "The Training of Educational Specialists for Emotionally Disturbed and Socially Maladjusted Children," In *N.S.S.E. Yearbook 1966: Social Deviancy Among Youth.* Chicago: University of Chicago Press, 1966. pp. 398–423.

Garvey, W. & Hegrenes, J. "Desensitization Techniques in the Treatment of School Phobia," *American Journal of Orthopsychiatry,* 1966, 36, 147–152.

Grossberg, J. "Behavior Therapy: A Review," *Psychological Bulletin,* 1964, 62, 73–88.

Hewett, F. "Teaching Reading to an Autistic Boy Through Operant Conditioning," *The Reading Teacher,* 1964, 17, 613–618.

Jersild, A. & Holmes, F. "Methods of Overcoming Children's Fears," *Journal of Psychology,* 1935, 1, 75–104.

Krasner, L. & Ullman, L. *Case Studies in Behavior Modification.* New York: Holt, Rinehart & Winston, 1965.

Lazarus, A. "The Elimination of Children's Phobias by Deconditioning," In H. Eysench ed. *Behavior Therapy and the Neuroses.* New York: Pergamon Press, 1960. pp. 114–122.

Levitt, E. E. "Results of Psychotherapy with Children: An Evaluation," *Journal of Conseling Psychology,* 1957, 25, 189–196.

Lewis, W. "Continuity and Intervention in Emotional Disturbance: A Review," *Exceptional Child,* 1965, 31, 465–475.

Lovaas, I. "Building Social Behavior in Autistic Children by Use of Electroshock," *Journal of Experimental Research in Personality,* 1965, 1, 99–109.

Marshall, H. "The Effect of Punishment on Children: A Review of the Literature and a Suggested Hypothesis," *Journal of Genetic Psychology,* 1965, 106, 108–133.

Meyer, W. & Offenbach, S. "Effectiveness of Reward and Punishment as a Function of Task Complexity," *Journal of Comparative and Physiological Psychology,* 1962, 55, 532–534.

Penny, R. O. & Lupton, A. "Children's Discrimination Learning as a Function of Reward and Punishment," *Journal of Comparative and Physiological Psychology,* 1961, 54, 449–456.

Quay, H. "Some Basic Consideration in the Education of Emotionally Disturbed Children," *Exceptional Child,* 1963, 30, 27–31.

Redl, F. "Crisis in the Children's Field," *American Journal of Orthopsychiatry,* 1962, 32, 759–780.

Redl, F. "The Concept of Punishment," in N. Long, W. Morse & R. Newan eds *Conflict in the Classroom.* Belmont, Calif.: Wadsworth, 1965.

Sears, R., Maccoby, E. & Levin, H. *Patterns of Child Rearing.* Evanston, Ill.: Row Peterson, 1957.

Slack, C. "Experimenter-Subject Psychotherapy: A New Method for Introducing Intensive Office Treatment for Unreachable Cases," *Mental Hygiene,* 1960, 44, 238–256.

Solomon, R. "Punishment," *American Psychologist,* 1964, 19, 239–253.

Stevenson, H., Weir, M. & Zigler, E. "Discrimination Learning in Children as a Function of Motive-Incentive Conditions," *Psychological Report,* 1959, 5, 95–98.

Warren, A. "All's Quiet in the Backroom," Paper read at the Council for Exceptional Children, Wichita, Kans., Oct., 1965.

White, M. & Harris, M. *The School Psychologist.* New York: Harper, 1961.

Williams, C. D. "The Elimination of Tantrum Behavior by Extinction Procedures," *Journal of Abnormal and Social Psychology,* 1959, 59, 269.

Wolf, M., Risley, T. & Mees, H. "Application of Operant Conditioning Procedures to Behavior Problems of an Autistic Child," *Behavior Research and Therapy,* 1964, 1, 305–312.

Wolpe, J. *Psychotherapy by Reciprocal Inhibition.* Stanford, Calif.: Stanford University, 1958.

Zimmerman, E. & Zimmerman, J. "The Alternation of Behavior in a Special Classroom Situation," *Journal of Experimental Analysis of Behavior,* 1962, 5, 59–60.

Applying "Group" Contingencies to the Classroom Study Behavior of Preschool Children[1]

Don Bushell, Jr.,
Patricia Ann Wrobel,
and Mary Louise Michaelis

EDITORS' QUESTIONS:

1. Is reliance upon extrinsic rewards, such as those utilized in this study, a desirable practice? Discuss the advantages and disadvantages of such a motivational technique.

2. Assume the existence of an especially widespread undesirable behavior. Make suggestions for alleviating the problem through the implementation of a strategy combining the techniques suggested by Clarizio and Yelon with a system of group response contingencies.

3. Can the Modified Reward Preference Assessment Procedure advocated by Cartwright and Cartwright help increase the effectiveness of a behavioral modification system which utilizes group contingencies? If not, explain why not. If so, indicate how it can do so and specify any limitations inherent in such an application of this instrument.

4. Evaluate the research design of the experiment reported in this article. Include in your analysis an examination of the following procedures:
   a. The practice of never giving a token when it was asked for regardless of the quality of the work concurrently presented.
   b. The conscious avoidance of the examination of another pupil's work in the immediate vicinity of a student who had just been rewarded.
   c. The demonetization of the tokens as a means of making participation in the special event noncontingent.
   d. The clandestine removal of the pupils' accumulated tokens on the eve of their remonetization.

5. A teacher should realize that no event impinging upon a pupil's consciousness is devoid of consequences. Consider item "d" in question 4. What sort of affective learning might be expected to result from this occurrence?

1. This study was carried out as a part of the program of the Webster College Student Behavior Laboratory, and preparation of the report was supported in part by the Institute for Sociological Research, The University of Washington. The authors gratefully acknowledge the able assistance of the observers who made this study possible: Alice Adcock, Sandra Albright, Sister Eleanor Marie Craig, S. L., Jim Felling, and Cleta Pouppart. We are particularly indebted to Donald M. Baer who encouraged us to commit this study to paper and subsequently gave thoughtful criticism to the manuscript. Reprints may be obtained from Don Bushell, Jr., Dept. of Human Development, University of Kansas, Lawrence, Kansas 66044.

The experimental analysis of behavior has concentrated on the examination of responses emitted by a single subject. Recently, extensions of this research have begun to deal with groups of individuals. Behavioral research with adult psychiatric patients (Ayllon and Azrin, 1965), and retarded children (Birnbrauer, Wolf, Kidder, and Tague, 1965) has indicated that certain operant techniques can be applied effectively well beyond the "artificial" conditions of the experimentally isolated subject.

In most group situations it is not practical to program individually special contingencies for the responses of each group member. Uniform criteria must be designed according to which a number of individuals are to be rewarded or punished. Schools, prisons, hospitals, business, and military organizations all maintain systems of response contingencies which are quite similar for all the individuals of a certain category within the organization. The objective of this research was to determine whether operant techniques may be applied to a group of individuals with effects similar to those expected when a single subject is under study. The specific behavior under analysis was the study behavior of a group of preschool children.

The dependent variables were behaviors such as attending quietly to instructions, working independently or in cooperation with others as appropriate, remaining with and attending to assigned tasks, and reciting after assignments had been completed. Counter examples are behaviors such as disrupting others who are at work, changing an activity before its completion, and engaging in "escape" behaviors such as trips to the bathroom or drinking fountain, or gazing out the window. To the extent that the first constellation of behaviors is present and the second is absent, a student might be classified as industrious, highly motivated, or conscientious; in short, he has good study habits.

Method

Children and Setting

The subjects were 12 children enrolled in a summer session. Three other children were not considered in this report because they did not attend at least half of the sessions due to illness and family vacations. Four of the 12 children were 3-yr old, two were 4-yr old, five were 5-yr old, and one was 6-yr old. These 10 girls and two boys would be described as middle class; all had been enrolled in the preschool the preceding spring semester, all scored above average on standardized intelligence tests, and all had experienced some form of token system during the previous semester.

Classes were conducted from 12:45 to 3:30 p.m., five days a week for seven weeks. A large room adjoining the classroom afforded one-way sight and sound monitoring of the class. The program was directed by two head teachers who were assisted for 25 min. each day by a specialist who conducted the Spanish lesson. All of the teachers were undergraduates.

Daily Program

Data were collected in three phases during the first 75 min. of each of the last 20 class days of the summer session. During the first 20 min., individual activities were made available to the children for independent study, and the amount of social interaction, student-student or student-teacher, was very slight. The next 25 min. were devoted to Spanish instruction. The interaction pattern during this period was much like that of a typical classroom, with the teacher at the front of the assembled children sometimes addressing a specific in- dividual but more often talking to the entire group. The remaining 30 min. were given over to "study teams," with the children paired so the one more skilled at a particular task would teach the less skilled. Composi- tion of the groups and their tasks varied from day to day according to the developing skills of the children.

Following this 75 min., a special event was made available to the children. Special events included: a short movie, a trip to a nearby park, a local theater group rehearsal, an art project, a story, or a gym class. The special event was always 30 min. long and was always conducted outside the regular classroom. The children were not told what the activity would be for the day until im- mediately before it occurred.

Token Reinforcement

The tokens, colored plastic washers about 1.5-in. in diameter, served as a mone- tary exchange unit within the classroom. As the children engaged in individual activities, Spanish, and study teams, the teachers moved about the room giving tokens to those who appeared to be actively working at their various tasks, but not to those who were not judged to be attending to the as- signment at the moment.

To minimize unproductive talking about the tokens, the teachers avoided mentioning them. Tokens were never given when re- quested. If a child presented a piece of work and then asked for a token, the request was ignored and additional work was provided if needed. Similarly, the presentation of tasks was never accompanied by any mention of tokens, such as, "If you do thus and so, I will give you a token." The tokens were simply given out as the children worked and, where possible, the presentation was accompanied by such verbal statements as "good,"

"you're doing fine, keep it up," "that's right," *etc.* The teachers avoided a set pat- tern in dispensing the tokens so that their approach would not become discriminative for studying. They would watch for appro- priate behavior, move to that child, present a token and encouragement, then look for another instance not too nearby. During Spanish, the two teachers were able to present tokens for appropriate responding to the children who were assembled in front of the Spanish teacher. During study teams the teachers presented tokens as they cir- culated from group to group, and also at a checking session at the end of the period. Here, the student-learner recited what had been learned and both children were given tokens according to the performance of the learner. Each teacher distributed from 110 to 120 tokens during the 75 min.

The tokens could be used to purchase the special-event ticket. The price varied from 12 to 20 tokens around an average of 15 each day so the children would not leave their study activities as soon as they acquired the necessary amount. Children who did not earn enough to purchase the special-event ticket remained in the classroom when the others left with the teachers. There were no recriminations or admonishments by either the teachers or the students, and the one or two children left behind typically found some toy or book to occupy themselves un- til the rest of the class returned. After the special event, additional activities enabled the children to earn tokens for a 3:00 p.m. snack of cookies, ice cream, milk, or lemon- ade, and a chair to sit on while eating. To- kens could be accumulated from day to day.

As tokens became more valuable, theft, borrowing, lending (sometimes at interest), hiring of services and a variety of other eco- nomic activities were observed. No attempt was made to control any of these except theft, which was eliminated simply by providing the children with aprons which had pockets for the tokens.

Observation and Recording Procedures

The four principal observers were seated in an observation room. Each wore earphones which enabled audio monitoring of the class and also prevented inter-observer communication. On a signal at the beginning of each 5-min. period, each observer looked for the first child listed on the roster and noted that child's behavior on the data sheet, then looked for the second child on the list and noted its behavior; and so on for each child. All observers were able to complete the total observational cycle in less than 3 min. During the 75 min. of observation, the children's behavior was described by noting what the child was looking at, to whom he was talking, and what he was doing with his hands. Fourteen daily observations of each child by each observer produced 672 items of data each day.

Criteria were established by which each behavioral description on the data sheets could be coded as either "S," indicating study behavior, or "NS," indicating non-study behavior. Behaviors such as writing, putting a piece in a puzzle, reciting to a teacher, singing a Spanish song with the class, and tracing around a pattern with a pencil were classified as "S," if they were observed in the appropriate setting. Descriptions of behaviors such as counting tokens, putting away materials, walking around the room, drinking at the fountain, looking out the window, rolling on the floor and attending to another child, were classified as "NS." Singing a Spanish song was scored "S" if it occurred during the Spanish period when called for, but "NS" if it occurred during an earlier or later period. Similarly, if one child was interacting with

another over instructional materials during the study teams period, the behavior was labeled "S," but the same behavior during another period was classified "NS."

If a given child's behavior was described 14 times and eight of these descriptions were coded "S," then the amount of study time for that child was 8/14 for that day. The amount of study behavior for the entire class on a given day was the sum of the 12 individual scores.

Time-Sampling Validity Check

Time-sampling assumes that, in a given situation, the behavior observed at fixed spacings in time adequately represents the behavior occurring during the total interval. To check the validity of this assumption, a fifth observer described the behavior of only three children much more frequently. At the beginning of each 15-sec. interval an automatic timing device beside the fifth observer emitted a click and flashed a small light. The observer then described the ongoing behavior of the first of the three target children of the day, noting essentially the child's looking, talking, and hand behaviors. The procedure was repeated for the second child, then the third. At the onset of the next 15-sec. interval, the sequence was repeated. The tape ran continuously. Consequently, during the same interval when the principal observers made 14 observations, the fifth made slightly more than 300 observations of each of the three children. This procedure was used during nine of the 20 experimental sessions, and the three children chosen for this type of observation varied.

The data sheets completed by the four regular observers and the tapes recorded by the fifth observer were coded each day by the four principal observers who assigned either an "S" or "NS" to each description. Coding was accomplished independently by each observer without consultation. The fifth observer did not participate in classifying any of the tape descriptions.

Design

The study, a within-group design, consisted of three stages. During the first stage, participation in the special event was contingent upon the purchase of the necessary ticket with tokens. After nine days under these conditions, participation in the special event was made noncontingent. During the seven days of the noncontingent stage, the children were presented with special-event tickets and snack tickets as they arrived for school. Tokens and verbal statements of praise and encouragement were still given for the same behaviors as during the first phase, but the tokens no longer had any purchasing power. All the privileges of the classroom were available to every child regardless of how much or how little study behavior he or she displayed.

The decision to continue dispensing tokens but devalue them by providing everything free was made in order to retain all of the original procedures except the contingent special event. Had the tokens been given on a noncontingent basis at the beginning of each session, or eliminated entirely, this might have altered the behavior of the teachers toward the children throughout the remainder of the session.

After the sixteenth day of the study, the aprons containing the accumulated tokens were "sent to the cleaners" and all of the tokens were removed. As the children arrived the next day and asked where their tickets were, they were told they would have to buy them. When the children noted that they couldn't because they had no tokens, the teachers responded by saying: "Perhaps you can earn some. Your (activity —name) is over there." Thus, for the final

four days, the last days of the summer session, the initial conditions were restored with special-event and snack tickets again being made contingent upon tokens acquired by the students for study behavior.

Results

Figure 1 shows that study behavior was influenced by whether or not the special event was contingent upon it. During the first nine-day stage, offering the special event contingent on study behavior resulted in an average score for the class as a whole of 67%. During the noncontingent stage, the observed study behavior declined 25 percentage points over seven days to a low of 42%. Restoring the original contingencies on Day 17 was associated with a 22% increase in study behavior over that of the previous day.

Because the study behavior data were derived from observational measures, a number of checks were made to establish the reliability of the procedures. First, the total class score obtained by each observer for each day was compared to the scores of the other three observers. The vertical lines at each point in Fig. 1 describe the range of group scores obtained by the four observers each day. Inspection of these lines indicated that the same pattern was described even if the summary class score for any given day was drawn at random from the four available scores. Indeed, the data of any one, or any combination, of the four observers presented the same pattern with respect to the effects of contingent reinforcement upon study behavior.

The fact that the behavior descriptions of each day were coded within a few hours after they were obtained might have been an additional source of error. A description might have been coded "NS" on Day 15 and

"S" on Day 19 simply because the observer expected study behavior to increase during the final contingent stage. To check for such effects, four new coders were empaneled nine months after the study was completed. These new coders had no knowledge of the details of the original investigation. They were trained to read behavioral descriptions like those appearing on the original data sheets and assign an "S" or "NS" to each according to the criteria outlined in the previous section. Once they agreed within 5% on the independent scoring of a given data sheet, they were each given nine of the original sheets.

The data sheets given to the new coders were in scrambled order with all dates and other identifying marks obscured so they had no way of determining which stage a sheet came from even if they understood the significance of the experimental conditions. Sheets from Days 3, 4, 5, 12, 13, 14, 18, 19, and 20 (three from each stage) were recoded in this fashion. The procedure guaranteed that the expectations of the coder would not influence the scores obtained. The comparison of the original scores and those obtained by the new coders are shown in Fig. 2.

As a further check on coding bias, two of the original observers were recalled after a nine-month interval to recode one set of four data sheets from each of the three

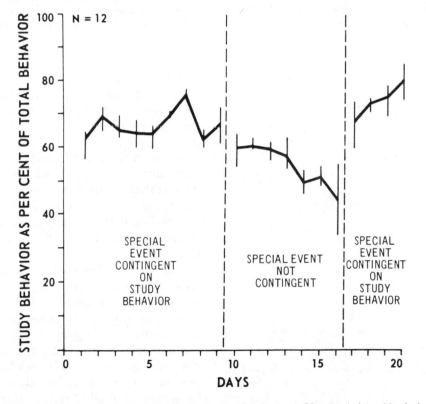

Figure 1 Mean per cent of 12 children's study behavior over 20 school days. Vertical lines indicate the range of scores obtained by the four observers each day.

stages of the study, 12 sheets in all, also presented in random order. These two observers each recoded the descriptions of one of the other observers and their own data sheets completed at the time of the original study. The results are also shown in Fig. 2 for Days 2, 11, and 17. These points, marked Δ, indicate that the results obtained by having the original observers recode their own and someone else's data do not differ from those obtained when newly trained coders score the original data. In all cases the scores obtained described the effects of contingent and noncontingent reinforcement in the same way.

The comparison of the total score for the three target children obtained by the regular method and the tapes is shown in Fig. 3 and supports the validity of the 5-min. time-sampling technique.

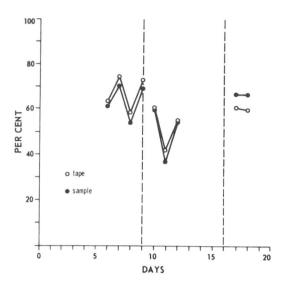

Figure 3 Mean study behavior of various trios of children based on taped observations each day compared with written time-samples during the same period.

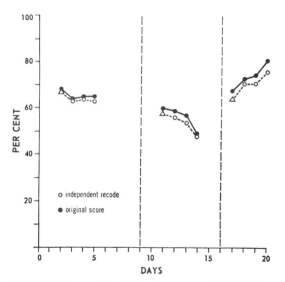

Figure 2 Mean study behavior scores obtained by original observers compared with scores obtained by a panel of coders nine months after the completion of the study. Δ indicates scores obtained by two of the original observers who recoded the original data sheets nine months after the completion of the study.

The data describing the effects of the different contingencies upon each of the three instructional styles (individual activities, group instruction, teams), failed to demonstrate that this was an important dimension in the present study. Day-to-day variability was greater for these smaller periods than for the entire session, but in all cases the proportion of study behavior dropped similarly in the absence of the contingent special event and rose during the final four days.

Just as the day-to-day variability increased as the analysis moved from the whole class to periods within each day's class, individual study behavior was more variable than the aggregate data for all 12 children. It is to be expected that students of different age, sex, and educational background will perform differently in comparable settings, but all 12 records shown in Fig. 4 indicate that noncontingent reinforcement was less effective in sustaining study behavior than contingent reinforcement. There was no case in which an individual student displayed more study behavior during the second stage of the study than was displayed during the first and third stages.

Discussion

The results indicate that the contingent special event controlled much of the study behavior. In the time available it was not possible to continue the noncontingent state until study behavior stabilized. With such an extension, study behavior might have gone lower.

A token system has much to recommend it from a practical standpoint, for there are many school activities (recess, early dismissal, extra-curricular events) which might be employed to develop and maintain higher levels of study behavior. Further, the classroom teacher responsible for the behavior of many students can manage a token system, but faces some difficulty in relying solely on verbal praise and attention as reinforcers. Behavior modification with social reinforcement requires constant monitoring of the subject's responding (Baer and Wolf, 1967). This can be done only on a very limited scale in a classroom by a single teacher.

The day-to-day variability in individual records requires further study. At first

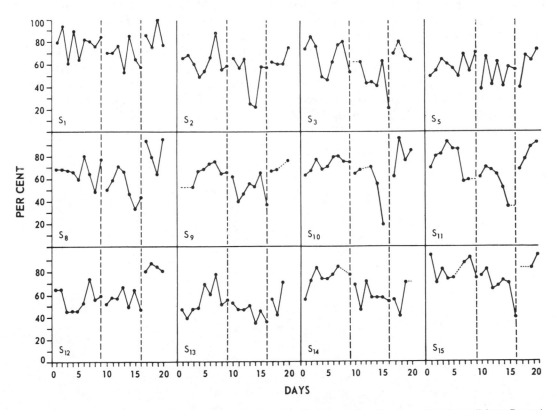

Figure 4 Per cent of each individual child's behavior classified as study behavior under all conditions. Dotted lines without points indicate absence.

glance it would appear that the individual fluctuations could indict the smoother curve of the group as resulting from the canceling effect of numerous measurement errors at the individual level. However, the several measurement checks suggest that other factors may have been more important in explaining the variability. For example, the practice of allowing the children to accumulate tokens from day to day may have produced some variability. It allowed the children to work hard and lend one day, and loaf and borrow the next; work hard and save one day, loaf and spend their savings the next. This would tend to produce a smooth curve for the group, since not everyone could lend at the same time nor could all borrow at once. The present practice in the preschool is to remove all tokens from the children's pockets after each day's session.

The next approximation toward a useful classroom observational technique will require additional measures to determine the effects of the students' changing behavior on the attending and helping behavior of the teachers. This work is now in progress.

It may be concluded that: (1) practical reinforcement contingencies can be established in a classroom; (2) the effects of various contingencies can be ascertained by direct observational techniques where the use of automated recording equipment is not practicable.

REFERENCES

Ayllon, T. and Azrin, N. H. "The Measurement and Reinforcement of Behavior of Psychotics," *Journal of the Experimental Analysis of Behavior,* 1965, 8, 357–383.

Baer, D. M. and Wolf, M. M. "The Reinforcement Contingency in Preschool and Remedial Education." In Robert D. Hess and Roberta Meyer Baer eds. *Early Education: Current Theory, Research, and Practice.* Chicago: Aldine. In press.

Birnbrauer, J. S., Wolf, M. M., Kidder, J. D., and Tague, C. E. "Classroom Behavior of Retarded Pupils with Token Reinforcement," *Journal of Experimental Child Psychology,* 1965, 2, 219–235.

The Self-Fulfilling Hypothesis and Educational Change

Arthur P. Coladarci

EDITORS' QUESTIONS:

1. Discuss the deleterious effects upon learning achievement of the self-fulfilling hypothesis.
2. Identify specific diagnostic procedures which would help the teacher avoid the formulation of self-fulfilling prophecies and assist her in identifying pupils who have fallen prey to this phenomenon.
3. Assess the feasibility of using a motivational system based on the Modified Reward Preference Assessment Procedure for enhancing a pupil's self-concept.
4. What self-fulfilling hypotheses have you been guilty of? Suggest means of avoiding such practices in the future.

26

Arthur P. Coladarci, "The Self-Fulfilling Hypothesis and Educational Change," *The California Journal for Instructional Improvement,* IX, No. 3 (October 1966), 146–150. Reprinted with the permission of *The California Journal for Instructional Improvement.*

Early in the present century, a distinguished American sociologist gave formal utterance to a social theorem that was probably understood at some level of consciousness centuries earlier. "If men define social situations," said W. I. Thomas, "they become real in their consequences." This theorem contains two propositions. First, and implied, is that we frequently respond to situations in terms of the *meanings* we invest in them rather than in terms of the "objective" aspects of the situations. The second and more critical proposition is that, having defined a situation in a given way, we may so act as to make the original definition become true—even if it were false. This, then, is the self-fulfilling prophecy: an erroneously based prediction that becomes true *because it is acted upon with the assumption that it is true; i.e.,* the prophecy fulfills itself.

Perhaps an immediate example is needed to clarify this admittedly obtuse definition. Consider the extremely topical prophecy, "If Negroes move into a white, middle-class neighborhood, property values will go down." If I, a white, middle-class neighbor, so define the situation and have some like-minded neighbors, the first intrusion of a Negro resident may produce a "sell-at-any-price" scramble and, surely enough, "property values go down." The situation was falsely defined but became true *because I acted as if it were true.* Tragically, it was I who caused the lowering of property values, not the new resident.

To summarize the phenomenon in Merton's words: "The self-fulfilling prophecy, is, in the beginning, a *false* definition of the

Dr. Coladarci is Professor of Education and Psychology at Stanford University. This article is based on a paper presented at the Governor's Education Conference on Educational Issues in a Changing World, Kaanapali, Maui, Hawaii, November 20, 1965.

situation evoking a new behavior which makes the originally false conception come *true.* The specious validity of the self-fulfilling prophecy perpetuates a reign of error. For the prophet will cite the actual course of events as proof that he was right from the very beginning."[1]

There are, of course, self-destroying prophecies—the "suicidal prophecy"[2]—but we are not concerned with them here. It is also true that there are self-fulfilling prophecies that do not necessitate the assumption of a *false* definition of the situation. These, also, are outside our attention for the moment—although every educator should remind himself of the one offered by Goethe in one of the most moving lines of Germanic poetry:

> "If you treat an individual as he is, he will stay as he is, but if you treat him as if he were what he ought to be and could be, he will become what he ought to be and could be."

The focus of attention in this paper is on prophecies arising from false, or possibly false, definitions of situations; to these I turn again.

As you either already know or can now guess, the self-fulfilling prophecy can be found in the domain of pedagogy. Indeed, my thesis is that such prophecies not only pervade our profession but, in many instances, have become so ritualized that their identification is extremely difficult. I wish further to argue that these prophecies are status-conserving; they may preclude, in fact, at the level of educational operations, whatever educational changes are defined as possible, in principle, at the level of intellectual strategy and institutional policy.

Let me describe what I interpret to be some common prophecy-inviting situations in education. These are drawn, I must confess, from my own sinful past. They may

prompt others to identify further situations and instances of more local relevance. The remedy for the illness (if such it be) is beyond my allocation of time and space and probably beyond my allocation of competence.

The uncritical use of measures of "intelligence" and its congeners ("scholastic ability," "aptitude," "talent," etc.) offers one of the most pregnant of self-fulfilling prophecy situations. Consider the following pedagogical parable. Mrs. Jones, school teacher, is expecting a list of her new fifth grade pupils with the IQ's for each contained thereon—which she will use to make three ability groupings ("Ravens," "Robins," and "Bluebirds," of course). She receives, at that moment, a list of her new pupils with the locker numbers assigned to each. Unfortunately, this list is untitled and she assumes that she has the IQ's she has been waiting for. Mrs. Jones makes her three groups, assigning children with low locker numbers to the "Ravens," high locker-numbered pupils go to the "Bluebirds," and the "Robins" comprise those children with locker numbers in the 95-110 range. She then proceeds to "enrich" and "challenge" the "Bluebirds," hold "average expectations" for the "Robins," and "protect" and "non-frustrate" the "Ravens." And, lo and behold, the groupings "prove" to be correct —at the end of the first semester, the Ravens have made less progress than the Bluebirds! The correlation between locker numbers and school success is consistent with research findings (.50, of course). Is this story merely apocryphal? Probably. Could it have happened? Possibly.

Another major breeding ground for self-

1. Robert K. Merton, *Social Theory and Social Structure,* Free Press, 1957, p. 423.
2. R. M. MacIver, *The More Perfect Union,* The Macmillan Co., 1948.

fulfilling hypotheses is the domain of achievement test scores and teachers' grades. Having observed that John Pupil performs low in arithmetic, as evidenced by scores and grades in that curricular area, Mary Teacher is frequently tempted to conclude that "John will have difficulty in arithmetic in the future." Given this definition of the situation, Mary Teacher may so act as to make it certain that John will not make dramatic growth in arithmetic. How? By making John satisfied with his lower level of competence (*i.e.,* John builds his own self-fulfilling prophecy), "protecting" him from more difficult material. When *all* of the available pupil information is brought together for the uncritical teacher in that "contract with destiny," the cumulative record, such an uncritical teacher may build self-fulfilling hypotheses so strong as to defy either identification or destruction. How often, for instance, have you heard a phrase of this order: "John is a C student"?

The foregoing discussion is not to gainsay the value and necessity of tests. I firmly believe in and support their use. The point of concern is the uncritical or unsophisticated use made of such tests at the level of pupils and teachers.

For my third error-inviting area I am indebted to whoever made the statement, "State Departments of Education will not change." It is easy, and even fashionable to equate governmental complex organizations with rigidity and immobility. It may be that the charge is correct. On the other hand, if the definition of such departments as "unchangeable" is false *but is acted on as true,* change can take place only with great difficulty, if at all.

Perhaps the most subtle and powerful self-fulfilling hypotheses in pedagogy arise in connection with social-ethnic-racial phenomenon—as they also do in non-pedagogical areas. There is little doubt in my own mind that Negro-Americans, as a group, do less well in school than white-Americans partially *because* teachers expect them to do less well. I will not belabor the point further since it is probably obvious. If you are doubtful, examine closely the school-related differences among social, ethnic or racial groups and see if they do not also conform to the social stereotypes we learned at somebody-or-other's knee. Then, consider, as an additional parameter of the situation, the meaning of James Baldwin's advice to his nephew: "The trouble with you is that you are beginning to believe what the white folks say about you."

What I suggest above does not exhaust the range of possible sources for self-fulfilling hypotheses. They include the areas of sex differences ("girls are more verbal than boys"), supervision ("Mary Teacher will never learn how to control a class"), administration ("Teachers do not have useful new ideas"), school-home relations ("Parents are the last people who should have children"). The examples given, however, may suffice to clarify the meaning of the self-fulfilling hypothesis, its relevance to educational practice, and its conservative power in attempts to bring about institutional changes.

Can anything be done to reform this variety of human error? Yes and no. In the case of educators who have formed and need logic-tight categories for viewing people—and have practiced these categories for a generation—I am not sanguine. In the case of the rest of the profession, it may be sufficient, or at least heuristic, merely to realize that self-fulfilling prophecies exist in the behavior of many educators—and even, perhaps, in ourselves.

Rules, Praise, and Ignoring: Elements of Elementary Classroom Control[1]

Charles H. Madsen, Jr.,
Wesley C. Becker,
and Don R. Thomas

EDITORS' QUESTIONS:

1. Discuss ways in which a knowledge of the causal relationship between teacher behavior and pupil behavior can assist the teacher in providing an environment more conducive to learning.

2. Give examples which illustrate how teachers may unintentionally reinforce disruptive pupil behaviors.

3. Why, in your opinion, did a combination strategy involving rules, ignoring and praising prove to be the most effective of all approaches attempted in the study reported by this article? State your answer in terms of motivational effectiveness.

4. Is the technique denoted in question 3 applicable to learnings in the affective domain? Could it, for example, be effective in dealing with racial prejudice or encouraging honesty? Support your conclusions.

Modern learning theory is slowly but surely increasing its potential for impact upon social problems. As problems in social development and interaction are more closely examined through the methods of experimental analysis, the importance of learning principles in everyday life becomes clearer. The potential contribution of these developments to childrearing and education appears to be especially significant. This report is a part of a series of studies aimed at demonstrating what the teacher can do to achieve a "happier", more effective classroom through the systematic use of learning principles. The study grows out of a body of laboratory and field research demonstrating the importance of social reinforcers (smiles, praise, contact, nearness, attention) in establishing and maintaining effective behav-iors in children. Extensive field studies in experimental nursery schools by Wolf, Bijou, Baer, and their students (*e.g.,* Hart, Reynolds, Baer, Brawley, and Harris, 1968; Allen, Hart, Buell, Harris, and Wolf, 1965; Bijou and Baer, 1963) provided a background for the extension of their work by the present authors to special and typical elementary classrooms. In general, we have

1. We wish to express our appreciation to the teachers involved, Mrs. Barbara L. Weed and Mrs. Margaret Larson, for their cooperation in a study which involved using and applying procedures which at times made their teaching duties very difficult. Gratitude is expressed to the Director of Elementary Education, Unit District #116, Urbana, Illinois, Dr. Lowell M. Johnson, and to the principals of Thomas Paine and Prairie Schools, Richard Sturgeon and Donald Holste. This study was supported by Grant HD-00881-05 from the National Institutes of Health. Reprints may be obtained from Wesley C. Becker, Bureau of Educational Research, 284 B Education Bldg., University of Illinois, Urbana, Illinois 61801.

found to date that teachers with various "personalities" and backgrounds can be trained systematically to control their own behavior in ways which will improve the behavior of the children they are teaching. (Becker, Madsen, Arnold, and Thomas, 1967). We have also found that teachers can "create" problem behaviors in the classroom by controlling the ways in which they respond to their pupils (Thomas, Becker, and Armstrong, 1968; Madsen, Becker, Thomas, Koser, and Plager, 1968). It is hoped that field studies of this sort will contribute to more effective teacher training.

The present study is a refinement of an earlier study of Becker *et al.* (1967), in which the behavior of two children in each of five classrooms was recorded and related to experimentally controlled changes in teacher behaviors. The teachers were instructed and guided to follow a program which involved making classroom rules explicit, ignoring disruptive behaviors unless someone was getting hurt, and praising appropriate classroom behaviors. Under this program, most of the severe problem children under study showed remarkable improvements in classroom behavior. However, that study lacked certain controls which the present study sought to correct. First, the teachers in the earlier study were in a seminar on behavior theory and practice during baseline conditions. Some target children improved during baseline, apparently because some teachers were beginning to apply what they were learning even though they had been requested not to do so. Second, public relations and time considerations did not make it possible to introduce the components of the experimental program one at a time (rules, ignoring, and praise) to better study their individual contributions. Third, a reversal of teacher behavior was not attempted. Such a reversal would more

conclusively show the importance of teacher's behavior in producing the obtained changes. Fourth, extensive recordings of teacher behavior under all experimental conditions were not undertaken in the earlier study. The present study attempted to deal with each of these problems.

Method

Procedures

Teachers in a public elementary school volunteered to participate in the study. After consultation with teachers and observation of the children in the classroom, two children with a high frequency of problem behavior were selected for study in each class. Previously developed behavioral categories (Becker *et al.*, 1967) were modifed for use with these particular children and baseline recordings were made to determine the frequency of problem behaviors. At the end of the baseline period the teachers entered a workshop on applications of behavioral principles in the classroom which provided them with the rationale and principles behind the procedures being introduced in their classes. Various experimental procedures were then introduced, one at a time, and the effects on the target children's behaviors observed. The experiments were begun in late November and continued to the end of the school year.

Subjects

Classroom A. There were 29 children in Mrs. A's middle-primary (second grade) room who ranged in school progress from mid-first-grade level to early-third-grade level. Cliff and Frank were chosen as the target children.

Cliff was chosen because he displayed no interest in school. In Mrs. A's words, "he would sit throughout entire work periods fiddling with objects in his desk, talking, doing nothing, or misbehaving by bothering others and walking around the room. Lately he has started hitting others for no apparent reason. When Cliff was required to stay in at recess to do his work, he would complete the work in a short time and it was usually completely accurate. I was unable to motivate him into working on any task during the regular work periods." Cliff is the son of a university professor who was born in Europe and immigrated when Cliff was 5-yrs old. Cliff scored 91 on an early (CA 5-3) intelligence test. This score was discounted by the examiner because of language problems. His group IQ scores rose steadily (CA 5-9, IQ 103; CA 6-2, IQ 119; CA 7-1, IQ 123). His achievement scores indicated a low second-grade level at the beginning of the present study. Cliff was seen by the school social worker throughout the entire first grade and throughout this entire study.

Cliff was observed early in the year and it was noted that he did not respond once to teacher's questions. He played with his fingers, scratched himself repeatedly, played in his desk, paid no attention to the assignment and had to stay in at recess to finish his work. Almost continually he made blowing sounds and talked to himself. On occasions he was out of his seat making noises and talking. He would leave the room without permission. Before the study began the observers made the following notes: "What a silly kid, writing on the bottom of his shoes, writing on his arms, blowing kisses at the girls. He was vying for the attention of the girl behind him, but she ignored him. . . . Poor Cliff! he acts so silly for his age. He tried to talk to the other kids, but none of them would pay attention to him. . . . Cliff seems concerned with the little girl beside him (girl behind him last week). He has a sign on his desk which reads, 'Do you love me?'. . . ."

Frank was described by his teacher as a likable child. He had a record of misbehavior in the classroom and intense fighting on the playground. He was often out of his seat talking to other children and did not respond to "discipline". If someone was reprimanded for doing something, Frank would often do the same thing. Test scores indicated an IQ of 106 (Stanford-Binet) and achievement level just under beginning second grade at the start of school (average California Achievement Test scores 1.6 grades). The school psychologist noted that Frank's mother was a person "who willingly permitted others to make decisions for her and did not seem able to discipline Frank." Father was absent from the home during the entire year in the Air Force.

Classroom B. Twenty children were assigned to Mrs. B's kindergarten room. Two children were observed initially; one moved from the community shortly after baseline was taken, leaving only Stan for the study.

Stan was described as coming from a truly pathetic home environment. The mother was not married and the family of four children subsisted on state aid. One older brother was enrolled in a special class for the educable retarded. At the beginning of the year, Stan's behavior was characterized by the teacher as "wild." She reported that, "Stan would push and hit and grab at objects and at children. He had no respect for authority and apparently didn't even hear directions. He knew how to swear profusely, and I would have to check his pockets so I would know he wasn't taking home school equipment. He would wander around the room and it was difficult to get him to engage in constructive work. He would frequently destroy any work he did rather than take it home."

The difficult home situation was made manifest during the month of March. Stan had been absent for two weeks and it was

Table 1
Behavioral Coding Categories for Children

I. Inappropriate Behaviors

A. *Gross Motor*. Getting out of seat, standing up, running, hopping, skipping, jumping, walking around, moving chair, *etc.*

B. *Object Noise*. Tapping pencil or other objects, clapping, tapping feet, rattling or tearing paper, throwing book on desk, slamming desk. Be conservative, only rate if you can hear the noise when eyes are closed. Do *not* include accidental dropping of objects.

C. *Disturbance of Other's Property*. Grabbing objects or work, knocking neighbor's books off desk, destroying another's property, pushing with desk (only rate if someone is there). Throwing objects at another person without hitting them.

D. *Contact (high and low intensity)*. Hitting, kicking, shoving, pinching, slapping, striking with object, throwing object which hits another person, poking with object, biting, pulling hair, touching, patting, *etc.* Any physical contact is rated.

E. *Verbalization*. Carrying on conversations with other children when it is not permitted. Answers teacher without raising hand or without being called on; making comments or calling out remarks when no questions have been asked; calling teacher's name to get her attention; crying, screaming, singing, whistling, laughing, coughing, or blowing loudly. These responses may be directed to teacher or children.

F. *Turning Around*. Turning head or head and body to look at another person, showing objects to another child, attending to another child. Must be of 4-sec duration, or more than 90 degrees using desk as a reference. Not rated unless seated. If this response overlaps two time intervals and cannot be rated in the first because it is less than 4-sec duration, then rate in the interval in which the end of the response occurs.

G. *Other Inappropriate Behavior*. Ignores teacher's question or command. Does something different from that directed to do, including minor motor behavior such as playing with pencil or eraser when supposed to be writing, coloring while the record is on, doing spelling during the arithmetic lesson, playing with objects. *The child involves himself in a task that is not appropriate*. Not rated when other Inappropriate Behaviors are rated. Must be time off task.

H. *Mouthing Objects*. Bringing thumb, fingers, pencils, or any object in contact with the mouth.

I. *Isolate Play*. Limited to *kindergarten* free-play period. Child must be farther than 3 ft from any person, neither initiates or responds to verbalizations with other people, engages in no interaction of a non-verbal nature with other children for the entire 10-sec period.

II. Appropriate Behavior

Time on task; *e.g.*, answers question, listens, raises hand, works on assignment. Must include whole 10-sec interval except for Turning Around responses of less than 4-sec duration.

reported that his mother was taking her children out of public school and placing them in a local parochial school. Investigation by school personnel indicated that Stan's mother had moved the children into a relative's home and had gone to the hospital to have another illegitimate baby. A truancy notice was filed for all four children including Stan. Following legal notice the children were returned to school.

Rating of Child Behavior

The same rating schedule was used in both classrooms except that Isolate Play was added to the list of Inappropriate Behaviors for the kindergarten. Since the children were expected to be involved in structured group activities during observation periods, going off by oneself to play with the many toys or materials in the room was considered inappropriate by the kindergarten teacher. Inappropriate Behavior was defined as the occurrence of one or more of the behaviors listed under Inappropriate Behavior in Table 1 during any observation interval.

Observers were trained in the reliable use of the rating schedule before baseline recordings began. Training consisted of practice in use of the rating schedule in the classroom. Two observers would each rate the same child for 20 min. and then return to the research office to compare their ratings and discuss their differences with their supervisor. Training was continued until reliability was above 80% on each behavior code. Training lasted approximately two weeks. Reliability was determined periodically throughout the study by dividing the number of agreements by the number of agreements plus disagreements. An agreement was defined as a rating of the same behavior class in the same observation interval. Average reliability over children, behavior classes, and days for the 69 occasions (out of 238) on which it was checked was 81%. Single day reliabilities ranged from 68% to 96%. Reliabilities were checked in each phase of the study.

Instructions to observers followed those used by Becker *et al.* (1967). In essence, the observers were not to respond to the children, but to fade into the background as much as possible. Teachers, as well as children, quickly learned not to respond to the observers, although early in the study one observer was attacked by a kindergarten child. The observer did not respond to the behavior and it quickly disappeared. Experimental changes were initiated without informing observers in an attempt to control any observer bias. However, the changes were often dramatic enough that observer comments clearly reflected programmed changes in teacher's behavior.

The target children were observed for 20 min. per day, three days a week. In the middle-primary class, observations were taken when the children were engaged in seat work or group instruction. In the kindergarten class, observations were made when structured activities, rather than free play, were expected. Each observer had a clipboard, stopwatch, and rating sheet. The observer would watch for 10 sec. and use symbols to record the occurrence of behaviors. In each minute, ratings would be made

in five consecutive 10-sec. intervals and the final 10 sec. would be used for recording comments. Each behavior category could be rated only once in a 10-sec. interval.

The primary dependent variable was percentage of intervals in which an Inappropriate Behavior occurred. Since the varieties of Inappropriate Behavior permitted a more detailed analysis with the schedule used, the presentation of results is focussed on them, even though functionally their converse (Appropriate Behavior) was the main behavior being manipulated.

Ratings of Teacher Behavior

Ratings of teacher behavior were obtained to clarify relationships between changes in teacher behavior and changes in child behavior. Recordings of teacher behavior were also used by the experimenters to help the teachers learn the contingent use of Approval and Disapproval Behaviors. The teacher rating schedule is presented in Table 2. Teacher behaviors were recorded by subclasses in relation to child behaviors. That is, the record would show whether a teacher response followed Appropriate child classroom behavior or whether it followed one of the categories of Inappropriate Behavior. Responses to all children were rated. Teacher behavior was scored as the frequency of occurrence of a specified class of behavior during a 20-min. interval. Teacher ratings were either recorded during one of the periods when a target child was being rated by another observer, or immediately thereafter when only one observer made both ratings. Teacher behavior was rated on the average of once a week, except during experimental transitions, when more frequent ratings were made. The number of days teacher behavior was rated under each condition is given in Table 3. Most recorded teacher behavior (about 85%) fell in the

Table 2

Coding Definitions for Teacher Behaviors

Appropriate child behavior is defined by the child rating categories. The teacher's rules for classroom behavior must be considered when judging whether the child's behavior is Appropriate or Inappropriate.

I. Teacher Approval following Appropriate Child Behavior
  A. *Contact.* Positive physical contact such as embracing, kissing, patting, holding arm or hand, sitting on lap.
  B. *Praise.* Verbal comments indicating approval, commendation or achievement. Examples: that's good, you are doing right, you are studying well, I like you, thank you, you make me happy.
  C. *Facial attention.* Smiling at child.

II. Teacher Approval following Inappropriate Child Behavior
  Same codes as under I

III. Teacher Disapproval following Appropriate Child Behavior
  A. *Holding the child.* Forcibly holding the child, putting child out in the hall, grabbing, hitting, spanking, slapping, shaking the child.
  B. *Criticism.* Critical comments of high or low intensity, yelling, scolding, raising voice. Ex-

amples: that's wrong, don't do that, stop talking, did I call on you, you are wasting your time, don't laugh, you know what you are supposed to do.
  C. *Threats.* Consequences mentioned by the teacher to be used at a later time. If _____ then _____ comments.
  D. *Facial attention.* Frowning or grimacing at a child.

IV. Teacher Disapproval following Inappropriate Child Behavior
  Same codes as under III.

V. "Timeout" Procedures[a]
  A. The teacher turns out the lights and says nothing.
  B. The teacher turns her back and waits for silence.
  C. The teacher stops talking and waits for quiet.
  D. Keeping in for recess.
  E. Sending child to office.
  F. Depriving child in the classroom of some privilege.

VI. Academic Recognition
  Calling on a child for an answer. Giving "feedback" for academic correctness.

[a]These are procedural definitions of teacher behaviors possibly involving the withdrawal of reinforcers as a consequence of disruptive behaviors which teacher could not ignore.

Verbal Approval or Disapproval categories. For this reason we have used the term *Praise* interchangeably with Approval Behaviors and *Criticism* interchangeably with Disapproval Behaviors.

Reliability of measures of teacher behavior was checked approximately every other rating day (21 of 42 occasions for the two teachers) by dividing the agreements as to time interval and behavior codes by the agreements plus disagreements. Average reliability over behavior classes, teachers, and days was 84% with a range from 70% to 96% for individual day measures.

Experimental Conditions

In the middle-primary class (Class A) the experimental conditions may be summa-

rized as consisting of *Baseline;* introduction of *Rules; Rules* plus *Ignoring* deviant behavior; *Rules* plus *Ignoring* plus *Praise* for appropriate behavior; return to Baseline; and finally reinstatement of *Rules, Ignoring,* and *Praise.* In the kindergarten class (Class B) the experimental conditions consisted of *Baseline;* introduction of *Rules; Ignoring* Inappropriate Behavior (without continuing to emphasize rules); and the combination of *Rules, Ignoring,* and *Praise.*

The various experimental procedures were to be used by the teachers for the classroom as a whole throughout the day, not just for the children whose behavior was being recorded, and not just when observers were present.

Baseline. During the Baseline period the

Table 3
Teacher Behavior-Averages for Experimental Conditions (Frequency per 20-min Observation)

Teacher A Behavior Classes	*Experimental Conditions*					
	Baseline I	*Rules*	*Rules + Ignore*	*Rules + Ignore + Praise I*	*Baseline II*	*Rules + Ignore + Praise II*
Approval to Appropriate	1.2	2.0	0.0	18.2	2.5	12.5
Approval to Inappropriate	8.7	0.8	2.0	1.2	4.0	5.1
Disapproval to Inappropriate	18.5	20.5	15.7	4.1	9.8	3.5
Disapproval to Appropriate	0.9	0.7	1.0	0.3	0.9	0.0
Timeout	3.3	1.4	1.7	0.4	0.0	0.1
Academic Recognition	26.5	23.6	46.3	52.4	45.4	45.6
Days observed	15	8	3	11	4	9

Teacher B Behavior Classes	*Baseline*	*Rules*	*Ignore*	*Rules + Ignore + Praise*
Approval to Appropriate	19.2	14.1	19.3	35.2
Approval to Inappropriate	1.9	0.9	0.3	0.0
Disapproval to Inappropriate	16.9	22.1	10.6	10.8
Disapproval to Appropriate	0.0	0.0	0.0	0.0
Timeout	1.5	1.5	0.3	0.4
Academic Recognition	14.5	5.1	6.5	35.6
Days observed	8	6	6	10

teachers conducted their classes in their typical way. No attempt was made to influence their behavior.

Rules. Many people would argue that just telling children what is expected should have considerable effect on their behavior. We wished to explore this question empirically. Teachers were instructed individually and given written instructions as follows:

"The first phase of your participation in the use of behavioral principles to modify classroom behaviors is to specify explicit rules of classroom conduct.

When this is done, there is no doubt as to what is expected of the children in your classroom. However, do not expect a dramatic shift in classroom control, as we all know that knowing the prohibitions does not always keep people from "sin." This is the first phase in the program and inappropriate behavior should be reduced, but perhaps not eliminated. The rules should be formulated with the class and posted in a conspicuous location (a chart in front of the room or a special place on the chalkboard where they will not be erased). Go over the rules three or four times asking the class to repeat them back to you when they are initially formulated and use the following guidelines:

"(a) Make the rules short and to the point so they can be easily memorized.

"(b) Five or six rules are adequate. Special instructions for specific occasions are best given when the occasion arises. Children will not remember long lists of rules.

"(c) Where possible phrase the rules in a positive not a negative manner (for example, "Sit quietly while working," rather than, "Don't talk to your neighbors"). We want to emphasize positive actions.

"(d) Keep a sheet on your desk and record the number of times you review the rules with the class (strive for at least four to six repetitions per day). Remember that young children do not have the retention span of an adult and frequent reminders are necessary. Let the children recite the rules as you ask them, rather than always enumerating them yourself.

"(e) Remind the class of the rules at times other than when someone has misbehaved.

"(f) Try to change no other aspects of your classroom conduct except for the presentation of the rules at appropriate times."

Teacher tally sheets indicated that these instructions were followed quite explicitly. The average number of presentations of rules was 5.2 per day.

Ignoring Inappropriate Behavior. The second experimental phase involved Ignoring Inappropriate Behavior. In Class A, repetition of rules was also continued. Individual conferences to explain written instructions were given both teachers. Both teachers were given the following instructions:

"The first aspect of the study was to make expectations explicit. This you have been doing over the past few weeks. During the next phase of the study you should learn to *ignore* (do not attend to) behaviors which interfere with learning or teaching, unless of course, a child is being hurt by another, in which case use a punishment which seems appropriate, preferably withdrawal of some positive reinforcement. Learning to ignore is rather difficult. Most of us pay attention to the violations. For example, instead of ignoring we often say such things as the following: "Johnny, you know you are supposed to be working"; "Sue, will you stop bothering your neighbors"; "Henrieta, you have been at that window for a long time;" "Jack, can you keep your hands off Bill"; "Susie, will you please sit down"; "Alex, stop running around and do your work"; "Jane, will you please stop rocking on your chair."

"Behaviors which are to be ignored include motor behaviors such as getting out of seat, standing up, running, walking around the room, moving chairs, or sitting in a contorted manner. Any verbal comment or noise not connected with the assignments should also be ignored, such as: carrying on conversations with other children when it is not permitted, answering questions without raising hands or being called on, making remarks when no questions have been asked, calling your name to get attention, and extraneous noises such as crying, whistling, laughing loudly, blowing noise, or coughing. An additional important group of behaviors to be ignored are those which the student engages in when he is supposed to be doing other things, *e.g.,* when the child ignores your instructions you are to ignore him. Any noises made with objects, playing with pencils or other materials should be ignored, as well as taking things from or disturbing another student by turning around and touching or grabbing him.

"The reason for this phase of the experiment is to test the possibility that attention to Inappropriate Behavior may serve to strengthen the very behavior that the attention is intended to diminish. Inappropriate Behavior may be strengthened by paying attention to it even though you may think that you are punishing the behavior."

Praise for Appropriate Behavior. The third phase of the experiment included individual contacts with teachers to encourage and train Praising of Appropriate Behavior. The Praise instructions to the teachers were as follows:

"The first phase included specifying explicit rules, writing them on the board and reviewing them 4-6 times per day. The second phase was designed to reduce the amount of attention paid to behaviors which were unwanted by ignoring them. This third phase is primarily directed toward *increasing* Appropriate Behaviors through praise and other forms of approval. Teachers are inclined to take good behavior for granted and pay attention only when a child acts up or misbehaves. We are now asking you to try something different. This procedure is characterized as "catching the child being good" and making a comment designed to reward the child for good behavior. Give praise, attention, or smile when the child is doing what is expected during the particular class period in question. Inappropriate Behavior would not be a problem if all children were engaging in a great deal of study and school behavior, therefore, it is

necessary to apply what you have learned in the workshop. Shape by successive approximations the behavior desired by using praise and attention. Start "small" by giving praise and attention at the first signs of Appropriate Behavior and work toward greater goals. Pay close attention to those children who normally engage in a great deal of misbehavior. Watch carefully and when the child begins to behave appropriately, make a comment such as, "You're doing a fine job, (name)." It is very important during the first few days to catch as many good behaviors as possible. Even though a child has just thrown an eraser at the teacher (one minute ago) and is now studying, you should praise the study behavior. (It might also decrease the rate of eraser throwing.) We are assuming that your commendation and praise are important to the child. This is generally the case, but sometimes it takes a while for praise to become effective. Persistence in catching children being good and delivering praise and attention should eventually pay off in a better behaved classroom.

"Some examples of praise comments are as follows:

I like the way you're doing your work quietly (name).
That's the way I like to see you work _____.
That's a very good job _____.
You're doing fine _____.
You got two right _____, that's very good (if he generally gets no answers right).

"In general, give praise for achievement, prosocial behavior, and following the group rules. Specifically, you can praise for concentrating on individual work, raising hand when appropriate, responding to questions, paying attention to directions and following through, sitting in desk and studying, sitting quietly if noise has been a problem. Try to use variety and expression in your comments. Stay away from sarcasm. Attempt to become spontaneous in your praise and smile when delivering praise. At first you will probably get the feeling that you are praising a great deal and it sounds a little phony to your ears. This is a typical reaction and it becomes more natural with the passage of time. Spread your praise and attention around. If comments sometimes might interfere with the ongoing class activities then use facial attention and smiles. Walk around the room during study time and pat or place your hand on the back of a child who is doing a good job. Praise quietly spoken to the children has been found effective in combination with some physical sign of approval.

"General Rule: Give *praise* and *attention* to behaviors which facilitate learning. Tell the child what he is being praised for. Try to reinforce behaviors incompatible with those you wish to decrease."

The teachers were also instructed to continue to ignore deviant behavior and to repeat the rules several times a day.

Additional training given teachers consisted of: (a) discussion of problems with suggested solutions during weekly seminars on behavior analysis, and (b) specific suggestions from the experimenter on possible alternative responses in specific situations based on the experimenter's observations of the teachers during experimental transitions, or based on observer data and notes at other times when the data showed that the teachers were not on program.

Additional cues were provided to implement the program. Cards were placed on the teachers' desks containing the instructions for the experimental phase in which they were engaged.

Reversal. In Class A the final experimental conditions involved an attempt to return to Baseline, followed by a reinstatement of the *Rules, Praise,* and *Ignore* condition. On the basis of the earlier observations of Teacher A, we were able to specify to her how frequently she made disapproving and approving comments. The success of this procedure can be judged from the data.

Results

Percentage of observation intervals in which Inappropriate Behaviors occurred as a function of conditions is graphed in Fig. 1 and 2. Major changes in Inappropriate Behaviors occurred only when Praise or Approval for Appropriate Behaviors was emphasized in the experimental procedures. A t test, comparing average Inappropriate Behavior in conditions where Praise was emphasized with those where Praise was not emphasized, was significant at the 0.05 level ($df = 2$).

Before examining the results more closely, it is necessary to inspect the data on teacher behavior. Table 3 gives the frequency of classes of teacher behaviors averaged within experimental conditions. Since day-to-day variability of teacher behavior was low for the measures used, these averages fairly reflect what went on.

Introduction of Rules into the classroom had no appreciable effect on Inappropriate Behavior.

Ignoring Inappropriate Behaviors produced inconsistent results. In Class A the

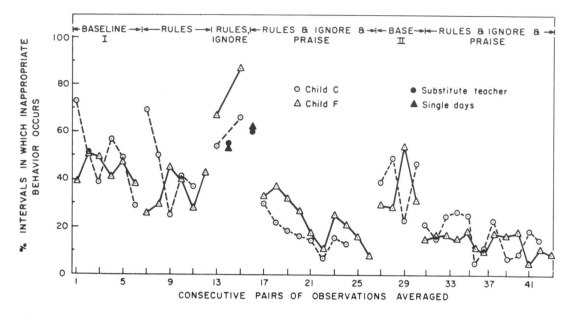

Figure 1 Inappropriate behavior of two problem children in classroom A as a function of experimental conditions.

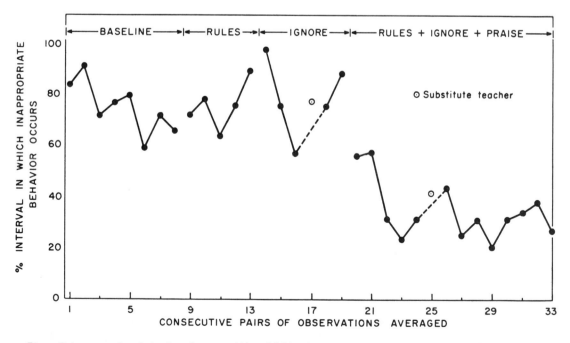

Figure 2 Inappropriate behavior of one problem child in classroom B as a function of experimental conditions.

children clearly became worse under this condition; in Class B little change was apparent. Both teachers had a difficult time adhering to this condition, and Teacher A found this phase of the experiment very unpleasant. Table 3 shows that Teacher A was only able to reduce critical comments from an average of one per 1 min to an average of three in 4 min. Teacher B cut her critical comments in half. In view of these difficulties, the present results cannot be taken as a clear test of the effects of responding with Disapproval to Inappropriate Behaviors.

The failure to eliminate Disapproval Reactions to Inappropriate Behaviors in Phase Three of the experiment, adds some ambiguities to the interpretation of the Phase Four data for Teacher A. The Rules, Ignore, and Praise condition for Teacher A involved both a reduction in critical comments (Ignoring) as well as a marked increase in Praise. As demonstrated previously (Becker *et al.,* 1967), this combination of procedures is very effective in reducing inappropriate classroom behaviors, but we still lack a clear isolation of effects. The data for Teacher B are not confounded with a simultaneous shift in frequency of Disapproval and Approval Reactions, but they are made less interpretable by a marked shift in Academic Recognition (defined in Table 2) which occurred when the shift in Praise was made. Since Academic Recognition does not show any systematic relations to level of Appropriate Behaviors elsewhere in the study, we are not inclined to interpret this change as showing a causal effect. A best guess is that the effective use of Praise gave the teacher more time to focus on academic skills.

The reversal operation for Teacher A quite clearly shows that the combination of Praising and Ignoring exerts a strong control over Appropriate Behaviors.

As with Academic Recognition, no attempt was made to control how frequently the teacher used procedures labelled "Timeout" (defined in Table 2). The frequency data reported in Table 4 indicates that during Baseline, Teacher A, especially, used "Timeout" procedures to try to establish control (usually turning off lights until the children were quiet). The changes in the frequency of use of "Timeout" procedures are not systematically related to the behavior changes graphed in Fig. 1 and 2.

In summary, the main results indicate: (a) that Rules alone had little effect in improving classroom behavior, (b) the functional status of Ignoring Inappropriate Behavior needs further clarification, (c) the combination of Ignoring and Praising was very effective in achieving better classroom behavior, and (d) Praise for Appropriate Behaviors was probably the key teacher behavior in achieving effective classroom management.

The effects of the experimental procedures on individual classes of behavior for the two children in Class A are presented in Table 4. The data in Table 4 illustrate that with a few exceptions the effects on individual classes of behavior are similar to those for Inappropriate Behavior as a whole.

Discussion

Technical Considerations

The problems of gaining good data and maintaining adequate experimental control in an ongoing classroom in a public school have not all been recognized as yet, much less solved. The greatest difficulty encountered was that of maintaining stable control over some important variables while others were being changed. When these variables involve aspects of teacher behavior, the problem becomes one of helping the teacher maintain discriminative control over her

Table 4

Percentage of intervals in which behaviors occur: averages for two children in classroom A by experimental conditions.

Behavior Classes[1]	Experimental Conditions					
	Baseline I	Rules	Rules + Ignore	Rules + Ignore + Praise I	Baseline II	Rules + Ignore + Praise II
Inappropriate Behavior[2]	46.8	39.8	68.5	20.5	37.6	15.1
Gross Motor	13.9	11.3	32.7	5.9	15.5	4.1
Object Noise	3.5	1.4	1.3	0.5	1.9	0.8
Disturbing Other's Property	3.3	1.8	1.9	0.7	0.7	0.3
Turning Around	21.6	9.9	11.4	9.1	12.8	7.6
Verbalizations	12.0	16.8	21.8	6.5	8.0	3.5
Other Inappropriate Behavior	10.9	7.8	16.5	3.9	7.8	2.6
Mouthing Objects	5.5	2.9	3.5	0.7	0.2	0.1

[1] *Contact* occurred less than 1% of the time and is not tabulated here.

[2] The sum of the separate problem behaviors will exceed that for Inappropriate Behavior, since the latter measure does not reflect the possibility that more than one class of problem behaviors may occur in an interval.

own behavior. Daily feedback from the experimenter, based on the observer ratings, can help in this task (*i.e.,* show the teacher the up-to-date graph of her behavior). Also, providing the teacher with a small counter to help monitor her own behavior can be helpful (Thomas, *et al.,* 1968). Most difficult to control in the present study was teacher's Disapproving Reactions to Inappropriate Behaviors during the Ignore Phase of the experiment. Teacher A became very "upset" as her classroom became worse. One solution to this problem might be a pre-study in which the teacher is trained in effective management techniques, and then taken through a series of short periods where both Approval and Disapproval are eliminated and one or the other reinstated. The teacher would then have confidence that she can effectively handle her class and be better able to tolerate short periods of chaos (if such periods did occur). She would also have had sufficient training in monitoring

her own behavior to permit more effective control.

No attempt was made to program the frequency of various classes of Academic Recognition behaviors. Since such behavior may be important in interpreting results, and was found to vary with some experimental conditions, future work should strive to hold this behavior constant also.

The present study emphasized the importance of contingencies between student and teacher behaviors, but did not measure them directly. While producing similar effects on two children in the same classroom and one child in another classroom, and showing correlated changes in teacher behaviors (including a reversal operation), more powerful data are potentially obtainable with a different technology. Video-tape recordings could enable the use of present coding techniques to obtain contingency data on all classroom members over longer observation periods. Just as the children adapted to the presence of observers, a class could be adapted to the presence of a TV camera man. Costs could be trimmed by saving only some sample tapes and reusing others after reliability ratings are obtained. The current observation procedures (short of having an observer for each child) cannot readily be extended to include simultaneous coding of teacher and child behavior without over-taxing the observers. The present findings, and related studies in this series, are sufficiently promising to warrant an investment in more powerful recording equipment.

Teacher Reactions

Teacher A. Initially, Mrs. A generally maintained control through scolding and loud critical comments. There were frequent periods of chaos, which she handled by various threats.

When praise was finally added to the program, Mrs. A had these reactions: "I was amazed at the difference the procedure made in the atmosphere of the classroom and even my own personal feelings. I realized that in praising the well-behaved children and ignoring the bad, I was finding myself looking for the good in the children. It was indeed rewarding to see the good rather than always criticizing. . . . I became convinced that a positive approach to discipline was the answer."

Teacher B. During Baseline Mrs. B was dispensing a great deal of praise and approval to her classroom, but it was not always contingent on Appropriate Behavior. Her timing was wrong and inconsistencies were apparent. For example, on one occasion two children were fighting with scissors. The instigator was placed under a table away from the rest of the class and left there for 3 min. After 3 min Mrs. B took the child in her arms and brought her back to the

group even though she was still emitting occasional loud screams. Mrs. B would also ignore behavior for a period of time and then would revert to responding to Inappropriate Behavior with a negative comment; she occasionally gave Approval for Inappropriate Behavior. The training given in seminar and discussions with the experimenter led to an effective use of contingencies. Teacher B was also able to use this training to provide instructions and training for her aide to eliminate problems which arose in the final phase of study when the aide was continuing to respond to Disruptive Behaviors.

Changes in the Children

Cliff showed little change until Mrs. A started praising Appropriate Behavior, except to get worse during the Ignore phase. He was often doing no academic work, talking to peers, and just fiddling away his time. It took considerable effort by Mrs. A to catch Cliff showing praiseworthy behavior. As the use of praise continued, Cliff worked harder on his assigned tasks, learned to ignore other children who were misbehaving, and would raise his hand to get teacher's attention. He participated more in class discussions. He was moved up to the fastest arithmetic group.

Frank showed little change in his "hyperactive" and "inattentive" behaviors until praise was introduced. Frank responded rapidly to praise. After just two days in the "praise" phase, Frank was observed to clean his desk quietly and quickly after completing a handwriting assignment. He was able to finish a task and study on his own until the teacher initiated a new activity. He began to ask for extra assignments and volunteered to do things to help his teacher. He had learned to sit quietly (when appropriate), to listen, and to raise his hand to participate in class discussion, the latter occurring quite frequently.

Stan slowly improved after contingent praise was instituted, but some of the gains made by Mrs. B were in part undone by the teacher aide. The aide was described as playing policeman and it took special efforts by the teacher to get her to follow the program. Mrs. B summarized the changes in Stan as follows: "Stan has changed from a sullen, morose, muttering, angry individual into a boy whose smile seems to cover his whole face." He became very responsive to teacher praise and learned to follow classroom rules, to pay attention to teacher-directed activities for long periods of time, and to interact with his peers in a more friendly way.

Implications

This replication and refinement of an earlier study by Becker, *et al.* (1967) adds further confidence to the assertion that teachers can be taught systematic procedures and can use them to gain more effective behaviors from their students. Unless teachers are effective in getting children "ready to learn", their technical teaching skills are likely to be wasted. Knowledge of differential social reinforcement procedures, as well as other behavioral principles, can greatly enhance teachers' enjoyment of the profession and their contribution to effective development of the students.

The reader should note that while we formally recorded the behavior of a few target children, teacher and observer comments indicated dramatic changes in the whole "atmosphere" of the classroom and in the teachers' enjoyment of their classes.

REFERENCES

Allen, K. E., Hart, B. M., Buell, J. S., Harris, F. R., and Wolf, M. M. "Effects of Social Reinforcement on Isolate Behavior of a Nursery School Child," In L. P. Ullmann and L. Krasner eds. *Case Studies in Behavior Modification.* New York: Holt, Rinehart, & Winston, 1965. pp. 307–312.

Becker, W. C., Madsen, C. H., Jr., Arnold, Carole R., and Thomas, D. R. "The Contingent Use of Teacher Attention and Praise in Reducing Classroom Behavior Problems," *Journal of Special Education,* 1967, 1, 287–307.

Bijou, S. W. and Baer, D. M. "Some Methodological Contributions from a Functional Analysis of Child Development," In L. P. Lipsitt and C. S. Spiker eds. *Advances in Child Development and Behavior.* New York: Academic Press, 1963. pp. 197–231.

Hart, Betty M., Reynolds, Nancy J., Baer, Donald M., Brawley, Eleanor R., and Harris, Florence R. "Effect of Contingent and Non-Contingent Social Reinforcement on the Cooperative Play of a Preschool Child," *Journal of Applied Behavior Analysis,* 1968, 1, 73–76.

Thomas, D. R., Becker, W. C., and Armstrong, Marianne. "Production and Elimination of Disruptive Classroom Behavior by Systematically Varying Teacher's Behavior," *Journal of Applied Behavior Analysis,* 1968, 1, 35–45.

Madsen, C. H., Jr., Becker, W. C., Thomas, D. R., Koser, Linda, and Plager, Elaine. "An Analysis of the Reinforcing Function of 'Sit Down' Commands," In Parker, R. K. ed. *Readings in Educational Psychology.* Boston: Allyn and Bacon (in Press).

Recommended Readings: Promoting Learning through Motivation and Reinforcement Strategies

Becker, W. C., Thomas, D. R. and Carnine, D. *Reducing Behavioral Problems: An Operant Conditioning Guide for Teachers.* Urbana, Illinois: ERIC Clearinghouse on Early Childhood Education, November, 1969.

Brown, Duane. *Changing Student Behavior: A New Approach to Discipline.* Dubuque, Iowa: Wm. C. Brown Company Publishers, 1971.

Catania, Charles A., ed. *Contemporary Research in Operant Behavior,* Glenview, Illinois: Scott, Foresman, 1968.

Filip, Robert T., ed. *Prospectives in Programming.* New York: The Macmillan Co., 1963.

Gnagey, William J. *The Psychology of Discipline in the Classroom.* New York: The Macmillan Co., 1968.

Hokanson, J. E. The *Physiological Bases of Motivation.* New York: John Wiley & Sons, Inc., 1969.

Johnson, Lois V. and Bany, Mary A. *Classroom Management: Theory and Skill Training.* New York: The Macmillan Co., 1970.

Kuethe, James L. *The Teaching Learning-Process.* Glenview, Illinois: Scott, Foresman, 1968.

Logan, Frank A. *Introduction to Learning and Motivation.* Dubuque, Iowa: Wm. C. Brown Company Publishers, 1970.

McDonald, Blanche and Nelson, Leslie W. *Successful Classroom Control.* 2nd ed. Dubuque, Iowa: Wm. C. Brown Company Publishers, 1959.

Morse, William C. and Wingo, Max G. *Classroom Psychology: Readings in Educational Psychology.* Glenview, Illinois: Scott, Foresman, 1970.

Reese, Ellen P. *The Analysis of Human Operant Behavior.* (Psy. Self-Sel. Ser.) Dubuque, Iowa: Wm. C. Brown Company Publishers, 1967.

Reynolds, George S., ed. *Contemporary Experimental Psychology.* Vol. 1: *Instinct, Learning and Motivation.* Glenview, Illinois: Scott, Foresman, 1971.

Rosenthal, Robert and Jacobson, Leonore *Pygmalion in the Classroom.* New York: Holt, Rinehart and Winston, 1968.

Russell, L. Ivan *Motivation.* Dubuque, Iowa: Wm. C. Brown Company Publishers, 1971.

Schmuck, Richard and Schmuck, Patricia *Group Processes in the Classroom.* Dubuque, Iowa: Wm. C. Brown Company Publishers, 1971.

Ullman, L. P. and Kransner, L., eds. *Case Studies in Behavior Modification.* New York: Holt, Rinehart and Winston, 1965.

Valett, R. E. *Modifying Children's Behavior.* Palo Alto, California: Fearon Publishers, 1969.

Utilization and Management
of Multi-Media for Teaching

In order to assist the classroom teacher in carrying out the important task of improving the quality of classroom instruction, particular attention must be paid to the effective utilization of audiovisual media.

Allen states that the major consideration in choosing suitable media for teaching is the relative effectiveness of the materials in achieving the desired instructional objective. He sets up guidelines designed to help the teacher in selecting the type of instructional media most effective for the accomplishment of specific learning skills. Through the use of a table each type of instructional medium was rated low, medium, or high according to the effectiveness of each in accomplishing a particular learning objective. Also of significance to the classroom teacher is his presentation of a step-by-step procedure for making the most effective use of instructional media in teaching an art lesson.

Recognizing the importance of matching instructional media to specific learning skills, Hartley has provided the teacher with a list of toys, play materials and equipment appropriate for the development of specific skills and abilities, understandings and aesthetic expressions. In addition, the author matches the list of materials and equipment to the interests and developmental levels of children from preschool years to preteens.

Several studies of the effectiveness of audiovisual materials are reviewed by Wendt and Butts. The audiovisual materials under investigation are motion pictures, filmstrips, slides and transparencies, pictorial illustrations and graphic materials, recordings and radio, and three-dimensional materials. Studies concerning interaction between learners and materials and the utilization of audiovisual materials are also reviewed. It is pointed out by the authors that some researchers suspect that learner characteristics are related to the effectiveness of teaching materials rather than to the nature of the materials themselves or the manner in which audiovisual materials are used.

The importance of matching materials to the specific needs and abilities of the learner is the subject of the article by Weinthaler and Rotberg. In this selection they describe a system for selecting instructional materials based upon an inventory of learning abilities and skills. The method is discussed in two parts—selecting materials for individuals and selecting materials for groups of children. Though the article is directed toward teachers of the handicapped, it carries vast potential for applicability in regular classrooms.

A thorough study of this section is expected to prepare the student to:

1. Develop criteria for the selection of instructional media.
2. State a specific type of learning and choose the most effective instructional materials for its accomplishment.
3. Make an inventory of audiovisual aids and match each instrument with the developmental levels of individual children from nursery school to Grade 4.
4. Devise a system for the selection of instructional materials which is based upon an inventory of the learner's abilities and skills.
5. Design a procedure for the effective utilization of instructional media for teaching a skill in a particular subject-matter area.
6. Create a number of teacher-made audiovisual materials and assess the effectiveness of each in achieving desired instructional objectives.

Media Stimulus and Types of Learning

William H. Allen

EDITORS' QUESTIONS:

1. Explain what is meant by the statement "At this stage of our knowledge, one might conclude that the use of films, projected still pictures, television and programmed instruction in the presentation of factual information adds little to student learning, and they are probably no more effective than such conventional types as print and oral presentation." Does this conclusion coincide with your own view? Support your answer with evidence from research and other related readings. Does this statement point to the inconclusiveness of evidence concerning the relative effectiveness of the use of media in promoting certain types of learning? If so, how are you to direct your behavior with regard to the utilization of media for instructional purposes?

2. Discuss the major considerations involved in the use of educational media.

3. How can a teacher judge the effectiveness of alternative instructional materials? Develop a set of criteria for the selection of instructional media.

4. Make a chart showing a match between instructional objectives and instructional media. Select the media that are most effective in contributing to the accomplishment of each of the designated learning objectives.

5. Read carefully the procedures suggested by the author for the use of instructional media in teaching. Devise similar procedures for the teaching of arithmetic or some other subject-matter area.

28

William H. Allen, "Media Stimulus and Types of Learning," *Audiovisual Instruction*, XII, (January 1967), 27–31. Reprinted with the permission of the National Art Education Association, The Association for Educational Communication and Technology, *Audiovisual Instruction* and William H. Allen.

Characteristics of the Instructional Media

The key to the selection of the appropriate instructional media to use in any particular teaching situation is the relative effectiveness of that medium in accomplishing the desired educational objective.

In other words, given a specific instructional goal, what is the best means of reaching it? Interestingly enough, in education there is little experimental evidence to point the way for the making of these instructional decisions. This is true at every level of teaching and in every subject-matter area. It is true in the teaching of art, and it is true in the application of audiovisual instructional media to the teaching process. Gagné and Bolles observed, "relatively little of a systematic nature is known about how to promote efficient learning in practical situations" (6). And Gage stated that "the limited usefulness of learning theory in education has long been acknowledged" (3). This does not mean, of course, that we know nothing about selecting appropriate media

267

for instruction in specific tasks. It is just that this knowledge has not been systematically organized into a useable set of operational procedures that might be applied to the teaching of art.

Over the entire range of art teaching you have, at different times, a variety of educational objectives. We will not argue the relative merits of the objectives in this paper, for this is your responsibility as art educators, and your literature is filled with discussions of this problem. Our task here is to relate the audiovisual instructional media to the accomplishment of these various objectives. This is a difficult task and has never been systematically applied to instructional media selection for art education. So the following attempt must be treated as very tentative at this time. It is presented here in the hope that art teachers will draw from it suggestions for instructional media implementation and not as a fully developed guideline to be arbitrarily applied to the se-

lection of instructional materials. In *Table 1* a very rough and preliminary rating is given for the effectiveness of different instructional media types when used to accomplish six different learning objectives. It is suggested that this evaluative grid be used jointly with the following explanation of the media-objectives relationships. Those teachers who want to obtain a more comprehensive background in the determination of learning objectives and their relationships to instructional techniques are referred to the writing of Gagné (4, 5) and Mager (14).

1. *Learning factual information.* This includes information such as names, dates, events, terms, definitions, etc., all of which have concrete referents. In the teaching of art these might include such tasks as learning the facts of art history, terminology, or facts about art media.

An abundance of audiovisual media research points to the effectiveness of films,

Table 1
Instructional Media Stimulus Relationships to Learning Objectives

INSTRUCTIONAL MEDIA TYPE:	LEARNING OBJECTIVES:					
	Learning Factual Information	Learning Visual Identifications	Learning Principles, Concepts and Rules	Learning Procedures	Performing Skilled Perceptual-Motor Acts	Developing Desirable Attitudes, Opinions & Motivations
Still Pictures	Medium	HIGH	Medium	Medium	low	low
Motion Pictures	Medium	HIGH	HIGH	HIGH	Medium	Medium
Television	Medium	Medium	HIGH	Medium	low	Medium
3-D Objects	low	HIGH	low	low	low	low
Audio Recordings	Medium	low	low	Medium	low	Medium
Programed Instruction	Medium	Medium	Medium	HIGH	low	Medium
Demonstration	low	Medium	low	HIGH	Medium	Medium
Printed Textbooks	Medium	low	Medium	Medium	low	Medium
Oral Presentation	Medium	low	Medium	Medium	low	Medium

filmstrips, television, and programed instruction in meeting this educational objective (1). Unfortunately, however, although the research indicates that these audiovisual materials are effective, it does not tell us specifically what types of audiovisual media are indicated under what kinds of teaching conditions. That is, we have no evidence that would help us choose from a variety of materials that *particular* instructional medium that would be most effective. At this stage of our knowledge, one might conclude that the use of films, projected still pictures, television, and programed instruction in the presentation of factual information adds little to student learning, and they are probably no more effective than such conventional types as print and oral presentation. On the other hand, films and projected still pictures do contribute greatly to the interest level of learners and provide a useful variety in the teaching. It should be pointed out that television is a *carrier* of information to the learner and probably possesses no particular characteristic that would make it more effective than any other instructional medium in teaching factual information. The characteristics of the television image are identical to that of sound motion picture image, but with significant degradation in picture quality. The educational differences between the sound motion picture and television are those related to the method of image display, the control that can be exercised by the teacher in using them, and the system of distribution of the images. From the standpoint of the teaching function, they appear to be the same. (However, Marshall McLuhan (15) would disagree, claiming that television is a different medium with different instructional characteristics just because of such features as degraded image and difference in display.) Research with programed instruction (17, 18) indicates that factual information may be efficiently taught with teaching machines or programed textbooks, but not necessarily more so than with other instructional methods. The use of three-dimensional objects or demonstrations probably is of little instructional value in the learning of facts as such.

2. *Learning visual identification.* This learning task will involve the use of visual cues to discriminate one element from another and will require the identification and naming of objects, words, or symbols. This type of task is one of the most common performed by human beings. In the teaching of art it might include such tasks as identifying shapes and forms, learning the characteristics of different art forms, recognizing works of art, "seeing" the various visual aspects of the environment, or discriminating among different shades and tones of colors. It would be expected that this learning objective would play a significant role in art education.

It has been shown that in instructional situations where the initial presentation stimulus is similar to the performance or behavior in the final task to be learned, high positive transfer will occur (2, 6, 8, 12, 16). It is to be expected that such a condition would prevail in the learning of visual discriminations in art education. This means that the stimulus representations of the associations to be learned should be made as much like the stimuli in the performance or behavior in the final task as possible. It is apparent that conventional *printed* or *lectured* verbal stimuli have only symbolic similarity to visual identification learning tasks and would not be expected to transfer optimally to the final task situation. On the other hand, high amounts of positive transfer may be expected from *pictured representations* (such as films, slides, flat pictures) of stimulus objects where the final task performance requires *crucial* knowledge of these objects (7). The purpose of visuals of this kind is to practice, in the learning situation, the response needed in the performance situation. Gropper has called these "criterion visuals" because the "use of visual presentations appears to be desirable in those subject matters in which visually perceived physical objects and events are integral parts of the criterion situation" (9). That is, the learner should be able to observe, describe, interpret, or reconstruct the precise content presented in the instruction.

It would appear, then, that audiovisual instructional media that closely represent the physical characteristics of this material being taught should be effective in the teaching of visual discriminations. Those instructional media particularly high in this quality are sound motion picture films, filmstrips, slides, photographic illustrations, and three-dimensional objects. Interestingly enough, however, little audiovisual media research has looked specifically at this problem. Rather, the research has tested the effects of stimulus materials that have mixed objectives; thus, it is not possible to determine the specific relationships of the instructional media used to accomplish a specific objective. The best we can do at this point is to say that the theory strongly indicates that instructional media of a representational nature would be highly effective in the teaching of visual identifications.

3. *Learning principles, concepts and rules.* This task involves the learning and understanding of relationships among things or events, the meaning of rules, or the principles pertaining to the functioning of different kinds of operations. In the teaching of art, this objective would be associated with learning of principles governing color or the understanding of the concepts underlying the various schools of art.

There is little experimental research with projected materials or television learning on this particular objective. However, a recent study by Gropper (10) used the programed instruction mode to study the learning of science concepts and principles on the basis of either visual (pictorial) or verbal (print) presentation alone. Gropper found that when a totally *visual* (pictorial) presentation of the concept to be learned *preceded* a verbal (print) presentation of the same concept, the learning was significantly greater and took significantly less learning time than when the *verbal* presentation *preceded* the visual one. The importance of this study, for our purposes here, are twofold. First, it represents a systematic attempt to develop a *strategy* of instructional media use by manipulating certain variables and controlling others to arrive at a generalizable conclusion. Second, it presents some very convincing evidence in support of the effectiveness of visual (pictorial) presentations.

4. *Learning procedures.* This task involves learning to carry out a sequence of acts or operations in the proper order. In the teaching of art, these might be the learning of the procedure for the making of a silk screen print or the procedure to follow in preparing art media for use. Because of the fairly simple nature of the *order* of most art procedures, this learning objective may not be as important as the others. There is no recognizable audiovisual research relating directly to this problem, but it might be expected that sound motion pictures, televised instruction, programed instruction, and demonstrations would be the educational media most apt to enhance such learning.

5. *Performing skilled perceptual-motor acts.* This task involves the use of simple and complex perceptual-motor skills for performing a manipulation task. In the teaching of art, this might entail the learning of proper manipulative techniques with art

media such as the handling of tools, water-color washes, etc.

There is little doubt about the effectiveness of films in teaching perceptual-motor skills, particularly when students are given opportunities for active participation during the presentation process (1, 11, 13). Studies using the repetitive 8mm film-loop for skill training have demonstrated the efficacy of this promising instructional technique (19). For the art teacher who wishes to develop specific perceptual-motor skills and to give students an exemplary model to follow, there would appear to be a sound research base for the employment of motion picture films, particularly if they are used creatively (stopping for practice, repeating, etc.) rather than merely as one-way one-time communication media. If the teacher will use the repetitive 8mm film-loop and build in opportunity for student participation, skills learning will probably be greatly enhanced.

6. *Developing Desirable Attitudes, Opinions, and Motivations.* This task relates to the enhancement of the learner's preference for a particular point of view, idea, practice, or course of action, and requires the involvement of his drives, wishes, or needs. In the teaching of art, this might involve the development of awareness of the aesthetics of artistic presentation or the desire to engage in art activities. There is limited research evidence pointing to the superiority of any specific medium of instruction; but it would appear that a variety of different kinds of stimuli, presenting the learner with many dimensions of the subject, would be most likely to lead to the development of desirable attitudes.

Making Proper Use of Instructional Media in Teaching

In the previous section and in *Table 1* some rough guidelines were presented as aids to the proper selection of instructional media under different conditions of learning. It is suggested that the following step-by-step procedure be used in order to make the most effective application of instructional media to art teaching:

1. *State the exact behavior to be expected of the learner.* In other words, as a result of your teaching of a specific lesson or sublesson, precisely what will the student be expected to learn or what skill to perform? This should be stated in very specific behavioral terms (5, 14).

2. *Identify the type of learning objective being met by the instruction.* Descriptions of types as they relate to art education are presented in the preceding section. These types are also the column listings in *Table 1.*

3. *Write down the particular "instructional event" that will occur* (such as, "Introduce the art materials for silk screen printing" or "Demonstrate the procedure for silk screen printing"). From *Table 1* select the appropriate instructional media options (such as "demonstration procedure" or "film of procedure").

4. *Determine availability of the instructional media* to meet the educational objective (from school materials, audiovisual catalogs, personal resources, etc.).

5. *Determine availability of equipment* needed for presentation of indicated material. *Table 2* shows the relationship of equipment to instructional media, the considerations required in production of materials, the general availability of the equipment under normal instructional conditions, and a rough measure of equipment cost.

6. *Arrange for preparation of unavailable instructional media and/or obtain access to needed equipment.*

The preceding six steps may appear to be unnecessarily detailed, and the art teacher,

Table 2
Equipment/Media Relationships and Considerations

Instrument	Media Used	Materials Production Considerations	Availability of Facilities and Equipment	Equipment Cost
1. Filmstrip or slide projector	35mm filmstrips or 2x2 slides	Inexpensive. May be done locally in short time.	Usually available. Requires darkened room.	low
2. Overhead transparency projector	Still pictures and graphic representations	Very inexpensive. May be done locally in short time.	Available. May be projected in light room.	low
3. Wall charts or posters	Still pictures	Very inexpensive. May be done locally in very short time.	Available. No special equipment needed.	very low
4. Motion pictures (projection to groups)	16mm motion picture (sound or silent)	Specially-produced. Sound film is costly and requires 6-12 months time.	Usually available. Requires darkened classroom.	moderate
5. Motion picture projection as repetitive loops (8mm silent) to individuals	8mm motion picture film (silent)	Special production normally necessary. May be produced as 16mm film alone or locally at low cost and in short time.	Not normally available. Will need to be specially procured to meet requirement of instructional program.	low per unit, but moderate for groups
6. Magnetic tape recorder	1/4″ magnetic tape	Easy and inexpensive. Usually produced locally.	Available	low
7. Record player	33 1/3, 45 or 78 rpm disk recordings	Need special recording facilities. Usually commercially made.	Usually available	low
8. Display area	3-D models	May vary in complexity and in difficulty of production. Component parts easy to obtain.	Available	varies from low to high
9. Television (closed-circuit)	Live presentations. Motion picture film. Videotape recordings. Still pictures.	Normally requires large and skilled production staff.	Not normally available	moderate to high
10. Teaching machines & programed textbooks	Programed material	Some programs available commercially. But will normally be specially prepared for course.	Not normally available	low per unit, but moderate for groups
11. System combinations	Television. Motion pictures. Still pictures. Audio recordings.	Complex. Probably will be done locally to meet specific requirements.	Not normally available	moderate to high

of course, will not be able to follow them for every lesson. They were presented, however, in the belief that if the teacher has a clear conception of his objectives and the behavior expected from his students, he will be able to make more intelligent media selections. This method substitutes a procedure that uses reasoned choice based on some set of standards for a procedure that operates merely on the basis of what materials are available. As a result, the quality of instruction should be improved.

REFERENCES

1. Allen, William H. "Audio-Visual Communications." In Chester W. Harris (editor), *Encyclopedia of Educational Research.* Third Edition. New York: Macmillan, 1960. pp. 115–37.

2. Carpenter, C. R. "A Theoretical Orientation for Instructional Film Research." *AV Communications Review.* 1:38–52; Winter, 1953.

3. Gage, N. L. "Theories of Teaching." In Ernest R. Hilgard (editor), *Theories of Learning and Instruction.* Sixty-Third Yearbook of the National Society for the Study of Education, Part I. Chicago: The Society, 1964.

4. Gagné, Robert M. *The Conditions of Learning.* New York: Holt, Rinehart and Winston, 1965.

5. Gagné, Robert M. "The Analysis of Instructional Objectives for the Design of Instruction." In Robert Glaser (editor), *Teaching Machines and Programed Learning, II: Data and Directions.* Washington: Department of Audiovisual Instruction, National Education Association, 1965. pp. 21–65.

6. Gagné, Robert M., and Bolles, Robert C. "A Review of Factors in Learning Efficiency." In Eugene Gallanter (editor), *Automatic Teaching: The State of the Art.* New York: Wiley, 1959.

7. Gagné, Robert M., and Foster, Harriett. "Transfer to a Motor Skill Practice on a Pictured Representation." *Journal of Experimental Psychology.* 39:342–55; 1949.

8. Gibson, James J. "A Theory of Pictorial Perception." *AV Communication Review.* 2:3–23; Winter, 1954.

9. Gropper, George L. "Why is a Picture Worth a Thousand Words?" *AV Communication Review.* 11:75–95; July–August, 1963.

10. Gropper, George L. "Learning from Visuals: Some Behavioral Considerations." *AV Communication Review.* Spring, 1966.

11. Hoban, Charles F. and van Ormer, Edward B. *Instructional Film Research, 1918–1950.* Technical Report No. SDC 269-7-19, Instructional Film Research Program, Pennsylvania State College, Port Washington, L.I., N.Y.: U.S. Navy Special Devices Center, 1950.

12. Hovland, C. I. "Human Learning and Retention." In S. S. Stevens (editor), *Handbook of Experimental Psychology.* New York: Wiley, 1951.

13. Lumsdaine, A. A. "Instruments and Media of Instruction." In N. L. Gage (editor), *Handbook of Research on Teaching.* Chicago: Rand McNally, 1963. pp. 583–682.

14. Mager, Robert F. *Preparing Objectives for Programed Instruction.* San Francisco: Fearon Publishers, 1962.

15. McLuhan, Marshall. *Understanding Media.* New York: McGraw-Hill, 1964.

16. Osgood, C. E. *Method and Theory in Experimental Psychology.* New York: Oxford University Press, 1953.

17. Schramm, Wilbur. *The Research on Programed Instruction: An Annotated Bibliography.* Bulletin 1964 No. 35, OE-34034. Washington: Office of

Education, U.S. Department of Health, Education, and Welfare, 1964.

18. Silberman, Harry F. "Self-Teaching Devices and Programed Materials." *Review of Educational Research.* 32:179–93; April, 1962.

19. Wendt, Paul R., and Butts, Gordon K. "Audiovisual Materials." *Review of Educational Research.* 32:141–55; April, 1962.

Toys, Play Materials and Equipment[*]

Ruth E. Hartley

EDITORS' QUESTIONS:

1. Using as a guide the criteria which you have developed for the selection of instructional materials, evaluate the list of toys, play materials and equipment presented in this article.

2. Make an inventory of instructional materials and match each to the developmental levels of children (Nursery through Grade 4) and to specific learning objectives.

3. Discuss the effects on the creativity and originality of teachers and children of the availability of ready-made commercial instructional materials. Does the availability of such materials rob teachers and pupils of the vast learning opportunities provided by creating or improvising their own instructional materials?

4. Select a commercial toy or game which children like to play, for example, Candy Land game, Monopoly or Bingo game. Modify this toy or game for use as an instructional device for teaching a specific learning objective to a child or a group of children in nursery, kindergarten or early primary grades.

5. Create two or three instructional materials. Identify the age level for which each is most appropriate and the specific learning objectives that each can help accomplish.

29

"Toys, Play Materials and Equipment," by Ruth E. Hartley. From CHILDHOOD EDUCATION, November 1968, Vol. 45, No. 3. Reprinted by permission of Ruth E. Hartley and the Association for Childhood Education International, 3615 Wisconsin Avenue, N.W., Washington, D.C. Copyright © 1968 by the Association.

Preschool Years (3, 4, 5)

For Motor Play

Toys and play equipment encouraging motor activity can be most important in strengthening and developing large muscle coordination and helping lay the foundations of concepts of space. Among these are rocking horses; vehicles to ride *in* such as replicas of fire engines, cars, Irish mail-cars, propelled by pedals; vehicles to ride *on,* such as tricycles; wheeled toys to push and to pull, such as wheelbarrows and wagons. Also appropriate are large hollow blocks, swings, slides, balancing boards, see-saws, box-ladders, doorway gyms (rings or bars)

and jungle gyms. Where space is available, a rope ladder to be attached to a tree or a landing net to be thrown over a triangular support and pegged securely down is an excellent choice.

"Slow" roller skates of wood or metal, sleds, small skis and beginner's ice skates can also serve the older preschooler where the terrain permits. Balls to throw or roll and beanbags are useful. Play tunnels or kegs to

Ruth E. Hartley is professor of Human Development and director, Human Development Program, The University of Wisconsin-Green Bay, Wisconsin.
*Adapted from *The Complete Book of Children's Play,* by Ruth E. Hartley and Robert M. Goldenson (New York: Thomas Y. Crowell Company, 1963).

crawl through and cloth "houses" that fit over a card table encourage the use of muscles not necessarily involved in using other toys. Plastic wading pools and large, light, inflatable water toys that float offer variety.

All play equipment must, of course, be graded to the size and skill of the child. Particularly during the preschool years, when growth is rapid, adjustable items are preferable to fixed-size items if they are equally sturdy and otherwise as satisfactory.

For Manipulation and Construction

The foundations of future understanding of mathematics and physics are laid in early play with manipulation and construction materials. An ample and varied supply of these types of materials may be closely associated with realizing the full intellectual potential of the child. To some extent their selection for the preschool years depends on what has been available to the child earlier. These recommendations are based on the assumption that the children being served have had adequate experience during the first three years of life with objects which they could manipulate according to their skill levels.

Blocks are basic manipulative materials for the preschool ages. Unpainted, hardwood "kindergarten" blocks are the type of choice, the first "set" to contain rectangular units, square half units, longer double units, and small triangles. As the child learns to handle these adeptly (perhaps around four to five years of age), other shapes should be added: quadruple units, large triangles, short pillars, half-circles, quarter circles and arcs to serve as bridges. Accessories extend the play possibilities of the blocks. Small replicas of vehicles, animals and people are all useful. The people and animals should be stable; the people should bend easily, in ways appropriate to their use.

Small colored blocks are useful for table-top play. For three- and four-year-olds, small blocks of identical shapes but different sizes and colors, blocks of different shapes but identical colors (several colors), blocks identical in both color and shape but differing in size—these are useful for sorting games, which help develop size, form and color concepts and the ability to classify. Also useful for this purpose are containers with differently shaped or colored openings, into which matching objects are to be inserted, as are color cones for younger children and mosaic blocks and pegboards for those slightly older. Allied to these are simple, framed wooden puzzles to be put together, graded according to age, and picture lotto games that require matching.

For other small-muscle activity, Threes like large beads to string on colored shoelaces, punched cards to lace with yarn (and blunt large-eyed needle), wooden shoes to lace, and large screw- and hook-sets to manipulate.

Some table games are suitable for Fives—parcheesi, Chinese checkers, dominoes, card games like "Old Maid." Letter stencil sets, anagram sets and sets of interlocking segments that can be put together to form letters or numbers give helpful preparation for the academic tasks just ahead.

Simple construction sets of the Tinker-Toy variety are suitable around four or five years, as are a worktable with clamps and suitable accessories; a small sturdy claw hammer (6 to 10 ounces); a small crosscut saw; monkey-wrench; pliers; screwdriver; screws; three-, four- and sixpenny nails and pieces of soft wood or hard board to use them on.

Finally, materials for waterplay should be supplied for a kind of manipulative play that is also important in other ways. These might be a large container for water (a tub or large plastic container), straws, soap flakes for bubbles, food coloring, bubble pipes, objects to measure fluids with, objects of different sizes and shapes for pouring fluids from one to the other, sponges, funnels, sieves, small floating toys. A sandbox or sandtable, with accessories similar to those recommended for blockplay and waterplay, also serves needs to master and to build.

For Creative and Expressive Play

We usually think of creative materials as serving the child's emotional development; however, they also encourage intellectual development by giving opportunities for experimentation, exploration and self-knowledge. Crayons, the most frequently used, are probably the least useful for these functions. A freestanding easel, newsprint paper to paint on, large brushes and a supply of poster paints would be a desirable gift for any preschooler who does not otherwise have access to similar materials. Clay, preferably ready mixed for home use, Plasticine, fingerpaint and fingerpaint paper would all be desirable additions if a child does not have them. For the very young, large, thick crayons are appropriate. For older preschoolers who show manual deftness, magic markers in a variety of colors encourage further experimentation. A large blackboard and a supply of colored chalks extends the child's repertoire.

For more structured expression, the following are useful: a flannel-surfaced board and felt cutouts in a variety of shapes and colors; a flexible plastic sheet and colored plastic pieces that cling to it; pregummed dots, strips, squares, circles, triangles of colored paper. A pair of blunt scissors and sheets of colored paper, paste, and a variety of small objects and bits of materials for making collages give even more scope.

Among the latter are buttons, bits of sponge, shells, seeds, beads, cake decorations, colored macaroni, colored pebbles, feathers.

To encourage experimentation and creativity with sound, a variety of percussion instruments are suitable. These might be songbells, tambourines, tone blocks, gourds, rattles, cymbals, rhythm sticks, chimes, triangles, and hand drums like tom-toms. A record player that the child himself can manage, with appropriate records, would make a splendid gift for the five-year-old.

For Imitative and Dramatic Play

The greatest variety of toys come under this heading. Dolls and household equipment of all kinds belong here: cribs, bathinettes, carriages, laundry equipment for doll clothes, ironing board and iron, small tables and chairs, unbreakable dishes, toy stoves and sinks, pots and pans, infant feeding bottles, toy cleaning equipment, "shaving" sets, "makeup" kits—any toy a child can use to imitate domestic activity. For imitation of nondomestic activities, costumes and accessories abound: stick-ponies with reins (for the youngest), doctor's kit, nurse's outfit, cowboy and cowgirl costumes, lineman's belt with tools, police badge and handcuffs, storekeeper's apron, milkman's carrier and bottles, ballet tutus, etc., the choice to be dictated by the child's interest. Replicas of articles related to all phases of public adult life are welcome and appropriate: cars and specialized vehicles of all sizes, dump trucks, steam shovels, snowplows, tractors, planes, helicopters, trackless trains, sailboats and other boats. Vehicles should be large enough so that their movable parts can be controlled easily by small hands. They should be very sturdy and the working machinery really able to do the job they are supposed to do. Four- and five-year-olds will especially appreciate these. For three-year-olds, objects need not be realistically detailed. The five-year-old wants realism.

Fives also delight in small objects: tiny replicas of the objects of daily living, like doll-house furniture, and scale dolls; household paraphernalia, models of fruits and meats, vehicles built to scale of doll-house people. If a doll house is acquired, it should open from the top on a single level. Barnyard items and animals in scale add to the fun.

For all preschool ages, a large inflated weighted figure made to be pounded and punched is invaluable for letting off steam.

For Encouraging Intellectual Interests

Intellectual curiosity in the young is encouraged by having something to focus on and to get into direct contact with. For this purpose, the following make fine additions to play materials: small aquarium with a few hardy fish; ant colony with ants behind glass; seeds and pots with soil for planting and small gardening tools; weathervane; collection of various types of magnets and iron filings; hourglass; thermometer; play clock with movable hands and real clock; prisms; tuning fork; scales; ruler; yardstick; tape measure; abacus; play money.

Early School Years (6, 7, 8)

One cannot make a sharp distinction between the needs of adjacent years. Many objects of interest to Fives are also appropriate for older children. The following lists are suggested on the assumption that the child being considered already has the items mentioned earlier. The items are mentioned in a general chronological order, starting with the interests of the younger children; but in all instances the specific interests of the in-dividual child have to be increasingly consulted.

For Developing Skill

Jump rope, scooter; bicycle (size-graded); lightweight bat and softball; baseball catcher's mitt; boxing gloves; pogo stick; basketball hoop and ball; tetherball and stand; punching bag and stand; badminton set; pingpong set; small tennis racquet and tennis balls (for eight-year-old); swimming accessories (water gogles, flippers); regular roller skates, ice skates; skis; football, helmet, shoulder pads; Carom board; hoop to roll; ringtoss; shuffleboard; pick-up sticks; top; yo-yo; jacks and marbles; tenpins; horseshoe pitching set; bow and arrows with suction heads; magnetic dart set; kites; gliders; camping tent.

For Construction and Manipulation

Jig-saw puzzles (age-graded); wirecutters; brace and bit; coping saw; augur bits; hand drill; hand plane; wood files and rasps; brads; two- and sevenpenny nails; erector set (no engine); building sets made up of "logs" or interlocking "bricks"; model plane or boat kits (simple, skill-graded); leather and plastic braiding materials; leathercraft materials, precut at first; square loom and loops; heddle loom (small); scissors; paper punch; stapler; jewelry-making kits; pipe-cleaners; construction paper.

For Creative and Expressive Activities

Hand puppets; metallic surfaced paper in many colors; elaborate crayon sets with many colors; sketch pads and drawing paper; pastels; water-color crayons or pencils; magic markers; self-hardening clay; shells; other materials for collages; wind instruments—harmonica, song flute, ocarina, recorder; xylophone; autoharp; drums with drumsticks.

For Imitative and Dramatic Play

Paper dolls; dolls with hair; doll clothes with simple fastenings; doll furniture; doll feeding set (sterilizer, etc.); pastry and cooking sets, with real food mixes; realistic toy refrigerator and storing cabinets; scale-model vehicles and machinery, such as dumptrucks, towing cars, etc., flying planes and helicopters (no engines); large working models of road-building, hauling, agricultural machinery; wooden trains with tracks; mechanical trains; walkie-talkie; stockade, fort and frontier sets; working toy sewing machine; cash register; equipment for playing store; conventional doll house; costumes for fantasy characters (spaceman, circus queen, ballerina, ring master, etc.); astronaut helmets; make-up and disguise kits; magic tricks.

For Intellectual Growth and Special Interests

Barometer; magnifying glass; field glasses; camera; scrap-books; photo albums; coin folders; stamp albums; toy typewriter; typesetting printing sets (large type); air pump and bellows for experiment; additional measuring aids—compass, plumb line, level; sundial checkers; lotto; trading games (Monopoly, etc.); card games (Hearts, Menagerie, Space Race, etc.); table games with simple rules and scores; tiny items for collectors—animals, figurines, dishes, boxes, costume dolls, etc.

Preteens (9, 10, 11, 12)

The items suggested below are to be considered in addition to those in the previous section. Many items in the latter hold continuing interest, even for older children.

For Developing Skills

Any of the sports items suggested in the earlier section, upgraded for size and skill; hockey equipment; mat, for mat wrestling; baseball equipment; real archery set; snorkel; volleyball; jackstraws; tiddlywinks; tennis racquet and balls; tetherball.

For Manipulation and Construction

Bent-wire puzzles; materials for kite-making; paraffin, wicks for candle-dipping; cloth, thread, needles, simple patterns to make small articles; split wood, reed, raffia for basket-making; calfskin or steerhide, heavy needles, thongs for leathercraft; woodburning set; metalworking set; electric assembly kit (for buzzers, bells, lights, electromagnet); soldering iron; large hammer; tri-square; working steam engine; miniature attachments for steam engine (fan, grindstone, etc.); erector set with engine; put-together kits (electric clock; crystal radio; models of cars, trains, planes, ships); stiff plastic sheets, etching tools, strong knife, shell-jewelry set; plastic flower kit; large crochet hook and heavy thread; samplers, towels and materials for simple embroidery.

For Creative and Expressive Activities

Puppet theatre; marionettes and stage; tools for carving wood, soap, sculpstone (quarter-inch chisel, gouges, veining tools); armatures and tools for clay sculpture; nonfiring glazes for pottery; small potter's wheel; plaster of Paris; casein paint; water color paint, sketchpad; metalcraft tools, molds, blanks and enamels; tin shears, tin, wood, cardboard, paint, thread for making mobiles.

For Imitative and Dramatic Play

Little-girl dolls, teen-type dolls with wardrobes; mannequin sewing set; doll accessories such as wigs, hair-setting equipment, additional clothing outfits; mix-your-own perfume sets; manicure sets; electric trains and accessories; remote-control vehicles; model cars and planes with engines; auto-racing equipment; garage sets.

For Special Interests and Intellectual Exercise

Microscope; telescope; sky charts; mineralogy set; kit for hydroponics; soil-testing kit; chemistry set; aids for serious collectors of butterflies, stamps, minerals, coins; real typewriter; printing press (circular drum type); scale car models for collectors, costume dolls, national and period, for collectors; adult-type card games of the simpler sort (rummy, casino, etc.); magnetic and electric table games; detective table games (Clue, etc.); word-building games (Scrabble, etc.); practical joke items; how-to science books, giving directions for simple experiments; books of riddles and puzzles.

Audiovisual Materials

Paul R. Wendt
and Gordon K. Butts

EDITORS' QUESTIONS:

1. Discuss the findings of research concerning the effectiveness of audiovisual materials in achieving objectives in particular subject-matter areas. How can you account for the lack of conclusive evidence concerning the use of audiovisual materials and their effectiveness in promoting learning? Discuss some of the limitations of the research designs used by investigators and other factors which might have altered the results of each study.

2. Considering the inconclusive findings of research in this area, justify your continued use of audiovisual materials for teaching. Support your answer with research and other related readings.

3. Cite some research studies to show that the characteristics of the learner are related to the effectiveness of teaching materials. Are results conclusive or inconclusive? What implications do these studies have for the utilization of audiovisual materials for instructional purposes?

4. Discuss some research studies concerning the relationship between the method of using audiovisual materials and learning effectiveness. What do these research findings mean to you as a classroom teacher?

5. Based upon your knowledge of the findings of research, devise a procedure for selecting media for instruction.

Paul R. Wendt and Gordon K. Butts, "Audiovisual Materials." *Review of Educational Research*, XXXII, No. 2 (April 1962), 141–155. Copyright by American Educational Research Association, Washington, D.C. Used by permission.

Increasingly in recent years, research in audiovisual materials and methods of teaching has been paced by the rapid rise of television, language laboratories, and programmed instruction, all of which have now won their place in other chapters of this issue of the *Review*. Research in the administration of audiovisual materials, including facilities and equipment, and in motion-picture production is also not covered in this chapter. The studies reviewed are organized in somewhat the same manner as in the April 1956 *Review* chapter by Allen (1956) in that the general headings, Effectiveness of Audiovisual Materials, Learner Characteristics, and Utilization, are employed.

A few specialized summaries are useful. Research studies completed, so far, under Title VII of the National Defense Education Act were reviewed by Norberg (1961) and by VanderMeer (1961) in two issues of *AV Communication Review*. Moldstad (1961) reported on doctoral dissertations in the audiovisual field. Literature on training aids was summarized by Saul and others (1957). An indexed bibliography of human engineering reports was published by the Special Devices Center (1956). May and

Lumsdaine (1958) wrote on their series of experiments on films and still pictures. Greenhill (1957) brought together research in the Instructional Film Research program on the use of films in clinical psychology.

Effectiveness of Audiovisual Materials

In spite of the diversion of much research talent into investigating television and programmed instruction, considerable research is still being carried on, with novel emphasis, in the regular audiovisual means of instruction. Emphasis in this chapter is placed on the major studies, as measured by conclusiveness and scope.

Motion Pictures

Increasing attention has been paid to testing the effectiveness of long series of films planned to be used in sequence and often providing a major part of classroom instruction. Wendt and Butts (1960) tested a series of 54 films on world history in grade 9 classes in seven schools. In each school, one teacher taught an experimental class and a control class. The experimental classes saw the films; the control classes did not. In all other respects, each teacher attempted to treat her control and her experimental class alike. The seven schools ranged from moderately large to moderately small. While the control classes took the usual full year to complete the course, the film classes covered the same subject matter in one semester. A criterion test in the subject given immediately at the end of the instruction showed no significant difference between control and experimental classes. Cottle (1960) did an auxiliary study in this same situation and found the effect of the world-history films was equally good for both high and low achievers.

Anderson and Montgomery (1959) tested a series of 162 physics films in 16 classes in one experimental and one control school. No significant difference was found between the two groups on a criterion test. The authors hypothesized that the lack of difference may have resulted from the superior training of the control teachers. Noall and Winget (1959) conducted a similar experiment with the same series, as part of the staff-utilization studies of the National Association of Secondary-School Principals. They used three large, three medium, and four small schools as the experimental group and a similar grouping of schools for control. Too much variation among schools hampered analysis, but among the medium-sized schools the control classes were significantly better. No significant difference was determined by a criterion test in the larger or the smaller schools. There were no differences by ability levels. The authors concluded that the films did not improve instruction but that they were as good as classroom teaching. There seemed to be an over-all loss of interest in the field of physics in the experimental group. The same series of physics films was tested by Wittich, Pella, and Wedemeyer (1960). There were no significant differences in achievement between the experimental and control groups in immediate recall, but after three months, the particular control group incorporated to assess a possible Hawthorne effect retained more. What was interpreted as a Hawthorne effect seemed to increase the scores of the control group.

Another series of 160 chemistry films (each of 30-minute duration) was investigated by Anderson, Montgomery, and Moore (1961). They used 590 high-school students in 33 classes with nine teachers. Of 17 comparisons, 8 favored the nonfilm group, whereas 3 favored the film group. In a similar study, Popham and Sadnavitch

(1961) used 149 physics films and 132 chemistry films. Six schools served for the filmed physics and nonfilmed chemistry instruction and six schools for the nonfilmed physics and filmed chemistry. The investigation concluded that the achievement performance of the nonfilm group in physics was significantly superior to the film group. There was no significant difference between the two groups in chemistry. For neither series was there a significant interaction of teacher method with the level of student intelligence. Although all students in both subjects showed a more unfavorable attitude toward both subjects at the conclusion of the study than at the beginning, the attitudes of members of the film groups were significantly more unfavorable than those of students of the nonfilm groups. Sadnavitch and Popham (1960) have also reported upon an attitude scale developed particularly for filmed courses.

Schenberg (1961) used the chemistry series for the in-service training of 19 chemistry teachers. He concluded that films can improve the effectiveness of instruction of both experienced and inexperienced teachers and that correct use of the films would raise the level of supervision. Smith and Anderson (1958) made a further analysis of data of a previously reported experiment showing a significant achievement increase from films for high-ability and low-ability students, but not for the group of intermediate ability. They hypothesized that this difference might have resulted from different learnings. Therefore, they divided their criterion test items into *fact* items and *principle* items and reran the statistical analysis. They found no significant difference.

It might be noted that the flurry of experiments involving long series of films was a far cry from the early days of film experimentation, when it was somehow presumed that the showing of one film might have a measurable effect on the achievement of students. Teaching by television undoubtedly inspired the creation of some of these film series; in fact, the physics film series was a direct by-product of broadcasting. The question that had persisted over the years—what a teacher would be able to accomplish with pupils if he had all the films he needed—was answered in part by this familiar *saturation* experiment. Judging from feelings of teachers and pupils resulting from all the physics and chemistry film-series research, the saturation point was exceeded when 30 minutes of film was shown each day for many months.

S. Cohen (1960) provided a fifth-grade teacher with 14 pieces of equipment and noted that the use of audiovisual materials increased almost ninefold. In the college setting, Caspers (1956) found that achievement gains increased with the number of films used in a psychology course.

An investigation of films used with special film readers and a magnetic sound-track projector was carried out by Witty and Fitzwater (1957) with grade 2 children in six schools. Regular instruction was used in the first semester; integrated audiovisual materials were added in the second. A somewhat greater gain in reading skill was made during the experimental period than during the control period. There were also other benefits, such as faster reading rate, more related reading, more class discussion, and evidence of learning to work more effectively.

The very intensive use of films not only provided a test of the saturation hypothesis but also tended to change the status of films from a supplementary aid to a complement to the work of the live teacher. Duval and others (1960) taught two technical courses in the Navy without the presence of instructors. One course consisted of 4 half-hour lessons recorded on slides with tape-recorded commentary; the other was recorded in 21 half-hour sound motion pictures. Each course was also taught by an instructor. In both cases, the recorded instruction was as effective as the regular instruction and acceptable to the trainees, although they preferred a live instructor. The cost of the sound motion pictures, produced economically, was less than for the slides and tape. This experiment reaffirms the results of a few previous studies, which indicated that motion pictures, at least in certain circumstances, could assume the total teaching load. Although earlier research also showed that the effectiveness of a film could be much increased through proper utilization by a live teacher, considerations of economy might suggest giving up this added benefit and letting the films speak for themselves.

The evaluation of films for the teaching of skills represented a continuation of the research in these areas during the previous decades. Stein (1958) used film loops for instruction in beginning typing at the high-school level. The film-loop class typed more rapidly, but the control class typed more accurately; both differences were very significant.

Drury (1959) taught beginning tumbling to college freshmen by instructor demonstration, by drawings, and by motion pictures. Four easy and four difficult stunts were taught to all classes. The author found no differences traceable to difference in method or degree of difficulty of the stunt; but he also found that increasing the number of showings in successive class periods was more effective than just one showing, especially with the easier stunts. Hirsch (1957) tested eight 8-minute films on as-

pects of marksmanship, available on continuous projectors, to trainees on the rifle range as compared to the efforts of the best instructors. The results were nonsignificant, possibly because the superiority of the instructors narrowed the difference.

In the study of visual aids in dental training, Yock and Erlandson (1958) taught part of the porcelain jacket and crown technique by three methods: film alone, demonstration alone, and film and demonstration together. The combined film and demonstration method was significantly better than the film-alone method, which might possibly be explained by the very small groups of eight or nine who saw the demonstrations, in contrast to the customary large demonstration groups.

Filmstrips, Slides, and Transparencies

Dworkin and Holden (1960) compared four 15-minute sound filmstrips with a regular classroom lecture for 120 graduate engineering students in two matched groups. The teacher who gave the classroom lecture also wrote and recorded the filmstrip script. There was no significant difference in learning between the two methods, although 40 percent of the filmstrip students wished that they could have asked questions. A comparison of commercial filmstrips with illustrations cut from magazines was made by Sprague (1955) in sixth-grade and seventh-grade science classes. No differences were found by material or by sex, and no differences by level except that high-level students learned more from the commercial filmstrip. McBeath (1961) used 20 sixth-grade classes matched in four groups on four variables to test these ways of presenting a sixth-grade social studies lesson: (a) a silent captioned filmstrip, (b) a captioned filmstrip with a recorded narration, (c) a 16mm sound filmograph, and (d) a sound filmstrip with a filmograph sound track. On immediate and delayed retention tests, there were no significant differences among the four methods. But further analysis showed interaction between sex and method: the highest gains were scored by boys who saw the captioned filmstrip with narration, the lowest gains by girls who saw the filmograph.

In a basic study of the nature of learning from photographs, Lubin and Wilson (1956) used six black-and-white and six color pictures showing handicapped children. These were shown to an experimental group of 20 severely handicapped children and also to 20 normal children. Each child was asked to write a story about each picture, and the score was a numerical count of the words in each story. The verbal productivity of the handicapped children was significantly higher than that of the normal children, presumably because of the closer identification with the children in the pictures. The handicapped group also showed more reaction than the normal group to the color pictures, but only if the color pictures were presented second and not first.

Variations in mode of representation of pictures were also tested by Ryan and Schwartz (1956). Their four modes consisted of a photograph, a shaded drawing, a line drawing, and a cartoon. The criterion of effectiveness was the speed of recognition of details in the picture. Photographs were made of the following: (a) a human hand in four different positions; (b) a row of five electrical knife switches, with a different switch closed in each of four pictures; and (c) a cutaway model of the valves of a steam engine at four different stages of the cycle. Each of the resulting 12 photographs was copied in (a) line drawing, (b) shaded drawing, and (c) cartoon. All 48 pictures were then reduced to 2 x 2-inch slides and projected tachistoscopically in an ascending series of longer exposures. The presentation

was randomized. The results showed that the recognition rank orders were significantly different, as follows: the cartoon was best and the line drawing worst; the photograph and shaded drawing were about equal.

Goehring (1956) developed a feasible film-slide test to measure the ability at the college level to apply scientific method to the area of mechanics in high-school physics. Chance (1961) used 200 transparencies and 800 overlays in teaching engineering descriptive geometry to freshmen engineering students, 104 of whom were divided between this method and the usual instruction with the chalkboard. The transparency group did significantly better at the end of the course than the chalkboard group. Moreover, it was determined that approximately 15 minutes of each 60-minute class lecture could be saved by the transparency medium. As indicated by the total number of questions, attentiveness was greater in the experimental group. Both instructors and students preferred this method.

Two types of transparencies, static and animated, were used by Silverman (1958) to teach facts about three kinds of firearms to 150 male college students. The animated devices were classified by the number of moving parts. The same tape-recorded lectures were given to all groups. No differences between static and animated transparencies were observed with a paper-and-pencil test, but significant differences did appear with the performance tests. The number of moving parts in the animated transparencies did not make a difference.

Pictorial Illustration and Graphic Materials

Experimentation with still pictures during the period under review showed promising increased interest in more basic research in production variables and in what might be called the psychological characteristics of pictures, as well as continued interest in field studies in classrooms. Boyd and Mandler (1955) tested the reactions of grade 3 children to animal and human stories in pictures. Each child was asked to write a story about each picture, and the stories were analyzed by eight variables of productivity and indexes of ego-involvement. Although 74 percent of the children preferred animal over human stories, statistical analysis showed that the human stories had much greater effect on the eight variables. Bloomer (1960) showed fourth-, fifth-, and sixth-graders pictures varying in three styles and three themes. The styles were line drawing, shaded drawing, and color wash drawing. The picture themes were pleasant, unpleasant, or neutral. Preference was for color, pleasant, and neutral pictures. However, when asked to write stories, most students selected the line drawings and the unpleasant pictures as subjects.

Ferguson (1959) made a tape recording of the free responses of 60 nursery-school and kindergarten children to 10 pictures of common objects such as a horse, a train, and a dog. Action pictures elicited, roughly, twice as many responses as nonaction pictures; the qualitative analysis of the words used showed the action pictures also elicited a larger number of verbs.

Weintraub (1960) studied the effects on selected reader-comprehension abilities of stories for a basal reader presented to five classes of grade 2 children without pictures, with pictures but without text, and with both pictures and text. The result favored the first presentation at the 5-percent level of significance. Further analysis revealed, surprisingly, that it was the poor readers who contributed mainly to this difference.

A statistically valid and reliable scale of photographs was developed by Byrom (1957) to be used for the appraisal of learn-ing influences in industrial-arts shops. In teaching engineering drawing, Hepler (1957) found that orthographic projection followed by a pictorial presentation was superior to pictorial presentation followed by orthographic projection.

Declarative, imperative, and interrogative captions on still pictures were tested by Butts (1956) in grade 8 classes in six schools. The pictures were identical in every other respect. The declarative captions were found to be significantly better than the other two.

Tannenbaum and Fosdick (1960) reported one of the few studies on the effect of photographic technique on still pictures. In this study, Fosdick used four angles of lighting on four subjects and had 14 sections of college students rate them on a semantic-differential scale. In the evaluation, only the 45-degree angle was significantly different. The authors stated that "the original suspicion that lighting from below would create an unfavorable judgment proved to be unfounded" (p. 259).

Two studies were concerned with the process of identification in looking at pictures. Bevan, Secord, and Richards (1956) had 15 male college-fraternity members rate full-face photographs of each other on 29 facial characteristics. They were also asked to identify the person in their group they would (a) most like to be and (b) least like to be. The control group consisted of 15 similar students at another university. No significant differences were found in any of the comparisons. The authors concluded that neither liking nor disliking had an effect on perception of the features as shown in the photographs. Working with a rather small sample of 15 men and 16 women in a small liberal arts college, Chambers (1957) confirmed his hypothesis that persons tend to like photographs of individuals who they believe have traits like their own and to dislike those who appear to have opposite traits.

Controlled experimentation with graphics still remains meager except for four studies reported by Vernon (1957 a, b, c, d). The subjects ranged from elementary-school children to boys and girls aged 15 to 19 and included members of the Air Force. Three of Vernon's four experiments showed no advantage for using charts, graphs, or pictures with a text; at the very least, a text should accompany the graphical methods. Vernon found that, contrary to the popular impression, considerable intelligence and education were needed to learn from graphs and charts. Mixed results were obtained by Glazener (1958) in using charts to teach beginning mechanical drawing. Richter (1956) asked subjects to draw charts used in biology and found that the accuracy with which the charts were prepared did have some relationship to both the amount and quality of learning of biological subject matter.

Recordings and Radio

The rise of language laboratories seems to have spurred experimentation with tape recordings, whereas radio has been overshadowed by the dominance of television. Another of the projects of the National Association of Secondary-School Principals was reported by Gibson (1960). Grade 7 spelling was taught by tape alone over a public-address system to some members of 15 classes; their classmates served as a control. The difference in favor of the tape method alone was highly significant, but further analysis showed this to be almost entirely due to the presence of high-ability groups; the low-ability groups did not profit from tape recordings.

Popham (1961) played 34 taped college lectures to 55 students divided between experimental and control groups and matched by the *Miller Analogies Test.* Each taped lecture was followed by 20 minutes of discussion. There was no significant difference in teaching facts about research, research interpretations, or research design.

Employing 296 high-school students in 10 classrooms to test auding ability in English and German, Gideon (1956) used tapes, pictures, and records in the experimental sections. She found that the teaching method employed made no significant difference in the results but that the audiovisual materials provided an interesting focus for students.

The value of tapes when used only for lesson reviews was studied by Edgerton (1961). Classroom lectures totaling 826 minutes were made available to 229 trainees. About one-half of the trainees listened to the reviews, but showed no superiority in the course examinations. Newman and Highland (1957) taught radio to Air Force trainees for five days through use of supervised reading by recordings integrated with the workbook and by recordings accompanied by slides. No important differences were noted, but the length of the lessons may have had an important influence. Johnston (1961) compared tape recordings teamed with large posters, with conventional instruction involving lectures and laboratory in a college class in general psychology lasting 12 weeks and consisting of 18 sections. Each of the four instructors taught both an experimental and a control section to control the teacher variable. The conventional method proved superior to the experimental one.

Three-Dimensional Materials

An experimental and a control group of pupils in grade 5 were set up by Erickson and Chow (1961) to test some effects of using portable typewriters. It was found that their use did not affect academic achievement or spelling, but there was a significant improvement in capitalization, punctuation, speed of composition, and quantity of written work. Similarly, Reddell and DeVault (1960) used an abacounter, a calculator, and teacher-made aids to help children in grade 5 with arithmetic over a five-month period. The dependent variables were (a) measure of arithmetic reasoning, (b) fundamentals, and (c) general achievement. In reasoning and achievement, the two commercial devices were significantly better; but in fundamentals, the abacounter was superior to the other two methods.

In training students to thread a 16mm sound projector, Trubov (1956) found that it was important to give a lecture on the principles of the machine but that it made no difference whether he used a mock-up or an actual projector or whether the equipment was demonstrated.

A total of 1900 aircraft maintenance technicians was used by Swanson and Aukes (1957) to teach fuel, hydraulic, and rudder control systems by means of (a) operating mock-up, (b) nonoperating mock-up, (c) cut-away mock-up, (d) animated panels, (e) charts, and (f) symbolic diagrams. There was no significant difference among the devices when a lecture was given with them. However, when the lecture was omitted, significant differences were found in immediate recall (but not in delayed recall) for the hydraulic and rudder control systems, but not for the fuel system.

L. Cohen (1959) had one member of each of 63 pairs of high-school seniors construct 22 models in studying solid geometry. Constructing models did not help in final achievement in the subject. Johnston (1956) used 106 college students of general electricity over a period of two years to determine the superiority of teacher demonstrations over shop activities.

Additional References: Ball (1959); Carlson (1959); Fell (1959); Knapp (1960); Lambert (1959); Owens (1956); Porter (1956); Redemsky (1959); Smith (1960); Twyford (1958, 1960); Villa (1960).

Learner Characteristics

More researchers have developed the suspicion that the characteristics of the viewer have more to do with the efficacy of teaching materials than the characteristics of the materials themselves or the manner of their use. A development during the past few years has been the increase in interest by psychologists in the interaction between learners and materials.

Maccoby, Wilson, and Burton (1958) studied the eye movements of subjects of both sexes watching motion pictures to determine whether each sex tends to watch a character of the same sex. The subjects were 48 college students, equally divided by sex, who were shown two 3-reel feature films containing test scenes in which one character of each sex was on the screen. Eye movements were timed by an observer, not recorded on an eye camera. Surprisingly, men did tend to watch male characters on the screen significantly more than women subjects did. Data for women characters were not given. The authors called attention to the many variables in the film which could emphasize sex character differences. In a related investigation, Maccoby and Wilson (1957) performed an identification study on 25 classes of grade 7 pupils who were shown two 20-minute episodes of a movie serial featuring an upper-middle-class boy and lower-class boy. Identification was inferred from the subjects' preference between these two characters. It turned out that the boys tended to identify with the class to which they aspired rather than with the class to which they belonged. They remembered more of the content of the film related to their identification. After showing another film in which the two primary characters were a boy and a girl, the authors found that boys remembered more aggressive content from the film than girls, but girls remembered more "girl alone" content; results from later recall were approximately the same. The authors made many more detailed analyses. If the basic assumption of identification is accepted, the results would provide many clues for further experimentation.

Krebs (1958) used only two films with an experimental group to determine whether showing of the films would be associated with a more homogeneous perception of the specific learning situation than that found for the nonfilm control group. His hypothesis was confirmed, although he stated that similar changes in larger groups would be more difficult to determine. To find out whether the viewer's learning from the film depends on his perception of its usefulness to him, Greenhill and McNiven (1956) showed three films to 473 high-school seniors and then had them respond to a scale of perceived usefulness drawn up by the authors. On this basis, they concluded that the more an individual perceives himself using the content of the film, the more he will learn from it. In another quantitatively oriented study, Merrill and McAshan (1960) developed a prediction system for the learning of facts and skills from a film and for the determination of attitude changes with which its showing could be associated.

Denny (1958) used a series of unspecified films to reduce the frustration level of 249 grade 8 pupils, as compared to a control group. In terms of the measures furnished by the *California Test of Personality, Intermediate Series, Form A,* significant gains in ad-

justment were made in the area of personal adjustment (but not social adjustment), primarily by girls rather than boys and by those pupils scoring high in intellectual measures. Using a smaller group of nine adolescent boys, Iscoe, Mims, and White (1957), in a similar manner, employed 12 films and concluded subjectively that motion pictures offer a promising means of getting at the underlying maladjustments of emotionally disturbed children.

Using small groups of 10 experimental and 10 control nursery-school children, Lövaas (1961) exposed them to five-minute aggressive and nonaggressive films and then allowed them to play with either aggressive or nonaggressive toys. As expected, exposure to aggressive films was associated with a tendency to play with aggressive toys, and experience with nonaggressive films was related to the amount of play with nonaggressive toys. Working with adult psychiatric patients, Whitmyre (1959) observed, in general, no difference in overt behavior during the showing of various types of feature films. However, patients having greater contact with reality showed more emotionally disturbed reactions to films than the more seriously ill patients.

In the complex business of fitting teaching materials and methods to learners, it is to be hoped that more researchers will take an interest in the field of learner characteristics and their relation to specific teaching materials.

Additional References: Fritz (1957); Horowitz and Fromer (1960).

Utilization

A number of the experiments reported above could also be listed here as a test of ways in which the materials were used, but for the sake of brevity they will not be repeated under this category. The two to be reviewed, therefore, are primarily concerned with the manner in which the materials are used in teaching. Staudohar and Smith (1956) used a feature film on discipline with 850 trainee airmen divided into groups given (a) a lecture before the film, (b) a lecture after the film, (c) a lecture before and after the film, and (d) no lecture. The criterion test was an attitude scale of 16 items developed with a sample of 311 trainees. There were no significant differences among the four methods. Carter, Moss, and Wilson (1961) worked with 104 educable mentally retarded children, showing them seven short films on health and safety in these three versions: (a) narration, (b) no narration, but with synchronized voices of children, and (c) no sound, but with encouragement from the interviewer for the children to make loud, unrestrained, and frequent comments on the film. A control group did not see the film. No significant differences resulted.

From a consideration of the several studies reviewed it may be concluded that research activities are progressing at a rapid pace. It is also apparent that much of the research is highly specialized, even though the substantive aspects cut across many fields of endeavor in the behavioral sciences.

Additional References: Adkins (1961); Roper (1956); Salley (1957); Siegel (1956).

BIBLIOGRAPHY

Allen, William H. "Audio-Visual Materials." *Review of Educational Research* 26: 125–56; April 1956.

Anderson, Kenneth E., and Montgomery, Fred S. "An Evaluation of the Introductory Physics Course on Film." *Science Education* 43: 386–94; December 1959.

Anderson, Kenneth E.; Montgomery, Fred S.; and Moore, Sid F. "An Evaluation of the Introductory Chemistry Course on Film." *Science Education* 45: 254–69; April 1961.

Bevan, William; Secord, Paul F.; and Richards, James M. "Personalities in Faces: V. Personal Identification and the Judgment of Facial Characteristics." *Journal of Social Psychology* 44: 289–91; 1956.

Bloomer, Richard H. "Children's Preferences and Responses as Related to Styles and Themes of Illustration." *Elementary School Journal* 60: 334–40; March 1960.

Boyd, Nancy A., and Mandler, George. "Children's Responses to Human and Animal Stories and Pictures." *Journal of Consulting Psychology* 19: 367–71; October 1955.

Butts, Gordon K. *An Experimental Study of the Effectiveness of Declarative, Interrogative, and Imperative Captions on Still Pictures.* Doctor's thesis. Bloomington: Indiana University, 1956. 155 p. Abstract: *Dissertation Abstracts* 16: 2400–2401; No. 12, 1956.

Byrom, John M. *The Development of a Scale of Photographs for the Appraisal of Learning Influences in Industrial Arts Shops.* Doctor's thesis. University Park: Pennsylvania State University, 1957. 173 p. Abstract: *Dissertation Abstracts* 18: 116–17; No. 1, 1958.

Carter, Lamore J.; Moss, Roy B.; and Wilson, Mamie T. "A Comparative Study of the Effectiveness of Three Techniques of Film Utilization in Teaching a Selected Group of Educable Mentally Retarded Children Enrolled in Public Schools in Louisiana." (Abstract) *AV Communication Review* 9: A16–A17; July-August 1961.

Caspers, Wesley. *An Experimental Evaluation of Certain Motion Picture Films in Selected Educational Psychology Classes in Kansas Colleges.* Doctor's thesis. Minneapolis: University of Minnesota, 1956. 239 p.

Abstract: *Dissertation Abstracts* 16: 1105–1106; No. 6, 1956.

Chambers, Jay L. "Identification with Photographs of People." *Journal of Consulting Psychology* 21: 232–34; June 1957.

Chance, Clayton W. "Experimentation in the Adaptation of the Overhead Projector Utilizing 200 Transparencies and 800 Overlays in Teaching Engineering Descriptive Geometry Curricula." (Abstract) *AV Communication Review* 9: A17–A18; July-August 1961.

Cohen, Louis. *An Evaluation of a Technique To Improve Space Perception Abilities Through the Construction of Models by Students in a Course in Solid Geometry.* Doctor's thesis. New York: Yeshiva University, 1959. 108 p. Abstract: *Dissertation Abstracts* 21: 1136; No. 5, 1960.

Cohen, Samuel. "Classroom Experiment Shows 'Saturation' AV Gets Results." *Educational Screen and Audiovisual Guide* 39: 324–29; July 1960.

Cottle, Eugene. *An Experiment Using World History Films with Selected Tenth Grade Pupils: Implications for the Improvement of Teaching with Motion Picture Films.* Doctor's thesis. Carbondale: Southern Illinois University, 1960. 138 p.

Denny, Earl W. *A Study of the Effectiveness of Selected Motion Pictures for Reducing Frustration in Children.* Doctor's thesis. Seattle: University of Washington, 1958. 111 p. Abstract: *Dissertation Abstracts* 19: 3170–71; No. 12, 1959.

Drury, Francis A. *An Evaluation of Visual Aids in the Teaching of Tumbling.* Doctor's thesis. Iowa City: State University of Iowa, 1959. 102 p. Abstract: *Dissertation Abstracts* 20: 949–50; No. 3, 1959.

Duval, D. P., and others. "The Effectiveness, Acceptability, and Feasibility of Technical Training Courses Recorded on Sound Motion Pictures and Slides plus Tape."

(Abstract) *AV Communication Review* 8: 312; November-December 1960.

Dworkin, Solomon, and Holden, Alan. "An Experimental Evaluation of Sound Filmstrips vs. Classroom Lectures." (Abstract) *AV Communication Review* 8: 157; May-June 1960.

Edgerton, Harold A. "The Acceptability and Effectiveness of the Casual Use of Auditory Training Aids." (Abstract) *AV Communication Review* 9: 77; January-February 1961.

Erickson, Lawrence W., and Chow, Cletus. "The Manual Portable Typewriter as a Tool of Learning with Fifth Grade Elementary School Pupils." (Abstract) *AV Communication Review* 9: 232; July-August 1961.

Farmer, Ronald J. *The Effect of Selected Film Sequences on Individuals Toward Nature and Art Forms.* Doctor's thesis. University Park: Pennsylvania State University, 1958. 141 p. Abstract: *Dissertation Abstracts* 19: 1615–16; No. 7, 1959.

Ferguson, Marian Nelson. "A Comparison of the Chain Associations of Nursery School and Kindergarten Children to Action-Picture Stimuli." *Audio-Visual Communication Review* 7: 310–11; Fall 1959.

Gibson, Mrs. R. E. "Final Report on the Westside High School Teaching by Tape Project." *Bulletin of the National Association of Secondary-School Principals* 44: 56–62; January 1960.

Gideon, Sara B. *Aural Comprehension or Auding in Secondary School German.* Doctor's thesis. University Park: Pennsylvania State University, 1956. 158 p. Abstract: *Dissertation Abstracts* 17: 274–75; No. 2, 1957.

Glazener, Everett Ruthven. *An Experimental Determination of the Value of Selected Visual Aids in Teaching Beginning Mechanical Drawing.* Doctor's thesis. University

Park: Pennsylvania State University, 1958. 128 p. Abstract: *Dissertation Abstracts* 19: 2878–79; No. 11, 1959.

Goehring, Harvey J., Jr. *Construction and Validation of a Film Slide Test To Measure Ability To Apply Scientific Method in a Selected Area of High School Physics.* Doctor's thesis. Pittsburgh: University of Pittsburgh, 1956. 243 p. Abstract: *Dissertation Abstracts* 17: 110–11; No. 1, 1957.

Greenhill, Leslie P. "Application of Sound Motion Pictures to Research in Clinical Psychology." *Audio-Visual Communication Review* 5: 529–38; Fall 1957.

Greenhill, Leslie, and McNiven, Malcolm. "Relationship Between Learning and the Perceived Usefulness of a Film." *Audio-Visual Communication Review* 4: 255–67; Fall 1956.

Hepler, Earl R. *Order of Presenting Orthographic Projection and Pictorial Representation and Its Effect on Achievement in Engineering Drawing.* Doctor's thesis. Columbia: University of Missouri, 1957. 232 p. Abstract: *Dissertation Abstracts* 17: 2222–23; No. 10, 1957.

Hirsch, Richard S. "Experiments in Rifle Marksmanship Training—Film Experiment." (Abstract) *Audio-Visual Communication Review* 5: 552; Fall 1957.

Iscoe, Ira; Mims, Jean; and White, Paul. "An Exploration in the Use of Personal Adjustment Motion Pictures as a Psychotherapeutic Medium." (Abstract) *Audio-Visual Communication Review* 5: 550–51; Fall 1957.

Johnston, John L. *Teacher-Demonstration Versus Shop Activities in the Teaching of Electricity: An Experimental Comparison.* Doctor's thesis. Columbia: University of Missouri, 1956. 210 p. Abstract: *Dissertation Abstracts* 16; 2105; No. 9, 1956.

Johnston, Roland E., Jr. *Magnetic Recordings and Visual Displays as Aids in Teaching Introductory Psychology to College Students.* Philadelphia: Drexel Institute of Technology, May 1961. 62 p.

Krebs, Robert E. *The Effects of Educational Films on Student Perceptions.* Doctor's thesis. Gainesville: University of Florida, 1958. 136 p. Abstract: *Dissertation Abstracts* 19: 1030; No. 5, 1958.

Lövaas, O. Ivar. "Effect of Exposure to Symbolic Aggression on Aggressive Behavior," *Child Development* 32: 37–44; March 1961.

Lubin, Nathan M., and Wilson, M. O. "Picture Test Identification as a Function of 'Reality' (Color) and Similarity of Picture to Subject." *Journal of General Psychology* 54: 31-38; January 1956.

McBeath, Ronald J. "A Comparative Study of the Effectiveness of the Filmstrip, Sound Filmstrip, and Filmograph for Teaching Facts and Concepts." (Abstract) *AV Communication Review* 9: A24–A25; July-August 1961.

Maccoby, Eleanor E., and Wilson, William C. "Identification and Observational Learning from Films." *Journal of Abnormal and Social Psychology* 55: 76-87; July 1957.

Maccoby, Eleanor E.; Wilson, William C.; and Burton, Roger V. "Differential Movie-Viewing Behavior of Male and Female Viewers." (Abstract) *Audio-Visual Communication Review* 6: 307-308; Fall 1958.

May, Mark A., and Lumsdaine, Arthur A. "Attention Directed to Parts of a Film." *Learning from Films.* New Haven, Conn.: Yale University Press, 1958. Chapter 7, p. 84–106.

Merrill, Irving R., and McAshan, Hildreth H. "Predicting Learning, Attitude Shift, and Skill Improvement from a Traffic Safety Film." *AV Communication Review* 8: 263–74; November-December 1960.

Moldstad, John. "Doctoral Dissertations in Audio-Visual Education: Supplement

III." (Abstract) *AV Communication Review* 9: 220–29; July-August 1961.

Newman, Salter E., and Highland, Richard W. "The Effectiveness of Four Instructional Methods at Different Stages of a Course." (Abstract) *Audio-Visual Communication Review* 5: 562: Fall 1957.

Noall, Matthew F., and Winget, Lerue. "Staff Utilization Studies Help with Education: B. The Physics Film Project." *Bulletin of the National Association of Secondary-School Principals* 43: 183–95; January 1959.

Norberg, Kenneth D. "The First of the Title VII Reports—A Review." (Abstract) *AV Communication Review* 9: A5–A14; July-August 1961.

Popham, W. James. "Tape Recorded Lectures in the College Classroom." *AV Communication Review* 9: 109–18; March-April 1961.

Popham, W. James, and Sadnavitch, Joseph M. "The Effectiveness of Filmed Science Courses in Public Secondary Schools." (Abstract) *AV Communication Review* 9: A28–A29; July-August 1961.

Reddell, William D., and DeVault, M. Vere. "In-Service Research in Arithmetic Teaching Aids." *Arithmetic Teacher* 7: 243–46; May 1960.

Richter, Marion. *Drawing and Learning in Biology: The Relationship Between Pupils' Drawings of Visual Aids and Their Learning in Biology.* Doctor's thesis. New York: Columbia University, 1956. 118 p. Abstract: *Dissertation Abstracts* 16: 2090–91; No. 9, 1956.

Ryan, T. A., and Schwartz, Caryl B. "Speed of Perception as a Function of Mode of Representation." *American Journal of Psychology* 69: 60–69; March 1956.

Sadnavitch, Joseph M., and Popham, W. James. "Measuring Attitudes Toward Filmed Courses." *AV Communication Review* 8: 286–88; November-December 1960.

Saul, Ezra V., and Others. "A Review of the Literature Pertinent to the Design and Use of Effective Training Aids." (Abstract) *Audio-Visual Communication Review* 5: 565–66; Fall 1957.

Schenberg, Samuel. "An Experiment in the Use of Films for the Inservice Training of High School Chemistry Teachers, October 6, 1959 to February 6, 1960." (Abstract) *AV Communication Review* 9: 76; January-February 1961."

Silverman, R. E. "The Comparative Effectiveness of Animated and Static Transparencies." (Abstract) *Audio-Visual Communication Review* 6: 238–39; Summer 1958.

Smith, Herbert A., and Anderson, Kenneth E. "An Inquiry into Some Possible Learning Differentials as a Result of the Use of Sound Motion Pictures in High School Biology." *Science Education* 42: 34–37; February 1958.

Special Devices Center. *Bibliography of Human Engineering Reports.* (Unclassified) NAVEXOS P-1491. Port Washington, N.Y.: Special Devices Center, Office of Naval Research, 1956. 18 p.

Sprague, Newton G. *A Comparative Study of the Effectiveness of Filmstrips and Flat Pictorial Material.* Doctor's thesis. Bloomington: Indiana University, 1955. 156 p. Abstract: *Dissertation Abstracts* 17: 312–13; No. 2, 1957.

Staudohar, Frank T., and Smith, Robert G., Jr. "The Contribution of Lecture Supplements to Effectiveness of an Attitudinal Film." *Journal of Applied Psychology* 40: 109–11; April 1956.

Stein, Sarah C. *An Experimental Study of the Use of Motion Picture Film Loops in the Instruction of Beginning Typewriting.* Doctor's thesis. Los Angeles: University of

Southern California, 1958. 252 p. Abstract: *Dissertation Abstracts* 19: 3253–54; No. 12, 1959.

Swanson, Robert A., and Aukes, Lewis E. "Evaluation of Training Devices for B-47 Fuel, Hydraulic and Rudder Power Control Systems." (Abstract) *Audio-Visual Communication Review* 5: 563; Fall 1957.

Tannenbaum, Percy H., and Fosdick, James A. "The Effect of Lighting Angle on the Judgment of Photographed Subjects." *AV Communication Review* 8: 253–62; November-December 1960.

Trubov, Herman. *An Experimental Study of the Effectiveness of a Mock-Up of the 16 Millimeter Motion-Picture Projector for Teaching the Threading of the Projector for Maximum Transfer.* Doctor's thesis. Syracuse, N.Y.: Syracuse University, 1956. 159 p. Abstract: *Dissertation Abstracts* 16: 1861; No. 9, 1956.

VanderMeer, A. W. "Ten Recent Title VII Reports: A Perspective." (Abstract) *AV Communication Review* 9: A35–A44; November-December 1961.

Vernon, M. D. "The Use and Value of Graphical Material with a Written Text." (Abstract) *Audio-Visual Communication Review* 5: 565; Fall 1957. (a)

Vernon, M. D. "The Use and Value of Graphical Methods of Presenting Quantitative Data." (Abstract) *Audio-Visual Communication Review* 5: 566; Fall 1957. (b)

Vernon, M. D. "The Value of Pictorial Illustration." (Abstract) *Audio-Visual Communication Review* 5: 564–65; Fall 1957. (c)

Vernon, M. D. "The Visual Presentation of Factual Data." (Abstract) *Audio-Visual Communication Review* 5: 564; Fall 1957. (d)

Weintraub, Sam. *The Effect of Pictures on the Comprehension of a Second Grade Basal Reader.* Doctor's thesis. Urbana: University of Illinois, 1960. 92 p. Abstract: *Dis-*sertation Abstracts 21: 1428–29; No. 6, 1960.

Wendt, Paul R., and Butts, Gordon K. *A Report of an Experiment in the Acceleration of Teaching Tenth Grade World History with the Help of an Integrated Series of Films.* Carbondale: General Publications, Southern Illinois University, 1960. 9 p.

Whitmyre, John W. "Psychiatric Patients' Audience Reactions to Types of Motion Pictures." (Abstract) *Audio-Visual Communication Review* 7: 237–38: Summer 1959.

Wittich, W. A.; Pella, Milton O.; and Wedemeyer, C. A. "The Wisconsin Physics Film Evaluation Project." (Abstract) *AV Communication Review* 8: 156; May-June 1960.

Witty, Paul, and Fitzwater, James P. "An Experiment with Films, Film-Readers, and the Magnetic Sound Track Projector." (Abstract) *Audio-Visual Communication Review* 5: 554–55; Fall 1957.

Yock, Donald, and Erlandson, Forrest. "The Effectiveness of Visual Aids in Dental Teaching." *Journal of Educational Research* 52: 11–15; September 1958.

ADDITIONAL REFERENCES

Adkins, Gale R. "A Study of Certain Factors That Influence the Use of Radio Broadcasts and Recordings in Public School Classrooms." (Abstract) *AV Communication Review* 9: 158; March-April 1961.

Ball, Charles E. *Filmed Demonstrations for Individual Arts: Sound Motion Pictures of Selected Industrial Arts Demonstrations Which May Be Used as a Teaching Device.* Doctor's thesis. New York: New York University, 1959. 138 p. Abstract: *Dissertation Abstracts* 20: 1283; No. 4, 1959.

Carlson, Frederic R. *The Design, Production, and Evaluation of a Vocational Guidance Film on Occupations for the Quincy School System.* Doctor's thesis. Boston: Boston

University School of Education, 1959. 130 p. Abstract: *Dissertation Abstracts* 21: 2529; No. 9, 1961.

Fell, John L. *A Comparison Between Sponsored and Educational Motion Pictures: A Study of High School Biology Films Issued in the United States in 1955.* Doctor's thesis. New York: New York University, 1959. 123 p. Abstract: *Dissertation Abstracts* 20: 223; No. 1, 1959.

Fritz, John O. *Film Persuasion in Education and Social Controversies: A Theoretical Analysis of the Components Manifest in Viewer-Film Involvement as They Affect the Viewer's Urge To Further Inquiry into Social Controversies.* Doctor's thesis. Bloomington: Indiana University, 1957. 426 p. Abstract: *Dissertation Abstracts* 17: 2221; No. 10, 1957.

Horowitz, Milton W., and Fromer, Robert. "A Set of Discriminable Surface Colors and Symbols for Coding in Animated Training Panels." (Abstract) *AV Communication Review* 8: 79; Winter 1960.

Knapp, Austin C. *An Analysis of Trends in Selected Graduate Audiovisual Education Programs.* Doctor's thesis. Bloomington: Indiana University, 1960. 146 p. Abstract: *Dissertation Abstracts* 21: 2631; No. 9, 1961.

Lambert, Charlotte L. *A Film for Teaching Selected Sport Skills to Elementary School Children.* Doctor's thesis. Iowa City: State University of Iowa, 1959. 144 p. Abstract: *Dissertation Abstracts* 20: 2137–38; No. 6, 1959.

Owens, Blanche Elizabeth. *A Film on Fundamental Procedures in Physical Education for Elementary School Classroom Teachers.* Doctor's thesis. Iowa City: State University of Iowa, 1956. 128 p. Abstract: *Dissertation Abstracts* 16: 1633; No. 9, 1956.

Porter, Lorena R. *Construction of a Film as an Aid for Teachers of Primary Physical Education.* Doctor's thesis. Iowa City: State

University of Iowa, 1956. 74 p. Abstract: *Dissertation Abstracts* 16: 1633–34; No. 9, 1956.

Redemsky, Louis W. "Student Evaluation of Films Used in College Social Studies." *Audio-Visual Communication Review* 7: 3–13; Winter 1959.

Roper, Keith I. *The Utilization of Industry-Sponsored Instructional Materials by Colorado High School Chemistry Teachers.* Doctor's thesis. Boulder: University of Colorado, 1956. 211 p. Abstract: *Dissertation Abstracts* 17: 2884–85; No. 12, 1957.

Salley, Homer E. *A Study of the Use of 16mm Films by Community Organizations with Special Attention to the Louisville Free Public Library as a Source of Films for Such Groups in Louisville, Kentucky.* Doctor's thesis. Bloomington: Indiana University, 1957. 227 p. Abstract: *Dissertation Abstracts* 17: 2201–02; No. 10, 1957.

Siegel, Helene F. *A Study of Teachers' Use of Business-Sponsored Instructional Materials in Selected Elementary Schools.* Doctor's thesis. Detroit: Wayne University, 1956. 118 p. Abstract: *Dissertation Abstracts* 16: 1643; No. 9, 1956.

Smith, Karl U. "The Scientific Principles of Textbook Design and Illustration." *AV Communication Review* 8: 27–49; Winter 1960.

Twyford, Loran C. "Michigan Educational Film Libraries." (Abstract) *Audio-Visual Communication Review* 6: 231; Summer 1958.

Twyford, Loran C. "Operations Research on Instructional Films." (Abstract) *AV Communication Review* 8: 156; May-June 1960.

Villa, Alfred L. *Educational Factors That Influence Decisions To Produce Instructional Films.* Doctor's thesis. Boston: Boston University School of Education, 1960. 204 p. Abstract: *Dissertation Abstracts* 21: 2640–41; No. 9, 1961.

The Systematic Selection of Instructional Materials Based on an Inventory of Learning Abilities and Skills

Judith Weinthaler
and Jay M. Rotberg

EDITORS' QUESTIONS:

1. Evaluate the system presented in this article for the selection of appropriate instructional materials.

2. Devise two methods for selecting materials for instruction—one for an individual child and another for a group of children. Incorporate some of the procedures suggested by the authors.

3. Implement the procedure you have devised for selecting materials for an individual child. Assess the effectiveness of your system.

4. Implement the procedure you have written for a group of children. Evaluate your procedure. Make changes or alterations as necessary.

Judith Weinthaler and Jay M. Rotberg, "The Systematic Selection of Instructional Materials Based on an Inventory of Learning Abilities and Skills," *Exceptional Children,* XXXVI, No. 8 (April 1970), 615–619. Reprinted with the permission of the Council for Exceptional Children and the authors.

Considerable attention has been focused on the availability and selection of materials for instructing the handicapped. Although substantial progress has been made in publicizing and disseminating these materials, little emphasis has been given to establishing a system for selecting materials according to particular learning abilities. Often, material is chosen at random from available catalogs or on the basis of a few children's needs rather than the diverse needs within a classroom. Selection often also tends to be based solely on subject matter. This practice leads to either an overabundance or a lack of materials in a particular category, since one type of material cannot cover the complete range of learning abilities. In addition, how materials may be modified to teach various skills and how the presentation and response may be adapted to many different learning abilities are often not considered.

A system for selecting appropriate materials based on an inventory of learning abilities is described here. From such an analysis, the materials can be matched to the specific needs and abilities of the children who will use them.

The system will be discussed in two parts: its application to selecting and modifying materials for a particular child and its use in choosing materials for groups of children with varying learning abilities. The selection procedure uses the same set of variables to analyze the learning abilities of a single child or a group of children and the

Judith Weinthaler is Learning Disabilities Specialist, Brookline Public Schools, Brookline, Massachusetts and Consultant, New England Instructional Materials Center, Boston University; and Jay M. Rotberg is Assistant Professor of Education, Department of Special Education, Boston University and Associate Director, New England Instructional Materials Center, Boston University, Massachusetts.

type of problem for which the material is best suited.

Selecting Materials for Individuals

With the heightened demand for instructional materials and their increased production and dissemination, education has often focused upon the material as the prime variable and first step in the teaching process. In working with handicapped children, however, the child's abilities should be evaluated first; only then can the appropriate materials be selected. The teaching process should begin with a determination of the learner's profile through a complete evaluation of his assets and deficits. From this profile, general remedial approaches should be determined, the teaching tasks specified, and the components placed in a logical developmental sequence beginning with the child's readiness and interest levels.

In addition to a learner's profile, a materials' profile, based on a similar analysis, should also be formulated. By comparing the two profiles, the best materials for each part of the teaching task can be selected, and the concept of diagnostic teaching (basing remediation on an initial and ongoing evaluation) can be effectively used.

Both of these profiles are compiled by using the six specific variables already employed in analyzing diagnostic and remedial learning tasks or activities: level of the task, modality of reception, modality of expression, types of psycholinguistic processes, the number of modalities, and the content of the task. These six variables are further explained by the following outline:

I. Level of the Task (according to a developmental hierarchy of learning experiences)
   A. Sensation—most concrete, earliest, basic level of functioning
   B. Perception
   C. Memory
   D. Symbolization
   E. Conceptualization—most abstract, highest level of functioning
II. Modality of Reception (information is received through one or more of the following channels)
   A. Auditory
   B. Visual
   C. Tactile
III. Modality of Expression
   A. Auditory-oral (phonemes, words, environmental sounds, etc.)
   B. Motor-tactile-kinesthetic (gestures, pointing, marking, matching, drawing, writing, etc.)
IV. Psycholinguistic Process
   A. Reception
   B. Association
   C. Expression
V. Number of Modalities (involved in the reception-association-expression sequence of a task)
   A. One modality—aural oral (listening and speaking)
   B. Two modalities—aural motor (listening and writing)
VI. Content of the Task (may be characterized by whether it is verbal or nonverbal and social or nonsocial)
   A. Verbal nonverbal content
      1. Verbal: involving both the auditory and visual modalities—phonemes, letters, words, both oral and printed. The word "cat" either printed or heard is considered verbal task content.
      2. Nonverbal: other means of communication and symbolization such as pictures, gestures, objects, environmental sounds, and numbers. A picture of a cat is nonverbal task content.

B. Social nonsocial content
   1. Social: meaningful part of a child's environment such as environmental sounds and pictures.
   2. Nonsocial: nonmeaningful part of an environment such as pure tones, nonsense figures, nonsense syllables, or words.

Using the above variables, a profile of the learner's assets and deficits and a complementary materials profile is constructed, forming a Learner-Material Match. In a Learner-Material Match, the materials should capitalize upon the child's assets as well as strengthen his areas of weakness.

To illustrate an appropriate match, let us assume that a child has a deficit on the perceptual level, primarily in the auditory modality of reception and expression; in the visual modality, however, his abilities are relatively intact. In terms of task content his problem is verbal in nature. Let us also assume the teaching task is to strengthen the child's auditory discrimination. The material selected should not only involve an oral exchange, but also capitalize upon his visual strengths. Therefore, materials on the perceptual level should be selected which employ visual cues and motor gesture responses.

To illustrate an inappropriate Learner-Material Match, let us assume that a learner's profile consists of deficits in visual perception of verbal material and auditory strengths, while the materials' profile consists of nonverbal, nonsocial visual perceptual material (discrimination between meaningless designs) requiring visual motor responses. Although this material is on the correct hierarchy level, it is not appropriate for two reasons. First, its nonverbal and nonsocial task content is unrelated to the child's verbal problem; and second, it does not capitalize upon the child's auditory or tactile strengths. If the profiles are not matched, the instructional materials will probably not relate directly to the child's total learning needs. When both remediation and materials selection are not based on the diagnostic evaluation, the concept of diagnostic teaching is of little value.

Selecting Materials for Groups

The concept of a Learner-Material Match for individual children can also be applied to choosing materials for groups of children found, for example, in clinics, classrooms, and learning centers. Assuming that the individual profiles will vary, the first step is to establish a general framework of group learning abilities as a basis for selecting a master materials library. This collection must cover a wide range of learning abilities because the materials best suited for each child will be drawn from it. For example, in training two children with different auditory perceptual problems—one with strengths and one with deficiencies in visual perception and visual motor abilities—two types of materials are necessary: a type which capitalizes on the first child's visual perceptual strengths and another type which does not overemphasize visual input or visual motor response for the second child.

Discussion of Learning Abilities Framework

The six variables used for individual diagnostic purposes form the basis for selecting the master collection and developing a general framework of learning abilities. The major headings in this framework are perception, memory, and symbolization-conceptualization—three of the five levels of the task hierarchy. Because remediation at the sensation level is more of a medical than educational concern, this level has not been included. The task levels of conceptualization and symbolization are combined because, although theoretically distinct, they are difficult to separate in the teaching process; both levels involve higher mental processes and require significantly more integration than the perceptual or memory levels.

Modalities of input are the subheadings and are followed by more specific breakdowns of learning abilities with specific suggestions for materials. Under the primary learning modalities of vision and audition, the additional variables of modality of expression and task content should be considered as often as possible.

Since the following outline of the learning abilities framework is merely a guide to a more efficient selection of materials based on a systematic inventory of learning abilities, little attempt has been made to include examples of all of the theoretically possible combinations of the six variables.

1. Perception
   A. Auditory Perception
      1. Gross discrimination
         a. Nonverbal: tapes, records, pictures, noisemakers, environmental sounds.
         b. Verbal: lists and/or pictures of dissimilar whole words having different initial, medial, and final sounds—banana-telephone, mailman-rosebud.
      2. Fine discrimination
         a. Nonverbal: sounds involving finer and more subtle discrimination—bells, animals, horns, footsteps, voices.
         b. Verbal: lists of morphemes and phonemes involving subtle discriminations—money-monkey, men-mend, fine-vine, house-mouse, bell-ball, s-d, s-c, d-b—phonics cards, and games.
   B. Visual perception
      1. Discrimination
         a. Form and shape discrimination
            (1) Nonverbal: two and three dimensional objects, numbers, geometric forms, shape and number templates and inserts, peg boards.
            (2) Verbal: two and three dimensional letters, letter stencils, templates, tactile letters, and block words (discrimination of word configurations).
         b. Color discrimination—objects and cards for matching, sorting, pasting
         c. Size discrimination
            (1) Nonverbal: graduated cylinders, nesting boxes, three dimensional numbers.
            (2) Verbal: two and three dimensional letters and words varying in height and length.
      2. Constancy
         a. Nonverbal: objects, pictures, numbers varying in size, shape, position of viewing, color, and texture.
         b. Verbal: letters, words, sentences varying in size, shape, position, color, context, and texture; visual tracking of letters and words; varying styles

of letters and anagrams; words printed on paper of varying colors.

3. Part-whole relationship
   a. Nonverbal: form puzzles, single figure and picture puzzles, toys and objects to construct and assemble, fraction insert puzzles, cuisinaire rods, parquetry blocks, balance scale, abacus.
   b. Verbal: letter puzzles, letters to cut up, word builders (linking letters), sentence builders, syllabication lists and cards.
4. Figure ground
   a. Nonverbal: objects for sorting, hidden figure pictures, picture tracking exercise.
   b. Verbal: symbol and word tracking exercises, hidden letter and word exercises, reading frames.
5. Visual motor
   a. Fine motor: stencils, templates, construction toys, arts and crafts activities, programed handwriting exercise books, bean bag and ring toss games, jacks, paints, throwing and catching games, nuts and bolts, acetate overlays, grease pencils, writing frames, corrective pencils, daily living materials such as buttons, zippers, ties, and eating utensils.
   b. Gross motor: records for body movement development, trampoline, walking boards, climbing ropes and bars, barrels, balance boards, medicine ball, staircase, and other playground equipment.
C. Body perception (laterality, body image, body schema)—dolls, pictures of humans, people puzzles, manikin, mirror, balance board, trampoline, walking board, videotapes, polaroid cameras, film strips, records for developing body image
D. Temporal perception—real clocks and calendars, teaching clocks and calendars, pictures to emphasize significant events and seasons, stories involving temporal sequences of events, rhythm instruments and activities, materials for estimation of temporal duration such as a timer and a stopwatch, and equipment for pouring liquids and drawing to music
E. Social perception—pictures portraying various facial expressions and emotions, cause-effect pictures, picture interpretation activities, group games

II. Memory
A. Auditory
   1. Recall—pictures to aid recall of auditory commands and sentence repetition; art projects and games for following directions; games stressing auditory recall; objects and pictures for rapid naming
   2. Sequencing
      a. Nonverbal: tapes with sequences of environmental sounds and instrumental sounds using real objects and pictures to accompany tapes; buzzer boards; and pattern cards.
      b. Verbal: picture cards and word lists for training sequences of initial, medial, and final sounds and auditory blending of sounds; letters and cards to reinforce the recall of sequences of sounds and words; programed exercises for au-

diovisual equipment; dual track tape recorders.

B. Visual
1. Recall—objects, pictures, numbers, words, and letters to be recalled; flash cards, programed worksheets, tachistoscope or tachistoscopic attachment for overhead projectors
2. Sequencing
    a. Nonverbal: beads for stringing, numbers for sequencing, different shaped blocks and designs.
    b. Verbal: manipulative block letters for imitation of sequential patterns, exercises for matching letter sequences.

III. Symbolization-Conceptualization
A. Oral language (verbal symbols)
1. Reception (listening)—materials geared to teaching nouns, parts of speech, sentence structure, and concepts or categories not requiring a spoken response to confirm the child's understanding of the information presented; real objects for manipulation; pictorial representations of nouns, verbs, adjectives, and prepositions; film strips, lotto games, language development kits, stories to be read
2. Expression (speaking)—walkie talkie sets, tape recorder, dual track tape recorder, phonics mirror, large action pictures, hand and finger puppets, stimulation cards

B. Written language (verbal)
1. Reception (reading)—reading materials using whole, phonetic, linguistic, and tactile-kinesthetic methods; reading clinics; exercises for reading comprehension, concept and vocabulary building, and following directions; independent high interest, low vocabulary reading
2. Expression (writing)—learning abilities not involving visual motor coordination, but including spelling, sentence formulation, productivity, and level of ideation
    a. Programed spelling workbooks, sentence building cards, tape recorders, and picture sequences to increase written productivity.
    b. Typewriters, letter charts, wide lined paper, letter stamp sets (aids which should be provided since this category does not deal with visual motor coordination).

C. Arithmetic (nonverbal symbols)—number lines, stepping stones, counting objects, boxes, frames, ladders, abacus, flash cards, place value charts, fraction boards, programed workbooks, real and play money, number charts, and stamp sets

Summary

Failure to establish a systematic framework of learning abilities often results in a random selection of instructional materials based on factors such as availability of catalogs, learning profiles of a limited number of children, or subject matter alone. This type of selection rarely relates to the child's needs and abilities. Without the appropriate materials, the remedial teaching process is impeded. Only by establishing such a systematic framework can materials be selected to insure a Learner-Material Match and, therefore, to insure the full application of the concept of diagnostic teaching.

Recommended Readings: Utilization and Management of Multi-Media for Teaching

Allen, Andrianna "Criteria for Selecting Gifts," *Childhood Education* 45 (1968): 118–121.

Allen, William H. "Audio-Visual Materials," *Review of Educational Research* 26 (1956): 125–156.

Apter, Michael J. and Boorer, David "Skinner, Piaget and Frobel: A Study of Programmed Instruction with Young Children," *Programmed Learning* 6 (1969): 164–177.

Austin, James T. "Videotaping as a Teaching Tool," *Exceptional Children* 35 (1969): 557.

Brown, James W., Lewis, Richard B. and Harcleroad, Fred F. *A-V Instruction: Materials and Methods.* New York: McGraw-Hill Book Co., Inc., 1959.

Brown, R. A. and Brown, M. R. "New Horizons in Materials," *Instructor* 76, (1967): 109–110.

Cole, Barry G., ed. *Television.* New York: The Free Press, A Division of the Macmillan Co., 1970.

Erickson, Carlton W. *Fundamentals of Teaching with Audiovisual Technology.* New York: The Macmillan Co., 1965.

Filep, Robert T., ed. *Prospectives in Programming.* New York: The Macmillan Co., 1963.

Glaser, Robert, ed. *Teaching Machines and Programmed Learning. 11: Data and Directions.* Washington: Department of Audiovisual Instruction, National Education Association, 1965.

Haney, John and Ullmer, Uldon J. *Educational Media and the Teacher.* Dubuque, Iowa: Wm. C. Brown Company Publishers, 1970.

McIntyre, Robert B. "Evaluation of Instructional Materials and Programs: Applications of a Systems Approach," *Exceptional Children* 37 (1970): 213–220.

Mehl, Marie A., Mills, Hubert H., Douglass, Harl R. and Scobey, Mary-Margaret *Teaching in the Elementary School.* 3rd ed. New York: The Ronald Press Co., 1965.

Miller, L. P. "Materials for Multi-Ethnic Learners," *Educational Leadership* 28 (1970): 129–132.

Nelson, Leslie W. *Instructional Aids: How to Make and Use them.* 2nd ed. Dubuque, Iowa: Wm. C. Brown Company Publishers, 1970.

Oates, Stanton C. *Audio Visual Equipment Self-Instruction Manual.* 2nd ed. Dubuque, Iowa: Wm. C. Brown Company Publishers, 1970.

Pincus, M. and Morgenstern, F. "Graphs in the Primary Grades," *The Arithmetic Teacher* 17 (1970): 499.

Russell, Roger W. *Frontiers in Psychology.* Glenview, Illinois: Scott, Foresman, 1964.

Suppes, Patrick "The Uses of the Computer in Education," *Scientific American* 215 (1966): 206–220.

Wittich, Walter A. and Schuller, Charles F. *Audiovisual Materials: Their Nature and Use.* 3rd ed. New York: Harper & Row, Publishers, 1962.

PART
THREE

Combining Strategies for Individualized Instructional Programs

INTRODUCTION

Introduction to Part III

The fact that no two individuals are alike —that each learns at his own speed, in his own style and in accordance with his own unique motivational structure—has received lip service by many. Recently, however, there appears to be a sincere, mounting dissatisfaction with the practice of requiring pupils to learn the same subject matter at the same time, in the same manner and at the same rate, using the same instructional materials, through exposure to the same teaching technique. The technological age has intensified the realization that the dream of achieving quality education for each learner can become a reality. As a consequence, individualized instructional programs have mushroomed throughout the country.

Beck and Bolvin acquaint the reader with the Reading Program for Individually Prescribed Instruction (IPI) conducted at the University of Pittsburgh in cooperation with the Baldwin-Whitehall School District. An approach to individualizing reading is vividly illustrated and discussed in their article.

Of particular interest to the classroom teacher is the example of an individualized lesson in science for nonreaders in Grades K-3 presented by Lipson. He also discusses five aspects of the individualized science program: instructional systems and use of tests, objectives of instruction, use of direct experience as the basis of instruction, individualized lessons for nonreaders and results of the program.

Deep presents an individualized instructional system called the Program for Learning in Accordance with Needs (PLAN). In his presentation he discusses the meaning of individualized instruction and shows the difference between computer-assisted instruction and computer-managed instruction. He points out ways in which the computer can assist the classroom teacher in individualizing instruction. The change in the teacher's role resulting from the implementation of the PLAN approach is also considered.

The interesting example of computer-assisted instruction described by Fejfar illustrates how computers, that many schools already possess, can be converted, through programming alone, into effective teaching machines. He indicates how the particular program described provides for the implementation of generally accepted learning principles. Fejfar points out the need for further research and poses a number of questions for investigation. One of the important features of this article is the illustration of the combination of instructional strategies with the aid of the computer to enhance learning for each child.

In order to realize some of the benefits of computer technology, it is not necessary to actually use a computer. Berry shows how some techniques of computer programming can be utilized by the classroom teacher. Using as an example the teaching of counting to first graders, the author demonstrates how computer simulation can assist the teacher and the child in understanding the various mental operations involved in programming a learning task.

The article of Kapfer, "An Instructional Management Strategy for Individualized Learning," is designed to help the teacher in developing procedures for individualized instruction. Learning packages for use by each child comprise the important elements of this strategy. A common characteristic of each package is the provision for self-pacing.

After studying Part III, it is expected that the student will be able to:

1. Illustrate the interrelatedness of the essential components of the teaching process.

2. Demonstrate the desirability of combining several strategies for effective teaching.

3. Analyze the nature of individualized instruction.

4. Participate in the development of a program for individualized instruction.

5. Develop her own original strategies for individualizing instruction.

A Model for Non-Gradedness: The Reading Program for Individually Prescribed Instruction

Isabel L. Beck
and John O. Bolvin

EDITORS' QUESTIONS:

1. Identify the components of the Individually Prescribed Instruction program (IPI).
2. Discuss the four stages of the IPI linguistic approach to reading.
3. Evaluate the IPI Reading Curriculum on the bases of the criteria you have established in your study of the previous sections of this book for the following areas:
   a. method used for stating objectives
   b. assessment procedures
   c. classroom management
   d. utilization of audiovisual materials.
4. What provisions does the program have for matching reinforcement techniques to the characteristics of the learner? For instance, it is stated that the students work independently on prescribed materials and that if a student needs help, he can ask for help from the teacher or teacher aides. What provisions are made for reinforcing the learning of children who do not voluntarily seek help and who may not even be aware of their need for help?
5. Compare this program with other individualized programs in reading. What are the advantages of this program over other programs? What are its disadvantages?

32

During the past four years the Learning Research and Development Center at the University of Pittsburgh in cooperation with the Baldwin-Whitehall School District has been involved in designing, developing, and implementing curricula for a program to individualize instruction in reading, mathematics, and science. Approximately 250 children in kindergarten through sixth grade along with the teaching staff at the Oakleaf Elementary School are involved in the program called Individually Prescribed Instruction (IPI).

The IPI Project represents an investigation into the problems encountered in in-dividualizing instruction and involves the development of a program for achieving this goal. The definition of individualization that serves as a basis for the project is that individualization of instruction implies the provision for planning and implementing an

Mrs. Beck is a Research Assistant and Director of the Curriculum Staff in Reading, Learning Research and Development Center, University of Pittsburgh, Pittsburgh, Pennsylvania.
Dr. Bolvin is an Associate Professor of Education and Associate Director of the Learning Research and Development Center, University of Pittsburgh. In addition, Dr. Bolvin is the Director of the Individually Prescribed Instruction Project, Learning Research and Development Center, University of Pittsburgh, Pittsburgh, Pennsylvania.

individualized program of studies suited to each student's learning needs and his characteristics as a learner. The essential aspects of individualization that are of major concern to the project staff at the present stage of development are: 1) individualization of rate at which students proceed through a carefully sequenced set of objectives for a given subject; 2) mastery of subject-matter content by individuals as they proceed through a set of objectives; 3) self-direction, self-evaluation, and self-initiation on the part of the learners; and 4) devising individualized techniques and materials of instruction. All these aspects are predicated upon the fact that individualized instruction entails determining what the child knows in a given area at a particular time and what he is ready to learn.

The IPI model for individualization consists of the following components: 1) sequentially established curricular objectives in each area stated in behavioral terms, 2) procedures and processes for diagnosis of student achievement in terms of the objectives of the curriculum, 3) materials for individualizing learning to provide a variety of paths for attainment of mastery of any given objective, 4) a system for individually prescribing the learning tasks that the student is ready to undertake, 5) the organization and management of individualization as it relates to the total school environment, and 6) strategies for continuous evaluation and feedback of information for teacher decision-making.

Curriculum

The IPI reading curriculum is based on an analysis of recent thinking in the field. After reviewing the alternatives available, a linguistic approach to reading was selected.

This approach suggests four stages of reading: 1) pre-reading, 2) decoding, 3) comprehension and skills development, and 4) independent reading.

Stages

The pre-reading stage emphasizes the behaviors needed to begin the decoding process. Included in this stage are teaching the letter names and some letter sounds, identifying groups of letters as words, and auditory blending. During the pre-reading stage, the child is guided through the IPI system and taught to manage the materials that assist him in learning to read.

The *Sullivan Associates Programmed Reading* published by McGraw-Hill Book Company is the major instructional material used during the decoding stage. It was selected because it is based, in general, on a linguistic approach and because it permits the child to proceed at his own rate. During this decoding stage comprehension skills receive attention through small group teacher-directed situations.

Comprehension and skills development emphasize "reading for meaning." The pupil objectives in the third stage assume decoding, and develop the comprehension skills with stress on literal, interpretative, and evaluative comprehension.

The last stage, independent reading, assumes that the pupil uses the decoding and comprehension skills to read in areas of his interests and needs. Although it is possible to think of these stages as analytically discrete, they are not; they overlap. Some independent reading occurs at the decoding stage, comprehension skills are practiced at the decoding stage, and comprehension skills continue to be developed in the independent stage. The label for each stage only states the primary emphasis of that stage. Table I is a graphic representation of these stages of development.

Objectives

The key aspect of the curricula for the Individually Prescribed Instruction Project is the careful specification of behavioral objectives. The IPI reading curriculum contains approximately 400 behavioral objectives arranged by area of study (e.g., literal comprehension, vocabulary development) and sequenced by difficulty. There are 13 areas of study on 11 levels of difficulty. The intersection of an area of study with a level of difficulty is called a unit. Table II represents a scope and sequence chart indicating the areas of study and the number of objectives for each unit.

Some objectives appear at several levels of difficulty. However, the selection to which the objective applies varies. An example of this is the objective that asks a student to state in his own words the main idea of a selection. This particular objective appears on six levels of difficulty. However, each time it appears the text to which the objective is applied is longer, the readability is more difficult, and the content (e.g., fiction, non-fiction, science) varies. In this sense, the conditions for which the objective applies are considered in sequencing the curriculum. Thus, the pupil is refining his use of the skill as he proceeds through the levels.

Diagnostic Instruments

A vital ingredient of an individualized program is the diagnostic instruments for determining to which levels, units, and ob-

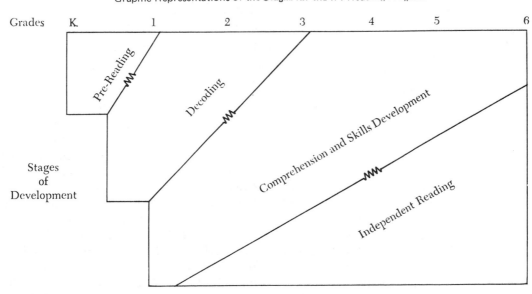

Table 1
Graphic Representations of the Stages for the IPI Reading Program

Table 2
Number of Objectives in Each Unit
in Individually Prescribed Instruction Reading

Area of Study	Level										
	A	B	C	D	E	F	G	H	I	J	K
Visual Discrimination	12	–	–	–	–	–	–	–	–	–	–
Auditory Discrimination	2	2	–	–	–	–	–	–	–	–	–
Phonetic Analysis	–	–	3	6	4	5	6	–	–	–	–
Structural Analysis	–	–	4	7	11	12	6	3	3	3	5
Vocabulary Development	–	4	4	4	3	3	5	2	4	2	2
Literal Comprehension	5	4	4	3	3	4	4	5	3	2	2
Interpretative Comprehension	5	8	5	5	3	4	5	6	6	5	8
Evaluative Comprehension	2	3	4	2	5	4	4	5	4	2	5
Organizational Skills	–	–	–	–	–	7	5	3	6	5	6
Library Skills	3	2	3	2	2	4	6	5	5	2	–
Reference Skills	–	4	1	3	4	7	6	5	4	4	2
Oral Reading	–	2	1	1	–	–	–	–	–	–	–
Related Reading	6	4	2	–	–	–	–	–	–	–	–

jectives a pupil should be assigned. Four types of diagnostic instruments have been developed for the reading program. These include the placement test, the unit pretest, the curriculum-embedded test, and the unit post-test.

The placement test is given at the beginning of each academic year and to children upon transferring into the school. A pupil's performance on the placement test assists the teacher in determining the initial starting unit for that student. Once this starting unit has been determined, the student is assigned the pretest for that particular unit. This instrument measures the child's proficiency in each objective within the unit. When a pupil demonstrates the desired proficiency for any of the objectives within a unit, he is not assigned work for that objective. For any objective in which the pupil does not demonstrate mastery, he is assigned a sequence of work.

The curriculum-embedded test is a check to assist the teacher and student in determining when the pupil should move on to the next objective within a unit. If a child

fails to show mastery on the curriculum-embedded test, additional work is assigned. After the additional assignment is completed, another curriculum-embedded test is administered. When the pupil completes the assigned work within a unit, and when his performance on the curriculum-embedded tests indicates competence, he is given a post-test for the unit. The post-test is a parallel form of the pretest.

Materials

Materials for individually prescribed instruction have been selected and developed to teach each of the objectives. As much as possible, these materials provide for some degree of self-study. They lead the child from what he knows to what he needs to know to progress through the curriculum. Where possible, existing materials that meet these criteria were identified and when necessary, modified. Where the demands of the objectives were such that commercial materials were not readily available or easily modified, the Learning Research and Development Center's staff and the IPI teachers have written the necessary materials. An example of the adaptation of commercial materials is the present use of *Sullivan Associates Programmed Reading.* In attempting to implement the first 14 or 15 books of this series in an individualized program, it was necessary to develop approximately 500 short recordings to introduce sounds, new words, dictation exercises, and other instructional and auditory requirements of the program. As a result of adapting this program, it was possible to reduce by approximately 50 percent the amount of work assigned in each of the 14 books.

Another example of the adaptation of available materials are staff prepared worksheets that have pupils go to a particular commercial source and read a specified selection. After reading the selection, the child returns to the worksheet and answers staff prepared questions or performs a variety of staff prepared activities. In other words, commercial reading selections are used, but the instructional strategies are determined by the staff.

Presently throughout the program there is considerable reliance on worksheets; tape and disc recordings; programmed materials; individual readers; selected materials from reading kits such as SRA, Macmillan Reading Spectrum; as well as manipulative devices such as the language master. The program contains approximately 4,000 staff prepared workpages and 600 staff prepared disc recordings and response sheets.

Although there is an emphasis on self-instruction, this is not the only instructional technique employed. In some instances, it is necessary and desirable for the teachers to present new ideas and processes; this is done in small and/or large groups as well as individually. The major difference of group instruction as employed in an individualized program is that the groups assemble for a particular purpose and usually remain intact for only short periods of time.

Individual Prescriptions

The keystone of the IPI system is the individual pupil's prescription or daily lesson plan. On the basis of the teacher's diagnosis of the student's abilities and placement test results, the lesson plan for each child lists the materials to be used and the instructional techniques to be employed for a particular objective. In writing the prescription, the teacher takes into account such factors as: 1) the achievement of the student as it relates to the curriculum, 2) the general maturity of the child, 3) certain learner characteristics as they relate to the particular tasks, and 4) the student's present degree of self-direction and self-initiation. Prescriptions are prepared prior to the scheduled time for reading instruction and are organized for ease of distribution as the class begins.

Classroom Management

The students in the primary classes begin work independently on prescribed materials. In the case of a first grader working primarily in the decoding portion of the program, the child often begins by listening to one or two records prepared to go with a series of student response sheets. These records introduce new sound symbols, review previously taught sound symbols, and introduce new words. After completing this auditory introduction, he will then work in his reading book which, at the present time, is a modified version of *Sullivan Associates Programmed Reading.* His prescription tells him how far to proceed in this book before checking with his teacher. Most of the students can proceed through the prescribed materials with a minimum of teacher direction and instruction. However, when assistance is needed the student can obtain help from either the teacher aides or the teacher, depending on the nature of the assistance needed. When the child has completed this portion of his assignment, the teacher generally brings together five to 10 students and conducts a group reading lesson. The emphasis during the individual aspect of the program is on the decoding processes, while the emphasis during the group lesson is on oral reading and comprehension.

The reading program for students in the intermediate grades is also divided into two major areas—basic skills development and reading skill utilization. An example of the management of the basic skills portion follows: A student ready to begin work at Level E—Literal Comprehension, is assigned a pretest covering the three objectives for this unit. These objectives are:[1]

1. List in written form the events of a given story or article in the order of occurrence.
2. Answer, in written form, true-false statements that require recall of direct statements in a printed text.
3. Copy the sentence from a story which provides proof for the answer to a given question.

If results of the pretest indicate that a child needs work assigned for Objective 1, his prescription would list the tasks that are appropriate for him for this objective. These would be listed as: E-LC-1, pages 2, 3, 4. The student would then go to the materials center and pull the sheets corresponding to these assignments. His first assignment as listed on assignment sheet 2 would be: "Go to the SRA Reading Laboratory 1C in the Learning Center. Find the story, 'Smart Lit-

tle Rooster,' Olive 15 and read it." After completing this assignment the student checks his answers against an answer key. If he has questions concerning interpretations or errors that he made, he sees the teacher. If he has no questions, he proceeds to the next assignment. The next assignment might be a selection from a Basal reader. It often happens that the teacher gives the child a more open assignment within an objective permitting him to read any three or four selections from the material available for the objective.

As the student follows his daily prescription and works through his assignments, the teacher moves throughout the class checking student progress and giving assistance as needed. The information gained from this interaction plus the information obtained from the child's successes and difficulties with the assigned materials are the bases for the next days prescription. About one-half of the child's reading time is spent on the activities just described. These activities comprise the skills development area.

The other half of the intermediate reading program involves skill utilization activities. Here the student is involved in applying and integrating previously learned skills to tradebooks, textbooks, magazines, and newspapers. Depending upon the child's placement in the skills development area he is assigned to a small group. In this group he is introduced to a variety of reading sources, shares interpretation of mutually read selection with others, is introduced to some of the classics, and is provided with opportunities for purposeful oral reading. Also, during part of this time, he is given the freedom to select what he wants to read. As

1. Individually Prescribed Instruction Reading Curriculum. Working Paper No. 28. Pittsburgh, Pennsylvania: Learning Research and Development Center, University of Pittsburgh, September 1, 1967.

the child progresses the amount of time spent in directed activities decreases, while the time spent in independent reading increases. The main difference between the extremes of directed reading and independent reading is the amount of control of the child's reading activities by the teacher.

Data Collection

An essential aspect of individualized instruction is the provision for charting the progress of each student as he moves through the curriculum and the availability of these reports for teacher use. This information is necessary for individual prescriptions and classroom organization. The data to be used for prescription writing should include: 1) general ability level in the given subject, 2) the degree of mastery or lack of mastery in each skill in the particular unit assigned to the student, 3) information related to the child's progress in previous units directly related to the skills in the present unit, 4) detailed information related to the pupil's progress as he moves through the various tasks related to the particular skill or objective assigned, and 5) general learning characteristics of the pupil as they relate to the assigned task.

Information needed by the teacher for day-to-day classroom organization must include: 1) level, unit, and skill of each pupil in the class; 2) the approximate length of time (days) the student has been working in a given skill; and 3) the next immediate skill for each pupil in the class. With this information the teachers can organize the classes for small and large group discussion, peer-group discussions, or individualized tutoring. The availability, accuracy, and format of these reports is essential to the success of IPI as an operating system.

A program for computer-assisted management for the project has been developed and will become operational in September, 1968. With the implementation of this management system, teachers will be able to obtain more quickly relevant information on a particular student, reports as to how many and which students are working in the same units or objectives, and daily summaries of the progress of each student. Additional functions of this system will be added as the teachers and staff are able to suggest further needs.

An Individualized Science Laboratory

Joseph I. Lipson

EDITORS' QUESTIONS:

1. Describe the taped demonstration lesson on magnetism for nonreaders. Replicate this lesson using a five-year-old child as your subject. Assess the effectiveness of the procedures used.

2. Suggest ways of modifying the lesson to enhance learning achievement.

3. Develop an individualized lesson in mathematics for a five-year-old nonreader. Tape a lesson designed to teach a pupil to distinguish shapes of objects such as squares, circles and triangles. Use as a guide the taped demonstration lesson presented in this article. Implement your plan using a kindergarten child as a subject. Assess the results achieved and revise the lesson as necessary.

4. Discuss the different aspects of the individualized program in science for nonreaders. Point out the desirable elements of the program.

Joseph I. Lipson, "An Individualized Science Laboratory," *Science and Children*, Vol. 4, (December 1966), 8–12. Reprinted with the permission of the National Science Teachers Association.

The Learning Research and Development Center at the University of Pittsburgh is creating individualized science laboratory lessons. These lessons are part of an experimental project to examine innovative methods of individualized instruction in the elementary school. Reading, mathematics, and science are the subjects to which individualization procedures have been applied. The project has been underway in a Baldwin-Whitehall School (suburban area of Pittsburgh, Pennsylvania) of 220 pupils during the school years of 1964–65 and 1965–66.

Thus far in science, the project has focused upon the problems of instruction with nonreaders in grades K-3. Lessons for the K-6 grades will be instituted eventually. In the individualized system each student in a class of fifteen may be doing a different experiment. To permit each nonreading student to interact with the materials of his lesson, tape recorded voice directions, and questions are used. These tape recorded lessons are put onto an endless belt cartridge much like those being used in automobile tape systems. A sample lesson is presented on the opposite page.

A Typical Lesson

At the beginning of a class each student receives a tape cartridge and a plastic box containing the materials for his lesson. The

The author is affiliated with Learning Research & Development Center, University of Pittsburgh, Pittsburgh, Pennsylvania.

The research and development reported herein was performed pursuant to a contract with the United States Office of Education, Department of Health, Education, and Welfare under the provisions of the Cooperative Research Program.

33

children then take their tape and materials to a carrel. Each carrel has a tape repeater with earphones as well as a work surface; The tape repeater has easily accessible ON and OFF buttons; and once the cartridge has been plugged into the tape repeater, the child starts and stops the tape by pushing these buttons. After a direction has been given which requires a student response, a bell rings (tape recorded sound of a bell); and when the student hears the bell, he stops the tape and complies with the directions given. It is important to note that while the tape is off, the student can take as long as he likes to comply with the directions. No pressure is ever exerted to have the student turn the tape back on before he feels ready in his own mind. The child can explore the materials or convince himself of an observed effect. This freedom for the student is an important result of the philosophy of the program.

To clarify how the lessons work, let us use as an example the first lesson in magnetism. This lesson is designed (1) to show that a magnet attracts some objects and does not attract others, (2) to teach the student to be able to sort objects into two classes: those that a magnet does attract and those that a magnet does not attract. In a sense these operations define what a magnet is to the child, and in future lessons other objects will be identified as magnets if they behave similarly.

The materials for this lesson are thumb tacks, paper clips, marbles, pennies, rubber bands, stones, pieces of cardboard, nails, eight cardboard dishes, and a small red horseshoe magnet.

Using this taped demonstration as an illustration of the form and style of presenting the lessons, the following aspects of the program can now be discussed: (1) The instructional system and use of tests, (2) The instructional objectives of the program, (3) The reason for using direct experience as the

---

Students begin their lesson on magnetism as they listen to the taped instructions given below

1. Hello. I am going to tell you to do some things. The teacher will help you, too. First, we will practice. After you stop the machine, stand up, put your finger on your nose, and turn around. **BELL**

2. That was very good. Now, after you stop the machine, shake your head three times. **BELL**

3. Very good. Now you will do some things to learn something new. After you stop the machine, find the dish of thumb tacks. **BELL**

4. After you stop the machine this time, find the dish with paper clips. **BELL**

5. This time I will ask you to find two things. Find the dish with buttons and the dish with pennies. **BELL**

6. Now find the dish with rubber bands and the dish with some stones in it. **BELL**

7. We are almost finished finding things. Find the dish with the pieces of cardboard and the dish with some nails. **BELL**

8. The only thing left on the table that you have not found is called a MAGNET. A magnet can pick up some things, but there are some things it cannot pick up. We will try to find out what things it will pick up and what things it won't pick up. The magnet is painted red to help you find it. Find the magnet. **BELL**

9. That was very good. Now take the magnet and try to pick up the thumb tacks in the dish with the magnet. Touch the thumb tacks with the magnet. **BELL**

10. If some stick to the magnet, take them off the magnet, and put them in the dish. **BELL**

11. Touch the paper clips with the magnet. If any stick to the magnet, put them back in the dish. **BELL**

12. Touch the marbles with the magnet. **BELL**

13. Touch the pennies with the magnet. **BELL**

14. Touch the rubber bands with the magnet. **BELL**

15. Touch the stones with the magnet. **BELL**

16. Touch the nails with the magnet. **BELL**

17. Now put all the dishes that have things that stuck to the magnet on one side of the table. If you are not sure, use the magnet to see if the things in the dish will stick to the magnet. Remember, put all the things that stuck to the magnet on one side of the table, away from the other dishes. **BELL**

18. Now check all the things that did not stick to the magnet to make sure that none of them do stick to the magnet. **BELL**

19. Check all the things that did stick to the magnet to make sure that they really do stick to the magnet. **BELL**

20. That was very good work. Now find the paper with the pictures. **BELL**

21. Put an X on the pictures of the things that stuck to the magnet. **BELL**

22. After you stop the machine this time, do not start it again. Goodbye. **BELL**

basis of instruction, (4) The reason for developing individualized lessons for non-readers, (5) Results.

1. Instructional Systems and Use of Tests

In the individualized laboratory it is important that each child has mastered all prerequisite skills and that the students not be required to undergo formal instruction in learning areas that they have mastered already. This means that testing is very important, but it is not testing to assign a grade or to either reward or punish the student. The tests are for the purpose of diagnosis so that work can be properly assigned. In the science program the tests are now performance tests with actual materials since the objectives are phrased in terms of operations with materials.

Pre-tests have the nature of transfer lessons in which a problem is posed and no assistance is given in the solution. Since the children have not had the lessons prior to the pre-tests, the actual lesson materials may be used. After a group of lessons has been completed, a post-test is administered with new materials. For example, if a lesson involved sorting buttons, the post-test might deal with sorting playing cards. This change of materials is designed to prevent memorization of the responses asked.

The actual tests have gone through three phases. Initially, group pencil and paper tests were used. These were not satisfactory because they did not indicate the students' ability to perform operations with real objects. The other extreme of performance tests was then tried. This called for an adult to watch a single student perform each test. The procedure had to be dropped because it involved too much time and disrupted class schedules.

A compromise testing system resulted.

The tests are put on tape so that the students can perform them individually. The tests are constructed so that materials must be manipulated in order to answer the questions. After determining the answer the student must record his answer on paper. For example, in the lesson on magnetism, the test might have the materials in a box and the student would be asked to sort the objects into a group which the magnet attracts and a group of objects which the magnet does not attract. After the student has completed his task, he would be referred (by the tape voice) to a sheet of paper with pictures of the objects in the box. The student would then be asked to put an X on all the objects which the magnet attracted. The paper could then be scored later.

In order to place the student into the program, a rough-scale performance test is administered at the beginning of the school year to indicate the general level at which the student becomes unable to perform the objectives of the lesson sequence. Typically, a child stops being tested when he misses three items in succession. The student is then pre-tested in greater detail in the units for which he showed uncertain mastery. After the pre-test results are analyzed, individual laboratory lessons are assigned. After all the assigned lessons in a unit are completed, a post test is administered. If some items are still not being handled adequately by the student, the student either takes the appropriate lessons over again or he talks with the teacher in order to clear up his difficulty. As yet there is no remedial sequence of lessons to help a student who has trouble the first time around. However, the lessons are sufficiently redundant that a student who goes through all of the lessons on a concept usually encounters a theme several times in his instruction.

A typical unit consists of about fifteen lessons; and in each unit there will be from one to three lessons which we call transfer lessons. These are problems which go beyond the scope of the planned curriculum, and test whether the student can apply his learning to a new previously unseen situation. A major instructional sequence consists of about 60-75 lessons. When a sequence (e.g. Discrimination, Sorting, and Classification; Magnetism; Light; Symmetry and Measurement) is completed, a final examination is given which tests the kind of ability the student carries with him into his other activities.

2. Objectives of Instruction

The instructional objectives have gone through two important modifications. During the first year, 1964, the project produced approximately 45 taped lessons in magnetism and 30 taped lessons in light. These areas of science were chosen because they are topics usually included in the elementary school science curriculum and because some of the equipment problems looked more manageable in these areas. The main concern the first year of the project was to learn *how* to write lessons using the individualized tape medium so that students would understand them. It was important to discover what size step could be taken from lesson to lesson, what degree of freedom could be allowed in the lessons, and what degree of structure would be required. The lessons were really designed for the prereader, but during the first year the same lessons were used for all students. (grades 1-6)

The magnetism lessons begin with simple phenomena of permanent magnets and progress to include beginning electromagnetic effects. The student is shown that an electromagnet's strength increases (a) as the number of turns of wire increase (holding the core material and total wire length constant), (b) as the core material is changed from air to iron, and (c) as the number of fresh batteries supplying current increases.

The light lessons initially tackle the concept of light as an observed phenomenon by having the student identify objects which can be seen in an otherwise dark room (candle, luminous dial, flashlight bulb, etc.). The students are told that these objects emit light. Then they are asked to discriminate between things that can only be seen when light shines on them and things which can be seen because they emit light. From here the lessons explain the properties of light and eventually reflections, refraction, color properties, and image formation are observed through direct experience.

In the second year of the experiment the objectives were re-considered. In looking about the field of elementary school science, two programs seemed to have the most cohesive educational philosophy behind them. These were the AAAS program, *Science—A Process Approach* and the units of the *Science Curriculum Improvement Study* under Robert Karplus at Berkeley, California. Their lessons were adopted and modified so that they could be used with the project's equipment and procedures.

The immediate problems of the Learning Research and Development Center are to generate a set of lessons which work for the majority of the students in the school and to eliminate technical, logistic, and language problems from the system. Each school year requires a minimum of 75 lessons so that the entire elementary school sequence encompasses about 1000 lessons. Not all of these lessons require tapes since we have found that a printed script is chosen by competent readers once the novelty of the tapes has worn off.

A longer term problem is to develop a comprehensive elementary school program which has a reasonable chance of adoption and execution in the public schools. This comprehensive program must, in addition to the laboratory experiences, include the following:

1. Stories which will allow the student's laboratory experiences to fit into a larger context.

2. Lessons which draw upon the experiences of all children in order to develop a concept or reveal a pattern in the children's experiences which they might not have perceived.

3. Vocabulary development through interesting but, perhaps, scientifically irrelevant material which familiarizes the children with the sound and configuration of the words which will later be defined by experience and observation.

4. A library of science books, of audiovisual materials, and of science materials.

5. A continuing sorting and refining of the laboratory lessons in order to arrive at a sequence of lessons which will have proven value.

Verbal learning (Nos. 1 and 3 above) can be useful as long as it is not allowed to masquerade as scientific learning. The point must be stressed that verbal learning is a coding and communications device and that the scientific learning resides in the mastery of content and process in contact with the world of direct experience.

As a result of experience and analysis of the elementary school science problem, the project has arrived at the conclusion that it is advantageous to use sequences of content objectives in addition to the process objectives of the AAAS and the conceptual themes of the SCIS.

3. Direct Experience

Confusion between the symbol and the abstraction which the symbol represents plagues many areas of learning although it is particularly inappropriate in science. In science the truth of an idea is established by observation of nature. Arguments are resolved by appeal to experiment, and ideas are abstracted from many observations. It must be obvious that this natural recourse of science to direct experiment and observation is especially important to the learning of children. It takes many encounters with dogs for young children to learn what a dog is. This classification ability comes long after the child can say the word, *dog*. On the other hand, the ability to answer the question, "What is a dog?" with the statement, "A dog is a carnivorous mammal," will have little to do with knowing what a dog is.

On the other side of the problem many adults think that certain concepts are difficult for children simply because they seem esoteric to the adults. To children most things they are learning are esoteric until they become familiar with them. If adequate instances and examples are provided many concepts can be learned through direct experience which adults might think difficult (e.g. symmetry or refraction) for the children.

A favorite instance occurred when a visitor asked a class of first graders at Oakleaf, "What happens when the north pole of one magnet comes near the north pole of another magnet?" A first grader replied, "They repel each other." The visitor thought that he had trapped the youngster into giving a memorized verbal response and said, "Repel, that's a good word. What does it mean?" The boy answered, "I can't tell you, but I will demonstrate it for you." This instance illustrates the irreducible use of language as a means of coding and communication as well as the use of direct experience to enable a child to attain a concept. An elementary school science program must have a solid base in the experiences which define concepts. The number of instances and experiences which different children must have in order to form a concept which is resistant to confusion or forgetting must be determined by much observation and evaluation.

4. Individualized Lessons for Nonreaders

The project has generated several questions: "Why go to the trouble of making science lessons for nonreaders? Why not just wait until they are older, can read directions, and can bring more powerful intellectual tools to the problems?" "Why do you have *individualized* lessons when it would be so much easier to have teacher demonstrations and teacher-directed lessons?" These can be answered in the following ways.

Why Lessons for Nonreaders?

The reason for such lessons is that young children have the ability to learn important concepts in science which will interact with their later learning. As Karplus and others have pointed out, if children's common sense expectations are allowed to grow without guidance and structure in the early years it will be difficult to develop relationships among concepts in later learning. Experiences with college students reveal instance after instance in which the student's intuitive expectations seriously interfere with what is being taught.

Why Individualize Lessons for Nonreaders?

The purpose in this approach lies partly in the experiment being conducted and in the dimensions of individualized instruction which are being explored. However, there are some clear reasons for attempting to individualize science lessons. The difference

in scientific ability and background is often great. A few children do not know the names of the common colors. Yet, others have scientifically trained fathers and mothers who have informally enriched the education of their children with books and materials. This causes the pace of the students to vary. Any allowance in the school schedule for different completion times for an experiment must move any science program in the direction of the project. Even when a lesson is taught to a homogeneous group, some students will learn what was intended in the time allowed while others will not. Nevertheless, as soon as additional instruction is provided for those who did not master the objective, the program will once more move in the direction of the project.

While some logistic and technical problems are magnified by these procedures, the number of duplicate sets of materials the project must produce has lessened. Since the children do not all reach the same experiment at the same time as few as three sets of equipment for each experiment are needed. The use of earphones and carrels allows some interaction between children but seems to cut down distraction and allows the children to focus upon their problems.

5. Results

There are some conclusions which can be stated about the program and the performance of the children.

Science is by far the best-liked subject in the curriculum. The students are eager to read science books after exposure to the program. Fourth, fifth, and sixth graders had exposure to the program last year but not this year. Almost all of the fifth and sixth grade students when interviewed, said that they liked the individualized program better than the group program they are having this year.

The light lessons proved interesting and appropriate to the fourth through sixth grade children, but difficult for the younger children. An interesting comparison was made between these students and some college freshmen from the University of Pittsburgh. A comparison test was made when some physics instructors saw one of our tests and commented that they wished that entering freshmen knew the material covered in the test. Since we had been looking for a comparison group, it was decided to use a college freshman English class which included students with a wide variety of intended majors and a wide variety of high school science backgrounds. The results of the comparison need some qualification. The college students had not had their science for at least a year and only the best elementary school students got far enough in the lessons to take the test. On the other hand, none of the elementary school students had completed the lessons they were being tested on and the college students were supposedly a mature, highly selected group.

The most positive conclusion to be drawn is that the teaching of concepts by direct experience enabled the elementary school children to perform as well or better than college students who had covered much of the same material through a textbook approach in high school.

Thus, it can be seen through the testing program that there is verification students can do the things that the program expects them to do. If concepts attained through direct experience are indeed more resistant to forgetting than purely verbal learning, then there should be a high degree of retention of performance from year to year. Some indication of this was discovered when the magnetism placement tests were administered to the second- and third-grade students who had been exposed to the magnetism lessons the year before. The results indicated a high degree of retention.

All of the above does not mean that the project has initiated a significant or successful science program. The task is too great and the program is too experimental and young for any such statement. Comparison groups of children reaching for the same objectives in other ways are not yet available. The program does have the feature that the instructional procedures are so different and so controlled that they may help to define the optimal means of instruction at the same time that they provide data for the improvement of instructional materials for the future.

The Computer Can Help Individualize Instruction

Donald Deep

EDITORS' QUESTIONS:

1. Discuss the meaning of individualized instruction. Compare the definition presented by this author with the definitions suggested by other authorities.

2. Distinguish between computer-assisted instruction and computer-managed instruction. In a computer-managed system, what is the role of the computer in providing for individualized instruction?

3. What advantages are made available by the PLAN (Program for Learning in Accordance with Needs) approach which are not afforded by other approaches with which you are familiar? Provide specific examples.

4. Discuss the different uses of the computer in PLAN. Suggest some other ways that the computer can assist the classroom teacher.

5. How does the implementation of the PLAN program affect the role of the classroom teacher?

34

Donald Deep, "The Computer Can Help Individualize Instruction," *The Elementary School Journal,* Vol. 70, No. 7 (April 1970) pp. 351–358. Published monthly October through May *by* the University of Chicago Press with the Department of Education and the Graduate School of Education of the University of Chicago. © 1970 by the University of Chicago. All rights reserved. Reprinted with the permission of the University of Chicago and Donald Deep.

In this article I hope to accomplish four main objectives:

To explain the difference between computer-assisted instruction and computer-managed instruction

To define and discuss individualized instruction.

To describe one individualized instructional system—Program for Learning in Accordance with Needs (PLAN)

To point out the function of the computer in (PLAN) (1).

In computer-assisted instruction the pupil is faced with the computer and works directly with it. The computer teaches, or administers, the pupil's instruction. At Oakleaf Elementary School, just south of Pittsburgh, where Individually Prescribed Instruction originated and is still being ex-perimented with, a terminal was connected to a computer in upstate New York. The purpose of this operation was to give pupils practice in basic facts in addition, subtraction, multiplication, and division. The pupil set his own time interval between questions. The interval ranged from two seconds to fourteen seconds, and the pupil decreased the time as he became more proficient. He sat in front of a typewriter and watched for the questions being typed out by the computer. An example:

Terminal: 4 x 6 =
Pupil's response: 24 (by typing digits 2 and 4).
Terminal: 5 x 7 =
Pupil's response: 35.

If the pupil typed out the wrong answer, the

terminal replied, "No, try again." If the pupil missed again, the terminal replied: "No, here is the correct answer . . ." and then asked the pupil another question. However, the missed questions were stored in a special cell for that pupil and were asked again during the same session or the next session.

Pupils from Grades 2 through 5 used portions of the computer-assisted instruction program, and careful records were kept to determine whether the program was helpful. The researchers at Oakleaf contended that if pupils could improve their basic facts, then indirectly performance in the over-all mathematics program would improve. Slowness in providing answers to basic facts slowed down mathematics progress in other types of problems. The study compared the experimental group with a control group and showed a slight significant difference in favor of the experimental group, which used the terminal.

No two pupils received the same program. Questions were fed randomly and included those from the "special cell," which the pupil had missed previously. If the pupil continued to miss question after question, the terminal would reply, "Ask for help!" One ingenious second-grader did ask for help by typing H E L P. But behind every ingenious pupil there could be a wise programmer, and in this instance there was one who programmed a reply, "Sorry, I cannot give you that kind of help, see your teacher." This operation is considered to be computer-assisted instruction.

The Computer and the Teacher

In computer-managed instruction the computer helps the teacher. It comes into the instructional program behind the teacher and serves as an aid. In computer-managed instruction the computer assists the teacher; it does not instruct the pupil as in computer-assisted instruction. Some critics complain that *managed* is the wrong word, for, whatever the approach, the teacher is still the manager in the classroom. The teacher certainly is still in charge of the classroom, but in this article I shall refer to the computer's function as *computer-managed instruction*.

If there was any doubt about the longevity of computers, the night of July 20, 1969 certainly should have erased it. Computers were used extensively in landing man on the moon and returning him safely to earth. It is estimated that close to sixty thousand computers have been installed in the USA. The vast majority are being used outside the field of education.

If there is any fear that the computer will replace school administrators and teachers, that apprehension should be eradicated. The computer is being brought into the scene to allow administrators of schools to act as administrators, not as clerks, and to allow teachers to teach, which is their prime purpose for being in schools. Even though differentiated study materials, audiovisual equipment, teacher aides, and television use of the computer have been introduced into the classroom, success or failure of the instruction still rests with the teacher. The classroom teacher is still the most important ingredient in our instructional recipe. If we get better and more efficient administrators and teachers, the pupils coming out of the schools will be better prepared to take their place in society.

Individualized Instruction

Educators across the United States are being challenged to individualize all instruction in all elementary and secondary schools for all pupils. The theme certainly is *individualized instruction,* and the computer is going to play a major role in assisting schools to truly individualize their programs. But let's define what we mean by *individualized instruction.* According to one definition individualized instruction occurs whenever a teacher plans and conducts with each pupil a program of studies that is specifically tailored to his learning needs and characteristics. In individualized instruction each individual pupil is the starting point for all instructional decisions. The educational resources such as objectives, diagnostic tests, materials and equipment, instructional time, instructional setting, and the instructional method are manipulated to meet the individual need of pupils.

Many educators and laymen believe that in individualized instruction the pupil is either working independently or being tutored. On occasion the pupil does work independently and does receive tutorial help from the teacher. But group instruction also occurs. Whenever several pupils have the same needs, the teacher instructs the children in a group and then disbands it. Instructional groups are temporary and are formed only to teach those things to those pupils who, at a given time, have the same needs and would benefit from the group setting.

A distinction needs to be made between administrative grouping and instructional grouping. It is necessary and practical to assign a group of pupils to a teacher, but within that administrative group certain instructional groups must be formed to meet individual needs. However, the majority of group settings in our schools function to instruct groups, not individuals. William Shanner, of the American Institute for Research, says: "The strategy of group instruction is to move the curriculum through students. One of the main differences between individualized instruction and group instruction is whether you are moving the curriculum or whether you are moving the students. With individualized instruction you move the students, not the curriculum" (2).

Ability grouping is presently the most common way of dealing with individual differences, but research studies show that ability grouping does not overcome the problem of individual differences. Actually ability grouping segregates children along class lines, stigmatizes and discourages the children in low groups, and lessens the progress of children in low groups (3).

School systems are taking a critical look at ability groupings and are attempting to eliminate them altogether. Computer-managed instruction is brought into the limelight to help schools individualize their instruction. Computer-managed instruction does include group instruction, but a special type of group instruction that allows true individualization to occur, group instruction that is not permanent, but temporary (five minutes, twenty minutes, one hour, and so on).

One Individualized System

PLAN (Program for Learning in Accordance with Needs) was initiated in September, 1967 by a joint effort of the American Institutes for Research and Westinghouse Learning Corporation, with the co-operation of thirteen school districts (4). PLAN is an individualized educational system designed to provide each pupil with a program of studies geared to his needs, abilities, and interests. Mathematics, language arts, social studies, and science are presently being individualized in Grades 1, 2, 3, 5, 6, 7, 9, 10, and 11. In September, 1970 Grades 4, 8, and

12 will be added to complete the range from 1 through 12. In the near future, other subject areas such as art, music, and industrial arts will be added to the system.

PLAN has six goals:

1. Pupil's personal formulation of goals.

PLAN assists the pupil in developing to his full potential, in making decisions relative to his educational and occupational future, and in providing information about his interests and possible leisure-time activities.

2. Pupil's personal development.

PLAN helps the pupil adjust to difficult situations, gives him responsibility in carrying out tasks, and encourages him to be creative and to show initiative when confronted with a special need.

3. Pupil's social development, which includes social adjustment, sensitivity to others, group orientation, and adaptability to rules and conventions.

4. Pupil's development of basic skills and abilities, which includes reading with comprehension, expression of oneself, and logical thinking on conflicting issues.

5. Pupil's acquisition of knowledge, concepts, and principles and ability to transfer these to new problems.

6. Pupil's management of his educational behavior.

PLAN encourages pupils to be self-directed learners and to be responsible for their education and personal development.

PLAN has five major components that assist the pupil in attaining these goals. These components are:

1. Comprehensive set of educational behavioral objectives.

These objectives are observable and are to be achieved by the pupil under certain conditions by meeting an acceptable performance score.

2. Teaching-learning units.

These are designed to teach the objectives and to take into account the different learning styles and interests of pupils.

3. Tests.

The purpose of all tests in PLAN is to provide information for correct decision-making.

4. Guidance and individual planning system for each pupil.

This system is designed to aid the pupil in learning about adult activities and roles with respect to both avocations and occupations. The system is designed also to help the pupil to learn the significance of his developed abilities and interests.

5. Evaluation system.

An IBM 360 Model 50 computer is programmed to score tests used in monitoring the development of each pupil, to keep files on the experience and progress of each pupil, and to evaluate the effectiveness of teaching-learning units and guidance and planning procedures for each pupil.

How Does PLAN Work?

In September each PLAN pupil receives his program of studies for each subject area. A program of studies is a list of modules in a subject area which is to be completed by the pupil in a year's time. The program of studies is individualized for each pupil and is based on the pupil's past achievement, his academic goals, his vocational goals, his interests, his style of learning in an individualized setting, and state or local school district requirements. Of course, not all six factors are applicable to the program of studies of pupils in elementary schools.

During the first week of school PLAN pupils are busily meeting with their teachers to discuss their program of studies and possible modifications. Actually, the program of studies can be altered at any time during the year. Also, during the first week the pupils complete their orientation, which consists of diagnostic tests and information pertinent to their role in PLAN.

After a pupil has completed his orientation program, he begins work in the first module in his program of studies. A module is a set of instructional objectives that the pupil is expected to achieve. The manner in which he achieves these objectives depends on the teaching-learning unit the computer suggests or the pupil chooses. Teaching-learning units are designed to accommodate learning differences among pupils. The units provide alternate paths for the pupil to take to achieve the objectives. The module objectives never change; the way a pupil achieves these objectives depends on his teaching-learning unit. One teaching-learning unit may be designed for a pupil who is an excellent reader; another for a pupil who, judging from his past performance, does well with manipulative devices; another for a pupil who needs to be directed step by step in his achievement of objectives; and another for a pupil who is independent and resourceful and likes to find his own resources and make his own decisions about what he needs to do to attain the objectives.

Once a pupil has worked through a teaching-learning unit (usually about two weeks) he takes the module test. If the test results indicate mastery, the pupil can proceed to the next module in his program of studies. If he fails one objective or more, the pupil and the teacher meet to decide on the next action. This could be the assignment of a different teaching-learning unit, a review of the same teaching-learning unit, peer assistance, or tutoring by the teacher.

Little, if anything, is kept secret from the PLAN pupil. He is well aware of what is expected of him and how much time is allotted for completion of his assignments, for he participated in the planning. He is also aware of the flexibility provided under teaching-learning units and other instructional resources.

Someone entering a PLAN classroom would see pupils in a variety of activities. Some pupils might be engaged in discussions in large groups or small groups. Some pupils might be engaged in independent study. Some might be taking module tests. Some pupils might be working with a tutor or might be in a counseling session with the teacher. Some pupils might be listening to a tape or a record. Others might be viewing a filmstrip or a film, or conducting experiments. Room arrangement and organization of materials are important to the success of a PLAN classroom and are stressed in the teacher training conference. Pupils know what they can and cannot do in the individualized setting. They are responsible for retrieving their study materials or equipment and returning them after use.

PLAN teachers have devised their own way of helping pupils signal their need for assistance. Some have pupils raise their hands. Some have pupils raise a distress signal on the desk. Some may have pupils write their names on chalkboard. You seldom see PLAN pupils standing in line waiting for teacher assistance because of the flexibility built into the program. In the majority of PLAN classrooms pupils are allowed to seek out peer assistance any time the need arises. Although the teacher is available to all pupils, she will not instruct each pupil each day. She plans her day to work with certain pupils at certain times and to check the progress of the other pupils.

In a self-contained fifth-grade classroom, pupils may be working on any one of the four subject areas and may switch at any desirable time. Many of these pupils plan their own weekly and daily schedule. A pupil may spend the whole morning on mathematics and the whole afternoon on science. He may spend the next day on language arts and social studies. The important thing is that the pupil is involved in his schedule and goal assignment.

The Role of the Computer

The teacher's role in the PLAN classroom is one of an educational diagnostician, instructional system manager, instructor, small- and large-group discussant, counselor, and planning strategist. The computer handles the clerical and the other non-professional tasks. The computer frees time for teacher-student instruction by being responsible for the clerical tasks that teachers usually carry out. The computer is not a thorn in the teacher's side, but assists her each day in making correct educational decisions about each of her pupils. In no instance in PLAN does the computer assume a teaching role. The role of the computer is to make PLAN efficient and economical. At the present time the computer performs the following functions:

1. Records the pupil's learning and academic history. Keeps a record on how best an individual learns.

2. Records the pupil's present program of studies. Makes modifications and recommends certain modules for pupils.

3. Scores all module tests and examinations and provides the results to the teacher and the pupil. Suggests the next module to be taken. Indicates objectives missed so that the pupil does not have to repeat the entire module.

4. Monitors the progress of the pupil daily. Progress cards are submitted on a weekly basis. Progress reports, including report cards, are sent back periodically.

5. Compares available learning materials and pupil's successes with those materials. Results can be used in making future recommendations for other pupils.

6. Provides backup support for the teacher so that the amount of teacher-student instructional time is maximized. The pupil can use his time in a flexible way. He can work on different teaching-learning units at the same time. The computer suggests to the teacher what action she needs to take today, what pupil groups need to be called together, what special materials are needed, and so on.

7. Assists in the formative evaluation of PLAN. The type of evaluation needed in education is a formative one, rather than an over-all single evaluation. A formative evaluation would evaluate the components of an instructional system such as objectives, the progress of the teacher, and the materials. We have finally recognized that all educational programs are tentative. Unfortunately, too many tentative programs have become permanent. With this idea in mind, the computer can eliminate antiquated, unsatisfactory, or spoiled educational products. The computer can play an important role in this formative evaluation of our present educational programs.

In conclusion, the computer and computer-managed instruction systems can be expected to play a major role in transforming the educational process by assisting the teacher and making individualized education possible—a long overdue school need.

NOTES

1. Donald Deep. "The Computer Can Help Individualize Instruction." Speech given at the School Leadership Institute, University of Akron, Akron, Ohio, August 5, 1969.

2. William Shanner. "Evaluations of Mastery Level in Systems of Individualized Instruction." Paper read at the Los Angeles Seminar Systems in Education, Los Angeles, California, July, 1968.

3. Glen Heathers. *Encyclopedia of Educational Research.* New York: Macmillan, 1970 (fourth edition).

4. Bethel Park School District, Bethel Park, Pennsylvania; Hicksville Public School District, Hicksville, New York; Penn Trafford School District, Harrison City, Pennsylvania; Pittsburgh Public Schools, Pittsburgh, Pennsylvania; Quincy Public Schools, Quincy, Massachusetts; Wood County Schools, Parkersburg, West Virginia; Archdiocese of San Francisco, Department of Education, San Francisco, California; Fremont Unified School District, Fremont, California; San Carlos Elementary School District, San Carlos, California; San Jose City Unified School District, San Jose, California; Santa Clara Unified School District, Santa Clara, California; Sequoia Union High School District, Redwood City, California; Union Elementary School District, San Jose, California.

A Teaching Program for Experimentation with Computer-Assisted Instruction

James L. Fejfar

EDITORS' QUESTIONS:

1. Discuss the teaching program described in this article. To what extent does it provide for individual differences in pupils' skills and abilities?

2. Explain how the different psychological or pedagogical principles listed in the article were provided for by specific aspects of the computer-assisted instructional system.

3. Discuss the role of the classroom teacher in connection with a system of computer-assisted instruction. Is her role greatly altered by the introduction of this strategy? Explain.

4. Assess the feasibility of implementing a system of computer-assisted instruction, such as that described by the author, in your own school. Considered from the standpoint of economic efficiency, would the advantages to be gained from such a program justify its cost of implementation? Substantiate your answer.

5. Draft a proposal for a system of computer-assisted instruction for teaching a particular skill in another subject-matter area. Detail the instructional technique you wish the computer to employ. Specify the exact pupil-computer interactions required. Analyze your proposal to determine its congruity with accepted principles of learning.

James L. Fejfar, "A Teaching Program for Experimentation with Computer-Assisted Instruction," Reprinted from the *Arithmetic Teacher,* March 1969 (Vol. 16, pp. 184–188), © 1969 by the National Council of Teachers of Mathematics. Used by permission.

Although many perspicacious mathematics teachers are interested in learning more about computer-assisted instruction (CAI), the high costs and relative inaccessibility[1] of these sophisticated systems have afforded little opportunity for firsthand experience with this technological advance which will surely have far-reaching effects on education. Recently, however, a program has been developed which will "convert" a small general-purpose computer, available at many schools and campuses, to an electronic teaching machine capable of teaching skills with facts of both multiplication and addition.[2] It is hoped that the dissemination of this program will lead to improved pupil achievement, increased teacher and parental interest in innovation, and the enhancement of research opportunities in other places as it has at Indiana State University.

James Fejfar was formerly an associate professor of mathematics at Indiana State University. He is now an associate professor of elementary education at the University of Nebraska, where he teaches graduate and undergraduate courses and works with student teachers.

1. The IBM Corporation, for example, apparently plans to produce only 50 of its 1500 series, CAI System. These are experimental and have been placed specifically for research.

2. The author wishes to thank Dr. Roger W. Elliott, now of Texas A & M University, who did the computer programming, and Indiana State University, which provided the funds for this research project.

The computer used in the development of this program was the IBM model 1130 with a modification level-four monitor. The program itself can be used, however, with slight modifications, on any computer with a FORTRAN IV compiler and a console typewriter. It can also be adapted to other languages.

The remainder of this article will describe the teacher-learning situation resulting from use of the system, give a rationale for some of its various aspects, briefly relate some observations concerning its use, and discuss research potentialities.

The Teaching-Learning Situation

This teaching system is designed to enhance the learner's speed and accuracy with the addition of multiplication facts by providing practice and immediate feedback. Optimally, this program would be used after appropriate concepts have been developed through classroom activities.

The computer randomly selects examples from subsets of the facts, which are arranged in a presumed order of increasing difficulty, presents them to the student via the console typewriter, and waits for a response. The student then types in an answer and the machine reacts. This feedback can simply be the typing of another problem if the answer was correct, or the correct answer and repetition of the same problem if the given answer was incorrect. Social reinforcers, i.e., words of reprimand or praise, can also be presented at the option of the teacher-researcher. The system can also offer a review of questions answered incorrectly, along with an initial presentation of those facts which may have been omitted because of the randomizing process for choosing examples. A report card which summarizes the lesson is printed at the end of each session. Subsequent sessions may begin at the level of difficulty encountered at the previous termination or at the initial level.

Since all communication between the learner and the electronic teacher is by typewriter, a written transcript of each lesson is available for inspection by the "real" teacher. A part of a typical first lesson is presented below. All of the typing except the answers ("2," "14," and "12") was done automatically by the computer.

HELLO MARY,
I AM A COMPUTER. I CAN DO MANY THINGS. I CAN TYPE AND I CAN READ SOME MESSAGES THAT YOU GIVE ME BY TYPING. I CAN ALSO DO PROBLEMS CORRECTLY AND I CAN HELP YOU BECOME VERY GOOD AT ARITHMETIC. I WILL ASK YOU TO DO SOME EXAMPLES. IF YOU ARE CORRECT I WILL GIVE YOU ANOTHER QUESTION. IF YOU ARE WRONG, I WILL TELL YOU THE ANSWER AND THEN REPEAT THE QUESTION. IF YOU ANSWER A QUESTION FIVE TIMES WITHOUT A MISTAKE, I WILL RETIRE THAT QUESTION. IF YOU MISS A QUESTION THREE TIMES I WILL NOT ASK IT AGAIN TODAY. MY OPERATOR WILL HELP YOU WITH THE KEYBOARD. NOW, LET US BEGIN.

$$\begin{array}{r} 2 \\ \times 1 \\ \hline 2 \end{array}$$ VERY GOOD, MARY

$$\begin{array}{r} 6 \\ \times 2 \\ \hline 14 \end{array}$$ WRONG, 12 IS THE RIGHT ANSWER.
DO NOT GET CARELESS

$$\begin{array}{r} 6 \\ \times 2 \\ \hline 12 \end{array}$$ RIGHT, KEEP UP THE GOOD WORK

Each session continues in the manner indicated above until completion or termination by the computer operator. Completion is achieved when the learner has responded correctly ten consecutive times to questions at each level of difficulty. The first of these levels contains all of the facts with 1, 2, or 5 as a factor or addend; the next the 0's, 3's, 4's, and 6's; the last level contains the 7's, 8's, and 9's. The computer begins a lesson by randomly selecting an example from the first level. The example can be presented in two ways, e.g.,

$$7 \quad \text{or} \quad 1$$
$$\underline{\times 1} \qquad \underline{\times 7}$$

The remainder of the lesson depends upon the student. Correct responses elicit a new item, and incorrect responses bring forth the correct answer and the repetition of the incorrectly answered item. After ten consecutively correct responses, which do not always occur, items from the second list augment the selection set, and the procedure

is repeated. If a student answers the same *item* correctly five consecutive times, the item is retired and this message is typed:

CONGRATULATIONS, THIS PROBLEM
WILL NOT BE ASKED AGAIN TODAY.

If, on the other hand, a learner misses a particular example three times, the example is retired (to diminish the practicing of the incorrect response) and this message is typed:

WRONG AGAIN, YOU NEED HELP WITH THIS
PROBLEM. I WILL NOT ASK IT AGAIN TODAY.

REPORT CARD FOR JIM

DIGITS COLUMN IS THE NUMBER OF CORRECTS. HUNDREDTHS COLUMN IS THE NUMBER OF TRIES. MINUS INDICATES THAT THE PROBLEM HAS BEEN RETIRED.

	0	1	2	3	4	5	6	7	8	9
0	101	101	101	101	202	101	202	101	101	101
1	101	101	101	101	101	101	101	101	101	101
2	101	101	101	101	101	101	202	101	101	101
3	101	101	101	101	303	101	101	101	101	101
4	101	404	101	—505	101	101	101	202	101	101
5	101	303	101	101	101	202	101	202	202	202
6	202	101	101	101	101	101	101	101	504	101
7	202	101	101	201	202	101	101	101	201	101
8	202	202	101	101	202	101	101	101	201	101
9	202	101	101	101	101	101	101	202	101	101

THE NUMBER OF CONSECUTIVE CORRECTS

	0	1	2	3	4	5	6	7	8	9
0	1	1	1	1	2	1	2	1	1	1
1	1	1	1	1	1	1	1	1	1	1
2	1	1	1	1	1	1	2	1	1	1
3	1	1	1	1	3	1	1	1	1	1
4	1	4	1	5	1	1	1	2	1	1
5	1	3	1	1	1	2	1	2	2	2
6	2	1	1	1	1	1	1	1	4	1
7	2	1	1	1	2	1	1	1	1	1
8	2	2	1	1	2	1	1	1	1	1
9	2	1	1	1	1	1	1	2	1	1

TOTAL TRIES = 134
TOTAL CORRECTS = 130
PROBLEM QUESTIONS
  6 × 8
  7 × 3
  7 × 8
  8 × 8

Figure 1 A Report Card

Psychological or Pedagogical Principles	Related Aspect of the Program
Learning should be individualized as much as possible.	Choice of problems depends on the students' previous responses. Students work at a self-determined rate. Computer can call students by name.
Skills are developed through repetitive practice with feedback.	Items can be repeated through the randomization process. Items are retired only after five consecutively correct responses. Feedback is presented after every response.
Immediacy of feedback enhances learning.	Knowledge of results or feedback is presented immediately after a student writes an answer.
Continued practice with mastered items can be boring and thus detrimental to learning.	Mastered items are retired.
Learning tasks should progress from easy to hard.	Items are presented in categories based on difficulty.
Incorrect responses should be extinguished.	Verbal reprimands can be given for incorrect responses. Correct answers are given for items answered incorrectly, and these questions are immediately repeated.
Positive and negative social reinforcers (praise and reprimand) have an effect on learning, and this effect varies with the individual.	Phrases of praise and reprimand are available; and either, or neither, or both can be used.
Results of learning sessions should be available in an easily used form.	The report card and the type-written lessons are available.
The learning situation should be challenging and interesting.	The computer seems to be intrinsically interesting to children. The students progress quickly to levels where they are challenged.

The computer operator can call for the previously described review sequence at any time prior to termination or completion.

The last phase of each lesson is the printing of a so-called report card (Fig. 1), which is a summary of the lesson. It lists the frequency of presentation and the number of consecutively correct responses for each item and indicates whether or not an item has been retired. The number of items presented is also reported, along with the total number of correct responses and a list of all problems answered incorrectly.

The factors or addends are given in the vertical column at the extreme left and the top horizontal row. Thus it is seen that 8 X 6 was presented 5 times and was answered correctly 4 times. The report card has been very effective for diagnostic and remedial purposes and in analyzing student progress.

Rationale

Because skills are such a great part of mathematical learning at all levels and because of the limitations of the computer available, it was decided to begin this experimentation with a program for developing speed and accuracy. As is shown by the chart above, well-known principles from psychological and pedagogical theory form the basis for various aspects of this CAI system.

Observations

The program has been used in a teaching situation about 200 times by elementary school children of various ages, grades, and backgrounds. Observations and interviews have resulted in modifications in the program. Other apparent results are these:

1. The students had very little difficulty in communicating with the computer through the typewriter console.
2. Students were very enthusiastic about this kind of instruction.
3. The use of the system does lead to improvement in multiplication.

The system seems to fascinate and motivate the pupils. They eagerly volunteer for computer sessions even during the noon hour. A group of 20 fourth graders with a history of difficulties in arithmetic answered an average of 107 items per twenty-minute teaching session. Only one of these students appeared to find the session too long. One fifth-grade girl worked for eighty minutes without interruption. In a pilot study conducted during May 1967, 5 fourth and fifth graders who had four CAI sessions showed gain scores of from 12 to 43 percent on timed pretests and posttests over the 100 multiplication facts, while the scores of their classmates who did not have this instruction remained relatively constant.

As would be expected, the results of the sessions were varied. For instance, one boy not in the groups described above seemed to learn as the result of CAI but did not retain this knowledge. There were also differences in the rate and amount of achievement. Experiences with the system do indicate, however, that it is capable of carrying out its primary function—to teach.

Potential Research

Although general principles from psychology and pedagogy were employed in the development of this program, specific applications were necessarily based on experience and intuition rather than on statistical evidence. Almost every phase of the program could be modified and the results of this modification studied. Questions relating to the amount of repetition, the optimal number of correct or incorrect responses required to retire an item (if items should be retired), and the extinction of incorrect responses should be answered in order to perfect the program. More general questions such as those relating to the length of sessions and the amount of time between sessions should be studied. The answers would not only lead to improved programs but would supplement the existing knowledge about the teaching of mathematics. For instance, the author is presently seeking to determine if the use of social reinforcers can enhance the learning of pupils with certain personality characteristics. The results could not only have implications for CAI program writers but for classroom and methods teachers as well.

Teachers and administrators will soon be making important decisions regarding this mode of instruction. Although some of these decisions will involve computer hardware, the more important decisions will be with regard to the pedagogy. Although a variety of research developments have already taken place, problems are still unsolved. What subject matter should be taught? Should the teaching sequences be expository, inductive, or both? If both, in what proportion and when? Do the children learn to think and solve problems, or do they just learn to parrot responses? Can concepts be taught by computers? How does the role of the "live" teacher change when some or most of the instruction is by computer? These and other questions require answers from educators. Experience is needed in order to begin the formulation of the answers. The program presented through this article is not sophisticated enough to help answer all of these questions. Furthermore, since the system can be used by only one learner at a time, research designs involving large numbers of students might be difficult to implement. The program does, however, represent a starting point for firsthand experience with CAI.

REFERENCES

Bork, Alfred M. *Using the IBM 1130.* Reading, Mass.: Addison-Wesley, 1968.

Bright, Louis, *et al.,* "There is a Computer in Your Future," *American Education,* III (November 1967), 12–15.

Davis, Robert B. (ed.). *The Changing Curriculum: Mathematics.* Washington, D.C.: Association for Supervision and Curriculum Development, 1967, pp. 1–4.

Hanson, Carroll. "Giants in the Schoolhouse," *Phi Delta Kappan,* XLIX (November 1967), 114.

McCammon, Mary. *Understanding Fortran.* New York: Thomas Y. Crowell Co., 1968.

Zinn, Karl L. "Computer Technology for Teaching and Research in Education," *Review of Educational Research,* XXXVII (December 1967), 618–34.

Pretending to Have (or to Be) a Computer as a Strategy in Teaching[*]

Paul C. Berry

EDITORS' QUESTIONS:

1. Assess the value of pretending to have or to be a computer in discovering the interrelatedness of the essential components of the teaching-learning process.

2. Explain how the use of program flow charts can assist the teacher in planning instruction.

3. Cite the advantages which accrue from getting pupils to do the programming themselves.

4. In this article the experimenter employed a role-reversal technique to assist pupils in programming. What are some of the advantages of this approach?

5. Construct a flow chart for the identification of four different geometric figures: Square, rectangle, triangle and circle. Devise and implement an instructional procedure based upon the insights you have gained from this activity.

Paul C. Berry, "Pretending to Have (or to Be) a Computer as a Strategy in Teaching," *Harvard Educational Review,* 34, Summer 1964, 383–401. Copyright © 1964 by President and Fellows of Harvard College. Used by permission.

The flurry of interest in curriculum development, with its new math and new science and its projects in reading, social studies, and English, has brought together three sorts of people far more often than ever before. One of these three is the teacher. The second is the scholar, who now periodically deserts his laboratory or study to try to explain to teachers and thence to children what he feels are the exciting and the fundamental ideas of his discipline in the modern age. The third is the psychologist (with or without the prefix "educational"), who is charged both with suggesting how the new ideas are to be conveyed to children and with testing afterwards whether they have been learned.

At the heart of most of the new curriculum efforts is an attempt to instill in children a way of thinking, both a general approach to a subject and the detailed steps of the various operations involved in mastery of that subject. The psychologist is constantly insisting to the teacher and the scholar, "You specify the behavior, and I'll tell you how to produce it or test for it." For the scholar, intent upon getting children really to understand some portion of his thinking or technique, specifying the precise component mental operations turns out to be surprisingly difficult. He finds that he can not clearly explicate the processes of his own thinking, nor can he recall how his present style of thinking was built up. Simi-

[*]Work reported here was conducted as part of the program of the School Mathematics and Science Center of the University of Minnesota, supported by Grant GE-3 from the National Science Foundation.

larly, the psychologist, while more confident that complex thinking must be achieved through the integration of many smaller component mental operations, is also very remote from a detailed understanding of the human thinking mechanism.

Therefore, faced with the practical problem of educating children to new mental operations, we are still searching for ways to break down the global descriptions of the activities of each curriculum into smaller components that make more manageable elements in a program of instruction. There is one group of people to whom the problem of breaking up complex acts into smaller components, or of assembling some set of simple acts into one much more complex act, is very familiar. These are the persons who write the sequences of instructions, called programs, for electronic computers. (This meaning of "program" is independent of the word as it is used in "programmed instruction.") I believe that some of the techniques of the computer programmer can be borrowed by the educator as a means for making much more explicit what component skills go into a complex act and how the components are linked together. This suggestion does not assume that children's brains resemble electronic machines but merely that mental tasks are information-processing operations and share that characteristic with operations that are programmed for computers.

For the inexperienced, writing the program that gets a computer to carry out even a simple operation can be a chastening experience. Computers, being intolerant of ambiguity and devoid of common sense, go ahead and do just what they are told. The resulting absurdities frequently reveal the shortcomings of badly stated instructions. Like programmed instruction, computer programming requires explicit statement of all of the steps involved in a complex behavior. However, computer programming goes beyond explicit statement of the details and provides a precise and testable model for assembling all of the component operations into a total more complex behavior. This permits verification not only that the various steps are clearly stated, but also that they are all present and accounted for and are effectively connected together. For this reason, writing a computer program is a very instructive way to start thinking about teaching. Fortunately, it is writing the program that is the most useful part of the procedure, so that you can do it even when you can't afford a real computer on which to run the program or even if you refer to operations which are impractical with existing computers.

When the teacher tries to produce a computer program (or at least the flow diagram of a program) as a way of specifying the details of an activity that is to be taught, he is pretending to *have* a computer on which the program might eventually be run. It is also possible to involve children in the task of programming; if the children themselves construct the program, they may share some of the benefits of increased awareness of what goes on in complex activities that they otherwise take for granted. Since children can't be expected to handle a real computer, this has to be arranged otherwise. The teacher can get children to give their instructions to him, and he can then carry them out in very literal fashion, thus pretending to *be* a computer.

We can distinguish three possible ways in which it is useful to imagine a computer program for a mental operation that we want to teach:

1. The teacher pretends to have a computer for which he writes a program that provides the operations of whatever task he

is interested in, in whatever way seems simplest or most logical. This is useful in making clear the logical structure of the task.

2. The teacher pretends to have a computer for which he prepares a program which as far as possible represents the actual skills, errors, weaknesses, and virtues of human (or child) performance. Such a program in some sense is a description of the child's performance. Comparing the program for what children seem to do with what is logically required to do the work well then offers a way of identifying needs for training.

3. The teacher pretends to be the computer, letting children build up their own programs by successive approximation. They may thus obtain much greater insight into the activity they are programming and (hopefully) greater ability to modify their own operations to make them appropriate to the task at hand. Even if they don't reap this benefit, the teacher may see to what extent the children have explicit control over the operations and what implicit assumptions may limit their performance.

In order to illustrate these educational uses of an imaginary computer, we will present an example taken from work of the Minnesota School Mathematics and Science Center on elementary arithmetic. A mathematic example is in some ways unfortunate because it might give the impression that an imaginary computer is suitable only for mathematical tasks, or only for tasks for which there are fairly simple algorithms. Such an impression would be false, for computer programming is being extended more and more widely into fields that are not at all mathematical. Pioneering work on computer "thinking" was done by Simon, Newell, and Shaw (1958). While this work started with mathematical-logical games and problems, it has been extended much more generally to such topics as computer

thinking (Feigenbaum & Feldman, 1963), computer use of natural language (Garvin, 1963), and computer simulation of personality (Tomkins and Messick, 1963). But these are areas that are quite complex. For our illustration we will use a most elementary example: first graders' counting.

First let's get a computer to count, then let's compare children's counting with our program, and then let's get children to generate programs for counting. In doing this, we do not intend to explore the significance of counting in the development of more general concepts of number and measurement. Without an effective understanding of the logical nature of counting, it may be possible to count correctly and still fail to reach effective conclusions about the equivalence of sets or about the direction of differences of inequalities or even about making change correctly. Fairly accurate simple counting without any appropriate application is reported among 4-6 year olds by Piaget (1941, part II) and in the review by Lovell (1961, pp. 31–52). For the purpose of this paper, we will simply examine the steps and operations required to give a precise answer to the question, "How many?" without going into the uses to which this information is put.

The function of counting is to identify a symbol that denotes the size of the set of things counted. This is done by matching the members of the set one-to-one with the members, taken in order, of an agreed upon arbitrary set, the integers. The name of the last integer which can be matched is the required symbol. Whenever another set must be established equivalent (i.e. equal in number of members) to the first set, this can be done by matching members of the new set one-to-one to the integers taken in order until the previously identified symbol is reached. For the purposes of this example, we refer only to the counting of finite sets, even though mathematicians regard certain infinite sets as countable in the sense that they can be matched one-to-one with the (infinite) set of the integers.

The actual operations required to carry out our description are implied within it, but it may take some reflection to discover all of the sub-steps necessary to produce effective counting.

Counting by Computer

The basic operation of counting is to run through the integers one by one. A counter or resister of the computer passes through a series of states corresponding to the various symbols for integers. This is achieved by successively adding 1 to the number in the counter. Computers are wired so that addition is a primitive operation, and adding 1 to an integer automatically produces the symbol for the next integer in order. Under these circumstances, the task is to make sure that one step of the counter is made for each of the items to be counted.

A standard flow diagram to count items in a designated region of computer storage might look like Figure 1. Here, items that have been stored are identified by their locations, or addresses, to use computer parlance. These addresses are consecutively numbered, each location having its own unique number, and the computer is told to count only those items between the number designating the first address and the number designating the last address. The particular address that the computer is working on at any particular moment is known as the "working address." In order for the computer to identify the items to be counted, it must be told the nature of the identifying attribute, that is, the "criterion."

This tiny program already identifies some of the sub-operations for counting. The program has these features:

1. It specifies the symbol with which to start counting (at zero, before any are counted).
2. It specifies where to start looking for things to count.
3. It specifies when to stop looking for things to count.
4. It has a plan to generate new places to look for things to count.
5. It specifies how to tell when a location that is examined contains something that should be counted.
6. It advances a counter by 1 for each new item counted.

The essential feature of one-to-one matching between the steps of the counter and the items to be counted is obtained here indirectly because this routine is certain to search every location once and only once. This systematic search is obtained in the same way that the stepping of the counter itself is obtained, by using the computer's built-in adding capability to increment the counter and the working address. However, when we are interested in teaching counting to children, no such capability can be assumed. How might it be built up? Can a computer count if it is not allowed to use the operation ADD for these two functions?

Random Search Counting

If you can't search in order through all the locations, one approach might be to search the locations at random. Sooner or later this procedure would search all of the possible locations. Then the problem would be to avoid counting some of them twice. It would be possible to mark any item once it has been counted or to mark any location once it has been examined. Then the routine would skip over items it found checked off

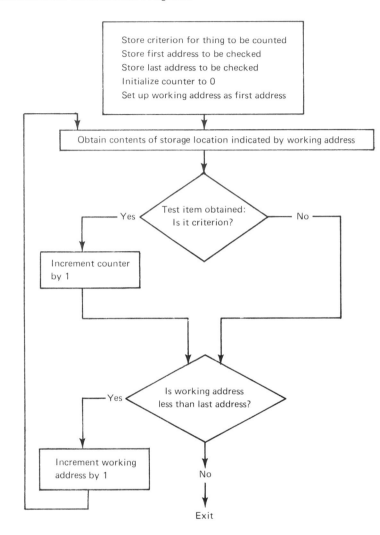

Figure 1 Elementary computer flow to count all items meeting a criterion within a specified storage range.

from its previous work. Such flow is indicated in Figure 2.

By eliminating the systematic search, we have identified another necessary feature for a counting program:

    7. It can check off items that are counted so that none is counted twice.

Broad Scan
Even though the random search outlined in Fig. 2 may come up with the right answer if given enough time, it has no way of knowing that the answer is correct. It is sure that no items have been counted twice, but it is not sure that no item has been left uncounted. There seems to be no way to do this without either an orderly search or a list of all possible locations to be searched.

It would be quite possible to wire a computer or write a subroutine to detect nonzero condition in a large block of storage. (In

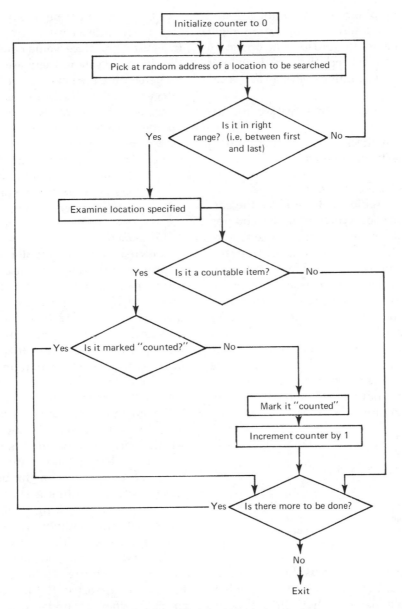

Figure 2 Random search for items to be counted.

computer parlance, a "subroutine" is a miniature program-within-a-program, a set of simple operations which can thereafter be treated as a unit and which give the effect of a new primitive operation in addition to those originally built into the machine.) If a non-zero bit were detected, systematic search would then be required to decide where it was. Under these conditions, the routine could empty out all the storage it searched and then check to see whether the storage was completely empty. If not empty, it could keep plugging away until it found everything. This sort of an operation might be compared to the broad-scan operation used by people to check that a parking lot is empty without counting each stall as a separate item.

This generates another feature for the program:

8. It can check off to see that nothing is left unexamined.

The Symbol Sequence List

The next problem is to produce the correct sequence of symbols in the counter. Children, of course, cannot produce this sequence in the built-in way that computers do. If addition is not wired in, or if we abstain from using addition as a primitive operation, it is still possible to program a computer to count. This can be done by looking up a list of paired items. For any symbol now in the counter the same symbol is identified on the list, and the symbol there paired with it is taken as the next symbol. This list does not need to be constructed in order (see Figure 3).

0 – 1	2 – 3
1 – 2	0 – 1
2 – 3	4 – 5
3 – 4	3 – 4
4 – 5	1 – 2
5 – 6	5 – 6
List stated in order	List stated without ordering

Figure 3

With either of these lists the counter can always be advanced to the next symbol. Since people have no built-in ability to know the order of the symbols which name the integers, we generate the next requirements for the counting program:

9. There must be in storage (memory) a list specifying for every integer-symbol what symbol follows it.

10. There must be a way of searching the integer list.

In a system of place-value notation, such as the decimal system, there are precise rules for generating the next integer for any given integer, so that if storage contains these rules, only the symbols from 0 up to the number–base (0-9, in the decimal system) need appear explicitly on the list.

11. For counting beyond 9, either the list must be extended, or rules must be stated for the generating of symbols for larger numbers.

Precautions

It is customary in computer programming to provide a routine with fuses which stop the work if an impossibly difficult task is presented. If the number of items is so large that counting would take a great deal of time or exceed the length of the stored lists, we might want the routine to quit. Or if the marks which we use to indicate that an item has been counted are not distinguishable, we might want to abandon the attempt. Or if the storage could not be emptied out, we might want to prevent the use of a routine which depended upon emptying everything in order to decide that counting is finished. Some of these fuses might be set up as checks before counting is started.

A programmer writing a subroutine will also specify the conditions for entry into the routine. These conditions are not part of the routine, but rather a guide in selecting occasions for which the routine is appropriate. For counting, this is the list of rules that specifies when or under what conditions counting is the appropriate operation. A perfectly working routine will be useless unless it can be called for when appropriate.

12. It requires a list of conditions under which the routine should be called.

This preliminary exercise in programming a computer to count has already generated a quite lengthy list of subroutines or features that must be provided. For the instructor these are the skills that must be assumed or provided if the final performance is to be produced reliably by a student.

Features Observed in Children's Counting

If we examine the counting behavior of children, we can now classify a number of their aberrations simply as failures to build in one or another of the essential features 1-12 listed above.

Earliest Counting

I do not know of a systematic study of the pre-counting behavior of children, although Piaget (1941) alludes to this topic. Based on my own informal observations, it appears that children's earliest counting exhibits two rather distinct procedures. For very small quantities a name is learned for the configuration of simple numbers. No stepping procedure is employed at all. Thus "one" is certainly recognized in this way, and so may be "two," "three," and even "four." Beyond this it gets harder for the child to recognize the patterns under rearrangement, and the process is generally abandoned and replaced by the stepping algorithm. (Note in this connection that, quite apart from numerals, all human languages also contain grammatical provision to distinguish between "one" and "more than one," and a number of languages also distinguish among one, two, and many or even one, two, three, and many. See Greenberg, 1963, p. 74.) To present a program that does this sort of counting we would need a pattern recognition device, something that is still a difficult problem in computers, but which people do with ease.

Early Rote Counting

Children fairly early acquire the impression that counting involves the recitation of a list and that the list is somehow related to an array of objects. At this stage, then, the child is:

(1) Building up an entry routine for counting.
(2) Building up the list of numerals.
(3) Not bothering with the matching, stopping, and checking requirements.

This behavior produces pseudo-counting in which the child chants numbers, at first in a rather garbled order. Note that according to our description of a good counting program most of these activities are essential to the eventual acquisition of counting.

Errors of Counting Among First Graders

The earliest situations presented to children for counting are generally constructed so that successful counting can be achieved without the child's using any systematic check-off routine of the items counted. If a child counts the number of marbles in a cup, he may be shown how to put the contents on the table and return the marbles one by one to the cup. This makes highly salient the important step of one-to-one matching. It also means that the child needs no procedure to check off the marbles (putting them into the cup does that) and no procedure to check verify the end (putting them into the cup does that too since he can effortlessly scan a table top to see that no marbles remain on it). Similarly, other early counting exercises present things in a row, so that the left-right strategy used for reading will reliably check off all the items and reveal when the last item has been checked. Children appear to make use of this strategy without appreciating its significance.

When children are presented counting

tasks that do not lend themselves to automatic check-off of the items, errors are produced because of the failure to adopt a check-off strategy. In particular, children may fail to use the check-off systems built into their earlier exercises because check-off was provided there by the task and not by anything the child had to do.

Some Observations of Children's Counting

During the fall of 1963 I presented some counting problems to first grade children. The children were not typical but were chil-

dren of neighboring University of Minnesota faculty members who happened to be handy. The sessions were tape recorded. The excerpts that I quote here are not random samples of their work, but rather are selected to illustrate some of the more interesting possibilities of the method.

First example. A six-year old child was presented with a 20 x 20 squared board on which 42 checkers were arranged and was asked to tell how many checkers there were (see Figure 4).

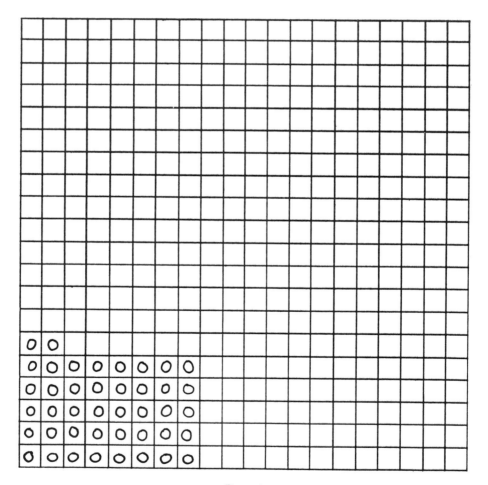

Figure 4

The conversation included the following:

Child: Am I allowed to move them?
E: Yes.
Child: Can I take them right off the board?
E: If you want to.

He started pushing them off the board, counting aloud as he went. After "twenty-seven" his counting had gotten so far ahead of his moving the checkers that he stopped, looked lost for a moment, said "twenty-eight," and went on more slowly. His total was 43. Although he counted in correct sequence, and although he had no doubt about when he was finished, he slipped in matching the symbols to the checkers. It appears that, describing the child's actions as a program, a loop was set up as in Figure 5a,

which degenerated with automatization to the short loops shown in Figure 5b.

Frequently repeated short loops like this one tend to be short-circuited, both by children and by adults. With frequent rapid repetition the operations of moving the checkers and incrementing the counter begin to be performed concurrently, each apparently independently conditioned to the signal that the task is not yet done. This destroys the sequence of the earlier loop (Figure 5a). A part of the loop, incrementing the counter, becomes conditioned to its own previous execution, thus getting out of phase with the successive removal of items to be counted. This is particularly easy to do with counting, where calling the numerals

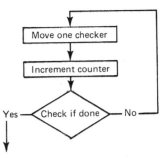

Figure 5a Count and Check-off Loop

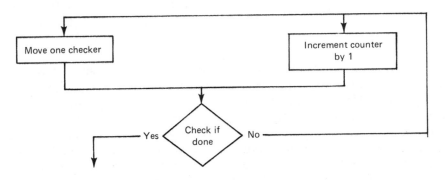

Figure 5b Automatized Loop

in order is already a highly practiced sequential response. Such a flow is not found in present digital computers, which do only one thing at a time, although it could be imitated by a time-sharing routine.

Describing this child's action as a program would require inclusion of the matching of the counter to the items (even though that went wrong in this case). It also reveals a well-established numeral list and a check-off procedure that involves removing the items completely, presumably to facilitate the decision to stop counting when the last checker is done. It was not clear whether the child appreciated the significance of his plan to remove the checkers bodily from the board.

Second example. Another child, also six years old, was given the same problem but was told that he could not remove checkers from the board. He did not attempt to move them at all (although he could just as well have shifted them to the other side of the board for check-off) but counted by pointing to each in turn.

> E: Why did you do that one next?
> Child: I've done these here, so now I'm doing this one.

Apparently, he knew that those counted once should not be counted again. He started counting at the bottom row, went all the way across it, then up the first column, and then looped back.

> E: How do you know which ones you've done?
> Child: I remember them. I started here [points], and then I did these, and then I came down here and did these.

His order of counting the checkers is shown in Figure 6. He hit some checkers twice, others not at all, and produced the answer 46.

There was a check-off routine here, but it was not an effective one. The child was attempting to remember each checker and

could not do it. He did not substitute any other means for identifying which checkers had been counted and which remained uncounted.

Third example. The child reported in the first example was given the same example six months later and revealed a much more sophisticated strategy, apparently learned in the interval. He first counted the number of checkers in the bottom row. He found 8. He started moving checkers from the row above until there were 10 in the bottom row, 6 in the row above. Then he moved checkers from the row above that until the second row had 10. He continued until all the checkers were in four rows of 10, with two standing above. He said "42."

Apparently this child had developed an efficient strategy in several ways, since he counted out only the first row and then matched the remaining rows without counting them. The strategy matched the decimal number system, so that he said 42 without ever producing all of the intervening symbols. Despite the efficiency of this counting procedure, the way he moved the counters was not optimally efficient, since he moved them out of a row that he subsequently refilled. When the test was repeated with 42 beans in a bowl, he took out the beans but no longer used the decimal arrays and returned to the method used in the first example. It appears that the sub-routine of grouping and matching was learned in the context of the arrays provided by the squared board. Possibly it was seen as an exclusive alternative to the removal procedure for check-off. Since the beans could not be discriminated in the bowl, he removed them. But removing them was the check-off procedure used before, and having once started that, he made no further search for other procedures.

Selecting the Routine

This example suggests an important additional aspect about children's counting programs: they do not have a master algorithm that deals with all counting situations with which they are familiar, but several separate ones for different situations. Presumably there is some prior decision routine which for each problem selects one of the counting routines. This might be done by simply picking out attributes of the situation and having a list of the various counting plans associated with one or another attribute. Effective counting in many situations, however, might depend on having a well-developed routine for selecting the operations appropriate to the situation and on checking that all the logical requirements are met.

The development of a routine to select counting procedures would be faciliated by a process which makes explicit all the separate functions involved in counting and their contribution to the total performance.

29	28									
40 / 12	41 / 13	44 / 18	38 / 27	37	36	35				
42 / 11	45 / 14	15 / 19	46 / 26	39 / 43		34				
10	15	20	25			33				
9	16	21	24	30	31	32				
8	7 / 17	22 / 6	23 / 5	4	3	2	1			

Figure 6 Record of counting by a six-year-old for the distribution of checkers shown in Figure 4

For this purpose, we may want to get children to see more explicitly the function of different parts of their procedures where usually they take these for granted. This can be done by getting them to prepare the program.

Getting Children To Do The Programming

It is difficult to get small children to draw up a complex plan in advance. But the advantages we have enjoyed by pretending to program may also be obtained by the child (at least to an extent) by jumping right into a procedure in which his instruction statements alone guide the action. The child gives the instructions, and the experimenter carries them out as literally as he can. Or he may deliberately misinterpret ambiguous instructions in order to make the ambiguity apparent.

The experimenter explains the procedure to the child as follows: "Now we will play at a special way of doing counting. I'm going to pretend that I don't know anything at all about how to count. I'll have some things in front of me, and I am supposed to count them. You have to tell me what to do. I am pretending to be very stupid and my memory is very bad, so you have to tell me each little thing to do, one at a time, and then I will do whatever you say."

Fourth example. Experimenter had a tray of about 30 beans scattered more or less randomly. The child was a six year old first grader.

Child: Pick a bean.
(Experimenter singles out a bean to look at but does not touch it.)
Child: Say the first number. That is "one."
E: One.
Child: Remember that.
E: You want me to remember it? I have a very bad memory. If you want me to remember it, I'd better write it down.
Child: OK, write down 1. (E writes down 1).
Child: Pick another bean.
E: I don't understand.
Child: Pick out a bean. The way you did before.
E: OK. I've got a bean.
Child: Write down the next number.
E: Where?
Child: Write it where you wrote that other one. Cross out the first one and write this instead.
(E crosses out the 1.)
E: What am I supposed to write now?
Child: Write the next number.
E: I don't know the next number.
Child: The next number is 2. Write 2. Now go back and do it again.
(This continues until 7 beans have been counted.)
Child: What bean are you counting?
(E points to it.)
Child: Is that the same one you counted before?
E: I don't know.
Child: You don't know! You're supposed to keep track of them.
E: You didn't say that.
Child: Well, it's no good if you don't keep track of them.
E: What should I do now?
Child: We'll just have to start over. Pick out a bean.
E: OK.
Child: No, really pick it up. (E picks it up.) Write down 1. Pick out a bean.
E: What am I supposed to do with this bean in my hand?
Child: Just keep holding it. Pick out a bean.
(E holds out the bean already in his hand.)
Child: No, not that one, pick out a bean *that's on the tray.*
(E picks out a bean from the tray, adding it to the first one in his hand.)
Child: Write down the next number, which is 2.
(This continues until all are counted.)

In this example the child was probably never in any doubt about how to proceed, but his instructions were initially too elliptical to be useful in guiding the experimenter. He made check-off much more explicit than it was before.

Fifth example. The experimenter placed on the table a large gear-wheel with about 20 teeth. The child was the same six-year-old.

Child: Pick out one of those teeth.
E: OK, I've got one.
Child: No, put your finger on it. (E complies.)
Child: Write down 1. No, use your other hand. Put the other hand on the gear so you can write with the other hand. Now move your finger to the next gear. Put down 2 where you had 1. Now move your finger to the next gear. Put down 3. Now move your finger to the next gear. (E moves to adjacent tooth but backs up, returning to the one counted before.) No, no, you can only go forward. Move to the next one forward from where you were. (E complies.)
(This procedure continues until the count is at 24.)
Child: Something's wrong. You've gone too far. You're going around again.
E: What's wrong with that? You didn't say anything about that.
Child: No, you aren't supposed to go around again. Just do them all once.
E: Well, what should I do now?
Child: Where did you start?
E: I don't know.
Child: We'll just have to start over. Now this time make a mark where you start.
(E makes a pencil mark on the gear.)
Child: Now write down 1. Move forward to the next gear thing.
(After a while.)
Child: Have you come to the mark yet?
E: I didn't notice.
Child: Well, it doesn't matter, but keep looking for the mark. When you get to it, we have finished.

The child made explicit the need for a stop-decision and the role of marking as a signal that all are counted. This routine took advantage of the natural array of the teeth around the gear wheel.

Sixth example. In programming the computer we made explicit the need for a list of integers. The following fragment shows that the child was forced into much the same procedure.

Child: Write down the next number.
E: I don't know what that is.
Child: Well, what number have you got now?
E: I've got 6 written here.
Child: Well, 7 comes after that. Write down 7.
E: You'll have to tell me what to write down every time.
Child: All right.
E: Why don't you tell me how you get the next number to write down, and I'll be able to do it myself.
Child: Well, 7 comes after 6.
E: Yes, but how do you know that?
Child: You just know it, that's all.
E: How can I get to know it too?
E: You'll just have to learn it.
E: But I can't remember things.
Child: Well, I'll tell you all the numbers right now, and you write them down. Then you will know all of them.
E: OK.
Child: 1, 2, 3, 4, 5, 6, 7, 8, 9, 10, 11, 12, 13, 14, 15, 16, 17, 18, 19, 20, 21, 22, 23, 24, 25, 26, 27, 28, 29, 30, 31 . . . that's really enough, you won't need more than that.
(At the next instance.)
Child: Write down the next number.
E: What is it?
Child: Look on your list.
E: What should I look for?
Child: Look for the next number.
E: How can I? I don't know what it is.
Child: What was the last number you had?
E: 7.
Child: Look for that, then.
E: I've found it.
Child: Write down what comes after it; that's right, 8.

Thus the child, under the pressure of the inadequacy of his own instructions, invented the same list procedure as we used in the program, except that his depended upon the order in the array of numbers in the list.

Extending the Method

It would be possible to make the task more difficult and the program more general if the child were unable to see the task on which the experimenter was working. This would certainly force explicit consideration of the selection of a routine. It would also be possible to record the instructions generated during one such session and attempt to use them in another session. In this fashion the child could build up a more general and more explicit program, just as is done by the machine programmer. It is possible to imagine the separate instructions stored in discrete places, the locations connected together by a sort of map. Such a map would represent the flow diagram used in programming computers and yet would be a familiar concept to children who often play games that involve following a route across a board according to the throw of a die.

In the examples presented here, detailed specification is provided for quite fine steps of a small task. There is no reason that the steps could not be either finer still, or much larger. One could write a program for a much more complex task (e.g. marketing, or inventory) in which counting was treated as a simple operation which could be called without further explanation of its details. Nor is it necessary that the task involve mathematics. Specifying the operations and providing the map that links them together in an operating sequence could be done for tasks that involve no mathematical procedure whatever, provided (and this is the important point) that a clear way to state the directions is possible.

Summary

The explicit statement of procedures required for programming a computer is suggested as a model:

1. To specify components of a task,
2. To compare the features of children's performance with what is logically required for the task, and
3. To show the child how to make his own instructions explicit by doing the programming himself and seeing its consequences.

Elementary counting among first graders is presented as a miniature example of these procedures, but it is believed that they are far more generally applicable.

REFERENCES

Feigenbaum, E. A. and Feldman, J., eds. *Computers and Thought.* New York: McGraw-Hill, 1963.

Garvin, P. L., ed. *Natural Language and the Computer.* New York: McGraw-Hill, 1963.

Greenberg, J., ed. *Universals of Language.* Cambridge: M.I.T. Press, 1963.

Lovell, K. *The Growth of Basic Mathematical and Scientific Concepts in Children.* New York: Philosophical Library, 1961.

Newell, A., Shaw, J. C., and Simon, H. A. "Elements of a Theory of Human Problem-solving." *Psychol. Rev.* 1958, *65,* 151–166.

Piaget, J. *La genèse du nombre chez l'enfant.* Geneva, 1941, Translated as: *The Child's Conception of Number.* London: Routledge and Kegan Paul, 1952.

Tomkins, S. S. and Messick, S., eds. *Computer simulation of Personality.* New York: Wiley, 1963.

An Instructional Management Strategy for Individualized Learning

Philip G. Kapfer

EDITORS' QUESTIONS:

1. Discuss the assumptions of the instructional management strategy for individualized learning. React to each assumption and qualify your position.
2. Describe the components for individualized instruction contained in the learning packages. Compare these with other components for individualized instruction in the IPI and the PLAN. What are some of the elements that these approaches have in common? How are they different?
3. Assess the feasibility and applicability of this program in teaching young children at the nursery, kindergarten and Grade 1 levels.

Philip G. Kapfer, "An Instructional Management Strategy for Individualized Learning," *Phi Delta Kappan*, XLIX, No. 5, (January 1968), 260–263. Reprinted with the permission of Phi Delta Kappa, Inc. and Philip G. Kapfer.

A frequent goal of the administrator is to integrate the essential components of instruction—the teacher, the learner, and that which is to be learned. The problem of integrating these components for the purpose of individualizing instruction is the central concern of this paper.

An instructional management strategy developed at Valley High School, Las Vegas, Nevada, is potentially effective for any school whose staff is attempting to individualize instruction, regardless of the type of schedule being used. To be genuinely effective in the school for which it was designed, however, the strategy was developed within the context of the four phases of instruction which have been advocated by innovators such as Bush, Allen, and Trump. These phases include large-group instruction, small-group instruction, laboratory instruction, and independent study.

Educators should cease to be concerned primarily with the technical problems of team teaching and flexible scheduling. Rather, they should get to the heart of the matter—the opportunities to individualize instruction *provided by* these innovations. The reader may or may not feel that the technical problems of team teaching and flexible scheduling have been solved; yet progress has certainly been made toward their solution. Agreement can be reached, however, that the problems of individualizing instruction have *not* been solved.

One key to providing for individualized instruction is the preparation of individualized learning units or packages. Such learning packages are the major elements of the instructional management strategy proposed here, and will be discussed following presentation of the strategy.

Mr. Kapfer (1965, Ohio State University Chapter) is curriculum and research director, Valley High School, Las Vegas, Nev.

349

Assumptions

If a strategy for individualizing instruction is to be effective, it should begin with the currently existing program as perceived by teachers and pupils. In devising the strategy used at Valley High School, several assumptions were made concerning the perceptions of teachers and pupils, and concerning the schedule.

The first assumption, that *the pupil's responsibility is to learn and the teacher's responsibility is to make available to the pupil that which is to be learned,* places responsibility for the teaching-learning process where it belongs. The teacher does not cover a course, but rather uncovers it; he does not need to cover —or talk about—everything that is to be learned by the pupil.

A second assumption concerns the individuality of the pupil. *The subject matter of a course must be appropriate to the learner* with reference to (1) the pace of instruction, (2) the level of difficulty of the instructional material, (3) the relevance of the instructional material to reality as perceived by the pupil, (4) the pupil's level of interest, and (5) the individual learning style of the pupil.

Both the common and the individualized experiences of the pupil result from a third assumption which is related to the schedule: *The size of a group, the composition of a group, and the time allotted to a group should be appropriate to the purposes of the group.* The common experiences which every pupil in a given course should have are primarily a function of large-group instruction. Pupil-centered discussion of large-group presentations may occur in scheduled small-group instruction. Individualized, self-paced, quantity- and quality-monitored learning (that is, the use of learning packages with built-in self-correcting mechanisms) may occur in the laboratory phase of the course. In addition, the laboratory phase should include oppor-tunities for student interaction and should provide directly for the independent study phase of the individualized instructional program.

A fourth assumption of the instructional management strategy is that *before truly individualized instruction can become a reality, learning packages are needed which will provide for self-paced rather than group-paced instruction.*

The Strategy

The instructional management strategy is based on, but does not adhere strictly to, the principles of Program Evaluation and Review Techniques (PERT). In a PERT network diagram, an *activity* is a time-consuming element of a project which is represented on a network as a line between two *events*.

An event is a specific, definable accomplishment in the project plan, which is recognizable as a particular point in time when activities start and/or finish. An activity cannot be started until the event preceding it has been accomplished. A succeeding event cannot be accomplished until all activities preceding it are complete.[1]

The strategy is presented as a network diagram in Figure 1. The network is designed to show a sequence in which the pupil will attain an adequate *background* so that he is able to perceive problems and ask questions. The result of his questioning will be internal generation of a problematic *confrontation.* Through study and research the

1. *PERT Time Fundamentals.* Las Vegas, Nevada: Edgerton, Germeshausen & Grier, Inc., undated, p. 3.

Figure 1 The Instructional Management Strategy Network Diagram for Self-Paced Learning

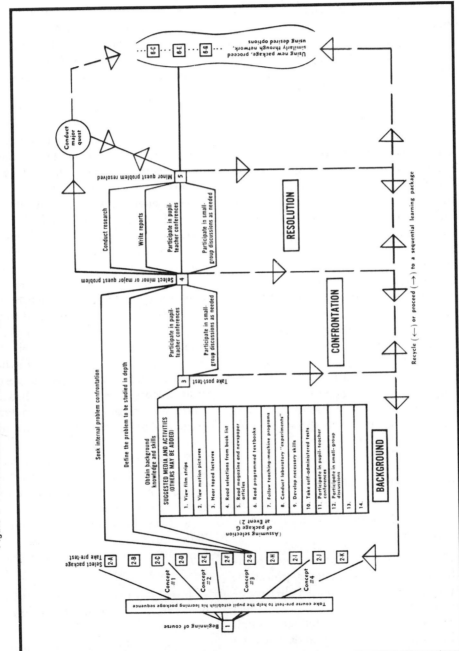

pupil will achieve *resolution* of the problem which he chose for investigation. Thus the sequence in the network is from achievement of *background* to problem *confrontation* to problem *resolution*.

Recycling, for some pupils and for some instructional objectives, may occur at various stages as indicated by arrows in the network. Thus, although the instructional management strategy may be thought of as a design for concept attainment through discovery or problem solving, it is not restricted to this interpretation. In the discovery interpretation of the strategy, the pupil might not be given a statement of the concept under study; rather, he would discover it for himself. In the presentation interpretation, a statement of the concept may be given to the pupil at the beginning of the learning package. In either case, the activities and events *following* Event 3 (see Figure 1) represent an inquiry approach. The activities surrounding Events 4 and 5, those involving minor and major quest, give the pupil the opportunity to become a researcher, and in the process of resolving problems the pupil learns information-seeking techniques. When the decision is made to proceed to a sequential learning package, options similar to those just outlined are available to the pupil.

Preparing Learning Packages

Learning packages usually include the following eight ingredients for individualizing instruction:

1. *Concepts* are abstractions which organize the world of objects, events, processes, structures, or qualities into a smaller number of categories.

2. *Instructional objectives* tell the pupil what he will have to be able to do when he is evaluated, the important conditions under

which he will have to perform, and the lower limit or quality of performance expected of him.[2]

3. *Multi-dimensional learning materials* of varying difficulty are cited from commercial sources, whenever possible, and include a variety of media which require use of as many different senses as possible.

4. *Diversified learning activities* provide alternative approaches for achieving the instructional objectives, and include such activities as large group and small group instruction, field trips, model building, drama productions, games, laboratory experiments, role playing, pupil-teacher conferences, reflective thinking and the like.

5. *Pre-evaluation* is designed to assess the extent to which the pupil has already achieved the instructional objectives as a result of his earlier learning experiences. Pre-evaluation enables the pupil to invest his time wisely in areas in which he is weak.

6. *Self-evaluation* is designed to assist the pupil in determining his own progress toward achieving the instructional objectives. Self-evaluation, the results of which indicate the pupil's readiness for post-evaluation, occurs after the pupil has used the multi-dimensional learning materials and participated in diversified learning activities.

7. *Post-evaluation* is designed to assess the extent to which the pupil has achieved the instructional objectives as a result of his learning experiences.

8. *Quest* includes problem confrontation, delimitation, research, and resolution. Quest is a pupil-initiated and self-directed learning activity.

Integration of the above eight curricular elements in the form of learning packages

2. Robert F. Mager, *Preparing Instructional Objectives.* Palo Alto, Calif.: Fearon Publishers, 1962, p. 52.

can serve as an important advancement in providing for self-paced learning through individualized instruction. An experimental course, Human Relations—an Interdisciplinary Study, which is currently under way at Valley High School, is based on the instructional management strategy. One of the learning packages developed for the course is reproduced below in the form in which it is available to students. Only the pre- and post-tests have been omitted here due to space limitations.

LEARNING PACKAGE TOPIC:
STEREOTYPING[3]

I. CONCEPT STATEMENT

Stereotyping is a learned behavior which results in loss of individuality for members of a stereotyped group or institution.

II. INSTRUCTIONAL OBJECTIVES

A. From his own experiences, the student will be able to define the term "stereotype" and give at least five examples of stereotyping. He will be able to explain how such thinking restricts his effectiveness in human relationships.

B. Given six general headings and related terms, the student will write the response which he freely associates with each term. By looking at himself or at someone he knows, he then will be able to explain the degree of validity of his free association responses.

1. Physical appearance
   a. red hair
   b. blonde
   c. blue-eyed
   d. fat
   e. tall and dark
2. Geographical location
   a. Southerners
   b. Las Vegans
   c. New Englanders
   d. San Franciscans
   e. Westerners
3. Occupation
   a. doctors
   b. lawyers
   c. truck drivers
   d. musicians
   e. school teachers
4. Age
   a. teen-agers
   b. over 30
   c. over 65
   d. Old Shep
   e. kindergarten
5. Socioeconomic level
   a. hicks
   b. snobs
   c. happy
   d. unhappy
6. Racial, religious, and ethnic groups
   a. Pollacks
   b. Mormons
   c. Irish

III. LEARNING MATERIALS AND ACTIVITIES*

A. Scan—current news media.

B. View—"Common Fallacies About Group Differences," 15-minute 16 mm. film, McGraw-Hill.

C. View—"High Wall," 32-minute 16 mm. film, McGraw-Hill.

D. View—"None So Blind," color filmstrip with sound, Anti-Defamation League of B'nai B'rith.

E. Read—Robert P. Heilbroner, "Don't Let Stereotypes Warp Your Judgment," Anti-Defamation League of B'nai B'rith (pamphlet).

F. Read—Raymond W. Mack and Troy S. Duster, "Patterns of Minority Relations," Anti-Defamation League of B'nai B'rith (pamphlet).

G. Read—Earl Raab and Seymour Lipset, "Prejudice and Society," Anti-Defamation League of B'nai B'rith (pamphlet).

H. Read—William Van Til, "Prejudiced—How Do People Get That Way?" Anti-Defamation League of B'nai B'rith (pamphlet).

I. Read—Howard J. Ehrlich (ed.) *Theory Into Practice,* special edition, available from Anti-Defamation League of B'nai B'rith.

J. Read—William Peters, "Why Did They Do It?" *Good Housekeeping,* June, 1962.

3. Charles A. Silvestri and Kathleen Harrell, *Human Relations—An Interdisciplinary Study.* Las Vegas, Nev.: Valley High School, 1967, unpaged.

*The student selects from the suggested learning materials and activities those which he needs in order to achieve the instructional objectives. He is neither restricted to these suggestions nor expected to use all of them.

K. Read—G. M. Morant, *The Significance of Racial Differences.* Paris, France: UNESCO, 1958, 47 pp.

L. Read—Arnold Rose, *The Roots of Prejudice,* Paris, France: UNESCO, 1958, 35 pp.

M. Read—David Westheimer, *My Sweet Charlie.* Garden City, N.Y.: Doubleday, 1965, 255 pp.

IV. SELF-TEST

A. Define "stereotype" and give at least five examples of stereotyping. Explain how the thinking represented in each of your examples restricts one's effectiveness in human relations.

B. List your free response to each of the following terms: blond, teacher, teen-ager, parent, Mexican, truck driver, farmer, fat, red. Are your responses accurate? Explain.

V. SELF-TEST KEY

Answers on the self-test will vary. After checking your performance with the objectives and discussing your answers with other students, if you still are in doubt about acceptability you should discuss the answers with one of your instructors.

VI. QUEST SUGGESTION

Select a common stereotype and describe the process of generalization by which this stereotype might have developed. Can you find any evidence to support or refute your description?

Summary

The instructional management strategy is designed to assist teachers in establishing stepwise procedures for achieving individualized instruction. The important elements in the strategy are learning packages designed for use by individual pupils. Identification of the important concepts and instructional objectives which are to be taught by means of these packages will permit the establishment of hierarchical schemes around which the curriculum may be organized, K-12 and even higher. The packages may take many forms, but a common characteristic of each is the provision for self-pacing. As a result, the pupil is enabled to progress at his own best rate, thus avoiding the familiar difficulties of group-paced instruction.

Recommended Readings: Combining Strategies for Individualized Instructional Programs

Bell, Norman T., Starkes, David D. and Hunt, James G. *Self-Instructional Program in Educational Psychology.* Glenview, Illinois, 1970.

Bentley, Joseph *Learning Through Discovery.* Dubuque, Iowa: Wm. C. Brown Company Publishers, 1972.

Darrow, H. F. and Howes, M. V. *Approaches to Individualized Reading.* New York: Appleton-Century-Crofts, 1960.

Fischer, B. B. and Fischer, L. "Toward Individualized Learning," *The Elementary School Journal* 69 (1969):298–303.

Fry, Edward B. *Teaching Machines and Programmed Instruction: An Introduction.* New York: McGraw Hill, 1963.

Howes, Virgil M. *Individualization of Instruction: A Teaching Strategy.* New York: The Macmillan Co., 1970.

————. *Individualizing Instruction in Reading and Social Studies: Selected Readings on Programs and Practices.* New York: The Macmillan Co., 1970.

————. *Individualizing Instruction in Science and Mathematics: Selected Readings on Programs, Practices and Uses of Technology.* New York: The Macmillan Co., 1970.

Jasik, Marilyn "Breaking Barriers by Individualizing," *Childhood Education* 45 (1968):65–74.

Matthews, Charles C., Good, Ronald G. and Phillips, Darrell G. *Student-Structured Learning in Science: A Program for the Elementary School Teacher.* Dubuque, Iowa: Wm. C. Brown Company Publishers, 1971.

Miel, Alice, ed. *Individualizing Reading Practices: Practical Suggestions for Teaching.* No. 14. New York: Bureau of Publications, Teachers College, Columbia University, 1958.

Moore, R. E., "Individualized Math," *School and Community* 54 (1968):20–21.

Parker, Don H. *School for Individual Excellence,* New York: Thomas Nelson and Sons, 1963.

Petrequin, Gaynor *Individualizing Teaching Through Modular Flexible Programming.* New York: McGraw Hill, 1968.

Postlethwait, S. N., Novak, Joseph and Murray, H. T., Jr. *The Audio-Tutorial Approach to Learning—Through Independent Study and Integrated Experiences.* Minneapolis, Minn.: Burgess Publishing Co., 1969.

Ramsey, I. L. and Wiandt, S. L. "Individualizing Elementary School Science," *School Science and Math* 67 (1967):419–427.

Schubert, Delwyn G. and Torgeson, Theodore L. *Improving Reading Through Individualized Correction.* Dubuque, Iowa: Wm. C. Brown Company Publishers, 1969.

Sharpe, William F. and Jacob, Nancy L. *An Introduction to Computer Programming Using the BASIC Language.* Rev. Ed. New York: The Free Press, A Division of the Macmillan Co., 1971.

Shulman, Lee S., ed. *Learning by Discovery: A Critical Appraisal.* Chicago, Illinois: Rand McNally, 1966.

Thomas, J. I. "Individualizing Instruction in the Social Studies," *The Social Studies* 60 (1969):71–76.

Veatch, Jeannette *Individualizing Your Reading Program: Self-Selection in Action.* New York: Putnam, 1959.

Younie, William J. *Instructional Approaches to Slow Learning.* New York: Teachers College Press, 1967.

PART
FOUR

The Process of Evaluation

Evaluation of Educational Programs

Section 1
Evaluation of Educational Programs

Any program of evaluation must consider the major responsibility placed upon the school by society. The primary purpose of schools is the promotion of all aspects of growth of each learner. Evaluation in education, therefore, must consider the extent to which this objective is being realized. Viewed in this light, the process of evaluation acquires a broad and complicated nature calling for the best efforts of everyone involved in the education of children.

The purpose of evaluation as viewed by Patterson is threefold and may be described as summative, comparative or formative. She also indicates that evaluation procedures may be characterized as product-oriented or process-oriented in accordance with the type of variables selected for investigation. Emphasis is given the necessity of selecting objectives which can serve as criteria for evaluation and of using evaluative procedures which are congruent with the type of variables being measured. The advisability of developing evaluation programs that are sufficiently flexible to accomodate changes in priorities or objectives is also considered.

Jenkins points out that since the classroom is the place in school where most learning experiences occur it is important that methods be devised which can be used by the classroom teacher for evaluating the effectiveness of classroom activities. Therefore, he provides the classroom teacher with some background on the components of evaluation and some guidelines for evaluating classroom practices and programs.

The purpose of the article of Farr and Brown is to develop an awareness on the part of the student of how evaluation can be used as an aid to decision making for effective instruction. The different types of decisions that a teacher makes, such as assessing pupils' needs, devising monitoring procedures and determining progress toward the mastery of ultimate objectives, are illustrated through the use of an example—the teaching of a reading vocabulary.

The social-emotional climate in the classroom is related to the promotion of children's learning. Since the teacher, to a large extent, sets the atmosphere in the classroom, Withall provides her with a technique for assessing classroom climate through the use of the Social-Emotional Climate Index. Instructions for the use of this instrument are also furnished.

Cognizant of the influence of the classroom environment upon the learning of each child, Harms encourages the teacher to look at the environment from the child's point of view. An evaluation checklist grouped into four categories—physical environment, interpersonal environment, activities to stimulate development and scheduling—is provided in order to help the teacher identify strengths as well as problem areas that need improvement in her classroom setting.

The student, after reading this section and the recommended readings, is expected to be able to:

1. Critically analyze the nature of evaluation and its components.

2. Demonstrate each type of evaluation through simulated teaching or micro teaching.

3. Write program objectives and specify two or more appropriate evaluation instruments for each.

4. Devise strategies for evaluating classroom climate and physical environment.

5. Develop assessment procedures for evaluating the effectiveness of classroom activities and programs.

Analyzing Early Childhood Education Programs: Evaluation

June M. Patterson

EDITORS' QUESTIONS:

1. Critically analyze each of the instruments suggested by the author for assessing pupils' learning achievement.

2. Discuss the use of observation, interviews, questionnaires and rating scales for determining instructional effectiveness. What other instruments would you, as a teacher, like to have used in evaluating your performance? Give reasons for your choices.

3. What is the appropriate role of parents in the evaluative process? Make suggestions for increasing the value of parental participation in evaluation programs.

4. State the rationale underlying process-oriented evaluative procedures. Make suggestions for a more systematic implementation of this approach.

5. Standardized tests are frequently used as instruments for evaluation. Indicate ways in which the use of these tests is often abused and suggest techniques for analyzing test results which would enhance the value of these instruments to the classroom teacher.

6. Analyze the criteria for evaluation stated by Patterson. Do these encompass the entire range of educational objectives? What alterations or additions would you make? State your reasons for each change.

38

June M. Patterson, "Analyzing Early Childhood Education Programs: Evaluation," *Educational Leadership,* XXVIII, No. 8 (May 1971), 809–811. Reprinted with the permission of the Association for Supervision and Curriculum Development and June M. Patterson. Copyright © 1971 by the Association for Supervision and Curriculum Development.

Whether or not program evaluation is a clearly articulated aspect of an early childhood education program, evaluation will take place. It may be as casual as a conversation between parents as they meet in the store and exchange views on what is, or is not, happening in the school program; or it may be more formalized, perhaps a conference between supervisor and teacher to discuss the progress of children.

In any case, some type of evaluation is taking place whenever people assess the quality of the educational program. If the evaluation is to be an integral part of the education program, decisions regarding its purpose, criteria, procedures, and instrumentation will be made as a part of the total program planning, rather than at the end of the year or in isolation from other program decisions.

Purpose of the Evaluation

The general purpose of evaluation is to determine whether or not what is expected to happen has happened or is happening. This purpose provides a general framework for evaluation which accommodates all empirical questions regarding the effectiveness of a given program designed to accomplish specified objectives. It is important to make a distinction between empirical questions, the answers to which are based on empirical data, and value questions, the answers to which require judgments of desirability and of value positions. Value questions must be dealt with in deciding on program objectives and procedures; empirical questions deal with what actually happened, whether desired or not.

A given evaluation may be viewed as either process- or product-oriented and its purpose described as summative, comparative, or formative.[1] *Process evaluation* is focused on the program procedures, on the setting in which the program takes place, and especially on the behavior of the adults who participate. The main questions asked concern the nature of materials and equipment, the plant and physical space, and adult roles, especially whether adults are functioning as intended. *Product evaluation* has to do with outcomes and questions whether the program achieved what it was supposed to accomplish.

Process evaluation is seldom carried out systematically. Product evaluation, while often systematic, is seldom sufficiently comprehensive in terms of time span covered and variables considered; nor is such evaluation usually well enough focused on significant variables.

Summative evaluation is most common. Here the purpose is simply to determine to what extent a program has fulfilled its intended product goals (for example, did the children enrolled change as much as hoped for?). A second form of product-oriented evaluation is *comparative evaluation,* in which two or more programs are contrasted in terms of their effects on children.

A large independent research effort might be involved in which the particular aspects of each program to be compared are specified in detail, and the main canons of experimental research are followed. A third purpose for evaluation often involves both product and process emphases. In *formative evaluation* the purpose is to facilitate decision making by feeding back information into an ongoing program. Information is collected on these two questions: Are the students showing signs of responding and changing in the direction of program objectives? Have the intended program procedures been implemented?

Two general points should be made before going on to specific aspects of evaluation. The first is that one important index of the extent of instruction differentiation may be found in the degree to which it carries on both initial diagnostic assessment of pupil status and continuing evaluative assessment of the amount of change or development, especially as related to specific program procedures. This information is also one index of the program's adaptability to different kinds of children and different environmental conditions.

The second point is accountability, which is relevant to both the purposes and the procedures of evaluation. Every educational program has many constituencies to which it is accountable. Generally, some form of reporting (that is, summative evaluation) is essential, although the particular form of the report may vary among constituencies. Therefore, data should be available for reports appropriate to the needs for which such reports are made. Examples of con-

[1]See: Michael Scriven. "The Methodology of Evaluation." In: R. Tyler, R. Gagné, and M. Scriven. *Perspectives of Curriculum Evaluation.* Chicago: Rand McNally & Company, 1967.

stituents are: children, parents, teaching staff, school administration, and funding agencies.

Criteria Used for Evaluation

Evaluation, even the most casual, matches observation to a model and makes a judgment regarding the exactness of fit between the two. The model may be clearly defined, such as some of those used in Follow Through programs, or it may be loosely defined and, in fact, take on a definition as a result of the evaluation process. In either case, it is necessary to decide what program variables are to be used to describe and define the model and the program. These variables or objectives set the criteria which may be used in the evaluation. The following are examples of variables which may be used to describe models and programs:

1. Expected outcomes in terms of children's behavior change or learning and development, as indicated in program objectives
2. Implementation of program procedures, including
   a. Staff behaviors (teachers, aides, specialists, etc.)
   b. Materials and equipment available and ways utilized
   c. Nature and arrangements of physical space and plant
3. Extent and quality of parent and community involvement.

Procedures and Implementation

The time schedule for collecting data is determined, in part, by the purpose of the evaluation. In general, one of the following three procedures can be used to describe any given evaluation data collection time schedule:

1. Data collected at one point in time. This schedule allows a comparison of the model expectation and the program at a specified point in time.

2. Data collected at two points in time, as exemplified by the classical pre- and post-test schedule. This schedule allows an analysis of change and a comparison of the observed change and the expected change, as defined by the model.

3. Longitudinal evaluations, generally, collect data at critical points over a long period of time (that is, more than a year). The critical times are specified by the model. This schedule allows an analysis of change, as in 2 above, but with a greater degree of sophistication.

A program evaluation may use many types of instruments to collect data. Instruments should be appropriately related to the variables (that is, criteria) which define the model and the program. Any given evaluation may select instruments of the following general types, depending on the purpose of the evaluation:

1. Instruments for use in determining the progress of the children (cognitive, affective, and perceptual-motor domains)
   —Standardized tests (group or individual)
    Achievement tests
    Developmental tests
    Intelligence tests
    Readiness tests
   —Teacher (staff) constructed tests
   —Observations by staff, parents, children, specialists
   —Interviews and questionnaires

(including self-reporting questionnaires) completed by staff, children, parents, specialists
—Children's products

2. Instruments for use in determining the effectiveness of staff behavior
—Observations
—Interviews
—Questionnaires
—Rating scales

3. Instruments for use in determining the effectiveness of the learning environment
—Observation of organization of the physical plant and space
—Observations and questionnaires regarding the use of materials and equipment

4. Instruments for use in determining the quantity and quality of parent involvement
—Interviews
—Questionnaires
—Observations

5. Instruments for use in determining the quantity and quality of community involvement
—Interviews
—Questionnaires
—Observations.

In planning for program development, one may find that it is desirable to provide for an assessment of the program evaluation. As the early childhood education program evolves and develops, so should the evaluation component. It may be necessary periodically to monitor the evaluation to be certain that it is relevant to the ongoing program. As objectives or priorities change, the evaluation procedures, including instruments, should change to maintain the meaningful match between the program and its evaluation.

Planning for Classroom Evaluation of Educational Programs

Jerry A. Jenkins

EDITORS' QUESTIONS:

1. What are the purposes of evaluation indicated by Jenkins? Compare and contrast these purposes with those enumerated by Patterson.

2. How does precise statement of instructional objectives in terms of specific observable behavioral outcomes enhance the effectiveness of evaluative techniques? Indicate instances in which another method of stating objectives might be preferable and justify your view.

3. How should the question of costs be handled in evaluation? Suggest criteria for determining whether costs are reasonable or excessive. Are the attitudes of the businessman or the economist concerning cost minimization applicable to educational endeavors? Substantiate your conclusions.

4. Assess the advisability of bringing in an outside evaluation specialist or of delegating the task of analyzing the results of an evaluation to such an expert. Can you discern the obvious advantages of such a procedure? What are some of its potential disadvantages?

5. Consider Stufflebeam's definition of evaluation as quoted by Jenkins. Viewed in this perspective, is evaluation a recent phenomenon? State the importance of a scientific approach to decision making in the structuring of evaluation programs.

6. Make suggestions for building flexibility into evaluation programs. Indicate how implementation of your recommendations would enhance the capacity of such programs to accommodate changes in priorities or objectives.

Jerry A. Jenkins, "Planning for Classroom Evaluation of Educational Programs," *Contemporary Education,* XLII, (October 1970), 25–27. Reprinted with the permission of the author and Indiana State University.

Growing public pressure for educational accountability, that is, evidence to support continued allocation of resources to the various school programs and activities, is bringing increased importance to the development and implementation of effective evaluation designs. Recent efforts have focused primarily on system-wide or school-wide evaluations with attention given to practically all major factors which exist within school curricula. Little attention has been devoted, however, to devising methods which the typical classroom teacher can follow in evaluating the effectiveness of intraclassroom activities. This is a strange paradox because the classroom is the place where most learning experiences are provided the children by schools.

Because of this situation, teachers, supervisors, and principals, who willingly concede the importance of classroom evaluations to education, are not certain

Jerry A. Jenkins, Research Associate, Institute for Educational Research, Downers Grove, Illinois.

how to undertake them in their own settings. As a result, few elementary and secondary educators even attempt program evaluations.

Evaluation may be operationally defined as the process of acquiring, analyzing, and using information for making decisions associated with planning, programming, implementing, and re-cycling program components and activities.[1] Its purposes are to facilitate continual improvement of an educational program and to assess the effectiveness of the program at its conclusion.

Evaluation in this sense does not need to be quite as "scientific" as usually conceived in research activities.[2] This is not to say that one should not use the most scientific, the most generalizable design he is able to (within the constraints in which he is operating) in planning and undertaking his evaluation, but he need not be concerned with the theoretical aspects of the outcomes. The results of the evaluation, however, may lead to subsequent research efforts to investigate the "whys."

In order to serve the needs of educators, evaluation may be dichotomized into two components. They are *formative* and *summative*.[3]

Formative evaluation is an ongoing dynamic process where information is added continuously, organized systematically, and analyzed periodically. The information gathered is such that it provides for deciding whether to continue, terminate, modify, refocus efforts, or link phases of a program. It accomplishes this through measuring the extent to which operationally defined objectives are being attained, comparing the measurements with predetermined standards, and by making rational analyses of the outcomes.

Summative evaluation utilizes the information provided in the formative states to determine whether the classroom project was successful in reaching its objectives. Although similar in many respects to formative evaluation, the summative component is primarily concerned with painting a detailed picture of the overall efforts and results of the project.

With this background in mind, the following steps are suggested for initiating and undertaking evaluations of classroom programs and practices:

1. A teacher who has an activity or a program which he would like to evaluate should initially attempt to formulate as concisely as possible the questions for which answers are desired. For example, an elementary teacher may be interested in assessing the effectiveness of a new elementary science program which is underway in his classroom. Questions that he might be interested in investigating include: (1) To what extent is the program attaining its stated objectives? (2) Is there any difference in the extent to which this program is attaining its objectives as compared with other science programs within the school and the extent to which they are attaining their objectives? (3) Are the objectives of the various programs congruent with those desired by the teachers? (4) Do the students enjoy the science programs? and (5) How effective are the various programs in terms of per pupil costs of the programs?

2. With the proposed questions clearly in

1. Daniel S. Stufflebeam, "The Use and Abuse of Evaluation in Title III," *Theory Into Practice,* June, 1967, p. 129.

2. Robert E. Stake, "Generalizability of Program Evaluation: The Need for Limits," *Educational Product Report,* February, 1969, p. 39.
3. *Ibid.,* p. 40.

mind, the teacher should meet with other teachers, his departmental or immediate supervisor, and his school principal to present the questions and find out whether other teachers would be interested in participating in the evaluation and to obtain administrative support for the evaluation.

3. The teacher and/or teachers participating in the evaluation would then list the program objectives or goals operationally to describe precisely what outcomes should result from the program in terms of changes in pupil behaviors. For example, returning to the questions stated above, an objective of the science program might be, "Given a set of objects, the child should be able to classify them into categories according to size, shape, color, or structural configuration."

4. At this time, the teacher may decide to peruse other research or literature relative to his questions. He may find, for example, that his particular concerns have already been assessed in another educational setting. The reported results may lead the teacher to decide that he does not need to replicate all or part of the study with his own students. On the other hand, the teacher may decide to go ahead and develop the evaluation within his own setting.

5. If possible, the teacher should arrange to meet with a research or evaluation specialist before proceeding further. The purpose of this meeting is to obtain expert advice in developing an evaluation design that will measure the success of the educational program in reaching each stated goal.

At this meeting, the teacher should be able to describe the program components, the objectives, and the questions to be answered by the evaluation. One outcome of this might be the modification, deletion, or addition of objectives and/or questions.

When they have been outlined to the satisfaction of both the evaluation specialist and the teacher, the evaluation strategy itself will be detailed.

6. As the design evolves, deadlines for various activities should be established. It should include a delineation of task responsibilities if more than one person is to be involved in the evaluation. Such a plan will prevent duplication of efforts, gaps in activities, and a lack of coordination of endeavors. The design may also include a training session for whoever has responsibility for gathering the data.

The evaluation design itself is nothing more than a detailed plan of investigation. It may be viewed as being a blueprint to be followed. It includes such elements as identification of the variables to be examined, sampling procedures to be followed (where appropriate), measurement devices to be used in getting the requisite data, and the analysis to be conducted on the data. In our example, there are at least three factors to be considered: (1) achievement of children on science tests, (2) attitudes toward science, and (3) costs in terms of money, time, and efforts devoted to the programs.

In some instances the data may take the form of information gained from observations of behaviors. In other cases, information may be acquired using non-reactive unobtrusive measures, such as estimating pupil attitudes through determining the amount of time the children participate in science-related activities of their own choosing, examining the number of science-related books they may check out of the school library, or through reports of personal hobbies related to science which the children develop on their own.

7. Once the design and measurement problems are resolved the teacher could

then conduct the evaluation carefully following the procedures selected and obtaining whatever assistance he might need from time to time from the evaluation specialist. Careful attention should be given so that strict adherence to the evaluation strategy is maintained.

8. At pre-selected phases of the evaluation, data should be gathered by those designated in the evaluation design and analyzed in accordance with the plans. It should be emphasized that if the analysis is of a statistical nature it ought to be done by a trained specialist rather than by the person who collects the data. There are several reasons for this. First, there are many pitfalls in statistical analysis open to those who are not aware of them. Often, the most obvious techniques may be inappropriate because of the form of the data or the methods used when gathering the data. Greatest assurance of the validity of an analysis is gained when it is accomplished by an expert. Secondly, the specialist generally has available efficient methods and equipment such as computers for analyzing the data. Lastly, the analyst is impartial and can provide an objective and an accurate interpretation of the results.

9. Following the analysis the evaluation specialist should meet with the teacher, supervisors, and principal to discuss the findings and the implications and to make future projections concerning the program as a result of the information gained from the evaluation.

10. As data are obtained and modifications of the program occur, all persons who are interested in the various aspects of it should be informed of the findings that result. At the conclusion of the program when summative information is available, a report of the program and the evaluation results should be prepared and disseminated to all who might be interested.

In conclusion, the purpose of this article has been to provide classroom teachers with some background concerning the components of evaluation of an educational program and to provide general guidelines for undertaking an evaluation. Evaluations are not undertaken for their own sakes. They are designed to make information available to individuals so that they can make intelligent decisions regarding the future directions of those programs. If evaluation is not undertaken, what other options are available for making educational decisions?

Evaluation and Decision Making*

Roger Farr
and Virginia L. Brown

40

EDITORS' QUESTIONS:

1. Explain what is meant by "evaluation as an aid to decision making."
2. Discuss the example given in Figure 1 of this selection. How does evaluation assist the teacher in making instructional decisions?
3. Which of the fourteen "possible samplings of performance" listed in Figure 1 may be regarded as diagnostic procedures?
4. Consider the terms "diagnosis" and "evaluation." Are they synonymous? How are they different?
5. Devise a method of gathering information about each child in your class.

Roger Farr and Virginia L. Brown, "Evaluation and Decision Making," *The Reading Teacher,* XXIV, (January 1971), 341–346, 354. Reprinted with permission of the International Reading Association and Roger Farr.

Teaching children to read is a process which involves continuous decision making, not only by teachers, but by many different persons and agencies. State departments of education decide upon teacher certification requirements. Local school boards, superintendents, principals, reading coordinators, and consultants work cooperatively to decide on the best use of available money, the need for special teachers, the suitability of particular programs, and so on. The classroom teacher is also vitally concerned with these questions. Perhaps more importantly, however, she works with crucial decisions regarding the individual child. She determines which skills are to be taught to specific children and the functional reading level and interests of each child. The list of instructional decisions made by classroom teachers is infinite.

The decision situation is not new to educators. However, most instructional decisions are made by forfeit; that is, by not recognizing that a decision can be made or by not being aware of possible alternatives. The usual forfeit "decision" involves continuation of a practice whether or not it is the most appropriate procedure for the situation. Other decisions are made on the basis of limited or biased information; or they are made after consulting "expert" opinion, with little regard to the needs and problems of a specific situation.

The Evaluation Concept

The desirability of making rational educational decisions based upon the needs and criteria of a particular educational setting is obvious. What is not so obvious is the pro-

*Supported in part by EPDA OEG 0-9-247053-3589-721.
Roger Farr is with Indiana University, Bloomington. Virginia Brown is with the University of Minnesota at Duluth.

cess for accomplishing this task.

Traditional structured research is too cumbersome and insensitive to the problems of program implementation to be of much value in daily instructional decision making. Re-definition of the concept of evaluation as a process to aid in educational decision making would seem to hold greater possibility for assisting those directly concerned with improvement of the classroom situation. This broader definition of evaluation is somewhat different from the restricted concepts of evaluation either as a testing program, or as a determination of the value of something, where these activities have not led to appropriate program changes.

The purpose of the present discussion is to acquaint the practitioner with some of the implications of the use of evaluation as an aid to decision making. The article can only introduce the concepts, but the authors recommend that this introduction become the impetus for further study. Suggested references include Scriven (1967), Stake and Denny (1969), and Stufflebeam (1969).

Much of the recent development of the evaluation concept has resulted from the decision-making requirements of the Elementary and Secondary Education Act (ESEA), primarily Titles I and III. This initial development emphasis has been placed upon evaluation as a tool for administrators.

Implications for the Teacher of Reading

While the administrative application of evaluation concepts is appropriate and vital, it is within the classroom that the most important decisions regarding instruction are made. It is in this setting that the potential resides for helping children become competent and interested readers, or for handicapping them in skill development and "turning them off" from reading as a lifetime habit. Because of the crucial nature of classroom decisions, it seems most appropriate to describe the application of an evaluation model in that setting.

Reading programs which emphasize flexible grouping, individualized instruction, and continuous pupil progress are compatible with and depend on the dynamic concept of evaluation being proposed here. They are likely to involve choice points before, during, and after an instructional sequence, with each point emphasizing a different decision.

At first glance, the evaluation process described below would seem little different from what is done many times each day in thousands of schools throughout the country. However, a careful examination of usual classroom practices reveals that evaluation is *not* used as an aid to making decisions. One of the major impediments to this development is that much of the educational environment militates against precise descriptions of instructional objectives and identification of procedural alternatives. Despite the restrictions of the educational milieu, the development of rational instructional decision making is the responsibility of the classroom teacher. In order to develop useful evaluation programs, teachers must state specific behavioral objectives; they must relate these objectives to classroom procedures; they must recognize alternatives to procedures and objectives; they must develop criteria for making decisions; and they must develop various methods for collecting the information needed for making decisions. Through this development evaluation will provide the practitioner with data for the professional power to remove some of the organizational malfunctions which tend to dissipate instructional energy.

An example of decision settings for further discussion is outlined in Figure 1. The specific example is concerned with decisions regarding the teaching of vocabulary for a story the children are to read.

The figure presented is a simplified example. The samples of behaviors suggested are limited and intended only to be representative. While the purpose of each of these evaluation settings may seem obvious, it is probably best to have these purposes clearly stated in order to avoid misinterpretation.

Decision Types

Although *Determining Mastery* of the "ultimate" objectives is placed last in the chart format, the consideration of the longer range objectives should precede any selection of a particular unit because it is within this context that all other decisions are made.

The purpose of *Assessing Needs* is to identify the students for whom the particular skill development and practice materials are needed and are appropriate. This assessment would include gathering information concerning whether students were already able to decode the new vocabulary. It would also include a determination of students' prerequisite skills for undertaking the new task. In addition, teachers should gather information regarding the students' backgrounds, both educational and social, which would help to guide the teacher in selecting or developing appropriate procedures.

The purpose for *Monitoring Procedures* is to cause the teacher to assess the flexibility or suitability of her own practices. The cliché about teaching the program rather than the children is appropriate for this area. If a teacher is inexperienced in alternatives available to teach a required skill, it may be that the purchase of several teacher editions or professional books or publications would

be a wiser investment than an abundance of copies of pupil texts. Inservice training possibilities may also be discovered when monitoring procedures; in addition, a reorganization of curriculum resources may be indicated; and perhaps a newly determined staff need for a "finder and organizer of curriculum resources" may be identified in order to make instructional resources available and retrievable by the practitioner.

Sometimes teaching procedures are so subtle that an outside observer is necessary to assist with assessment. Word-by-word reading might be occurring because the activities seldom include discussion of key ideas, or perhaps because having each word "right" is being reinforced rather than reading for understanding.

Monitoring Growth toward intermediate objectives allows children to move ahead when a particular skill has been mastered or determines that additional or different practice material is needed. This feature deals especially with the problem of pacing. Unless pacing is completely individualized, several points should be considered. Those who have mastered the skill need alternative activities that are more reinforcing than doing more of the same activity. If additional help is needed, it should be determined whether the help is in understanding the process or practice in different settings to promote mastery or generalization. Some teachers use unobtrusive error analysis procedures for making this kind of discrimination, perhaps asking the child to tell what he is doing. Again, curriculum alternatives should be available, but this time for the child.

Finally, a return to monitoring growth toward *Ultimate Objectives* is made to assess growth in the overall behavior that is being developed: the students' progress toward becoming more powerful readers.

Figure 1 Types of Decisions

	Decision types			
Elements of planning	*Assessing needs*	*Monitoring procedures*	*Monitoring growth intermediate objectives*	*Determining mastery toward ultimate objectives*
Objective	Students should recognize in context or in isolation the words needed to read this story.	To teach so that children will be able to pronounce these words when they see them in print and will be able to supply appropriate meaning of content in which words appear.	The children will be able to pronounce these words when they see them in print and will be able to supply appropriate meaning of content in which words appear.	1. Same as monitoring. 2. Students' approach to reading tasks. 3. Independent reading development.
Decision alternatives	1. Which children need to learn the words? 2. Alternate activities for those who do not need the instructional unit?	1. What kind of introduction, practice work, etc., is needed for recognizing, pronouncing and understanding these words? 2. Evidence that the procedures were followed?	1. Which students have mastered the objective? What will they now do? 2. Which students need additional work, and what kind of assistance do they need?	1. Does the nature of the work seem to promote broad goals? 2. Which children need a different type of activity? What kind?
Possible samplings of performance (tests)	1. List words on board and ask children to use them in sentences. 2. Matching test. 3. Evidence from past activities. 4. Pupil self-checklist, etc.	1. Checklist of teacher behaviors planned and carried out. 2. Tape recording as feedback. 3. Modification of lesson plan if one is pre-set, etc.	1. Monitoring of oral reading and discussion. 2. Teacher-made exercise for pupil-teacher discussion. 3. Review of workbook practice if appropriate. 4. Pupil-pupil, or teacher-pupil discussion, etc.	1. Unit test. 2. Observation of other reading behavior. 3. Interest inventory, etc.

Implementing Evaluation

It is essential that the teacher and those who support classroom activities recognize the importance and opportunities of the major sequences of decisions within the broad program. It is equally important that they are able to operationalize each portion of the sequence. This aspect involves clear statements of objectives; delineation of instructional procedures and alternatives, being careful to make clear the relationship of procedures to objectives; and the statement of criteria for recognizing that the objective has either been met or to determine what else is necessary to secure its attainment.

What has been described here may be called "merely good teaching," and in fact this model does place the teacher in a role as planner who makes rational decisions regarding an educational environment which is likely to provide an optimal learning situation. Evaluation in the classroom necessitates much preplanning and critical thinking. Teachers may plead that this time should be spent in activities other than evaluation. Evaluation, however, can be a vital guide for planning instruction; as a monitoring system to determine the nature of assistance for teachers as well as students; and as a system for insuring student success. Viewed in this manner the only concern should be that it would be wasteful of the time and energy of both teacher and children *not* to begin systematic evaluation.

Many attempts to implement evaluation procedures at the classroom or program level have met with only limited success. Sometimes the teacher is unable or unwilling to state objectives in relation to the complexities of the total program. In addition, if the teacher competencies described above have not been part of an effective pre- or in-service program, teachers will be required to "shop" for appropriate training

programs, school districts, or materials to assist in developing their competencies.

It is also possible that other concepts such as traditional testing or grading practices are incompatible with evaluation. In this case the instructional staff should examine contradictory policies and begin to set priorities.

Finally, and related to the previous concern, unless the teacher receives full support from administrative and supervisory personnel, evaluation practices can neither survive nor flourish. As long as teachers continue to be rewarded by administrators, supervisors, and instructional materials for providing non-individualized, inflexible instruction, it is improbable that they will feel confident enough to work through the problems involved in setting up a classroom evaluation system.

In addition to providing a climate for encouraging evaluation, there is currently a dearth of guides for decision rules, a lack of appropriate measurement devices, and limited understanding of the nature of the reading process. However, these limitations will not halt reading instruction, and they should not prevent the development of evaluation as a process for providing information for making decisions.

It is quite possible that the plea for accountability will lead educators into accepting inappropriate goals, procedures, and outcomes all based upon inappropriate evaluation. The potential disaster of "commercial accountability" can be avoided only as teachers of reading address themselves to the problems of self-evaluation and self-improvement by providing evidence of professional accountability.

REFERENCES

Scriven, M. "The Methodology of Evaluation," in B. O. Smith, ed. *Perspectives of*

Curriculum Evaluation. Chicago: Rand McNally and Company, 1967. pp. 39–83.

Stake, R. E., and Denny, T. "Needed Concepts and Techniques for Utilizing More Fully the Potential of Evaluation," In R. W. Tyler, ed. "Educational Evaluation: New Rules, New Means," *The Sixty-eighth Yearbook of the National Society for the Study of Education* 1969, 370–390.

Stufflebeam, D. T. "Evaluation as Enlightenment for Decision Making." In W. H. Beatty, ed. *Improving Educational Assessment.* Washington D.C.: Association for Supervision and Curriculum Development, 1969, pp. 41–73.

Evaluation of Classroom Climate

John Withall

41

EDITORS' QUESTIONS:

1. How does the nature of the classroom climate affect learning progress? What is the contribution of the teacher in the evolution of the classroom climate?

2. Discuss the rationale for using the teacher's verbal behavior as a means of assessing the social-emotional climate which prevails in a classroom.

3. Using a tape recorder, or with the assistance of another student, prepare a tally sheet categorizing your own verbalizations in a micro teaching episode. Does your own subjective assessment of the classroom climate coincide with that expected on the basis of your observed verbal behavior? Analyze any discrepancy noted between the expected and the observed climate and identify the factors you believe to be responsible for the lack of correspondence.

4. Discuss the dangers inherent in reliance upon any one evaluative technique to the exclusion of all others.

5. Describe ways in which you can modify your own verbal behavior in order to foster a classroom climate that is more conducive to learning.

Interactions and Confrontations

The climate or atmosphere pervading a situation, be it a classroom or other milieu where two or more human beings are gathered together, is a commonly experienced phenomenon. We have all heard of or experienced the situation in which it is claimed one could "feel" the tension; the air was "electric"; the emotional atmosphere was such one felt he could cut it. Social-emotional climate can be viewed as the affect or emotional tone that accompanies interactions and communications of human beings in groups. It is the pervasive feeling that is the accompaniment or ingredient of the diverse interactions. It seems to influence the problem-focus, satisfaction, esprit

John Withall is professor of Educational Psychology and head, Department of Secondary Education, Pennsylvania State University, University Park.

de corps and productivity of the members and their group.[1]

If we try to analyze this feeling tone in diverse settings, it becomes clear that our antennae or sensors are picking up many minuscule behavioral cues from those present. These cues communicate the level of emotional tension or ease. Furthermore, these behavioral impingements on you or me have an influence on us as we settle into the interactive field. If the situation is charged with "negative" affect, we pick up innumerable little behaviors that evidence concern, distress, a feeling of psychological threat, malaise, hostility, or frustration and the like. These clues include such behaviors as a taut face, narrowed eyes, tense shoulders, uneasy stirrings, side glances, mutterings, asides, on-the-edge-of-the-seat postures, and the rest. If the situation is charged with "positive" affect, then we pick up cues and behaviors that include open or shining eyes, easy or relaxed postures, smiles and chuckles, quiet and relaxed voice tone, timbre and volume—in general, easy behaviors, insofar as facial expressions, bodily postures and verbalizations are concerned.

Classroom Climate

In the classroom we take it for granted that the teacher is placed there for special reasons. The major responsibility of the teacher is to facilitate the learning of the learners in his class. This is so whether the learners comprise a group of four-year-olds, twelve-year-olds, twenty- or seventy-year-olds. He cannot escape this responsibility with impunity.

To fulfill his responsibility of creating a psychologically liberating environment to enable the learners to learn (namely, to change their perceptions, attitudes and hence their behaviors) the teacher, or

facilitator of learning, has to engage in professional behaviors. What are some of these professional behaviors?

Professionals and Their Behaviors

Like all professionals the teacher engages in behaviors to fulfill his facilitative functions vis-a-vis his target population. The lawyer engages in his professional ploys and strategies, just as does the architect, the physician and the educator in order to aid, help, ameliorate the condition or problems of his client. These behaviors in the case of all genuine professionals are witting and deliberate. They are guided by a rationale derived from the discipline or science of law, architecture, medicine or pedagogy. In addition the true professional constantly monitors his behaviors in terms of their impact on the target, whether it be people or materials. These professional behaviors are aimed at helping to enhance and inform the target individual or groups in their aims, purposes, need and tension reduction. We assume that the professional behaviors of the teacher or instructor are aimed at nurturing and enhancing the learners' (1) inquiry, problem-solving and conceptualizing skills; (2) coping skills and competency with

---

[1]"Climate represents the general emotional factor present in each individual's complex of feelings arising out of shared experience and interpersonal interaction. Climate considered as [both] an affect-concomitant and a resultant of interaction between persons may be thought of as reflecting, to some extent, the degree of comprehension and acceptance of each other's goals and needs.

"Operationally climate may be defined as influencing the sense of common purpose of a group of individuals, the meaningfulness of the group or individual problem, the degree of objectivity with which the problem is attacked, and the degree of self-involvement or participation by the individual. Climate probably affects the degree of freedom, spontaneity and range of roles available to each individual within the limits set by the problem and the group. . . ." John Withall, "The Development of a Technique for the Measurement of Social Emotional Climate in Classrooms." Unpublished doctoral dissertation, The University of Chicago, September 1948, p. 32.

respect to handling their own and others' emotions, concerns and needs.

Teachers' Verbalizations Represent Behaviors

We have found that the verbal behavior of the teacher can be taken as representative of the total syndrome of behaviors used by the teacher in fulfilling his professional responsibility. We have also found that the verbalization of teachers can be categorized according to stated criteria of the Climate Index.*

Everything that you or I say as a teacher can be placed in one of seven categories.[2] On the basis of the pattern of verbalizations one can decide whether the teacher's behaviors are learner- or teacher-oriented. Learner-oriented verbalizations (Categories 1, 2 and 3) comprise positive verbal reinforcement, acceptant, and problem-structuring statements or questions by the teacher. Teacher-oriented statements (Categories 5, 6 and 7) comprise negative verbal reinforcement, reproving and denigrating, or teacher self-supportive statements and questions. The other category of verbalization (Category 4) seems neither to help nor hinder either learner or teacher.

Assessing Climate

By placing each statement or question (thought unit) of a teacher in turn in one of the seven categories, a pattern of verbalization emerges. One way to assess the climate in a situation is to compute an Index of the climate by dividing the total number of statements that fall into Categories 1, 2 and 3 by the total number of statements that fall into Categories 5, 6 and 7. The resultant number is the climate Index. If the number of statements altogether in the three learner-oriented categories is 25 and the number in the teacher-oriented categories is 25, the resultant Index is 1.0. If the number of verbalizations in the learner-centered categories is 50 and the number in the teacher-centered 25, the resultant is 2. If the number of statements in the teacher-centered categories is 50 and the learner-centered statements number 25 the resultant is .50. Thus a number larger than 1.0 by this computation denotes a climate that is liberating for the learners and enhancing of their inquiry, hypothesis-stating and testing, and coping skills. A number less than 1.0 indicates a climate that is hindering of both the learning efforts (cognitive domain) and coping activities (affective domain) of the learners.

Another procedure is simply to compute the percentage of statements that fall into Categories 1, 2 and 3 by dividing the number of statements in those three categories by the total number of statements in Categories 1, 2, 3 and 5, 6 and 7 (omitting Category 4) and multiplying by 100. Hence, in the first cited case, 25 verbalizations in Categories 1, 2, 3 and 50 altogether in Categories 1, 2, 3 plus 5, 6 and 7, the result is 50%. In the second case, with 50 verbalizations in 1, 2, 3 and 75 in 1, 2, 3 and 5, 6, 7, the result is 66-2/3%.

Self-Evaluation of Teacher Verbalization Pattern and Follow-up

Once the teacher (after 12 or so hours of training) has developed skill in reliably and objectively using the Climate Index, he should make a tape recording of any of his classes. He should then categorize his ver-

---

*See Social-Emotional Climate Index: Criteria of Teacher-Statement Categories and Frame of Reference appended.
[2]John Withall, "The Development of a Technique for the Measurement of Social Emotional Climate in Classrooms," *Journal of Experimental Education* (March 1949), Vol. XVII, No. 3.

balizations and examine the proportions that fall not only into the learner-oriented (1, 2, 3 categories) and the teacher-oriented (5, 6, 7 categories) but also make note of the explicit proportion, category by category, of his verbalizations. By this we mean that he should identify the number and percentage of his statements falling into each of the categories[3] (in order of importance):

No. 2 (acceptant and clarifying)
No. 3 (problem-structuring)
No. 1 (approving and commending)
No. 6 (reproving and deprecating)
No. 5 (controlling)
No. 7 (teacher self-supportive)

After the teacher has identified reliably and objectively the proportion of his verbalizations falling into the learner-oriented and teacher-oriented categories and after he has noted the proportion of his verbalizations falling into each (excepting No. 4) of the categories, he should then, with the help of a trusted colleague or friend, begin to develop some hypotheses regarding the contributions (negative or positive) his verbalizations are making to the overall climate in his classroom and on the facilitative or hindering vectors of those verbalizations with regard to his learners. After this diagnosis has been made remedial activities may be identified and implemented. This is the most difficult part of the operation. This is where the pay-off comes.

Conclusion

By means of the Climate Index, which has been used to observe teachers' verbal behaviors in elementary schools, secondary schools and colleges, one can reliably and validly categorize the verbalizations of the teacher. On the basis of this analysis of the teacher's verbalizations, an evaluation of the climate in a classroom can be made. There is research evidence[4,5,6,7] that the social-emotional climate in any teaching-learning situation is related to the quality of the problem-solving, inquiring and coping activities of the learners.

Social-Emotional Climate Index

John Withall

Criteria of Teacher-Statement Categories
1. *Learner Supportive* statements or questions

These are teacher-statements or questions that express agreement with the ideas, actions or opinions of the learner or that commend or reassure the learner. Agreement is frequently expressed by a monosyllabic response such as "Yes," "Right," "Uh-huh," and the like. Commendation or reassurance may be stated in terms of

a. class-accepted criteria or goals or
b. the private goals and subjective criteria of the teacher.

---

[3]Statements that are placed in category 4 are all customarily ignored in computation and evaluation once they have been categorized. They represent situation-structuring verbalizations, administrative detail statements, polite amenities, and verbatim repetition. Category 4 verbalizations tend to be irrelevant to the climate phenomenon and to the facilitative or non-facilitative operations of the teacher.
[4]Kenneth G. Vayda, "A Study of the Relationship Between Classroom Social-Emotional Climate and Group Problem-Solving Behavior in Elementary School Children." Unpublished doctoral dissertation. The Pennsylvania State University, University Park, 1967.
[5]William F. Alexander, "An Investigation of the Effects of Teacher Verbal Behavior as Categorized by Withall's Climate Index on the Development of Certain Manipulative Skills in Grades 7, 8 and 9. Unpublished doctoral dissertation. The Pennsylvania State University, University Park, 1969.
[6]Hugh V. Perkins, "Climate Influences Group Learning," *Journal of Education Research* (1951) 45, pp. 115–19.
[7]Ned A. Flanders, "Personal-Social Anxiety as a Factor in Learning." Unpublished doctoral dissertation, The University of Chicago, Illinois, 1949.

The *dominant intent* of these statements or questions is to *praise, encourage* or *bolster the learner.*

2. *Acceptant* or *Clarifying* statements or questions

These are teacher-statements or questions that either

   a. accept, that is, evidence considerable understanding by the teacher of, or

   b. clarify, that is, restate clearly and succinctly in the teacher's words the ideational or the feeling content of the learner's statement. The *dominant intent* of these teacher-responses is *to help the learner* to gain insight into his problem, that is, define his "real" problem and its solution in more operational terms.

3. *Problem-Structuring* statements or questions

Problem-structuring responses by the teacher offer facts or ideas or opinions to the learner about

   a. phenomena

   b. procedures

in a nonthreatening and objective manner. These responses contain NO element of advising or recommending the adoption of certain ideas or procedures. Problem-structuring responses are frequently posed as questions that seek further information from the learner about the problem confronting him; or they may be statements that offer information to the learner about his problem. The learner is free to accept or to reject in part or in entirety the facts or opinions that are presented to him. Problem-structuring responses may be questions that the teacher asks (1) to further increase her own understanding of what the learner has said or (2) to increase the precision of the learner's statement of the problem. Problem-structuring responses are problem-centered rather than either teacher or learn-

er-centered; nevertheless, they do tend to sustain the learner by facilitating his problem-solving activities.

4. *Neutral* statements evidencing no supportive intent

These statements are neither teacher-sustaining, learner-sustaining nor problem-centered. They constitute a small percentage of the total teacher-responses. These responses include statements in which the teacher: (1) questions herself aloud; (2) repeats verbatim a statement that the learner just made; (3) uses a polite formality, etc. Statements having to do with administrative procedure—the room in which the class will meet, the hour at which a conference will occur (especially after consensus has been achieved), fall into this category.

5. *Directive* statements or questions

These are teacher-statements or questions that advise the learner regarding a course of action or his future behavior and which narrowly limit his choice or offer no choice. These statements recommend to the learner the facts or procedures that the teacher proffers him. These statements or questions convey the impression to the learner that the teacher expects and hopes that he will follow her prompting and that she will approve if he does. The *intent* of these responses is to have the learner take up the teacher's point of view and pursue a course of action that she advocates.

6. *Reproving, Disapproving* or *Disparaging* statements or questions

By means of these statements a teacher may express complete or partial disapproval of the ideas, behavior and, to her, personality weaknesses of the learner. The teacher's internalized societal values largely enter into these responses. By means of these statements some teachers believe they are fulfilling their responsibility of inculcating in young people society's standards of acceptable and desirable behavior and achievement. The *intent* of these statements is

a. to represent to the learner societal values as the teacher sees them;
b. to admonish the learner for unacceptable behavior and to deter him from repeating it in the future;
c. to impress on the learner the fact that he has not met the criteria for successful achievement that the teacher accepts.

7. *Teacher-Supportive* statements or questions

These are statements or questions in which the teacher refers to herself and expresses a defensive attitude or refers to her present or past interests, activities or possessions with the purpose of reassuring herself and of confirming her position or her ideas in the eyes of those around her. The *dominant intent* of these teacher-responses is to *assert*, to *defend*, or to *justify* the teacher. Statements in which the teacher perseverates on an idea, belief or suggestion would fall in this category. By "perseveration" is meant a persisting in, a reiteration of, and a rigid advocacy of an idea or opinion by the teacher despite additional data being presented to her that calls for a re-examination of the original idea or opinion.

A Frame of Reference and Procedure To Facilitate Categorization of Teacher-Statements[8,9]

Each teacher-statement contains *one* of two dominant kinds of intent. These are either

a. intent to sustain the teacher and his behavior (teacher-centered statements) or
b. intent to sustain the learner and his behavior (learner-centered statements and issue-centered statements are included under this intent).

By analysis of both the *Context* and the *Content* of a teacher statement it may be possible to determine whether the dominant intent of a statement is to sustain the teacher or the learner.

Once the dominant intent of a teacher-statement has been ascertained, one can proceed to determine the technique by which the support is conveyed.

1. If the statement is intended primarily to *sustain the teacher*, one or possibly a combination of the two following techniques may be used:

   a. reproof of the learner (category 6)
   b. directing or advising the learner (category 5).

   Frequently the intent of the statement is to sustain the teacher yet neither of the above techniques is used. In that event the statement is simply a self-supportive remark that defends the teacher or evidences perseveration in support of the teacher's position or ideas. (category 7)

2. If the intent of a statement is to *sustain the learner* then one or possibly a combination of the two following techniques may be used:

   a. clarification and acceptance of the learner's feelings or ideas (category 2)
   b. problem-structuring statements (category 3).

   Frequently the intent of a statement is to sustain the learner yet neither of the above techniques is used. In that event the statement is simply one that reassures, commends, agrees with or other-

[8]John Withall, "The Development of a Technique for the Measurement of Social-Emotional Climate in Classrooms," *Journal of Experimental Education* (March 1949), Vol. XVIII, No. 3.
[9]John Withall, "Impact on Learners of Climate Created by the Teacher"—film. (University Park, 16802: Bureau of Audio-Visual Services, The Pennsylvania State University).

wise sustains the learner (category 1). Infrequently a teacher-statement may have no dominant intent to sustain either the teacher or the learner. If the statement represents neither of the techniques in the two intent areas nor gives evidence of being one of the more general kinds of supporting statements then the statement can be considered to have no intent to support and should be placed in category 4.

Recourse to the learner-statement or behavior before and after a teacher response, particularly when one encounters a statement in which the intent is difficult to ascertain, is sometimes helpful in categorizing the teacher's statements.

Tally Sheet for Categorizations of Teacher-Verbalizations

Social Emotional Classroom Climate Teacher:						
Observer: Date: Subject:						
Category 1 Commendatory	Category 2 Acceptant	Category 3 Problem-Structuring	Category 4 Neutral	Category 5 Directive	Category 6 Reproving	Category 7 Teacher-Supportive

Evaluating Settings for Learning

Thelma Harms

EDITORS' QUESTIONS:

1. Develop a procedure for the evaluation of the learning environment which takes into account all of the following factors:
   a. verbal behavior of the teacher
   b. availability and accessibility of materials
   c. organization of physical facilities
   d. provision for interpersonal activities
   e. opportunities for self-expression and individual development
   f. structuring and scheduling of learning experiences.

2. How can the checklist provided by this article assist the teacher in developing and using instructional strategies that are consistent with both the educational environment and the capabilities and needs of learners.

3. Identify the questions in the checklist which you consider extremely valuable and indicate why you feel as you do.

4. Use the checklist to identify deficiencies in your own classroom, or if you are not presently teaching, visit an elementary classroom and discover the areas in which it is deficient. Make recommendations for overcoming the shortcomings noted. In view of the many constraints under which educational processes function, *for the purposes of this exercise only*, concentrate on changes which can either be immediately implemented or which require little or no monetary outlay to accomplish.

5. To what extent does the checklist assist the teacher in assessing the availability of opportunities for affective learning and the development of psychomotor skills? Cite, as examples, specific items which support your conclusion.

It is very helpful during an evaluation to look at the environment from a child's point of view. To a child, everything that is present in a setting is a stimulus. He responds to what is really there, not only to what we as adults are aware is there. The way people treat him is as real a part of his environment as the materials on the shelves or the space provided for block building. The teacher's tone of voice, the way she walks and her facial expression contribute to the overall atmosphere. Similarly, the child's interaction with other children is an important component of the school setting. Everything present in the environment, even the spacial arrangement, communicates to the child how to live in that setting.

Thelma Harms, M.A., is currently Head Teacher at the Harold E. Jones Child Study Center of the University of California at Berkeley. She is also an Instructor through the University of California Extension Division and is pursuing a doctorate in Early Childhood Education.

Materials that are in good condition and placed far apart on open shelves tell a child that the materials are valued, that they are meant to be considered, and that a child may take them off the shelf by himself. When they are taken off the shelf, they leave a big, empty space so it is easy to put them back where they belong. What kind of a message does a child get from open shelves crowded with an odd assortment of materials, few with all the pieces put together? What kind of a message does he get from a closed cupboard?

Physical environment is a powerful means of communication. To sensitize yourself to physical environment, set yourself the task, every time you walk into a new setting, of reading the messages contained in the room arrangement. The room with a speaker's stand in front of rows of chairs tells us something about the predicted relationship of teacher to student, and student to student in the class. Chairs in a circle imply another kind of learning interaction.

Children respond to the messages given to them by the physical environment, the activities and the time schedule, so we must become increasingly aware of the total environment we are creating for them. Often problems occur because contradictory messages are being simultaneously sent out by the different components making up the environment. The teacher may be trying to prevent running and sliding while the large, slick expanse of floor in the center of the room is inviting the children to run and slide. Improvement in the children's use of materials in that situation might require a reorganization of the physical environment rather than improvement in interpersonal skills or changes in activities or time schedule. In another school, however, the physical environment may be well defined, the interpersonal atmosphere warm and accept-

ing, but the children may need the challenge of more complex activities, or they may need longer periods of unbroken time to become involved in the activities offered. Each setting for learning needs to be looked at individually because it is a unique combination of children, staff and setting.

Suggestions for Using the Check List

The following list of questions is organized into four categories. Each category contributes in a major way to the environment as experienced by the child. The questions are meant to help you identify both strengths and problems in your own setting. Many schools have found it helpful to give each staff member a checklist to think about for several days before the evaluation meeting. Then, when the entire staff meets, each person is prepared to share his observations and suggestions.

Evaluation Checklist

The Physical Environment

1. Can quiet and noisy activities go on without disturbing one another? Is there an appropriate place for each?
2. Is a variety of materials available on open shelves for the children to use when they are interested? Are materials on shelves well spaced for clarity?
3. Are materials stored in individual units so that children can use them alone without being forced to share with a group?
4. Are activity centers defined so that children know where to use the materials?
5. Are tables or rug areas provided for convenient use of materials in each activity center?
6. Is self-help encouraged by having

materials in good condition and always stored in the same place?

7. Are cushioning materials used to cut down extraneous noise—rug under blocks, pads under knock-out bench?

8. Are setup and cleanup simple? Are these expected parts of the child's activity?

9. Have learning opportunities been carefully planned in the outdoor area? Painting, crafts, block building, carpentry, gardening, pets, sand and water all lend themselves to learning experiences outdoors.

10. Is the children's work displayed attractively at the child's eye level?

11. Do the children feel in control of and responsible for the physical environment?

The Interpersonal Environment

1. Is there a feeling of mutual respect between adults and children, children and children?

2. Is the physical environment enough under control so that the major part of the adults' time is spent in observing or participating with children?

3. Can children engage in activities without being disturbed or distracted by others?

4. Do adults observe children's activity and intervene only when it is beneficial to the child?

5. Do adults have "growth goals" for each child based on the needs they have observed in each child? Is individualized curriculum used to reach these goals?

6. Do children feel safe with one another?

7. Is competition avoided by arranging materials in individual units, limiting the number of children participating in an activity at one time, insuring the

fairness of turns by starting a waiting list on which the child can see his name keeping his place in line?

8. Do the adults show children how to help themselves? Are children encouraged to learn from one another?

9. Are there opportunities for children to play alone, participate in a small group, and participate in a large group?

10. When limits are placed, do adults use reasoning and consistently follow through? Are limits enforced?

11. Are the adults models of constructive behavior and healthy attitudes?

12. Is there an overall warm interpersonal environment?

Activities to Stimulate Development

1. Are there many opportunities for dramatic play: large housekeeping corner, small dollhouse, dress-up clothes for boys as well as girls, puppets?

2. Is there a variety of basic visual art media: painting, drawing, clay, salt-flour dough, wood-glue sculpture, fingerpaint, collage?

3. Is music a vital part of the program: records, group singing, instruments, dancing?

4. Is language stimulation varied: reading books, games with feel boxes, flannel board stories, questions and answers, conversation, lotto games, classification games? Are limits enforced through verbal control and reasoning?

5. Are there small manipulative toys to build eye-hand coordination and finger dexterity?

6. Are there some opportunities to follow patterns or achieve a predetermined goal: puzzles, design blocks, dominos, matching games?

7. Do children do real things like cooking, planting seeds, caring for animals?

8. Are field trips planned to give experi-

ence with the world around us? Is there adequate preparation and follow-up after trips?

9. Are there repeated opportunities for children to use similar materials? Are materials available in a graded sequence so that children develop skills gradually?

10. Are children involved in suggesting and planning activities? How is free choice built into the program?

11. Are new activities developed by teachers as they are suggested by the interests of individual children?

12. Is the range of activities varied enough to present a truly divergent curriculum? Are there opportunities for learning through exploration, guided discovery, problem solving, repetition, intuition, imitation, etc.? Is there provision for children to learn through their senses as well as verbally?

Schedule

1. Is the time sequence of the school day clear to both teachers and children?

2. Has the schedule been designed to suit the physical plan and particular group of children in the school?

3. Are long periods of time scheduled to permit free choice of activities and companions?

4. Are other groupings provided for in the schedule, e.g., small group activities one to one adult-child contacts, larger group meetings, etc.?

5. Is the schedule periodically reevaluated and modified? Are changes in schedule and the reasons for these changes made clear to both staff and children?

Extending Your Experience

Visiting other schools and using the checklist as an observation guide is a good way to extend your experience. There are also some helpful films and books you might want to use as resource materials. A selected list of films, books and pamphlets to extend your experience with environment follows:

FILMS

"My Art is Me." Univ. of California Film Media Center, Berkeley, Calif.

"Organizing for Free Play." Project Head Start, Office of Economic Opportunity, Washington, D.C.

BOOKS

Almy, Millie C. *Ways of Studying Children.* New York: Teachers College Press, Columbia University, 1959.

Ashton-Warner, Sylvia. *Teacher.* New York: Simon & Schuster, 1963.

Pitcher, E. G., Lasher, N. G., et al. *Helping Young Children Learn.* Columbus, Ohio: Charles E. Merrill Books, 1966.

Read, Katherine. *The Nursery School: A Human Relations Laboratory.* Philadelphia: W. B. Saunders Co., 1971.

PAMPHLETS

"Space, Arrangement, Beauty in School." #101, Association for Childhood Education International, 3615 Wisconsin Ave., N.W., Washington, D.C. 20016.

"Let's Play Outdoors." #101, National Association for the Education of Young Children, 1834 Connecticut Ave., N.W., Washington, D.C. 20009.

"Nursery School Settings—Invitation to What?" #102, NAEYC.

"Space for Play: The Youngest Children." #111, NAEYC.

"Housing for Early Childhood Education." Bull #22-A, ACEI.

Recommended Readings: Evaluation of Educational Programs

Allen, P. M. "Student Evaluation Dilemma," *Today's Education* 58 (1969): 48–50.

Baker, R. L. "Curriculum Evaluation," *Review of Educational Research* 39 (1969): 339–358.

Conklin, K. R. "Educational Evaluation and Intuition," *Educational Forum* 34 (1970): 323–332.

DiLorenzo, L. T. and Salter, R. "An Evaluation Study of Prekindergarten Programs for Educationally Disadvantaged Children: Followup and Replication," *Exceptional Children* 35 (1968): 111–120.

Dizney, Henry *Classroom Evaluation for Teachers.* Dubuque, Iowa: Wm. C. Brown Company Publishers, 1971.

Ebel, Robert L. "Prospects for Evaluation of Learning," *The Bulletin of the National Association of Secondary School Principals* 52 (1968): 32–42.

Flanagan, J. C. "Evaluating Educational Outcomes," *Science Education* 59 (1966): 248–251.

Gronlund, Norman E. *Measurement and Evaluation in Teaching.* New York: The Macmillan Co., 1970.

Guba, E. G. "The Failure of Educational Evaluation," *Educational Technology* 9 (1969): 29–38.

Harrison, A. and Scriven, E. G. "Does Evaluation Preclude Learning?" *School and Community* 56 (1970): 24–25.

Karmel, Louis J. *Measurement and Evaluation in the Schools.* New York: The Macmillan Co., 1970.

Lien, Arnold J. *Measurement and Evaluation of Learning.* 2nd ed. Dubuque, Iowa: Wm. C. Brown Company Publishers, 1971.

Lindvall, C. M. and Cox, Richard R. (with the collaboration of John O. Bolvin). *Evaluation as a Tool in Curriculum Develop-*ment: The IPI Evaluation Program. Chicago, Illinois: Rand McNally & Company, 1970.

McFarland, Susan J. and Hereford, Carl F. *Statistics and Measurement in the Classroom: A Book of Readings.* Dubuque, Iowa: Wm. C. Brown Company Publishers, 1972.

Nelson, Clarence H. *Measurement and Evaluation in the Classroom.* New York: The Macmillan Co., 1970.

Noll, Victor H. and Noll, Rachel P., eds. *Readings in Educational Psychology.* 2nd ed. New York: The Macmillan Co., 1968.

Palardy, Michael J. *Elementary School Curriculum: An Anthology of Trends and Challenges.* New York: The Macmillan Co., 1971.

Rauch, Sidney J. "How to Evaluate a Reading Program," *The Reading Teacher* 24 (1970): 244–250.

Scriven, M. *The Methodology of Evaluation.* AERA Monograph Series on Curriculum Evaluation, 1967. No. 1, 39–83.

Simpson, Ray H. *Teacher Self-Evaluation.* New York: The Macmillan Co., 1966.

Stufflebeam, D. S. "The Use and Abuse of Evaluation," *Theory Into Practice* 6 (1967): 126–133.

Taylor, Peter and Cowley, Doris *Readings in Curriculum Evaluation.* Dubuque, Iowa: Wm. C. Brown Company Publishers, 1972.

Tyler, Ralph, Gagné, Robert M. and Scriven, Michael *Perspectives of Curriculum Evaluation.* Chicago, Illinois: Rand McNally & Co., 1967.

Wilhelms, F. T. "Evaluation as Feedback." In F. T. Wilhelms, ed. *Evaluation as Feedback and Guide.* Washington, D.C.: Association for Supervision and Curriculum Development, 1967, 2–17.

The Need for
Accountability in Education

A topic that is causing a great deal of controversy in educational circles today is the need for educational accountability. The concept of accountability has to do, primarily, with the evaluation of the extent to which resources, human and otherwise, contribute to the achievement of desirable educational outcomes. Since resources, in all except completely automated processes, do not produce results without human intervention, efforts in connection with accountability have concentrated upon the establishment of responsibility for results on the part of those charged with the task of achieving educational objectives. Just exactly *who* is to be held accountable, for *what, where, when* and *how* are questions that remain to be answered. Efforts to establish accountability are currently moving in two directions at the same time: (1) toward the development of systems of accountability within existing institutional arrangements, utilizing present staff and other educational resources and (2) toward the hiring out of

instructional processes through "performance contracting." Both of these tendencies are examined in the selections which comprise this section.

A critical look at the question of accountability is presented by Mills and Mills. They concede the inevitability of accountability, but suggest that certain preparatory steps must be taken before functional systems of accountability can be successfully implemented. Emphasis is given the need for attention to economic and managerial considerations in establishing and maintaining accountability—especially the need for adequate communication. A participative approach to the development of systems of accountability is advocated for the purpose of motivating acceptance, cooperation and personal commitment on the part of those affected.

Harms, in *Specifying Objectives for Performance Contracts,* likens educational performance contracts to product and service contracts of industry and the professions—

387

a major feature of which is proof of performance as a prerequisite of payment. He delineates a number of considerations which must be taken into account in specifying objectives for both product output systems and process performance systems. The importance of selecting appropriate assessment devices and of developing reliable monitoring procedures is also considered.

A guide for the drafting of performance contracts is outlined by Mayrhofer. He identifies certain specifications which should be included in a binding agreement and issues a number of warnings concerning potential problem areas. Particular attention is given the desirability of utilizing performance contracting as a means of developing the "in-house" capability to continue those practices resulting in enhanced learner performance.

After a thorough analysis of both the selections and the recommended readings provided in this section, the student should be prepared to:

1. Assess the relevance of accountability to her role as a classroom teacher.
2. Distinguish between product output systems and process performance systems and be able to adjust her performance to coincide with the emphasis of either approach.
3. Propose ways in which greater control over educational resources can be provided the classroom teacher without diminishing administrative authority.
4. Make suggestions for establishing accountability at the instructional level.
5. Take part in the preparation of a proposal for a performance contract.
6. Cooperate with fellow teachers, students, administrators and other interested parties in the development of a system of accountability that is feasible, efficient and just.

A Critical Analysis of the Concept of Accountability

Belen C. Mills
and Ralph A. Mills

EDITORS' QUESTIONS:

1. Apply the concept of opportunity cost to the selection of a particular instructional medium.

2. What can you do to influence the type of system of accountability that is adopted by your school system? Make specific suggestions, and indicate ways of gaining support for your ideas.

3. To what extent should the desires of parents, students and other interest groups be taken into consideration in the developing of educational objectives? Support your answer.

4. Do you agree with the authors that there are inherent difficulties in attempting to judge teaching effectiveness in terms of pupils' learnings? If not, why not? If so, offer suggestions for overcoming such difficulties.

5. Evaluate the feasibility of the participative approach advocated by the authors for establishing accountability. What modifications do you recommend? Support your answer.

6. Clarify your own thinking concerning accountability by writing a proposal for the establishment of a system of accountability geared to the unique needs of your own school system. Be sure to specify who should be held accountable, and to stipulate procedures for implementation (including criteria for the evaluation of performance, techniques for disseminating information and provisions for insuring equitable application).

43

Currently, a topic of great concern, among educators, is the subject of educational accountability. The purpose of this paper is to examine the nature of, and need for accountability, and to indicate some of the issues which must be resolved before a viable system of accountability can be established.

The Nature of Accountability

It is important that accountability not be confused with accounting—at least not in the sense of "bookkeeping." For many years, educators have been able to account for expenditures with a great deal of facility. The true accountant, however, is considerably more than a bookkeeper. He not only ascertains how money has been spent, but provides, through summarization and analysis, the bases for managerial decisions. It is in this light of the accounting process that accountability should be viewed. The dis-

Belen C. Mills is Assistant Professor of Elementary Education, Florida State University, Tallahassee and author of *Understanding the Young Child and His Curriculum*, New York: The Macmillan Co. (1972).
Ralph A. Mills is Supervisor of Instruction, Georgia Center for Continuing Education, The University of Georgia–Waycross Center, where he teaches courses in business and economics.

covery of a reliable procedure for determining the cost of a unit of education would enable the classroom teacher and the administrator to seek ways of either achieving comparable progress at a lower cost, (thus freeing funds for ancillary applications), or else to attain a greater level of efficiency for the same cost.

The concept of accountability is not limited to accounting, however, but encompasses the entire scope of management and economics. The concept of opportunity cost is particularly relevant. The simplest working definition of opportunity cost is "what one must give up in orde. to undertake a particular course of action." It is not necessarily a dollars-and-cents measure. For example, if one decides to implement the "open-concept" organizational structure, there are no doubt numerous benefits to be derived. However, its implementation precludes the enjoyment of any benefits which might have accrued from the utilization of an alternative structuring (except for those benefits that are common to both approaches). Good management, whether in education, hospital administration, military logistics or industry, requires the application of economics, sociology, political science, psychology, accounting and intuition—and a great deal more. However, in a dollars-and-cents world where even blood and water have their respective prices, the economics of education is becoming one of the crucial variables in the educational process.

In designing any system of educational accountability, one should be mindful of the economic constraints under which he operates. Resources—physical, financial, instructional, administrative and informational—are always limited, whereas the demand for educational services and the demand for improvement in the quality of these services are virtually unlimited. Therefore, the economic question involved is "How can the educational system best satisfy the demands made upon it by society, students, and educators themselves, with the resources it has or can reasonably expect to obtain?" It is not a question of sacrificing professional ethics and quality education on the altar of materialism—which must never be permitted—but rather the problem of obtaining the greatest possible benefit through the most efficient utilization of available means.

Accountability has occasionally been referred to as a new theory of education. Deterline(3) has pointed out that it is not theoretical. It should also be asserted, most emphatically, that neither is it new! A degree of accountability has always existed in education. Given that the fundamental aim of any educational process is to equip the student to adjust to the exigencies of a dynamic environment, thus enabling him to assume his rightful place as a desirable and productive member of society, one elemental unit of accountability is predetermined. Ultimately, the one held accountable on behalf of the entire educational system is the individual student. In the event of educational failure—whether officially recognized or unrecognized—he is the one who pays! The current emphasis upon educational accountability has resulted, in part, from a recognition of the basic unfairness of such a practice. If there is any connection whatever between teaching and learning, we are partially to blame for student failures, and must share the responsibility! It is high time we abandoned the "some-must-fail" philosophy (an outgrowth of the adoration of the bell-shaped curve), stopped using the classroom as a screening device for identifying education's rejects and concentrated our efforts on helping each student to achieve his optimum potential thereby enabling each student to succeed.

The Need for a Viable System of Accountability

Today, primarily from the youth of this nation, one frequently hears the charge that formal education is irrelevant. Further, student unrest, uprisings and demands for specifically-oriented programs bear evidence to student awareness of the failure of the contemporary educational system to meet the needs of at least some of its constituents. Ever more rapidly, a *de facto* bilateral system of accountability is emerging in education as students seek to gain, by every possible means, the power to evaluate their evaluators.

This process is more noticeable on college campuses, but even within the scope of elementary and secondary education its influence is felt. It is not uncommon to read of instances in which groups of disgruntled parents have been very articulate in their criticism of educational practices and results. Some have even gone so far as to physically take over schools. Lessinger(7) tells of one instance in which this occurred and indicates that some parents feel that rank amateurs can do no poorer job of conducting a school than the self-styled professionals who, under more normal circumstances, perform that function. Moreover, the constituencies of many school districts have refused to vote additional funds for educational purposes in spite of increasing costs and the need for better facilities as well as additional staffing. When queried, many voters respond that they are dissatisfied with the results obtained by the particular educational system, and do not intend to vote for additional funding until evidence of improvement is provided. It matters not that these individuals may have no tractable conception of the kind of results they might consider desirable, the crucial funding is missing nonetheless.

It would appear, therefore, that the appropriate question to be posed by educators is not "Should we be subject to a system of accountability?" It should be obvious, in view of current circumstances that this is not a matter of choice. Given the undeniable *fact* of accountability, they must decide whether to be content to submit to evaluation by those outside the profession, or to seek to develop a system of internal accountability that is noticeably superior to any external alternative thus insuring that evaluation is performed by those who are best qualified for the task.

Crucial Issues for Consideration

More realistic, and potentially more valuable, questions which might be asked would include the following:

1. What objectives are both desirable and feasible?
2. What are the appropriate criteria for evaluation?
3. What procedures can be developed for the evaluation of affective learning?
4. How can the effects of administrative policies and procedures upon educational achievement be determined?
5. Who should be charged with the responsibility for setting standards?
6. Can intangible and future results of the educational process be measured? If so, how?
7. Can a system of accountability be devised that will justify its costs of development and administration?

8. What agency, individual or group of individuals could most objectively and efficiently perform the evaluation function?

9. Can standardized criteria that are applicable to all school systems be developed?

10. What safeguards are necessary in order to preserve academic freedom?

These and many other questions must be considered before a system of accountability in education can become a reality.

Providing answers to all of these questions cannot possibly be accomplished within the scope of a paper such as this. Nevertheless, a number of these and related questions will now be considered in a somewhat more detailed manner in order to ascertain some of the factors which must be taken into consideration in attempting to provide answers.

The Need for Effective Communication and Participation

A great deal has been written in an attempt to answer the first question, "What objectives are both desirable and feasible?" Some of these efforts concern themselves with the identification of the discrepancy between "what is" and "what should be."(4) Many different but related techniques have been suggested for the determination of appropriate goals—for example, needs assessment, system analysis, national assessment and the like.(5) It seems to be assumed, generally, that educational administrators will be the primary initiators of such procedures. Such an approach fails to take into account the nature of education as a service activity—one which serves a complex and varied constituency. At least six groups should be given the opportunity to

have their opinions considered in the determination of educational objectives, namely: the business community, parents of pupils, the general public, the various professional and union organizations in education, classroom teachers and the students themselves. If the opinions of any of these groups are ignored, one runs the risk of losing its cooperation and support. For example, the business community may prefer not to employ graduates of an educational system the goals of which it views as irrelevant. Professional associations or teachers' unions may resist what they consider the imposition of externally–determined goals. Parents and other taxpayers may refuse to provide necessary funding because they are dissatisfied with both stated objectives and educational results. Finally, classroom teachers and students may give less than full cooperation because of a lack of personal commitment—a lack which might well have been avoided had they been allowed to participate in the development of the objectives they were expected to achieve.

While a participative approach is apt to provide numerous insights concerning the desirability of certain objectives, it is not very likely to be particularly valuable in assessing the feasibility of the goals proposed. There is usually a considerable discrepancy between what people would like to have and what they are willing to pay for—and the latter, as often as not, defies prediction. However, it may be that such an approach will be helpful in fostering an awareness, on the part of the participants, of the costs involved in developing quality educational programs and in enhancing their willingness to assume the responsibility of meeting these costs. Ultimately, however, the question of feasibility must be decided through the use of a technique that is capable of identifying the most efficient method of utilizing existing resources to achieve desired objectives. A number of procedures for attempting this have already been developed and are being utilized. Among them are the Planning, Programming, Budgeting System (PPBS)—a procedure for discovering the relationships between desired results and the costs of achieving them for various alternative approaches—and various other methods–means selection techniques involving a combination educational-engineering/economic-feasibility approach. Systems analysis (including both mission analysis and task analysis) has also been found to be a useful tool in assessing the feasibility of proposed objectives.(5)

The Problem of Behavioral Objectives

It is sometimes alleged that the requirements of accountability necessitate the statement of performance objectives in behavioral terms. While the effectiveness of such an approach has not yet been fully determined, the statement of desired results in terms of precise, observable behaviors under specified conditions does, at least in some instances, facilitate the evaluative process. However, there are some limitations of such an approach that should be considered. Some learnings may not lead to observable behavior within the period of observation. Learnings within the affective domain are not directly observable, may lead only to changes in attitudes and *never* manifest themselves in overt behavior, and even if they do, it may be difficult to determine the underlying motivation for a particular act. There are at least three inherent difficulties that are apt to be encountered in connection with any attempt to judge teaching effectiveness in terms of pupils' learnings:

1. Some learning may have taken place which cannot be detected, for example, cognitive learning which does not result in observable behavior and learnings occurring within the affective domain. Also, the results of learning are not limited to the school experience and behavioral modification may take place only after twenty years or so even though it is the result of a cumulative process, the first step of which occurred during the child's sojourn as an elementary pupil.

2. Things are not always what they seem. A particular response may appear to be indicative of complex processes of thought when, in fact, it is the mere parroting of *borrowed wisdom*.

3. The connection between teaching and learning has not yet been clearly established. A particular pupil may learn not because of, but *in spite of* the teacher's influence. On the other hand, even the best efforts of master-teachers may be ineffective in motivating learning in a particular child.

Notwithstanding the difficulties inherent in the utilization of behavioral objectives, there are certain advantages afforded by their use. Observed behavior does constitute an indication, however imperfect it may be, of whether learning has taken place. When statements of behavioral objectives are sufficiently precise, it is relatively easy to determine how closely observed behavior approximates targeted behavior.

An Equitable System of Evaluation

"What should be the scope of the accountability process?" is almost certain to be an unpopular question but one which needs to be asked. It is closely related to another question: "Who should do the evaluating?'' These questions have already been answered by some. Their answer is: "Let *me* evaluate *him* and not vice-versa!'' Hence, we find members of school boards and legislators advocating a crackdown on classroom teachers, members of the public demanding that school boards be held accountable, administrators preparing detailed plans for the establishment of accountability in all areas of their supervisory domain and individual teachers and spokesmen for teachers' unions and professional associations speaking out against the unfairness of accountability aimed at teachers alone. One is tempted to inquire: *"Where does the buck stop?"* If accountability is "The product of a process in which an agent, public or private, *entering into a contractual agreement to perform a service will be held answerable for performing according to agreed upon terms, within a stipulated time period and with a stipulated use of resources and performance standards,"* (2) then *everyone* even remotely connected with as important an activity as education *should be* subject to accountability. But this very definition of accountability indicates the difficulty of attempting to implement accountability immediately under existing circumstances. To begin with, "agreed upon terms" have never been adequately detailed, stipulations concerning resource use leave much to be desired and performance standards have only recently begun to receive the attention that will be required in order to rescue them from the realm of subjectivity. The phrase "agreed upon terms" is especially worthy of attention because it denotes a need for a participative approach to accountability. No one, be he a member of the school board, a superintendent, a reading specialist, a university professor or an elementary teacher, should be held accountable for the achievement of certain specified objectives unless he is concurrently given a degree of control

over resources that is sufficient to permit him to accomplish these objectives. If we may be permitted to borrow a concept from Law, no *reasonable prudent man* may be expected to agree to terms which do not specify such a degree of control.

Questions like "Who should be charged with the responsibility of setting standards?", "What agency, individual or group of individuals could most objectively and efficiently perform the evaluation function?" and the like have to do not only with efficiency but with fairness or equity as well. It would not be especially helpful to establish a system of accountability for the purpose of preventing teachers from proceeding on the basis of intuition if the criteria established for evaluating their performance consisted of the principal's intuitive insights. His subjective "feelings" might or might not be superior to those of any particular teacher.

Suggested Preparatory Steps for the Implementation of Accountability

In order to foster the efficient functioning of whatever system of accountability is adopted, it is suggested that the following five preparatory steps be taken prior to its implementation:

1. Secure agreement concerning desirable and feasible objectives.
2. Establish performance standards that are acceptable to those charged with the responsibility of meeting such standards.
3. Determine whether the proposed system of evaluation is considered equitable by those it affects.
4. Establish an evaluative agency composed of representatives of all levels of endeavor subject to accountability, making sure that there are ac-

ceptable criteria for both the selection and the removal of members.

5. Provide an effective feedback mechanism to disseminate information so that all those affected are provided knowledge of the policies and regulations adopted.

If successful, these procedures could lead to the realization of a situation not unlike the *rule of law* wherein adherence to standards is maintained because the governed consider those standards fair and just and those who refuse to be governed by generally accepted standards of conduct are not permitted to continue endangering the rest of society. The analogy between standards of performance and law breaks down, of course, when the type of incentive pay sometimes utilized in connection with performance contracting is considered. There can hardly be works of supererogation if the least that is required of each is that he do his best. Law enforcement agencies are not given to paying bonuses to those who refrain from committing burglary or running stop signs. If, however, teachers are to be subject to disciplinary procedures for failure to meet minimum standards, considerations of equity may require that they also be rewarded for significantly exceeding such standards. Incentive pay for teachers may be advantageous provided that money is an effective motivator (several studies tend to indicate that other incentives provide stronger motivation) and difficulties in measuring achievement can be overcome.

In conclusion, accountability is a fact of life. We can neither stop it, nor escape it. However, if it does not turn out the way we would like it to, we will have only ourselves to blame. We should insist that *all* assume their portion of responsibility and be willing to accept our own share. Economic and managerial considerations are believed to be of paramount importance in developing systems of accountability, but only to the extent that they serve desirable educational purposes. A participative approach is believed to be a superior method of developing and implementing systems of accountability and suggestions have been offered for insuring that the approach adopted is equitable for all concerned. Nevertheless, many questions must still be resolved before an efficient system of accountability can become a reality. The solution of these problems and the ultimate establishment of such a system or systems will require the best efforts of all concerned.

REFERENCES

1. Atkins, J. M. "Behavioral Objectives in Curriculum Design: A Cautionary Note," *The Science Teacher.* May, 1968. pp. 27–30.

2. Bair, Medill "Developing Accountability in Urban Schools: A Call for State Leadership," *Educational Technology.* January, 1971. pp. 38–40.

3. Deterline, William A. "Applied Accountability," *Educational Technology.* January, 1971. pp. 15–20.

4. Johnson, W. Frank "Performance Contracting with Existing Staff," *Educational Technology.* January, 1971. pp. 59–61.

5. Kaufman, Roger A. "Accountability, a System Approach and the Quantitative Improvement of Education—An Attempted Integration," *Educational Technology.* January, 1971. pp. 21–26.

6. Lessinger, Leon M. "Accountability and Curriculum Reform," *Educational Technology.* May, 1970. pp. 56–57.

7. ———. "Robbing Dr. Peter to 'Pay Paul': Accounting for Our Stewardship

of Public Education," *Educational Technology.* January, 1971. pp. 11–14.

8. ———. "Teachers in an Age of Accountability," *Instructor.* June-July, 1971. pp. 19–20.

9. Macdonald, James B. and Wolfson, Bernice J. "A Case against Behavioral Objectives," *The Elementary School Journal.* December, 1970. pp. 119–128.

10. Ojemann, Ralph H. "Should Educational Objectives be Stated in Behavioral Terms?" *The Elementary School Journal.* February, 1968. pp. 223–231.

11. Wagoner, David E. "Do you Know Anything at All about How Well or How Much Your Teachers Teach?" *American School Board Journal.* August, 1970. pp. 21–22.

12. Wilson, John O. "Performance Contracting—An Experiment in Accountability," *Instructor.* June-July, 1971. pp. 21–22.

Specifying Objectives for Performance Contracts

H. M. Harmes

44

EDITORS' QUESTIONS:

1. How does a product output system differ from a process performance system? Give examples of instances in which each approach would be preferable to the other. State your rationale in each case.

2. Do you agree with the author that it is not possible to transcend the standards of performance required by a process performance contract, and that, therefore, no bonuses should be paid for excellence, but penalties should be imposed for doing less well than the design requires? Qualify your response.

3. What benefits, if any, are likely to be derived from hiring out instruction by means of performance contracting that are not easily obtained by a more efficient employment of existing staff and other educational resources? Support your answer.

4. Recommend criteria for evaluating performance under a product output system. Do the same for a process performance system. Which is the more difficult? Why?

5. Suppose elementary school teachers were not employed by school systems, but, instead, were offered performance contracts. What specifications would you require the contract to include before you would be willing to sign it? Justify each requirement.

H. M. Harmes, "Specifying Objectives for Performance Contracts," *Educational Technology*, XI, No. 1 (January 1971), 52–56. Reprinted with the permission of *Educational Technology*.

Performance contracts may deal with either of two basic types of expected output —product or process. Product output contracts specify in detail expected learning but generally do not specify the processes to be used to attain it. On the other hand, process output contracts specify a set of processes to be put into operation.

Educational product output contracts are analogous to industry contracts which call for the delivery of products. Construction of a thousand pairs of shoes, five thousand tires, or one hundred transistor radios are examples of product outcomes.

Educational process contracts are analogous to service contracts of professions and industry. An attorney contracts his services to perform certain legal operations. A security firm furnishes guards for a bank. A surgeon contracts to perform an operation to save the life of his patient. All of these contractors are to be paid whether or not the desired outcomes of the processes they implement are realized.

The major difference between product output contracts and process output contracts, then, lies with the conditions specified as outcomes. In education, if the expected outcome is that a group of stu-

H. M. Harmes is director of the School Service Center, Division of Continuing Education, Florida Atlantic University, Boca Raton.

dents will test a year higher in reading achievement, then the contract defines a product output. If, on the other hand, the expected outcome is that a group of students will have received 80 hours of instruction following the procedures specified by a specific instructional system, then the contract is a process output contract. The agency which lets the contract assumes that it will get at least a minumum amount of product output if the desired processes are implemented.

In a sense, normal teacher work contracts are process output contracts. To be sure, the exact processes to be implemented are not specified in a teacher's contract. However, it has been assumed by most school agencies that teachers who were employed under the terms of the contract would use the *best* processes known to the teaching profession to accomplish the objectives that the agencies had in mind. Most professional contracts are of this nature. The physician, the attorney, the architect, the accountant and others are paid to implement the best processes known to their professions.

Regardless of the reasons for performance contracting and performance financing, the major idea behind them is that the agency which enters into a contract will receive the product or services which it desires or it will not pay for them. Procedures of performance contracting mean that the requirements of the contract must be carefully delineated in order that the contracting agency will know when it should make payment and the contractor will know what he must do in order to receive payment. To achieve the required degree of specificity, each contract must contain certain critical elements. There are four:

1. *Objectives of the contract.* Each performance contract must spell out in detail what is to be accomplished by the contract, either in terms of product or of processes to be implemented.

2. *Student entry characteristics.* Both the school agency and the contractor must know the specific type of student who is to be transformed by the instructional program.

3. *Resources.* Resources to be committed to the performance financing contract must be carefully spelled out. Resources consist of three things: operating resources, capital resources and time resources.

4. *Constraints.* Both the contractor and the school agency should be fully aware of those things that must be done or must *not* be done, apart from fulfilling the objectives of the contract, in order to meet the intent of the school agency in issuing the contract.

All of these ingredients are absolutely essential in any performance contract which is going to be successful. However, only techniques of specifying objectives will be treated here.

Specifying Objectives for Product Output Systems

Early efforts of performance contractors —beginning late in 1969—were aimed at the production of learning as output, and payments were made on the basis of evidence that learning had occurred. Generally, learning was specified in terms of increased scores on standardized achievement tests.

Probably the best known project of this type was that which took place in Texarkana in 1969–70. There the contractor was paid if the students reached specified levels of test score increase, and was paid a reduced amount or not at all if the student did not achieve the increase.

In this type of contract the objective is,

quite simply, to increase test scores to a specified level. From the test scores the contracting agency then infers that the students have learned what was intended. In the case of Texarkana, tests were given in reading and mathematics. Consequently, the contractor knew that his objective was to increase the standardized achievement test scores of the students in these two subject areas.

Notice that, in this particular case, the objective was to increase test *scores*. The contractor was to receive full payment if a student's test score on a standardized test was 1.0 year higher at the end of the instructional program than it was at the beginning. This amount of increase was the objective of the contractor. It was not that the students would achieve any particular math skills. The objective which was spelled out in the contract was that the students would *test* higher at the end than they did at the beginning.

This type of objective has certain advantages and disadvantages. It is certainly easy to determine if the students have attained the objective or not. It is as simple as administering an achievement test before and after the program. The method is simple and explicit.

However, the contractor for the Texarkana project was accused of raising the students' test scores by including test items in instructional materials. Apparently this was viewed by the contracting school agency and many educators as a breach of the contract, and the professional ethics of the contractor were also questioned.

Reaction was swift. Across the United States contracting school agencies specified that performance could be measured by any one of several different achievement tests, thereby making it virtually impossible for the contractor to teach to a particular

achievement test. This practice raises some very serious questions in turn.

It is known that standardized achievement tests which purport to measure achievement in a subject area do not correlate perfectly with one another. It is possible that a student who is administered two different achievement tests in a single subject area may test two or three grade levels apart on the two tests. It is also possible that a student who is administered two different forms of the same test will achieve two or three grade levels apart on the two forms. Publishers of standardized tests readily admit that these conditions obtain, and they state that standardized achievement tests were never meant to be sufficiently reliable to measure individual student progress.

Is it reasonable, then, to hold a contractor responsible for increasing individual achievement test scores when a wide range of tests is to be used to measure achievement and when the tests are all unreliable? On the other hand, if a single achievement test form is designated as a measuring device, how can the contracting agency assure itself that the contractor is not teaching memorization of responses to achievement test items? It can't. It would seem that disadvantages of accepting standardized achievement test scores as evidence of product output considerably outweigh the advantages of specificity and ease of administration.

A better way to specify product output is in terms of specific behavioral objectives. Behavioral objectives specify the class of behavior that the student will exhibit when he has learned that which is intended by the contracting agency. Specifying product output in terms of behavioral objectives increases options for development of many different specific assessment procedures rather than limiting the process to one test or combination of tests that are uncorrelated with one another. This calls for "criterion-referenced" measurement, rather than "norm-referenced" measurement.[1]

Robert Mager[2] gave the basic outline for this type of instructional objective. His criteria for the preparation of instructional objectives were given more specific and concrete form by the author in *Behavioral Analysis of Learning Objectives*.[3] Very simply, a behavioral objective specifies the class of behavior in which the student will engage, the conditions which will be given to him for exhibiting that behavior, and the degree of proficiency he will show in order to indicate that he has learned what is intended.

The following is a properly stated behavioral objective in the area of mathematics:

Given 40 random addition algorisms of sums of 18 or less, the student will solve each within a period of three minutes.

The purpose of this objective is to determine whether or not any particular student knows his addition combinations. He must know them from memory or he will not be able to solve the 40 problems within a three-minute period. Because the addition algorisms to be given to the student can be drawn at random from all algorisms of sums of 18 or less, the student must learn *all* of the addition algorisms of sums of 18 or less. If a student misses even one, he has not met this objective.

It is obvious from the objective that an infinite number of tests could be devised to determine whether or not any particular student had met the objective. Therefore, it would be impossible for a contractor to teach toward items of a particular test. Performance of the contract would be measured by the performance of students who achieved the objective. This type of contract objective makes it possible to determine

what the student has actually learned. It is far superior to making inferences from nebulous and unreliable standardized achievement test scores.

Any instructional objective may be stated in behavioral terms. Quite obviously, a number of behavioral objectives are needed to ascertain the degree of learning in any given subject area. These objectives may be developed solely by the contracting agency or by the contracting agency in cooperation with potential contractors.

Development of sequences of behavioral objectives is an extremely difficult task. Perhaps that is why it has been avoided by school systems prior to the advent of performance contracting. It is much more difficult to develop sequences of behavioral objectives than it is to specify achievement in terms of standardized achievement tests. Yet, *such specification gives school officials an opportunity to state exactly what they want out of the instructional programs provided by their school systems,* whether or not they engage in performance contracting.

When behavioral objectives specify output, a possible way of determining when payment should be made would be for an independent evaluation agency to maintain assessment personnel at the project site. The assessment personnel would be satisfactory to both the contractor and the school system and would have at their disposal a number of assessment procedures required to determine if any students had achieved an objective at a particular point in time. At his option, the contractor could send to the as-

1. Popham, W. James *et al. Criterion-Referenced Measurement.* Englewood Cliffs, New Jersey: Educational Technology Publications, 1971.
2. Robert Mager. *Preparing Instructional Objectives.* Palo Alto: Fearon Publishers, 1962.
3. H. M. Harmes. *Behavioral Analysis of Learning Objectives.* West Palm Beach, Florida: Harmes and Associates, 1969.

sessment personnel a student to be assessed on a particular objective. If the student met the objective, the assessment personnel would certify that fact to the school agency and payment could be made to the contractor. Or, the contractor could accumulate a number of credits for objectives accomplished and receive payment when the amount due him reaches a predetermined figure.

The assessment agency could receive payment on the number of assessments it administered, the amount to be paid by the school agency when the student meets the objective assessed and by the contractor when the student fails to meet the objective. Because assessment is a valuable part of the learning process, i.e., students learn from taking tests, the assessment agency would actually be contributing to the performance objectives of the contractor. Therefore, the contractor could utilize the assessment agency to give tests to the extent that taking tests contributed to the instructional process. If many assessments were to be given, then the assessment agency would receive more money than if a few assessments were to be given.

Specifying Objectives for Process Performance Systems

Unlike product output performance agreements, process performance agreements do not require the contractor to show that the students have learned that which was intended. Rather, they require the contractor to implement and operate a process which is assumed to produce desired learning outcomes.

Let's take an example. *Science: A Process Approach* is an elementary school level program developed by the American Association for the Advancement of Science

(AAAS).[4] Manuals which explain the program define intended student learnings in more or less behavioral terms and give descriptions of activities, instructional materials, and assessment procedures. Scanty research indicates that perhaps as many as 80 percent of the students achieve 80 percent of the program objectives when they are implemented as described in the manuals.

A school system might decide that it would like to have its students learn the objectives of the AAAS program. If so, the system would have two routes to follow for performance contracting. It could specify that a contractor would be held responsible for students learning the objectives of the program. This would, therefore, be a product output performance contract. On the other hand, *because some information is known about what product the processes of* "Science: A Process Approach" *will produce,* it would be reasonable and feasible to contract for implemention and operation of the program. In this case, the contracting school agency would have control over both the outcomes of the learning system and the methods used to achieve those outcomes.

Defining the objectives of a process performance contract takes on dimensions that are different from those of product contracts. As the best type of objective for product contracting defines how it will be determined that students have learned, the best type of objective for process contracting defines how it will be determined that a process has been, or is being, *operated as intended.* Both types must be so specific that they are subject to the least possible chance of misinterpretation. Objectives in both types of contracts are critical to the structure

4. American Association for the Advancement of Science. *Science: A Process Approach.* Rochester: Xerox Education Division, 1967.

of the contract because, if payment is to be made for performance, it must be determined exactly what performance is wanted and when it has been received.

An important step in setting a process objective is to identify those characteristics of the program that make it a program. In other words, what conditions must be present in order for it to be said that the program is truly implemented and in operation? Characteristics in five areas must be specifically identified and delineated.

1. Learning objectives for students.
2. Characteristics of students for which the program is designed.
3. Materials and methods of instruction for reaching the objectives with the intended target population.
4. Techniques for assessing student learning.
5. Internal and external management specifications.

As they are now designed, most instructional "programs" do not have all of these elements. Therefore, it will be necessary to supply missing elements as the performance objective is developed.

Let's continue with the AAAS science program, as an example, by assuming that a goal is to operate it in Elementary School X during the 1971–1972 school year. This program meets more of the required program characteristics than most programs. It does have specific learning objectives, detailed descriptions of instructional materials and methods, and techniques of assessment of student learning. However, it lacks sufficient descriptions of characteristics of students for whom the program is designed and both internal and external management specifications.

What is known, then, can be incorporated into the process objective.

At the end of the 1971–1972 school year, students in Elementary School X will have received instruction in science according to the procedures described in the manuals for *Science: A Process Approach.*

If all requirements for program design were met and were described in the manuals, the objective statement could end with the addition of monitoring procedures. Because the program is not complete, however, answers to certain questions must be included in the process objective. How much time must be included in the process objective? How much time must be devoted to the process and how must it be arranged? What type of student will be treated? What will the teacher be doing when the program is in operation?

Let's arbitrarily answer these questions and add them to the process objective.

At the end of the 1971–1972 school year, students in Elementary School X will have received instruction in science according to the procedures described in the manuals for *Science: A Process Approach.* To achieve this, not more than one lesson or activity will be conducted on any day for any student. Each qualified student who is in attendance 160 days or more will receive instruction in at least 150 lessons or activities as defined in the manuals. Students who are in attendance fewer than 160 days will receive instruction as follows:

140-159 days of attendance at least 130 lessons or activities

120-139 days of attendance at least 110 lessons or activities

0-119 days of attendance no minumum limit of activities

Each lesson or activity will meet the following time requirements:

	Minutes	
	At Least	Not More Than
Kindergarten	20	35
Grade 1	30	45
Grade 2	35	50
Grade 3	45	60

Instruction will be conducted in groups of not more than 30 members nor fewer than 15 in spaces allowing at least 25 square feet of area per pupil. Each group will be led by one adult teacher who will be present for at least the minumum time of each lesson. Groups will be formed on random assignment from age brackets, as follows, to receive instruction in program graded activities indicated:

Age at Beginning of year	Program Level
5.0 - 5.9	A
6.0 - 6.9	B
7.0 - 7.9	C
8.0 - 8.9	D

Only students who have tested I.Q.'s of 75 or higher will receive this program. Each must also have full use of at least three limbs and have sight and hearing within the limits described as normal by a physician who will be agreed upon by the contractor and the school agency.

Once an objective of this nature is formulated for a process performance agreement, the remainder of the contract is completed in a manner similar to that involved in development of product performance agreements. Commitments of capital and operating resources and constraints are added.

Special attention must be given, however, to the methods by which performance will be monitored. Products can be and are measured at a point in time. Processes, on the other hand, take place over a span of time. Unless one wishes to continuously monitor an instructional process, a very time-consuming and expensive thing to do, he must devise techniques whereby the process is sampled at points in time or during short time spans. From this sampling, it is then inferred that the process taking place between samples is similar to the samples of it.

An example may help to clarify what is meant. *Science: A Process Approach* manuals indicate that students must engage in the processes of science to learn the intended

objectives. Many student activities are described for individual lessons. Also, there are descriptions of activities that are to be led by the teacher. It can be assumed that (1) students will be discussing science topics with each other some of the time; (2) students will be working on science activities but will not be discussing, nor listening to discussion, some of the time; (3) students will be discussing science topics under the direction of the teacher some of the time; and (4) students will be listening to the teacher discuss science topics some of the time.

Although it is not defined in the manuals, assume that internal management requirements of the program are established so that categories (3) and (4) combined are not more than 40 percent nor less than 25 percent of total program time.

Procedures will then need to be devised to determine the degree to which this requirement is met. Obviously, total monitoring would require as much time and almost as many resources as are committed to the operation of the program. Therefore, a sampling technique is indicated to effect efficiency in the monitoring process. Also, the technique must result in reliable data.

Edmund J. Amidon and Ned A. Flanders[5] have devised a technique of interaction analysis which utilizes trained observers to classify interaction during classroom discussions into three main categories: teacher talk, student talk, and silence or confusion. A classroom observer also records the amount of time devoted to each category. Research indicates that the technique is very reliable when trained observers are used.[6]

5. Edmund J. Amidon & Ned A. Flanders. *The Role of the Teacher in the Classroom.* Minneapolis: Association for Productive Teaching, 1967.
6. Edmund J. Amidon & John B. Hough (Eds.) *Interaction Analysis: Theory, Research, and Application.* Reading, Massachusetts: Addison Wesley Publishing Company, 1967.

In the example under discussion, a monitoring process which utilizes the Flanders system might well be agreed upon by both parties to the process performance agreement:

> The contractor will maintain video tape recordings of all lessons conducted during the 15 work days immediately prior to any current date of the agreement. Any and all tapes requested by the Analysis Evaluation Company, an independent firm, will be surrendered to it for a period not to exceed 15 work days, when they will be returned to the contractor.
>
> The Analysis Evaluation Company will select, using random sampling techniques, 100-110 tapes and apply the Flanders scale of interaction analysis to them.

Once proper monitoring procedures are defined, penalties for discrepancies existing between program requirements and observed performance may then be included in the agreement. Unlike product performance agreements, it is not possible to include bonuses for "better" performance in a process performance agreement. The objective is to implement the process and operate it within the parameters designed for it. It is not possible to achieve objectives beyond that, nor to do "better" than the process was designed to do. Therefore, penalties may be imposed only for doing less well than the design, i.e., failure to operate within the program specifications.

An Opinion

In the long run, a process performance agreement in education may be more palatable to professional people in education than those which require product performance. It is well known that it is not possible for either businesses or individuals to teach someone something just because they want to do so. All instructional processes operate with some degree of unreliability. The purpose of performance contracting and financing should be to implement and operate *the best programs that are known.*

No one holds physicians responsible, financially or otherwise, for losing patients, as long as they use practices that have been researched and accepted by the profession. Attorneys expect to receive their fees when they lose well-prepared cases. Why should educators, particularly public school educators, be singled out and be asked to guarantee results from instructional programs which are unreliable to varying degrees?

Perhaps it is because there has been so little definitive research done in instruction, and so little requested by educators, that it is impossible to support with evidence the contention that any instructional program is the best practice for anyone under any circumstances. Perhaps it is because the public and school boards which are responsible to the public don't know what to think about the professional practices of educators when they observe five teachers teaching the same subject to students of similar characteristics in the same school at the same time using five widely different approaches, and each teacher claiming his is the best. Not only that, in many cases the approaches not only differ from one another, they also differ from any program approach described *anywhere.*

Perhaps, losing faith in the ability of educators to select, implement and operate the best programs, school boards are beginning to see product output performance as their only recourse for securing the best programs for their clients, the public.

Hopefully, the product output performance contracting and financing movement will have that effect by forcing educators to ask for, receive and utilize definitive research into effective instructional processes.

Factors to Consider in Preparing Performance Contracts for Instruction

Albert V. Mayrhofer

EDITORS' QUESTIONS:

1. Explain the importance of the "turnkey feature" of performance contracts advocated by the author.

2. Considering the fact that if a contractor fails to perform he will not be paid, evaluate the contention that the contractor should, nevertheless, be required to post a performance bond.

3. Assume a situation in which an outside contractor provides an instructional system but utilizes the existing instructional staff to implement it. Assume further, that participation by teachers is voluntary but that, as a condition of participation, each teacher must agree to follow specified procedures exactly and to use only the materials provided by the contractor. Suppose, finally, that the system proves unsatisfactory. Assess the potential effects upon pupils, teachers and authority relationships between participating teachers and the administration.

4. Suggest procedures for using performance contracts for improving instructional effectiveness and developing the capacity to continue implementing those procedures which enhance learning achievement even after the contract has expired.

45

Albert V. Mayrhofer, "Factors to Consider in Preparing Performance Contracts for Instruction," *Educational Technology*, XI, No. 1 (January 1971), 48–51. Reprinted with the permission of *Educational Technology*.

A contract is a legal agreement in which one party promises to deliver goods or services to another party for a consideration of value. Thus, any contract has performance of a promise as its essence and redress in the event of violation.

The term "performance contracting" is used rather than "contracting" because it better describes the intent—measured acquisition of skills, knowledge or attitudes. A contract could be effected in which one would agree to deliver resources. The practice of using contracts for the delivery of resources has been in common practice in the schools for many years. The schools have made contracts with architects and building firms for facilities, with caterers for food service, with administrators for administering, and with teachers for teaching. All of these are based on the delivery of resources, and they are good for that purpose. But the major charge of the schools is that our young shall learn, that their behavior should be somehow different as a result of having spent time in school. The public has a right to expect that our youth shall, as a result of the resources contributed, be better prepared to take their place in a free and open society as free people, contributing both to their personal and to the general

Albert V. Mayrhofer is assistant to the associate commissioner of education, U.S. Office of Education.

welfare. This expectation assumes a change in behavior on the part of students, based on the acquisition of requisite knowledge, skills and attitudes.

As in any well-constructed contract, the performance contract will, among other things, stipulate the gains promised, criteria of acceptable evidence, modes of proof, time, processes, conditions, costs, logistics and *guarantees.* If the contract is to be institution-building, to increase the capacity of the school to meet its burdens, the contract will include a turnkey feature. The contractor will guarantee to do those things which will, upon termination of his activities, leave the capacity *within the schools* to continue the good practice responsible for improved learner performance. In order to document the degree to which the promises have been fulfilled and payment made, an outside, independent, educational audit should be mandatory. Without this provision, accountability for results is meaningless.

Performance contracting for direct student instruction is a relatively new experience for the public schools. Contracting for the instruction of teachers and administrators is not new.

Because it is a new practice, the district which entertains this institution-building device must be politically and socially astute. This is an operation with which the district will have to live. It must, at this time, be prepared to turn to its advantage the media coverage which will increase the rate of communication of friend and foe alike. The increased interest of the client which results will be turned to advantage or liability, depending on the management capability of the staff.

Experience would dictate the wisdom of beginning a performance contract with a very general statement of purpose and jus-

tification. This would not be grossly different from the types of things included in present grant application proposals. It should correspond to statements in the grant proposal, if outside funds are to be the source of dollars, in order that orderly correspondence can be achieved. It might include a statement of desire to improve student reading or mathematics performance and state that this is an educationally and fiscally sound approach. It should say that the contractor does in fact have something of value to offer at a good price. It should include a general comment on the agreement of the contractor to be accountable for results.

The document should indicate the district's decision that the contractor's service is educationally, politically, socially and economically sound in terms of established goals, philosophy and operating principles.

Potential spinoff benefits should be included in general language. Benefits to the district of inservice training, sharpened and more relevant evaluation and cost benefit data can be mentioned. These are the kinds of things the media have time for, because the general public can understand and will want to know about these aspects. A statement of district intent to add the resources of the private sector to those of the school in improving the learning of their children is important. The public has, in general, little sympathy with the "white hat-black hat" game which we have played for too many years.

One might next make a general, protective statement concerning the source of funding. This aspect will be considered in precise detail later in the document, but it is good practice to set the general constraints early. The funding might be federal, state, private, local, or a combination of any of these sources.

Since a performance contract is an agreement, a written set of mutual promises so definite with respect to price, quantity, standards, time and place of performance that an independent group can adequately assess fulfillment, precise statement of what each party proposes to do and what he expects from the other is now appropriate in this sequence. The intent of each party should be detailed, and the mutual areas of responsibilities should be clearly documented.

A note of caution is made at this point to the educator. The private sector, because of a performance oriented experience as fundamental as survival, will be astute in *not promising more than it can deliver.* Educators have quite different experiences. Delivery on vague promises of intent and direction, with no survival consequences except for superintendents, has not been the educator's experience. For these reasons, the educator must be very careful to promise only that which *he* can deliver. A pragmatic assessment of his logistic and personnel capability must be made if the school is not to overpromise and cause an operational failure during or after the contract. This caution must be considered in a continuum beginning with the framing of a "Request for Proposal" and extending through the "turnkey" phase. Request for Proposal and the turnkey phase will be treated in more detail later in this article.

Among the mutual promises each party makes are the specific student achievements guaranteed, how they will be measured, and acceptable modes of proof. The total payment schedule should be addressed in terms of amount and payment times. These should include precise "Reduction Criteria" and amounts, as well as "Incentive Criteria" and amounts. Note that the term "reduction criteria" is used rather than "penalty" because it is more specific. One pattern of contract surpasses the achievement guaranteed by the contractor at a fixed price, and a reduction of the fixed price if student performance does not meet the guaranteed level. Regardless of whether a formula involves a fixed fee with incentives and reductions, a fixed fee on an all-or-none basis, or any other pattern, an offset agreement should be stipulated. In the event that a reduction or incentive is indicated from evaluation evidence at a point which does not give the district sufficient lead time to handle the required paperwork, the reduction or incentive may be made against the next payment period amount. This might be easier said than done if it is not a stipulation of the contract.

The consideration of demurs is relevant at this point in a contract sequence. One such demur might address money from a federal grant. If the funding source is federal, any and all payments should be made subject to the federal grant conditions, delivered amount, and periods of fiscal delivery. It is also wise to stipulate that payments under the contract will not involve 100 percent of the grant. This reinforces the upper limit set on the flat fee or flat fee plus incentive, and also protects the additional funds within the total project for other needed district activities from becoming a lure to the contractor. Such a lure could become a problem to the district. If these conditions are stipulated, valuable time and effort will be safeguarded, and a smoother operation will result.

Since the guarantee has been delineated, specifically for payment purposes, it is apropos now to restate the performance guarantee in terms of target population, the procedures to be used, the places, times, conditions and specific treatment of measuring instruments and alternatives concerning modes of proof. When this is accomplished, very precise payment and responsibility terms can be stated. Either tables or formulas can now be presented. Whatever the means by which these processes are described and mutual promises made, the language should be sufficiently clear that a group of persons with twelfth grade mathematics and reading ability, having read it, will agree with the authors in detail.

Logistics is an area which, if unaddressed, will lead to disaster in the turnkey phase and can severely limit the immediate progress of the operation. For this reason, it is good judgment to specify management personnel and data flow systems. Who is the project director? What is his authority? Is there to be one for the district and one for the contractor? If an adequate needs assessment has been performed and a system technology employed, hard data will be available for negotiating optional responses. Agreement on management personnel, forms, reporting times and streams, authority and responsibility nets can be approached on a more rational basis and interfaced with school district operation. It is wise at this juncture for the person delegated the responsibility for the planning of the performance contract to remember the superintendent. The superintendent may have delegated the responsibility but, since he is the legal point at which the "buck" stops, he should be kept fully informed. His advice and counsel should be sought at critical points. Do not expect him to make rational responses unless the project is displayed in a way that programmatic options are visible and alternatives are possible.

This sequence would now require that teacher competence be addressed. Whether the district or the contractor is responsible for teaching personnel, the instructional staff should be competent to work with the children and resources within the system specified. This is necessary in fairness to the children, the teachers, the contractor and the public. Teacher preservice and inservice training should be provided, and teachers should be tested to determine if, in fact, they have acquired the competence to successfully engage in the endeavors. All too often, teachers have been "thrown to the wolves." They have, in good faith and high spirit, engaged in "projects" with little or no understanding or skill. Performance contracting calls for dedicated *competence.* Teachers should be consulted at this stage. Specifications should be set for the criteria of competence both for beginning and continuance in the endeavor. Criteria for removal and replacement of a teacher, without reflection on the teacher, should be specified. Within these criteria statements should be a written agreement that teachers will not engage in the use of alien material, processes or conditions *without the written permission of the project director.* If, in a teacher's judgment, other materials and activities are dictated, and the teacher can support the position, the agreement of the project director and the contractor is negotiable. No teacher has the right, however, to unilaterally intervene with alien procedures and revise a system which is legally agreed to and by which a contractor will receive reimbursement. Since, in most cases, the teachers involved in this kind of operation will be volunteers, making this known initially, as a condition of participation, should require no more than a signed agreement by each teacher assenting to this requirement of the contract.

The next item to be addressed is a calendar of events and specification of total contract time in detail. Protection of the project and the contractor should be stipulated in terms of time and results. What about Acts of God, strikes, fires, lightning and tornadoes? The contractor cannot be held accountable if the children are not engaged in the learning system. The public institution has not been held accountable for results, but a performance contractor *will* be. If a district expects a contractor to enter an agreement, this area will have to be addressed fairly—and contingencies specified.

The problems surrounding data must be addressed. What rights does the contractor have to statistical data, both during and at the completion of the contract? Will the identity of child, teacher and school be protected? Invidious comparisons can be made by people with inadequate backgrounds. Protection is needed. However, since data indicating success of the contractor is worth money to that contractor as advertising, it is not wise to be so protective that a lever to lower the cost of the operation is overlooked. Good, practical judgment within the constraints of standard professional ethics is all that is required. Judgment and documented, ethical practice are pointed to here rather than common convention because common convention arises from experience, and educators have no experience with this. Application of common convention would run the risk of being counterproductive and inappropriate. It is in the enlightened self-interest of educators to be cooperative in dealing with the contractor selected.

With all of the foregoing negotiated and stipulated, a summary of funding constraints is in order, with some additional specifications. The payment criteria, amounts and time can be summarized. Statements of the normal and tolerable limits on fund non-delivery can be specified and liability described. Suppose the source of funds is federal and some catastrophe ter-

minates the project money? A liquidated damage clause is helpful in such a case. Such items as "successors and assignees" should be covered. If the corporation loses its key management people through some unfortunate circumstance, much difficulty could accrue to the project. Specifically detailing interest with respect to successors, assigned heirs and executors could do much to solve problems if they should arise and will, in any case, allow for more undistracted activity of the school management people.

Subcontracting constraints can be detailed to the degree deemed appropriate by the district personnel. It is important to think through the ramifications. Problems arising after the signing of a contract without constraints could cause no end of problems.

A protection for the project people, based on exclusivity of funding, is worth including. A restatement of the source of funds, a reference to methods, means and criteria of payment, and a statement which prohibits the contractor from billing anyone in the district for anything except as described in the contract is good protection to have. A "hold harmless clause" would also be appropriate.

A specification which, depending on many circumstances, might be appropriate is a performance bond. Ownership and possession specifications concerning materials, facilities and equipment is not hard to cover legally. The management of the delivery of service to the children should be protected as well as district financial interests. For this reason, a performance bond should be considered. Decision criteria would include the degree of capitalization of the contractor and the reliability and performance record of the contractor in question. This kind of decision should be stipulated in the general "boiler plate" which details purchase options, extended payments, and who owns and possesses what and when.

Depending on the kind of contract contemplated, the area of data responsibility will be addressed to a minor or major degree. What about patent, copyright and publication rights arising from the endeavor? Will a story or a history of the project be written? Who is to do this? Who owns it? What about materials produced or equipment modified or invented? Who disseminates data? Whoever disseminates the data should be provided the requisite resources, or major interference with other duties will occur.

Another "boiler plate" consideration is litigation. Many firms are chartered in states which extend desirable conditions. These conditions may not extend to the school district. A statement should specify that local, state and federal law is incorporated by reference and that any and all litigation, should there be any, will be brought in the school district's home state.

The future financing of the district demands that there be included a materials and equipment future cost escalation and the delivery clause. A statement should specify that future costs shall rise no more than the contractor can justify by his cost increases. The time period might cover the amortization life of the last item delivered under the contract. This clause is worthless unless a clause guaranteeing delivery of the specified equipment or material is also included.

If a school district addresses these and other considerations in a binding agreement with a contractor, and the children learn, this in itself will not make the exercise cost effective nor educationally sound. One of the main purposes of performance contracting is to assist renewal and reform within the district. The performance contract should confer on the district the capability of extending the benefits received by the target population to all appropriate students. This increases the capability of the district relative to its burden. This is what a "turnkey feature" is all about. The contractor should be bound to do those things which make it possible for the district to extend and expand the service *independently of the contractor* upon termination of the contract. This is the part of the contract which has the most enduring performance guarantee. Performance of these specifications by the contractor should be paid for on a flat rate, with "motivating" reduction clauses for partial or total nonperformance. The logistics specifications of this feature of a contract are beyond the scope of this article. Likewise, the logistics specifications for the production of the "Request for Proposal" are beyond the scope of this article. Since the "Request for Proposal" is the instrument which does or does not secure a socially, politically and fiscally responsible performance contract, it is suggested that the district secure the services of a management support group to assist in its construction and the management of the proceedings. There are groups which can furnish teams of people who have the knowledge, experience and attitudes to assist school districts in a successful engagement in the area of performance contracting with a turnkey feature. It is my belief that school people will have to engage the services of organizations such as these until they develop or acquire the "in-house" capability, which events demonstrate they do not now possess.

Performance contracting holds enormous promise for the children of this nation and the institutions charged with their learning. It is, however, no panacea which can be applied formula-wise by the ignorant and inexperienced, no matter how intelligent and dedicated.

Recommended Readings: The Need for Accountability in Education

Areen, Judith and Jencks, Christopher "Education Vouchers: A Proposal for Diversity and Choice," *Teachers College Record* 72 (1971):327–335.

Bair, Medill "Developing Accountability in Urban Schools: A Call for State Leadership," *Educational Technology* XI (1971): 38–40.

Bhaerman, Robert D. "Accountability: The Great Day of Judgment," *Educational Technology* XI (1971):62.

Carpenter, M. B. *Program Budgeting as a Way to Clarify Issues in Education.* Rand Corporation, July, 1968.

Cleland, D. I. and King, W. R. *Systems Analysis and Project Management.* New York: McGraw-Hill Book Co., 1968.

Cook, D. L. "Management Control Theory and the Context for Educational Evaluation," *Journal of Research and Development in Education* 3 (1970):13–26.

Daniel, Fred K. "Moving Toward Educational Accountability: Florida's Program," *Educational Technology* XI (1971): 41–42.

Deck, Linton L., Jr. "Accountability and the Organizational Properties of Schools," *Educational Technology* XI (1971):36–37.

Deterline, William A. "Applied Accountability," *Educational Technology* XI (1971):15–20.

Duncan, Merlin G. "An Assessment of Accountability," *Educational Technology* XI (1971):27–30.

Ginzberg, Eli "The Economics of the Voucher System," *Teachers College Record* 72 (1971):373–382.

Garvue, Robert J. "Accountability: Comments and Questions," *Educational Technology* XI (1971):34–35.

Johnson, Frank W. "Performance Contract-

ing with Existing Staff," *Educational Technology* XI (1971):59–61.

Katzenbach, E. L. *Planning, Programming, Budgeting Systems: PPBS and Education.* The New England School Development Council, March, 1968.

Kaufman, Roger A. "Accountability, A System Approach and the Quantitative Improvement of Education—An Attempted Integration," *Educational Technology* XI (1971):21–25.

Lessinger, Leon M. "Teachers in An Age of Accountability," *Instructor* 80 (1971):19–20.

——— "Robbing Dr. Peter to 'Pay Paul': Accountability for Our Stewardship of Public Education," *Educational Technology* XI (1971):11–14.

McCann, Walter and Areen, Judith "Vouchers and the Citizen—Some Legal Questions," *Teachers Record* 72 (1971):389–404.

Provus, M. "Evaluation of Ongoing Programs in the Public Schools." In R. W. Tyler, ed. *Educational Evaluation: New Roles, New Means.* Chicago: University of Chicago Press, 1969.

Roueche, John E. "Accountability for Student Learning in the Community College," *Educational Technology* XI (1971): 46–47.

Straubel, James "Accountability in Vocational-Technical Instruction," *Educational Technology* XI (1971):43–45.

Stufflebeam, D. S. "Toward a Science of Educational Evaluation," *Educational Technology* 8 (1968):5–12.

Sweigert, R. L. *Need Assessment-The First Step Toward Deliberate Rather than Impulsive Response to Problems.* California State Department of Education, 1968.

Temkin, S. A. *A Comprehensive Theory of*

Cost-Effectiveness. Philadelphia: Research for Better Schools, Inc., 1970.

"Three Reports of Performance Contracting Now in Action," *Instructor* 80 (1971):23–26.

Voegel, George H. "A Suggested Schema for Faculty Commission Pay in Performance Contracting," *Educational Technology* XI (1971):57–59.

Wilson, John "Performance Contracting: An Experiment in Accountability," *Instructor* 80 (1971):21–22.